WITHDRAWN

η. ___

THE CENSUS OF ELPHIN 1749 WITHDRAWN

COIMISIÚN LÁIMHSCRÍBHINNÍ NA hÉIREANN

The Census of Elphin 1749

Edited by

Marie-Louise Legg

with a statistical analysis by

Brian Gurrin

DUBLIN

IRISH MANUSCRIPTS COMMISSION

2004

Designed and typeset
by Tony Moreau
in Times

ISBN 1 874 280 738

Printed by ColourBooks Limited
Baldoyle Industrial Estate
Dublin 13

CONTENTS

CONTENTS — CONTINUED

List of Maps **Page**

List of Tables

ACKNOWLEDGEMENTS

We are very grateful to James McGuire, James Kelly, Toby Barnard, Ray Gillespie, Robert Mills, Librarian of the Royal College of Physicians of Ireland, Ray Refaussé and Susan Hood of the Representative Church Body of the Church of Ireland, David Dickson and members of the Irish history seminar at TCD, and Richard Smith and the Cambridge Group for the History of Population and Social Structure; Tom Desmond and the staff of the National Library of Ireland; the staff of the Friends' Historical Library, Dublin; Ed Finn and the Leitrim-Roscommon website. We also thank David Fleming, Dorothy Porter, Joanna Bourke; the staff of the London Library; Tom Legg, Máire Kennedy at the Gilbert Library, Dublin, Bernadette Cunningham and the staff of the Royal Irish Academy, Edward McParland, Kevin Nowlan, W.E. Vaughan, Jacqueline Hill and John Regan for their help.

We are both grateful to the Irish Manuscripts Commission for their generous grant towards supporting the statistical analysis of the census.

The National Archives of Ireland have kindly given permission for the publication of the manuscript, and David Craig, Aideen Ireland and the staff have been very helpful over a long period of time.

Marie-Louise Legg
Brian Gurrin

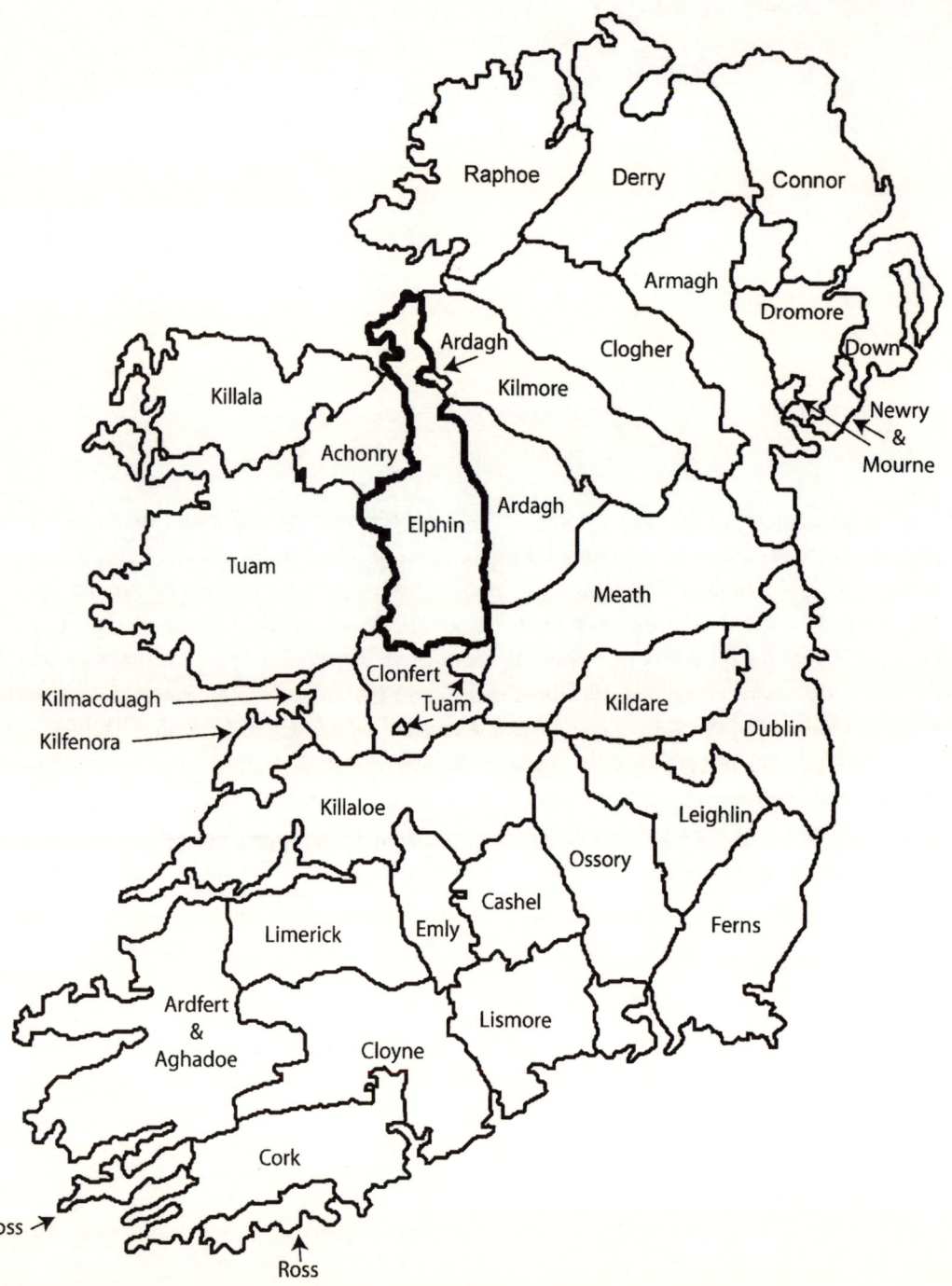

Figure 1 The dioceses of Ireland

INTRODUCTION

Bishop Edward Synge's census of the diocese of Elphin in 1749 has been in the National Archives of Ireland for over 60 years.[1] Its completeness, and the detail of occupations, status and households that it includes is unique. Synge's census gives us an insight into rural Ireland in the mid-eighteenth-century because, as well as counting Roman Catholics and Protestants, he included much other valuable information. From it, we know about the occupation and religion of heads of households, the size of their family, the size of their households and who had servants and how many. His census provides statistical, demographic and social data for a part of the country, and at a time, for which there is very little other material available. There are no 1660 poll-tax records for County Galway and parts of County Sligo; no hearth-tax records for County Galway or County Roscommon for the 1660s; and almost no 1766 census material.

Edward Synge[2] was installed in the diocese of Elphin in 1740 on the death of bishop Robert Howard (1730-40). The Church of Ireland clergy were occasionally instructed by the Irish parliament and the Irish administration in Dublin Castle to undertake enquiries in their dioceses. Howard's diocesan papers are revealing of the kind of statistical and demographic enquiries that were sought. These include reports on the state of Roman Catholicism, a list of mass houses, and returns (made in 1725) to queries about parishes. On his arrival in Elphin, Synge received copies of these from the Howard estate and also a report written by Howard on the state of popery, possibly his response to the inquiry instituted by the Irish House of Lords in 1731.[3]

Since Synge did not embark on his census on instruction from Dublin, and his letters, notably those to his daughter,[4] are uninformative, the only concrete evidence we have about his initiative is a letter from Lord Chief Baron Willes to the Earl of Warwick, written during Willes's tour of Ireland in 1761.[5] Synge had told Willes that he had been 'curious' about the proportion of Roman Catholics to Protestants in his diocese. Synge believed, almost certainly wrongly, that the state of Roman Catholicism in his own diocese reflected the situation across the whole of Ireland. There is also some evidence about the history of Synge's interest in compiling a census. In about 1746, he met Charles Varley, an agriculturalist from Yorkshire who had come to Ireland to seek his fortune. Synge invited Varley to stay with him at Elphin and to advise on his agricultural improvements. Twenty-five years later, Varley wrote a pamphlet in which he outlined proposals

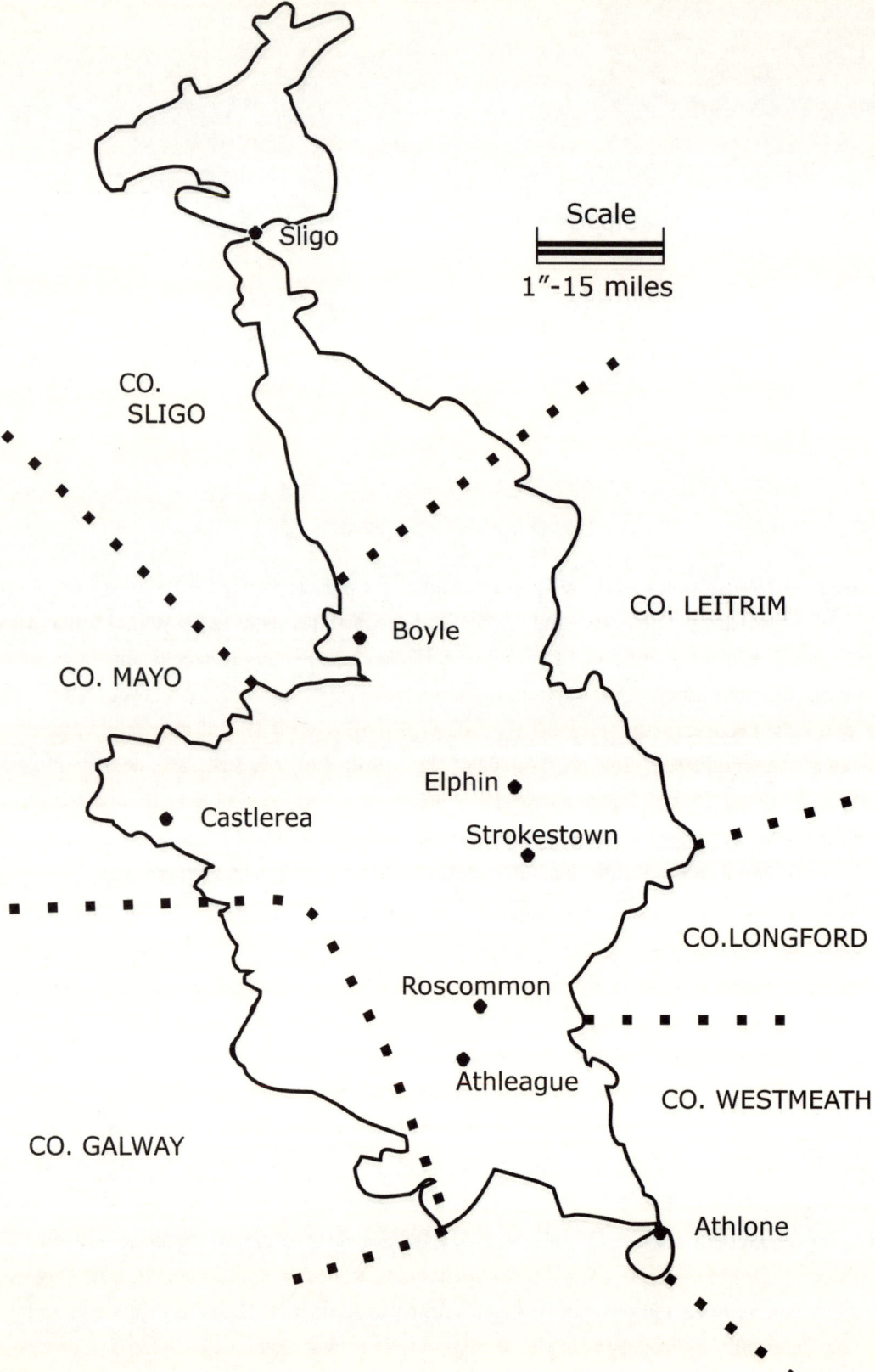

Figure 2 Diocese of Elphin with principal towns

for a census (to be conducted by churchwardens) which would count the numbers of Roman Catholics and Protestants, the acres of tilled and untilled land and the yearly rent of each parish. To this end, he printed a tabulated form for churchwardens to copy. Varley claimed that the purpose of the census was 'for enacting constitutional laws',[6] but given their friendship in the 1740s, the similarity between Synge's own census and Varley's later proposal is significant, since it suggests that the bishop may also have anticipated that his census would inform the legislature and future policy.

There is a further possibility. In 1749 an act was passed to ensure that proper salaries were paid to parish clerks. This may have been the spur for Edward Synge to order a census of the inhabitants of the diocese to ensure the correct amount was paid.[7]

The entries upon which Synge's census was calculated were completed on a form specially designed and printed for the purpose. These forms contained 12 columns with headings of county, place of abode (that is, town or townland), the names of the householder (and in some cases their wives or other relations living in the same house), the occupation and religion of the householder, their children under and over 14[8] and their servants, male and female.[9]

The 1731 report on the state of popery had been undertaken by high sheriffs, chief magistrates and clergy. To carry out his initiative, Synge appealed to his clergy and their churchwardens.[10] They were used to undertaking tasks of this kind as they were charged with applotting the parish rates and with valuing each house within the parish. The organisation of the census forms and (in many cases) the neat handwriting, means it is improbable that they were completed on the spot by the enumerator, and it is reasonable to suppose that Synge instructed his clergy at his visitation in July 1748, and that they in turn delegated to their churchwardens. The information they collected was received and copied by the incumbent on to the printed forms which were returned to Synge. Not every clergyman used this form. The return for the parish of Kiltoom was written on both sides of hand-drawn pages, smaller than the original forms. The clergyman who completed the entries for the parish of Baslick had great difficulty in entering the figures, putting them in the wrong column and crossing them out. Erasures are frequently made by smudging the erroneous entry and it has been difficult to determine in some instances whether the smudge was intentional or accidental.[11] These mistranscriptions underline the probability that the information was transcribed from another sheet.

Churchwardens and their clergymen appear to have had different conceptions of how to complete Synge's form. Rather than writing out the whole names of wives and others in the household, some used systems of enumeration with symbols to indicate those who were married or widowed. Symbols were sometimes used to indicate mixed marriages. In the parish of Kilbride a symbol was used to indicate those whose husbands worked as domestic servants to gentlemen. Similarly, not all of the clergy were very numerate. Most of them totalled up the pages as they went along. But counting the final totals often proved challenging. All these totals were checked and corrected by Edward Synge who was drawn on occasion to make intemperate comments on the arithmetical competence of his clergy.

Despite the problems encountered in its completion, comparison has been made between the census and the hearth-tax returns for 1753 for County Roscommon. There were 6211 hearths liable for tax returned for County Roscommon in 1749, and 8780 in 1753. Synge's Elphin census records ca.13,200 families in the county[12] which suggests that the diocesan census is a more accurate record of the numbers of houses, and therefore of the number of people. In the hearth-tax returns, pauper houses, 'new' houses, barracks, hospitals, schools, and public buildings are not included because they were not taxable. Widows were exempted on production of a certificate of their status. Synge's census, by contrast, has widows' houses, though not barracks, gaols, schools and public buildings.[13] However, the hearth-money collectors' walks may have covered houses which were not included in the census, such as the detached parts of parishes, as in the case of the parish of Ballynakill in County Sligo, which were difficult for the parish enumerators to reach.[14]

Synge received the completed census forms at the visitation on 12-13 July 1749, the date on the census manuscript. At least two of his clergy were absent from the visitation because of illness, and subsequently sent on their parish returns for Killyon and Termonbarry to Synge in September at his Dublin house in Kevin Street.[15]

Fulfilling Synge's request was a major undertaking for the clergy of Elphin, given that most of them had the charge of a number of parishes. Of the 69 parishes in the diocese, only six can be definitely identified as having a resident clergyman. One clergyman lived in east County Longford.[16] Only two of the Elphin clergy had the charge of a single parish; two had seven parishes each. Six parishes had no clergyman at all.

The physical geography of the country cannot have helped, with bad roads, and rivers, loughs and mountains cutting across the country.[17] The diocese of Elphin ran from north to south from County Sligo down to that part of Athlone west of the river Shannon in County Roscommon. It covered over 700,000 statute acres, of which some 34,000 acres (5 per cent) was water. Within the parishes there were 1485 townlands.[18] Fifty parishes were in County Roscommon, eleven parishes were in north-east County Galway and twelve parishes were in north-east County Sligo (Figure 3).

The population of the diocese as shown in the census can be fixed at approximately 76,484 people. Of these, 9.73 per cent were Protestant (including Presbyterians and a small group of Quakers). According to Willes, Synge found that there were 24 Roman Catholics to one Protestant in County Galway. Elsewhere, which he said was 'tolerably well inhabited by protestants', there were 11.25 Catholics to 1 Protestant. Synge was near in his estimation: in the County Sligo section, nearly 50% of the inhabitants were Protestant, whereas in the County Galway section the Protestant population was just over 5% of the total population. Mapping the census reveals that Synge was right when he told Willes of the geographical difference in the distribution of Roman Catholics and Protestants (Figure 4).

The occupations given ranged from gentleman to beggar, from popish priest to dogtrainer. A total of 245 occupations are listed. It is clear this overstates the total number as the categories overlap. For example, Roman Catholic priests can be entered as 'priest', or as 'popish priest' or as 'parish priests'. Church of Ireland clerks are also 'clerks' or 'church clerks' or 'vestry clerks', which is a different occupation.[19] Many householders are defined, not by occupation but by tenure: 'tenants', 'cottiers', 'cottagers', 'landholders' and 'freeholders'. Middlemen, who certainly existed, are invisible. Moreover these terms were not always used precisely: a cottier, who might also be called a tenant, was one who held a small holding limited by a year's tenure. Landholders might equally have been cottiers or tenants.

The census is based on two divisions of land: parishes and townlands. Townlands are defined units of economic activity.[20] The need to study his diocese in more minute detail than that provided by parish boundaries may have led Edward Synge to use this accepted and convenient measure. Both parish and townland are convenient here for the purpose of analysis of economic activity.

To get a sense of the economy of the diocese, it is worth analysing occupations by classifying them according to the 'Occupations of Ireland' divisions in the 1841 census of Ireland.[21] The sectors present in 1749, nearly a century earlier, embraced manufacturing (which, with 77 separate types of occupation, is by far the greatest in variety), professional and public sector employments (50), agriculture (32), dealing (25),

1 Aghanagh
2 Ahamlish
3 Ahascragh
4 Ardcarn
5 Athleague
6 Athlone St Peter's
7 Aughrim
8 Ballintober
9 Ballynakill,Co. Galway/Co. Roscommon
10 Ballynakill,Co. Sligo
11 Ballysumaghan
12 Baslick
13 Boyle
14 Bumlin
15 Cam
16 Clooncraff
17 Clonfinlough
18 Clontuskert
19 Cloonygormican
20 Creeve
21 Drumatemple
22 Drumcliff
23 Drumcolumb
24 Dunamon
25 Dysart
26 Elphin
27 Estersnow
28 Fuerty
29 Kilbegnet
30 Kilbride
31 Kilbryan
32 Kilcolagh
33 Kilcooley
34 Kilcorkey
35 Kilcroan
36 Kilgefin
37 Kilglass
38 Kilkeevin
39 Killadoon
40 Killasolan
41 Killeroran
42 Killian
43 Killinvoy
44 Killukin
45 Killummod
46 Kilmacallan
47 Kilmactranny
48 Kilmacumsy
49 Kilmeane
50 Kilmore
51 Kilnamanagh
52 Kilross
53 Kilteevan
54 Kiltoom
55 Kiltrustan
56 Lissonuffy
57 Ogulla
58 Oran
59 Rahara
60 Roscommon
61 Shancough
62 Shankill
63 Sligo,St John's
64 St. John's
65 Taghboy
66 Tawnagh
67 Termonbarry
68 Tibohine
69 Tisrara
70 Tumna

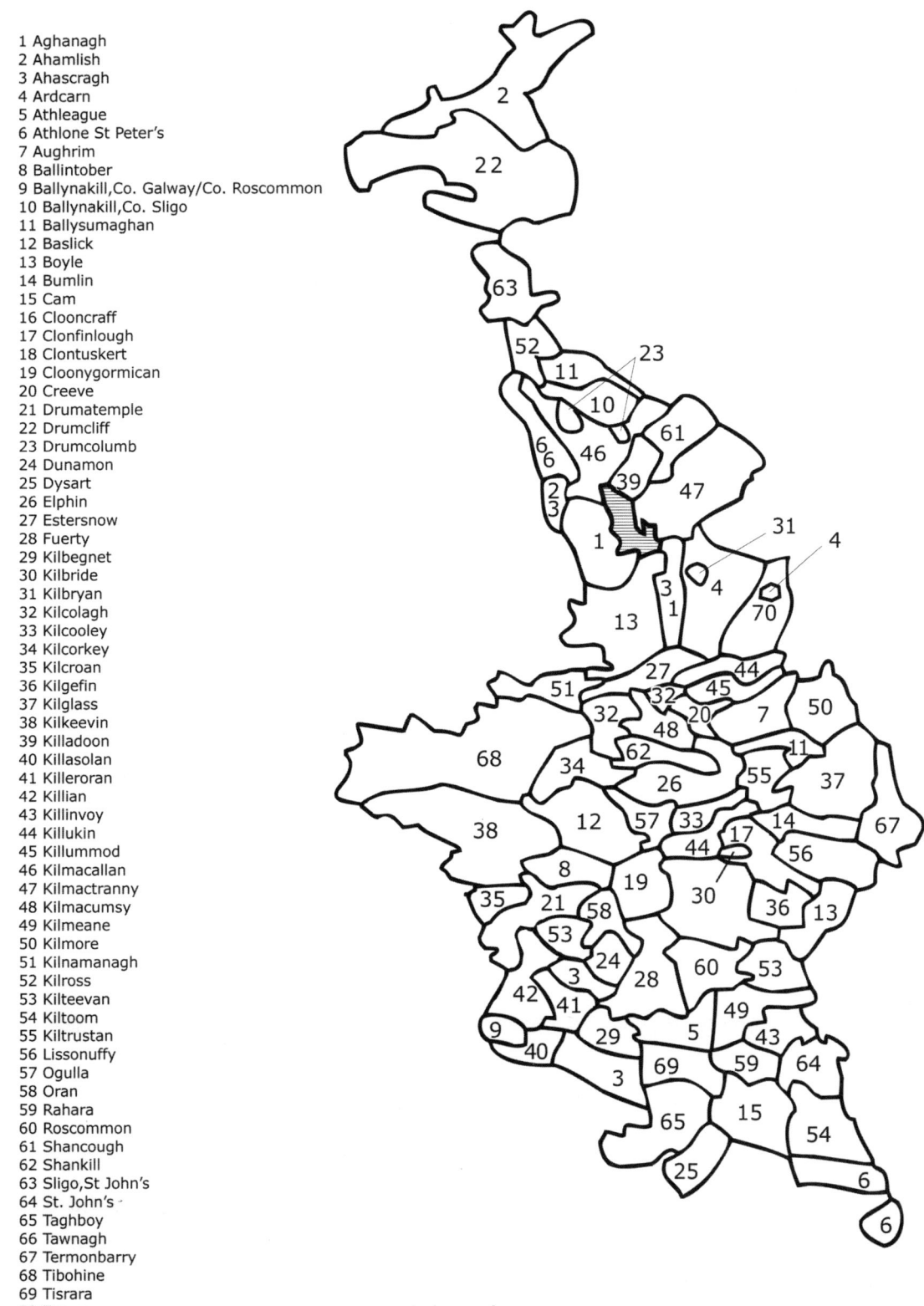

Figure 3 The parishes of the diocese of Elphin

domestic service (11), building (10), transport (5), mining (2), and industrial service (2). The poor comprise 12 classes; another six were soldiers or outpensioners. Seven occupations cannot be classified as they are illegible or unclear. The actual numbers of people working in the 32 identifiable occupations in agriculture outstripped those engaged in manufacturing; the diocese was overwhelmingly agricultural. Similarly, domestic service, with large numbers of servants stretching from the gentry houses down to the dwellings of labourers, employed more people than both manufacturing and dealing, which were concentrated in the larger towns (Figure 2). One group that appears occasionally cannot be firmly fixed. The peripatetic hawkers and hucksters appeared at fairs and patterns and then moved on. Pedlars and tinkers probably travelled from house to house.

Despite the great range of soil types, contemporary observers of the Elphin diocese saw that much of the area was well suited to agriculture. Synge's predecessor Robert Howard noted that the diocese was in a 'very rich deep country... pleasant enough...'.[22] Charles Varley concurred: from Lanesborough to Roscommon, Elphin, Boyle, and Castlerea down to Ballinasloe outside the diocese, the land was said to consist of 'deep loamy soil; at about three feet deep is a rich limestone gravel, which they raise and lay on as manure'.[23] Willes described County Roscommon as 'a very fine county and has most noble and rich pastures... [with] a prodigious quantity of bullocks and sheep'.[24] Most of the land was limestone, covered with areas of bog. The conjunction of the two made cultivation possible, as dressing the peaty land with limestone corrected its acidity.[25] It did not, in practice, generate effective farming as, in Varley's opinion, Roscommon farmers were 'great slovens in husbandry...their land is so good it makes them idle'. They seldom housed their cattle and made little use of dung.[26] The large areas devoted to grazing meant there were limited opportunities for men and women in tillage.[27]

What the census cannot show is the full reality of rural life. The land may have been good, but the living conditions of the peasantry appalled travellers. Varley claimed that three-quarters lived in 'little huts or cabins built of sods and covered with rushes ... not sufficient to keep out a shower of rain ... perhaps inhabited by eight or ten men, women and children, half-naked'.[28] Irish towns did not impress visitors or new residents: Robert Howard called Elphin in 1730 'a dirty Irish town', while Sligo was said to have only 15 slated houses in 1738.[29] Boyle may have been better because of the activities of the King family who built a grand new house in the town in the 1720s.[30] But, despite Isaac Weld's description of Boyle as 'more remarkable for improvement than ... the whole county', large quarters of these towns were miserable. Weld presents a picture of Boyle's Irishtown as a scene of 'human misery and debasement', and of people in Roscommon living in wretched hovels with dunghills at their doors.[31] Synge was active in the mid-1740s in building a new palace at Elphin,[32] but he says nothing of improving the town itself.

The census opens up the various worlds that co-existed in the diocese in the mid-eighteenth-century. In preparing this edition, the information on families and households has been supplemented from the archives of the King family of Boyle, the Pakenham-Mahons of Strokestown, the Croftons of Mote, the Coopers of Markree, and the O'Haras, Temples and Wynnes of Sligo.[33] Account books of the Pakenham-Mahons and the letters of bishop Synge reveal the differing levels of trading in the area.

The descendants of the Roman Catholic gentry of the seventeenth-century were still present in 1749 in the townlands their ancestors had occupied before 1641. The heads of these families had not always been degraded to landless peasantry and are described as 'gentleman'. Using the contemporary letters of Charles O'Conor of Belanagare, and modern work by Hugh Fenning and Francis Beirne on the Roman Catholic diocese of Elphin in the eighteenth-century, not only can Roman Catholic priests be traced but also the laity

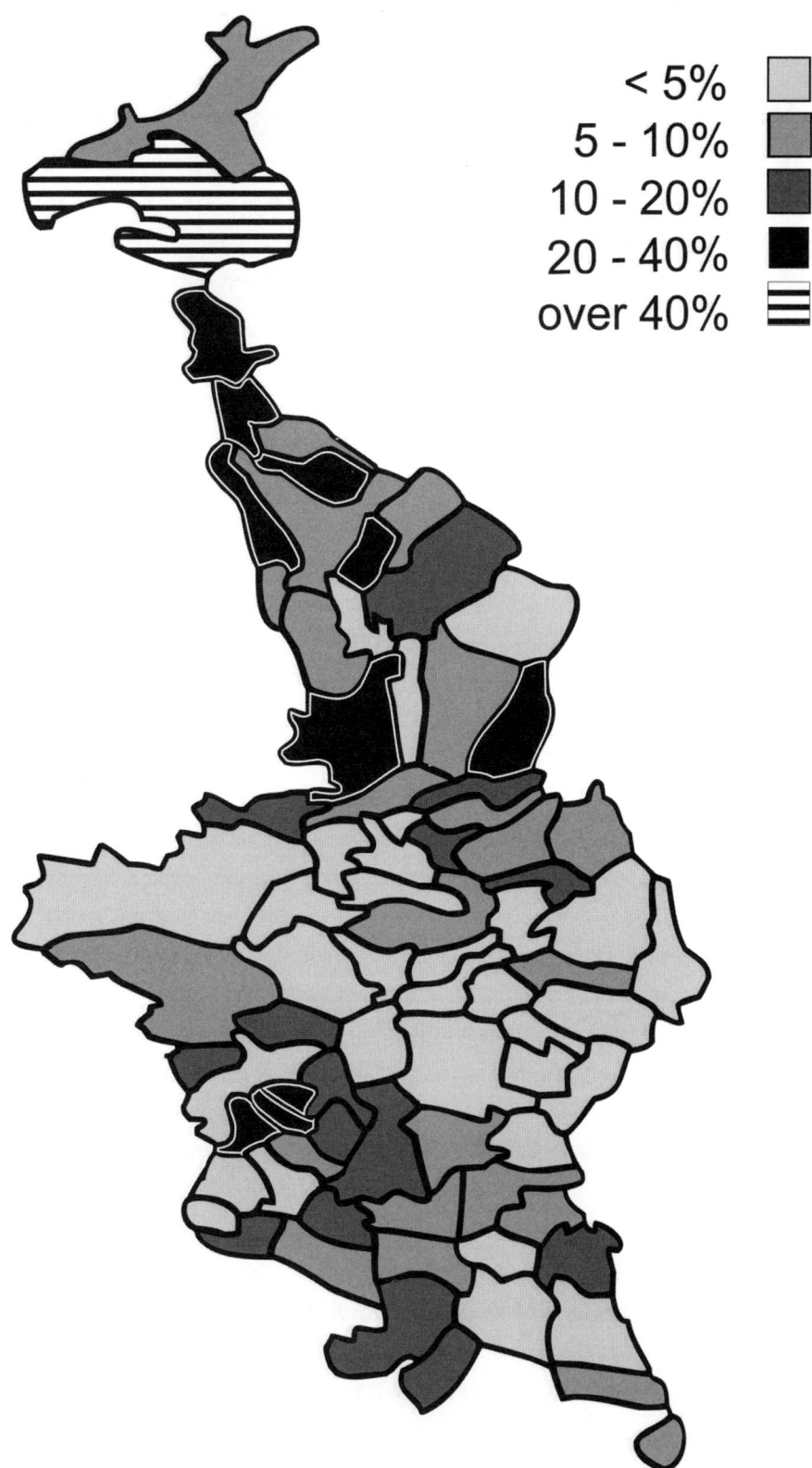

Figure 4 Geographical distribution of Protestants in the diocese of Elphin, 1749

< 5%
5 - 10%
10 - 20%
20 - 40%
over 40%

who were engaged in Roman Catholic politics.[34] In 1748, many of the gentry and merchants signed papers in support of a candidate for the bishopric of Elphin. The occupations of the lay supporters of the candidature of the Rev. William (alias Augustine) O'Kelly, prior of St. Mary's, Roscommon to succeed his uncle Patrick French as bishop of Elphin are an indication of the extent of the Roman Catholic gentry community. Three Roman Catholic gentlemen, two shopkeepers, a distiller, a merchant and five farmers signed this petition in July 1748.[35]

Except for the town of Sligo, where Protestants were in the ascendant in commerce and trade, merchants and traders were overwhelmingly Roman Catholic in other towns in the diocese. This is consistent with Dickson's separation of activities between Protestants who engaged in the main in municipal politics and foreign trade (as in Sligo), and Roman Catholics who pursued processing, provisions, construction and service industries.[36] In a diocese like Elphin, remote from Dublin and with less patronage and wealth, Roman Catholics had greater opportunities for advancement in the rural inland towns.

Catholics were in the majority in the towns of Roscommon, Boyle and, to a lesser extent, in Sligo. In Roscommon town, Roman Catholics outnumbered Protestants by 63.18 per cent. Legislation provided that when it came to appointing to offices normally held by Protestants, Catholics could be appointed when suitable Protestants were not available. Roscommon had a Roman Catholic bailiff, gaoler and turnkey.[37] In Boyle, by contrast, all the posts which were awarded by patronage were held by Protestants, and the same was true, with one possible exception, of Sligo.[38] Of professional posts in Boyle and Sligo the apothecaries were Protestant, but in Roscommon they were Roman Catholic. Boyle had a Roman Catholic doctor, Sligo a Protestant doctor. There were no schoolmasters in Boyle; there were five Protestant schoolmasters in Sligo.

Inevitably the skilled trades present a more varied scene. The specialists - the cabinetmakers, confectioners, glaziers, glovers, saddlers, shoemakers and watchmakers - in Sligo were largely Protestant, as they were also in Boyle. Sailors in Sligo were 7 to 4 Protestant, which may have reflected the sea captains' preference to choose their crew from those they knew personally.[39] In all three towns, skilled shoemakers were almost all Protestant; unskilled broguemakers were Roman Catholic. Weavers in the towns, where they may have been planted by improving landlords, were confessionally divided half and half. In Boyle, half the weavers were Presbyterian, but Roman Catholics dominated the retail trades and service industries – the shopkeepers, merchants, and the various traders who supplied the wool and linen industries. This is consistent with Dickson's view that these industries both drew unskilled countrymen to towns and gave openings to a new Catholic middle-class.[40] Again, membership of merchant guilds and constraints on land-owning may have restricted such growth in Sligo.[41]

There was no Quaker monthly meeting within the Elphin diocese and the Quakers who lived there were members of the monthly meeting based in Moate, County Westmeath. We have no information on a Presbyterian congregation in the area at this period, though there was a considerable community of Presbyterians in the parishes of Boyle and Kilmeane.

There were particular factors which lay behind the economic prosperity of Boyle and Roscommon. The town of Boyle was owned by the King family and their influence is reflected in the fact that 22.09 per cent of Boyle householders were members of the Church of Ireland. There was also a substantial (10.07 per cent) Presbyterian community. Boyle may have been the site of a linen factory which Robert Stephenson said had been set up by a London company of merchants, but which had failed because of cost.[42] To build the better houses in the towns there were carpenters, glaziers and stonecutters. The King family had been granted the right to hold a market in Boyle on eight days in the year[43] and, to support the trade coming in, there were inns, butchers, carmen, dealers, merchants, millers, peddlers, smiths and a skinner. There was a gauger present to levy taxes on traders. Many of those living and working in the town also farmed land in the town parks. The combination of trading and agriculture revealed by the census shows a town that was prosperous and probably growing in size.[44] The greater gentry would, as we know bishop Synge did, depend on Dublin for wigs, gloves, shoemakers and tailoring. They would not have patronised the town for fashionable goods. But the lesser gentry and the more prosperous tradesmen and farmers in the locality used Boyle as a centre for conspicuous consumption, especially on market days.

In contrast, Roscommon, despite being an assize town, had little in the way of consumer goods. In the mid-seventeenth century the great Norman castle was semi-destroyed and by the mid-eighteenth century it was uninhabited. The loss of that centre of power partially accounts for the decline of Roscommon by the mid-eighteenth-century. The main cause was that the absentee earls of Essex owned the town and much local land. They also drew income from town tolls. None of this money was used to develop the town. Even in 1835, there was no resident magistrate or municipal officer, no watch, and no lights. This was attributed to this lack of investment by the landlord.[45] In Roscommon, there were fewer tradesmen selling the goods that were desired by those wishing to be up to date. There was one wigmaker and a few tailors but there were no shoemakers, only broguemakers, and there was only one inn. Despite its judicial importance, the town's population was much smaller than that of Boyle, and a lower proportion (18.41 per cent) were Protestant.

Away from churches and labour, the census throws light on rural leisure. There were no bookshops, but pedlars would have sold chapbooks.[46] Music was pervasive. Fourteen parishes have pipers, and two of them have two pipers.[47] Two parishes also have fiddlers, another a dancing master and another a music master. These entertainers, together with the enormous numbers of alehouses and inns, show that, out of season and in the dark evenings, music was an essential accompaniment to spare time.[48]

It is not known whether Edward Synge took the census any further, except to cite it as he did when he talked to Edward Willes in 1761. He may well have used its data in speeches in the House of Lords since, like his father before him, he was anxious to convert Roman Catholics by education and reasoned persuasion. However, conversion by education would have been an insuperable task for the clergy of Elphin.

Bishop Synge's census is a document of major importance. It provides an insight into life in a lesser-known part of Ireland. With its concentration on people, their religion, their occupations, their families and their households, it will help all those who want to understand the makeup of eighteenth-century rural Ireland.

Marie-Louise Legg
London, May 2004

NOTES

1. National Archives of Ireland (henceforth N.A.I.), MS 2466.

2. Edward Synge (1691-1762) was born in Inishannon, County Cork, the eldest son of Edward Synge (1665-1742), archbishop of Tuam. He entered TCD in 1706 and took BA in 1709. He was briefly a Fellow of the College. He was ordained and became vicar of St Audoen's, Dublin and in 1727 of St Werburgh's, Dublin. After being chancellor of St Patrick's from 1726-30, he was installed as bishop of Clonfert in 1730 and translated to Cloyne in 1732. He went to the diocese of Ferns and Leighlin in 1734 and was translated to Elphin in 1740. He served on the Linen Board and was a governor of Dr Steevens' Hospital. He died in Dublin in 1762 and was buried in St. Patrick's Cathedral.

3. *Irish House of Lords Journal*, iii, (Dublin, 1779), pp. 169, 486.

4. Marie-Louise Legg (ed.), *The Synge Letters: Roscommon to Dublin, 1746-1752* (Dublin, 1996).

5. James Kelly (ed.), *The Letters of Lord Chief Baron Willes to Lord Warwick 1757-1762,* (Aberystwyth1990), pp.93-4.

6. Charles Varlo [Varley], *Schemes offered for the Perusal and Consideration of the Legislature* (London, 1775), pp.176-7.

7. The heads of a bill were discussed by the Privy Council in March 1749 and approved (National Archives Public Record Office, Privy Council Registers (henceforth N.A., P.R.O) PC2/101 ff 480,490). The act (*An Act for amending continuing and making more effectual the several Acts now in force in this Kingdom for the more easy recovery of Tythes and other Ecclesiastical dues of small value and also for the more easy providing and maintenance for Parish Clerks*) was 23 Geo II, c.xii. I am grateful to Dr. T.C. Barnard his assistance on this point.

8. A possible reason for a separate column for children over 14 might have been due to the passing of an act which provided that the children of any barrister, six-clerk, attorney, or solicitor who married a Roman Catholic woman and who educated his children under 14 as Roman Catholics should be deemed to be a Roman Catholic and barred from practising his profession. (*An Act for the Amendment of the Law in relation to Popish Solicitors; and for remedying other Mischief in relation to the Practioners in the several Courts of Law and Equity,* 7 Geo.II, c.v).

9. The enumerator for the parishes of Kiltrustan and Bumlin squeezed in extra notes on those named. A couple were 'newly marrid'; another couple had 'run away' and a man had 'gon to the City of Galway'. Widow Hodson was said to be 100 years old (Census ff.75, 76, 83.).

10. Synge told Willes that the census had been conducted by his churchwardens. The 1766 census was collected by Church of Ireland ministers, parish constables and tithe-proctors (*Willes Letters,* p.95; David Dickson, Cormac Ó Gráda and S. Daultrey, 'Hearth Tax, Household size and Irish population change 1672-1821', *R.I.A. Proc.,* 82C, (1982), p.146).

11. For problems of census enumerators' transcription see Dickson, Ó Gráda, Daultrey, op.cit., p.145.

12. Dickson, Ó Gráda, Daultrey, op.cit., p. 148.

13. Paupers were those whose house and land were worth less than 8 shillings per annum and whose personal property was worth less than £4. Widows were exempted on presenting a certificate. There was a barrack master in Sligo town but no details of soldiers stationed there (Dickson, Ó Gráda, Daultrey, op.cit., pp., 138-141; Census, f.401).

14. The parish of Ballynakill was divided between County Roscommon, County Galway and County Sligo. The detached part in County Sligo was about 40 miles distant from the rest.

15. Forms that were sent to Synge in Kevin Street, Dublin were for the parishes of Killyon and Termonbarry.

16. Thomas Palmer prebendary of Termonbarry lived at Glanmore between Ballymahon and Keenagh, County Longford (*Synge Letters*, p.7).

17. The Rev.William Harrison of Strokestown was drowned crossing a deep ford in November 1740 (N.L.I., Lodge's Obituaries of the Clergy of Ireland taken from Armagh Library, MS 2678/13).

18. See Appendix I. These figures must be considered as approximate. Parish and townland boundaries tended to be fluid until boundaries were fixed by the Ordnance Survey in the nineteenth century. The 1851 census boundaries used here may well not match those of 1749. Many of the eighteenth-century townlands have not survived or may have been renamed (Brian Gurrin, *Pre-census Sources for Irish Demography* (Dublin, 2002) p.24).

19. Parish clerks were appointed by the incumbent and had to assist in the performance of religious services; vestry clerks were elected by the parish (W.A. Holdsworth, *The Handy Book of Parish Law*, (1995 reprint of original edition London, 1859) p. 19) (henceforth Holdsworth).

20. Paul Connell, Denis A. Cronin and Brian Ó Dálaigh (eds.), 'Introduction' to *Irish Townlands: Studies in Local History* (Dublin 1998), p.10.

21. Agricultural, Building, Dealing, Domestic Service, Industrial, Mining, Manufacturing, Professional and Public, Transport, Paupers. (L.A. Clarkson, E. Margaret Crawford, M.A. Litvack (eds.), *Occupations of Ireland 1841 vol IV Connaught* (Queen's University Belfast, 1995)).

22. Robert Howard to Hugh Howard, 18 July 1730 (N.L.I., Wicklow Papers PC 227).

23. Charles Varley, *A New System of Husbandry* (York, 1770).

24. *Willes Letters*, p.96.

25. Estate surveys have frequent references to poor land which could be reclaimed because there is limestone 'on the spot' (N.L.I., Survey of lands owned by Rt. Hon. Joshua Cooper, 1788, MS 21 F 2/9).

26. Varley, *A New System of Husbandry*, ii, 30-1.

27. *Willes Letters*, p.96.

28. Varley, *New System of Husbandry,* iii, 210-12.

29. Robert Howard to Hugh Howard, 18 July 1730 (N.L.I., Wicklow Papers PC 227); John Irwin to Lord Palmerston, 30 January 1738 (Southampton University, Hartley Library, Broadlands Papers, MS BR143/37).

30. The seventeenth-century house was destroyed by fire (Anthony King-Harman, *Kings of King House* (Bedford 1996), p.16).

31. Weld attributes much of this misery to the middleman, to the convention of short leases and, in the case of Roscommon, to the absentee earl of Essex who spent nothing on the town. (See below p.xix). (Isaac Weld, *Statistical Survey of the County of Roscommon* (Dublin 1832), pp.188, 196, 198, 397, 400 (hereafter cited as Weld, *Roscommon*)).

32. *Synge Letters*, p.xvii.

33. N. L. I., Pakenham Mahon Papers, MS 16 M 14-16; N.L.I., King Papers, MS 16 F 9; N.L.I., Mountrath Papers, MS 2793; N.L.I., Cooper Papers, MS 21 F 2; N.L.I., Wynne Papers, MS 750; N.L.I., Crofton Papers, MS 21 F 23 (1-16); Southampton University, Broadlands Papers.

34. Robert E. Ward, John F. Wrynn, and Catherine Coogan Ward (eds.), *Letters of Charles O'Conor of Belanagare: A Catholic Voice in Eighteenth-Century Ireland* (Washington, D.C. 1988); Francis Beirne (ed.), *The Diocese of Elphin: People, Places and Pilgrimages* (Blackrock, 2000); Hugh Fenning, 'The Diocese of Elphin 1747-1801', *Collectanea Hibernica*, 36, 37, (1994-5), pp.159-73, and 'Clergy Lists of Elphin 1731-1818', *Collectanea Hibernica* 38, (1996), pp. 145-55.

35. The gentry were Daniel O'Conor of Clonalis, Michael O'Connor of Twomona (Timoney), and Denis O'Conor of Belanagare. The shopkeepers were Roger O'Connor of Ballykagher, Roger O'Connor of Roscommon; Thadeus O'Flyn of Castlerea merchant, Hugh O'Hanly of Roscommon,distiller, and Charles O'Connor of Ballaghbuy, Terence McDermott of Ballyglass, John McDermott of Highlake, Richard Plunkett of Lackane and Daniel O'Hanly of Kilglass, farmers (Fenning, 'Diocese of Elphin', op.cit., pp.163-4).

36. D. Dickson, 'Catholics and Trade in Eighteenth-Century Ireland: an Old Debate Revisited 'in T.P Power and Kevin Whelan (eds.), *Endurance and Emergence: Catholics in Ireland in the Eighteenth-Century* (Dublin, 1990), pp.87-9.

37. A gaoler is in charge of the gaol; the turnkey is his subordinate and is in charge of the keys of the prisoners' cells.

38. The exceptions were boatmen in Sligo. Boatmen were normally customs officers, but in this case this may not have been so.

39. For a discussion of the relationship between officers and crew in the eighteenth-century navy, see N.A.M. Rodger, *The Wooden World: an anatomy of the Georgian Navy* (London 1988), p.119.

40. Dickson, 'Catholics and Trade...', p.89.

41. Dickson, 'Catholics and Trade...', pp. 89, 91.

42. Robert Stephenson, *The Reports and Observations made to the ... Trustees of the Linen Manufacture for the years 1760 and 1761....* (Dublin, 1762), p.62.

43. *Report of the Commissioners appointed to inquire into the state of fairs and markets in Ireland* HC 1852-3 (1674) XLI.74. (Hereafter cited as *Report ... fairs and markets*).

44. In 1749, the census has 258 households in Boyle; in 1830, there were 497 houses in the town (Weld, *Roscommon*, pp. 189-90).

45. *Reports from Commissioners on Municipal Corporations in Ireland* HC 1835, xxvii, 415-6.

46 Niall Ó Ciosáin, *Print and Popular Culture in Ireland 1750-1850* (Basingstoke, 1997), pp. 59-60.

47. A piper could also be used as a town crier. In 1743, Charles O'Hara paid a piper $6^{1}/_{2}$d to proclaim a lost horse (N.L.I., O'Hara Papers, MS 36,324/2).

48. In 1779, Arthur Young observed that dancing was so universal that there were 'everywhere itinerant dancing-masters to whom the cottars pay sixpence a quarter for teaching their families' (A.W. Hutton, (ed.), *Arthur Young's Tour of Ireland (1776-1779)* (2 vols, London, 1892), ii, 147).

49. *General Alphabetical Index to the Townlands and Towns, Parishes and Baronies of Ireland* (Dublin, 1861 reprinted Baltimore, 2000) (Hereafter cited as *General Alphabetical Index*).

50. In the manuscript he instructed the binder that 'The particulars [are] to be plac'd in the same order in the Book in which they lye in this paper' (Census, f. 365).

51. It is listed in Joshua Cooper's 1762 catalogue of Synge's books and manuscripts (Farmleigh House, Castleknock, County Dublin).

EDITORIAL NOTE

In transferring the census to a data base, every effort has been made to record the entries as they appear in the manuscript. Except for the text itself, the spelling of parish and townland names follow that used in the 1851 census. An introductory profile has been written of each parish, giving information on its physical geography, its Church of Ireland incumbent and its occupations. This is presented in italics at the beginning of each parish entry.

The manuscript census has 447 pages, bound in stamped reverse calf. The text was ordered by Synge himself.[50] The order starts with his own parish of Elphin and ends with Ahamlish, County Sligo, the most northerly parish in the diocese. There are 24 pages devoted to parish totals, either singly or in groups. These totals were the only statistics abstracted from the census.

The manuscript of the census did not share the fate of that of many other early censuses. It was a private document, and it remained in private possession for many years after its compilation. After Synge's death in 1762, the volume went with his library to Joshua Cooper of Markree, County Sligo who married Synge's only surviving child Alicia in 1758.[51] The manuscript was in Markree Castle library in 1913 when the books were rearranged by Bryan Cooper. It was later sold to S. Fenning, the Dublin bookseller who in turn sold it to the Public Record Office of Ireland in 1939.

We are very grateful to David Craig, the Director of the National Archives, and to his staff for their assistance in preparing this edition and for permitting access to the original manuscript, which is not available to the public.

The data text of this Census can be accessed electronically at www.irishorigins.com, the website run by Eneclann in partnership with origins.net, on a subscription basis.

AN EXAMINATION OF THE 1749
CENSUS OF THE DIOCESE OF ELPHIN

The loss of Irish census and census-substitute materials stored in the PRO in 1922 has presented substantial challenges for Irish demographic historians as the destruction has meant that relatively little early demographic material remains extant. Even with the commencement of decennial statutory censuses in the early part of the nineteenth century the situation is hardly better as few enumerators' schedules have survived. In the vast majority of cases all that remain today of the pre-1901 censuses are the published returns to parliament. The situation with census-substitute material for the period prior to the commencement of the statutory census series is worse as surviving census-substitute material is both rare and typically incomplete. Aside from a handful of tax rolls and summaries and the occasional attempt at a census, usually aimed at determining the success or otherwise of official attempts to contain the growth of popery, there is little material of any consequence available to the demographer studying pre-Union Irish population trends and levels.[1]

In England parish registers have proven to be a fruitful source for the generation of population back-projection estimates but such records are rarely suitable for use in the Irish context.[2] In the case of the records of the Church of Ireland, the available registers usually provide information on communities which were numerically small outside of Ulster and the environs of Dublin. Furthermore, following the disestablishment of the Church of Ireland, legislation was introduced defining parish registers as public records, which ensured their availability to the public.[3] As a result many of the registers were lodged in the PRO in the decades following disestablishment where they eventually perished in 1922. Registers of other denominations – Presbyterian registers for parts of northern and eastern Ulster and Catholic registers for most of the country outside of Dublin and parts of Ulster – notionally more appropriate tools for demographic analysis in the Irish context, are equally unsuitable for such analysis because the records, with some few exceptions, seldom commence prior to 1800.[4] Although some stoic Irish historians have endeavoured to extrapolate demographic trends from various parish registers, these efforts have been sporadic and usually centred on Ulster.[5]

Unlike England where, at least until the religious-worship 'census' of 1851,[6] counting the people served economic and social purposes, in Ireland from the seventeenth century onwards counting the people was strongly linked with the religious question. In the aftermath of the Williamite victory, penal legislation was passed that aimed to make membership of the Established Church economically and socially advantageous by imposing disabilities on Catholics. Questions concerning the numerical strength of Catholicism in the country exercised the minds of many in positions of power and thus prompted a variety of attempts – official and unofficial – to determine religious trends during the seventeenth and eighteenth centuries.

Conducting a census was both time consuming and expensive, and in most cases these early censuses were held as an adjunct to standard official enquiries. The typical religious census was conducted by instructing hearth-tax and poll-tax collectors to include religious estimates of the tax-paying population in the abstracts that they returned to the exchequer. It is known that national ethnic or religious enumerations were conducted in Ireland in 1660, 1732, 1764-5 and 1766. All of these censuses were conducted using tax collectors as enumerators, with the exception of the 1766 inquiry which was implemented by the Church of Ireland clergymen.

Aside from these national inquiries small-scale, local censuses were also occasionally taken. As with the national enumerations these returns could be compiled by tax-collecting officials, but it was more typical for them to be made by local Church of Ireland clergy. The best of these local surveys is the census of the diocese of Elphin held in 1749, on the instruction of Bishop Edward Synge. This census is a formidable example of early modern enumeration and was the most comprehensive conducted in Ireland during the eighteenth century. The census has been little studied to date, which is surprising because the sheer wealth of information that can be garnered from this census is immense. Its importance is further reinforced because the geographic area covered by the census – an extensive part of eastern Connaught – corresponds with a part of the country for which there is a paucity of pre-nineteenth century demographic material. The census facilitates a minute inquiry into the lives of the inhabitants and the identification of key demographic details which illuminate the shade of mid-eighteenth-century Elphin.

As with all eighteenth-century population estimates, some areas were better enumerated than others and the parishes of Elphin and Ogulla, for instance, seem to have been carefully enumerated – as one would expect, being the home parishes of the bishop. It seems reasonable also to presume that the degree of accuracy with which each parish was enumerated was influenced by various factors including, for instance, the quality of the roads in the parish, the size of the parish, the enthusiasm of the enumerating official, the remuneration available to the enumerating official, the prevailing weather at the time the census was conducted, the proportionate size of the Protestant population and the relationship between the various denominational groups and between the local inhabitants and the local landlords. As there is little surviving documented evidence available to clarify these unknowns, any estimate of the accuracy of the parish returns can be little more that speculative.

Nonetheless, it is clear from the data that at the time the census was conducted the diocese of Elphin was overwhelmingly Catholic. Only four religions, Catholic, Church of Ireland, Presbyterian and Quaker, are recorded in the census and unsurprisingly Catholics were significantly the most numerous denominational group, comprising 89.7 per cent of the 16,841 recorded householders. Among the Protestant religions, the Church of Ireland was denominationally dominant, comprising 96 per cent of the 1,742 Protestant households. Presbyterian householders are only recorded in five parishes, all of which are located in north County Roscommon. It is not clear if the enumerators were requested to record the specific Protestant religions in their returns and if they were not this would have inflated the Protestant (Church of Ireland) count to the detriment of Presbyterians and other Protestant denominations. Table 1 summarises the religion of the householders in each parish in the diocese:

Table 1 - Religion of households per parish in the diocese of Elphin, 1749.

Parish	Presbyterian	Church of Ireland	Catholic	Quaker	Total	% Prot.	% Cath.
Aghanagh		16	122		138	11.6	88.4
Ahamlish		15	266		281	5.3	94.7
Ahascragh		18	321		339	5.3	94.7
Ardcarn		44	317		361	12.2	87.8
Athleague		23	248		271	8.5	91.5
Athlone		81	286		367	22.1	77.9
Aughrim		26	275		301	8.6	91.4
Ballintober		14	192		206	6.8	93.2
Ballynakill		12	170		182	6.6	93.4
Ballysumaghan		14	70		84	16.7	83.3
Baslick		2	325		327	0.6	99.4
Boyle	43	67	390		500	22.0	78.0
Bumlin		82	296		378	21.7	78.3
Cam		5	303		308	1.6	98.4
Clooncraff		4	118		122	3.3	96.7
Cloonfinlough		9	321		330	2.7	97.3
Cloontuskert		5	159		164	3.0	97.0
Cloonygormican		10	267		277	3.6	96.4
Creeve		2	60		62	3.2	96.8
Drumatemple		7	130		137	5.1	94.9
Drumcliff		105	467		572	18.4	81.6
Drumcolumb		32	123		155	20.6	79.4
Dunamon		6	70		76	7.9	92.1
Dysart			62		62	0.0	100.0
Elphin		36	365		401	9.0	91.0
Estersnow	1	13	108		122	11.5	88.5
Fuerty		26	292		318	8.2	91.8

Table 1 (Continued) - Religion of households per parish in the diocese of Elphin, 1749.

Parish	Presbyterian	Church of Ireland	Catholic	Quaker	Total	% Prot.	% Cath.
Kilbegnet		6	284		290	2.1	97.9
Kilbride		22	497		519	4.2	95.8
Kilbryan	11		60		71	15.5	84.5
Kilcolagh		1	69		70	1.4	98.6
Kilcooley		3	137		140	2.1	97.9
Kilcorkery		1	98		99	1.0	99.0
Kilcroan		6	90		96	6.3	93.7
Kilgefin		5	278		283	1.8	98.2
Kilglass		12	476		488	2.5	97.5
Kilkeevin		62	485		547	11.3	88.7
Killadoon		8	106		114	7.0	93.0
Killeroran			69		69	0.0	100.0
Killian			183		183	0.0	100.0
Killinvoy		13	155	4	172	9.9	90.1
Killosolan		13	134		147	8.8	91.2
Killukin (Boyle)		29	145		174	16.7	83.3
Killukin (Roscommon)		2	143		145	1.4	98.6
Kilmacallan		40	211		251	15.9	84.1
Kilmactranny		12	220		232	5.2	94.8
Kilmacumsy			148		148	0.0	100.0
Kilmeane		23	99		122	18.9	81.1
Kilmore		30	247		277	10.8	89.2
Kilnamanagh	8		89		97	8.2	91.8
Kilross		27	89		116	23.3	76.7
Kilteevan		7	139		146	4.8	95.2
Kiltoom		8	156		164	4.9	95.1
Kiltrustan		22	175		197	11.2	88.8
Kilummod		7	100		107	6.5	93.5
Lissonuffy		15	299		314	4.8	95.2
Ogulla		1	184		185	0.5	99.5
Oran		3	111		114	2.6	97.4
Rahara		4	94		98	4.1	95.9
Roscommon		73	470		543	13.4	86.6
Shancough		8	62		70	11.4	88.6
Shankill		2	115		117	1.7	98.3
Sligo		416	882		1,298	32.0	68.0
St John's		17	202		219	7.8	92.2
Taghboy		4	168		172	2.3	97.7
Termonbarry		4	154		158	2.5	97.5
Tawnagh		11	76		87	12.6	87.4
Tibohine	4	30	690		724	4.7	95.3
Tisrara		19	241		260	7.3	92.7
Tumna		31	146		177	17.5	82.5
Total	**67**	**1,671**	**15,099**	**4**	**16,841**	**10.3**	**89.6**

The numerical dominance of Catholics in the diocese is clear from table 1. The Protestant proportion of the total number of householders in each parish only exceeded 20 per cent in six parishes and in only one parish, Sligo, did this proportion exceed 30 per cent. Five of these six parishes are in the northern part of the diocese (three are in County Sligo), the exception being the largely urban parish of Athlone in the far south.[7] In common with other eighteenth-century censuses, the clustering of Protestants in urban areas is evident in this census, with the parishes containing the principal urban areas having substantial Protestant populations. Sligo in particular had a very significant Protestant community, comprising nearly half of all householders inhabiting the town.

Table 2 - Householders in the principal urban areas in the diocese of Elphin, 1749.

Parish	Householders				% Prot.	% Cath.
	Presbyterian	Church of Ire	Catholic	Total		
Athlone		73	176	249	29.3	70.7
Boyle	26	57	175	258	32.2	67.8
Castlereagh		42	134	176	23.9	76.1
Elphin		15	57	72	20.8	79.2
Roscommon		44	195	239	18.4	81.6
Sligo		322	354	676	47.6	52.4
Total	**26**	**600**	**1,214**	**1,840**	**34.0**	**66.0**

Although the census reported a diocese in which 90 per cent of the householders were Catholics it should be noted that a census organised by a bishop of the Established Church may have tended to underestimate the Catholic proportion of the population. At this time Catholics were suspicious of the motives of zealous Protestant officials arriving at their doors seeking information.[8] Questions concerning the number of children in their family, the occupation of the householder or the presence of servants in the house could all be seen by suspicious minds as invasive interferences, a prelude to increased taxation, or worse.[9] It is not improbable, therefore, that the numerical dominance of Catholics in the area was even greater than that reported in this census.

As noted above, in 1732, some years previous to Synge's census, the hearth-tax collectors, on the instigation of the Irish House of Lords, inquired into the denominational makeup of the inhabitants in their walks. If inquiries by officials associated with the Established Church were unwelcome in the mid-eighteenth century, inquiries by tax-officials were viewed with even more suspicion and the data from eighteenth century Irish tax-based censuses typically underestimate the true Catholic proportion of the population and grossly underestimate the population as a whole. If, however, the 1732 census is compared with Synge's census it is surprising to find that the denominational proportions reported by both censuses are quite similar. The 1732 census enumerated households rather than population and table 3 compares the comparable data for these two censuses for a number of baronies.

It should be noted that the 1732 census was barony-based whereas Synge's enumeration was diocese-based. Thus some of the baronial data in table 3 are not strictly comparable as the equivalent data are not provided in the 1749 census in respect of parishes outside the diocese of Elphin. There is, for example, no 1749 data for the parish of Kilronan in Boyle barony as that parish is in Ardagh diocese. However despite the omission of some few parishes from the 1749 figures an unmistakeable pattern is evident. The religious data reported by Synge's census closely match the data reported in the early 1730s by the hearth-tax collectors, and in some cases the later census reports a higher Protestant proportion of the population than that recorded in the 1732 enumeration. As eighteenth-century tax-based censuses typically overestimated the Protestant population this must raise some concerns about the accuracy of the Elphin census.

Table 3 – Comparison of the aggregate household data in the 1732 and 1749 censuses.

Barony	1732 census				1749 census			
	Prot.	Cath.	% Prot.	% Cath.	Prot.	Cath.	% Prot.	% Cath.
Killian	25	579	4.1	95.9.	3	315	0.9	99.1
Roscommon	131	1,472	8.2	91.8	176	2,157	7.6	92.4
Ballintober	173	1,903	8.3	91.7	158	2,419	6.1	93.9
Boyle	196	1,480	11.7	88.3	246	1,266	16.3	83.7
Ballymoe (Rosc.)	23	303	7.1	92.9	23	485	4.6	95.4
Athlone total	244	2,667	8.4	91.6	224	2,285	8.9	91.1
Carbury	401	1,579	20.3	79.7	536	1,615	24.9	75.1
Tirerrill	158	967	14.0	86.0	168	1,080	13.5	86.5
Total	**1,351**	**10,950**	**11.0**	**89.0**	**1,534**	**11,622**	**11.7**	**88.3**

Source (1732 data): An abstract of the number of Protestant and Popish familys as returned to the hearth money office anno 1732 (Lambeth Palace Library, MS 1742, ff 47v-48).

Of course the fact that a householder was of a particular religion did not necessarily mean that all the residents in the house followed that same religion. In the first instance, while inter-church marriages were uncommon in the diocese they were not unknown and in any inter-church household the religion of some or all of the children may have differed from that of the householder. Furthermore, Protestant households, by dint of their greater proportional wealth, exhibited a greater tendency to employ servants. While it seems likely that Protestant households preferred to employ Protestant servants in the main, the numerical weakness of the Protestant population in the area in the mid-eighteenth century meant that there were insufficient numbers of Protestants available for service. This greater tendency for Protestant households to contain Catholics than for Catholic households to contain Protestants indicates that the Protestant position was even weaker than the household count presented in table 1 suggests.

Table 4 - Parish population counts, per denomination, in the diocese of Elphin, 1749.

Parish	Protestant houses				Catholic houses				Total			
	Prot.	Cath.	Tot.	HF	Prot.	Cath.	Total	HF	Prot.	Cath.	Total	HF
Aghanagh	55	18	73	4.56	7	510	517	4.24	62	528	590	4.28
Ahascragh	72	34	106	5.89	0	1,355	1,355	4.22	72	1,389	1,461	4.31
Aughrim	124	44	168	6.46	12	1,168	1,180	4.29	136	1,212	1,348	4.48
Ahamlish	57	27	84	5.60	2	1,067	1,069	4.02	59	1,094	1,153	4.10
Ardcarn	182	72	254	5.77	8	1,333	1,341	4.23	190	1,405	1,595	4.42
Athleague	95	24	119	5.17	9	895	904	3.65	104	919	1,023	3.77
Athlone	367	62	429	5.30	23	1,165	1,188	4.15	390	1,227	1,617	4.41
Ballintober	71	33	104	7.43	15	845	860	4.48	86	878	964	4.68
Ballynakill	62	22	84	7.00	3	857	860	5.06	65	879	944	5.19
Ballysumaghan	58	11	69	4.93	0	284	284	4.06	58	295	353	4.20
Baslik	17	8	25	12.50	6	1,507	1,513	4.66	23	1,515	1,538	4.70
Boyle	521	145	666	9.94	58	1,632	1,690	4.33	579	1,777	2,356	4.71
Bumlin	298	88	386	4.71	45	1,152	1,197	4.04	343	1,240	1,583	4.19
Cam	18	13	31	6.20	0	1,309	1,309	4.32	18	1,322	1,340	4.35
Clooncraff	23	18	41	10.25	3	511	514	4.36	26	529	555	4.55
Cloonfinlough	39	36	75	8.33	1	1,316	1,317	4.10	40	1,352	1,392	4.22
Cloontuskert	11	17	28	5.60	0	628	628	3.95	11	645	656	4.00
Cloonygormican	34	31	65	6.50	9	1,481	1,490	5.58	43	1,512	1,555	5.61
Creeve	8	2	10	5.00	0	244	244	4.07	8	246	254	4.10
Drumatemple	43	23	66	9.43	0	638	638	4.91	43	661	704	5.14
Drumcliff	454	141	595	5.67	30	1,987	2,017	4.32	484	2,128	2,612	4.57
Drumcolumb	175	56	231	7.22	9	535	544	4.42	184	591	775	5.00
Dunamon	30	8	38	6.33	1	347	348	4.97	31	355	386	5.08
Dysart	0	0	0	NA	1	269	270	4.35	1	269	270	4.35
Elphin	137	57	194	5.39	26	1,880	1,906	5.22	163	1,937	2,100	5.24
Estersnow	81	8	89	6.85	8	473	481	4.45	89	481	570	4.67

Table 4 (Continued) - Parish population counts, per denomination, in the diocese of Elphin, 1749.

Parish	Protestant houses				Catholic houses				Total			
	Prot.	Cath.	Tot.	HF	Prot.	Cath.	Total	HF	Prot.	Cath.	Total	HF
Fuerty	109	71	180	6.92	9	1,174	1,183	4.05	118	1,245	1,363	4.29
Kilbegnet	25	5	30	5.00	14	1,098	1,112	3.92	39	1,103	1,142	3.94
Kilbride	109	80	189	8.59	3	2,388	2,391	4.81	112	2,468	2,580	4.97
Kilbryan	45	5	50	NA	0	234	234	3.90	45	239	284	4.00
Kilcolagh	5	3	8	8.00	0	293	293	4.25	5	296	301	4.30
Kilcooley	10	11	21	7.00	0	741	741	5.41	10	752	762	5.44
Kilcorkery	1	7	8	8.00	0	606	606	6.18	1	613	614	6.20
Kilcroan	20	17	37	6.17	6	413	419	4.66	26	430	456	4.75
Kilgefin	12	14	26	5.20	0	1,049	1,049	3.77	12	1,063	1,075	3.80
Kilglass	50	28	78	6.50	6	2,050	2,056	4.32	56	2,078	2,134	4.37
Kilkeevin	221	131	352	5.68	59	2,011	2,070	4.27	280	2,142	2,422	4.43
Killadoon	36	2	38	4.75	1	408	409	3.86	37	410	447	3.92
Killinvoy	71	35	106	8.15	7	710	717	4.63	78	745	823	4.90
Killeroran	0	0	0	NA	0	274	274	3.97	0	274	274	3.97
Killian	0	0	0	NA	2	969	971	5.31	2	969	971	5.31
Kilmeane	107	49	156	6.78	0	545	545	5.51	107	594	701	5.75
Killosolan	47	24	71	5.46	1	601	602	4.49	48	625	673	4.58
Killukin - Boyle	132	41	173	5.97	4	724	728	5.02	136	765	901	5.18
Killukin - Rosc.	7	5	12	6.00	6	783	789	5.52	13	788	801	5.52
Kilmacallan	186	53	239	5.98	2	912	914	4.33	188	965	1,153	4.59
Kilmactranny	43	21	64	5.33	2	825	827	3.76	45	846	891	3.84
Kilmacumsy	0	0	0	NA	0	972	972	6.57	0	972	972	6.57
Kilmore	135	51	186	6.20	25	1,083	1,108	4.49	160	1,134	1,294	4.67
Kilnamanagh	37	16	53	NA	2	388	390	4.38	39	404	443	4.57
Kilross	120	39	159	5.89	3	347	350	3.93	123	386	509	4.39
Kilteevan	20	18	38	5.43	2	590	592	4.26	22	608	630	4.32
Kiltoom	37	27	64	8.00	2	665	667	4.28	39	692	731	4.46
Kiltrustan	82	32	114	5.18	3	732	735	4.20	85	764	849	4.31
Kilummod	47	9	56	8.00	3	446	449	4.49	50	455	505	4.72
Lissonuffy	35	16	51	3.40	0	1,246	1,246	4.17	35	1,262	1,297	4.13
Ogulla	3	1	4	4.00	0	902	902	4.90	3	903	906	4.90
Oran	12	2	14	4.67	7	594	601	5.41	19	596	615	5.39
Rahara	19	7	26	6.50	0	483	483	5.14	19	490	509	5.19
Roscommon	298	109	407	5.58	33	2,057	2,090	4.45	331	2,166	2,497	4.60
Shancough	44	11	55	6.88	3	318	321	5.18	47	329	376	5.37
Shankill	13	6	19	9.50	15	650	665	5.78	28	656	684	5.85
Sligo	1,505	278	1,783	4.29	64	3,221	3,285	3.72	1,569	3,499	5,068	3.90
St John's	88	48	136	8.00	8	939	947	4.69	96	987	1,083	4.95
Taghboy	16	12	28	7.00	3	705	708	4.21	19	717	736	4.28
Tarmonbarry	18	10	28	7.00	12	743	755	4.90	30	753	783	4.96
Tawnagh	58	19	77	7.00	1	304	305	4.01	59	323	382	4.39
Tibohine	140	56	196	6.53	15	2,941	2,956	4.28	155	2,997	3,152	4.35
Tisrara	85	42	127	6.68	13	1,049	1,062	4.41	98	1,091	1,189	4.57
Tumna	154	44	198	6.39	7	607	614	4.21	161	651	812	4.59
Total	**7,234**	**2,453**	**9,687**	**5.80**	**619**	**66,178**	**66,797**	**4.42**	**7,853**	**68,631**	**76,484**	**4.54**

Note: HF columns show the mean houseful size in each parish – the total number of inhabitants divided by the total number of households.

As is shown in table 4, the total population of the diocese, as estimated by this census, was 76,484.[10] Of these 76,484 persons, 7,853 were Protestants (of one form or another) whilst the remaining inhabitants (68,631) were Catholics. Thus, by Synge's census, Protestants accounted for no more than 10.3 per cent of the total population of his diocese, with Catholics accounting for the remaining 89.7 per cent. Furthermore, the census recorded a total of 9,687 persons inhabiting the Protestant households. Of these, however, more than 25 per cent were Catholics (2,453 persons). In sharp contrast, the Catholic households contained 66,797 persons, but less than one per cent of this total - 619 persons - were Protestants.

In the 1970s, F.J. Carney, on analysing 1821 census material from five Irish counties, suggested that there are different measures for household-size which stem from the various definitions of the household. A household, for instance, can be defined on the basis of 'shared residence, shared activities, or blood and marriage ties'. Bearing this in mind, Carney suggested that there were three appropriate measures of the size of co-resident domestic groups which can be used to examine typical census-type data.[11] These three measures of the size of co-resident domestic groups are:

- houseful size (the total number of all inhabitants in a house)
- household size (all the members of a household directly or indirectly related plus their servants)
- family size (all the members of a household related by blood or marriage).

In large measure the Elphin data is sufficiently good to allow for the use of some of these variables to determine the size of co-resident domestic groups in mid-eighteenth-century east Connaught. On the basis of the definitions presented above, the mean houseful size must either equal or exceed both the mean family size and the mean household size and the mean household size must equal or exceed the mean family size. Carney states that, on average, family size was always 90 per cent of the household within a narrow range and he points out that compared with English households, Irish households were larger. For the data sample examined by Carney he found the following:

Table 5- Mean houseful, mean household and mean family size for parts of five Irish counties, 1821.

Co-resident domestic group	Mean size (persons)	Range (persons)	Galway (N = 506)
Mean houseful size	5.68	5.45 – 5.86	5.86
Mean household size	5.45	5.26 – 5.60	5.60
Mean family size	5.05	4.86 – 5.25	5.25

Note: Galway data are shown because of its proximity to Elphin (Carney, 'Aspects of pre-famine Irish household size', p. 36).

For convenience, and because there is probably some under-recording of lodgers and inmates, the houseful and family size definitions are the most appropriate measures of household size when considering the Elphin data. No significant benefit accrues from using the household size definition because its value differs only minutely from the houseful size value in most parishes in the diocese. Ultimately, Carney concluded that there was a positive correlation between the largest household and family sizes and higher socio-economic status. This was accounted for by the greater tendency of wealthy families to employ servants. As will be seen, this finding is borne out in the Elphin data, where relatively richer Protestants had significantly larger households than had Catholics.

In terms of houseful size, in Elphin in 1749 it is clear that Protestant households were substantially larger than were Catholic households. The mean houseful size for the entire diocese was 4.54, which is significantly lower than the 5.68 determined by Carney from the 1821 census (table 5).[12] However Catholic houseful size was only 4.42 – contrasting starkly with Carney's figures – whereas the comparable figure for Protestants households was 5.80.[13] It was stated earlier that the greater likelihood of Protestant households employing servants explained some of this houseful-size differential and this clear tendency is shown in table 6. In total, the census records 855 Protestant servants and 8,489 Catholic servants in the entire diocese. The 15,099 Catholic households were recorded as employing less then one servant for every two households – 220 Protestant and 6,537 Catholic servants – whereas the Protestant households employed a mean average of 1.5 servants per household. In addition, the 220 Protestant servants employed by Catholic households account for just 3 per cent of the total number of servants employed by Catholics but by contrast 75 per cent of the servants employed by Protestant households were Catholic.

Although table 6 does show the increased tendency for Protestant families to employ servants it is worthwhile remembering that an eighteenth-century understanding of whom constituted 'a servant' may not have been as precise as it is today. In fact, in early censuses and tax returns family members are sometimes recorded as being servants – particularly when it was suspected by the populace that the purpose of the inquiry was to identify possible revenue returns for future taxation purposes.[14]

Thus, the larger houseful size of Protestant households can be easily and logically accounted for. Interestingly, however, Protestant families also tended to be marginally larger than their Catholic equivalents. This is in keeping with the findings of most eighteenth-century religious censuses and inquiries although some of this difference may be explained by the propensity of Catholics to mislead the enumerators - another 'unknown' than cannot be accurately estimated in the case of this census. The typical family recorded in the census was small, and in no parish did the mean size of Catholic families exceed 5.

Table 6 - Employment of servants in the diocese of Elphin, 1749, per denominational group.

Households	Number of households	Prot. servants	Cath. servants	Total	Servants per house
Catholic	15,099	220	6,537	6,757	0.45
Protestant	1,671	627	1,899	2,526	1.51
Presbyterian	67	7	46	53	0.79
Quaker	4	1	7	8	2.00
Total	**16,841**	**855**	**8,489**	**9,344**	**0.55**

Table 7 – Mean family size per denominational group in diocese of Elphin, 1749.

Parish	Total number of family members (excluding servants)			Mean family size		
	Protestant	Catholic	Total	Prot.	Cath.	Total
Aghanagh	59	463	522	3.69	3.80	3.78
Ahascragh	74	1,319	1,393	4.11	4.11	4.11
Aughrim	115	1,042	1,157	4.42	3.79	3.84
Ahamlish	50	1,037	1,087	3.33	3.90	3.87
Ardcarn	180	1,193	1,373	4.09	3.76	3.80
Athleague	97	871	968	4.22	3.51	3.57
Athlone (St. Peters)	354	1,047	1,401	4.37	3.66	3.82
Ballintober	68	773	841	4.86	4.03	4.08
Ballynakill	55	758	813	4.58	4.46	4.47
Ballysumaghan	55	258	313	3.93	3.69	3.73
Baslick	22	1,373	1,395	11.00	4.22	4.27
Boyle	488	1,519	2,007	4.44	3.89	4.01
Bumlin	307	1,096	1,403	3.74	3.70	3.71
Cam	16	1,266	1,282	3.20	4.18	4.16
Clooncraff	22	450	472	5.50	3.81	3.87
Cloonfinlough	44	1,199	1,243	4.89	3.74	3.77
Cloontuskert	19	570	589	3.80	3.58	3.59
Cloonygormican	35	1,159	1,194	3.50	4.34	4.31
Creeve	8	230	238	4.00	3.83	3.84
Drumatemple	39	566	605	5.57	4.35	4.42
Drumcliff	461	1,894	2,355	4.39	4.06	4.12
Drumcolumb	175	488	663	5.47	3.97	4.28
Dunamon	28	323	351	4.67	4.61	4.62
Dysart	0	265	265	NA.	4.27	4.27
Elphin	123	1,503	1,626	3.42	4.12	4.05
Estersnow	72	461	533	5.14	4.27	4.37
Fuerty	122	1,136	1,258	4.69	3.89	3.96
Kilbegnet	25	1,077	1,102	4.17	3.79	3.80
Kilbride	112	2,065	2,177	5.09	4.15	4.19

Table 7 (Continued) – Mean family size per denominational group in diocese of Elphin, 1749.

Parish	Total number of family members (excluding servants)			Mean family size		
	Protestant	Catholic	Total	Prot.	Cath.	Total
Kilbryan	46	226	272	4.18	3.77	3.83
Kilcolagh	5	280	285	5.00	4.06	4.07
Kilcooley	9	649	658	3.00	4.74	4.70
Kilcorkery	4	431	435	4.00	4.40	4.39
Kilcroan	26	374	400	4.33	4.16	4.17
Kilgefin	20	965	985	4.00	3.47	3.48
Kilglass	48	2,004	2,052	4.00	4.21	4.20
Kilkeevin	246	1,838	2,084	3.97	3.79	3.81
Killadoon	36	366	402	4.50	3.45	3.53
Killinvoy	68	618	686	4.00	3.99	3.99
Killeroran	0	248	248	NA.	3.59	3.59
Killian	0	761	761	NA.	4.16	4.16
Kilmeane	93	441	534	4.04	4.45	4.38
Killosolan	53	575	628	4.08	4.29	4.27
Killukin – Boyle	133	654	787	4.59	4.51	4.52
Killukin – Rosc.	7	664	671	3.50	4.64	4.63
Kilmacallan	176	844	1,020	4.40	4.00	4.06
Kilmactranny	45	756	801	3.75	3.44	3.45
Kilmacumsy	0	720	720	NA.	4.86	4.86
Kilmore	131	979	1,110	4.37	3.96	4.01
Kilnamanagh	40	362	402	5.00	4.07	4.14
Kilross	116	326	442	4.30	3.66	3.81
Kilteevan	23	543	566	3.29	3.91	3.88
Kiltoom	47	632	679	5.88	4.05	4.14
Kiltrustan	90	666	756	4.09	3.81	3.84
Kilummod	35	391	426	5.00	3.91	3.98
Lissonuffy	49	1,174	1,223	3.27	3.93	3.89
Ogulla	3	719	722	3.00	3.91	3.90
Oran	10	494	504	3.33	4.45	4.42
Rahara	17	435	452	4.25	4.63	4.61
Roscommon	282	1,855	2,137	3.86	3.95	3.94
Shancough	43	277	320	5.38	4.47	4.57
Shankill	13	488	501	6.50	4.24	4.28
Sligo	1,423	3,093	4,516	3.42	3.51	3.48
St John's	81	872	953	4.76	4.32	4.35
Taghboy	16	664	680	4.00	3.95	3.95
Tarmonbarry	22	654	676	5.50	4.25	4.28
Tawnagh	50	284	334	4.55	3.74	3.84
Tibohine	139	2,746	2,885	4.09	3.98	3.98
Tisrara	87	989	1,076	4.58	4.10	4.14
Tumna	143	582	725	4.61	3.99	4.10
Total	**7,100**	**60,040**	**67,140**	**4.08**	**3.98**	**3.99**

Table 7 shows the mean family size per parish as indicated by the census data. For the purpose of this calculation it was presumed that families comprised all persons enumerated in the census except servants.[15] As can be seen, the substantial difference in houseful size between Catholic and Protestant families, as shown on table 4, is not similarly manifested in family-size figures, implying that the difference in houseful size between Catholic and Protestant families was almost exclusively caused by Protestant households employing more servants. The mean family size for both Protestant (4.08 persons) and Catholic (3.98 persons) families is lower than the 5.05 determined by Carney for the 1821 census (table 5). However, Carney's figures are for a period when the population of the country had been soaring for two generations and was approaching a zenith, which accounts for at least some of the difference.

Mirroring this near uniformity in the mean size of families between the two denominational groups is the similarity between the distribution of people per family in Catholic and Protestant families. The distribution of family-sizes for the diocese, shown in table 8, demonstrates that the median size of a family among both Protestant and Catholic households was 4. Among Protestant households more than half of all families had three, four or five members, while the corresponding proportion for Catholic families was 43 per cent. Large families were something of a rarity throughout the diocese – less so for Protestants than Catholics – with only 0.7 per cent of Protestant and 0.1 per cent of Catholic families having more than ten members. The two largest families, one Protestant and one Catholic, recorded in the census both had 15 members.

Table 8 - Distribution of family-sizes and household-sizes for the diocese of Elphin, 1749.

Size	Families			Housefuls		
	Protestant	Catholic	Total	Protestant	Catholic	Total
1	107	475	582	63	374	437
2	339	2,241	2,580	204	1,674	1,878
3	319	3,417	3,736	239	2,987	3,226
4	326	3,840	4,166	276	3,506	3,782
5	254	2,713	2,967	248	2,766	3,014
6	185	1,492	1,677	189	1,930	2,119
7	106	589	695	160	1,001	1,161
8	61	223	284	112	489	601
9	27	64	91	80	185	265
10	6	32	38	50	97	147
11	8	10	18	28	41	69
12	2	0	2	21	16	37
13	0	1	1	17	10	27
14	1	1	2	8	11	19
15	1	1	2	10	5	15
> 15	0	0	0	37	7	44

The distribution in size of the entire household (the houseful) is less uniform, as is to be expected given the distribution of servants amongst the denominational groups illustrated in table 6. Although the median houseful-size is 4 for both Catholic and Protestant households, the distribution of houseful size among Protestant households is skewed towards larger households relative to Catholic households. This is shown clearly in table 9. While 75 per cent of Catholic households were recorded as having less than six members the corresponding figure for Protestants was 59 per cent. At the other end of the scale, 14.5 per cent of Protestant households had more than 8 members but only 2 per cent of Catholic houses were of a similar, large size.

Table 9 - Distribution of family-size and household-size (houseful) among selected size groups.

Size	Families			% of the total for the denomination		Households			% of the total for the denomination	
	Prot.	Cath.	Total	Prot.	Cath.	Prot.	Cath.	Total	Prot.	Cath.
1 – 3	765	6,133	6,898	43.9	40.6	506	5,035	5,541	29.1	33.4
4 – 5	580	6,553	7,133	33.3	43.4	524	6,272	6,796	30.1	41.5
6 – 8	352	2,304	2,656	20.2	15.3	461	3,420	3,881	26.4	22.7
9 – 10	33	96	129	1.9	0.6	130	282	412	7.4	1.9
11 – 15	12	13	25	0.7	0.1	84	83	167	4.8	0.6
> 15	0	0	0	0.0	0.0	37	7	44	2.1	0.1
3 – 5	899	9,970	10,869	51.6	66.0	763	9,259	10,022	43.8	61.3

It was noted earlier that inter-church marriages were uncommon in the area at the time of the census. All denominations, but particularly the Protestant churches, baulked at the prospects of inter-church marriages because they feared losing members to other congregations. However, in an area such as Elphin where Protestants were so dramatically outnumbered by their Catholic contemporaries the difficulties facing Protestants in finding a marriage partner of their own church made inter-church marriages necessary. This was not as great a problem for Catholics. A summary of inter-church marriages in the census is shown in table 10.[16]

Table 10 – Inter-church marriages in the diocese of Elphin, 1749.

Householder's rel.	Inter-church marriages	No. of households	% of total in inter-church marriages
Presbyterian	6	67	9.0
Protestant	85	1,671	5.1
Quaker	0	4	0.0
Catholic	53	15,099	0.4
Total	**144**	**16,841**	**0.9**

Perhaps surprisingly, Presbyterians exhibited the greatest tendency to involve themselves in inter-church marriages, with almost 9 per cent of Presbyterian householders recorded in the census being married to Catholics. In fact, in all cases where Protestants, be they Presbyterians or Established Church, were involved in an inter-church marriage the other spouse was a Catholic. Nowhere in the census is there evidence that Presbyterians or Protestants had spouses of a Protestant denomination different to their own. This is surprising and is probably more a reflection of the quality of the data than a commentary on the contemporary state of inter-church marriage in the diocese.

The census data also suggests that Protestant churchmen were right to be concerned about the issue of inter-church marriage as many of the children in such unions were raised as Catholics (see table 11). The families of the 91 inter-church marriages involving Protestant (Established Church or Presbyterian) householders contained 128 protestant and 78 Catholic children. This meant that 38 per cent of the children in these inter-church families were raised in a faith other than that of the householder. A similar picture is evident when the religion of the families of the inter-church marriages with Catholic householders is analysed. In this case, the 53 Catholic families contained 81 Catholic (60 per cent) and 54 Protestant children.

Table 11 - The distribution of family members in inter-church marriages, Elphin diocese, 1749.

Parish	Protestant households — Inter-church marriages	Religion of children Prot.	Religion of children Cath.	Catholic households — Inter-church marriages	Religion of children Prot.	Religion of children Cath.	Total — Inter-church marriages	Religion of children Prot.	Religion of children Cath.
Ardcarn	8	10	2	2	0	4	10	10	6
Athleague	1	0	1	1	4	4	2	4	5
Aughrim	3	3	3	1	1	1	4	4	4
Ballintober	2	6	0	1	0	2	3	6	2
Boyle	6	6	10	7	14	11	13	20	21
Bumlin	11	13	8	10	2	17	21	15	25
Clooncraff	1	1	0	1	2	0	2	3	0
Cloonfinlough	3	8	4	0	0	0	3	8	4
Cloontuskert	4	6	4	0	0	0	4	6	4
Cloonygormican	5	9	0	1	0	0	6	9	0
Drumcliff	0	0	0	1	5	0	1	5	0
Dunamon	0	0	0	1	0	5	1	0	5
Elphin	1	2	0	2	2	0	3	4	0
Fuerty	8	17	13	4	2	5	12	19	18
Kilbegnet	0	0	0	1	0	2	1	0	2
Kilbryan	1	0	0	0	0	0	1	0	0
Kilcorkery	1	0	2	0	0	0	1	0	2
Kilcroan	3	5	6	0	0	0	3	5	6
Kilgefin	2	0	6	0	0	0	2	0	6
Kilglass	0	0	0	1	4	2	1	4	2
Kilkeevin	8	12	12	9	14	10	17	26	22
Killukin (Rosc.)	0	0	0	1	2	0	1	2	0
Kilmore	6	11	3	4	1	9	10	12	12
Kilnamanagh	2	0	0	1	1	0	3	1	0
Kiltoom	0	0	0	1	0	1	1	0	1
Sligo	11	12	1	2	0	3	13	12	4
Tarmonbarry	1	0	3	1	0	5	2	0	8
Tibohine	3	7	0	0	0	0	3	7	0
Total	**91**	**128**	**78**	**53**	**54**	**81**	**144**	**182**	**159**

It may be supposed that in the eighteenth century the religion of the children in inter-church marriages was either largely determined by the mother or else that males were raised in the religion of the father and females raised in the religion of the mother. Unfortunately the data in the census does not facilitate the easy verification of either of these hypotheses for the diocese of Elphin. In the case of the former proposition – that the religion of the mother played a major part in determining the religion in which the children were reared – one can only say that this does not seem to have been a general rule, as in a substantial proportion of the inter-church families the children were not raised to practice the religion of their mother. In the case of the latter hypothesis (that the religion in which the children were reared was determined by their sex), as the sex of children is not recorded in the census one cannot say for sure if the children's religions match those of either of the parents. However, the data suggests that only 8 of the 91 Protestant and 7 of the 53 Catholic lead inter-church marriages contained children of more than one religion. If the girls in an inter-church marriage were to be raised in the religion of their mother and the boys were to take the religion of their father then it would be expected that a far higher proportion of inter-church marriages would contain children with more than one religion. Thus, in all likelihood it seems as if the issue of the children's religion was a matter of choice for the individual families in these inter-denominational unions.

CONCLUSION

Following this 1749 census, the next censuses that aimed of to inquire into the religious makeup of the area were the national religious censuses ordered by the House of Lords in 1764 and 1766. Unfortunately the data for Elphin diocese collected during these censuses have been virtually totally lost.[17] After the 1760s a national census did not inquire into the religious persuasion of the population until a religious query was included in the 1861 statutory census.[18] The population of the diocese as found by this census exceeded 200,000 people, as is shown in table 12.

Table 12 - Population of the diocese of Elphin in 1861 as reported by the census of that year.

County	Cath.	Prot.	Pres.	Meth.	Quak.	Others	Total	% Cath.	% non-Cath.
Galway pt	20,669	395	43	10	0	3	21,120	97.9	2.1
Sligo pt	40,508	5,045	610	596	0	183	46,942	86.3	13.7
Roscommon pt	128,391	5,004	250	115	2	53	133,815	96.0	4.0
Diocese total.	189,568	10,444	903	721	2	239	201,877	93.9	6.1

Source: The census of Ireland for the year 1861, pt. iv: Reports and tables relating to the religious professions, education, and occupations of the people, vol. i [3204-III], H.C. 1863, lix, i, pp 487-513, 534-53.

Dickson *et al.*` have suggested that the national population for 1749 may have been of the order of 1.95 – 2.28 million people.[19] The 1861 census estimated the national population figure at 5.799 million.[20] If Dickson *et al*'s lower estimate is considered, the national population increased by a factor of 3 in the century or so after 1750. Based on the 1749 census for Elphin (table 4) the population of the diocese of Elphin increased by a factor of 2.65 in this same period, which is at least comparable with the probable equivalent national figure.

Unquestionably, the 1749 census is to some extent deficient. Indeed it could not be otherwise considering the social, political and administrative state of Ireland at the time it was compiled. However, as it is an enumeration of an area of Ireland for which there are no comparable surviving data and as it was compiled with considerable care, it is of boundless worth to eighteenth-century historians. It is without question a formidable example of early Irish census taking which contains untold rewards for historians who take the time to explore its hidden secrets. It requires a far more comprehensive treatment than it has received in this brief introduction. In fact it deserves no less.

Brian F. Gurrin*

Brian Gurrin is a Ph.D student at NUI Maynooth. He acknowledges the support of the Irish Research Council for the Humanities and Social Sciences.

NOTES

1. See E. M. Crawford, *Counting the people, a survey of the Irish censuses, 1813-1911* (Dublin, 2003) and Brian Gurrin, *Pre-census sources for Irish demography* (Dublin, 2002).

2. E. A. Wrigley and R. S. Schofield, *The population history of England, 1541-1871: a reconstruction* (Cambridge, 1989).

3. Greágóir Ó Duill, 'Church records after disestablishment', *The Irish Archives Bulletin*, 5 (1975), pp 10-22.

4. For an introduction to Presbyterian records see Christine Kinealy, 'Presbyterian church records' in James Ryan (ed.), *Irish Church Records* (2nd ed., Dublin, 2001), pp 69-105 and for an introduction to Roman Catholic records see James Ryan, 'Catholic Church records' in Ryan, *Irish Church Records*, pp 107-38.

5. Examples include William Macafee, 'The colonisation of the Maghera region of South Derry during the seventeenth and eighteenth centuries', *Ulster Folklife*, 23 (1977), pp 70-91; William Macafee and Valerie Morgan, 'Mortality in Magherafelt, County Derry, in the early eighteenth century reappraised', *Irish Historical Studies*, 23 (1982-3), pp 50-60; Colin Thomas, 'Family formation in a colonial city: Londonderry, 1650-1750', *Proceedings of the Royal Irish Academy*, 100C, no. 2 (2000), pp 87-111.

6. See B. I. Coleman, *The Church of England in the mid-nineteenth century, a social geography* (London, 1980), pp 5-7 for a brief introduction to this inquiry.

7. This parish is more commonly known as St Peter's but is called Athlone in the census.

8. Even as late as the 1821 census there were concerns that Catholics were reluctant to participate in the census as they 'feared they were to be decimated or banished, as if in the time of Cromwell, to some bog or desert if found too numerous, than that any measures were to be adopted for the improvement of their condition' (J.K.L., *Letters on the state of Ireland* (Dublin, 1825), p. 96).

9. In the 1764 hearth-tax census an example of Catholics managing to avoid enumeration in a religious census is available from east-Donegal when the hearth-tax collector Down Cope noted that 'I do believe there are many others who I cannot find who are poor & most of them Papists' (P.R.O.N.I., T/808/15261, f. 22v).

10. This figure was not actually reported by the census as, presumably on account of either poor instructions to the enumerators or lack of interest by the enumerators, no wives were specified in twenty-eight parishes. To arrive at this figure, therefore, it is necessary to adjust the total population figure in the census upwards to account for this deficiency. As there is no way of knowing what exact proportion of the householders in these deficient parishes had spouses it has simply been assumed that all male householders, unless they are explicitly stated as being widowers or bachelors, had spouses. This adjustment results in the addition of approximately 4,400 persons to the total population count. While this may slightly overestimate the population of the enumerated houses it is very unlikely to overestimate the actual population of the diocese as many houses will have been omitted as a result of poor registration and many children, servants and extra adults will likely have avoided being included in the population-count figures.

11. F. J. Carney, 'Aspects of pre-famine Irish household size: composition and differentials' in L. M. Cullen and T. C. Smout (ed.), *Comparative aspects of Scottish and Irish economic and social history, 1600-1900* (Edinburgh, n.d.), pp 32-5.

12. Typically eighteenth-century population estimates were made by multiplying house-counts by an estimate of the mean number of people per house. The most common estimate of mean household size used for this operation was 5. This estimate of mean household size for Elphin, approximately 4.5, is smaller than the figure that was commonly used.

13. The contrast between the Elphin data and the 1821 census figures for the Galway parishes (table 1) is even more evident. The Galway figures presented by Carney show a mean houseful size of 5.86 persons which is almost 1.5 persons per house more than the mean houseful size for Catholic houses.

14. See, for example, S. T Carleton, *Heads and hearths: the hearth money rolls and poll tax returns for Co. Antrim, 1660-69* (Belfast, 1991), p. 176.

15. See Carney, 'Aspects of pre-famine Irish household size', pp 32-46 for a detailed explanation of family size. Although this assumption may not be quite correct as some of the columns included in the family total may include lodgers and some of the servants may be family members it is the best assumption that can be made considering the presentation of the data.

16. There are another 81 families which contain both Catholic and Protestant children but for which there is no indication that the parents were of differing religions. This may indicate a deficiency in the census.

17. The only known surviving data for Elphin are the parish aggregate figures for Ahamlish parish in north County Sligo from the 1766 census (N.A.I., MS 2471).

18. In 1834 a Commission on Public Instruction used the 1831 census returns as the basis for a religious enumeration. The data for Elphin is available in *First report of the commissioners of public instruction, Ireland*, H.C. 1835 [45], xxxiii, pp 15d-28d.

19. David Dickson, Cormac Ó Gráda and Stuart Daultrey, 'Hearth tax, household size and Irish population change, 1621-1821', *Proceedings of the Royal Irish Academy*, 82C, no. 6 (1982), p. 156.

20. *The census of Ireland for the year 1861*, pt. iv, p. 10.

THE CENSUS OF ELPHIN 1749

ELPHIN, COUNTY ROSCOMMON

INTRODUCTION: *The town of Elphin was the seat of the bishop of the diocese. The parish covered 12,544 statute acres and was in the barony of Roscommon[1]. Lewis[2] says nothing about the quality of the land but we know from Edward Synge's letters that he grew barley, corn, oats and many vegetables, including fruits such as peaches and strawberries.[3] To encourage the linen industry in his area Synge, who was a trustee of the Linen Board, received grants for flax seed, wheels, reels and looms.[4]*

A hundred years after bishop Robert Howard had described Elphin as 'a bad dirty Irish town',[5] Isaac Weld wrote of its 'ranges of squalid and miserable hovels.[6] Charles Varley, Synge's agricultural advisor, described the soil as rich and loamy overlying a stratum of limestone, which was dug out and laid as a top dressing.[7] Apart from the bishop, the schoolhouse, the deanery and the residences of professional men, the poor lived in cabins thatched with rushes.[8] A patent was issued in 1618 to the bishop of Elphin to hold a fair every Wednesday and he was also granted the right to hold a market four times a year in May, June, September and December.[9]

The carpenter, sawyer and masons were probably employed by Synge, as he was still building his new palace in 1749. However he did not employ the local smiths, and nor did he use the Elphin wigmaker.[10]

Bishop Hodson's Grammar School in the town was founded by bishop John Hodson in ca. 1700. Oliver Goldsmith's mother Ann Jones was the daughter of the Rev. Oliver Jones, the first master of the school. It is curious that the census does not mention the master of the school in 1748-9, who would have been John Gunning.[11]

The incumbent was the dean of Elphin, the Rev Alexander Gunning. The patron was the King.

OCCUPATIONS

Ale seller	3	Farmer	112	Schoolmistress	1
Apothecary	1	Fowler	1	Servant	73
Beggar	3	Gentleman	4	Servants, household	463
Blind	1	Gleasor	1	Shepherd	2
Broguemaker	3	Glover	1	Shoemaker	5
Butcher	5	Herd	1	Shopkeeper	2
Cadger	2	Housekeeper	1	Smith	6
Carpenter	5	Knitter	1	Spinner	8
Cleric	2	Labourer	59	Surveyor	1
Constable	2	Maltster	2	Tailor	6
Cooper	1	Mason	3	Turner	1
Cottener	1	Merchant	1	Victualler	2
Cottier	14	Miller	3	Weaver	21
Dealer	3	Piper	1	Wigmaker	1
Distiller	1	Saddler	1		
Doctor	3	Sawyer	1		

Com~Ros common Parish of	Place of Abode	Names and Religion	Proffession	Children under 14		Children above 14		Men Servts		Women Servts	
				Prot.	Paps.	Prot.	Paps.	Prot.	Paps.	Prot.	Paps.
Elphin	Elphin	Andw Monaghan & wife	Servt.				3				
		Pat Lough & wife	Labr.				1				
		George Murphy and wife	Labr.				2				
		Farr: Beirne & wife & John Kelly	Labr.		2						
		Owe: Killeline Prot & wife Pap	Weaver			2		2			
		Ab: Chanonhouse & wife Prot	Weaver		2						
		Patt: Kelly & wife	Labr		3		1				
		Pat Gillgrishe & w & father & mother	Labr.		1						
		Darby Lenaghane & 2 sisters[12]	Labr.								
		Jon Lanaghan & W:	Labr.								1
		Alexr Dowell - [13]	Gent:					1	‡		1
		Laur: Geagan & W:	Taylor								
		Bry: Geenty & Wife	Aleseller				3				
		Jas: Comyn -									
		Widow Day -					3				
		Wid: Connaghton									
		Ricd Healy & Wife	Miller		2		2				
		Pet. Brolon & Wife	Labr.		2		2				
		Ed. Gormly & wife	Labr.		2		1				
		Mar: Horan & W:	Servant		1					1	
		Fardy Moran & Wife	Labr.		1		1				
		Matt Murtagh[14] & wife & mother	Labr.		1		3				
		Wi: Hawkes Prot[15]		2				1			2
		Andw Martyn & mother	Distiller					3			2
		Jas: Crawford[16] & wife Prot	Carpenter		1			2	1		1
		Luke Feeny & w:	Aleseller						1		1
		Walter Barritt & Wife	Broguemaker				3		3		
		Jon Chananhouse Prot:	Weaver		0		4				
		Rob: Tweed & wife Prot	Weaver								
		Andw Comyn Pap:	farmer		0		4		1		2
		Geo Higgin and son in law	Shoemaker		3		1		1		1
		John Green & wife & mother	weaver		2				1		1
		Andw. Lynch Pap:	Shopkeeper								
		Ed: Thomson & & wife & father Pro:	Weaver		2				1		1
		Wid: Bourke & Wid Moran									
		Pat: Lackery	broguemaker				2				
		Jon O Brien & wife	Shopkeeper		3					2	1
		Hugh Stafford[17] - Prot									
		& mother Pap[18]	Apothecary						2		2
		Prot 12 Pa 62		2	27	2	34	5	22	0	17
f.2 Emlagh		G:Oulaghan & wife[19]	Labr.		3				1		
		B Martyn -	Do		1			2		2	
		Mic: Concanon	Do		2				1		
		Pat: Diffily & wife & mother	Do		2				1		
		Rog:: Oulaghan & W	Do		2				1		1
		Jon Padine & w:	Do		2				2		

Note in left margin: All Pa: except such as marked Prot

Com~Ros common Parish of	Place of Abode	Names and Religion	Proffession	Children under 14		Children above 14		Men Servts		Women Servts	
				Prot.	Paps.	Prot.	Paps.	Prot.	Paps.	Prot.	Paps.
All Pa: except such as marked Prot	Town of Elphin	Bry: Lenaghan	Do		3						
		B: Flanagan & W:	Herd		1				1		
		B. Mcmanus & w:	Mason		2			2			
		Geo: Burke & W:[20]	Labr.		2			2			
		Wid: Clark			1			3			
		Wid: McDermot									
		Wid: Connaughton					1				
		Wid: Keon					2				
		Thos. Keon & W:	Labr.		2						
		Pat: McManus	Do		3		1				
		Pat: Sheridan & W Sawyer			2		2				
		Den: Beirn & w:	Cottener				1				
		Lu: Reily & W:	Labr.				2				
		W: Flyn					1				
		Wid: Tweed & son & daughter in law Prot	Smith	1		2					
		Phil: Tweed & w Prot[21]	Smith								
		Pat: Killroy & w:	Taylor		1		2				
		Dom: McCormuck & w:	Labr.				6				
		Jon Keon & W:	Weaver		3		1				
		Rd M Cary Prot:[22]	Cleric	2				3		1	2
		Matt: Higgins & W:	Butcher		1						
		Ter: McKeon & wife	Weaver		1			1			
		Mic: Quin & wife	Labr.		1						
		Thady McDermot & w:	Labr.		1		1				
		Andw Young[23] & W: Prot	Fowler	2	0	1	0		0		
		Bry: Donnagher & wife	Labr.		2						
		Wid: Connaughton					1				
		Chas McManus	Labr.		2		1				
		Wife									
		Mother									
		Cor: McManus wife & mother	Labr.		2						1
		Ric: Boulton & W:	Labr.		3		2				
		Wid: Beirn			1		2				
		Dan: Killkenny & wife Labr.			1		2				
		Will: Martyn & W: Malster			3		2				
		Prot 8 Pa: 65		5	50	3	41	5	11	1	5
[f.3]Elphin	Elphin	Rose Carny widow Pap	Spenr.								
	Dito	Patrick Higgin & wife Pa:	Butcher		1						
	Dito	James Armstrong & wife Prot	Surveaor[24]	2							
	Dito	Peter Percevell & wife Pa:	Smith		2				3		
	Dito	Lareme Kelly & wife Pa:	Wigmakr		2				1		
	Dito	John Grimsby & wife Prot	Constable[25]			3					
	Dito	James Thomson & wife Prot	Weavr	3					2	1	
	Dito	Joshua Griffin & wife Prot	Farmr.	4					1		3
	Dito	Michael Kelly and mother Pa:	Tealer						1		
	Do	James Rogers & wife Pa:[26]	Shoemaker				1		2		
	Do	Rev.Alexander Gunning[27] & wife		1					1		3

Com~Ros common Parish of	Place of Abode	Names and Religion	Proffession	Children under 14		Children above 14		Men Servts		Women Servts	
				Prot.	Paps.	Prot.	Paps.	Prot.	Paps.	Prot.	Paps.
All Pa: except such as marked Prot	Do	Edward Garaghan & wife Pa:	Carpenter		1					1	
	Do	Symon Lanaghan & wife	Tailor		3						
	Do	Edward Gormly & wife Pa:	labour.		2						
	Do	Henry Houlding & wife Prot	Weaver						1		
	Do	Henry Magahy & wife Prot	Weaver	1							
	Do	Edmond Brennan & wife Pa:	Shoemaker								
	Do	Edmond Huefy and Alexander Dowell papt.	Weavers								
	Do	Mary McDonouogh. Widdow papt.	School mistress								
	Do	Patt Hill papt.	Labourer		2						
	Do	Mark McDermott & wife papt.	Labourer		2						
	Do	Bar: Connillan & wife papt.	Butcher		4		1				
	Do	John Connillan & wife papt.	Carpenter		2				1		1
	Do	Philip Connillan & wife papt.28	Butcher						1		1
	Do	Peter Dowell & wife papt.29	Smyth		2		1				
	Do	John Road & wife Prot.	Merchant	2					1		1
	Do	Rodmond Fahy & wife papt.30	Mason				2				1
	Do	Pat. Connillan & wife papt.	Sadler		1				1		1
	Do	Philip Farly & wife papt.	Aleseller		1		1		1		
	Do	Francis Banaghan & wife papt.	Tailor		2				3		1
	Do	Edward McManus Prot	Butcher								
	Do	Richard Tweed Pro & wife	Broguemaker						1		1
	Do	John Gaffrey widdower 31	Glover		1		2				
	Do	Ed: Hill	Labr.	1							
	Do	Rt. Rd. Lord Bishop of Elphin	Cleric					12		5	
	Do	Prot. 21. Pa- 44		14	28	3	8		21	6	12
[f.4]Elphin	Elphin Town	John Reeve papt & wife Prot	Weaver	1							
	Do	James Conner & wife Pa:	Servant						1		1
	Do	Owen Gormly & wife Pa:	Farmr.				3				
	Do	Thomas Sheridon & wife Pa:	Turner		3		1				
	Do	Alexander Doyle & wife Pa:	Farmr.				2				
	Do	Dinish Horly & wife Pa:	Meason		4		4				
	Do	Terence Gowrin & wife Pa:	Leabour.		4		1				
	Do	Thomas Vanwick & wife Prot	Weaver		3			3			
	Do	Thady Shananean & wife Pa:	Cadger32		2		1				
	Do	Richard Gary & wife Pa:	farmr.		3						1
	Do	Peggy Berin widow Pa:	Spiner		1						
	Do	James Reyly & wife Pa:	Leabour.				3				
	Do	Michael Higgins & wife Pa:	Leabour.		1				1		1
	Do	Thomas Higgins & wife Pa:	Leabour.		1						
	Do	John Talbert & wife Pa:	Leabour.		2						
	Do	Edmd Burk & wife Pa:	Leabour.		1						
	Do	Thady Morin & wife Pa:	Leabour.		1						
	Do	Thomas Higgins & wife Pa:	Leabour.		2						
	Do	Owen Dermott & wife Pa:	Leabour.		1		2				
	Do	Shiply Flanigin widow Pa:	Spinr				2				
	Do	Owen Callgin & wife Pa:	Tealer33								
	Do	Bryan Healy & wife Pa:	Leabour.		5						1

Com~Roscommon Parish of	Place of Abode	Names and Religion	Proffession	Children under 14		Children above 14		Men Servts		Women Servts	
				Prot.	Paps.	Prot.	Paps.	Prot.	Paps.	Prot.	Paps.
	Do	Bryan Eagan & wife Pa:	Leabour.				2				
	Do	Ann Cormuck Widow Prot	Spinr		3		1				
	Do	Michell Healy & wife Pa:	Leabour.		3						
	Do	Peggy Reedan widow Prot	Spinr.			2					
	Do	Rossy Henry widow Prot	Housekeepr			3					
	Do	Roger Carney & wife Pa:	Leabour.		2						
	Do	Paul Ferriss & wife Prot[34]	Weavr			1		2			
	Do	John Herissan & wife Prot	Weavr					2			
	Do	John Reed & wife Prot[35]	Gleasor[36]						1		1
	Do	Gregory Connr. & wife Pa:	Leabour.		2						1
	Do	Diniss Berin & wife Pa:	Leabour.		3		1				
	Do	Cormuck Caloughon & wife Prot	Coopr	1							
	Do	Ellizabeth Robson widow Prot	Spinr.			2					
	Do	James Carell & wife Pa:	Shoemakr		1						
	Do	Elizabeth Offerwhile widow Prot	nitter								
	Do	James Burk Pa: & wife Prot	malster			1					
	Do	Patrick Hamell & wife Pa:	Leabour.		2		2				
	Do	John Ferriss & wife Prot	Leabour.	1		2					
	Do	Richard Burke & wife Pa:[37]	Shoemakr								
		Pr 28 Pa 55 -		3	43	14	25	4	6	0	7
[f.5]Elphin	Glan Thomas	Roger Johnston & wife Pa:	Servt.		2		1				
		Willm Carny & wife Pa:	Servt.		3		1		1		1
		Pat Scally & wife Pa:	Servt.		2		1		1		1
		Walter Kelly & wife Pa:	Servt.		2				1		1
		Cavin Headin Widow Pa:	Spinr		4		3				
		Mathw.Callow & wife papt	Servt.		4		2				
		Owen Connor & wife papt	Sheepherd		3		1		1		1
		Patt.Scally & wife papt	Servt.		1				1		1
		Thos.Muldowney & wife papt	Servt.		2				1		1
		James Connolly & wife papt	Servt.		1				1		1
		Patt Carny & wife papt	Servt.		1				1		1
		Owen Scully & wife papt	Servt.						1		1
		John Connor & wife papt	Servt.		3		1		1		1
		Michl.Shanagh & wife papt	Servt.		2		1		1		1
		Fran.Connor & wife papt	Sheepherd		1				1		1
		Dinis Murry & wife papt	Servt.		3		1		1		1
Do	Comoge	John Shomane & wife papt	Farmr.		3				1		1
		John Ellison & wife papt	Farmer	2				1			1
		Patt.Shannane & Sistr.	Farmr.						1		1
		Owen Shannane & wife papt	Servt.		1						1
		Mattw.Hicks papt	Doctor						1		1
		Michael Crolly & wife papt	Servt.		1						1
		Andrew Shanod & wife papt	Servt.		2						1
		John Coslane & wife papt	Piper		2						
Do	Cornetstown	Michael Owens & wife papt	Servt.		2						1
		John Buttler & wife papt	Beggrs.								
Do	Boyanagh	Hugh Scally & wife papt	Cotter		1						
		Danl Connor & wife papt	Cottr.		1		2				1
		Michael Connor & wife papt	Cottr.				2				

All Pa: except such as marked Prot

Com~Ros common Parish of	Place of Abode	Names and Religion	Proffession	Children under 14		Children above 14		Men Servts		Women Servts	
				Prot.	Paps.	Prot.	Paps.	Prot.	Paps.	Prot.	Paps.
		Bryan McMurry & wife papt	Cottr.		1						
		Laghlin Lough & wife papt	Cottr.						1		1
		Patt.King & wife papt	Cottr.		4		2				
		Mable Moony widow papt	Spinster								
		Patt. Rock & wife papt[38]	Smith		6		1		1		1
		Peter Lassan papt.	Labourer		1		2				
		Michl. Lyn & wife papt	Labr.								
		Luke Dooly & wife papt	Cottr.								1
		Cavin Scally & wife papt	Spinser		2						
		Wm Gallagh & wife papt	Cottr.		2						
		Hugh Carty & wife papt	Labr.		3						
		Elizth.Brady Widow papt.	Beggr		2						
		Pa 76			3	70		21	19		25
[f.6]Elphin	Flask	Owen Morris & wife papt	Vittler		3		2		1		1
		Arthur Wilkins & wife papt	Farmr.				2		1		1
		Bridget Kevin Widw. papt	Spinstrs.		3		1				
		Patt.Scally & wife papt	Cotter		3		1				
		Wm.Duhody & wife papt	Cottr.		2						
		John Whilson & wife papt	Beggr.								
Do.	Rossmore	Thos.Higgins & wife papt	Cottr.		3						
		Luke Daly & wife papt	Servt.		2				1		1
		Wm.McAndrew & wife papt	Servant		2						1
Do.	Ross Begg	Peter Purser & wife papt	Farmr.		3		2		1		2
		Denis Byrne & wife papt	Farmr.		4		2				
		Patt.Gorman & wife papt	Farmr.		3		2				
		Thady Hughes & wife papt	Farmr.						1		1
		Patt. Kenny & wife papt	Farmr.						1		1
		Thady Shannon & wife papt	Farmr.		2						1
		David Doughly & wife papt	Farmr.		1						1
		Connor Shannone & wife papt	Farmr.		3		1				
		Patt.Cormuck & wife papt	Farmer		3						1
		Patt Moran & wife papt	Farmer		3						1
		Peter Conelly & wife papt	Farmr.		1				1		1
		Denis Shannane & wife papt	Miller		3						1
		Owen McDermott & wife papt	Farmr.		2		1		1		1
		Dan. Connane & wife papt	Labr.								1
		Jon.Conelly & wife papt	Labr.		2						
		Bridgt Hary Widow	Spinner		3		1				
Do.	Runoghue	John Power & wife papt	Farmr.		3				1		1
		Thos.McDonough & wife papt	Farmr.		3						1
		Fran.Connan & wife papt	Cotter		2						1
		Mark McDermott & wife papt.	Cottr.		1				1		1
Do.	Dingowan	Bryan Flanigan & wife papt.	Servt.		3						1
		Jams.Connor & wife papt.	Servt.						1		1

Com~Ros common Parish of	Place of Abode	Names and Religion	Proffession	Children under 14		Children above 14		Men Servts		Women Servts	
				Prot.	Paps.	Prot.	Paps.	Prot.	Paps.	Prot.	Paps.
	Caronurlar	George Hicks & wife papt[39].	Farmer	2		1			1		1
		Laughln. Morin & wife papt.	Servant		3						
		Ed.McLoughlin & wife papt	Servant		6		1		1		1
		Hugh Kelly Pap:	Cottr.				2				
		Edmd. Kelly & wife papt	Farmr.				2		1		1
		Hugh Ward papt:	Miller						1		1
		Pat: Burn & wife papt			4				1		1
		Owen Sculloge & wife papt	Cadger		2				1		1
		Pro. 0 Pa: 73			80		10		18		29
[f.7]Elphin	Ballymuny	Peter Digenan and wife papt.	Farmer		2		3		1		1
		Chancs.Renalch & Wife papt.	Farmr.		3		1		1		1
		Peter Renold & Wife papt.	Farmer		3		3		1		1
		Wm.O'Bryan & Wife papt.	Farmr.		1		2		1		1
		John Flanigan & Wife papt.	Weavr				3		1		1
		Terence Flanigan & Wife papt.	Farmr.		2		2		1		1
		Petr.Elwood & Wife papt.	Farmr.		3		3		1		1
		Martin Elwood & Wife papt.	Farmer		2		1		1		
		Stephn. Elwood & Wife papt.	Farmr.		3		1				1
		Edmond Renolds & Wife papt.	Farmer						1		1
		John Higgins & Wife papt.	Weaver		1						1
Do.	Killucuan	Frans.Heverin & Wife papt.	Gent		2				1		3
		Michl.Dowlon & Wife papt.	Servt.		3		1		1		1
		Michl.McDowne & Wife papt.	Servt.		1				1		1
		Darby Freely & Wife papt.	Servt.		1		2		1		1
	Toberowry	Pat. Murphy & Wife papt.	Servt.		2		2		1		1
		Patt.Mullane & Wife papt.	Servt.		2						1
		Denis McGan & Wife papt.	Servt.		3						
		Wm.Donellan & Wife papt.	Labr.				2				
	Flask More	John McNeal & Wife papt.	Servant		2				1		1
		Frans.Daly & Wife papt.	Servt.		5		3		1		
		Pat.Higgins & Wife papt.	Servt.		2		1		1		1
	Cloon Quin	Mrs Win. Chapman Prot	Servt.						4		1
		Chars.Clabby & Wife papt.	Carpentr.	1	2				1		2
		Michl.Farrell & Wife papt.	Carpentr.						1		2
		Domk.Lutton & Wife papt.	Servt.		1		3		1		1
		Thos.Coughlan & Wife papt.	Servt.		1				1		1
		Cormk.Fenny & Wife papt.	Servt.		2		2				
	Cloone Cranon	Jon.Branon & Wife papt.	Servt.						1		1
		John Casserly & Wife papt.	Servt.		2				1		1
		Michl.Branon & Wife papt.	Vittlr.		1				1		
		Patt. Birn & Wife papt.	Servt.		4						
	Cartron	Luke Wholoughan & Wife papt.	Farmer		1		4		1		1
		Darby Healy & Wife papt.	Farmr.						2		2
		Thos.Healy & Wife papt.	Labr.		1		1		1		1
	Tansyfield	John Kelly & Wife papt.	Gardiner						1		1
		Edmd.Burke & Wife papt.	Dealer		2		2			[ms damaged]	
		Manus Hopkin & Wife papt.	Farmr.				3				
		Edmond Burke & Wife papt.	Farmr.		2		2				

Com~Ros common Parish of	Place of Abode	Names and Religion	Proffession	Children under 14 Prot.	Children under 14 Paps.	Children above 14 Prot.	Children above 14 Paps.	Men Servts Prot.	Men Servts Paps.	Women Servts Prot.	Women Servts Paps.
		Mary Mealis Widow	Spinr.		1						
		Darby Caserly & Wife papt.	Servt.								
		Prot 1 Pa: 79		63	47		34				30[?]
[f.8]Elphin	Raheens	Lawr.Kildery Widowr papt.	Servt./widow		2						2
		Chars Lenon Widr. papt	Servt.				2				2
		Denis Banaghan & Wife papt.	Servt.		2						2
	Cloghr Begg	Mr.David Digenan & Wife papt.	Doctr.						2		2
		Patrk.Nash & Wife papt.	Servant		2						1
		Michl.Hughes & Wife papt.	Servt.		2						1
		Wm.Leanane & Wife papt.	Servt.								1
		Patt.Leanane & Wife papt.	Servt.		2						1
		Jane Nash Widw. Papist	Servt.				2				
	Cloghermore	John Croghan & Wife papt.	Farmer						1		2
		Martin Croghan & Wife papt.	Farmr.		1						1
		Cormick Morris & Wife papt.	Weaver		2		1				
		John Reagan & Wife papt.	Farmr.		3		2				
		Richd.Mullane & Wife papt.	Farmr.								1
		Chars.Feeny & Wife papt.	Farmr.		3				1		1
		Peter Hughes & Wife papt.	Farmr.		1				1		1
		Herbert Conane & Wife papt.	Farmr.		2		1				
		Edmond Farrell & Wife papt.	Farmr.		2				1		1
		John Hughes & Wife papt.	Farmr.		2				1		1
		Patt.Kean & Wife papt.	Farmr.		3				1		1
		Jno.Dillon & Wife papt.	Farmr.		1		1			1	
		Danl.Farrell & Wife papt.	Farmr.		2				2		1
		Carbry Byrn & Wife papt.	Constable[40]		1				2		1
	Cartron	Michl.Shannon & Wife papt.	Farmr.		3		1		1		1
		John Donash & Wife papt.	Farmr.		1		1		1		1
		John Igoe & Wife papt.	Farmr.		1				1		1
		Ambrose Shannon Wdr. Pap	Farmr.				3		1		1
		Teady Common & Wife papt.	Farmr.		3				1		1
		And. Shannon & Wife papt.	Farmr.						1		1
		John Brabson & Wife papt.	Farmr.		3				1		1
		Jams.Shannon & Wife papt.	Farmr.		3				1		1
		Frans.Shannon & Wife papt.	Farmr.		1				1		1
		Thos.Dockery & Wife papt.	Farmr.		3				1		1
		Mathw.Shannon & Wife papt.	Farmr.		2				1		1
		Daniel Common & Wife papt.	Farmr.		3				1		1
		Patt.Conlan & Wife papt.	Farmr.		2				1		1
	Ballymuny	Danl.Killkelly & Wife papt.	Farmr.				2		1		1
		Patt.Elwood & Wife papt.	Farmr.				2		1		1
		Carbry Egan & Wife papt.	Farmr.		1				1		1
		Owen Shannon & Wife papt.	Farmr.		5				1		1
		Richd.Digenan papt.	Farmr.				3		1		1
		Pa: 77			61		23		31		36
[f.9]Elphin	Loughteask	Jams.Nary & Wife papt.	Farmr.		3				1		1
		Jams.Nowland & Wife papt.	Farmr.		2		1		1		1
		Frans.Ford & Wife papt.	Farmr.		2				1		1
		Math.Moran & Wife papt.	Farmr.		3				1		

Com~Ros common Parish of	Place of Abode	Names and Religion	Proffession	Children under 14		Children above 14		Men Servts		Women Servts	
				Prot.	Paps.	Prot.	Paps.	Prot.	Paps.	Prot.	Paps.
		Patrick Bradikin & Wife papt.	Farmr.		3				1		1
		Jams.Bradikin & Wife papt.	Farmr.		3				1		1
		Con.Moran & Wife papt.	Farmr.		2				1		1
		Jams.Bradikin & Wife papt.	Farmr.		3				1		1
		Barty Heely & Wife papt.	Farmr.								
		George Coollogh & Wife papt.	Farmr.		2		2				1
		Hugh Boyle & Wife papt.	Farmr.		3		3				
		Darby Dowell & Wife Pap.	Farmr.		2		2				1
		Hugh Markwell & Wife papt.	Farmr.		1		2				1
		Edmond Flanigan & Wife papt.	Weaver		4				1		1
		Petr.Banaghom & Wife Pap.	Blind		1		3				1
		Donl.Flangin & Wife Pap.	Farmr.		2		2				1
		Danl.Shile & Wife papt.	Doctor		1		1		1		1
		Cartron Hanigin widow pap	Spinner		2		3		1		1
		George Mills & Wife pap.	Farmr.		2				1		1
		Jerome Gannon & Wife pap.	Farmr.		1				1		1
		John Gannon & Wife pap.	Farmr.		2				1		1
		Terence Gannon & Wife papt.									
		Paule Winn & Wife pap.	Servt.		1				1		1
		Patric. Coningham & Wife papt.	Servt.								
	Killynagh	Denis Delane[41] & Wife Prot	Gentleman	2		1			1		1
		Milas Anderson & Wife papt.	Servt.				3		1		1
	Ownagh	Franc.Finegin & Wife papt.	Servt.								
		Luke Carny & Wife papt.	Servt.		2		1		1		1
	Clonmoghan	Tarance Mahon & Wife papt.	Labour		1						1
	Foxbourough	Bryan King & Wife papt.	Servant		3				1		1
		Petr. Owne & Wife papt.	Servant								
		Thady Flanigan & Wife papt.	Servant		4		1			1	
		Thad. Doulan & Wife papt.	Servant		4		1			1	
		Patt. Kearin & Wife papt.	Farmr.		1		1		1	1	1
	Killinagh	Patt.Keenyne & Wife papt.	Farmr.		1		1				1
	Comouge	Pattr. Hanly & Wife papt.	Farmr.		1				1		1
	Monylough	Michael Eagan & Wife papt.	Farmr.		1		1		1		1
		Comr Eagan & Wife papt.	Farmr.		1				1		1
		Roger Eagan & Wife papt.	Farmr.		1				1		1
		Jorine Flanigin & Wife papt.	Farmr.						1		1
		Roger Brouk & Wife papt.	Weavr.		1				1		1
		Conr. Bogoer & Wife papt.			3				1		1
		Pro:2 Pa 79		2	66	1	28		17	14	34
[f.10] Elphin	Tully	Bryan Lawder & wife pap.	Farmr.								
		John Dermott & wife pap.	Farmr.		2		1		1		1
		Roger Loum & wife pap.	Farmr.		2		1		1		1
		Danl.Kiely & wife pap.	Farmr.		1		1		1		1
		Edmond Ganon & wife pap.	Farmr.		2		2		1		1
		Thad Mangan & wife pap.	Farmr.				2		1		1
		Thoms. Sneal & wife pap.	Farmr.		2				1		1
		Barty Jeram & wife pap.	Farmr.						1		1
		Laughlin Conial & wife pap.	Farmr.		1				1		1
		William Small & wife pap.	Far.		2		1		1		1

Com~Ros common Parish of	Place of Abode	Names and Religion	Proffession	Children under 14 Prot.	Paps.	Children above 14 Prot.	Paps.	Men Servts Prot.	Paps.	Women Servts Prot.	Paps.
		John Conilan widow pap.	Farmr.						1		1
		Margett Dermott widow pap.	Spinner	1					1		
	Clonvillane	Thos.Hanly & wife pap.	Gent		2		3		1		1
		Edmd Doyle & wife pap.	Dealer				1				
		Thos. Casserly & wife pap.	Weavr.		1				1		
		Richd.Linan & wife pap.	Smith		3						
		Cholum Doyle & wife pap.	Dealr		4						1
		Owne Wollgan & wife pap.	Servnt.		2				1		1
		Thad. Killy & wife pap.	Servat.								
		Diacth Barrin & wife pap.	Servt.		1						1
		Pattr.Donelon & wife pap.	Servt.		2				1		1
		Bryan Flanigin & wife pap.	Servt.		3						
	Clonconny	Watt.Mccormick & wife pap.	Servt.		4						
		Roger Bradigin & wife pap.	Servt.						2		
		Roger Kelly & wife pap.	Servt.		1				1		
		Jams. Carly & wife pap.	Servat.		1						
		Patt.Conr. & wife pap.	Servt.		2						
		Jerm.Flanigin & wife pap.	Servt.		3						
		Robert Carly & wife pap.	Servant								
		Bragon Conry & wife pap.	Servt.		1						
		John Dermot & wife pap.	Servt.		2						
	Clouroghan	John Monah & wife pap.	Farmr.		2				1		1
		Owne Dermott & wife pap.[42]	Farmr.		2				1		1
		Thoms Hanly & wife pap.	Farmr.		1		1				1
		Martin Heriny & wife pap.	Farmr.		2		2		1		1
		Michell Mcgrath & wife pap.	Farmr.		1		2				1
		Coner. Moran & wife pap.	Farmr.		2						1
		William Dermott & wife pap.	Farmr.		2				1		1
		Bryan Hart & wife pap.	Farmr.		3				1		1
		John Ganon & wife pap.	Farmr.		3				1		1
		Bryan Moran & wife pap.	Farmr.								
		John Boughan & mother pap	Labr.& Spinr								
		Pa 80			62		17		23		25

[Verso f.10]

Number of Souls

	in Ogula	Prot 000	
	in Do	Pap 875	875
	in Shankill	Prot 17	428
	in Do	Pap 411	
	Killmacumsy	Pro 000	
	in Do	Pap:	987
	Killcorkey	Prot: 1	
	in Do	Pap: 533	533
Number of Souls	in Elphin Parish	Prot 148	1548
	in Do	Pap: [illegible]	
			4171

Total number of Prot -   166
Do of Papists -   4005
     4171

					Children under 14		Children above 14		Men Servts		Women Servts	
					Prot.	Paps.	Prot.	Paps.	Prot.	Paps.	Prot.	Paps.
Elphin	P. 1	12		64	Pr.	Pa.	Prot.	Pa.	Pr	Pa	Pr	Pa
	2	8		65	2	27	2	34	5	22	0	17
	3	21		44	5	50	3	41	5	11	1	5
	4	20		55	14	28	3	8	12	21	6	12
	5	0		76	3	43	14	25	4	6	0	7
	6	3		73	0	70	0	21	0	19	0	25
	7	1		79	0	80	0	20	0	18	0	29
	8	0		7?	0	63	0	47	0	34	0	38
	9	2		79	0	61	0	23	0	31	0	36
	10	0		80	2	66	1	28	0	17	14	34
					0	61	0	17	0	23	0	25
		67		692								
					26	550	23	264	26	202	21	228

		Pt.	Pa.
If the same Method			
be taken wth. the other	Ogula	3	898
above mentioned	Shankill	40	640
Parishes there will	Kilmcumsey	0	972
appear yt these are	Kilcorkey	1	614

NOTES

1. Including 426 acres of water (*General Alphabetical Index*).

2. Samuel Lewis, *Topographical Dictionary of Ireland* (2 vols, Dublin 1837) (hereafter cited as Lewis).

3. *Synge Letters*, pp. 84, 114.

4. *Synge Letters*, p.111, fn. 7.

5. Robert Howard to Hugh Howard, 18 July 1730 (N.L.I., Wicklow Papers PC 227).

6. Weld, *Roscommon*, p.396.

7. Varley, *A New System of Husbandry*, iii, 31-2.

8. Varley, op. cit., 78-9.

9. *Report...fairs and markets*.

10. *Synge Letters*, p.100.

11. Michael Quane, 'Bishop Hodson's Grammar School, Elphin', *Journal of the Royal Society of Antiquaries of Ireland*, 96, (1966) pp. 157-177.

12. Darby Lenaghan was a tenant of the Bishop of Elphin in 1740: Rent roll & leases of the plots of Elphin (N.L.I., Wicklow Papers PC 223/6/61 Box 7).

13. Alexander Dowell was a tenant of the Bishop of Elphin in 1740: Rent roll & leases of the plots of Elphin (N.L.I., Wicklow Papers PC 223/6/61 Box 7).

14. Matthew Murtagh was described by Bishop Synge as 'a sort of favourite'. Synge sent his son to Dublin in 1752 as he had 'a strange swelling in his breast' (*Synge Letters*, p.395).

15. Possibly the widow of the Rev. Lewis Hawkes, tenant of the Bishop of Elphin in 1740 (N.L.I., Wicklow Papers PC 223/6/61 Box 7).

16. James Crawford was employed by Edward Synge in the building of a new church (*Synge Letters*, p. 57).

17. Hugh Stafford was a friend of both Bishop Synge and Charles O'Conor of Belanagare for whom he acted as a go-between when they wanted to lend each other books. Stafford attended on Synge's servants but he was reluctant to trust his daughter, Alicia, to his care (*Letters of Charles O'Conor*, p.70).

18. Widow Stafford rented demesne land from the Bishop of Elphin (N.L.I., Wicklow Papers PC 223/6/61 Box 7).

19. Michael Hoologon rented Emlaghgare and Clonicarron from the Bishop of Elphin (N.L.I., Wicklow Papers PC 223/6/61 Box 7).

20. George Burk, illiterate labourer signed a receipt for the Rev. George Hanly in 1740 (N.L.I., Wicklow Papers PC 223/6/61 Box 7).

21. Phillip Tweed, locksmith was a tenant of the Bishop of Elphin in 1740 (N.L.I., Wicklow Papers PC 223/6/61 Box 7).

22. The Rev. M. Cary rented demesne land from the bishop of Elphin (N.L.I., Wicklow Papers PC 223/6/61 Box 7).

23. In service to Bishop Synge, who ordered a frock-coat for him in 1749 (*Synge Letters*, p. 121).

24. Parish surveyors were appointed by the vestry and were responsible for the repair and upkeep of all roads in the parish. The post was salaried. (Holdsworth, pp.37, 38).

25. Constables executed warrants issued by a justice of the peace and apprehended offenders. By 1749 the legislation that had stipulated that constables must be Protestant had lapsed (Holdsworth, p.32).

26. James Rogers was a tenant of the Bishop of Elphin in 1740 (N.L.I., Wicklow Papers PC 223/6/61 Box 7).

27. Alexander Gunning, son of Alexander Gunning and Mrs Nowland, was born in Dublin. He was admitted to TCD in 1729 and gained BA in 1734. He was collated vicar of Kilgefin in 1740. He married Elizabeth Hodson in 1747 and she died in 1751. His will was proved in 1793 (G.D. Burtchaell and T.U. Sadleir, *Alumni Dubliniensis: a register of the students, graduates, professors and provosts of Trinity college in the University of Dublin (1593-1860)* (Dublin 1935) (hereafter cited as *Alumni Dubliniensis*; *Synge Letters*, pp. 626, 48, 64,. 68, 304; A.E. Vicars, *Index to the Prerogative Wills of Ireland 1536-1810* (Dublin 1897) p.208 (hereafter cited as Vicars).

28. Philip Coneley, butcher was a tenant of the Bishop of Elphin in 1740 (N.L.I., Wicklow Papers PC 223/6/61 Box 7).

29. Peter Dowell, smith invoiced the estate of Robert Howard, Bishop of Elphin, 1740 (N.L.I., Wicklow Papers PC 223/6/61 Box 7).

30. Redmond Fahy, mason invoiced the estate of Robert Howard, Bishop of Elphin 1740 (N.L.I., Wicklow Papers PC 223/6/61 Box 7).

31. John Gaffry was a tenant of the Bishop of Elphin in 1740 (N.L.I., Wicklow Papers PC 223/6/61 Box 7).

32. A carrier, particularly of butter and eggs.

33. Assumed to be a tailor.

34. Paul Farris was a tenant of the Bishop of Elphin in 1740 (N.L.I., Wicklow Papers PC 223/6/61 Box 7).

35. John Read was a tenant of the Bishop of Elphin in 1740 (N.L.I., Wicklow Papers PC 223/6/61 Box 7).

36. Glazier.

37. Richard Burke was a tenant of the Bishop of Elphin in 1740 (N.L.I., Wicklow Papers PC 223/6/61 Box 7).

38. Patrick Rock witnessed the inventory of Robert Howard, Bishop of Elphin, 7 July 1740 (N.L.I., Wicklow Papers PC 223/6/61 Box 7).

39. George Hicks was a tenant of the Bishop of Elphin in 1740 (N.L.I., Wicklow Papers PC 223/6/61 Box 7).

40. Edward Synge refers to Carbry Byrn in a letter of 2 June 1749 (*Synge Letters*, p.97).

41. Denis Delane was a son of George Delane. He was educated in Dublin and entered TCD in 1723, aged 16 (*Alumni Dubliniensis*).

42. Owen Dermot labourer signed a receipt in July 1740 and was a tenant of the Bishop of Elphin in 1740 (N.L.I., Wicklow Papers PC 223/6/61 Box 7).

OGULLA, COUNTY ROSCOMMON

INTRODUCTION: *Ogulla is in the barony of Roscommon. It covers 6,213 statute acres.[1] The land included 'rich feeding bullock and sheepwalk ground'.[2] A patent to hold a fair in Tulsk four times a year was issued to Sir Richard Lane in 1664.[3]*

The town of Tulsk had been a stronghold of the O'Conors. The O'Conor Roe built a castle there in about 1406 and the O'Conor family owned at least one townland in 1641.[4] Michael Conner, a Roman Catholic gentleman of Timoney was one of nine surviving Conor/Conners in the parish.[5]

Tulsk was incorporated by Charles II in 1663. The corporation had a portrieve, 15 free burgesses and a commonalty who returned 2 MPs to parliament. Seven members of the Caulfeild family represented the constituency from 1692 and 1786. St George Caulfeild, attorney-general in 1749, lived in the parish of Dunamon and owned the borough at the time of the census.[6]

The parish was held with that of Elphin. The incumbent in 1749 was the Rev. Christopher Lloyd, who was installed in 1739 as dean and rector of Elphin and remained until his death in 1757.[7] The patron was the King..

OCCUPATIONS

Beggar	1	Merchant	1	Shopkeeper	1
Broguemaker	3	Miller	1	Smith	1
Cottier	138	Pumpmaker	1	Spinner	1
Farmer	10	Servant	4	Weaver	3
Gentleman	1	Servants, household	184	Wigmaker	1
Glover	1	Shepherd	2		
Labourer	1	Shoemaker	1		

Com~Ros common Parish of	Place of Abode	Names and Religion	Proffession	Children under 14		Children above 14		Men Servts		Women Servts	
				Prot.	Paps.	Prot.	Paps.	Prot.	Paps.	Prot.	Paps.
[f.11]Ogulla	Tulsk[8]	Thoms Naghtin & wife	Cotter		2						1
		Will. Nary & wife	Servt.								1
		John Kelly & wife	Mercht						1		2
		Thos.Connor & wife	Wigmaker				2				
		Thos.Kelly & wife									
		Jams. Tannyer & wife	Smith								
		Petr.Keah & wife			4						1
		Patt.Kelly & wife	Shoemaker		3				2		3
		Jams.Conway & wife	Miller		5						1
		Domk.Hear & wife	Broguemaker		2		2		1		1
		Brid.Fitzgerald & wife									
		Patt.Fox & wife			1		2				1
	Oldcalleland	Laro.Brett & wife			1						2
		Will.Kelly & wife	Smith		1		3				
		Jams.Stanlley & wife			2						
		Dick do. & wife			2						1
		Tern.Donagho & wife			1						1
		Thos. Gamlar & wife			2						
		Brayd.Eagan & wife			3		1				
		Widow Connor					1				
		Bryan Hanly & wife							1		1
		Lau.Kelly & wife					3				
		Mich.Croghan & wife			3						1
		John Dolan & wife									
		Widow Flyn			2						
		Petr Kohan & wife			6		1		1		1
		Laur.Connor & wife			3				1		1
		Fran. Do & wife			3						1
		Patt.Martin & wife			2						
		Thom. Kear & wife					2				
		Hugh Connor & wife			1						
Ogila	Ogila	Patt.Conelly & wife			3						
		Patt.Fanell & wife			3						
		Jo.Conilly & wife			1						
		Jam. Mullidy & wife			4						
		Frank Mullidy & wife			1						1
	Ogila	Widow Connor pap			2		1	┼			1
		Thom.Do. & wife			2		1				
		Patt. Bryan & wife			1						1
		Patt.Kelly & wife			1				1		1
		Franc.Kelly & wife			2				1		
		Pa: 79		0	69	0	19	0	9	0	24
[f.12]	Cornsleyrany	Cond. Gaffry & wife		3							
		Thos.McLangan & wife		2							
		Owen Do & wife							1		1
	Lisneane	Robt.Kelly & wife	Farmer				1		2		1
		Patt. Tiernan			2		1		2		1
		Thos.McDermott[9] & wife					2				
		Cath Givar widow					2				

Com~Ros common Parish of	Place of Abode	Names and Religion	Proffession	Children under 14		Children above 14		Men Servts		Women Servts	
				Prot.	Paps.	Prot.	Paps.	Prot.	Paps.	Prot.	Paps.
		Michl.Finan & wife	Labr.		1						
		Fran.Ash & wife			1						
	Carnekill	Robt.Hanly & wife			3		1				1
		Robt.Farrell & wife			1						
		Patt.Daly & wife							1		1
		Widow Kennedy			3		2				
	Kislree	Thom.Haydon & wife			2		1		1		1
		Fran.Igar & wife			2				1		1
	Ranagligh	John Kelly & wife			1						
		Con.Rower & wife			3		1				1
		Denis Goraghly & wife			3		1				1
		Tho.McDermott & wife			3		1				1
		John White & wife			2						
		Pet.Farrell & wife			3		1				
		Thady Cronan & wife			1						1
		Conr.Cormk & wife			2		1		1		1
		Patt.Conn & wife			1				1		1
		Nid. Cormk & wife			2				1		1
		Con.Daren & wife			1				1		1
		Pat.Casey & wife			2				1		1
		Thady Finy & wife	Weaver		3				1		1
		Carby Mason & wife	Broguemaker		1				1		1
		John Do & wife			2		1		1		1
Ogula	Timoney	Slip Conner & wife			3		1		1		1
		Michl.Connor[10] & wife	Gent				1		1		2
		Ned Corenus & wife					2				
		Gregory Mulloy & wife			2						1
	Ballymacinily	Thom.Talbott			3		1				1
		Cha.Bolan & wife			2						
		Sin.Talbott & wife	Broguemaker		2						
		Ja.Nally & wife	Cotter/labourer			2		1			
		Widow Faran	Widow								
		Widow Moran	Widow		2						
		Widow Riley & sister	Widow		3						
		Pa 74			69		22		18	0	24
[f.13]	Carinkill	Jams.Raulan & wife	Servt.		3		1		1		1
		Robert Farell & wife	Shopkr.		1				1		1
		Elizh.Kenidy widow	Spinner		3		2				
	Kilree	Thos.Headin	Servt.		2		1		1		1
		Franc. Igan & wife	Servt.		1		1		1		1
		John Kelly & wife	Shepard		1				1		1
	Rawnegligh	Michl.Phadin & wife	Farmer						1		1
		Cons.Headin & wife	Farmer		3		1		1		1
		Conr.Cormuck & wife	Farmr.		2		1		1		1
		Patt Conry & wife	Farmr.		1				1		1
		Ed.Cormuck & wife	Farmr.		2				1		1
		Con.Doram & wife	Farmer		1				1		1
		Hugh Coffy & wife	Farmr.		2				1		1
		Carby Mlgan & wife	Farmer		3				1		1

Com~Ros common Parish of	Place of Abode	Names and Religion	Proffession	Children under 14		Children above 14		Men Servts		Women Servts	
				Prot.	Paps.	Prot.	Paps.	Prot.	Paps.	Prot.	Paps.
		Tho. Feeny & wife	Weavr		3				1		1
		John Feeny & wife	Pumpmaker		2		1		1		1
		Steph.Conr & wife	Farmer		3		1		1		1
	Drimanagh	Conr.Diuginan & wife	Cotter				1		1		1
		Hugh Garnin & wife	Cotr		1				1		1
		Charl.Mory & wife	Cotr.		1						
		Edmond Greath & wife	Cottr		1				1		1
		Darby Naraghan & wife	Cotter						1		1
		Saml.Conilan & wife	Coter		3		1		1		1
		Nick.Feord & wife	Coter		1				1		1
		Patt.Feeny & wife	Coter						1		1
		John Bunnane & wife	Coter						1		1
		Domk.Corin & wife	Coter		2		1		1		1
		Owen Corin & wife	Coter		1						1
		Jams.Lync & wife	Cotter		2		1				1
		John Lync & wife	Cotter		2		2				
		Thoms. Mury & wife	Cotter		2				1		1
		Terince Bready & wife	Cotter						1		1
		Petter Hantin & wife	Cotter		1				1		1
		John Harly & wife	Cotter		1				1		2
		Thoms.Naughter & wife	Cotr						1		2
		Jams.Dound & wife	Cotter		1						
		Margrett Corane widow	Cotr		1						
		Patt.Grath widower	begr.								
		Martt.Nary & wife	Cotter		3				1		1
		Manis Nary & wife	Shepr.		2		1				
		Andr. Knavin prot	Cotter	2							1
		Pa 76		2	58		16		31		36

[Verso f. 12] There is an over return in Ogula of 11 families which I deduct in summing up the amount of the whole

Com~Ros common Parish of	Place of Abode	Names and Religion	Proffession	Children under 14		Children above 14		Men Servts		Women Servts	
[f.14]	Ogilla	Jos. Dorny & wife Pap	Cottier		2						
		Patt.Moffitt & wife Do	Do		2						
		Jos.Moffitt & wife Do	Do		2						
		Widow Conry do	Do		1						
		Domk.Oates & wife Do	Do		3						
	Ballybegg[11]	Luke Croshan & wife Do	Do				2				
		Ned Conolly & wife Do	Do		2						
		Petr.Conawhly & wife Do			1						
		Tom.Cooney & wife Do	Do				3		1		1
		Nr.Torney & wife Do	Do								2
		Tom McDrew & wife Do	Do				1				
		Owen Lenan Do	Do				3				
		Laughlin Kidyan & wife Do	Do				3				
		Mart.Nary & wife Do	Do		3						1
		Andr.Caveny & wife Do	Do		1						
		Manus Nary & wife Do	Do		3						
		Jos.Finawhty & wife Do	Do								
		Dudley Morris & wife Do	Do								
		Andr. Bones & wife Do	Do								
		Thos.Kear & wife	Do		2						

Com~Ros common Parish of	Place of Abode	Names and Religion	Proffession	Children under 14		Children above 14		Men Servts		Women Servts	
				Prot.	Paps.	Prot.	Paps.	Prot.	Paps.	Prot.	Paps.
		Thady Carty & wife Do	Do		2						
		Jos.Summachan Do	Glover		1						
	Driminah	Michl.Morewornagh & wife Do	Cottier		1				1		1
		Jams.Conway & wife Do	Do		2						
		Hey Garvin & wife Do	Do		1						
		Thom.Murry & wife Do	Do		1						1
		John Lyons & wife Do	Do		2						
		Conr.Dignan & wife Do	Do				1				
		Ned Masrah & wife Do	Do		1				1		1
		Darby Harrishan & wife Do	Do						1		1
		Patt.Feeny & wife Do	Do						1		1
		John Bannane & wife Do	Do		2				1		1
		Domk.Horan & wife Do	Do		2				1		1
		Owen Kereen & wife Do	Do		1						1
		John Lyne & wife Do	Do		2						1
		John Do & wife Do	Do		2				1		1
		Tho.Murry & wife Do	Do		2						1
		Tern. Bready & wife Do	Do						1		1
		Petr.Hanchiln & wife Do	Do		1				1		1
		Thos Washler & wife Do	Do						1		1
		Widow Careen Do	Widow								
		Pa: 76			45		13		11		18
[f.15] Ogulla	Laranon	John Kelly & wife					3				
		Jo. do & wife	Weaver		1				4		1
		Jams.Riley & wife									
		Peter Hagan & wife			1						
		Patt. Daly & wife			2		4				
		Cormuck Moran & wife									
		Franc Do & wife			3						
		Hen.Walsh & wife			1						1
		Matt.White & wife			3		3				1
	Carnagarrow	Widow Croghan			2		1				
		Thady Kelly & wife			1						1
		Patt.Kean & wife			2						1
		Edmd. Burke & wife			2						
		Peter Feeny & wife			2		3				
		Michl.McLean & w			3		1				1
		Peter Muldowny & wife			3		1				1
	Carne	Edmd.Kelly & wife			3						1
		Owen Kearing & wife			2						
		Larence Do & wife			2						
	Lismuliff	John Dillon & wife			4						1
		Bryan McCormuck & wife			3		2				
		Pa. 41			40		18		4		9

[1 blank page]

NOTES

1. Including a detached portion of 753 acres, and 56 acres of the river Shannon (*General Alphabetical Index*).

2. (N.L.I.,Clonbrock Papers, MS 19,672 pp. 37, 43, 54).

3. *Report...fairs and markets*.

4. J.J. Kelly, 'The Diocese of Elphin 1671-1717', *Irish Ecclesiastical Record*, xiv, no.2 (July-December 1893), p.1087; Turlough O'Connor Roe owned Cornsleyrane (R.C. Simington (ed.), *Books of Survey and Distribution being abstracts of various surveys and instruments of title 1636-1703*, Roscommon, (Dublin 1949). (Hereafter cited as *Books of Survey and Distribution*, Roscommon)).

5. Census, ff. 11, 12.

6. Census, f.244; Edith Mary Johnston-Liik, *History of the Irish Parliament 1692-1800 : commons, constituencies and statutes* (6 vols, Belfast, 2002), ii, 321. (Hereafter cited as *History of the Irish Parliament*).

7. N.L.I., J.B. Leslie, Elphin biographical succession list (1934), MS 5699, pp. 18, 142, 197. (Hereafter cited as Leslie, 'Elphin').

8. Described by Daniel Beaufort as 'a most wretched village' (Rev. D.A. Beaufort, 'Journal of a Tour through part of Ireland begun August 26th 1787',TCD MS 4026, 2/66). (Hereafter cited as Beaufort, 'Journal').

9. Thomas McDermott rented 'rich feeding bullock and sheep walk ground' from the Clonbrock estate in 1777 (N.L.I., Clonbrock Papers, MS 19,672 p. 43)

10. Michael O'Connor 'of Towmona' was a lay supporter of the Rev. William (alias Augustine) O'Kelly, prior of St. Mary's, Roscommon in 1748 to succeed Patrick French as Roman Catholic bishop of Elphin (Fenning, 'The Diocese of Elphin', p.166).

11. Lease from Edward Crofton to Danl Kelly of land at Ballybegg, 28 June 1723 (N.L.I., Crofton Papers, MS 8828/8).

SHANKILL, COUNTY ROSCOMMON

INTRODUCTION: *The parish of Shankill is in the barony of Roscommon, and is 2 miles south-west of Elphin. It covers 6,610 statute acres.*[1] *The land was thought to be good, but there was a large quantity of bog, and limestone was also quarried there.*[2]

The main landowner in the parish was Luke Dowell of Mantua. His fine palladian house has, like many, been attributed to Richard Castle. It is thought to have been built ca. 1747 by Oliver Grace who married the daughter and heiress of John Dowell.[3] *The large number of servants (29) living independently in the parish probably supplied not only the house at Mantua but also the demands of the neighbouring parish of Elphin, residence of the bishop.*

The parish was united with Kilmacumsy, Kilcooley, Killukin and Cloonygormican. The incumbent was the Rev. Oliver Cary who had been collated in 1731. The patron was the bishop.[4]

OCCUPATIONS

Butcher	1	Gentleman	2	Servant	29
Cottier	4	Herd	2	Servant, household	171
Cripple	1	Labourer	42	Shepherd	1
Dealer	2	Miller	3	Smith	2
Farmer	16	Pumpmaker	2	Spinner	2
Fiddler	1	Quilter	1	Tealar	1

Com~Ros common Parish of	Place of Abode	Names and Religion	Proffession	Children under 14		Children above 14		Men Servts		Women Servts	
				Prot.	Paps.	Prot.	Paps.	Prot.	Paps.	Prot.	Paps.
[f. 17] Shankill	Lanfoot	Edmd Eagan & wife pap	Labr.		3				1		1
		Hene.Sanders & wife pap	Labr.		3		1		1		1
	Killvoy	Math.Doffily & wife pap	Servt.						1		1
		Owen Feeny & wife pap	Servt.		2		1		1		1
		Jams Brillighan & wife pap	Servt.		1		1		1		1
		Joh. Bradly & wife pap	Servt.		3				1		1
		Michael Leapaghan & wife pap	Servt.		4				1		1
		Edmd.Larrinan & wife pap	Pumpmaker		5				1		1
		Patrick Gormly & wife pap	Tealar		3		5				1
		Walter Doyle & wife pap	Labr.		2		1		1		1
	Kilnebrady	Thom Shardwod & wife pap	Labr.		3		1		1		1
		Charls. Boran & wife pap	Labr.		1		1		1		1
		Bryan Haroughton & wife pap	Labr.		3				1		1
		And. Garry & wife pap	Labr.		2				1		1
		Jem. Flanigin widow pap	Quilter		1						
		James Carron & wife pap	Servt.		3				1		
		Conr. Kelly & wife pap	Labr.		3		1		1		1
		Danl. Dochry & wife pap	Labr.		2		1		1		1
		Patt. Kelly & wife pap	Servt.		1						1
		Owen Grily & wife pap	Labr.						1		1
	Fox Tail	Patt. Dowly & wife pap	Miller						1		1
		Cormick Murphy & wife pa			3		1			1	1
		John Bryan & wife pap	Farmr.		3		1			1	1
		Patt Bryan & wife pap	Labr.		3		2				
		Jams. Duany & wife pap	Butchr.		4					1	1
		Domk Dermott & wife pap	Labr.		4						1
		Cormuck Scally & wife pap	Labr.		1					1	1
		Jams. Neale & wife pap	Labr.		2					1	1
		Teranc. Neale & wife pap	Fidler		1					1	1
		Michael Duany & wife pap	Farmr.		3		1			1	1
		Conr. Coner & wife pap	Labr.		2		1			1	1
	Ballinaddy	Sileby Gaffry widow pap	Cullr.[?]							1	1
		Matt Brody & wife pap	Servt.		3		1			1	1
		Thom. Luby & wife pap	Servt.							1	1
		Domk Moran & wife pap	Servt.		3		1		1		1
		James Moran & wife pap	Servt.		2		2		1		1
	Carrowmore	Michael Conry & wife pap	Farmr.	2					1		1
		Thady Hull & wife pap	Labr.				2		1		1
		Thady Moran & wife pap	Labr. Jams.								
		Jams.Cormuck & wife pap	Farmr.		3				1		1
		John Cossare & wife pap			1						1
		Pro.2. Pa. 78		2	83		25		24	13	37
[f.18]	Carrowmore	Alex. Roach & wife papts	Labr.		1				1		1
		Thad Shanhod & wife pap	Labr.		2				1		1
		John Phadin & wife pap	Servt.								
		Darby Padyn & wife pap	Servt.		1						1
		John Bowton & wife pap	Labr.		1						1
		Sissey Brady widow	Miller		1						1
		Owne McDeigh & wife pap	Servt.		2				1		1

Com~Ros common Parish of	Place of Abode	Names and Religion	Proffession	Children under 14		Children above 14		Men Servts		Women Servts	
				Prot.	Paps.	Prot.	Paps.	Prot.	Paps.	Prot.	Paps.
		Owne McDeigh jr & wife pap	Servt.		1						1
		Bryn Donald & wife pap	Labr.		3						1
		Bridgett Rock widow			1		1				2
		Bryan Moran & wife pap	Smith		3						1
	Gortnagorr	Thady McDonagh & wife pap	Servt.		1						1
		Laughland Corran & wife pap	Dealr.		1				1		1
	Creeve	Bryan Doneagher & wife pap	Servt.		1				1		2
		Conr. Moran & wife pap	Labr.		1				1		1
		Thoms. Flanigin & wife pap	Servt.		3				1		1
	Carrowmongue	Jams Flanigin & wife pap	Farmr.		1				1		1
		Owin Dermott & wife pap	Farmr.		3						3
		Edmund Flanigan & wife pap	Farmr.		1				1		1
		John Moran & wife pap	Labr.		2				1		1
	Gortnegnanagh	Owne Moran & wife pap	Labr.		2				1		1
		Patt. Dermott & wife pap	Servt.		4				1		1
		Christy McDermott & wife papt	Servt.		1		2		1		1
	Tubermurry	Owne Spollon & wife pa	Miller		2				1		1
		John Farell & wife pa	Farmr.		3				1		1
		Jams. Farrel & wife pap	Labr.								
		John Farell & wife pap	Farmr.		2				1		1
		Conr. Cormick & wife	Farmr.		3				1		1
		Martin Conr & wife papt & wife pap	Labr.		3				1		1
		David Conry & wife pap	Farmr.		1				1		1
		Michael Burk & wife pap	Labr.		3				1		1
		Owne Conroy & wife pap	Pumpmaker								
		Catrin King & daught widow	Spinr.								
	Newtown	Charles Ronald & wife	Farmr.		1				1		1
		William Branan & wife pap	Farmr.		2		2		1		1
		Michell Brady & wife pap	Farmr.		3		1				1
		Patt Cononan & wife pap	Labr.						1		1
		Bryan Canonon & wife pap	Farmr.		2				1		1
		Mar. Moran & wife pap	Farmr.		3				1		1
		John Croughan & wife pap	Labr.		2						2
		Bryan Moran pap	A cripple								
		Pa: 79			67		6		25		41
[f.19] Shankill	Cloonasker	Peter Dealy & wife papt	Shepherd		3				1		1
		Ann Murphy & widow pap	Spinner				3				
		Thos Banaghan & wife pap	Dealer								
	Caldrimoran	Petter Dermott & wife pap	Servt.		3				1		1
		Bryan Biran & wife pap	Servt.								
		Philip Gormly & wife pap	Servt.		3						1
		John Dowd & wife pap	Servt.		3				1		1
		John Kelly & wife pap	Servt.		1						
	Ballyoughter	John Goldsmith[5] & wife prot.	Gentleman			5			2		2
		Michel Mullany & wife prot.	Servt.	2		2			1		1

Com~Ros common Parish of	Place of Abode	Names and Religion	Proffession	Children under 14		Children above 14		Men Servts		Women Servts	
				Prot.	Paps.	Prot.	Paps.	Prot.	Paps.	Prot.	Paps.
	All papists	Owne Cassily & wife pap	Servt.		3						
	that follow	Owne Conaghton & wife pap	Servt.		2				1		1
	in this page	Edmd Renold papt									
		Franc. Kelly & wife pap	Cottier		3		1				1
		Philip Gormly & wife pap	Cottier		2				1		1
		Daniel McGuire & wife pap	Cottier								1
	Rathroe	Thos. Sherrod & wife pap	Smith		2						1
		Bryan Harraghton & wife pap	Servt.		3		2				1
		Walter Doyle & wife pap	Cottier				2				
		Ger. Egan & w	Herd		1		3				1
	Mantua	Luke Dowell[6]	Gentleman						7		4
	Turlogh	Jas. Connor & w.			2		1				1
		Stephen Roach & Wife	Labr.		1		1				
		Joh. McDonagh & wife	Labr.		2		2				
		Jas. Sherrody & w	Labr.		2		1				1
		Darby Murtogh & wife	Labr.		3						1
		Owen McIrvine & wife	Labr.		4						1
		Pat. Conry & w	Labr.		3						1
		Pet. Hoen & w	Labr.				2		1		
		Joh. Maguire & w	Labr.		4				1		1
		Shep. Morris & w	Labr.		2				1		1
		Own. Tanisty & w:	Labr.		1		1				
		Ter. Hughes & w:	Labr.		3						1
		Jams. Sherody & wife	Herd		2		1		1		1
		Thady Berran & w:	Labr.		3		1				1
		Pa: 68		2	61	7	21		18		28

[1 blank page]

NOTES

1. Including 37 acres of water. There is a turlough at Mantua which covers 500 acres of water in winter (*General Alphabetical Index*; Lewis, 'Shankill, County Roscommon').

2. Lewis, 'Shankill, Co. Roscommon'.

3. (Mark Bence-Jones, *A Guide to Irish Country Houses* (revised edition, London 1988) 'Mantua House, Co. Roscommon'. (Hereafter, Bence-Jones, *Guide*).

4. Oliver Cary, son of Charles Cary. Educated at Carrick on (Shannon?) by Mr Manby. Entered TCD in 1720, aged 15 and took BA 1724. Became curate of Kilkeevan in 1729, rector of Cloonfinlogh 1731-42, rector of Killukin 1742-3, and prebendary of Kilcooley in 1743-67. In 1758 he became vicar of Enniscorthy, diocese of Ferns and rector of Rossdroit. He was precentor of Ferns 1767-77. Married Frances Southwell in Dublin. His will was proved in 1777 (Leslie, 'Elphin', p.183).

5. John Goldsmith, was a son of Robert Goldsmith a gentleman of Ballyoghter. He was tutored by a Mr Cugh of Strokestown and entered TCD in 1697, aged 18 (*Alumni Dubliniensis*).

6. Luke Dowell (c.1721-c.1755) was born at Elphin. He took BA at TCD in 1742. A tenant of Bishop Synge, he paid £3 a year rent. His will was proved in 1755 (N.L.I., Wicklow Papers PC 223(6); Vicars, p.142).

KILMACUMSY, COUNTY ROSCOMMON

INTRODUCTION: *The parish of Kilmacumsy is in the barony of Frenchpark, 4 miles north of Elphin. Its soil was gravel and limestone.*[1]

The living of Kilmacumsy was held with those of Shankill, Kilcooley, Killukin and Cloonygormican and Kilcorkey. The Rev. Oliver Cary was collated vicar in 1731 (see Shankill).

OCCUPATIONS

Farmer	60	Rider	1	Spinster/widow	11
Gentleman	1	Servant	31	Victualler	2
Labourer	38	Servants, household	250	Weaver	2
Piper	1	Smith	1		

Com~Ros common Parish of	Place of Abode	Names and Religion	Proffession	Children under 14 Prot.	Paps.	Children above 14 Prot.	Paps.	Men Servts Prot.	Paps.	Women Servts Prot.	Paps.
[f.21] Killmcumsy	Carrowcarn	Peter McDermott & Wife Pap	Farmr		3		1		1		1
		Laughln.Shanly & Wife Papt	Servt.		2				1		1
		John Feely & Wife Papt	Servt.		1				1		1
		Franc.Shannon & Wife Pap	Servt.		1				1		1
	Calltrough	Bryan Kelly & Wife Pap	Farmr						1		1
		Patt.Kenny & Wife Papt	Servt.		3				1		1
		John Shannon & Wife Pap	Servt.		4				1		1
		Michl Tanesty & Wife Pap	Servt.		1				1		1
		John Kenny & Wife Papt	Servt.		4				1		1
		Phelen Dermott & Wife Pap	Labr.		3						
		Michl.Bevin & Wife Papt	Servt.		3		2				
		Luke Walsh & Wife Papt.	Farmr.		4				1		1
		Paul Flanigin & Wife Papt.	Farmr.		4				1		1
		Patt.Byrn & Wife Papt.	Farmr.		3		1		1		1
		Mathw.Walsh & Wife Papt.	Farmr.		2				1		1
		John Shanly & Wife Papt.	Farmr.		2		1		1		1
		Rogr.McDermott & Wife Pap	Farmr.		1				1		1
		Patt.Bevin & Wife Papt.	Farmr.		2				1		1
		Rogr.Coony & Wife Papt.	Farmr.		1				1		1
		Char.Brian & Wife Papt.	Farmr.		1				1		1
		Hugh McDonogh & Wife Pap	Farmr.		2				1		1
		John Walsh & Wife Papt.	Labr.		2				1		1
		Farrell Flanigan & Wife Pap	Labr.		1				1		1
	Coroongh	Timothy Leanaghan & Wife	Farmr.		3				1		1
		Terce. McDermott & Wife Pap	Farmr.		3				1		1
		Wm.Conoughton & Wife Pap	Farmr.		2				1		1
		Patt.Horen & Wife Papt.	Farmr.		3		1		1		1
		Pat Leanaghan & Wife Papt.	Farmr.		1				1		1
		Edmd.Leanaghan & Wife Pap	Farmr.						1		1
		John Lambert & Wife Papt	Farmr.		1				1		1
		Alice McCormick widow Pap	Spinsr.		2						
		Eliz.Leanaghan wd. Papt	Spinsr.		4		1				
		Bridgt Digenan widw	Spinsr.		6		2				
		Edmd.Doyle Pap	Gent		1						1
	Shanbally	Robt. Cusick widr.	Farmr.				4		1		1
		Jno.Reily & Wife Papt.	Labr.		1				1		1
		Thos. Thonisk & Wife Pap	Servt.		2		1		1		1
		Mary Dowd wid Pap	Spinsr		3		1		1		1
		Jams.Bourn & Wife Pap	Servt.		2		1		1		1
		Darby Donnott & Wife	Servt.		2		1		1		1
		Darby Feally & Wife Pap	Labr.		3		1		1		1
[f.22] Killmcumsy	Killmcumsy	Franc.Brannon & Wife Papt	Farmer		2				1		1
		Char. Flanigan & Wife Papt	Farmer		3				1		1
		Patt.Whologhan & Wife Pap	Farmr.		3				1		1
		Tho.Moran & Wife Papt	Farmr.		5				1		1
		Owen Rynolds & Wife Papt	Farmr.		3				1		1
		Franc. Flanigan & Wife Papt	Farmr.		3				1		1

Com~Ros common Parish of	Place of Abode	Names and Religion	Proffession	Children under 14		Children above 14		Men Servts		Women Servts	
				Prot.	Paps.	Prot.	Paps.	Prot.	Paps.	Prot.	Paps.
		Jams.Duke & Wife Papt	Farmr.		2				1		1
		Laughln Flanigan & Wife Papt	Farmr.		1		1		1		1
		Conor Branan² & Wife Papt	Farmr.		2				1		1
		Teady Branan & Wife Papt	Farmr.		2		1		1		1
		Hugh Thorp & Wife Papt	Weaver		5		1		1		1
		Patt.Connell & Wife Papt	Labr.		3		1		1		1
		Michl.Whelaghan & Wife Papt	Labr.		4				1		1
		Thady Wholaghan & Wife Papt	Labr.		2				1		1
		Thos.Higgins & Wife Papt	Farmr.		3				1		1
		John Kelly & Wife Pap	Farmr.		2				1		1
		Patt.Dowd Papt.	Labr.								
		Patt.Connor & Wife Papt	Labr.		1				0		1
		Martin Moran & Wife Papt	Servt.		3				1		1
		Thos. Murphy & Wife Papt	Labr.		2				1		1
	Termore	John Martin & Wife Papt	Farmr.		3				1		1
		Patt Ore & Wife Papt	Labr.		3		1		1		1
	Lissnabull	Connor McDermott & Wife Papt	Servt.		3				1		1
		Mary McDermott widw.Pap	Spinsr.		1						
	Skenivar	Laghln Dowlan & Wife Papt	Servt.		3		1		1		1
		Patt.Keellen & Wife	Servt.		2				1		1
	Carrowintod	Toms.Flyn & Wife Papt	Servt.		3				1		1
		Chars.Diffilly & Wife Papt	Servt.		2				1		1
		Bryan Dowd & Wife Papt	Servt.		1				1		1
		Hugh Bradikin & Wife Papt	Smith		4				1		1
		Elinor Bratt widow Papt	Spinsr.		1		1				
		Dolly Byrne Widow papt	Spinsr.				2				
		Darby Daly & Wife Papt	Servt.		2						
	Carrowgarry	Edmd Moran & Wife Papt	Farmr.						1		1
		Connor Moran & Wife Papt	Farmr.		1				1		1
		Patt.Feely & Wife Papt	Farmr.		2				1		1
		Owen Connor & Wife Papt	Servt.		2				1		1
		Peter Brennan & Wife Pap	Vittlr.		2						
		Domk.Brannon & Wife	Labr.		6				1		1
		Patt.King & Wife Pap	Labr.		2						
		John Kearon & Wife Pap	Rider		4						
[f.23] Killmacumoy	Ardrologh	Mans.Brogan & Wife Papt	Servt.		3				1		1
		Jn.Hary & Wife Papt	Servt.		2		1		1		1
	Thurwough	John McGuire & Wife Papt	Farmr.		1				1		1
		Miles Moran & Wife Papt	Farmr.		3		1		1		1
		Jon.Moran & Wife Papt	Farmr.		1		1		1		1
		Jno.Morris & Wife Papt	Farmr.						1		1
		Mary Lorgan widw Papt	Spinsr.		4		4		1		1
	Carrowcolly	Patt. Bevin & Wife Papt	Farmr.		4		2		1		1
		Jams Quin & Wife Papt	Farmr.		4		2		1		1
		Thos. Moran & Wife Papt	Labr.		4		3		1		1
		Matthw.Bevin & Wife Papt	Labr.		3				1		1
		Luke Padyn & Wife Papt	Labr.		3		1		1		1
		Bryan Canna & Wife Papt	Farmr.						1		1
		Jams. Cahan & Wife Papt	Farmr.		2		1		1		1

Com~Ros common Parish of	Place of Abode	Names and Religion	Proffession	Children under 14 Prot.	Paps.	Children above 14 Prot.	Paps.	Men Servts Prot.	Paps.	Women Servts Prot.	Paps.
		Pet. Cahan & Wife Papt	Labr.						1		1
		Owen McDonough & Wife	Labr.		4		1		1		1
		Carbry Byrne & Wife Papt	Labr.		2		1		1		1
		Rogr. Connor & Wife Papt	Labr.		4		2				
		Thady Higgins & Wife Pap	Farmr.		3		2		1		1
		Wm.Higgins & Wife Papt	Farmr.		3		1		1		1
		Jams.Higgins & Wife Pap	Farmr.		1		1		1		1
		Mattw.Byrne & Wife Pap	Labr.		2				1		1
		Patt.Conry & Wife Pap	Labr.		3		2				1
		Ann Higgins & wife Pap	Spinsr.		2		1				1
		Jno.Bryan & Wife Papt	Labr.		4		7				1
		Jno McGarry & Wife Pap	Labr.		3		2				
		Patt.Comon & Wife ~~Labr~~	Labr.		1				1		1
		Thos Gaffry & Wife Pap	Farmr.		1		3		1		1
		Tady Flanigan & Wife	Farmr				3		1		1
		Owen Tresan & Wife Pap	Labr.		1		2		1		1
		Thos.Gaffry & Wife Papt	Farmr.						1		1
	Lissphilip	Patt.Moren & Wife Papt	Servt.		3		1		1		1
		John Moran & Wife Papt	Servt.		2		1		1		1
		Wm.Luby & Wife Papt	Servt.		3		1		1		1
		Thos. Dowd & Wife Papt	Piper		1				1		1
		Thady Burn & Wife Papt	Labr.		5		3		1		
		Owen Renolds & Wife Papt	Labr.		3		2				1
	Carrowgarry	Michl.Dermott Pap	Servt.		4		3		1		1
		Jno.Rowan & Wife Pap	Farmr.		2				1		1
		Jno.Fleming & Wife Pap	Farmr.		3		3		1		1
		Bryan O Brien & Wife	Farmr.								1
[f.24] Killmacumoy	Scormore	Morris Keating & Wife Pap	Farmr.		1				1		1
		Loughln Bain & Wife Pap	Farmr.		2				1		1
		Jams.Bain & Wife Pap	Farmr.		3				1		1
		Thady McDermott & Wife Pap	Farmr.		3		2		1		1
		Patt. Cran & Wife Pap	Farmr.		3		1		1		1
		Thady McDermott & Wife Pap	Victualler		2		1		1		1
		Tho Burke & Wife Pap	Labr.		1		1		1		1
		Edmd. Cran & Wife Pap	Labr.		2				1		1
		Matt.McLany & Wife Pap	Weaver		5		2				1
		Wm.Whaly & Wife Papt	Labr.		3		2		1		1
		Jams. Cran & Wife Pap	Labr.		1				1		1
		Elin McDermott Pap	Spinsr.			3		1			
	Gortnecligh	Patt.Cary & Wife Pap	Servt.		3				1		1
		Edmd McDermott & Wife	Farmr.				3		1		1
		Michl.Berne & Wife	Farmr.		3		2		1		1
		Andw.Bevin & Wife Papt	Labr.		4				1		1
	Lissphilip	Patt.Moren & Wife Papt	Labr.		3		1		1		1
		John Gowrin & Wife Pap	Servt.		2				1		1
		Conr.Garvin & Mothr. Pap	Labr.						1		1
		Jno.Gannon & Wife Pap	Labr.				1		1		1
	Lissmacool	Mathw. Gannon & Wife	Servt.		2		1		1		1
		Owen Gannon & Wife Pap	Servt.						1		1

Com~Ros common Parish of	Place of Abode	Names and Religion	Proffession	Children under 14		Children above 14		Men Servts		Women Servts	
				Prot.	Paps.	Prot.	Paps.	Prot.	Paps.	Prot.	Paps.
		Carin Gannon widow	Spinsr.		1		3				
		Edmond Clark & Wife Pap	Servt.		3		1		1		1
		Edmond Flanigan & Wife	Labr.						1		

NOTES

1. Lewis, 'Kilmacumsy'.

2. The estate of Connor Brannon of Kilmacumsy was proved in 1798 (Index to Administration Bonds, N.L.I. microfilm p.1731).

KILCORKEY, COUNTY ROSCOMMON

INTRODUCTION: *The parish of Kilcorkey is 2 miles south-east of French Park and is in the barony of Castlereagh. It covers 6102 statute acres. It was said to have excellent pasture, but that the land bordering the banks of the streams that flowed into Lough Gara was frequently flooded and consequently produced rank grass.[1] Belanagare was the residence of the O'Conor family and had markets five times a year, in January, March, May, August and November. The January market was noted for horses and pigs.[2] A fair was held three times a year in Kilcorkey.[3]*

The leading Roman Catholic was Denis O'Conor of Belanagare who was born in 1674 and married Mary O'Rourke, daughter of the Chief of Breffny. They were the parents of Charles O'Conor, the writer and antiquarian.[4]

The parish was a rectory. In 1749, the rector was the Rev. Oliver Cary who was collated in 1723. He held the living with those of Shankill, Kilcooley, Kilmacumsy, Killukin and Cloonygormican (see Shankill). The patron was the bishop.

OCCUPATIONS

Broguemaker	2	Plowman	1	Spinner	3
Cooper	1	Servant	45	Tailor	1
Farmer	28	Servants, household	175	Victualler	2
Gentleman	4	Smith	4	Weaver	7
Miller	1				

Com~Ros common Parish of	Place of Abode	Names and Religion	Proffession	Children under 14 Prot.	Paps.	Children above 14 Prot.	Paps.	Men Servts Prot.	Paps.	Women Servts Prot.	Paps.
[f.25] Killcorkey	Ballinagar	Denis O'Connor[5] & Wife Papt.	Gent				4		2		2
		Mathw. Nowin & Wife Papt	Servt		3						
		Willm.Concannon & Wife	Servt		1						
		Edmd. Kenedy & Wife Papt	Miller		1				1		1
		James Highland & Wife Pap	Smith		1				1		1
		Franc. Conolly & Wife Papt	Broagmakr.		2				1		1
		Chars.Gowrin & Wife Papt	Broagmakr.		1				1		1
		Thos.Conniff & Wife Papt	Plowman		1				1		1
		Wm.Fingle & Wife Papt	Servt		3						1
		Michl.Lowry & Wife Pap	Servt		4						
		Patt.Gall & Wife Papt	Cooper		1				1		1
		Edmd. Eagan & Wife Papt	Victulr		1				1		1
		Connor Flannigan & Wife	Farmr		3				1		1
		Bryan McVeigh & Wife	Servt		3				1		1
	Carrowreagh	Joseph Plunkett[6] & Wife	Gent		1						1
		Peter McGann & W	Servt		3						
		Franc.McNeal & Wife Papt	Servt		2						
		Patt.Callaghan & Wife Pap	Servt		4						1
		Darby Dockery & Wife Papt	Servt		2				1		1
		Lawce.Gormally & Wife Pap	Servt		4						1
		Charl.Comond & Wife Pap	Servt		2						1
		Terce.Conn & Wife Pat	Servt		2				1		1
		And.McDonnell & Wife Pap	Servt		3				1		1
		Pat.Casarrly & Wife Papt	Servt		1		2		1		1
		John McGowrin & Wife	Farmr		2		1		1		1
		Patt.Flin & Wife Papt	Farmr		2		1				1
		Bryan Gordin & Wife Papt	Farmr		2		1		1		1
		Bryan Dockeran & Wife	Farmr		2		1				1
		Danl.Bradly & Wife pa	Weaver		3		1		1		1
	Peake	Thady Keigher & Wife pap	Smith		0		2		1		1
		Domk.Hoaser & Wife pap	Farmr				2		1		1
		Edmund Smith & Wife pa	Farmr		1				1		1
		Mathw.Tully & Wife Pap	Farmr		1				1		1
		Mary Dermott Widow pa	Spinsr				2		1		1
		Elinor Dowell widw. Pap	Spinsr		1				1		1
		John Farrell & Wife Pap	Farmr				3				1
		Carin Roger Widow Pap	Spinsr								
	Killcorky[7]	Richd.Ruttledge[8]/Prot & Wife pa	Gent				2		2		2
		Mongon Sweeny & Wife Pap	Vict		1						
		Jno Kelly & Wife Pap	Weaver		2						
		Conor Hasler & Wife	Tailor						1		1
		Pro. 1. Pa 78			66		22		27		35
[f.26] Killcorky	Killcorky	Tho Eagan Papist	Smith						1		1
		Thady Hanly & Wife Pap	Constable						1		1
		Jno.McRownesson & Wife Pap	Servt		2				1		1
		Petr. Higgins & Wife Papt	Servt		2				1		1

Com~Ros common Parish of	Place of Abode	Names and Religion	Proffession	Children under 14		Children above 14		Men Servts		Women Servts	
				Prot.	Paps.	Prot.	Paps.	Prot.	Paps.	Prot.	Paps.
		John Mcand & Wife Papt	Servt		2				1		1
		Luke McRonofin & Wife Pa	Servt		2				1		1
		Michl. McDermott & Wife Papt	Servt		2				1		1
	Tully	Connr. Croghan & Wife Pap	Servt				4		1		1
		Michl. Harter & Wife Papt	Servt		2				1		1
		Andrew Conn & Wife Papt	Servt		1				1		
		Lewis Conry & Wife Pap	Servt		2						1
		Rob. Farrell & Wife Pap	Servt		3		4		1		1
		Danl. Conry & Wife Pap	Servt		3		1		1		1
		Danl. Sheill & Wife Pap	Servt		3		1		1		1
		Miles Reily & Wife Pap	Servt		2				1		1
		Patt. Carn & Wife Pap	Servt		3				1		1
	Braiscan	Patt.Plunkett & Wife Pap	Gent		3				2		2
		Luke Tresnan & Wife Pap	Servt		3		1		1		1
		Thos. Farrell & Wife Pap	Smith		3		1		1		1
		Jno. McLain & Wife Pap	Servt		2		1		1		1
		John Farrell & Wife Pap	Servt		2		1		1		1
		John Crofton & Wife Pap	Servt		2		2		1		1
		Mathw. Tully & Wife Pap	Weaver		3		2		1		1
	Ballyconbeg	John Brown & Wife Pap	Farmr		2		3		1		1
		Franc.Hanly & Wife Pap	Farmr		1				1		1
		Richd. Muldowne & Wife Pap	Farmr		2		3		1		1
		Patt.Lain & Wife Pap	Farmr		1		1		1		1
		Patt.Ward & Wife Papt	Weaver		1		1		1		1
		Bartly Heidian & Wife Papt	Farmr		3		1		1		1
		Hugh McGrah & Wife Pap	Farmr		2				1		1
		Patt.Birn & Wife Pap	Farmr		2				1		1
		Edmd. Manin & Wife Pap	Farmr		3		1		1		1
		Rogr. Scally & Wife Pap	Farmr		1				1		1
		Connor Scally & Wife Pap	Farmr		2				1		1
		Lawr.Dockery & Wife Pap	Farmr		3				1		1
		Jno.Ward & Wife Papt	Farmr						1		1
		Jno.Higgins & Wife Papt	Farmr		1		1		1		1
		Michl.Foord & Wife Pap	Weaver						1		1
		Thos.Dillon & Wife Pap	Weaver		3		1		1		1
		Bryan Moran & Wife	Servt		1				1		1
		Bryan Kelly & Wife	Servt		3		1		1		1
		Pa 80			78		31		41		42
[f.27] Killcorky	Rawnaclerg	Walter Stanton and Brother Papt	Farmers						1		1
		Bryan Master & Wife Pap	Farmr		1				1		1
		Owen Master & Wife Papt	Farmr						1		1
		Edmd.McCormick & Wife Papt	Farmr		1				1		1
		Edward Sansom & Wife Pap	Farmr		3				1		1
		James Flanigin & Wife Papt	Weaver		3		1		1		1
	Rawkinerly	Michl.Fox & Wife Papt	Servt		3		1		1		1
	Ballyconbeg	Edmd.Kelly & Wife Papt	Servt		3				1		1
		James Kelly & Wife Papt	Servt		2				1		1

Com~Ros common Parish of	Place of Abode	Names and Religion	Proffession	Children under 14 Prot.	Paps.	Children above 14 Prot.	Paps.	Men Servts Prot.	Paps.	Women Servts Prot.	Paps.
		John Harraughton. & Wife Papt	Servt		3				1		1
		Thos. Clark & Wife Papt	Servt		3				1		1
		Thos.Healy & Wife Pap	Servt		2		1		1		1
		Denis Kelly & Wife Papt	Servt		3				1		1
		Hugh Morin & Wife Papt	Servt		4				1		1
		Cormick Garvin & Wife Pap	Servt		3				1		1
		Patt.Ward & Wife Papt	Servt		2		1		1		1
		Thos. Houlton & Wife Papt	Servt		2		2		1		1
		Pa 34			38		6		17		17

[1 blank page]

NOTES

1. Lewis, 'Kilcorkey'.
2. Lewis, 'Belanagare'.
3. *Report...fairs and markets*.
4. Sir Bernard Burke, *Landed Gentry of Ireland* (London, 1958). (Hereafter cited as Burke, *LGI* (1958)).
5. Denis O'Conor married Mary, daughter of Tiernan O'Rourke, chief of Breffny. She died in 1760. They had eight children, the eldest of whom was Charles O'Conor (1710-1790) the antiquarian. Denis O'Conor was a lay supporter of the Rev. William (alias Augustine) O'Kelly, prior of St. Mary's, Roscommon in 1748 to succeed Patrick French as bishop of Elphin (Fenning, 'Diocese of Elphin', (1994), p.166).
6. Joseph Plunkett of Carurivagh was a lay supporter of the Rev. William (alias Augustine) O'Kelly, prior of St. Mary's, Roscommon in 1748 to succeed Patrick French as bishop of Elphin. (Fenning, 'Diocese of Elphin', p.166).
7. 'To be sett for a Term of Years from the first of May next the town and lands of Akeerin, Lissigallen and comms within Two miles of Roscommon and also the Town and lands of Killcorkey with a good Farm house and offices therein, within four miles of Boyle and four miles of Elphin, all in the County of Roscommon. Proposals will be received by Mr Wentworth Thewles Attorney at his house in Athlone... the lands will be shown by Mr Edward Hodson of Houndslow Heath, near Roscommon. N.B. All the said lands are Tythe and Quit-rent free' (*Dublin Courant*, 30 December-1 January 1746).
8. Richard Rutledge was a freeholder who supported John French in 1768 (N.L.I., Freeholders of Co. Roscommon 1768, MS 35,152).

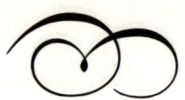

AUGHRIM, COUNTY ROSCOMMON

INTRODUCTION: *The parish of Aughrim is in the barony of Roscommon. It has 8254 statute acres and lies north-west of Elphin.*[1] *A section of the north-east boundary of the parish is bounded by the river Shannon. There are many small lakes, tracts of bog and woodland, and there were limestone quarries, with stone suitable for building. The land was mainly under tillage.*[2] *Most of the parish was owned by the St. George family.*

The parish minister was the Rev. George Blackburne. He held Aughrim together with the parishes of Clooncraff, Kilmore and Killummod. A new church was built in Aughrim in 1744.[3] *The parish had been held with that of Clooncraff from the 15th century. The patron was the bishop.*

OCCUPATIONS

Barber	1	Herd	17	Servant, household	150
Broguemaker	2	Innkeeper	3	Shoemaker	1
Carpenter	2	Magistrate	3	Smith	4
Clerk and Schoolmaster	1	Mason	3	Spinster	3
Cottager	118	Merchant	1	Tailor	8
Farmer	147	Pedlar	1	Weaver	13
Gentleman	3	Servant	3	Yeoman	3
Hatter	1				

Com~Ros common Parish of	Place of Abode	Names and Religion	Proffession	Children under 14 Prot.	Paps.	Children above 14 Prot.	Paps.	Men Servts Prot.	Paps.	Women Servts Prot.	Paps.
Aghrim	Lisdorn[4]	Jn. Crofton Esqr[5] & Wife	Magistrte.	3		3		3	1	2	4
	Ardsallagh	Joan Daly, Widow Papt.	Spinster		2		2				
		Danl.Hely Batchr. Papt	Carpentr.								
	Do-	Redmd.& Margt.Hellford Papt.	Cotager								
	Do-	Matt.& Sarah Tully Papt.	Smith		4						
	Do-	Paul & Sarah Carane Papt.	Cotagr.		3						1
	Do-	Michl. & Jane Trap Prot.	Weaver	1					1		
	Do-	Thady & Giles McSharry Pap.	Cotagr.		2						
	Do	Edmd. & Ellinr. Murphy Pap	Mason		2		1				
	Do-	Olivr. & Mary Smith Prot.	Servant	3		1					
	Do -	Eliz.Pilkington Widw. Prot		1							
	Do -	Jn. & Jane Smith Prot	Inn keeper	4							1
	Do -	Jn. & Ann Rogers Pap.	Cottager		3						
	Do -	Jam. & Ellinr. Crofton Pap.	Cottager		1				1		
	Do -	Winny McCormuck Pap Widow			1		2				
	Do -	Jn. & Joan Kelly Pap.	Cottager		3						
	Do -	Jam. & Brigt.Canane Pap	Cottager		5						
	Do -	Jn. & Brigt.McDonnell Pap	Cottager		3						
	Do -	Petr. & Mary Higgins Pap	Cottager		2						
	Do -	Char.Connor Batchr. Pap	Hatter								
	Ardboy	Pat. & Margt. Cannane Pap	Herd		1		1				
	Do -	Hugh & Hanna Hangly Pap.	Cottager				2				1
	Do -	Carbry & Catherine Beirn Pap	Cottager		1		1				2
	Do -	Joan McDermott Widw. Pap.					3				
	Do -	Barthw. Ann } Kelly Pap	Cottager		5						
	Do -	Thos. Cath. } Crofton Pap	Cottag		2				1		
	Do -	Thoms Brigt. } Pilkington Prot.	Mason			1					
	Do -	Michl. Brigt } Dowd Pap	Cottag								
	Do -	Owen Sisley } McDay Pap	Cottag		2						
	Do -	Willm Honor } Gowarty Pap	Cottager				2				
	Do -	Owen Brigt. } McDay Pap	Cottag								
	Lagane	Mrs Ann Birchall Widw. Pr.				1			1		1
	Do -	Richd Mary } Plunkett[6] Pap	Farmer				1	1			1

Com~Ros common Parish of	Place of Abode	Names and Religion	Proffession	Children under 14 Prot.	Children under 14 Paps.	Children above 14 Prot.	Children above 14 Paps.	Men Servts Prot.	Men Servts Paps.	Women Servts Prot.	Women Servts Paps.
	Do -	George⁷ / Ann } Begg Pap	Farmer								
	Do -	Brian / Margt } McDermott Pap	Cottager		2		1				
	Do -	Luke Crosby Widr. Pap	Cottagr.		2						
	Do -	Henry / Mary } Costelo Pap	Weaver		3			1			
	Do -	Luke Crosby	Cottagr.		2						
	Do -	Owen / Rose } Moran Pap	Cottagr.		1						
	Carrowreagh	John / Cath. } Dillon Pap	Farmer		3						2
	Do -	Thady / Mary } Lenaghan Pap.	Cottager		1		1				
		Prots 12. Papts 60		12	54	6	17	5	5	2	12
[f.29] Aghrim	~~Thady Maxwell~~ Carrowreagh	Thady Maxell Pap. batchelor	Smith								
	Enagh	Patrick / Margart. } Verdun Pap.	Servt.		4						
	Do -	Hugh / Mary } Oats Pap.	Taylor		3						
	Do -	Danl. Sweeny Batchelr. Pap.	Farmer								1
	Do -	Charles / Mary } Horan Pap.	Farmer		2						
	Do -	Owen / Mary } Flanigin	Do								
	Cornespineoge	Anthony / Brigit } McLaughlin Pap.	Do.		2				1		1
	Do -	John / Mary } Daly Pap.	Do.		3						
	Do -	Thos. Newheny Batchr. Pap	Do.						1		1
	Do -	Terence / Sarah } Kelly Pap.	Do.								1
	Do -	Dennis / Brigit } Morahan Pap	Do.								
	Ardleckny	Roger / Margart. } Lenaghan Pap	Cottag.		1						
	Do -	James / Ann } Gannan Pap.	Do		2						

Com~Ros common Parish of	Place of Abode	Names and Religion	Proffession	Children under 14		Children above 14		Men Servts		Women Servts	
				Prot.	Paps.	Prot.	Paps.	Prot.	Paps.	Prot.	Paps.
	Do -	Faughny / Winny Flanagan Pap	Servt								
	Do -	Willm. / Mary Roach Pap	Cottager								
	Do -	Matthw. / Ellinor Blachford Pap	Cottager		1						
	Do -	Robt / Margt Brown Prot. Pap	Cottager								
	Do -	Giles Beirn Widw.Pap									
	Do -	Danl.Duffily Batchr. Pap	Broagmaker								
	Do -	Martin / Mable Lavin Pap	Herd		3		2				
	Do -	Bryan / Mary Rutlege Pap	Farmer		1				1		1
Killnemunah		John / Mary Crosby Pap	Herd		2				2		1
	Do -	Owen / Cath. McDermott Pap	Cottagr.		2						
Lishugh		Margart.Gormuly Widw. Pap	Cottager		1		1				
	Do -	Thos / Eliz. Costello Pap	Cottager		3						
	Do -	Laughlin / Catherine McGawran Pap	Cottager		3						
	Do -	Danl.Murphy Batchr. Pap	Cottager								
Corlis		Cormk. / Honor McDermott Pap	Farmer		2				1		
	Do -	James / Mary Hill Pap	Do		1						
	Do -	Connor / Mary McDermott Pap	Do		2						1
	Do -	Edmd. / Eliz. Hoen Pap	Do		3				1		1
	Do -	Willm. / Sisley Duignan Pap	Do		3						
	Do -	More Walsh Widw Pap	Do				1				
	Do -	Margt. McDermott Widw. Pap	Do.				3				
	Do -	James / Mary Dunn Pap	Do		2		3				
Kilcarwran		Terence / Cather. Moran Pap	Cottager				1				1

Com~Ros common Parish of	Place of Abode	Names and Religion	Proffession	Children under 14		Children above 14		Men Servts		Women Servts	
				Prot.	Paps.	Prot.	Paps.	Prot.	Paps.	Prot.	Paps.
	Do -	Thos. Mary } Moran Pap	Do		2						1
	Do -	Willm. Mary } Egan Pap	Do		2						
	Do -	Jam. Oonah } Halfpenny Pap	Do						1		
	Do -	Patr. Mary } Halfpenny Pap			1						
		Do - Prots 1. Papts 70			54		11		7		10
[f.30] Aghrim	Carrow- nagleragh	Danl. Cather. } Baltany Pap	Farmer		2						
	Do -	Margaret Beirne Widow Pap.	Do		2		1				
	Do -	Charles Jane } McDermott Pap.	Taylor		1		1				
	Do -	Bryan Elinor } Conolly Pap	Weaver		1						
	Do -	Patrick Giles } Gormuly Pap.	Farmer		4		1		1		
	Do -	Connor Margaret } Conry Pap	Farmer		2						
	Do -	Hugh Honor } Callaghan Pap	Do		1						
	Do -	John Sisley } Quin Pap	Do								
	Do -	Danl. Clare } Balteny Pap	Do				1				
	Do -	John Brigit } Balteny Pap	Do								
	Do -	Patrick Winny } Costello Pap	Do		2				1		
	Do -	Edmd Cath. } Gannan Pap	Farmer		3						
	Do -	Dennis Margart. } Flynn Pap	Smith		1		1				
	Do -	Bryan Margart. } Gibulan Pap	Farmer								
	Do -	Hugh Oonah } Flaherty Pap	Do								1

Com~Ros common Parish of	Place of Abode	Names and Religion	Proffession	Children under 14		Children above 14		Men Servts		Women Servts	
				Prot.	Paps.	Prot.	Paps.	Prot.	Paps.	Prot.	Paps.
	Do -	Martin / Ellinor } Gibulan Pap	Do		2						
	Do -	Edwd. / Margart. } Gormuly Pap	Do		1						
	Do -	Lawrence / Mary } Gannan Pap	Do						1		
	Do -	Gilbt. / Mary } Gannan Pap	Do		2		1				
	Do -	Thoms. / Sarah } Skulloge Pap	Do		2						
	Do -	Charles Skullogue Widower	Taylor		5		1				
	Do -	Hugh / Mary } Skulloge Pap	Farmer		2						
	Do -	Danl / Mary } Gannan Pap	Do		2						
	Do -	Domnick / Mary } Gannan Pap	Do		1						
	Do -	Mary Burk Widw. Pap	Do		2						
	Do -	Peter / Catherine } Callaghan Pap	Do		2						
	Do -	Gilbt. / Sarah } Gannan Pap	Do		2						
	Do -	Charles / Ellinor } Hely Pap	Do				1		1		
	Do -	Murtagh / Brigit } Kane Pap	Do		3						
	Do -	Hugh / Mable } Jones Pap	Do		5		4				
	Do -	Bryan / Sarah } Neal Pap	Weaver				1				
	Do -	Edmd / Mary } Kennedy Pap	Farmer								
	Do -	James / Sarah } Kennedy Pap	Do				2				
	Do -	Bryan / Margaret } Ward Pap	Farmer		1						
	Do -	Michl. / Honor } Callaghan Pap	Weaver		2						
	Do -	John Duane Widowr. Pap	Broagmaker		1						
	Do -	Dennis / Honor } Gannan Pap	Farmer								

Com~Ros common Parish of	Place of Abode	Names and Religion	Proffession	Children under 14		Children above 14		Men Servts		Women Servts	
				Prot.	Paps.	Prot.	Paps.	Prot.	Paps.	Prot.	Paps.
	Do -	John Mary } Gannan Pap	Do		1						
	Do -	Edmd. Brigit } Callery Pap	Do		4						
	Do -	Roger Ann } Dockery Pap	Do		3						
		Papts 76			65		15		4		1
[f.31] Aghrim	Carrowna-gleragh	Michl Ann } Balteny Pap	Farmer		2						
	Do -	James Margart. } Neal Pap	Weaver		1						
	Do -	Danl. Winny } Nolan Pap	Farmer		1						
	Do -	James Margart } Callery Pap	Do		1						
	Do -	Thady Balteny Widowr.Pap	Do								
	Do -	John Mary } Kennedy Pap	Do								
	Do -	Alexr. Mable } McDonnell Pap	Do		2						
	Do -	Danl. Eliz. } Hely Pap	Do		2						
	Do -	Darby Honor } Dockery Pap	Do						1		1
	Do -	Dennis Brien Widowr.Pap	Do		4		2				
	Do -	Patrick Mary } Gannan Pap	Weaver								
	Do -	Peter Mary } Dockery Pap	Farmer		2						
	Lisavilly	Margt Beirn Widw. Pap	Spinster		1		1				1
	Do -	Thoms. Jane } Butler Pap	Farmer								2
	Do -	Patrick Honor } Butler Pap	Do		3						1
	Do -	John Mary } Higgins Pap	Do								
	Do -	James Elizab. } McDonnell Pap	Herd		3						
	Do -	Thady Mary } Kelly Pap	Taylor		2						

Com~Ros common Parish of	Place of Abode	Names and Religion	Proffession	Children under 14		Children above 14		Men Servts		Women Servts	
				Prot.	Paps.	Prot.	Paps.	Prot.	Paps.	Prot.	Paps.
	Do -	Cather.mcGuire Widw. Pap	Cottager		2		4				
	Do -	Hugh Cather.} mcGuire Pap	Cottagr.		2						
	Do -	Barthw. Brigit} Daly Pap	Do		1						
	Tullnahirk	Gilbert Mary} Ganly Prot	Yeoman			1			1		2
	Do -	John Winny} Costello Pap	Cottager		5		1				
	Do -	Austin Winny} Oolaghan Pap			3						
	Do -	Thady Brigit} Hanly Pap	Herd		1						
	Do -	Bryan Rose} McDermott Pap	Cottager		5		1				
	Drummoodan	Peter Brigit} Glaney Pap	Farmer		1						1
	Do -	Honr. Hely widw. Pap	Do		1		2				
	Do -	James Mary} Beirn Pap	Do		2						
	Do -	Peter Ann} Dolan Pap	Do		3						
	Do -	Michl. Mary} Dolan Pap	Do		1						
	Do -	Morgan Mary} Flaherty Pap	Do		2						
	Do -	Austin Joan} Conry Pap	Do		2		1				
	Do -	Owen Ellinor} Regan Pap	Do		1		3				
	Do -	Thoms Joan} Comyn Pap	Do		2		1				
	Do -	Darby Ann} Comyn Pap	Do		2					1	
	Do -	Danl. Mary} Clark Pap	Cottager		2						
	Ballagh	Michl. Mary} Mulick Pap	Herd		1						
	Do -	Thomas Mary-} Lehaghan Pap	Cottager		1						1

Com~Ros common Parish of	Place of Abode	Names and Religion	Proffession	Children under 14		Children above 14		Men Servts		Women Servts	
				Prot.	Paps.	Prot.	Paps.	Prot.	Paps.	Prot.	Paps.
	Do -	Arthr. Cather. } Cormuck Pap	Cottager				2				
		Prots 2 Pap. 73.			64	1	17		4		9
[f.32] Aghrim.	Currys	Michl. Margar. } Dunn Pap	Farmer		2						
	Do -	John Honor } Duignan Pap	Do								
	Do -	Hugh Mary } Hoen Pap	Do		3						
	Do -	Bryan Brigit } Maxwell Pap	Do								
	Do -	Thoms Elizab. } Hoen Pap	Do								
	Do -	Barthw. Joan } Hoen Pap	Do								
	Do -	John Cather. } Glancy Pap	Do		2		1				1
	Do -	Charles Honor } Dunn Pap	Do						1		1
	Do -	Michl. Brigit } Beirn Pap	Do		2				1		1
	Corclare	Thady Margar. } Muldoony Pap	Do		2						
	Do -	Patrick Mary } Waldron Pap	Do		4						
	Do -	Owen Ellinor } Glancy Pap	Do		3		1				1
	Do -	Michl. Ellis } Dunn Pap	Do		1						
	Do -	Peter Cather. } Mcoy Pap	Do		2						
	Do -	John Ganly Widowr Prot	Do	2		2			2		
	Do -	Charles Lavy } Stevens Prot.	Do	3							
	Do -	Richd Mary } Smith ~~Buchanan~~ Prot	Do	2		3					
	Do -	John Ellinor } Buchanan Prot	Do	1		2					
	Grange	Chidly Mary } Crofton[8] Prot.	Gent					2		1	1

Com~Ros common Parish of	Place of Abode	Names and Religion	Proffession	Children under 14 Prot.	Children under 14 Paps.	Children above 14 Prot.	Children above 14 Paps.	Men Servts Prot.	Men Servts Paps.	Women Servts Prot.	Women Servts Paps.
	Do -	Henry Crofton Prot	Cottager		1						1
	Do -	Mrs Susanna Crofton Prot.	widow			1		1	1	2	2
	Do -	Dominick } Daly Pap Elizab.	Herd		2		1				
	Do -	Edmund } Padin Pap Mary	Cottager		1						1
	Do -	Mary Oats Widw. Pap	Do				1				
	Do -	Laurence } Balteny Pap Brigit	Do		2						
	Lisnenoran	Michl. } Lavin Pap Cather.	Cottager		2						
	Do -	Ambrose } Beirn Pap Mary	Do		2		1				
	Do -	Joan Lenaghan wid. Pap	Do		1		1				
	Do -	Peter } Lenaghan Pap Mary	Do		2						
	Do -	James } Dermott Pap Ann	Do		1						
	Do -	Sisley Lenaghan Widw Pap	Do				1				
	Cloonfad	Martin } Brown Pap Alice	Farmer		2				2		2
	Do -	Owen } Magrah Pap Ann	Cottager		2				1		
	Do -	Daniel } Moran Pap Sarah	Do				1				
	Do -	Thady } Connilan Pap Margt.	Do				1		1		1
	Do -	Owen } mcDermott Pap Cather.	Do				4				
	Do -	Michl. } Lenaghan Pap Ann	Do				2				
	Do -	James } Morris Pap Sarah	Do		1		2				
	Do -	Patrick } Duigenan Pap Cather.	Do				1				
	Do -	Patrick } Glancy Pap Ellinor	Do		2						
		Prots 11 Pap. 63.		8	40	9	18	3	9	3	11
[f.33] Aghrim.	Cloonfad	Martin } Casker Pap. Eliza.	Cottager		1						

Com~Ros common Parish of	Place of Abode	Names and Religion	Proffession	Children under 14		Children above 14		Men Servts		Women Servts	
				Prot.	Paps.	Prot.	Paps.	Prot.	Paps.	Prot.	Paps.
	Cloonfad beg	Ross Reynolds widowr Pap.	Farmer				1		1		1
	Do -	Nicholas } Reynolds Pap. Cathar.	Do		1				1		1
	Do -	William } Beirn Pap. Brigit	Cottager		2						
	Do -	Francis } Beirn Pap. Joan	Do		1						
	Do	Dennis } Glancy Pap. Joan	Do		2		2				
	Do -	Laughlin } Glancy Pap. Brigit	Do		2						
	Killevoy	John } Waple Pap. Cathar.	Constable								
	Do -	Michl } Bohan Pap. Rose	Weaver		1		2				
	Do -	Mary Walsh Widow Pap.	Cottager						1		
	Do -	More Duignan Widw. Pap.	Do		2						
	Do -	Patrick } Moran Pap. Brigit	Do		1				1		
	Lacken	Patrick } Laughlin Pap. Mary	Herd		2		2				
	Do -	Peter } Redahan Pap. Mary	Cottager				2				
	Do -	James } Farrel Pap. Mary	Herd		2				1		
	Bryanbeg	Cormuck } Cannan Pap. Honor	Farmer		1		1				2
	Do -	Hugh } Ganly Pap. Margar.	Do				1				1
	Bryanmore	Patrick } Keelty Pap. Mable	Farmer		1		2				
	Do -	Terence } Killmartin Pap. Jane	Cottager		1						1
	Do -	Thady } Rorke Pap Brigit	Do								
	Loghboy	Thady } Conry Pap Honor	Farmer		2				1		
	Do -	Patrick } Conry Pap Sisley	Do		2						
	Killraddan	James Plunkett Prot 2 maiden sisters Pap.	Gent						1		2

Com~Ros common Parish of	Place of Abode	Names and Religion	Proffession	Children under 14		Children above 14		Men Servts		Women Servts	
				Prot.	Paps.	Prot.	Paps.	Prot.	Paps.	Prot.	Paps.
Do -	Lewis Ann McLaughlin Pap.		Mason		1						
Do -	Patrick Sisley FitzGerald Pap.		Cottager		2		2				
Do -	Owen Mary Dolan Pap.		Do		1						
Knock-negawna	William Ellinor Gilmuir Pap.		Inn-keepr.	1					1		1
Logitean	Henry Susanna Waple Pap.		Farmer		4				1		1
~~Patr~~ Do -	Patrick Catherin Gibulan Pap.		Do		4				1		
Do -	James Rose Keelty Pap.		Cottager		1				1		2
~~John Jane Th~~-Do -	John Jane Thompson Prot		Yeoman	1					1		
Do -	James Jane Thompson Prot		Farmer	4							1
Do -	Lancelot Susanna Thompson Prot.		Yeoman						1		
Do -	John Mary Thompson Prot.		Cottager	3		2					
Do -	Peter Margar Canane Pap.		Taylor		1		2				
Do -	Bryan Gurrum Duane Pap.		Herd		1						
Do -	Thomas Mary Mulkeran Pap.		Cottager		2						1
Do -	Michl Brigit Beirn Pap.		Do		3						1
Lisvaddy	John Frances Gryner Prot.		Yeoman	5							1
Do -	Andrew Sarah Petty Pap.		Cottager								
	Prots 15 Pap. 63.			14	44	2	17		13		16
[f.34] Aghrim	Belragh	George Jane Prot Begg Pap	Gent				3				1
	Do -	Ignatius Mary Begg Pap	Farmer		3				1		2
	Do -	Thoms Dillon Batchr Pap	Farmer						1		

Com~Ros common Parish of	Place of Abode	Names and Religion	Proffession	Children under 14		Children above 14		Men Servts		Women Servts	
				Prot.	Paps.	Prot.	Paps.	Prot.	Paps.	Prot.	Paps.
	Do -	Richd. Ellinor } Connell Pap	Cottager		2						
	Do -	Christopher Catherine } Bealagh Pap	Do		1						
	Do -	Bryan Mary } Kennedy Pap	Do		1						
	Do -	Michl. Margt. } Dolan Pap	Do		2						
	Do -	Miles Margart. } Callaghan Pap	Do								1
	Do -	John More } Banagher Pap	Do		5						
	Do -	Michl. Honor } Connor Pap	Do		3						
	Do -	Terence Margar } Gallagher Pap	Weaver		1						
Bolnamahul		James Mary } Glanagan Pap	Cottager		1						1
	Do -	Richd. Mary } Roach Pap	Miller		1						
	Do -	Maurice Sarah } Donnelly Pap	Cottager				2				
	Do -	Thoms. Elizab. } Hoen Pap	Do		1						
	Do -	John Mary } Guff Pap	Do								
	Do -	John Sarah } Roach Pap	Do		1						
Rodyn		Willm Mary } Callaghan Pap	Farmer		4						
	Do -	Richd. Margt. } Gibulan Pap	Do		2		1				
	Do -	Dennis Mable } Dockery Pap	Do		2		2				
	Do -	John Mary } Beirn Pap	Do		5						
	Do -	Farrel Elizab. } Gibulan Pap	Do		3		1				
	Do -	Connor Cather. } Hanly Pap	Cottager		1						

Com~Ros common Parish of	Place of Abode	Names and Religion	Proffession	Children under 14		Children above 14		Men Servts		Women Servts	
				Prot.	Paps.	Prot.	Paps.	Prot.	Paps.	Prot.	Paps.
	Do -	Patrick / Margar. Cooney Pap	Do		3						
	Do -	Francis / Jane Doyle Pap	Pedlar		2						
	Do -	Loughlin Beirn Widowr Pap	Farmer		1		1		1		
	Do -	Hugh / Mary Beirn Pap	Do		1						
	Carrickena	Owen / Susanna Loyd9 Prot	Magistrate	7				2	2	3	3
	Do -	Charles / Ann Harrison Prot	Servt.	3				1		1	
	Do -	Terence Pap / Jane Duane Prot	Cottagers	1	1						
	Do -	Owen / Mary Rorke Pap	Herd		4						
	Coolnehinshy	Michl. / Kather. Hanly Pap	Cottager		3		1				
	Do -	Cormuck / Mary Mihan Pap	Do		1						1
	Do -	John / Mary Lindon Prot.	Clerk10 and School master	3							3
	Rushill	George Blackburn Sd Parish	Minister					2			2
	Do -	Willm & his sistr Elizabeth Devenish Prot	Farmer								
	Do -	Bryan / Margar. Redahan Prot Pap	Servt	3					1		1
	Do -	Michl. / Ellinor Redahan Pap	Cottagers		3		1				1
	Do -	John Hanly Batchr. Pap	Do								1
	Do -	Dennis / Catherine Beirn Pap	Do		3						
		Prots 12 Pap. 64.			17	61	12	5	6	4	13
[f.35] Aghrim	Rushill	James / Honor Hanly Pap.	Cottager		3						
	Carricklum	Thady / Catherine Beirn Pap.	Herd		3					1	3
	Carrickallow	James / Mary Sherah Pap.	Herd							1	1
	Twomore	Elizab. Brown widw. Pap.	Cottager		1		1				1

Com~Ros common Parish of	Place of Abode	Names and Religion	Proffession	Children under 14		Children above 14		Men Servts		Women Servts	
				Prot.	Paps.	Prot.	Paps.	Prot.	Paps.	Prot.	Paps.
Do -	Walter / Mary } Costello Pap.		Weaver		4		1				
Do -	Willm / Joan } Hogg Pap.		Cottager		1						
Do -	Mary Kennedy widw. Pap.		Do		1		2				
Do -	Connor / Sarah } Sharcott Pap.		Do		3		2				
Do -	George / Ellinor } Verdun Pap.		Do		1		1				
Do -	Patrick / Mary } Berreen Pap.		Herd						1		
Do -	Thady / Mary } Culkeen Pap.		Cottager		2						
Do -	Peter / Ann } Duane Pap.		Do		2						
Do -	Patrick [11] / Ellinor } Dillon Pap.		Do		2						
Do -	Thoms. / Brigit } Maxwell Pap.		Smith		2		1		1		1
Aghrim	Maurice / Brigit } Walsh Pap.		Herd						1		
Do -	Patrick / Cather. } Caslon Pap.		Cottager		2						1
Do -	Brigit Kelly Widow Pap.		Do				4				
Do -	Bryan / Ann } Carroll Pap.		Do		2						
Knockneshan	Patrick / Brigit } Connilan Pap.		Herd		3						
Do -	Patrick Beirn		Popish Priest of sd. parish[12]								
		Papts. 36			32		12		5		7

[verso f. 35]

Aghrim			Papts men & women	505
The sums total of sd. Parish			Do Childn undr 14 414 over 14 119	533
Prott. men & women		53	Do Men Servts	53
			Do Women Servts	79
Prott Childn. undr. 14 51 over 14 18		69		———
Prott men Servts		13		1170
Do. Women Servts.		9		144
		———		———
		144		1314

NOTES

1. Including 134 acres of the river Shannon and 13 acres of small loughs (*General Alphabetical Index*).

2. Lewis, 'Aughrim'.

3. George Blackburne was born near Elphin, a son of Andrew Blackburne, *generosus*. He was educated at Bishop Hodson's School, Elphin by Samuel Griffin, and entered TCD in 1707 aged 16. He graduated BA in 1711. He was prebendary of Termonbarry, from which he resigned in 1743, when he was collated vicar of Aughrim. His will was proved in 1797 (*Alumni Dubliniensis*; Leslie, 'Elphin' pp. 63, 69; Lewis, p. 98).

4. John Crofton (ca 1571-1639) settled at Lisdorn, Aughrim where he built a castle and a house (H. Crofton, *Memoirs of the Crofton Family* (Dublin 1910), p.189. (Hereafter cited as Crofton, *Memoir*)).

5. John Crofton (d. 1764), son of George and Elizabeth Crofton and great-grandson of John Crofton (note 4), married Catherine French, daughter of John French of French Park. They had seven children. He was High Sheriff of Co. Roscommon in 1729 and died in 1764 (Crofton, *Memoir*, p.186; Burke *LGI* (1958)).

6. Richard Plunkett of Ligan was a lay supporter of the Rev. William (alias Augustine) O'Kelly, prior of St. Mary's, Roscommon in 1748 to succeed Patrick French as bishop of Elphin (Fenning, 'Diocese of Elphin', p.166).

7. A George and Mathew Begg were living at Bellragh in the mid-seventeenth-century (Seamus Pender (ed.), *A Census of Ireland circa 1659 with supplementary material from the poll money ordinances, 1660-1661* (Dublin 1939). (Hereafter cited as *Census of Ireland*)).

8. Chidly Crofton was born about 1744 and married Mary Peyton in 1744 (International Genealogical Index).

9. Owen Lloyd (1714-45) of Carrickenagh (Rockville). He married Susanna, daughter and heiress of Dr. Blackburn, Archbishop of York who brought Carrickenagh as part of her dowry. He became High Sheriff of Co. Roscommon in 1740 (Burke, *LGI* (1958)).

10. Parish clerks were either appointed by the incumbent or elected by the vestry (Holdsworth, p.18).

11. A Lucas Dillon was living at Towmore in the mid-seventeenth-century (*Census of Ireland*).

12. John Beirne was returned as the parish priest in Aghrim in the 1731 state of popery report (Beirne, (ed.) *Diocese of Elphin*, p .109).

KILMORE, COUNTY ROSCOMMON

INTRODUCTION: *The parish of Kilmore is in the barony of Ballintober North. It is 2 miles from Drumsna and covers 9,316 statute acres.[1] The river Shannon runs along its north and east sides, opening into Lough Bodarig. On the south side it is bordered by Lough Gillstown. Lewis says that one-fifth was waste and bog. The remainder was good arable and pasture land. Limestone of very good quality was quarried and used for building and for agriculture. Freestone was quarried for mill-stones. A fair was held three times a year in Dangan.[2]*

The Crofton family had owned land in the parish since the early seventeenth-century, but the major landlord in the parish was Sir Gilbert King of Charlestown who was a magistrate. In 1641, eleven townlands in the parish were owned or part-owned by the O'Beirne family. They survived in large numbers into the eighteenth century, when there were 42 heads of households called Beirne living in 16 townlands in the parish.[3] In 1814, there were only 3 slated houses, one roofed with stone flags and one with oak shakes.[4]

The living was a vicarage, and the incumbent was the Rev. George Blackburne who had been installed in 1743.[5] He held the parish together with those of Aughrim, Kilmore, Killummod and Clooncraff (see Aughrim) The patron was the Lawder family.[6]

OCCUPATIONS

Barber	1	Herd	8	Piper	1
Broguemaker	1	Innkeeper	1	Quack Doctor	1
Carpenter	2	Miller	1	Schoolmaster	1
Catholic priest	2	Lieutenant	1	Servant	3
Cooper	6	Magistrate	1	Servants, household	184
Cottager	123	Mason	1	Shoemaker	1
Esquire	1	Merchant	2	Smith	4
Farmer	92	Miller	1	Tailor	5
Gentleman	1	Parish Clerk	1	Weaver	7
				Wheelwright	2

Com~Ros common Parish of	Place of Abode	Names and Religion	Proffession	Children under 14 Prot.	Paps.	Children above 14 Prot.	Paps.	Men Servts Prot.	Paps.	Women Servts Prot.	Paps.
[f.36] Aghrim	Charlestown	Gilbert / Ann } King7 Prot	Magistrat	5				6	2	3	3
Killmore	Do -	John / Mary } Cormuck Prot	Innkeeper					1	2		3
	Ditto	John / Deborah } Denby Prot	Merchant	1					1		1
	Do -	Henry } Prot. / Mary } Pap. Stratford	Shoemaker						1		
	Do -	Willm / Jane } Lally Prot	Weaver	2		1					
	Do -	Charles / Sarah } Trotter Prot	Barber	3		2		1			1
	Do -	James / Mary } Cullinan Prot	Carpenter	3		1			1		
	Do -	Thady / Brigit } mcLaughlin Pap	Mason								
	Curry	Francis / Rose } Duignan Pap	Farmer		3		4				
	Do -	Patrick / Joan } Roach Pap	Cottager		1		1				
	Do -	John / Mable } Cox Pap	Do		3						
	Do -	Bryan / Brigit } Shanly Pap	Do				1				
	Do -	Ann Courtney widw. Prot	Do	2		2					
	Do -	Thady / Catherine } Beirn Pap	Do		3		3				
	Do -	Thoms / Brigit } Conry Pap	Do		1		2		1		
	Do -	Dennis / Sisley } Flynn Pap	Do						1		
	Do -	Barthw. / Winny } Hanly Pap	Do						2		
	Cloonteam	Terence / Brigit } Kelly Pap	Farmer				2		1		1
	Do -	Dominick / Ellinor } Cormuck Pap	Do				4				
	Do -	Bryan / Cather. } Kelly Pap	Do		1						

Com~Ros common Parish of	Place of Abode	Names and Religion	Proffession	Children under 14		Children above 14		Men Servts		Women Servts	
				Prot.	Paps.	Prot.	Paps.	Prot.	Paps.	Prot.	Paps.
	Corlare[8]	Bryan / Mary } Cox Pap	Farmer		3						
	Do -	Richd. / Mary } Beirn Pap	Do				3				
	Do -	Michl / Rose } Doyle	Do		3		1				
	Do -	Hugh / Elizab. } Doyle Pap	Do				2				
	Do -	Michl / Joan } Beirn Pap	Do		5		1				
	Do -	Connor / Mary } Beirn	Do		4		1				
	Do -	Luke / Caneen } Pap	Do		1		1				
	Do -	Roger / Brigit } Hand Pap	Do		1		3				
	Do -	Patrick / Mary } Cox Pap	Do		4		2				1
	Do -	Thady / Cather } Carney Prot	Smith	2					1		1
	Do -	Luke / Brigit } Doyle Pap	Farmer		1				1		1
	Do -	Thady Beirn Pap	Do		1						
	Do -	Terence / Catherin } Beirn Pap	Do		3						1
	Do -	Francis Beirn Pap	Do				2				
	Do -	John[9] / Brigit } Keenan Pap	Do		2		2				
	Do -	Thoms / Mary } Hanly Pap	Do		3						1
	Do -	John / Brigit } Dolan Pap	Do		2		2				
	Do -	Willm Beirn Pap	Do		1		3				
	Do -	James / Mary } Cox Pap	Do		2						
	Do -	William / Catherine } Regan Pap	Do		3		2				1
	Do -	Prots 16 Pap. 61.		18	51	6	42	8	14	3	13
[f.37]~~Aghrim~~	Corlare	Peter / Ellinor } Regan Prot.	Farmer								1
	Do -	Owen / Ellinor } Loyd[10] Prot.	Do	2		2					
	Do -	Jacob / Mary } Lally Prot.	Parish Clerk			2					
	Do -	Ann Hogg widow Prot	Farmer			3					1
		Francis / Elizab. } Beirn Pap	Do			1					1
	Do -	Thomas / Cather. } Develin Pap	Cooper						2		1

Com~Ros common Parish of	Place of Abode	Names and Religion	Proffession	Children under 14 Prot.	Children under 14 Paps.	Children above 14 Prot.	Children above 14 Paps.	Men Servts Prot.	Men Servts Paps.	Women Servts Prot.	Women Servts Paps.
	Do -	Thomas Cather. Kerregan Pap	Farmer	.	1						
	Killcock	John Winny Cullum Pap	Farmer		2						
	Do -	Bryan Magdalen Beirn Pap	Do		2		1				
	Do -	Roger Elizab. Beirn	Taylor		5		1				1
	Do -	Michael Catherine Cox Pap	Farmer		3						
	Do -	Patrick Ann Flanaghy Pap	Do		2						
	Do -	Michael Elizab. Lenaghan Pap	Do		3						1
	Do -	Michael Mary Beirn Pap	Do								
	Do -	Giles Beirn Widw. Pap.	Do				1				
	Do -	Michl. Mary Dolan Pap	Do								
	Do -	Mary Beirn Widw. Pap.	Do				3				
	Do -	Catherine Beirne Widw. Pap.	Do				3				
	Do -	Owen Mary Shanly Pap	Do		1						
	Do -	Mary Beirn Widw. Pap.	Do		1						
	Do -	John Mary Hanly Pap	Do								
	Tully	John Mary Teige Pap	Herd		3				1		1
	Do -	Owen McLaughlin Widowr. Pap.	Cottager		1		3				
	Do -	Neal Cather. McLaughlin Pap	Do		4						1
	Do -	William Margaret Glancy Pap	Do		1						
	Carrakeel	Connor Jane Mcguane Pap	Herd		1				1		1
	Clogher	Owen Horan Jane his wife Prot.	Parish Schoolmastr	2							
	Do -	James Mary Simpson Prot.	Weaver				3				
	Do -	Robert Ellinor Abraham Prot.	Cottager	1							
	Do -	Daniel Jane Beirn Pap.	Do		4		2				
	Do -	Charles Elizab. Conry Pap	Do		1		1				
	Do -	Owen Cather. McDruy Pap	Do		3						
	Do -	John Sisly Conry Pap	Do		4				1		

Com~Ros common Parish of	Place of Abode	Names and Religion	Proffession	Children under 14		Children above 14		Men Servts		Women Servts	
				Prot.	Paps.	Prot.	Paps.	Prot.	Paps.	Prot.	Paps.
	Do -	Charles/Mary Beirne Pap	Do		1						
	Do -	John/Sarah Maxwell Pap	Smith			3				1	
	Do -	John/Sarah Brien Pap	Cottager			3					
	Do -	Nicholas Prot/Margaret Pap Fitzsimmons	Do			1		3			
	Do -	Charles/Brigit Mcdermott Pap	Do			4		1			
	Do -	James/Margar. Gibulan Pap	Do								
	Do -	Eneas/Sarah McDonnell Pap	Do			2		1			
		Prots 14. Paps.60.		5	43	20	18	5	5	1	9
[f.38] Killmore	Clogher	Francis/Martha Riley Pap.	Cottager		1		2				
	Lowfield	James/Jane Lawder11 Prot.	Esquire					1	1	1	2
	Do -	Thady/Mary Beirn Pap	Cottager		1		1				
	Do -	Edmond/Margar. Tiernan Pap	Servt.		1				1		1
	Tuluscan	Thomas/Brigit Kelly Pap	Cottager		1						
	Do -	Peter/Margart. Moran Pap	Do		1		2				
	Do -	James/Dorothy Fitz Gerald Pap.	Do								
	Do -	Michl./Ellinor Prot Doherty Pap	Servt.	4					1		1
	Do -	Luke/Susanna FitzSimmons Pap.	Cottager		1						1
	Do -	Michl./Margart. Oats Pap.	Do		2						1
	Do -	John/Cather. Klabby Pap.	Do		2						
	Do -	Joan Shanly Widw. Pap	Do				1				
	Do -	Margart. Flanaghy widow Pap	Do				1				1
	Do -	Daniel/Brigit Cavenagh Pap.	Do		1		2				
	Killmore	Patrick/Honor Kelly Pap.	Do		2		1		1		
	Do -	Barthw./Honor Kelly Pap.	Do		2						2
	Do -	Michl/Ann Kelly Pap.	Do		2		2		2		2
	Do -	Charles Pap./Margery Prot Conry	Do		1						2

Com~Ros common Parish of	Place of Abode	Names and Religion	Proffession	Children under 14 Prot.	Paps.	Children above 14 Prot.	Paps.	Men Servts Prot.	Paps.	Women Servts Prot.	Paps.
	Moyglass	Hugh / Margaret } Doherty Pap/Prot.	Herd		5		1		1		
	Dangan	Darby / Jane } mcManus Pap.	Farmer				5		2		1
	Do -	Edmund / Margaret } Burke Pap.	Do		4		1		1		2
	Do -	Thomas / Mary } mcGarry Pap.	Cottager								
	Do -	Roger / Joan } Lenaghan Pap.	Do								1
	Do -	Margart. Duane Widw. Pap.			2						
	Do -	Martin / Margar. } Duane Pap/Prot.	Taylor		2						
	Do -	Noah / Cather. } Simpson Prot./Pap.	Weaver	4							1
	Do -	John / Mary } Beirn, Pap.	Cottager		2		1				
	Do -	John / Honor } Coghlan Pap.	Piper								
	Do -	Ann Kane Widw. Pap.	Cottager		1		1				
	Do -	Patrick / Ellinor } Judge Pap.	Do		1						1
	Do -	Michl. / Brigt. } Beirn Pap	Do		1						1
	Do -	Mary Cummin Pap.	Do		2		1		1		
	Ardnakinene	Nichs. / Mary } Kelly Pap	Do		1				1		1
	Do -	Philip / Honor } Halfpenny Pap	Do		2		1				
	Do -	Andrew / Sisley } Gibulan Pap	Do		1				1		
	Do -	Francis / Mary } Killbane Pap.	Do		3		2				
	Do -	Charles / Cather. } McNeal Pap.	Do		1						
	Cloonsellagh[12]	Hugh / Mary } Connor Pap.	Herd		4						
	Do -	Edmond / Mary } Beirn Pap.	Cottager		1						
	Do -	Connor / Joan Beirn } Pap.	Do		2		1				
		Prots. 7. Papts. 69.		8	53		26	1	13	1	21
[f.39] Killmore	Cloonsellagh	Thomas / Joan } Lenaghan Pap.	Cottager						1		
	Do -	Rose Lenaghan Widw. Pap.	Do				1				
	Do -	4 poor Widows Pap			3						
	Cloongrillan	Richard / Margart. } Nugent Pap.	Gent		3		3		3		2
	Do -	Michael / Ann } Duffily Pap.	Cottager		1		1				

56

Com~Roscommon Parish of	Place of Abode	Names and Religion	Proffession	Children under 14		Children above 14		Men Servts		Women Servts	
				Prot.	Paps.	Prot.	Paps.	Prot.	Paps.	Prot.	Paps.
	Do -	Peter / Brigit Lennon Pap.	Miller		1		1				
	Do -	Michl. / Ann Cox Pap.	Cottager		4						
	Do -	Daniel / Margart. Cavanagh Pap.	Do		1						
	Do -	Francis / Mary Cavanagh Pap.	Do								1
	Clooncommonmore	Daniel / Rose Hely Pap.	Cottager				1				
	Do -	Thady / Sisley McNiff Pap.	Do		2						
	Do -	Thady / Mary Mahon Pap.	Do		2		2				
	Do -	William / Margar. Cox Pap.	Do		2						
	Do -	Conor / Honor Kelly Pap.	Taylor		2		1		1		
	Do -	Barthw. / Mary Morahan Pap.	Cottager		2						
	Do -	John / Winny Glancy Pap.	Do								
	Skey	Connor / Ann Conry Pap.	Servt.		2		2		2		
	Do -	John / Sidney Cregg Prot.							1		
	Do -	William / Jane Kelly Pap.	Taylor								
	Do -	James / Elizab Guane Pap.	Cottager				1				
	Do -	Owen / Brigit McKanny Pap.	Do		3				1		1
	Do -	Hugh Egan Widowr Pap.	Do				1				1
	Ballycummin	James / Esther Honan Pap.	Farmer				3		2		3
	Do -	Michl. / Cather. Feeny Pap.	Cottager		4				2		
	Do -	Cormuck / Mary Cox Pap.	Do						1		
	Do -	Patrick / Mary Killeline Pap.	Do		2		3		1		
	Do -	Lawrence / Jane Loyd Prot.	Do	2					1		
	Do -	Danl. Honan batchr.Prot.	Farmer						2		3
	Do -	Owen / Sarah Glancy Pap.	Cottager				1				1
	Do -	Owen / Cather. Egan Pap.	Do		2						1
	Cartron	Margart. Beirn Widw. Pap.	Cottager		1		1				

Com~Ros common Parish of	Place of Abode	Names and Religion	Proffession	Children under 14		Children above 14		Men Servts		Women Servts	
				Prot.	Paps.	Prot.	Paps.	Prot.	Paps.	Prot.	Paps.
	Do -	Patrick Catherine } McKeen Pap.	Do		1		1				
	Do -	William Catherine } Clifford Pap.	Do		2						
	Do -	Michl. Mary } Beirn Pap.	Do								
	Do -	Domnick Mary } Lynch Pap.	Do		2						
	Do -	Thady Brigit } Beirn Pap.	Do		2						
	Do -	Mary Tiernan Widw. Pap.	Do				1				
	Do -	Willm. Margar. } Flanaghy Pap.	Do		2						1
	Do -	Carbry Ellis } Beirn Pap.	Do				1				
		Prots. 7. Papts. 70.		2	47		25		18		14
[f.40] Killmore	Cartron	John Sisley } Conry Pap.	Cottager								
	Do -	John Honor } Mulvihill Pap.	Do		2						
	Roo	Daniel Mary } Lennon Pap.	Herd		4						
	Meelick	Dennis Brigit } Beirn Pap.	Farmer		4						
	Do -	Owen Brigit } Beirn Pap.	Do		2		2				
	Do -	Terence Mable } Beirn Pap.	Do		2						
	Do -	Patrick Alice } Beirn Pap.	Do		2						
	Scrabbagh	Patrick Sarah } McGrah Pap.	Cottager								
	Do -	James Jane } Collum Pap.	Do		1						
	Corneflyne	Darby Ann } Lenaghan Pap.	Do		2						1
	Do -	James Brigit } Fox Pap.	Do		1		3				
	Do -	... Riley[13]	Popish priest						1		
	Do -	Edmund Joan } Cavenagh Pap.	Cooper								
	Do -	James Cather. } Martin Pap.	Cottager		2						
	Corrobane	Michl. Cather. } Rogers Pap.	Herd		5				1		1
	Do -	Margaret Cox Widw. Pap.	Cottager		2						
	Do -	John Rose } Kelly Pap.	Do		2						
	Do -	Farrell Mary } Godrick Pap.	Do								

Com~Ros common Parish of	Place of Abode	Names and Religion		Proffession	Children under 14 Prot.	Children under 14 Paps.	Children above 14 Prot.	Children above 14 Paps.	Men Servts Prot.	Men Servts Paps.	Women Servts Prot.	Women Servts Paps.
	Do -	Thomas Mary	} Manning Pap.	Do		1		2				
	Do -	Thady Margar.	} Kelly Pap.	Do		2						
	Cloon-shanagh[14]	Bryan Benoan	} Judge Pap.	Do		1						
	Do -	Bryan Brigit	} Beirn Pap.	Farmer								
	Do -	John Brigit	} Beirn Pap.	Do		1						
	Do -	Owen Cather.	} Beirn Pap.	Do		1						
	Munnyduff	James Winny	Prot. Fairly Pap.	Weaver	2							
	Do -	Michael Jane	McDermott Pap.	Farmer		1				1		2
	Do -	James Ellinor	Prot. Fairly Pap.	Weaver	1							
	Do -	James Mary	} Reynolds Pap.	Cottager		2						
	Do -	James Sisley	} McLaughlin Pap.	Broagmakr.		2						
	Do -	Owen Ann	} Beirn Pap.	Farmer				3				1
	Do -	Carbry Ellinor	} Beirn Pap.	Do		5		1		1		1
	Do -	Austin Honor	} Lennon Pap.	Cottager		2						
	Do -	Patrick Jane	} Beirn Pap.	Do		2						
	Do -	John Mary	} Beirn Pap.	Do		2						
	Do -	Philip Mary	} Gralton Pap.	Do		1		1				
	Do -	James Mary	} Steward Pap.	Cooper		1						
	Do -	Patrick Mary	} Long Pap.	Cottager		1						
	Do -	Luke Ann	} Conry Pap.	Do				1				
	Do -	James Elizab.	} Kennedy Pap.	Do								
	Do -	Owen Mary	} Shanahan Pap.	Do		1				1		1
		Prots. 2. Papts. 76.			3	57		13		5		8
[f.41] Killmore	Curgullin	William Mary	} Johnson[15] Prot.	Farmer	4				1	1	1	1
	Do -	John Mary	} Conry Pap.	Herd		5						1

Com~Ros common Parish of	Place of Abode	Names and Religion	Proffession	Children under 14 Prot.	Children under 14 Paps.	Children above 14 Prot.	Children above 14 Paps.	Men Servts Prot.	Men Servts Paps.	Women Servts Prot.	Women Servts Paps.
	Do -	Francis Mary } Beirne Pap.	Cottager		3						
	Do -	Patrick Elizab. } Kelly Pap.	Do		1					1	
	Do -	John More } Beirn Pap.	Do		1						
	Do -	Dudley Cather. } McDonnell Pap.	Carpenter		3						
	Do -	2 poor Widows Pap.									
	Knocknagawna	James Winny } Goolrick Pap	Farmer		3						
	Do -	Thomas Sarah } Stapleton Pap	Do								1
	Do -	John Cather. } Stapleton Pap	Do		2						
	Do -	Thomas Jane } Stapleton Pap	Do								
	Do -	Margart. Kelly Wdw. Pap.	Cottager		1						
	Do -	Luke Cather. } Beirn Pap.	Farmer								1
	Do -	James Ann } Stapleton Pap.	Do								
	Do -	Richard Cather. } Stapleton Pap.	Do		2						
		Owen Ellinor } Cormuck Pap	Do		1				1		
	Do -	Thomas Mary } Morahan Pap.	Do		1						
	Do -	Patrick Ellis } Keegan Pap.	Do								1
	Do -	James Dorothy } Riley Pap.	Do		2						1
	Do -	Roger Ellinor } Beirn Pap.	Do		4						2
	Do -	Bryan Jane } Beirn Pap.	Do		2						
	Do -	Patrick Dorothy } Beirn Pap.	Do		1						
	Do -	Lawrence Mary } McCormick Pap.	Do		1		2				
	Do -	Francis Honor } Beirne Pap.	Do		1						
	Do -	...... Cox Mary } Pap.	Do		2						
	Do -	Michael Brigit } Hanly Pap.	Do						1		1
	Cloonmane	Thomas Mary } Roach Pap.	Farmer		1						
	Do -	Martin Catherine } Lenaghan Pap.	Weaver		1						
	Do -	Lawrence Sarah } Lenaghan Pap	Farmer		2						

Com~Ros common Parish of	Place of Abode	Names and Religion	Proffession	Children under 14		Children above 14		Men Servts		Women Servts	
				Prot.	Paps.	Prot.	Paps.	Prot.	Paps.	Prot.	Paps.
Do -	Do -	Patrick Brigit Beirn Pap.	do		2						
	Do -	Edward Jane Prot Dillon Pap	Quack Doctor		2		1				
	Do -	Thady Mable Beirn Pap.	Farmer		2						
	Do -	Edward Ann Dillon Pap.	Mercht.		1		4		1		
	Do -	Darby Margart. Beirn Pap.	Farmer		2		1				1
	Clooncoan	James Mary Flanaghy Pap.	Taylor		1						
	Do -	James Mary Feeny Pap.	Cooper						1		1
	Do -	Sisley Beirn Widw. Pap.	Farmer			1					1
	Do -	Dennis More McKeon Pap.	Cooper						1		
	Do -	Patrick Brigit Connor Pap.	Farmer	1					1		
	Do -	James Honor McCabe Pap.	Do		2						1
		Prots 3. Papts. 75		4	53		9	1	7	2	13
[f.42] Killmore	Feeraghmore	William Honor Fihily Pap.	Herd		2				1		1
	Do -	Edmund Honor Keeghran Pap.	Cooper				1				
	Feeragh-beg	Andw. Jn. Martin Pap.	Farmer						2		2
	Do -	Richd. Martin[16] Pap.	Popish priest								
	Do -	Thady Brigit Rorke Pap.	Do		4						
	Do -	John Mary Mullanny Pap.	Cottager		2						
	Do -	Patrick Honor McGluy Pap.	Do		1						
	Do -	Art Margart. McCormuck Pap.	Do		1		2				
	Ardgallagher	Daniel Anne Kelly Pap.	Smith		2		1		1		
	Do -	Thomas Catherine Beirn Pap.	Do		1						1
	Do -	Michl. Mary Flanagan Pap.	Cottager		2						1
	Do -	Bryan Mary Cavenagh Pap.	Do		1						1
	Do -	John Ann Farrell Pap.	Do		1						
	Do -	Dennis Mary Collins Pap.	Do		2						

Com~Ros common Parish of	Place of Abode	Names and Religion	Proffession	Children under 14 Prot.	Paps.	Children above 14 Prot.	Paps.	Men Servts Prot.	Paps.	Women Servts Prot.	Paps.
	Do -	John Honor } Cavenagh Pap.	Do								
	Killteshinoge	James Jane } Caslon Pap.	Farmer		3						1
	Do -	Peter Mary } Caslon Pap.	Do		2						1
	Do -	John Cather. } Conry Pap.	Do		1						
	Do -	Thomas Honor } McVahy Pap.	Do		4		2				
	Do -	John Winny } Caslon Pap.	Do								1
	Do -	Charles Alice } Beirne Pap.	Do		2						
	Do -	Hugh Catherine } Beirn Pap.	Do		3		1				1
	Carowmore	Francis Dimna } Shanly Prot.	Lieutenant	3		2			1		1
	Do -	Joseph Mary } Watson Prot.	Weaver	3		2		1			
	Do -	James Margar. } McNiff Pap.	Cottager								
	Do -	John Rose } Kelly Pap.	Do		1						
	Do -	Domnick Joan } McNiff Pap.	Do		1						
	~~John~~ Do -	John Mary } Ward Pap.	Do								
	Do -	Patrick Mary } Cunningham Pap.	Do		2						
	Do -	Peter Jane } Doherty Pap.	Do		3						
	Do -	Michl. Honor } Halfpenny Pap.	Do		2						
	Do -	Philip Honor } Duane Pap.	Do		2						
	Ahairriscull	Edward Margart. } Collum Prot.	Wheelwright	4							1
	Do -	Bryan Mary } McNiffe Pap.	Farmer		1						
	Do -	Cormuck Mary } Lavin Pap.	Wheelwright		2						1
	Ranarooanah	Jane Acheson Widw. Prot.	Farmer			2			1		1
	Do -	John Brigit } Macoy Pap.	Cottager		1		3				
	Do -	James Elizab. } Guane Pap.	Do		1		1				
		Prots Papts 67		10	50	6	11	1	6		13

[verso f. 42]

Killmore

The sums total of sd. Parish

Prott. men & women		56	Papts. Men & women	478
Do. Childn. Undr. 14 50 over 22		72	Do Children undr 14.	368
Do. Men servts 11 Women Servts. 6		17	Do Child. Over 14.	146
		145	Do. Men Servts	70
			Do Women Servts	95
				1157
				145
				1302

NOTES

1. Less 917 acres of the river Shannon and small loughs. Lewis said that 1000 statute acres were waste and bog (*General Alphabetical Index;* Lewis, 'Kilmore').

2. *Report...fairs and markets.*

3. Cartron - John mcJames Birne, John Barnes and Carbry Oge; Clogher, Loghlin Oge McLaughlin Birne; Cloonteem - Bryan oge McBryen mcConnor Birne; Curry and Moyglasse - Wm. McTeige Birne; Dangan, Donogh McDonogh Birne; Feerahbeg and Feeraghmore - Bryan McDonogh Birne; Kilteshinoge, Bryan McDonogh Birne, Carbry Birne and Teige mc Onegrana; Knocknagawane, Scrabbagh - Danll Groome Birne (*Books of Survey and Distribution* Roscommon; Census ff. 38, 39, 40, 41, 42).

4. *The O'Beirne Family Journal*, 8 (January 2003), p.6. (www.obeirnefamily.mcmail.com).

5. Leslie, 'Elphin', p. 184.

6. Lewis, 'Kilmore'.

7. A James King was living in Charlestown in the mid-seventeenth-century (*Census of Ireland*).

8. 1 big bullock, 10 big cows and 81 cows, 126 sheep and rams were kept on Corlare townland in 1728 (N.L.I., King Papers relating to Charlestown and Elphin 1667-1787, MS 8472).

9. John Keenan kept 3 cows on Corlare townland in 1728 (ibid).

10. Owen Loyd rented 113 Irish plantation acres at Ballagh for 3 lives in 1747. The annual rent was £30. 'These lands are an estate in fee they pay a Crown Rent of 1pd p.acr.' (N.L.I., King Papers, MS 3125).

11. James Lawder married Jane Contarine, daughter of Thomas Contarine of Emlaghmore, parish of Oran (f.233). In 1779 James Lawder was murdered by his drunken servants with his wife present. It had been thought that he had money in a locked chest. (John Ginger, *The Notable Man: The Life and Times of Oliver Goldsmith* (London 1977), p.78).

12. Clonsillagh, parish of Kilmore was described as 'land with cold tillage and pasture', let to cottier tenants (N.L.I., Clonbrock Papers., Maps with lists of tenants' holdings 1777, MS 19,672).

13. James Riley took a doctorate at the Sorbonne. He died on 11 May 1760, aged 72 (Fenning, 'Clergy Lists', (1996) p.145, fn. 7).

14. Let to common tenants for £21 and 6 pound of hank yarn (N.L.I., King Papers 1747-1786, MS 3125).

15. William Johnson rented arable land and bog for three lives for an annual rent of £32. An estate in fee (N.L.I., King Papers, MS 3125).

16. Richard Martin died ca. October 1770 in Charlestown (Fenning, 'Clergy Lists', (1996) p.145, fn. 5).

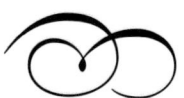

KILLUMMOD, COUNTY ROSCOMMON

INTRODUCTION: *The parish of Killummod is in the barony of Boyle. It is 3 miles south-south-west from Carrick-on-Shannon.[1] It covers 5,159 statute acres and has a number of small loughs and some bog. There is some good limestone.[2]*

The church of Ireland incumbent of Killummod and Clooncraff was the Rev. George Blackburn who lived at Rushhill in the parish of Aughrim. He held Killummod with Aughrim and Kilmore. (See Aughrim) The patron was the bishop. The rectory was impropriate in the King family.[3]

OCCUPATIONS

Aleseller	1	Herd	5	Servants, household	79
Chelsea pensioner	1	Merchant	1	Smith	1
Cottager	79	Miller	1	Weaver	2
Farmer	22	Officer on halfpay	1		

Com~Ros common Parish of	Place of Abode	Names and Religion	Proffession	Children under 14		Children above 14		Men Servts		Women Servts	
				Prot.	Paps.	Prot.	Paps.	Prot.	Paps.	Prot.	Paps.
[f.43] Killumod	Canrawer	Gilbt. Ann } Roycroft Prot.	Farmer	7				1	2	1	3
	Do -	Elizab.Roycroft Widw. Prot.	Do						1	1	
	Do -	James Ellinor } Roycroft Prot	Do	2					2		3
	Do -	Willm Ann } Cunningham Pap.	Cottager		2						
	Do -	Bryan Honor } Crien Pap	Do		4		1				1
	Do -	Francis Honor } Scott Pap	Do		1				2		2
	Do -	Michl. Mary } Murray Pap.	Do								
	Do -	Michl. Mary } Kelagher Pap	Do		2						
	Do -	Patrick Ann } Macot Pap.	Do				1				
	Do -	Patrick Winny } Ford Pap	Do		4						
	Do -	Philip Mary } Ford Pap	Do		3		2				1
	Cartron	Francis Ann } Nesbitt Prot.	Officer on halfpay	4		1		3		4	
	Do -	Patrick Catherine } Rice Prot.	Cottager	3							1
	Do -	Owen Sarah } Guane Pap.	Do		1				1		
	Do -	Bryan Ann } Padin Pap	Do		1		2				
	Do -	John Sarah } Bolan Pap	Do		3						
	Do -	Patrick Rose } Fox Pap	Do		3		1				
	Do -	Roger Sarah } Cunningham Pap.	Do		2						
	Do -	Andw. Mary } McDermott Pap	Do		1						
	Ballynvill	Ann Dermott Widw. Pap.	Farmer				3		1		2
	Do -	Tully Winny } Higgins Pap.	Herd				3				
	Cambo	John Christian } Morris Pap	Cottager		2						1
	Do -	Mark Honor } Carroll Pap	Do		1				1		
	Do -	Michl. Cather. } Brennan Pap.	Do								
	Do -	John Rose } Brennan Pap.	Do		1						

Com~Ros common Parish of	Place of Abode	Names and Religion	Proffession	Children under 14		Children above 14		Men Servts		Women Servts	
				Prot.	Paps.	Prot.	Paps.	Prot.	Paps.	Prot.	Paps.
	Carrowmore	Edmund Elizab. } Golding Pap.	Aleseller		1				1		1
	Do -	Thady Margar. } Haggedon Pap	Cottager		1						1
	Do -	James Mary } Killmartin Pap.	Do				1				
	Do -	Patrick Winny } Killmartin Pap.	Do		1						
	Do -	Thomas Brigit } Dormer Prot	Chelsea pensioner	1					1	1	
	Do -	Carbry Mary } Brennan Pap.	Cottager								
	Do -	Bryan Cather. } Brennan Pap	Do								
	Do -	John } Ellinor } Murray Prot.	Weaver	2		2		2			
	Cartron	Laughlin Mary } Beirn Pap	Cottager		2			1			
	Do -	Michl. Mary } Jones Pap.	Do		2						
	Do -	Michl. Mary } Fox Pap	Do		2				1		
	Do -	Danl. Ann } Kelly Pap	Do						1		
	Killnatreen	Bryan Sisley } McGarry Pap	Herd				2				
	Do -	Thoms. Rose } McGarry Pap	Cottager		1						1
	Do -	Connor Ellinor } Gralton Pap.	Farmer		3		4				
	Do -	Prots. 13 Papts. 65		19	44	3	20	7	14	6	18
[f.44] Killumod	Killinatreen	Anthony Elizab. } Daly Pap §	Farmer		4						
	Do -	Danl. Mary } Nary Pap	Do		2						
	Do -	Brigit Maxwell Widow Pap	Do				2				
	Do -	Michl. Sisley } Daly Pap.	Cottager								
	Killumod	Sisley Plunkett Widow Pap	Farmer		2		4	2			3
	Do -	Thoms. Cather. } Clark Pap	Herd		4				1		
	Do -	James Mary } Farrell Pap.	Cottager		1		1				
	Do -	Bryan Cather. } Mullkeran Pap.	Do		3						
	Do -	Connor Sisley } Oats Pap	Do		2						
	Do -	Miles Mary } Rogers Pap.	Do		4						

Com~Ros common Parish of	Place of Abode	Names and Religion	Proffession	Children under 14 Prot.	Children under 14 Paps.	Children above 14 Prot.	Children above 14 Paps.	Men Servts Prot.	Men Servts Paps.	Women Servts Prot.	Women Servts Paps.
	Do -	Mattw. Mary } Lennon Pap.	Do		3						1
	Carrowreagh	Patrick Ann } Hanly Pap	Do		2						
	Do -	Dennis Margart. } Horan Pap.	Do		2		3				
	Do -	Patrick Sarah } Scott Pap.	Do		1						
	Do -	Edmd. Jane } Clark Pap	Do				1				
	Do -	Ellinor Goghreen Widw. Pap	Do				1				
	Do -	Char. Garraghan Widowr. Pap	Do				3				
	Do -	John Mary } Coreem Pap.	Do		2						
	Do -	John Brigit } Clark Pap.	Do								
	Dackloon	Thady Ellinor } Redahan Pap	Farmer		2						1
	Do -	Michl. Sarah } Lenaghan Pap	Herd		2				1		
	Do -	Robert Eliz. } Tryner Prot	Cottager	2							
	Knockrow	Patrick Plunkett Widower Pap.	Farmer				1		3		2
	Do -	Bryan Jane } Redahan Pap	Cottager		3		2				
	Do -	James Brigit } Hanly Pap	Do								
	Do -	John Brigit } Morris Pap.	Do		5						
	Do -	Thady Mary } Coin Pap	Do		1						
	Do -	James Margt. } Morris Pap	Do		2						
	Do -	Patrick Ann } Ruan Pap	Do		4						
	Do -	Roger Margt. } Carly Pap.	Do				1				
	Do -	Terence Tiernan Widower	Do		1				2		
	Do -	John Brigit } Mahon Pap	Cottager		2		2				1
	Do -	James Honor } Crine Pap	Smith		1		1		1		
	Do -	William Giles } Common Pap	Herd		3				1		1
	Do -	Laughlin Elizabeth } Dowd Pap	Cottager		3						
	Do -	James Margt. } Renny Pap	Do								1
	Tannoor	Patrick Mary } McDermott Pap	Herd		3		1				

Com~Ros common Parish of	Place of Abode	Names and Religion	Proffession	Children under 14		Children above 14		Men Servts		Women Servts	
				Prot.	Paps.	Prot.	Paps.	Prot.	Paps.	Prot.	Paps.
	Do -	John} Winny} Egan Pap.	Cottager		2						
	Lisdaly	Ann Mulick Widw. Pap	Farmer				1				
	Do -	Connor} Sarah} Ford Pap	Farmer		3						1
		Prots 2. Papts. 71		2	69		24		11		11
[f.45] Killumod	Lisdaly	Patrick} Mary} Ford Pap.	Farmer		3				1		1
	Do -	Dennis} Cather.} Dugan Pap.	Do		2						
	Do -	Sarah Ford Widw. Pap.	Do				4				1
	Do -	Thomas} Elizab.} Philips Pap	Do								1
	Do -	Domnick} Mary} Noon Pap.	Do						2		1
	Do -	Luke} Mary} Glynn Pap.	Smith		2				1		1
	Do -	Garret} Rose} Farrell Pap.	Cottager		1						
	Do -	Peter} Sarah} Dempsy Pap.	Farmer		2						
	Do -	James} Mary} Behan Pap.	Do		2						
	Killappoge	James} Allice} Teige Pap.	Miller		4				1		1
	Do -	Patrick} Mary} Kelagher Pap.	Cottager		2						
	Do -	Dennis} Mary} Goolrick Pap.	Do				2				
	Do -	Thoms.} Honor} Brennan Pap.	Do		2						
	Do -	Thoms.} Honora} Moran Pap.	Do		~~2~~		2				
	Bunreagh	Charles} Jane} Beirn Pap.	Farmer		1						
	Do -	Edmd} Cather.} Glynn Pap.	Do		2						
	Do -	Thoms.} Ellinor} Goolrick Pap.	Do		1						
	Do -	Jon} Eliza} Connilan Pap.	Do		1		1				
	Do -	Thady} Brigit} Ford Pap.	Do		1						
	Do -	Paul} Mary} Beirn Pap.	Do								
	Do -	John} Cather.} Beirn Pap.	Do								

Com~Ros common Parish of	Place of Abode	Names and Religion	Proffession	Children under 14		Children above 14		Men Servts		Women Servts	
				Prot.	Paps.	Prot.	Paps.	Prot.	Paps.	Prot.	Paps.
	Do -	James / Sarah } Gihily Pap.	Do								
	Do -	Thoms. / Ellinor } Nelson Pap.	Do								
	Do -	Connor / Winny } Faughran Pap.	Do		1						
	Do -	Dennis / Ellionor } Balteny Pap.	Do		1						
	Do -	Peter / Elizab. } Connilan Pap.	Do		1				1		
	Do -	Mark / Brigit } Mullanney Pap.	Do		1			2	6̶		
Com~ Roscommon		Papts 53			30		11		6		6

NOTES

1. Less 300 statute acres of the water of the river Shannon and various loughs (*General Alphabetical Index*).

2. Lewis, 'Killumod'.

3.Ibid.

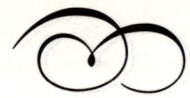

CLOONCRAFF, COUNTY ROSCOMMON

INTRODUCTION: *The parish of Clooncraff is in the barony of Roscommon, 5 miles north-east of Strokestown, and borders Lough Baffin. The parish covered 5,454 statute acres.*

The church of Ireland incumbent of Clooncraff was the Rev. George Blackburne who held it with the parishes of Aughrim, Kilmore, and Killummod (see Aughrim). The parish had been held with that of Aghrim and Killumod from the 15th century. The patron was the bishop. The rectory was impropriate in the King family.[2]

OCCUPATIONS

Cottager	35	Magistrate	1	Smith	1
Farmer	67	Merchant	1	Poor widow	1
Gentleman	3	Miller	1	Weaver	2
Herd	7	Servants, household	90		

Com~Ros common Parish of	Place of Abode	Names and Religion	Proffession	Children under 14		Children above 14		Men Servts		Women Servts	
				Prot.	Paps.	Prot.	Paps.	Prot.	Paps.	Prot.	Paps.
[f.45] Parish of Clooncraff	Cloonahey	John Margart } Conry Prot.	Magistrate	4		2		2	5		3
	Mosshill	John Elizab. } Conry3 Prot.	Gent.	5					2		4
	Drummod	Francis Catherine } Flanagan Pap.	Weaver		1				1		
	Do -	Winny Duane Pap.	a poor widow								
	Do -	Bryan Cassedy Widowr. Pap.	Farmer		2				1		
	Do -	Cather. McCabe Widw. Pap.	Do						1		1
	Do -	John Honor } Flanegan Pap.	Do								
	Do -	Francis Cather. } Flanegan Pap.	Do		1				1		
	Do -	Martin Sarah } Gowlan Pap.	Do		4						
	Do -	Martin Brigit } Kelly Pap.	Do		1						1
	Do -	Patrick Honor } Feeny Pap.	Do		2				1		
	Do -	Laughlin Catherine } Feeny Pap.	Do								
		Prots. 4. Pap. 17		9	11	2	1	2	11		9
[f.46] Clooncraff	Drummod	Michl. Honor } Fury Pap. Farmer		2							1
	Do -	Barthw. Mary } Reynolds Pap.	Do		4		2				1
	Do -	James Mary } Connilan Pap.	Do		3		1				1
	Do -	Peter Murphy widowr. Pap.	Do				1				
	Do -	John Jane } Hopkins Pap.	Do		1						1
	Do -	Owen Mary } Connilan Pap.	Do		2						
	Do -	Ullen Brigit } Conry Pap.	Do		2		2				
	Do -	John Sarah } Connilan Pap	Do		4						1
	Do -	Barthw. Brigit } Maly Pap.	Do		2						1
	Keillmore	Willm. Mary } Caneen Pap.	Farmer		2						1
	Do -	Mary Caslon Widw. Pap.	Do				3				
	Do -	Thady Lennan Widwr. Pap	Do				2				
	Do -	Patrick Brigit } Kelly Pap.	Do		2						1
	Do -	Dennis Mary } Caneen Pap.	Do		3						

Com~Ros common Parish of	Place of Abode	Names and Religion	Proffession	Children under 14		Children above 14		Men Servts		Women Servts	
				Prot.	Paps.	Prot.	Paps.	Prot.	Paps.	Prot.	Paps.
Do -	Michl. Honor } Hanly Pap.		Do		1						
Do -	Francis Mary } Hely Pap.		Do				2				
Do -	Bryan Jane } Keeneen Pap.		Do		2						
Do -	Edward Brigit } Tracy Pap.		Do		1						2
Do -	Sarah Costello Widw.Pap.		Do				2				
Do -	John Ellinor } Kelly Pap.		Do		2						
Do -	Edmond Mary } Desiby Pap.		Do		1						
Do -	Charles Margar } Killgannan Pap.		Do		2						
Do -	John Mary } Kelly Pap.		Do						1		1
Do -	Francis Sarah } Dowlan Pap.		Do		1				1		
Do -	Cormuck Joan } Connell Pap.		Do		2		1				
Do -	Bryan Mary } Caneen Pap.		Do		3						
Do -	Edmond Margar. } Hanly Pap.		Do		2				1		
Do -	Martin Ellinor } McDermott Pap.		Weaver		1				1		
Cloonshee	Luke Elizab. } Prot. Connor Pap.		Farmer	2					2		3
Do -	Thoms. Mary } Cox Pap.		Cottager		2						
Do -	Hugh Mary } Hanly Pap.		Do		2						
Curry	Roger Honor } Reynolds Pap.		Farmer		2						1
Do -	Roger Sarah } McManus Pap.		Do				3				
Do -	John Jane } Tracy Pap.		Do								
Do -	Cather. Beirn widw. Pap.				3		1				
Do -	Thoms. Giles } Chamberlain Pap.		Do		1						1
Do -	Owen Ann } Beirn Pap.		Do		2						
Lecarrow[4]	John Mable } McOwen Pap.		Do								
Do -	Martin Brigit } Beirn Pap.		Do		1						
Do -	Willm. Beirn widowr. Pap.		Do		1		2				1
	Prots. 1. Papts. 73			2	59		22		6		17

Com~Ros common Parish of	Place of Abode	Names and Religion	Proffession	Children under 14		Children above 14		Men Servts		Women Servts	
				Prot.	Paps.	Prot.	Paps.	Prot.	Paps.	Prot.	Paps.
[f.47] Clooncraff	Lecarrow	Patrick } Honor } Brennan Pap.	Farmer								
	Do -	Dennis } Ann } Murray Pap.	Do		5		3				
	Do -	Hugh } Joan } McKeon Pap.	Do		2		3				1
	Do -	Domnick } Mary } McKeon Pap.	Do								
	Do -	Lawrence } Margaret } McKeon Pap.	Do								
	Do -	James } Sarah } McKeon Pap.	Do		1						
	Do -	John } Sarah } Glynn Pap.	Do				1				
	Do -	James } Mary } McKeon Pap.	Do		2		3				1
	Do -	Francis } Ann } Beirn Pap.	Do								
	Cloonglasny[5]	John } Honor } Duane Pap.	Herd				1				
	Do -	Michl. } Cather. } Duane Pap.	Cottager		1						
	Do -	Darby } Mary } Donnellan Pap.	Do		1						
	Do -	Dennis } Elizab. } McNamarra Pap.	Herd		2		2		1		1
	Cloonkuscar	Patrick } Ann } McGawran Pap.	Herd		2				1		1
	Kinard	Barthw. } Margart. } Plunkett Pap.	Farmer		1				5		2
	Do -	Barnaby Plunkett Batchr. Pap.	Do						1		
	Do -	Willm } Elizab. } Foy Pap.	Cottager								
	Do -	Owen } Sisley } Carroll Pap.	Do		1		2				
	Carrakeel	John } Ann } Kelagher Prot.	Do	2							
	Do -	Ambrose } Jane } McDermott Pap.	Herd		2				1		1
	Do -	Bryan } Honor } Maxwell Pap.	Smith		2				1		
	Do -	Ambrose } Honor } Morris Pap.	Cottager		2						
	Do -	Peter } Mary } Duffily Pap.	Do		2						
	Cummin	John } Cather } Bohan Pap.	Farmer		2						
	Do -	Patrick } Cather. } Dowd Pap.	Do		2						1
	Do -	Margart. Kane widow Pap.	Do		2				1		

Com~Ros common Parish of	Place of Abode	Names and Religion	Proffession	Children under 14		Children above 14		Men Servts		Women Servts	
				Prot.	Paps.	Prot.	Paps.	Prot.	Paps.	Prot.	Paps.
Do -		Laughlin Joan } Bohan Pap.	Do		3		1				
Do -		Francis Mary } Conry Pap.	Do		2		1				
Do -		Owen Ann } Murray Pap.	Do		2						
Hey		William Margaret } O'Fallon Pap.	Gent.				2		2		2
Do -		Bryan Alice } Dowd Pap.	Cottager		1						

[verso f. 48]

Killummod

The sums total of wch. Parish are.

Prots. Men & Women -	1	Papts. Men & Women -	141
Do. Children under 14.	21	Do. Childn. Under 14	143
Do. Childn. Over 14	3	Do. Childn. Over 14	55
Do. Men Servts	7	Do Men Servts	31
Do. Women Servts.	6	Do Women Servts	35
	52		405

Clooncraff

Prots Men & Women in sd. Parish	8	Papts Men & Women in Sd Parish	220
Do. Childn. Under 14	14	Do. Childn undr. 14.	166
Do Children above 14	2	Do Childn. above 14.	61
Do Men Servts.	2	Do Men Servts	36
women Servts. None	26	Do Women Servts.	45
			528
			26
			554

	Prots	Papts
Aghrim Parish contains	144	1170
Killmore Parish	145	1157
Killumod Parish	52	405
Clooncraff Parish	26	528
	367	3260
		3627

for Aghrim & Killmore Parishes
see ye. Lists at ye. End of each.

[Edward Synge's hand]
N.B. the Sum of the popish Men & Women of the Parish of Killummod amounts to 189 for 65 + 71 + 53 = 189.

NOTES

1. Including 387 acres of the river Shannon, 207 acres of Lough Nablahy and 332 acres of smaller loughs (*General Alphabetical Index*).

2. Lewis, 'Clooncraff' '.

3. John Conroy (1704-69) collector of Cork was the sole legitimate son of Farfeasa Conry and Elizabeth Aylmer. He married Elizabeth Fowke, daughter and heiress of Robert Fowke of Mallow, Co. Cork. Their daughter Molly married Edmond Kelly of Churchborough in 1752. Farfeasa Conroy (1661-1746) of Carrowmore, near Roscommon was said to be the first member of the Conry family to convert to avoid penalties on holding land. Bishop Synge had no opinion of the Conry, later Conroy family.When John Conroy married Elizabeth Fowke, a young Cork heiress, came with her husband in 1749 to settle on Farfeasa Conry's farm at Carrowmore. When they arrived in Elphin they stayed at the local inn where 'all the *Canaille* of Conrys assembled to see their new Relation; and probably condemn'd to pass her days in a Caban. What a fall is this....' (*Synge Letters*, pp.xxxvii, 155-6; N.L.I., Wicklow Papers PC 223(6); Balliol College Oxford, Conroy Papers, item 13d)).

4. Arable and pasture land owned by the Mahon family (N.L.I., Pakenham Mahon estate maps 1745-1837, MS 16 M 15/3).

5. Cloonglassny was arable and pasture; the bottom land was coarse and sedgy which was flooded in winter. There was red bog (N.L.I.,Pakenham Mahon estate maps, MS 16 M 15/3).

TERMONBARRY, COUNTY ROSCOMMON

INTRODUCTION: *Termonbarry is in the barony of Roscommon, between Strokestown and Longford. It is 9,295 statute acres in size and is partly bounded by the river Shannon.[1] Lewis described it as being half 'inferior' arable and pasture land and half bog.[2]*

The poverty of the land is reflected in the occupations where there were no farmers or gentlemen but eighteen beggars and two retired old soldiers . A fair was held in Termonbarry four times a year, in February, May, August and in November, and a market was held in Ruskey every Wednesday.[3] Much of the land in the parish was the see land of the bishop of Elphin.[4]

The parish was a rectory in the patronage of the bishop of Elphin. The rector in 1749, also prebendary of Termonbarry, was the Rev. Thomas Palmer, who was instituted in 1743 and died in 1774.[5] He lived at Glanmore, County Longford. His curate was the Rev. William Wemyss who was also curate of Kilglass.[6] The patron was the bishop.

OCCUPATIONS

Beggar	20	Driver for rent	1	Servants, household	108
Clerk	1	Grass-keeper	1	Smith	3
Cottager	24	Herd	6	Tailor	4
Cottier	7	Old Soldier	2	Weaver	5
Doctor	1	Priest	1	Welder	83

Com~Ros common Parish of	Place of Abode	Names and Religion	Proffession	Children under 14		Children above 14		Men Servts		Women Servts	
				Prot.	Paps.	Prot.	Paps.	Prot.	Paps.	Prot.	Paps.
[f.49] Tarmonbarry	u Ballyto/hy	Willm. Graham & his wife Prot.	Grass-keeper	2		3			2		2
		Andrew Kennedy & his wife Pa:	Cottager		6				1		1
		Michael Murtagh & his wife Pa:	Cottr.		1				2		1
		Dennis Kelly & his wife Pa:	Cottr.		2		1		1		1
		Jon. Kelly & his wife Pa:	Cottr.		3				2		1
		Thady Kelly & his wife Pa:	Cottr.		1				1		1
		Laughlin Cox & his wife Pa:	Cottr.		5				1		1
		Pattrick Murtagh & his wife Pa:	Cottr.		4				1		1
		Darby Cormuck & his wife Pa:	Cottr.		1				2		
	Lack	Pattrick McGuane & his wife Pa:	Welder		1		3			1	
		Wm. Regan & his wife Pa:	Do		5						
		Miles Murtagh & his wife Pa:	Do		2						2
		Thos. Kelly & his wife Pa:	Weaver								
		Jas. Keane & his wife Pa:	Weaver		3		3				
		Michael Mcnamara & his wife Pa:	Welder		2				1		
		Jon. Cox & his wife Pa:	Cottager		4						
		Dennis Mcnamara & his wife Pa:	Welder		3				1		1
		Bryan Donigan & his wife Pa:	Welder					5			
		Peter Lyons & his wife Pa:	Do		1						
		Connor Mcnamara & his wife Pa:	Do		2						
		Jon. Mcnamara & his wife Pa:	Do		2		1				
		Connor Cox & his wife Pa:	Do				2				1
		Thos. Hallon & his wife Pa:	Do		1		1				
		Michael Kelly & his wife Pa:	Do		3				1		1
		Anthony Kelly & his wife Pa:	Do		2						
		Jon. Raney & his wife Pa:	Do		1						1
		Daniel Green & his wife Pa:	Do				2				1
		Thady McNamara & his wife Pa:	Do		2						1
		Widow Egan Pa:	Beggar		2		2				
		Widow Kilduff Pa:	Beggar				1				
		Widow Runey Pa:	beggar				2				
		Martin Cox & his wife Pa:	Herd								
	Cormagrine	Michael Casey & his wife Pa:	Welder		2						1
		Nicholas Casey & his wife Pa:	Do						1		1
		Luke Corkran & his wife Pa:	Doi		3						1
		Wm Cline & his wife Pa:	Herd								
		Thos. Hallon & his wife Pa:	Cottager		3						
		Owen Muldoon & his wife Pa:	Welder		4						1
In this Page	Total	73	total	2	71	3	23		17		22
[f.50] Tarmonbarry	Cornegrine	Widow Cline Pa:	Beggar				1				
	Derymilan	Jon. Teig & his wife Pa:	Herd		2				1		
	Newtown	Thos. Simpson & his wife Pro:	Smith	3		3			1		1
		Christopher Spallan & his wife Pa:	Welder						1		1
		Jas. Nowlan & his wife Pa:	Do		3						
		Thos. Carrinton & his wife Pa:	Do		2		3				

Com~Ros common Parish of	Place of Abode	Names and Religion	Proffession	Children under 14		Children above 14		Men Servts		Women Servts	
				Prot.	Paps.	Prot.	Paps.	Prot.	Paps.	Prot.	Paps.
		Thady Kilimade & his wife Pa:	Do			1		1			
		Cormuck Kilimade & his wife Pa:	Do		1						1
		Jon. Casey & his wife Pa:	Cottager								
		Peter Dolan & his wife Pa:	Welder		4				1		1
		Jon. Cox & his wife Pa:	Weaver		2		2				
		Wm. Casey & his wife Pa:	Welder		3						
		Bryan Hallon & his wife Pa:	Do		3				1		2
		Jas. Cunigam & his wife Pa:	Do		3				1		1
		David Spallan & his wife Pa:	Do		4						
		Gilbert fferrall & his wife Pa:	Do		3		2				
		Wm. Welch Pro his wife a Pa:	Do		3						
		Cormuck Casey & his wife Pa:	Cottager		1						
		Jas. Cahill & his wife Pa:	Welder		3		3				
		Jon Spallen & his wife Pa:	Do		3		2		1		
		Pat. Spallan & his wife Pa:	Do						1		
		Thos. Spallan & his wife Pa:	Do		1						
		Thady Casey & his wife Pa:	Do		3				1		1
		Jon. ffallan & his wife Pa:	Do		2		3				1
		Luke Cox & his wife Pa:	Cottager		1		1				
		Widow ffeney Pa:	beggar								
		Widow Bennett Pa:	beggar								
	Killbarry	Carbery fferrall & his wife Pa:	Welder		3				1		
		Laughlin Cox & his wife Pa:	Do				2		1		1
		Daniel Cox & his wife Pa:	Do		3						
		Pat. Cox & his mother Pa:	Do								
		Peter Duffely & his wife Pa:	Do		5						
		Jon. Cox & his mother Pa:	Do								
		Michael Cox & his wife Pa:	Taylor						1		
		Edmond fferrall & his wife Pa:	Welder		2		1				
		Jon Cox Pa: Do					3				1
		Wm. fferrall & his wife Pa:	Welder		3						
In this page	Total	70	Total	3	63	3	24		12		11
[f.51] Tarmonbarry	Killbarry	Owen Duffely & his wife Pa:	Welder		3						
		Pat. Cox & his wife Pa:	Do		1		1				
		Jane Cox widow	beggar		3		2				
		Catherine Cox	beggar		2						
	Cloonfad	Pattrick Mulligan & his wife Pa:	Herd		3		2				
	Kiltibeg	Daniel Keon & his wife Pa:	Herd				3				
	Ruskey	Jon. Huit & his wife Pro:	Cottager								
		Jon. Best & bror.	Old Soldiers								2
		Pat. Geelan Pa: & his wife Pro:	Cottager		5	0					2
		Miles Long & his wife Pa:	Do		6					1	1
		Phelim Hanly & his wife Pa:	Cottager		3	0	2	0			
		Hugh Duffely Pa:	Herd		2	0	3				
	Cloonmore	Andrew Stafford & his wife Pa:	Welder		2				0		1
		Jon. Cunlish & his wife Pa:	Do		3				1		1
		Jas. Kennedy & his wife Pa:	Do		1						1
		Pat. Gearty & his wife Pa:	Do		3		3		1		1

Com~Ros common Parish of	Place of Abode	Names and Religion	Proffession	Children under 14 Prot.	Paps.	Children above 14 Prot.	Paps.	Men Servts Prot.	Paps.	Women Servts Prot.	Paps.
		Morgan fferrall & his wife Pa:	a driver for rent &c[7].		3				2		1
		Laughlin Cassey & his wife Pa:	Welder		4		1				
		Ferrall Cox & his wife Pa:	Do		2		1				
		Wm. Regan & his wife Pa:	Do		1		2				
		Wm. Kelly & his wife Pa:	Do		3		2				
		Thady Connor & his wife Pa:	Taylor		3				2		1
		Jas. Cox & his wife Pa:	Welder		3				1		1
		Jas. fferrall & his wife Pa:	Do		2				1		
		Michael Mannin & his wife Pa:	Do		4		1				
		Hugh Galaher & his wife Pa:	Cottager		1						
		Jas. ffalland & his wife Pa:	Cottager								
		Pat. Igoe & his wife Pa:	Cottager				1				
		Dennis Cox & his wife Pa:	Welder								
		Owen Egan & his wife Pa:	Doctor		4						
		Jon. Callaghan & his wife Pa:	Cottager		2						
		Luke Nary & his wife Pa:	Welder						1		2
		Owen fferrall & his wife Pa:	Do								
		Thos. Igoe & his wife Pa:	Welder		3		2				
		Thos. fferrall & his wife Pa:	Do		2		1				
In this Page	Total	67			74		27		9	1	14
[f.52] Tarmonbarry		Jon. Gurlick & his wife Pa:	Welder		3						
		Wm. Bennet & his wife Pa:	Do		1		2				
		Peter Gurlick & his wife Pa:	Taylor		1				1		
		Jon. Murphy & his wife Pa:	Weaver		2		1				
		Richd. Bennet & his wife Pa:	Welder		2						
		Wm. Cox & his wife Pa:	Do		2		2				
		Jon. Gannon & his wife Pa:	Do		2						1
		Jas. Nary & his wife Pa:	Cottager		2						
		Thos. Nary & his wife Pa:	Welder		3		2				
		Stephen Jordan & his wife Pa:	Smith		1				1		2
		Owen Regan & his wife Pa:	Cottager		2		1				
		Fergus Hanly & his wife Pa:	Beggar								
		Dennis Cox & his wife Pa:	beggar		2						
		Pat. Mannin & his wife Pa:	Cottager		1						
		Darby O Bryan & his wife Pa:	Do		3						
		Wm. Dolan & his wife Pa:	beggar		2						
		Jon Kelly & his wife Pa:	Cottager		2						
		Daniel Kelly & his wife Pa:	Do								
		Francis fferrall & his wife Pa:	Do		2						
		Jon. Cox & his wife Pa:	Do								
		Wm. McVanny & his wife Pa:	Do		2						
		Jon. Moran & his mother Pa:	Do								
		Owen Cassedy & his wife Pa:	Doctor		1				1		1
		Michael Cunlish & his wife Pa:	Welder								
		Widow Hanly Pa:	Beggar		1		1				
		Widow Ganly Pa:	Do				2				
		Widow fflin Pa:	Do		1						
		Widow Nary Pa:	Do		1						

Com~Ros common Parish of	Place of Abode	Names and Religion	Proffession	Children under 14		Children above 14		Men Servts		Women Servts	
				Prot.	Paps.	Prot.	Paps.	Prot.	Paps.	Prot.	Paps.
	Corrane	Widow Bohon Pa:	Do		1						
		Widow Cassedy Pa:	Do								
		Widow Jordan Pa:	Do								
		Michael Cox & his wife Pa:	Welder		3				1		1
		Darby Hynes & his wife Pa:	Do								
		Bryan Cox & his wife Pa:	Do		1				1		
		Jon. Murtagh & his wife Pa:	Do								
		Wm. Carr & his wife Pro:	Weaver	3		1					
		Thady Connell & his wife Pa:	Welder				3				1
		Michael Servan & his wife Pa:	Do		1		1				
		Daniel Banan & his wife Pa:	Do		1				1		1
In this Page	Total	71		3	46	1	15		6		7
[f.53] Tarmonbarry	Corrane	Pat. Murphy & his wife Pa:	Welder		2						1
		Luke Hanly & his wife Pa:	Welder		3		3				
		Wm Kennedy & his wife Pa:	Smith		2						1
		Thos. Scally & his wife Pa:	Welder		4		2				
		Owen Bohan & his wife Pa:	Do		2						
		Gregory Trever & his wife Pa:	Taylor				1				
		Widow Bohun Pa:	beggar				1				
		Dorothy fferrall Pa:	beggar								
		[erasure]									
		Hugh Nerinny[8] & Thos. Lyons	Priest & Clerk								
In this Page	Totall	16			13		7				2

[In Edward Synge's handwriting]
Total of all ye. Pages – 297
making in the whole Parish — 776
September 1749

		297		8	267	7	96		44	1	56

[1 blank page]

NOTES

1. Including 755 acres of the river Shannon and 288 acres of water (*General Alphabetical* Index).

2. Lewis, 'Tarmonbarry'.

3. *Report....on fairs and markets*.

4. *Books of Survey and Distribution*, Roscommon.

5. Leslie, 'Elphin', p. 63.

6. William Wemyss was born in Edenderry, King's County and educated in Dublin. He entered TCD in 1709, aged 17 (*Alumni Dubliniensis*; Leslie, 'Elphin', p.221).

7. It was open to the landlord to distrain property on the tenant's land as a pledge for rent due. The bailiff could require a driver to drive livestock from a farm to a pound until the debt was paid (Matthew Dutton, *The Law of Landlords and Tenants in Ireland* (Dublin 1726) p. 536).

8. Hugh Nerinny (Nerney) died at Lissonuffy 31 May 1761 (Fenning, 'Diocese of Elphin', (1994) p.166).

KILGLASS, COUNTY ROSCOMMON

INTRODUCTION: *The parish of Kilglass is in the baronies of Ballintober North and Roscommon. It is 5 miles east of Strokestown on the way to Roosky, County Roscommon. It covered 7,168 statute acres, of which 1,400 acres were bog. Lewis said that the land was under tillage, with some quarries.*[1]

In 1641, the Hanly family owned five townlands in the parish.[2] *In 1749, 23 members of the Hanly family remained.*[3].

The incumbent was the Rev. Samuel Griffin who was instituted vicar in 1741 and the Rev. William Wemys was curate of Kilglass and Termonbarry from 1730[4] *(see Termonbarry). The patron was the bishop of Elphin. The tithes were impropriate in Lord Kingsland.*

OCCUPATIONS

Beggar	17	Illegible	1	Servants, household	82
Butcher	2	Maltster	1	Smith	7
Carpenter	1	Mason	1	Tailor	2
Catholic priest	1	Merchant	2	Tenant	105
Cooper	2	Miller	1	Tenant carpenter	1
Cottier	34	n/s	1	Tenant thatcher	1
Cow herd	4	Parish Clerk	1	Weaver	17
Farmer	13	Parish minister	1	Wheelwright	1
Gentleman	4	Piper	1	Widow	47
Gentlewoman	2	Pumpmaker	6	Widow gentlewoman	1
Herd	4	Saddler	1		

Com~Ros common Parish of	Place of Abode	Names and Religion	Proffession	Children under 14		Children above 14		Men Servts		Women Servts	
				Prot.	Paps.	Prot.	Paps.	Prot.	Paps.	Prot.	Paps.
Parish of Killglass [f.54] Killglass	~~Knock-Hall~~ Knock-Hall	Cathn. Mills Prot.	Gentwn.	2	0	5		3	3		3
		John Mills5 Prot.& wife	Gent.	2				1			
		Jams. Sharply Prot & wife	Tent.	5		1			1		1
		Hugh Callaghan Pt & wife	Tent.		2		1				
		Michl. Keenagen Pt & wife	Tent.								
		James Feeny Papt. & wife	Cottr.		1						
		Patk. Gaffny Papt. & wife	Taylor		2						
		John Gaffny Papt. & wife	Tent.		2						
		Edmd. Oaks Papt. & wife	Tent				1				
		Garrtt Beirne & wife	Tent						1		
		Dennis Gallagher & wife	Tent.		2						
		Mary McGuire	Widw.				2				
		Bryan Banane & wife	Tent				1				
		Owen Kieragen & wife	Tent.		1						
		Cathern ffeelan	Widw.		1						
		Michl. Hanane & wife	Tent.		1						
		Willm. Johnston & wife Papts	Beggar				2				
		Michl. Gaffny Papts & wife	Cottr.		2						
		John Nolan & wife papts	Maltstr.		1						1
		Michl. Carroll & wife	Beggar		2						
		James Keeragen Pt & wife	Tent.		1		2				
		John Keeragen Pt. & wife	Tent.		4						
		Patk. Keeragen Pt. & wife	Tent.		1						
		Mary Keeragen Pt	Widw.		3						
		John McGuire Pt & wife	Tent.		1		2				
		Abigal Clabby Pt.	Widw.				2				
		Patk. Cox papt & wife	Cottr.		2						
		Michl. Cox Papt. & wife	Weaver		2		1				
		Thady Dennigan & wife	Tent.		4		1				
		Mary Sweeny Papt.	Widw.		4						
		Darby Burn Pt & wife	Cottr.		2						
		Thoms. Dunnigan & wife	Weavr.		1		2				
		John McGuire Pt & wife	Widowr.				2				
		James Creag Papt. & wife	Tent.		2		1				
		John Lannan Papt & wife	Cottr.		1						1
		John Reily Papt. & wife	Cottr.		3						
		Sarah Keeragen	Widw.		1						
		Neal Keeragen & wife	Beggar		4						
		Darby ffeelan Pt & wife	Tent.		1						
		Laughlin Kelly Papt & wife Prot.	Tent.	~~2~~	0	2	2				1
		James Kelly Prot & wife									
[f.55] Killglass	Knock-Hall	Connor Killbanon & wife	Cottr.		2						
		Dorothy Corsey p	Widw.		1		2				
		Edmd. Hanane & wife	Carpentr.								
	Drummone	Andw Hanly Papt. & wife	Tent.								

Com~Ros common Parish of	Place of Abode	Names and Religion	Proffession	Children under 14		Children above 14		Men Servts		Women Servts	
				Prot.	Paps.	Prot.	Paps.	Prot.	Paps.	Prot.	Paps.
		Rich.Staunton & wife	Tent.		1						
		Edmd Hanly Papt. & wife	Beggar		1						
		Michl. Igo Papt. & wife	Tent		2		2				
		Willm. Igo Papt. & wife	Tent.				2				
		Peter Igo Papt. & wife	Tent.		3						
		Edmd. Nugent Papt. & wife	Cottr.		2						
		Mary Haneck Papt.	Widw.		2						
		Patk. Shanly Papt. & wife	Tent.				4				
		Thoms. Tully Papt. & wife	Tent.		1						
		James Shanly Papt. & wife	Tent.		2						
		Luke Tully Papt. & wife	Tent.		5						
		Mary Igo Papist	Widw.		2						
		Philip M'Guire & wife	Tent.		3		1				
		Honnr Igo Papt.	Widw.		1		1				
		Bartel Lannon Papt. & wife	Tent.		2						
		James Lannon Papist & wife	Tent.		2						
		Barbara McGuire papist	Widw.		2		1				
		Coll Monaghan Papt. & wife	Pumpmaker		2						
		Willm. Keragan Papt. & wife	Weaver								
		Cathn. Cox Papt.	Widw.		1		2				
	Runifarny	Michl. Gallagher Papt. & wife	Tent.		3						1
		Darby McGarry & wife papists	Tent.		3						
		John Donnelly Papt. & wife	Tent.		2						
		Daniel m'Laughlin & wife papists	Tent.		3						
		Michl. Cox Papt. & wife	Pumpmaker		3						
		Francis Cox Papt. & wife	Cottr.		1						
		Mary Gallagher papist	Widw.		2						
	Derrim'stirr	Bryan O Neal Papt. & wife	Tent.		1						
		James Dunnocho & wife Papist	Tent.		2						
		Daniel Feeny Papt. & wife	Tent.								
		Willm. Conry Papt. & wife	Beggar		1						
		Darby Feeny Papt. & wife	Cottr.		2						
		Thady Feeny Papt. & wife	Tent.				1				
		John Gallagher Papt. & wife	Tent.		3						
		Laughlin Feeny & wife	Tent.		3						
	Keilbogg	Willm Nary Papt. & wife	Cow Herd		3		1				
	Dooaune	Thos Hagan Pa Batchelr.	Farmer						1		1
[f.56] Killglass	Cawl	Francis Furce & wife Papist	Tent.				2				
		Patk. McGuire & wife Papist	Tent.		1						
		John Padeen & wife Papist	Tent.		1		1				
		Andw. Connr. Pa: & wife	Weavr.		4						
		Morris Roach & wife Papist	Tent.				2				
		James Reily Pa: & wife	Tent.		2						
		Edwd. Roach Pa: & wife	Piper		1						
		John Welsh Pa: & wife	Tent.		2						
		Thos. Tiernan Pa: & wife	Tent.		1						
		Farrell Berreen Pa & wife	Weavr.		1						
		Thos. Spilly Pa: & wife	Tent.		1						

Com~Ros common Parish of	Place of Abode	Names and Religion	Proffession	Children under 14 Prot.	Children under 14 Paps.	Children above 14 Prot.	Children above 14 Paps.	Men Servts Prot.	Men Servts Paps.	Women Servts Prot.	Women Servts Paps.
	Tully	Daniel Donnellan & wife Papists	Tent.		2						
		Darby McGuire & wife Papts	Tent.		2						
		Hugh Manion & wife Papts	Tent.		1						
		Bridgett Donnelly & wife Papts [sic]	Widw.		1		3				
		Thos. Flyn Pap & wife	Tent.		1		1				
		Thady Cox Pap: & wife	Tent.		2						
		Phelim Galaghr & wife Papts	Tent.		3		1				
		Bryan Reily Pa: & wife	Tent.		2						
		Daniel Sherridan & wife Papts	Tent.		2		3				
		Owen Reily Papts & wife	Tent.		2						
		Laughlin Cox & wife Papts.	Tent.		1		1				
		Mattw. Cormack & wife Papts	Tent.		2						
		Laurence Egan & wife Papts	Tent.		1						
		James Chapman & wife papist	Smith		1		3				
		William Stuart Pa: & wife	Tent.								
		Domnick Monaghan & wife Papts	Weaver		1						
		Patt. Hanly Papts & wife	Tent.		1						
	Ballymilan	Charles Stuart Pa: & wife	Tent.		1		3				
		Edwd. Hanly Papt. & wife	Farmer		1		3				
		Domnick Owens Papt	Mercht.		3		2				
		Henry Padeen & wife Papts	Tent.		2		1				
		Domnk Bercan Pa: & wife	Tent.		2						
		Willm. McGarry & wife Papts	Tent.		2		2				
		Luke McGarry & wife Papts	Tent.		2		2				
		Bridget Diffily Papt.	Widw.		1						
		Patk. Smith	Tent.		2		1				1
		Roger McDonnell & wife Papt	Tent.		2						
		Thady Cryne Pa: & wife	Tent.		1						
		Roger Flanigan & wife Papts	Tent.		1		2				
		Michl. Reynolds Pap:	Beggar		2						
[f.57] Killglass	Ballymilan	John Hanly Papt & wife	Smyth		2				1		1
		Willm. Nary Papt & wife	Tent.		1						1
		Brigit McGarry papist	Widw.				1				
		Thady Derrivan & wife Papts	Cooper		3		1				
		Barbra McGuire papist	Widw.				1				
		Cathrin Daly papt	Widw.				2				
	Moher	John Dunnacho & wife papts	Farmer						1		
		Thos. Spalan Papts & wife	Tent.		3						
		Bryan Bohelly Pat: & wife	Tent.		1						
		Patk. Connell pa: & wife	Tent.				2				
		Connr. McGuire & wife papts	Farmer				2				
		Terence Kelly Pa: & wife	Tent.		2						
		Bryan Ohara Pa: & wife	Tent.		2						
		Terence Feeh Pats	Beggar		3		2				
		John Dunnacho Pa: & wife	Tent.		2						
		Darby Spallan & wife papts	Miller		5						
		Manus Furee & wife	Tent.		1						

Com~Ros common Parish of	Place of Abode	Names and Religion	Proffession	Children under 14 Prot.	Children under 14 Paps.	Children above 14 Prot.	Children above 14 Paps.	Men Servts Prot.	Men Servts Paps.	Women Servts Prot.	Women Servts Paps.
		Ambrose Cassady & wife papts	Tent.		2		2				
		James Donnacho & wife papts	Tent.		1		3				
		Edwd. Furee & wife papts	Tent.		2		2				
		Daniel King & wife papts	Tent.		1						
		Connor Gannon & wife papts	Smyth		3		1				
		Edwd Flanigan wife Papts									
	Ballifeeny	Nich. Hawkes[6] Prot. & wife	Gent:n					2			2
		Tobias Nary & wife papts	Tent.		3						
		John Donnelly & wife papts	Tent.								
		James Connell & wife papists	Tent.		1						
		Francis Heely & wife papts	Tent.		1						
		Dennis M'Gee Pa: & wife	Tent.		1		1				
		Mark Lally Papt: & wife	Tent.		3		2				
		Hugh Reily Pa: & wife	Tent.		2						
		Bryan Beirn Pa: & wife	Tent.		4						
	Lagan Ragt.	John McGuire Pa: & wife	Smith		1				1		1
		William Nugent Pa: & wife	Farmer		2		1				
		Francis Hanly & wife papts	Mercht.		2		2				
		Michl. Geenty Pa: & wife	Smith		1						
		Dennis Connor & wife papts	Tent.		1						
		Martin Hoan & wife papts	Cottr.		1						
		James Fox & wife papts	Tent.		1		2				
		James Hanly Batchelr Papt.									
[f.58] Killglass	Delamr.Slatogh	Daniel Daly Papt. & wife	Tent.		1						1
		Hugh Reily Papt. & wife	Cottr.				1				
		Daniel Daily Papt. & wife	Tent.		1						
		Daniel Morris & wife papist	Tent.		2		1				
		Patk. Naughton Pa: & wife	Tent.		1		1				
		Francis Daly & wife papist	Tent.		1						1
		Thady O Brien Pa: & wife	Tent.		3						
		Bryan Padeen & wife papists	Beggar		4						
		Roger Mahon & wife papists	Farmer		2		1				
		Patrk. Mahon Papts & wife	Farmer		3		2		1		1
		Bridget McGuire papist	Widw.		2		2				
		James McGuire & wife papist	Cottr.		2						
		Laughlin Kelly & wife papists	Tent.		1						
		John Sharry Papt & wife	Tent.		1						
		Francis Honan & wife papist	Cottr.		1						
		Cathr. Derrinan papist	Widw.				3				
		Silvester Daly Pa: & wife	Tent.								
		Cathn. Hines papt.	Widw.								
		Patk. Deecan Pats & wife	Beggar		1		3				
		Charles Newcome & wife papists			1						
	Mahon Slatogh	Edmd Monaghan & wife papists	Farmer						1		1
		John Monaghan & wife papists	Tenant		2				1		1
		Thos Klince Papt. & wife	Tenant		2						
		Willm Cassidy Pap: & wife	Tent.		1		3				
		Thos. Carroll Papt: & wife	Cottr.		4						

Com~Ros common Parish of	Place of Abode	Names and Religion	Proffession	Children under 14 Prot.	Paps.	Children above 14 Prot.	Paps.	Men Servts Prot.	Paps.	Women Servts Prot.	Paps.
		Peter Shucran Papt: & wife	Cottr.		3		2				
		Luke McLooy Papt & wife	Beggar		3		1				
		Peter McLooy Papt & wife	Cottr.		2						1
		John Morris Papt. & wife	Cottr.								
		Mary Cassidy Papt	Widw.		1		3				
		Ch. Reily Papt & wife	Cottr.		2		1				
		Mary Murphy Pa:	Widw.		1		4				
		Darby Hanly Papt & wife	Tent.		2		2				1
		Edmd Reily Papt & wife	Cottr.		1		1				
		Hugh Carbry Pat: & wife	Cottr.		2						
		Conr. Monaghan & wife papists	Cottr.		1		2				
		Roger Deacon & wife papists	Cottr.		1		1				
		Willm Murphy & wife Papists	Cottr.		1						
		Mary Nary Pa:	Widw.		1						
		Henry Welsh Pa: & wife	Cottr.		2						
		Owen Kennedy & wife papists	n/s								
[f.59] Killglass	New Town	Patk. Skanlon Pa: & wife	Cooper		3		1		1		1
		John McGuire Pat & wife	Tenant		3		4				
		Art. McLoughlin & wife papists	Tent.		3		4				
		Patk. Connor Pa: & wife	Cottr.		1						
		Neal McLoughlin Pa: & wife	Tent.								
		James Kelly Papt & wife	Tent.		3						
		John Kelly Papt & wife	Tent.		2		2				
		Manus O Connell & wife papist	Tent.		2						
		Connor M'Guire & wife papist	Tent.		1						
		Daniel Conee Pat. & wife	Cottr.		1		3				
		Edmd. Kennedy Pa: & wife	Tent.								
	Coun Kell	Roger Hanly Pa: & wife	Tent.		3						1
		Darby Cox Papt & wife	Tent.		3						
		Simon Cox Papt.& wife	Cottr		3						
		Thos. Deleany & wife papist	Tent.		1		4				
		James Gibbon Pa: & wife	Tent.		3						
		Darby Bohelly & wife papist	Tent.		2						
	Slalogh Begg	Peter Hines Papt & wife	Tent.		1		1				
		John Derrownan Pa: & wife	Tent.		4						
		Hugh Daly Papt & wife	Tent.		3		1				
		Thos. Reily Pa: & wife	Tent.		1				1		1
		Peter Daly Papt & wife	Tent.		2				1		1
		Ellinor Cox	Widw.				1				
		Roger Murphy Pa: & wife	Cottr.		3						
		Pat. Dockery Papt & wife	Pumpmaker		2						
		Willm. Kelly Papt & wife	Tent.		1						
		Michl. Sweeny Pa: & wife	Tent.		1						
		Cathn. Reily Pa:	Widw.		4						
		Bridgett Reily Pa	Widw.		1						
		Mary McConnell papist	Widw.		4						
		Patk. Welsh Pa:	Beggar		4						
	Muckinagh	Bridget Lacy Pa:	Gentwomn.				2		2		3
		Thos. McDermott & wife papist	Cottr.		2						

Com~Ros common Parish of	Place of Abode	Names and Religion	Proffession	Children under 14		Children above 14		Men Servts		Women Servts	
				Prot.	Paps.	Prot.	Paps.	Prot.	Paps.	Prot.	Paps.
		Philip Donnelly & wife papist	Cottr.		1						
		Bridget Hanly papist	Widw.		2		2				
		Francis Geerty & wife papist	Cottr.		1		2				
		John Kennedy & wife papist	Cottr.		1		1				
		Thos. Farrell & wife papist	Cottr.		2		1				
		Mary Kennedy papist	Widw.		2		6				
		Owen Carroll & wife papist	Herd		2		1				
[f.60] Killglass	Mullogh M'Cormick	Owen Duignen & wife papist	Tent.		3						
		Bryan Green & wife papist	Tent.		4						
		John Green & wife papist	Weavr.		1		2				
		Thady Green & wife papist	Tent.		2		1				
		Cormack Morris & wife papist	Tent.		2						
		Thady Mee & wife papist	Tent.		2		2				
		James M'Donnell & wife papist	Tent.		2						
		Michl. Connilly & wife papist	Tent.		1		2				
		Patk. White & wife papist	Beggar		4						
		Pattk. M'Connell & wife papist	Weaver		4						
		Phelim Bartell Papist	Beggar		5						
		Roger Flaherty & wife papist	Tent.		2						
		Thomas Reily & wife papist	Tent.		2						
		Pat Gibbilan & wife papist	Tent.				1				
		Philip Diffily & wife papist	Tent.		1						
		Patt Reily & wife papist	Weavr.		3		1				
		Edmd Dennily & wife Protest	Tent.		3						
		John Dean & wife Protest	Tent.		2						
		Edwd Johnston & wife Protest	Tent.								
		Neal Gormly papist	Tent.		1		2				
		John Carroll & wife papist	Tent.		3		1				
		Owen Johnston & wife papist	Tent.	1							
		John Reily & wife papist	Tent.		2						
		James Kenny & wife papist	Tent.				1				
		Dennis Johnston & wife papist	Tent carpentr		1						
		Domnick Hanly & wife papist	Tent.		1		1				
		Martin Ward & wife papist	Wheelright		4						
		John Ruddy & wife papist	Tent.		2						
		Roger O Donnell & wife papist	Tent.		2						
		Hugh Golaghar & wife papist	Tent.		2						
		Dennis Mulogh & wife papist	Tent.		2						
		John Fallon & wife papist	Tent.		3						
	Aghimanane	Thady Hanly & wife papist	Cow herd				1				
		Dennis Connor & wife papist	Tent.		2		1				
		Dennis Berine & wife papist	Tent.		1						
	Rooaune	Thady Donallan & wife papist	Cow herd		1						
		Owen Feeny & wife papist	Tent.		1						
		Edmd Nary & wife papist	Tent.		1						
	Lagan Brennan	Daniel Brennan & wife papist	Farmer				1		1		1

Com~Ros common Parish of	Place of Abode	Names and Religion	Proffession	Children under 14 Prot.	Children under 14 Paps.	Children above 14 Prot.	Children above 14 Paps.	Men Servts Prot.	Men Servts Paps.	Women Servts Prot.	Women Servts Paps.
[f.61] Killglass	Lagan Brennan	Dennis M'Guire & wife papist	Tent.		2						
		Charles Clyne & wife papists	Tent.		1						
		Henry Page papist	Tent.		3		1				
		Patt Beirn & wife papists	Tent.		2						
		John Brannan & wife papists	Tent.		2						1
		Michl. Beirne & wife papists	Tent.		1						
		Edmd. Ridly papt	Tent.				1				
		William Page & wife papists	Tent.		3						
		John Calaghan & wife papists	Tent.		2						
		Dennis Flannigan & wife papists	Tent.								
		Owen Reily & wife papists	Tent.		4						
		Brigit Brannan	Widw.		2						
		Patt. Flannigan & wife papists	Tent.		2						
	Kellnaghmore	Terence Hagan & wife papists	Cow herd				3				
		William Clyne & wife papists	Tent.		2		2				
		Patt. Kelly & wife papists	Tent.		2		2				
		Luke Hagan & wife papists	Tent.		3						
		Cormack Hagan & wife papists	Tent.		2				1		
		Hugh Cassidy & wife papists	Tent.		1						
		Ann Gaffry	Widw.								
		Charles Galagher & wife papists	Tent.		1						
		Miles Welsh & wife papists	Tent.		1						
		Edwd Nary & wife papists	Tent.		2						
		Owen Galagher & wife papists	Tent.		1						
		John Nary & wife papists	Tent.				2				
		Francis Nary & wife papists	Tent.				2				
	Lecarrow	Daniel Hanly[7] & wife papists	Farmer		2		3		1		1
		Phelim M'Gan papist	Tent.				1				
		Winnifrid Flannigan papist	Widw.				4				
		Bryan M'Gan & wife papists	Tent.		2						
		Barbry Gearty papist	Widw.				2				
		Michl. Daly & wife papists	Weavr		1		2				
		Matthew Stafford papist	Tent.								
		Patt. Brown & wife papists	Tent.		1		1				
		Charles M'Dermott & wife papists	Tent								
		Owen Ganly & wife papists	Tent. & Thatcher				2				
		Carbry Beirn & wife papists	Tent.		1						
		James Duignan & wife papists	Tent.								
		Richd. Brown & wife papists	Tent.								
		Domnick Duignan & wife papists	Tent.		3		1				
	Kirlogh	Charles Conry[8] papist	Priest								1
[f.62]		Patt. Cullen & wife papists	Tent.		4		2				
		Bartil Cunningham & wife papists	Tent.		2						
		Peter Shary & wife papists	Tent.		2						

Com~Ros common Parish of	Place of Abode	Names and Religion	Proffession	Children under 14 Prot.	Paps.	Children above 14 Prot.	Paps.	Men Servts Prot.	Paps.	Women Servts Prot.	Paps.
	Killugan Killcegan[?]	Thos M'Gann & wife papists	Tent.		2						
		Ch: M'Gann & wife papists	Tent.		2						
		John Monaghan & wife papists	Tent.		3		2				
		Willm. Farrell & wife papists	Weaver		3						
		Patt Lorhan & wife papists	Tent.		1		1				
		Neal Lorhan & wife papists	Tent.		3		1				
		Patt: Coalman & wife papists	Tent.		1		1				
		Bryan Reily & wife papists	Beggar		5						
		Thady Cain & wife papists	Tent.		3		1				
		Martin Skinnan & wife papists	Tent.		3						
		Ellinor Skinnan	Widw.				2				
		Anthony Fox & wife papists	Beggar		3		1				
	Killgarow	Edmd Flaherty & wife papists	Tent.		3						
		Luke Dowell & wife papists	Tent.				1				
		John Cox & wife papists	Tent.		4						
		Darby Cox & wife papists	Tent.		1		2				
		Edwd Dockery & wife papists	Pumpmaker		2		2				
		Peter Hanly & wife papists	Tent.		3						
		Honr. Flaherty papist	Widw.				3				
		Patt. Ford & wife papists	Tent.		1						
		Roger Flaherty & wife papists	Tent.		2						
		Mary Reily papist	Widw.				3				
		Valentine Reily & wife papists	Tent.				2				
		Cormack Hanly & wife papists	Tent.				1				
		Connr Hanly & wife papists	Tent.				2				
		Bridgett m'Garry papist	Widw.				3				
		Willm Hanly & wife papists	Tent.		4						
		Roger M'Garry & wife papists	Tent.		2						
		Terence Reynolds & wife papists	Tent.		1		4				
		Thady Hanly & wife papists	Tent.		1						
		Mary Hanly papist	Widw.				3				
	Lavagh	Mr Francis Hanly protestant	Gent						2		2
		Thomas Chapman & wife papists	Smith		4						
		James Gulhean & wife papists	Tent.		4						
		Thady Gearty & wife papists	Tent.		4		1				
		Owen Reynolds & wife papists	Beggar		1						
		Patt. McDermot & wife papists	Tent.				3				
		Bryan Byran & wife papists	Tent.		3						
[f.63] Killglass	Lavagh	Thos. Costello & wife papists	Pumpmaker		2						
		Murtagh Flaherty & wife papists	Tent.		2						
		Laughlin Gaskin & wife papists	Tent.								
		John Ego & wife papists	Tent.		1						
		Luke Doyle & wife papists	Tent		2						
		Edwd Clyne & wife papists	Tent.		2		2				1
	Derrifucal	Carbry Beirn & wife papists	Tent.								
		Con Kelly & wife papists	Weaver		3						
		John Kelly & wife papists	Tent.		3						
		Ch: Kelly & wife papists	Tent.		4						

Com~Ros common Parish of	Place of Abode	Names and Religion	Proffession	Children under 14 Prot.	Children under 14 Paps.	Children above 14 Prot.	Children above 14 Paps.	Men Servts Prot.	Men Servts Paps.	Women Servts Prot.	Women Servts Paps.
		Patt. Treynor & wife papists	Tent.		2						
		Francis M'Cue & wife papists	Tent.		1						
		Martin Gibbilon & wife papists	Tent.		2						
		Bridgett Traynor papist	Weaver		3		3				
		Michl. Beirne papist	Tent.								
		Matt.Beirne & wife papists	Weavr.		2						
		Thos. Monaghan & wife papists	Tent.		4		2				
		Mary Narrant papist	Widw.				2				
		Michl. Cunnington & wife papists	Tent.		6						
	Keilgraffy	Bryan M'Donagh & wife papists	Tent.								
		Roger Murtagh & wife papists	Weavr.				1				
		William Connor & wife papists	Tent.		6		1				
	Barvally	Walter Morris & wife papists	Tent.		1		4				
		John Moran & wife papists	Sadler		2						1
		Luke Doyle & wife papists	Tent.		3		2				
	Gillstown	Mr John Stafford & wife protests	Gentn.						3		3
		Nicholas Stafford & wife papists	Tent.								1
		Kathn. Kilroy papist	Widw.		3						
		Ann McCormack	Widw.				1				
		Peter Gruine & wife papists	Tent.		1						
		Francis M'Guire & wife papists	Tent.		1						
		Kathn. Dockery [erasure]	Widw.		1						
		Patk. Lewis & wife papists	Tent.				2				
		Edwd Duffy & wife papists	Tent.		1						
		Michael McGuire & wife papists	Tent.		2						
		James Doolan & wife papists	Butcher		2						
		Francis Guskin & wife papists	Tent.								
		Margtt. Stafford papist	Widw.		2						
		Ch: King & wife papists	Tent.		3		1				
	Cargen	Rev. Saml. Griffin & wife	Parish minister	1				1	2		1
		Robt Onions & wife protestants	Clerk of ye Parish	2		3					
[f.64]	Cargen	Laughlin Beirn & wife papists	Tent.		2		1				
		Laurence Beirn & wife papists	Tent.		1						
		Patt. Hurracho & wife papists	Tent.		2						
		Bryan Mulligan & wife papists	Tent.		2						
		John Mulligan & wife papists	Tent.								
		Patt. Fallon & wife papists	Tent.		2						
		James M'Donnell & wife papists	Tent.		3						
		William Mullen & wife papists	Tent.		3						
		Edwd. Ford & wife papists	Weavr.		3						
		Laughlin Colally & wife papists	Tent.		1						
		Thos. M'Gan & wife papists	Tent.				1				
		John Carroll & wife papists	Butcher		2		3				
		Patt. Burge & wife papists	Tent.		1		1				
		Bryan M'Donnell & wife papists	Tent.		4						

Com~Ros common Parish of	Place of Abode	Names and Religion	Proffession	Children under 14		Children above 14		Men Servts		Women Servts	
				Prot.	Paps.	Prot.	Paps.	Prot.	Paps.	Prot.	Paps.
		Patt Hanly & wife papists	Tent.		1		2				
		Thos. Mullen & wife papists	Tent.		1						
		Francis M'donnell & wife papists	Tent.		3						
		Murtagh M'donnell & wife papists	Tent.		3						
		John Cryan & wife papists	Tent.		3						
		James Glancy & wife papists	Pumpmaker		3		1				
		William Phylican & wife papists	Tent.		3						
		John Roddy & wife papists	Tent.								
		Francis M'donel & wife papists	Tent.				1				
		John Lunneen & wife papists	Weavr.		2						
		Kathn. Cryan	Widw.		3		1				
		Thady Cox & wife papists	Tent.		2		2				
		Owen Hurrocho & wife papists	Tent.								
		John Mullen & wife papists	Tent.		3						
		Darby Mullen & wife papists	Tent.		3		1				
		Nick: Masters & wife papists	Mason		4		2				
		Peter Glyn & wife papists	Tent.		1						
		Laughlin Hurracho & wife papists	Tent.		3		2				
		Terence Gaffny & wife papists	Tent.		2		2				
		Arth. Mulligan & wife papists	Tent.		2		2				
		Mary M'dermot papist	Widw.								
		Michael M'Gragh & wife papists	Herd		2						
	Ballykillcline	Terence McGuire & wife papists	Tent.				4			1	
		Hugh Downy & wife papists	Tent.				2				
		Terence Beirne & wife papists	Taylor		4						
		Edwd. Downy & wife papists	Tent.		1		2				
		Hugh M'Guire & wife papists	Tent.		2		2				
[f.65] Killglass	Ballikillcline	Andw. Reynolds & wife papists	Tent.				3				
		Patt. M'Gragh & wife papists	[illegible]		2						
		Bryan Reynolds & wife papists	Tent.				1				
		Connor Beirne & wife papists	Tent.		2						
		Thos. M'Guire & wife papists	Tent.		2						
		Lawrence Beirne & wife papists	Tent.		1		2				
		Peter Beirne & wife papists	Tent.		1					1	
		Philip Reily & wife papists	Tent.		1						
		Carbry Beirn & wife papists	Tent.		2						
		Patt. Beirne & wife papists	Tent.		2						
		Patt. Coyle & wife papists	Tent.				1				
		Hugh Killroy & wife papists	Tent.		1		3				
		Patt. Stuart & wife papists	Tent.		1		1				
		Ch. Stuart & wife papists	Tent.							1	
		Patt. Clyne & wife papists	Tent.		2						
		Daniel Eigo & wife papists	Tent.		1						
		Barnaby Cormack	Tent.		3						
		Patt: Sharcody & wife papists	Tent.		1		1				
		Connor Eigo & wife papists	Tent.		1						

Com~Ros common Parish of	Place of Abode	Names and Religion	Proffession	Children under 14 Prot.	Children under 14 Paps.	Children above 14 Prot.	Children above 14 Paps.	Men Servts Prot.	Men Servts Paps.	Women Servts Prot.	Women Servts Paps.
	Cloonneen[9]	James Eigo & wife papists	Tent.		1						
		Terence M'connell & wife papists	Tent.		2						
		Morris Brackan papist	Smith		3						
		Redm'd M'Guire & wife papists	Tent.		2		2				
		Owen Mulligan & wife papists	Tent.				3				
		Michael Moran & wife papists	Herd		1						
		Martin Duffy & wife papists	Farmer		2		2	1			1
		Cormack Naughton papist	Tent.				4				1
		Darby Reynolds & wife papists	Tent.		3						
		Alex. Sweeny & wife papists	Tent.		2						
		Patt. Brennan & wife papists	Tent.		2						
		Darby Donelly & wife papists	Tent.		2						
		Edmd Donellan & wife papists	Tent.								
		Patt. Duffy & wife papists	Tent.		2						
		Owen Contrine & wife papists	Tent.		1						
	Corgowan	Edwd Stafford & wife papists	Farmer		4		2				
		Kath. Peirce	Widw. Gentwn		3						
		James M'Laughlin & wife papists	Tent.		2		1				
		William Masters & wife papists	Beggar								
	Moyglass	Richd. Ruttlidge & wife papists	Farmer		1		2				
		Connor Caring papist	Herd		2		1				
		Honnr. Langham papist	Widw.		1		3				

NOTES

1. Lewis, 'Kilglass'.

2. Aghamanaghan – Connor Oge mcFerdragh Hanly and Hugh Hanley; Ballymilan – Teige mcGillernow o Hanly; Knock-Hall – Dwaltagh mcDermot Hanley and farraghan mcHugh mcfforga Hanley; Rooaune – Dwaltagh mcDermot Hanley and Connor mcFerdoragh Hanly; Tully – Mlaughlin mcHugh o Hanly (*Books of Survey and Distribution* Roscommon).

3. Census, ff. 55, 56, 57, 58, 60, 61, 62.

4. Samuel Griffin was born in Elphin, the son of the Rev. Michael Griffin who was headmaster of Bishop Hodson's School. He entered TCD in 1725 at the age of 16. He went on to educate a large number of the clergy in Elphin during the period (*Alumni Dubliniensis*).

5. John Mills was born in County Roscommon and educated by Dr. Neligan. He entered TCD in 1739, aged 20. He graduated BA in 1743 (*Alumni Dubliniensis*).

6. Possibly the Nicholas Hawkes, attorney Exchequer who entered the King's Inns in 1734 (Edward Keane, P. Beryl Phair and T.U. Sadleir (eds.), *King's Inns Admission Papers 1607-1867* (Dublin 1982). (Hereafter cited as *Kings Inns Admission Papers*).

7. Possibly the Daniel Hanly of Kilglass who was a lay supporter of the Rev. William (alias Augustine) O'Kelly prior of St. Mary's, Roscommon in 1748 to succeed Patrick French as bishop of Elphin (Fenning, 'Diocese of Elphin', p.166).

8. Listed as parish priest in 1748 and 1756 (Beirne, (ed.) *Diocese of Elphin*, p.122).

9. Arable and pasture including half the river (N.L.I., Maps of lands in Boyle, Castlerea and French Park, MS 21 F 45/115).

LISSONUFFY, COUNTY ROSCOMMON

INTRODUCTION: *Lissonuffy is in the barony of Roscommon. It covers 11,665 statute acres.[1] The river Shannon bounds the parish on the east. The stone in the parish was particularly suitable for millstones with iron ore and coal on Slievebawn.[2] Members of the Branan/McBrenan family owned land in the parish in 1641.[3] Five members of the family were living in the parish in 1749, including a cottier, a constable, a friezemonger and a beggar. A widowed Roman Catholic gentlewoman, Eleanor Branan lived at Aghamore.[4]*

The parish had 28 beggars, of whom 19 were widows, which compared with other parishes was a large number. It may reflect the emphasis on manual occupations in the parish.

The incumbent in 1749 was the Rev. Richard Garrett who held the parish with those of Bumlin and Lissonuffy.[5]

OCCUPATIONS

Beggar	28	Friezemonger	2	Servant	2
Broguemaker	7	Gentleman	2	Servants, household	68
Butcher	1	Gentlewoman/widow	1	Shepherd	1
Carman	18	Herd	2	Sievemaker	1
Carpenter	2	Innkeeper	1	Smith	4
Chorewoman	1	Labourer	74	Tailor	4
Constable	1	Maltster	1	Tenant	41
Cottier	75	Matmaker	3	Tinker	1
Cowherd	9	Merchant	2	Turner	1
Fisherman	1	Mower	2	Weaver	6
Fowler	1	Pedlar	1	Wheelwright	5
Freeholder	2	Piper	1	Yarnbuyer	3
		Priest	1		

Com~Ros common Parish of	Place of Abode	Names and Religion	Proffession	Children under 14		Children above 14		Men Servts		Women Servts	
				Prot.	Paps.	Prot.	Paps.	Prot.	Paps.	Prot.	Paps.
[f.66]	Tullyvarran	Hugh Giles Gill Pap	Weaver		2		1				
		Fran. Winif.Cetane Do.	Labourer		3						
		John Ellen Burke Do	Cowherd								
		Darby Mary Regan Do	Do		2						2
		Will Anne Fahy	Inkeeper		4						1
		Luc. Joan Gahagan Do.	Cottier		3		2				
		Jon.Anne Maguane Do.	Broguemaker		3						
		Bryan Cath.Connel Do.	Carpenter		1						1
		Den.Mary Walsh Do.	Labourer				1				
		Edmd Mullen Widr. Do.	Taylor		2		2				
		Bry:Mary Conron Do.	Labourer		1						
		Jon. Mary McCabe Do	Do								
		Willm Anne Walsh Do.	Labourer		1						
		John Mary Kensey Do.	Piper		2		1				
		Giles Connor Wid.Do.	Beggar				1				
	Kilienoroe	Michl:Hon: Corker Do.	Smith		2		2				
		Thos.Rosalind Grine Do.	Labourer		4		2				
		Den: Neal widr. Do.	Do.		2						1
		Thos.Bridgt. Cretane Do.	Turner		2		1				
		Phelim Mary Mahar Do.	Labourer		2						
		Jon.Cath.Mahar Do.	Do.		5						
		Bry.Margt. Cox Do	Weaver		2						
		Martin Cox Batchr.Do	Labourer								
		Hugh Mary Felan Do.	Do.				1				
		Mich.Cath. Neal Do.	Do.		1						
		Thady Ellen Cox Do.	Do.		2		2				
	Corroghroe	Jon. Ellen Kelly Do	Cottier		4		2				
		Bryan Cath. Kelly Do	Pedlar		1						1
		Den. Cath. Ganan Do.	Cottier		2		2				
		Pat. Bridgt. Haly Do	Servants		2						
		Penelope Conry Wid: Do.	Beggar		1						
		Jn. Mary Grogan Do	Weaver		2		1		2		
		Redmd Margt. Dillon Do.			1		2				
		Jn. Mary Conry Do.	Cottier		2						
		Thos. Mary Geoghagan Do.	Labourer		2						
		Luc.Winnif. Neal Do.	Do.		2						1
		Pat. Mary Graly Do.	Weaver		2						
		Pat Joan Fannin Do.	Labourer		2						
		Mich. Margt. Cunningham Do	Do.								
		Dorothy Hanly Widw. Do.	Beggar								
Tot.	Papists	74			69		23		2		7
[f.67] Lissonuffy	Dillonsgehane	Wm Honr.Hanly Do.	Farmer		4		2				1
		Danl. Mary Moran Do.	Cotter		4		1				1
		Bry. Margt. Grine Do.	Cowherd				3				
		Jas Cath. Maguane Do.	Labourer		2						
	Dillonstrily	Hugh Dorothy Noon Pap.	Carman[6]				1				
		Roger Alice Magrine Do.	Cowherd				4				
		Edmd Jean Cretane Do.	Cottr.		3		2				
		Wm. Winif. Magrine Do.	Do.		1						
		Pat. Winif.Horoghoe Do.	Do.		2						
		Hugh Cat.Feeny.					3				

Com~Ros common Parish of	Place of Abode	Names and Religion	Proffession	Children under 14		Children above 14		Men Servts		Women Servts	
				Prot.	Paps.	Prot.	Paps.	Prot.	Paps.	Prot.	Paps.
		Corm. Martha Malony Do.	Beggar		2						
		Hugh Bridgt Noon Do.	Carman				4				
		Pat. Cath. Noon Do.	Do.				3				
		Darby Sarah Murray Do.	Do.				6				
		Pet.Sarah Green Do.	Labourer		3						
		Thos. Cat. Shanane Do.	Carman		1		3				
		Owen Mary Shanane Do.	Labourer		2						
		Laugh.Cath. Graly Do.	Do.				1				
		Bry. Anne Horoghoe Do.	Do.		2						
		Bridgt Grene Wid.Do.	Beggar		2						
		Jn.Winif. Shanane Do.	Carman		1						
		Darby Sarah Feeny Do.	Cottier		2		1				
		Pet.Winif. Murray Do.	Labourer		3						
		Rob Quin Widr. Do.	Beggar				1				
	Martins Trily	Den. Murry widr. Do.	Cottier				2				
		Luc. Cath. Murry Do.	Do.		2						
		Pat.Bridgt. Larany Do.	Broguemaker		1				1		
		Bry.Mary O Neal Do.	Cottier		3		1				
		Jon.Bridgt Feeny Do.	Beggars								
		Mary Nobbakin wid Do.	Cottier				3				
		Bry.Margt Flemming Do.	Broguemaker		1						
	Mt. Dillon	Jon.Teresa Dillon Do.	Gent.		1		1		3		3
		Chas.Eliza. Murry Do.	Cottier		1						
		Pat.Alice Green Do	Do.		2		2				
		Pat.Bridgt. Haly Do.	Do.		2						
	Drynogh	Wm.Cath Lynogh Do	Do.		1		2				
		Jn.Ann Kenny Do.	Do.		3						
		Laugh Mary Igoe Do.	Do.		1		2				
		Cath. Kenny widow	Beggar		2						
		Jas. Mary Duffy Do.	Cottier		1						
	Tot. Papists	75			55		48		4		5
[f.68] Lissonuffy	Mt. Dillon	Margery Igoe widow	Beggar				1				
		Jas.Mary Igoe Do.	Cowherd				1				
		Luc.Dorothy Maguane Do.	Broguemaker		3		1				
		Jas.Giles Hanly	Shepherd				1				
	KilmcNanay[7]	Nic.Anne Nerhenny Do.	Freeholder		2						
		Bry. Jane Murry Do.	Wheelright		2						1
		Pat.Mary Reynolds Do,	Tenant		2						1
		Thos.Hon. Reynolds Do.	Do.		1						
		Cath. Carly widow Do.	Do.				4				
		Jas.Anne Teig Do.	Do.		2						
		Mich.Anne Hogg Do.	Do.		3				1		
		Edw.Brigt. Smyth Do.	Do.		2		1				
		Laur:Alice Noon Do.	Do.				3				
		Morgan Bridgt. Noon Do.	Do.								
		Thos.Winif Scally Do.	Butcher				2				
		Mich.Cath. Murry Do.	Taylor		1						
		Roger Ellen Holmes Do.	Smyth				1				
	Granaghan Martin	Pat.Martha Dooly Do.	Tenant		2		3		1		1
		Gilb.Mary Grine Do.	Carman				3				
		Hugh Sarah Grine Do.	Do.		1						

Com~Ros common Parish of	Place of Abode	Names and Religion	Proffession	Children under 14 Prot.	Paps.	Children above 14 Prot.	Paps.	Men Servts Prot.	Paps.	Women Servts Prot.	Paps.
		Hugh Anne Cretane Do.	Tenant		2						
		Edmd.Bridgt. Nangle Do.	Carman				2				
		Hen.Mary Nangle Do.	Do.		2						
		Ter.Mary Fallon Do.	Labourer		2		1				
		Jon. Fallon Widr. Do.	Do.				1				
		Pat.Cath. Kensey Do.	Do.		2						
		Bridgt. Murry Widw. Do.	Cottier				3				
		Hugh Mary Murry Do.	Wheelright		3		3				
		Jon Anne Murry Do.	Do		3		2				
		Luc.Elen Murry Do.	Do		2						
		Jas.Cath. Killeen Do.	Tenant				3				
		Dom. Margt Teig Do.	Beggar				1				
		Pet.Hellen Murry Do.	Wheelright								
		Cath. Murry. widw. Do.	Beggar								
		Hon. Fallon widw. Do.	Cotter				1				
	Bunyerda	Jon.Winif. Nerhenny Do.	Tenant		3						
		Mich.Hon. McDermot Do.	Do				4				
		Wm. Sarah Kelly Do.	Frizemongr.		1		3				1
		Cath. McAndrew widw.Do.	Cotter				3				
		Thos.Hon. Feeny Do.	Do		2						
	Tot. Pap.	73			43		48		2		4
[f.69]	Bunyerda	Mich.Mary McAndrew Papist	Cotter		2						
		Bry.Margt Monaghan Do.	Do		3		1				
		Hugh Hon. Boyle Do.			3						
		Pat.Bridgt Geraghty Do.	Do		2		2				
		Jas. Rosal.Neal Do.	Carman		2						
	Aghamore[8]	Elen. Branan Wid: Do.	Gent.		2		3				
		Edmd. Mary Walsh Do.	Cotter		1						
		And. Eliz.Duffy Do.	Do.		1						
	Cordrohit	Hugh Winif. Kelly Do.	Tenant		1		2				
		Gerrad Mary Lyons Do.	Do.		2						
		Laugh.Eliz. Kerran Do.	Do.		3						
		Bry. Winif. Geraghty Do.	Do.		2						
		Laugh. Giles Farrel Do.	Do.				2				
		Bart.Hanna Harroghton Do.	Do.		1						
		Darby Giles Kimblohan Do.	Do.				2				
		Mary Hanly widw. Do	Do.		3						
		Jon.Mary Betty Do	Do.		1						
		Dom. Hon. Kelly Do	Do.		2						
	Doonicorneen	Susanna Cooper Protestt.	Farmer			2			1		1
		Edwd. Eliz.Cooper Do.	Do.	1							
		Hanna Cretane Widw.Papst.	Cotter		1		2				
		Ann Kimblohan Widw. Do	Do		1		3				
	Cregane	Owen Mary Dempry Do.	Do						1		
		Owen Ellen Quin Do.	Do.		2						
	Tureen	Pat Mary Southwell Do.	Tenant		1						1
		Hon. Moraghan Wid:Do.	Beggar				1				
	Ballyhobert	Darb.Hon. Campbelly Do.	Cotter		2						
		Mary McNeal Widw.Do.	Beggar		1						
		Mich. Bridgt.Hanly Do.	Cotter		1						
		Connor Mary Branan Do.	Do.		2						
		Jas. Ellen Branan Do.	Constable		1						

Com~Ros common Parish of	Place of Abode	Names and Religion	Proffession	Children under 14		Children above 14		Men Servts		Women Servts	
				Prot.	Paps.	Prot.	Paps.	Prot.	Paps.	Prot.	Paps.
		Hugh Joan Magneal Do.	Tenant		2						
		Jas.Margt.Magneal Do.	Do.		2						
		Charl.Cath. Ganane Do.	Do.		3						
		Ellen Hussy Widw, Do.	Cotter		1		2				
		Anne Heague Wid. Do.	Beggar				1				
		Bry.Sarah Quin Do.	Sievemaker		1						
		Bry.Bridgt.Branan Do.	Friezemonger		1						
		Den: Clary Do.	Labourer								
	Tot. Protestants	3		1	53		21	2			2
	Tot. Papists	65									
[f.70] Lissanuffy	Ballyhobert	Eliz. Beirne Widw. Papist	Beggar		2						
		Geo.Bridgt. Buchanan Protest.	Cotter	4							
		Nick.Bridgt. Hussy Do	Do.		1						
		Hon. Nanany Widw. Do	Do.		1		2				
		Hugh Winif. Geraghty Do	Do.				2				
		Bry.Bridgt. Nanany Do.	Do.		1						
		Margt. Clabby Widw. Do.	Do.				2				
		Jas.Eliz. Hussy Do.	Do.		2						
		Margt. McNeal Widw. Do.	Beggar		1						
		Thos.Margt. Emnogh Do.	Smyth		1						
	Lissafobble	Mich. Alice Maguire Do.	Cotter		1						
		Elen: Branan Do	Beggar								
		Edwd. Rebec: Gaynard Prot	Weaver	3							
		Thos.Ann O Hara Pap:	Taylor		1						
		Pat.Sarah Gilooly Do.	Labr.		4						
		Mart. Elen.Walsh Do.	Do		2						
		Hugh Judith Hanly Do.	Yarnbuyer		3						
		Mich.Joan Connel Do.	Cowherd				1		1		
		Roger Mary Owens Do.	Yarnbyer						1		1
		Lu.Cath. Duffy Do.	Cotter		1						
		Margt. Feely Widw. Do.	Do.		1		1				
	Lismehie	Jas Mary Duffy Do.	Do.		3						1
		Pat. Duffy[9] Do.	Priest-Clonf						1		1
		Den: Margt Duffy Do.	Mercht.		3						1
		Roger Mary Owens Do.	Cowherd		2						1
		Ann Barlow Wid: Do.	Beggar		1		1				
	Clooncarran	Thos.Sarah Duane Do.	Cowherd		2				1		
		Char. Mary Carlick Do.	Do.		2						
	Lissonuffy	Pet. Mary Donnellon Do.	Carman		1						1
		Fran. Bridg.Donellon Do.	Labourer								
		Edw. Bridgt.Turnan Do.	Yarnbuyer		3				1		
		Thad. Sarah Owens Do.	Carman				3				
		Jas.Mary Owens Do.	Do.		2						
		Const.Margt. Owens Do.	Do.		1						
		Mary Magneal Wid. Do.	Cotter		2		1				
	Caraward	Thos Cath.Daly Do.	Herd		1				1		
		Cath. McDonogh Widw. Do.	Beggar			2					
	Ballyduffy	Ter. Giles Dowel Do.	Tenant		1		1	1			
		Char. Anne Dowel Do.	Tenant		1			2			1
	Tot. Protestants	4		7	46		16	9			8
	Tot. Papists	67									

Com~Ros common Parish of	Place of Abode	Names and Religion	Proffession	Children under 14		Children above 14		Men Servts		Women Servts	
				Prot.	Paps.	Prot.	Paps.	Prot.	Paps.	Prot.	Paps.
[f.71] Lissonuffy	Ballyduffy	Morgan Cath. Webb Pap:	Tinker		3						
		Rich. Mary Burke Do.	Labourer		2						
		Edwd Penel.Teig Do.	Smyth		3						
		Elen. Maguire Wid: Do.	Beggar		1						
		Edmd Hon.Grissane Do.	Labourer		1						
		Danl.Bridgt. Brooder Do.	Do.		2						
		Edwd Mary Campbell Do.	Do.		2						
		Mat.Mary Carly Do.	Carman		2		1				
		Owen Rose Sweeny Do.	Labourer		1						
		Thos. Sarah Ganan Do.	Do.		2						
		Carbry Winif.Egan Do.	Do.		2		2				
		Austin Mary Dowel Do	Do.		1						
		Edwd Sweeny widr. Do.	Do.		2						
		Pat. Cath. Sweeny Do.	Do.		2						
		Miles. Winif. Sweeny Do	Do.		2		2				
		Bridgt.Bushel wid Do.	Chorewoman		3						
		Edw. Mary Egan Do	Taylor		2						
		Jas.Winif. Sweeny Do.	Labourer		3						
	Errew	Jas. Mary Moran Do.	Do.						1		1
		Morgan Hon. Casey Do	Do.		3						1
		Teig Mary Cox Do.	Do.		2				1		
		Cormick Hon: Grady Do.	Weaver		1						
		Pat. Hon. Casy Do	Labr.		4						
		Sarah Casy Widw. Do.	Do.		2		1				
		Pat. Margt. Murry Do.	Beggar								
		Bry. Mary Casy Do.	Labr.		2						
		Mich. Graly Wid: Do.	Do				1				
		Pet. Mary Graly Do.	Labr.		1						
		Bry: Cath: Murry Do.	Broguemaker								
		Jas. Casy Widr. Do.	Labr.		2						
		Teig. Cath.McKeegry Do.	Beggar								
	Derryhanilly	Char. Casy Widr. Do.	Do.								
		Owen Mary Farrel Do.	Tenant			4		1			1
		Bridgt.Maludy Wid: Do.	Beggar								
		Thos. Mary Casy Do.	Labr .		2						
		Fran. Mary Diffily Do.	Fisherman		2				1		2
		Jas. Hon. Millin Do.	Carpenter		5		2 .				
	Derryhubbert	Pat. Cath. Maguire Do.	Tenant		1		2		1		
	Cloonoe	Mich. Elen. Burke Do.	Cowherd		3						
		Mich. Bridget Murtogh	Cotter		1						1
	Tot. Papists.	72			71		12		4		6
[f.72] Lissonuffy	Cloonoe	Mich. Bridgt. Murtogh Do.	Cotter		1						
	Cogglekeeny	Jas. Mary McNamara Do	Do.		1						
		Thad. Giles Kinreen Do.	Do.		2						
		Thos Rider Widr. Do.	Do.		2		1				
		Pat. Eliz. Connel Do.	Do.		2						
		Pat. Bridgt. McNamara Do.	Do.		1						
		Jon. Bridgt. Boghlan Do.	Do.		2						
		Hugh Eliz. Carly Do.	Do.		2						
	Cogglemore	Dorothy Gill Widw. Do	Do.				2				

Com~Ros common Parish of	Place of Abode	Names and Religion	Proffession	Children under 14		Children above 14		Men Servts		Women Servts	
				Prot.	Paps.	Prot.	Paps.	Prot.	Paps.	Prot.	Paps.
		Wm. Sarah Gilooly Do.	Do.		2				1		
		Pat.Sarah Owens Do.	Do.		1						
		Const. Mary Owens Do.	Carman						1		
		Redmd. Ann Owens Do.	Do.		1						
		Hugh Winif.Kenny Do.	Labourer		2		4				
		Pat. Cath.Kenny Do.	Do.								
		Den. Sarah Moor Do.	Do.		2				1		
		Mat. Jane Kane Do.	Do.		1						
		Edmd. Alice. Kilmartin Do.	Do.		2		3				
		Joanna Smyth Widw. Do.	Do.				1				
		Ter.Jane Connor Do.	Do.		3						
		Mich. Mary Gillooly Do.	Do.		1		1				
		Jn. Bridgt. Duffy Do.	Do.								
		Roger Mary Hanly Do.	Do.		1		2				
		Lu. Anne Mullen Do.	Do.		1						
		Mary Roark Widw. Do.	Do.				1				
		Pet. Margt Cavecher Do.	Do.		2						
		Jas. Bridgt. Dinnegan Do.	Do.		1		1				
	Cogglestack	Mich. Cath. Toanry Do.	Do.		2						
		Pat.Mable Toanry Do.	Do.		3						
		Edw. Mary Lochan Do.	Matmaker		1						
		Connor Mary Lochan Do.	Do.								
		Jas. Sarah Fallon Do.	Broguemaker								
		Thady Cath. Flannegan Do.	Mower		4		1				
		Edw. Sarah Muloy Do.	Labr.		2						
		Edw. Mary Shaghnesy Do.	Mower		3						
		Char.Mary McLaughlan Do.	Labourer		3						
		Pat. Mary Lally Do.	Do.		2						
		Cath. Kelly Widw. Do.	Beggar								
		Mich. Bridgt. Lochan Do.	Matmaker		3						
		Luc. Bridgt Donnellan Do.	Labourer		2						
	Tot. Papists.	75			58		17		3		2
[f.73] Lissonuffy	Cogglestack	Jon.Anne Luane Papist	Labourer		1						
		Pat.Cath McManus Do	Do.								
		Mary Hanly widw. Do	Beggar		2						
	Tunereeva-comen New	Dudley Elen Mulroony Do	Tenant				1		1		1
		Widow Duffy Do	Do.		1						
		Pat. Mary Rush Do	Broguemaker		3						2
		Pet. Mary Lennon Do.	Tenant		4						
		Widow Maxwell Do.	Do.				3				
		Mich. Duffy Widw. Do.	Do.				3				
		Widow Lennon Do.	Do.				1				
		Darby Ellen Conry Do.	Do.		1						
		Widow Lennon Do.	Do.				3				
		Pat.Giles Barret Do.	Do.				1				
		Art.Eliz. Ford Do.	Do.				1				
		Jas Anne Rush Do.	Cotter		1		1				
	Aghadangen	Roger Anne Kaneen Do.	Herd		2		2		1		1
		Den. Cat. Shiell Do.	Cotter		2				1		1
		Thad. Mary Glinn Do.	Do.		3						

Com~Ros common Parish of	Place of Abode	Names and Religion	Proffession	Children under 14		Children above 14		Men Servts		Women Servts	
				Prot.	Paps.	Prot.	Paps.	Prot.	Paps.	Prot.	Paps.
		Jon. Elen. Connor Do.	Do.				3				
		Owen Anne Shiell Do.	Do.		2						
	Trineeseva-Lynch										
		Alex. Leyns Prot	Gent								
		Miss Margt. Lynch Pap									
		Miss Anne Lynch Do									
		Mr Pat. Lynch	Malster						1		1
		Patt Alice Scally Do.	Cotter		1				1		
		Widow Scally Do.	Beggar								
		Jon. Giles Lennon Do.	Cotter		4						
		Pat. Anne Mulroony Do.	Do.				2				
		Hugh Mary Kelly Do.	Do.		2						
		Edwd Cath. Bolan Do.	Do.				1				
		Darby Bridgt Bolan Do.	Do.		3						
		Walt. Elen. Walsh Do.	Fowler		2				1		
		Pat. Elen.Murphy Do.	Cotter		2						
	Cluggernah	Jon. Anne Neal Do.	Freeholder						1		3
		Bry. Anne Berne Do.	Cotter		3						
		Con.Mary Carly Do.	Do.								
	Tot. Protestants	1			39		22		7		9
	Tot Pap.	61									
	Tot Prot in Lissonuffy			8							
	Tot Pap.	562			454		205		33		41

[verso f.73]

Parish of Lissonuffy

Housekeepers	Children under 14	Children above 14	Men servants	Women servants
Tot. Prot - 8	8	–	–	
Tot Pap. 562	454	207	33	41

NOTES

1. Less 159 acres of the river Shannon and Loughanlea (*General Alphabetical Index*).

2. Lewis, 'Lissonuffy'.

3. Clooncarran - Con mcfferd mcBranan; Drynogh - Edmond mcLaughlin mcBranan; Lissafobble - Hugh mcConnor Boy mcBrenan (*Books of Survey and Distribution* Roscommon).

4. Census, ff. 69, 70.

5. Richard Garrett (d.1769) was admitted to TCD in 1727 and took BA in 1731. He was possibly the Richard Garrett who witnessed Archbishop Synge's will in 1740 (*Alumni Dubliniensis*; Leslie, 'Elphin', pp.111-12; Welply, Irish Wills, 12, p.6 (typescript in Society of Genealogists, London)).

6. Hugh Noon was employed by Bishop Edward Synge to take an unsatisfactory soup dish to Dublin. He returned with corks and 3 stone of glue (*Synge Letters*, p.25).

7. Owned by the Mahon family (N.L.I., Pakenham Mahon estate maps 1745-1837, MS 16 M 1).

8. Arable and pasture land (N.L.I., Pakenham Mahon estate maps 1745-1837, MS 16 M 15/8).

9. Patrick Duffy died in 1763. He held the parish of Lissonuffy with Clonfinlogh (Beirne, (ed.) *Diocese of Elphin*, p.120).

KILTRUSTAN, COUNTY ROSCOMMON

INTRODUCTION: *The parish was in the barony of Roscommon. It covers 6,339 statute acres. The land included a large area of bog, some quarries of 'excellent' limestone and limestone gravel and marl and at Tubberpatrick some 'very fine' potters earth. There was also some lead ore, but in 1837 it was not being worked.[1] The O Connor family had land in the parish in 1641.[2] In 1749, there were six Connor households in four townlands.[3]*

The rectory formed part of the prebend of Kilgoghlin. The incumbent in 1749 was the Rev. Richard Garrett who held the parish with those of Bumlin and Lissonuffy (see Lissonuffy). The Roman Catholic priest was Carbry Berne of Kilscagh.[4]

OCCUPATIONS

Beggar	11	Gentlewoman	1	Piper	1
Bleacher	1	Glover	1	Priest	1
Broguemaker	2	Herd	8	Servants, household	87
Carpenter	2	Mason	1	Smith	2
Cleric	1	Miller	2	Spinster	1
Cottier	144	Parish Registrar	1	Weaver	5
Farmer	7	Pedlar	1	Wheelwright	2

Com~Ros common Parish of	Place of Abode	Names and Religion	Proffession	Children under 14		Children above 14		Men Servts		Women Servts	
				Prot.	Paps.	Prot.	Paps.	Prot.	Paps.	Prot.	Paps.
Kiltristan [f.74]	Kildallogue	Thady Cat. McDermot Pap.	Cotter		3				1		
		Sim. Perdieu Prot.	Beggar								
		Fran. Sweeny Pap.	Cotter		3		2				
		Bar. Dermot Do.	Do.		2						
		Hu: Ma: Beirn Do.	Brogemakr		2				1		
		Pat. Cat. Cassidy Do.	Cotter		3						
		Ter. Elen. Dockra Do.	Do.		2						1
		Robt. Rose Creagg Prot	Wheelright			1			1		
		Walt. Eliz. Creagg Do.	Do								
		Rog. Margt. Gobbin Pap.	Cotter				1				
		Miles Bridgt. Kinree Do.	Do.				2				
		Hugh Jane Mullin Do.	Do.		2						
		Miles Burke Do.	Do.				1				1
		Den. Elen. Kenny Do.	Do.		1						
		Pat. Cat. Kenny Do.	Do.		2						
		Bry. Marg. Kenny Do	Do.				3				
		Hugh Keregan Do.	Do.		1		1				1
		John Garry Do.	Do.				3				
		Simon Margt. Gara Do.	Do.								
		Robt. Eliz. Cawfield Do.	Do.		2						
		Thad. Margt Cawfield Do.	Do.								
		Pat. Alice Cuningham Do.	Do.		1						
		Giles Coleman Do	Beggar								
	Dailoon	Laur. Cath. Berne Do.	Cotter		3						
		Mich. Sa. Berne Do.	Do.		3		1				
		And. Cath. Daly Do.	Do.								
		Pat. Cath. Murphy Do.	Smith		2						
		Miles Bridgt Kelly Do.	Cotter		2						
	Corscagh	Mich. Bridgt Heden Do.	Do.			1					
		Dan. Eliz. Diffily Do.	Do.			2					
		Bry. Margt Cannane Do.	Do.			5					
	Lavally[5]	Hugh Eliz. Digan Do.	Do.								
		Pet. Ma. Conner Do.	Do.		3				1		
		Thos. White Do.	Weaver		3				3		
		Thos. Gaffney Do.	Bleacher[6]						4		
		Mary Nary Do.	Cotter		5						
	Corry	Sarah Lennon Do.	Do.		5		2				
		Pat. Ma. Owens Do.	Do.		1						
		And. Cath. Conry Do.	Do.		2						
Tot Prot Housekeepers 5		Tot. Pap. Do 62			61	1	16		11		3
[f.75] Kiltristan	Corry	Thos. Ma. Conolly Do.	Cotter		4		3				
		Wm. Margt Mannin Do.	Do.		2						
		Jas. Cath. Mannin Do.	Do.								
		Den.Hon. Mannin Do.	Do.		3						
		Thady Mart. Mannin Do.	Do.		2						
		Chas. Ma. Dowd Do.	Do.		2		3				
		Wm Kelly widr. Do.	Do.				2				
		Bart. Anne Kelly Do.	Do.								

Com~Ros common Parish of	Place of Abode	Names and Religion	Proffession	Children under 14 Prot.	Paps.	Children above 14 Prot.	Paps.	Men Servts Prot.	Paps.	Women Servts Prot.	Paps.	
		Fran. Margt. Wholan Do.	Do.		1						1	
		Bry. Cath. Mulry Do.	Do.				2					
		Laugh. Inlihane Do.	Cotter									
		Jn. Elin. Mullin Do.	Do.		4							
	Carnagullah	Allen Eliz. Dowel[7] Do.	Farmer		3				1		1	
		Edmd. Anne Kelly Do.	Cotter				2				1	
		Pat Ma. Kelly Do	Do.		2							P
		Wm. Ma. Fallon Do.	Do.		3							
		Thady: Trassy Do.	Beggar									
	Tubberpatrick	Pet.Rose Finn Do.	Cotter		2						1	P
		Thos. Mary Finn Do.	Do.		1						1	
		Ow. Eliz. Kelly Do.	Glover						1			
		Wid. Ellen Kelly Do.	Spinster		1		2					
		Rich. Bridgt Kelly Do.	Cotter		2							
		Thad. Elen. Connor Do.	Smith									
		Thady Eliz Connor Do.	Cotter									newly marrid
		Den: Nary Do.	Beggar		1							
		Bry. Winif. Giblan Do.	Cotter		1		1					
		Geo. Cath. Kelly Do.	Do.		2						2	
		Rich. Bridgt. Kelly Do.	Do.		2						1	
		Lawr. Bridgt. Nary Do.	Do.		3						1	
		Cath. Giblan Wid. Do.	Do.				3	1				
		Char. Anne Berne Do.	Pedlar		3		2	1				
		Jas. Hon. Kelly Do.	Cotter		1				2		1	
		Edw. Bridgt.Nevin Do.	Do.		3							
		Thos. Hon. Concanon Do.	Do.		4		1					
		Laugh.Brid. Mannin Do.	Do.		3							
		Jn. Mannin Do.	Beggar									
		Pat. Cat. Slow Do	Cotter		3						1	
		Thos. Bridgt. Nary Do.	Do.		2						1	
		Bar. Cath. Conner Do.	Do.		1							
		Connor Kelly wid. Do.	Beggar									
		Jn. Hon. Feeny Do.	Cotter		4		2	1				
		Own: Mable Dulkeran Do	Beggar				1					
	Tot Pap	76			63		23			7	13	
[f.76] Kiltristan	Tubberpatrick	Owen Dowd Pap.	Beggar		1							
		Pet. Downy Do.	Piper		2							
	Cloncovanagh	Rich. Sus. Keague Prot.	Weaver	5		1			1			
		Laur. Cath. Carow Pap.	Cotter		2						2	
		Tha. Anne Kelly Do.	Do.		2		1		1			
		Jas. Giles Kean Do.	Weaver		2				1			
		And. Hon. Caven Do.	Do		3				2			
		Bart.Anne ~~Trassy~~Lenaghan Do.	Cotter				2					
		Wid:Ellen Gill Prot.	Farmer			4			1		1	
		Edwd Margt.Gill Do.	Carpenter	1								
		Mrs Atkinson Do	Farmer			1						
	Grange	Eliz. Conry Pap.	Beggar			1						
		Jas.Mary Fox Do.	Miller[8]		4				2			
		Jn. Bridgt. Conry Do.	Cotter									run away

Com~Ros common Parish of	Place of Abode	Names and Religion	Proffession	Children under 14		Children above 14		Men Servts		Women Servts	
				Prot.	Paps.	Prot.	Paps.	Prot.	Paps.	Prot.	Paps.
		Conr. Cath. Conry Do.	Do.		2						
		Mat. Lynch Widr. Do.	Do.		2		2	1			
		Char. Anne Conry Do.	Do.		3						
		Ow. Rose Dowell Do.	Do.		1						2
		Jn. Winif. McDermot Do	Do.		1						
		Pat. Hon. Conry Do.	Do.		2		1				
		Pat. Hon. Mannin Do.	Do.		1						
		Thad. Elen. Dowel Do.	Do.		2						
		Bart. Giles Foley Do.	Do.		2						
		Mary Foley Do.	Beggr.		1						
		Mary Mannin Do.	Cotter		2						
		Cath. Lenon Wid. Do.	Beggar				1				
	Ballyvahan	Jas. Ma. Dillon Do.	Cotter		3						
		Fran. Anne Reynolds Do.	Do.		2		1				
		Wid. Elen. Gilleesey	Do.		3						
		Dan. Bridgt. ~~Gilleeseey~~ McDermot Do.	Do.		2				1		
	Colclogernogh Killeegan	Far: Eliz Conry Prot.	Farmer			4			1		1
		Hugh Mar. Cassidy Pap.	Cotter								
		Edmd. Hon. Duffy Do.	Do.								
		Jas. Ma. Cassidy Do.	Do.								
		Hugh Ma. Cassidy Do.	Do.								
	Lissheen	Wid: Margt Hickes Prot.	Farmer			6		2	2		4
		Wid:Ruth Hickes Do.				2					
		Bry. Cath Somerville Pap.	Herd		3		1				
	LismcEgan	Darby Mary Connor Do.	Mason		1				1		
		Bry. Doroth: Dolan Do.	Cotter		2						
Tot Prot Housekeepers 11 Tot Pap Do 58				6	51	19	9	2	14		10
[f.77] Kiltristan	LismcEgan	Thos. Mable Maguire Do.	Cotter		2						
		Ter. Bridgt. Conry Do.	Do.		1						
		Pat. Cat. Conry Do.	Herd		3		2				
		Mich. Anne Ward Do.	Cotter		4		3				
	Killucloghane	Corm Ma. Davane Do.	Herd		1		3				
	Cordromin	Pat. Hon. Maguire Do.	Do.		1						
		Thos. Quinn Widr. Do.	Cotter		1						
	Kiltristan	Pat. Winif. Berne Do.	Do.		1		1				
		Jn. Conry & Wife Do.	Do.						1		1
		Carb. Elen Berne Do.	Do.				2				
		Michl. McDonagh Do.	Do.		2		1				
		Den.Ma. Crosbie Do.	Do.		3		1				1
		Laur. Dowell Do.	Do.		2						
	Doonardbeg	Char. Margt Magan Do.	Do.		1						
		Jn. Elen Appleby Prot	Carpenter			1					
		Bry. Anne Kelly Pap.	Cotter		1						
		Jn. Eliz. Dowd Do.	Do.		2						
		Mary Nerhenny Do.	Do.				1				
		Pat. Sar Conry Do.	Do.		2						
		Mich. Margt. Conry Do.	Do.		1		2				

Com~Ros common Parish of	Place of Abode	Names and Religion	Proffession	Children under 14		Children above 14		Men Servts		Women Servts	
				Prot.	Paps.	Prot.	Paps.	Prot.	Paps.	Prot.	Paps.
	Tullin	Mich. Bridgt. Whologhan Do.	Do.		2		1		1		1
		Jn. Cath. Berne Do.	Do.		1						
		Ant. Cath. Caroll Do.	Do.		1						1
	Letreen	Phil. Ma. Hanly Prot.	Farmer	2		4			1		
	Doonerdmore	Ow. Eliz. Kelly Do.	Herd		2		1				
		Darb. Jane Hay Do.	Do.						1		1
		Thos. Winif. Feeny Do.	Cotter				1				
	Caldragh	Pet. Naghlen Do	Do.				1				
		Den. Winif. Dowell Do.	Do.		1		3				
		Jn. Cath. Hill Do.	Do.				1		1		1
		Mick. Mable Kelly Do.	Do.		2						
	Cregagh	Jn. Anne Turner Prot.	Weaver	2							
		Pat. Eliz. Hanly Pap.	Cotter					1		1	
		Rogr Margt Connor Do.	Do.		0		2				
		John Mary Dalton Do.	Do.		1		2				
		Edw: Dalton Do.	Do.								
		Darby Branon Do.	Do.				1				
		Miles Hon. Berne Do.	Do.		1		1				
		Thos. Hon. Henry Do.	Do.				1				
		Geo. Berne Wid Do.	Do.				2				
		Tot Prot. 6 Tot. Pap 66		4	39	5	33	1	5	1	6
[f.78] Kiltristan	Cregah	Pat. Cat. Dowel Do.	Cotter		1						
		Pet. Dor. Conry Do.	Do.		1						
		Pet. Hon. Cassidy Do.	Do.		1		1				
		Pet. Ma. Haly Do.	Do.		2						
		Giles Berne Do.	Do.		3		2				
		Rick. Ma. Caten Do.	Do.		4						
		Jas. Giles Kenny Do.	Do.		1						
		Ma. Kennedy Do.	Do.				1				
	Kilscagh	Hen. Ma. Berne Do.	Farmer		2				2		2
		Carby Berne[9] Do.	Priest								
		Jn. Cat. Berne Do.	Cotter		2						
		Pat. Hon. Wuolohan Do.	Herd		3				1		1
		Jn. Margt. Feeny Do.	Cotter				1				
		Jas. Cath. Feeny Do.	Do.		2						
	Killegan	Hu. Ma. Cassidy Do.	Do.				1				
		Edm. Hon. Duffy Do.	Do.								
		Jas. Ma: Cassidy Do									
		Hu Mary Cassidy Do.	Do.								
	Creaghtae	Rich. Cath. Hickes Prot.	P:regis[10].			7		1	3	1	2
		Pat. Hon. Lanon Pap	Herd				1		1		
		Tho. Joan Murphy Do.	Brogemaker		2		1				
		Lau. Ma. Hickes Do.	Miller		2				2		3
	Largonroe	Jn. Winif. Toolon Do	Cotter		2		2				
		Corm. Hon. Lanon Do.	Do.		2		1				
		Miles Eliz. Ternan Do.	Do.				5				
		Thad. Cat. Gavin Do.	Do.		2				1		1
		Pat. Clare Kelly Do.	Do.		1						

Com~Ros common Parish of	Place of Abode	Names and Religion	Proffession	Children under 14 Prot.	Children under 14 Paps.	Children above 14 Prot.	Children above 14 Paps.	Men Servts Prot.	Men Servts Paps.	Women Servts Prot.	Women Servts Paps.
		Laur. Ellen. Kelly Do.	Do.	1							
		Mart. Brid. Stafford Do.	Do.	1							
		Pat. Ma. McCown Do.	Do.								
		Bry. Ma. McCormic Do.	Do.				2				
		Ow. Ellen McHugh Do.	Weaver	1			0				
		Miles Margt. Egan Do.	Cotter	0			3				
		Bry. Bridgt. Mcah Do.	Do.	2			2				
		Bry. Alice Toolon Do.	Do.	2			2				
		~~Tot. Prot~~ Miss Burk Prot.	Gent:								
		Tot. Prot Housekeepers 3		36	7	29		1	10	1	9
		Tot. Pap Do. 65									

[1 blank page. On verso]

Parish of Kiltristan

	Housekeepers	under 14	above 14	Men Servants	Women Servants
Prot	25	10	32	4	2
Tot Pap.	327	250	110	47	41

NOTES

1. Lewis, 'Kiltrustan'.

2. In Caldragh, Cregagh, and Donard (*Books of Survey and Distribution* Roscommon).

3. Census, ff. 74, 75, 77.

4. Census, f. 78.

5. Lavallamore and Lavallabeg were arable and pasture land (N.L.I., Pakenham Mahon estate maps, MS 16 M 15/5).

6. There was a bleachgreen on this townland (N.L.I., MS 16 M 15/5).

7. A James Dowell, gentleman, was living at Cnowingallagh in the mid-seventeenth-century (*Census of Ireland*).

8. In 1838 there was a corn mill and a tuck mill at Grange (Ordnance Survey 6":1 mile map County Roscommon 1838 Sheet 23).

9. Carbry O'Beirne was listed in 1748 as priest of Kiltristan and Bumlin. He supported the Rev. William (alias Augustine) O'Kelly, prior of St. Mary's Roscommon as bishop of Elphin (Beirne, (ed.) *Diocese of Elphin*, p.124; Fenning 'Diocese of Elphin' (1994-5), p.165).

10. Richard Hickes entered TCD in 1739/40. He does not appear to have taken BA. The parish registrar was responsible for all diocesan documents and accounts. In May 1747 Synge believed him to be a 'great R[ogue] ' and intended to proceed against him in the diocesan court. Hickes seems to have survived (*Synge Letters* p.31).

BUMLIN, COUNTY ROSCOMMON

INTRODUCTION: *Bumlin parish is in the barony of Roscommon. It lies south-east of Elphin and west of the Shannon. It is bounded on the north by the parishes of Kiltrustan and Kilglass, on the east by Termonbarry, on the south by Lissonuffy, and on the west by Cloonfinlough. The size of the parish was 6,582 statute acres.[1] The whole of the parish was in the ownership of the Mahon family, who built the house and town of Strokestown in the early eighteenth-century.*

Strokestown was both a market and post town on the road from Dublin to Ballina, 12 miles west of Longford. It held a fair every Friday.[2] The town is centred on Church Street, Bawn Street and Bridge Street, wide streets which cross each other, and the gates of Strokestown House (formerly Bawn House) form the end of Bawn Street at the east. The exceptionally wide street which runs through the town from east to west was the site of the market. Unusually, some of the streets are named. As a market town, Strokestown had the network of trades needed to support commercial activities. The carpenters, masons, plasterers, sawyer and builder were probably employed on the estate. This was a prosperous town in a prosperous parish.

The incumbent was the Rev. Richard Garrett (d.1769), who held the parish with those of Kiltrustan and Lissonuffy (see Lissonuffy). He did not live in the parish. The patron was the bishop.

OCCUPATIONS

Apothecary	1	Friezemonger	1	Sawyer	2
Barber	3	Gardener	2	Schoolmaster	1
Beggar	21	Gentlewoman	1	Servant	6
Breechesmaker	1	Hackler	1	Servants, household	179
Brewer	1	Herd	3	Shoemaker	3
Brickburner	2	Horseman	1	Skinner	3
Broguemaker	10	Horserider	1	Smith	4
Builder	1	Huckster	4	Snuffmaker	1
Butcher	5	Innkeeper	1	Spinster	4
Carman	13	Labourer	100	Stonecutter	1
Carpenter	7	Maltster	3	Tailor	6
Chorewoman	1	Mantua maker	2	Tanner	4
Clothier	1	Mason	8	Tenant	6
Constable	2	Merchant	6	Tobacco spinner	6
Cooper	5	Mower	1	Turner	2
Cottier	47	Plasterer	2	Weaver	16
Cottoner	1	Ploughman	1	Wheelwright	1
Currier	1	Rabbit catcher	2	Woodkeeper	1
Esquire	3	Saltmonger	1	Woodman	1
Farmer	4			Yarnbuyer	11

Com~Ros common Parish of	Place of Abode	Names and Religion	Proffession	Children under 14		Children above 14		Men Servts		Women Servts	
				Prot.	Paps.	Prot.	Paps.	Prot.	Paps.	Prot.	Paps.
Bumblin [f.79]	Newtown	Geo: Margt. Taylor Prot	Weaver	3	2				1		
		Jn. Margt. Higgins Pap.	Labourer								
		Widow Bridgt. Callaghan Do.	Do.				1				
		Sarah Tirrian Widw. Do.	Spinster				2				
		Jas. Bridgt Bruin Do.	Beggars		1						
		Bryan Mary Cretane Do.	Weaver		1		2				
		Mr Will. Wemys Prot:									
		Pat. Ellen Casy Pap.	Taylor		2						
		Susan Williams Widw. Do.	Beggar								
		Mich. Mary O Hara Do.	Weaver		2		2				
		Edwd Mary Donnellon Prot.	Plowman	1				1			1
		Jn. Celia Sharcot Pap.	Stonecutter		2						1
	Garuagh	Wm. Moraghan Widr Do.	Labourer				4				
		Bridgt Bolan Widw. Do	Do.		1						
		Denis Carrol Do.	Brewer								
		Ant. Cavecher Do.	Labourer								
	Glebe	Laur. Duffy Prot & Wife Pap.	Taylor				1				
		Bry. Bridgt. Carly Do.	Cotter		1		3				
		Pat. Eliz. Berreen Do.	Weaver		2						
		Bridgt. Connor Widw. Do.	Spinster	1		2					
	Farnbeg	Jn. Mary Holding Prot.	Farmer			2				1	
		And. Cat. Gilleesy Do.	Shoemaker	3		1					
		Alex. Margt. McDonnel Do	Plaisterer	3		1					
		Jn. Mary Holding Prot.	Yarnbyer	3		2					1
		Wm. Eliz. Lucy Do.	Cotter	1		1					1
		Bry. McDermot Prot & Wife Pap.	Do.		1		3				
		Bry. Mary Cunningham Pap.	Do.		2						
		Wm. Mary Coleman Prot.	Brickburner	2							
		Wm. Cath.Smyth Do.	Do.	1		1					
		Widow Jagoe Do.	Spinster	1		1					
		Rob. Mary Cackeside Do.	Carpenter								
		Wid: Robinson Do.				4	1	1			
		Danl. Elen. Donelly Pap.	Presser		3						1
		Mary Mahon wid Prot.	Tenant	3						1	
		Dan Brigt. Maluanaghly Pap.	Weaver		2		3				
		Peter Duffy Widr. Pap.	Proctor		1		2				
	Caslinode	Mr. Henry Cooper Widr. Prot	Farmer			2			2		2
		Dom. Bridgt. Connor Pap.	Carman		4		4		1		
		Darby Joan Lyons Do.	Do.		4				1		
	Tot Protestants Tot Papists	26 37		21	30	17	29	2	6	2	7
[f.80]	Caslinode	Dom. Winif. Finn Papists	Cotter								
		Thos. Rebec. Moffit Prot.	Weaver			1			1		
		Jn. Cath. Berne Pap	Carman		3						
		Wm. Rose Finn Pap.	Cotter		2		1				
		Ter. Mary Connor Do.	Do.				5				
		Jas. Joan Branan Do.	Do.				3				
		Margt Sarah Kennedy Do.	Do.		1						
		Dor. Kennedy Widr. Do.	Do.				1				

Com~Ros common Parish of	Place of Abode	Names and Religion	Proffession	Children under 14		Children above 14		Men Servts		Women Servts	
				Prot.	Paps.	Prot.	Paps.	Prot.	Paps.	Prot.	Paps.
	Cloonredoon	Lu. Mary Heverin Do.	Mason		2						
		Ter. Mary Brackan Do.	Carman		3				2		
		Jn. Hon. Carly Do.	Yarnbyer		1						
	Cloonrebracken	Jas. Mary Berne Do.	Herd						1		1
		Feeny Mary Carty Do.	Labourer		2						
		Phil. Margt. Connor Do.	Do.		1						
		Danl. Mary Keeregan Do.	Do.		2		2				
		Darb Mary Carly Do.	Do.		2		2				
	Scrimoge	Hugh Ellen Lanon Do.	Farmer						1		1
		Hugh Mary Ganly Do.	Cotter		3						
		Hugh Hon. Dolan Do.	Mason								
		Mary Flannigan Do.	Beggar								
		Jas. Hon. Farrel Do.	Mason		2				2		1
		Ow. Rose McDermot Do.	Cotter		2						
		Pat. Winif. Hanly[3] Do.	Carman		1		2				1
		Corm. Margt. Connor Do.	Labourr.		1						
		And. Mary Magrieve Do.	Weaver		3						
		Gilb. Bridgt. Hanly Do.	Carman		2						
		Jas. Ellen Lanon Do.	Tenant		2				1		1
		Con. Mary Lanon Do.	Smith		2		1				
		Con. Mary Casy Do.	Tailor		1				2		
		Thos. Elen Walsh Do.	Weaver		1						
		Hen: Cooper Prot. wife Pap.	Tenant	1							1
		Jn. Mary Lanon Pap.	Labourer		3						
		Pat. Margt Teig Do.	Do.		2		1				
		Bryan Dowel Do.	Mason				1				
		Jn. Bridgt. Feeny Do.	Brogemaker		1						
	Killenorden-more	Laugh Lyons Do.	Labr.		1		1				
		Den: Hon. Feeny Do.	Do.		1						
		Rogr Margt. Feeny Do.	Do.								
		Hugh Giles Lyons Do.	Do.		2						
	Tot. Prot 3 Tot Pap. 71			1	49	1	20		10		6
[f.81]Bumblin	Scrimoge	Thad. Hon.Flannigan Pap.	Labourer								
		Pat. Reynolds Widw Do.	Do.		1						
		Roger Mable Kelly Do.	Do.		2						
		Mick. Mable Maguane Do.	Brogemaker		1		1		1		1
		Fran. Giles Maguane Do.	Labourer		2						1
		Jn. Hon. King Do.	Do.		1		1				
		Jn. Winif. Maguane Do.	Do.		1						
		Edw. Bridgt. Branan Do.	Do.		1						
		Edw Sarah Feeny Do.	Do.		1						
		Jas. Mary Feeny Do.	Do.		1						1
		Pat. Margt. Spallon Do.	Do.		1						
		Thos. Hon. Madden Do	Turner		2						
		And. Winif. Davis Prot.	Weaver								
		Jas. Cath. McDonagh Do.	Beggars								
		Darby Hon. Nioge Do.	Do.								
	Mianagh	Dan. Bridgt. Cox Do.	Herd		2		1				

Com~Ros common Parish of	Place of Abode	Names and Religion	Proffession	Children under 14		Children above 14		Men Servts		Women Servts	
				Prot.	Paps.	Prot.	Paps.	Prot.	Paps.	Prot.	Paps.
	Kilmore	Mart Cath. Grace Do.	Cotters		1						
		Mart.Mary Grace Do.	Do.		2						
		Jn. Cath. Donnellan Do.	Do.		2						
		Jn. Anne Berne Do.	Do.		2						
		Mich. Hon. Cox Do.	Do.								1
		Widow Hon. Cox Do.	Do.				2				
		Jn. Mary Charly Prot.	Sawyer			3					
		Pat Elen Murry Do.	Cotter			3					
		Rich. Susan Smyth Prot.	Do.	5							
		Thos. Mary Grace Pap.	Do.								
		Jn. Hon. Berne Do.	Do.		1						
		Mich. Hon. Cox Do.	Do.								
		Wid. Fenneran Do.	Do.				1				
		Jas. Dor. Egan Do.	Do.		2						
		Mich. Eliz. Hanly Do.	Do.								1
		Jas. Cath. Lyons Do.	Do.		1						
		Mich. Hon. Lyons Do.	Do.		1						
		Bry. Anne Sharuane Do.	Do.		4						
		Jas. Margt. Lyons Do.	Do.		2						
		Lu. Anne Feeny Do.	Do.		2		1				
		Murt. Cath. Madden Do.	Do.		2		2				
		Pat. Anne Maglin Do.	Do.		2						
		Pat. Mullegan Do.	Carman								1
	Tot. Prot 6 / Tot Pap. 68			5	40	6	9		1		5
[f.82]	Kilmore	Jon. Eliz. Mulligan Pap.	Cotter						1		
		Fran Sarah Feely Do.	Do.		2		2				
		Mich. Joan Moran Do.	Do.		3						1
		Jas. Bridgt. Sharuane Do.	Do.		3						
		Darby Winif. Sharuane Do.	Do.				2				
		Ter. Margt. Lowry Do.	Do.				2				
		And. Bridgt. Hobbakin Do.	Do.		1						
		Laugh. Margt Keegan Do.	Turner		3		1				
		Pat. Sarah Donellon Do.	Woodkeeper		4		1				
		Jn. Mary Turner Do.	Cotter								
		Jn. Sarah Glinn Do.	Carpenter		4						
		Martin Mary Branan Do.	Labr.								
		Gilb. Hon. Higgins Do.	Do.		2						
		Nic. Donnellon Do.	Do.								
		Pat Coony Widr Do	Do		1		2				
		Jn. Jane Gilmor Prot.	Do.					1			
		Wid Magenis Do. Do.				1					
		Fran Alice Coleman Pap.	Broguemaker		3						
		Ter. Cath. McDermot Do.	Labr.		2		1				
		Ter. Cath. Sharuane Do.	Constable		2						
	Gortoose[4]	And. Bridgt. Grady Do.	Labr.		1						
		Pet. Mary Egan Do.	Do.		2		2				
		Con. Bridgt. Hagan Do.	Do.		1		1				
		Jn. Mar. Rose Maglin Do.	Do.								
		Mich. Mary Conollon Do.	Do.		1						

P

Com~Ros common Parish of	Place of Abode	Names and Religion	Proffession	Children under 14		Children above 14		Men Servts		Women Servts	
				Prot.	Paps.	Prot.	Paps.	Prot.	Paps.	Prot.	Paps.
		Dun. Bridgt. Maguire Do.	Do.		2						
		Mich. Mary Keelly Do.	Do.				3		1		
		Bry. Sarah Doogan Do.	Do.		4		2				
		Mich. Mary Mullegan Do.	Do.		2						
		Laugh Eliz McOwn Do.	Combmaker		2						
		Dom Anne Kelly Do.	Do.				1				
		Thos. Mary Flanerry Do.	Labr.		2						
		Jn. Bridgt Morris Do.	Do.		3		2				
		Edw. Bridgt Holmes Do.	Do.		3						
		And. Mary Moran Do.	Do.		3						
		Corm. Cath. Moran Do.	Do.		3		2				
		Dan. Cath. Hogan Do.	Do.								
		Thos. Anne Maglin Do.	Do.		3						
		Bry. Margt. Trassy Do.	Do.		2						
	Tot Prot 3 Tot Pap. 72				64	1	24	1	1		2
[f.83]	Gortoose	Rogr. Hanna Trassy Do.	Labr.		2						
		Miles Mary Maguane Do.	Do.		3						
		Wid. Cath.McDermot Do.	Do.		1		4				
		Rog. Elen Maguire Do.	Do.		1		1		1		1
		Wid. Cath. Carenton Do.	Do.				2				
	Cullegh	Pat. Elen. Malooly Do.	Do.				4				
		Owen Cath. Scully Do.	Do.		1						
		Jn. Winif. Dowd Do.	Carman								
		Walt. Cath. Wallis Do.	Labr.		1						
		Bry. Margt. Cox Do.	Cooper		1						
		Pet. Crawly Do.	Herd								
		Pat. Winif. Maguane Do.	Labr.		2						
		Phel. Hon. Maguane Do.	Do.		1						
		Fran. Bridgt. Fox Do.	Do.		2						
		Mich. Elen Gagan Do.	Do.		3		2				
		Thos. Hon. Grevey Do.	Do.		1						
		Robt. Mary Mullen Do.	Carman		6		2				
		Ant. Marg Giblen Do.	Labr.		2		1				
		Pet. Cath. Lyons Do.	Carman		4		3				
		Thad. Mary Cox Do.	Labr.		4						
		Thos. Margt. Fox Do.	Do.		2						
		Ter. Bridgt. Lyons Do.	Do.								
		Rog. Anne McDermot Do.	Do.		1						
		Mat Cat. Carlick Do.	Do.		4						
		Bry. Christi. Magrine Do.	Do.		2						
		Mich. Mary Rathan Do.	Do.		1						
		Wid. Eliz. Tully Do.	Beggar		1						
		Wid. Mary Ganly Do.	Do.		1						
		Edw. Cath. Sharcotty Do.	Weaver		2						
		Corm. Magrine Do.	Carman		1						
	Carenlass	Gilb. Mary Sharcot Do.	Labr.		1						
		Jas. Gahenny Do.	Do.								
		Alex. Ann Dowel Do.	Do.		2						
		Fran. Bridgt. Dowel Do.	Do.		2						

Com~Ros common Parish of	Place of Abode	Names and Religion	Proffession	Children under 14		Children above 14		Men Servts		Women Servts	
				Prot.	Paps.	Prot.	Paps.	Prot.	Paps.	Prot.	Paps.
		Mart Mary Magneal Do.	Do.		2						
		Jas. Elen. Magneal Do.	Do.		2						
		Pat. Giles Magneal Do.	Do.		1						
		Wid:Hodson (100 yrs. old)	Beggar								
	Mulliveheran	Jas. Winif Cox Do.	Cooper		2		1				
	Tot. Pap. Housekeepers 73				62		22		1		1
[f.84]	Mulliveheran	Thos. Mary Haly Do.	Labr.		2						
		Jn. Cath. Feeny Do.	Do.		1						
		Edw. Mary Maguire Do.	Tanner		1						
		Bryan Feeny Do.	Labr.								
		Fran. Hon. Feeny Do.	Carman								
		Pet. Mable Lanon Do.	Beggars								
		Wid. Sar: McDermot Do.	Do.		4		1				
		Con. Elen. Egan Do.	Do.		1		1				
	Upper Ballyfeeny	Wm. Jas. Hemsworth Prot.	Farmer	4		1		2	1		3
		Edmd Sar. Maglin Pap.	Cotter	4		1					
	Cordromin	Owen Mary Loorany Do.	Carpenter		1						
		Marc. Jane Cooper Prot:	Labr.	2							
		Lu. Mary Cox Pap.	Woodman		1						
	Stroakstown	Thos. Jane Mahon[5] Prot.	Esqr.	5				6	6	4	4
		Miss Elen. Mahon[6] Do.	Gent.							1	1
		Lu. Mahon Do.	Esqr.							1	
		Geo. Bridgt Cackeside Do	Do Servts								
		Jn. Mahon Do.	Esqr.								
		Dan Mar. Martin Do.	Do. Servts.	4						1	1
		Mary Frane Pap.	Mantua-maker								1
		Wm. Bridgt Crosbie Do.	Yarnbuyer								
		Geo. Mary Taaffe[7] Do.	Merchant		7				3		2
		Wm. Bridgt. Howard Prot	Tanner	3		2					
		Rick Celia Grevery Pap.	Carpenter		4		1		1		
		Corm Mary Hanly Do.	Yarnbuyer		1						
		Hen. Lyd. Hemsworth Prot.	Tanner	2					1	2	2
		Thos. Ma. Kilroy Pap.	Rabbitcatchr								
		And. Jon. Davis Prot.	Labr.								
		Pet. Cath. Gary Pap.	Tobacco spinner								
		Jas. Hon. Kelly Do.	Yarnbuyr.		2						
		Wid: Margt. Kelly Do.	Beggar		1						
		Edw. Mar. Monaghan Do.	Labr.		1		2				
		Edw. Margt. McDermot Do.				1					1
		Jn. Flannegan Prot.	Tanner						3		
		Wid. Mar. Mahon Pap.	Mercht				3		4		
		Thos. Bridgt. Larcon Do.	Skinner		4				2		
		Rog. Mary Burke Do.	Labr.				1				
		Mich Heague Do.	Skinner						2		
		Wm. Margt. Robinson Prot.	Weaver[8]	3					2	2	
	Tot. Prot. Housekeepers 22 Tot Pap. Housekeepers 40			22	35	3	11	10	26	8	16

Com~Ros common Parish of	Place of Abode	Names and Religion	Proffession	Children under 14		Children above 14		Men Servts		Women Servts	
				Prot.	Paps.	Prot.	Paps.	Prot.	Paps.	Prot.	Paps.
[f.85] Bumblin	Stroakstown	Thady Connor Pap. wife Prot.	Labr.								
		Wid: Lavender Prot.	Do.			1					
		Celia McLaughlin Pap.	Do.	1							
		Wid. Mary Scanlan Do.	Do.		2		1				
		Pat. Jud. Farrel Do	Apothecary		4				2		2
		Char. Connor Batchr. Do.	Builder								
	Newtown	Jas. Bridgt Egerton Do.	Carpenter		3						2
		Jn. Mary Spallon Prot.	Yarnbuyer	2							1
		Rich. Reb. Heague Do.	Tenant	1		2					
		Wid: Nerhenny Pap.	Cotter		1						
		Phil. Duffy Pap. Wife Prot	Labr.		3						
		Wid. Cath: Teig Pap	Beggar								
		Eliz. Duffy Do.	Do.				1				
		Hen: Holding Prot.	Tenant						1		2
		Dan. Mary Trassy Pap.	Cotter				3				
		Jas. Mary McLaughlin Do.	Do.		2						
		Jn. Sarah Daly Do.	Weaver								
		Hen. Folliot Prot. wife Pap.	Do.	2	2						
		Ow. Mary Carly Pap	Cotter		4						
		Jn. Tanner Prot. wife Pap.	Do.	2	1						
		Pat. Mary Mahon[9] Pap	Weaver		1				3		1
		Thos. Margt Mahon Do.	Labr.		2						1
		Ow. Elen. McDermot Do.	Do.		2						
		Mich.Eliz. Doosey Do.	Do.		2						
		Wid. Ma. Nary Do.	Do.		2		2				
		Jn. Hanna Branan	Do. Do.								
		Wid. Cat: Pritchard	Prot. Do.	1		1					
		Wid. Conry Pap.	Beggar				1				
		Hugh Anne Caveher Do.	Labr.				2				
		Thad. Bridgt. Caheny Do.	Do.		2						
	Bridge Street	Wid: White Prot.	Do.			1					
		Jn. Eliz. Whelan Do.	Horserider [?]	2							
		Jn. Duffy Pap. wife Prot.	Mower		1	1					
		Thos. Elen Gilroy Do.	Rabbitcatr								
		Bry. Elen. Connor Do.	Smith		4						1
		Jn. Bough Prot. wife Pap.	Huckster	2							
		Jn. Eliz. Creagg Prot	Constable	2							
		Jn. Cath. Cacheside Pap.	Carpenter	3					1		2
		Hugh. Hon. McCabe Do.	Friezemongr		2						
	Tot. Prot.	16		18	40	6	10		7		12
	Tot. Pap.	51									

Com~Ros common Parish of	Place of Abode	Names and Religion	Proffession	Children under 14		Children above 14		Men Servts		Women Servts	
				Prot.	Paps.	Prot.	Paps.	Prot.	Paps.	Prot.	Paps.
[f.86] Bumblin	Stroakstown	Mich.Anne Keogh Do.	Broguemaker								
		Jn. Mable Gara Do.	Tobacco spinr.								
		Dan. Hon. Ginty Do.	Carman								
		Mich. Eliz. Keogh Do.	Broguemaker								
	Puleneronylane	Bry. Ma. Murphy Do.	Malster	2		2					
		Bry. Sarah Heavy Do.	Tobacco spinr.		1						
		Wm. Mary Keogh Do.	Broguemaker		2						
		Roy. Bridgt. Gilban Do.	Labr.		2						
		Pet. Jane Long Do.	Smith		2						
		Bry. Giles Kilmartin Do.	Labr.		2						
		Jn. Mary McDermot Do.	Do.		1						
		Bry. Sar. Conollon Do.	Do.		3		1				
		Ow. Rose Keogh Do.	Brogemakr		2		1				
		Mich. Cusack Pap. wife Prot.	Gardener		1						
	Lisroy Street	Mich. Cat. Martin Prot	Horseman	2							
		Wid.Larkin Do.	Merchant								
		Hu. Nary Pap.	Beggar								
		Win. Nary Do.	Chorewomn.			1					
		Thos. Fran. Cowen Prot	Tenant	3							
		Mat. Bridgt. Conny Pap	Butcher		2						
		Wid. Sar. Branan Do.	Huckster				2				
		Bry: Branan Prot wife Pap	Inkeeper	3		2			2		
		Wm. Mar. Shanly Pap.	Mercht.		2						
		Jas. Joan Owens Do.	Labr.		3						
		Wid: Mary Dillon Do	Mercht.				3		1		
		Wid: Marg. Hanly Do.	Huckster		1		2				
		Pat. Jane Mahon10 Do.	Mercht.		3				2		
		Phil. Rose Connor Do.	Huckster		2						
		Tha: Anne Starrel Do.	Labr.		1						
		Rich. Bridgt. Lynch Do.	Yarnbuyr				1		1		
		Thos. Bridgt Darcy Do.	Do.		1						
		And. Cat. Barden Do.	Tobaccospinr.								
		Bry. Smyth Pap. Wife Prot	Wheelright		4						
		Edw: Smyth Pap. wife Prot.	Labr.		2		2			1	
		Jas. Mary Stuart Prot.	Tailor	2		1			2		
		Pat. Jane Mcaway Do.	Shoemaker	4					1		1
		Wid. Nixon Do.	Spinster			4					
		Jon. Ternan Pap. wife Prot	Labr.		1						
		Jn. Morris Prot. wife Pap.	Cooper	[erased]							
	Tot. Prot 13 Tot. Pap. 57			14	40	8	15		9	1	14
[f.87] Bumblin	Lisroyan Street	Wm. Sar. Morris Prot.	Weaver	1				1			
		Jn. Brid. Barton Do.	Do.	3				1			
		Phil. Brid. McDermot Pap.	Labr.		1						
		Edw. Cath. Cowan Prot	Do.			3					
		Wm. Margt. Gilmer Do.	Do.	1		2					
		Dan. Mar. O Brien Do.	Mason		2		1				

Com~Ros common Parish of	Place of Abode	Names and Religion	Proffession	Children under 14		Children above 14		Men Servts		Women Servts	
				Prot.	Paps.	Prot.	Paps.	Prot.	Paps.	Prot.	Paps.
		Wid: Thorp Prot	Beggr								1
	Church Street	Jn. Cat. Cowen Do.	Mercht[11].						1	1	1
		Dan. Martin Prot wife Pap.	an old servt.								
		Mich. Jane Cacheside Prot.	Carpenter	1					1		1
		Ow. Elen. Collagan Pap.	Shoemakr.		1	2			2		
		Den. Hon. Guan Do.	Tailor		1		1		1		1
		Robt. Mary Molloy Do.	Servants		2						1
		Jn. Cath. Bones Do.	Labr.								1
		Hugh Cath. McDermot Do.	Do.								
		Pet. Flannigan Widr. Do	Do.								
		Tha. Sar. McDonogh Do.	Malster		1		1				
		Pat. Margt Igoe Do.	Mason		1						2
		Jn. Hanna Creagg Prot	Breeches-maker	1							
		Jas. Bridgt. Slow Pap.	Cotter								1
		Pat. Cath. Flinn Do.	Saltmongr		2						1
		Edw. Rose Whitoath Do.	Mason		1				1		1
		Pat. Mulvy Pap.	Weaver								
		Mary Ward Do.	Servt.		1						
		Pet. Sar. Cane Pap.	Labr.		2						
		Bryn. Hon. McSwine Do.	Do.		2						
		Edw. Bridgt. Silke Do.	Do.		1				1		
		Corm. Ganly Pap: wife Prot.	Yarnbuyr.								1
		And. Dor. Cassidy Prot.	Barber								1
		Thos. Sa. Conreen Pap	Cotner		1						1
		Pat. Cat. Caveechar Do.	Tobaccospinr.		1				2		
		Edw Eliz. Sweeny Do.	Sawyer		1				1		
		Ow. Ma. Glancy Do.	Weaver								
		Mart. Margt. Daly Do.	Do.								
		Pat. Anne Halion[12] Prot.	Gardener	1		1					
		Wid: Brice Pap.	Labr.								1
		Hen. Dockra Pap wife Prot	Tailor		2	1			1		1
		Eliz. Barton Prot.	Spinster	1							
		Thos. Ellen Lally Pap.	Cooper		1				1		1
	Tot. Prot. 25 Tot. Pap. 47			9	24	9	3	2	12		17
[f.88]	Church Street	Thos Anne Maguire Pap.	Skinner		1						
		Mark Connor Do.	Barber						1		1
		Rich. Celia McDonogh Prot.	Schoolmasr	3		2	1				
		Char. Brid Mcdonogh Pap	Yarnbyer		1						
		Darb. Win. Hanly Pap.	Mason				1		1		
		Jn. Mary McDonogh Do.	Brogemaker								
		Edw. Ann Ginty Do.	Butcher		2				2		
		Jas. La. Branan Do.	Brogemaker		1						
		Pat. Elen. Sweeny Do.	Barber		3						
		Jas. Jane Davis Prot.	Cooper	2							
		Wm. Mary Black Do.	Smith	1		2					
		Wid: Hanly Pap.	Mantua-maker		2						
		Jas. Jane Cow Prot.	Hackler					1			

Com~Ros common Parish of	Place of Abode	Names and Religion	Proffession	Children under 14		Children above 14		Men Servts		Women Servts	
				Prot.	Paps.	Prot.	Paps.	Prot.	Paps.	Prot.	Paps.
		Wm. Cowen Widr. Do.	Labr.			1					
		Wid: Black Pap.	Do	4		1					2
		Laugh. Bridgt Lenaghan Do.	Tobaccospinr		2						
		Jas. Ellen Waldrom Do.	Butcher		1						
		Pat. Cas. Fahy Prot.	Currier	1				2			
		Con:Hon: Lanon Pap.	Butcher				2				
		Darb. Jane Gusheen Do.	Yarnbuyer		2						1
		Danl. Mary Sweeny Do.	Malster		1		2				
		Thad. Cat. Keogh Do.	Broguemaker		4		2		2		
		Chas. Gardiner Prot. wife Pap.	Butcher								
		Thos. Mary Conner Pap.	Snuffmaker		4						
		Phel. Mar. Connor Do.	Yarnbuyr								1
		Jon. Hamburgh Prot wife Pap.	Clothier			1					
		Jn. Murphy Pap. wife Prot.	Plaisterer		1						
	Tot. Prot	11		11	25	7	8	3	6		5
	Tot Pap.	36									
Tot in Bumblin Parish - Prot. 125				101		58		18	~~90~~	11	
Tot in Do -	Pap. 541				347		151		90		83

[verso f.88]

Parish of Bumblin

Housekeepers	Children under 14	Children above 14	Men servants	Women servants
Tot. Prot 125	101	98	18	11
Tot. Pap. 541	349	151	90	85

[verso f. 89]

A List of the Inhabitants in
Cloontouscort Kilgefin & Cloonfinlogh Parishes

Prots: 58
Paps: 3018
[Edward Synge's handwriting] Mr Garret

NOTES

1. Including 20 acres of water (*General Alphabetical Index*).

2. *Report ... fairs and markets*.

3. Used by bishop Synge in 1750 (*Synge Letters*, p. 164).

4. Gortoose townland was two-thirds soft wet bog impassable for cattle and the rest was arable and meadow with pasture (N.L.I., Pakenham Mahon estate maps, MS 16 M 45/4).

5. Thomas Mahon (1701-1782), the builder of Strokestown House, was the eldest son of John Mahon and Eleanor Butler. He was at Trinity College, Dublin in 1720 but did not take a degree. He was MP for Roscommon borough from 1740 to 1760 and for County Roscommon from 1761 to 1782. He was joint governor of County Roscommon in 1773. He was granted fairs at Strokestown in 1742. In 1735 he married Jane, daughter of Sir Maurice Crosbie (later Lord Brandon) of Ardfert, Co. Kerry (*Alumni Dubliniensis; History of the Irish Parliament;* Burke, *LGI* (1958)).

6. Will proved 1771 (N.L.I., Index to Diocesan Wills Elphin, microfilm p.1727).

7. 'One Taafe of Strokes-town' advised Edward Synge about the price of Swedish timber in 1749 (*Synge Letters* p.117).

8. Yarn was sent to William Robinson by the Mahon family in 1768 to be woven into diaper cloth (N.L.I., Pakenham Mahon Papers, household wages and account book, MS 5676).

9. Robert Stephenson, in his survey of the linen industry in County Roscommon, noted that Patrick, Dominick and Charles Mahon made sheetings, Doulais and Ozenbrigs and Pat and Dominick had built a bleach yard (Robert Stephenson, *Reports and Observations of Robert Stephenson... for the years 1760 and 1761* (Dublin 1761) p.60).

10. In 1761, Patrick Mahon, merchant of Strokestown, was a signatory of an address by the Catholic Committee to George III (*Letters of Charles O'Conor*, p.94).

11. John Cowen supplied wine to Thomas Mahon in the 1740s (N.L.I., Pakenham-Mahon Papers, MS 10,156/3).

12. Patrick Hallian was employed as a gardener by Thomas Mahon in 1734/5 (N.L.I., Pakenham Mahon Papers, account book, MS 5676/10).

CLOONTUSKERT, COUNTY ROSCOMMON[1]

INTRODUCTION: *The parish of Cloontuskert is in the barony of Ballintober South. It is bounded on the east and south by the head of Lough Ree and the river Shannon. It is one and three-quarter miles north west of Lanesborough in County Longford. The parish was 7,465 acres in size.[2] The main commercial centre was Ballyleague which had a fair once a year, the day after Trinity Sunday.[3]*

The parish was united with that of Cloonfinlogh from 1731, and the incumbent from 1741/2 was the Rev. Francis Bosquet.[4] It is not known where he lived. The patron was the bishop.

OCCUPATIONS

Ale seller	3	Cottier	137	Servants, household	67
Baker	1	Farmer	12	Shopkeeper	1
Beggar	8	Feathermonger	2	Smith	4
Broguemaker	9	Glover	1	Spinner	10
Butcher	1	Herd	5	Stonecutter	1
Carpenter	1	Innkeeper	1	Surgeon	1
Carrier	1	Labourer	29	Tailor	4
Constable	3	Maltster	1	Tenant	192
Cooper	2	Miller	1	Thatcher	1
Cottener	1	Piper	1	Weaver	12

Com~Ros common Parish of	Place of Abode	Names and Religion	Proffession	Children under 14 Prot.	Children under 14 Paps.	Children above 14 Prot.	Children above 14 Paps.	Men Servts Prot.	Men Servts Paps.	Women Servts Prot.	Women Servts Paps.
[f.89] Cloontouscort	Ballyleague	Thos. Norman Prot wi: Pap:	Inn-keeper	1					3		2
Do	Do	Wm. Norman Prot.	Shop-keeper								
Do	Do	Pat. Harvy & wi Paps:	Cotter								
Do	Do	John Harvy & wi Paps:	Tenant		6						1
Do	Do	Jas. Martin & wi Paps:	Malster		1				1		1
Do	Do	Mary McGuire Pap:	Cotter								
Do	Do	Pe. Hanly & wi Paps:	Labourer		1						
Do	Do	Anne Woods Paps	Beggar		2						
Do	Do	Jas. Moran & wi Paps:	Tenant		1						1
Do	Do	Eliz. Lacy Papist	Glover		1		2				
Do	Do	Mich. Hudson Prot wi: Papt.	Farmer	4			2		2		1
Do	Do	John Gibbons & wi Paps:	Tenant				1				1
Do	Do	John Hudson & wi Paps:	Weaver		2				1		
Do	Do	Wm. Godwell Prot: wi: Papt.	Weaver	1					1		
Do	Do	James Lyons Prot: wi: Papt.	Weaver		2						
Do	Do	Mary Martin Papt.	Baker								
Do	Do	Bryan Gill & wi Paps:	Butcher						2		3
Do	Do	Bryan Harvy & wi Paps:	ale-seller		1						
Do	Do	Ja. White & wi Paps:	Thatcher		2						
Do	Do	Mart Hobbikin & wi Paps:	Cotter		1						1
Do	Do	Pat. Flagherty & wi Paps:	Cotter		2		2				
Do	Do	Murt. Donagho & wi Paps:	Cotter		3						
Do	Do	Wm. Moran & wi Paps:	Cotter				3				
Do	Do	Ed. Pate & wi Paps:	Glover		2						
Do	Do	Ja. Egan & wi Paps:	Cotter		1				1		1
Do	Do	Margt.McGlochlin Pap	Cotter				1				
Do	Do	Pat. Gill & wi Paps:	Cotter		2						
Do	Do	Michl. Flyn Papt.	Beggar								
Do	Do	Ed. Kelly & wi Paps:	Labourer		1		2				
Do	Do	Danl. Hobbikin & wi Paps:	Cotter				1		1		
Do	Do	Cath. Cregg Papt.	Cotter				1				
Do	Do	Bar. Monaghan & wi Paps:	Labourer								
Do	Do	Cat. Caroon Papt.	Cotter		1		2				
Do	Do	Pe: McDonagh Papt.	Cotter				1				
Do	Do	Cicely McDonagh Papt.	Spinner								
Do	Do	Lu. Baron & wi Paps:	Tenant		1						
Do	Do	Catha. Lafy Papt.	Tenant		3		2				
Do	Do	Dan. Kelly & wi Paps:	Cotter		3						
Do	Do	Pierce Costello & wi Paps:	Weaver								2
Do	Do	James Kelly & wi Paps:	Cotter								
Do	Do	Wm. Salmon & wi Paps:	Broguemaker		4				1		
[f.90] Cloontouscort	Ballyleague	Gilb. Graly & wi Paps:	Weaver				1				
Do	Do	Laugh. Graly & wi Paps:	Cotter		1						
Do	Do	Peter Salmon Papt:	Cotter		2		1				
Do	Do	And. Moran & wi Paps:	Cotter		2						
Do	Cloonmustard	Fr. King & wi Paps:	Cotter				4				
Do	Do	Pat. Hanly & wi Paps:	Cotter		1						
Do	Do	Matt. Bellia & wi Paps:	Cotter		2						

Com~Ros common Parish of	Place of Abode	Names and Religion	Proffession	Children under 14		Children above 14		Men Servts		Women Servts	
				Prot.	Paps.	Prot.	Paps.	Prot.	Paps.	Prot.	Paps.
Do	Do	James Bellia Papt.	Labourer				1				
Do	Do	Thady Gill & wi Paps:	Cotter								
Do	Do	Denis Bonaghan & wi Paps:	Cotter		1		3				
Do	Do	Ja. Davis & wi Paps:	Farmer		3		1		3		4
Do	Do	Pat. Gill & wi Paps:	Cotter				1		1		
Do	Cloontouscort	Thos. Barlo Paps:	Cotter								
Do	Do	Pat. Barlow & wi Paps:	Cotter		2						
Do	Errinagh	Ed. Hanly & wi Paps:	Cotter		2						1
Do	Do	Char. Connor & wi Paps:	Cotter								1
Do	Do	Mich. Gill & wi Paps:	Weaver		2						
Do	Do	Mich. Caffry & wi Paps:	Cotter		5		1				
Do	Do	Pat. Graly & wi Paps:	Cotter		2						
Do	Gortgalline	Thady Hanly & wi Paps:	Aleseller								
Do	Do	Ja. McGrach & wi Paps:	Cotter				1				
Do	Do	Errold Hanly Papt.	Cotter				4				
Do	Do	Pat. Harvey & wi Paps:	Cotter		3		1				
Do	Do	Ja. Mackintree & wi Paps:	Cotter		3						
Do	Do	Joh. Mackintree & wi Paps:	Cotter		2						
Do	Do	Collogue Philips & wi Paps:	Cotter				2				
Do	Do	Sarah Bush Papt.	Cotter				1				
Do	Do	Darby Birn & wi Paps:	Labourer		1						
Do	Do	Dan. Kelly & wi Paps:	Tenant		3						
Do	Do	Apsty Lyons & wi Paps:	Weaver		1						
Do	Do	Bryan Mahon & wi Paps:	Cotter		1						
Do	Culleclych	Domi. Feely & wi Paps:	Farmer		5						1
Do	Do	Den. Kelly & wi Paps:	Tenant		3		1				
Do	Do	Sil. Hanly & wi Paps:	Tenant								
Do	Do	Rich. Casserly & wi Paps:	Tenant				3				
Do	Do	Ann Farrel Papt.	Tenant				3				
Do	Do	Fras. Hanly & wi Paps:	Cotter		1		1				
Do	Do	Pat. Staunton & wi Paps:	Cotter				1				
Do	Do	Pat. Scally & wi Paps:	Cowper		2						
Do	Do	Catha. Waters Papt.	Cotter				2				
Do	Moneene	Phe. Gallagher & wi Paps:	Cotter		1						
[f.91]Do	Do	Bryan Birn & wi Paps:	Cotter		2						
Do	Do	Catha. Callaghan Papt	Cotter								
Do	Do	John Murphy Papt	Cotter								
Do	Do	Ed. Murphy & wi Paps:	Tenant		4						
Do	Do	Thos. Farrel & wi Paps:	Smith				3				
Do	Coolshaughtiny	Ment. Brode & wi Paps:	Tenant		2						
Do	Do	John Scally & wi Paps:	Tenant		2						
Do	Do	Ja. Killine & wi Paps:	Tenant		1						
Do	Do	Hobert Farrel Papt.	Tenant								
Do	Do	Wm. Scally & wi Paps:	Broguemaker		2						
Do	Do	Dan. McGuire & wi Paps:	Tenant		1						
Do	Do	Terence McGuire Papt.	Tenant								
Do	Do	Ownagh McGuire Papt.	Spinner				1				
Do	Do	Ed. McGuire & wi Paps:	Tenant		1						
Do	Do	Dan. Hanly & wi Paps:	Tenant				4				

Com~Ros common Parish of	Place of Abode	Names and Religion	Proffession	Children under 14 Prot.	Children under 14 Paps.	Children above 14 Prot.	Children above 14 Paps.	Men Servts Prot.	Men Servts Paps.	Women Servts Prot.	Women Servts Paps.
Do	Do	Mary Flood Papt	Tenant				3				
Do	Do	Jas. Flanigan & wi Paps:	Tenant		2						
Do	Do	Th. Flanigan & wi Paps:	Tenant		1						
Do	Gallagh	James Conry Papt:	Tenant								
	Do	Sarah Conry Papt	Tenant				1				
Do	Do	Ma. Faghy & wi Paps:	Tenant		2						
Do	Do	Thos. Knilan & wi Paps:	Tenant		3						
Do	Do	Hob. Henly & wi Paps:	Tenant				1				
Do	Do	Bry. Hanly5 & wi Paps:	Tenant		2						
Do	Do	Thos. Knilan & wi Paps:	Taylor		1						
Do	Gardenstown	De. Daly & wi Paps:	Carpenter		1				1		2
Do	Do	Mi. Scally & wi Paps:	Brogue:maker		1		2				1
Do	Do	Cor. Connel & wi Paps:	Tenant		4		1		1		1
Do	Do	Bry. Nolan & wi Paps:	Labourer		1						
Do	Do	Pat. Nolan & wi Paps:	Labourer		1						
Do	Do	Denis Farrel Papt.	Tenant		1		1		1		2
Do	Do	Bridget Davis Papt.	Tenant		3		2				1
Do	Antrilo'Beg	Pat. Blakeney & wi Paps:	Tenant				1				
Do	Do	Marget. Hanly Papt.	Cotter				2				
Do	Do	Thady Gill & wi Paps:	Tenant		2				1		
Do	Do	Lu. Wallis & wi Paps:	Tenant				3				1
Do	Do	Andw. Gill & wi Paps:	Tenant		1						1
Do	Do	Joh. Casserly & wi Paps:	Tenant		2		2				
Do	Do	Darby Mony & wi Paps:	Tenant		1				1		1
Do	Do	Mary Gill Papt	Tenant				2				
Do	Do	Margt. Kilchal Papt	Tenant				1				
[f.92] Do	Do	Sarah Cavenagh Pap	Spinner								
Do	Do	Slany Cavenagh Papt.	Spinner								
Do	Do	John Cavenagh Papt.	Labourer								
Do	Ballycleare	John. Byrn & wi Paps:	Tenant		1						
Do	Do	Wm. Byrn & wi Paps:	Taylor		4						
Do	Do	Jon. Kery & wi Paps:	Tenant		3						
Do	Do	Pat. Kery & wi Paps:	Tenant		2						
Do	Do	Jas. Lafy & wi Paps:	Tenant		1						
Do	Do	Barw. Lafy & wi Paps:	Tenant		1						
Do	Do	Pe. Bush & wi Paps:	Carrier		1						
Do	Do	Wm. Hanly & wi Paps:	Tenant						1		1
Do	Do	Thos. Brenan & wi Paps:	Tenant		2						
Do	Do	Pat. Lafy & wi Paps:	Cotter		3						
Do	Do	Dom: Hanly & wi Paps:	ale:seller		1						
Do	Moher	Martn. Murry & wi Paps:	Weaver		5		4		2		1
Do	Do	Lau. Cormick & wi Paps:	Weaver		3				1		
Do	Do	Jon. Ratigan & wi Paps:	Tenant		1		1				
Do	Do	Jon. Farrel & wi Paps:	Tenant		2				1		1
Do	Do	Jon. Smith & wi Paps:	Cotter		2						
Do	Do	Jas. Fallon & wi Papt.	Cotter		1				1		
Do	Cloonadra	Thady Honen & wi Paps:	Cotter								
Do	Do	Andrew Ward & wi Paps:	Brogue:maker		1				1		
Do	Do	Thos. Casserly & wi Paps:	Constable		1				1		

Com~Ros common Parish of	Place of Abode	Names and Religion	Proffession	Children under 14		Children above 14		Men Servts		Women Servts	
				Prot.	Paps.	Prot.	Paps.	Prot.	Paps.	Prot.	Paps.
Do	Do	Eliz: Casserly Papt.	Spinner								
Do	Do	Rogr. Doghery & wi Paps:	Tenant		1						
Do	Do	Chrir: Farrell & wi Paps:	Tenant		1						
Do	Do	Jon. Farrel & wi Paps:	Tenant		1						
Do	Do	Pe. Scally & wi Paps:	Cowper		2						
Do	Do	Wm. Wallis & wi Paps:	Tenant							1	
Do	Do	Jon. McGuire & wi Paps:	Tenant		2						
Do	Do	Des. Kelly & wi Paps:	Labourer		1						
Do	Do	Pat. Glenan & wi Paps:	Tenant								
Do	Do	Wm. Scally & wi Paps:	Brogue:maker		1						
Do	Do	Jon. Kelly & wi Paps:	Tenant		2					1	
Do	Do	Jas. Hurracho & wi Paps:	Weaver		2					1	
Do	Do	Rob: Johnston & wi Paps:	Tenant		1						
Do	Do	Thos. Haly & wi Paps:	Beggar		2						
Do	Lissanriagh	Catha: Hanly Papt.	Tenant		1		1				
Do	Do	Joh. Nerheny & wi Paps:	Cotter		5		2				
Do	Do	Ed. Dean & wi Paps:	Cotter		2		2				
Do	Do	Jas. Mulveechely & wi Paps:	Herd		2						

The parish of Kilgefin begins here]

NOTES

1. In the manuscript, Cloontuskert and Kilgefin are run together.

2. Of which Lough Ree and the river Shannon covered 2384 acres (*General Alphabetical Index*).

3. *Report ... fairs and markets*.

4. Francis Bosquet was born in Lisburn and educated by a Mr Clark. He entered TCD in 1726 aged 18, and took BA in 1730. He was collated vicar of Cloonfinlogh, Cloontuskert and Kilgefin in 1742 (Leslie, 'Elphin', p. 123).

5. An Ed Hanly, gentleman, was living at Gallagh in the mid-seventeenth-century (*Census of Ireland*).

KILGEFIN, COUNTY ROSCOMMON

INTRODUCTION: *The parish of Kilgefin is in the barony of Ballintober South. The parish was 6,060 statute acres in size.*[1]

The parish was united with that of Cloonfinlogh from 1731, and the incumbent from 1741/2 was the Rev. Francis Bosquet (see Cloontuskert). The patron was the bishop.

OCCUPATIONS

Ale seller	3	Feathermonger	2	Smith	3
Baker	1	Herd	4	Spinner	5
Beggar	5	Innkeeper	1	Stonecutter	1
Broguemaker	4	Labourer	20	Surgeon	1
Constable	2	Miller	1	Tailor	2
Cottener	1	Piper	1	Tenant	135
Cottier	86	Servants, household	90	Weaver	2
Farmer	9				

Com~Ros common Parish of	Place of Abode	Names and Religion	Proffession	Children under 14 Prot.	Paps.	Children above 14 Prot.	Paps.	Men Servts Prot.	Paps.	Women Servts Prot.	Paps.
[f.93] Kilgefin	Corry	Pe. Gilhooly & wi Paps	Cotter		2						
Do	Do	Jon. Tonery & wi Paps	Cotter		2						
Do	Do	Jon. Donnel & wi Paps	Cotter		1						
Do	Do	Bry. Brenan & wi Paps	Herd		1				1		
Do	Do	Da. Fineron & wi Paps	Miller		3				1		
Do	Do	Thady Carrol & wi Paps	Cotter		1						1
Do	Cloonegearah	Thos. Coblay & wi Prot	Stone:cutter	3							
Do	Do	Jon. Coblay & wi Paps	Tenant		1						
Do	Do	Anne Coblay Papt.	Beggar		1		1				
Do	Do	Bry. Keenan & wi Paps	Beggar								
Do	Do	Jon. Compton Prot: wife Papt.	Tenant		1						
Do	Do	Hen. Compton & wi Paps	Tenant		2				1		1
Do	Do	Bry. Kilhooly & wi Paps	Tenant		2						
Do	Do	Bridget Carly Papt.	Tenant		2		1				
Do	Do	Mary McManus Papt.	Beggar								
Do	Do	Giles Cummaun Papt.	Cotter				6				
Do	Do	Rich. McCarra & wi Paps	Cotter				1				
Do	Do	Ed. Grenan & wi Paps	Tenant		6						
Do	Do	Cor. Mealiff & wi Paps	Tenant						1		
Do	Do	Red: Line Papt.	Labourer				2				
Do	Do	Roger O'Hara Prot wi Papt.	Tenant		2		3				
Do	Do	Pe. Fowkes & wi Paps	Tenant		1						1
Do	Do	Michl. Lyons & wi Paps	Tenant		1				1		
Do	Do	Ternan Murry & wi Paps	Cotter		1						
Do	Do	Hen. Rice & wi Paps	Labourer				1				1
Do	Do	Bry. Hopkins & wi Paps	Cotter		1				1		1
Do	Do	Cicely Holmes Papt.	Beggar								
Do	Do	Wm. Holmes & wi Paps	Cotter						1		
Do	Do	Ownagh Rourke Papt.	Spinner								
Do	Do	Honora Scally Papt.	Beggar								
Do	Do	Thady Donlon Papt.	Tenant				1				2
Do	Do	Ed. Donlan & wi Paps	Tenant		3				1		2
Do	Do	Pe. Donlan & wi Paps	Tenant		2						
Do	Do	Mar. Donlan & wi Paps	Tenant		2						
Do	Do	Jon. Mealiffe & wi Paps	Tenant		1						
Do	Do	Con. Mealiffe & wi Paps	Tenant				1				
Do	Do	Jon. Brenan Papt.	Cotter								
Do	Treily	Jon. Gill & wi Paps	Cotter		2		1				
Do	Do	Ter. Reily & wi Paps	Cotter		1						
Do	Do	Pat. Ganon & wi Paps	Cotter		1						
Do	Do	Sarah Connel Papt.	Cotter				1		1		
[f.94]Do.	Do	Jon. Macher & wi Paps	Cotter								
Do	Do	Own. Connor & wi Paps	Cotter		1		1				
Do	Do	Pe. Connor & wi Paps	Cotter		2						
Do	Do	Lau. Connor & wi Paps	Cotter				1				
Do	Do	Pat. Byrne & wi Paps	Cotter		1						
Do	Do	Ed. Mugan & wi Paps	Cotter								
Do	Kilmurtagh	Jon. Hanly & wi Paps	Farmer			1					
Do	Do	Eliz. Macher Papt.	Cotter				2				

Com~Ros common Parish of	Place of Abode	Names and Religion	Proffession	Children under 14 Prot.	Children under 14 Paps.	Children above 14 Prot.	Children above 14 Paps.	Men Servts Prot.	Men Servts Paps.	Women Servts Prot.	Women Servts Paps.
Do	Do	Bridget Brochan Papt.	Farmer				2				
Do	Do	Bry. Kenedy & wi Paps	Tenant	1			1				
Do	Do	Ed. Kenedy & wi Paps	Tenant	1			1				
Do	Do	Ed. Kenedy & wi Paps	Tenant	1					1		
Do	Do	Jas. Banaghan & wi Paps	Tenant	1							
Do	Do	Con. Banaghan & wi Paps	Tenant								
Do	Do	Bridget Fox Papt.	Cotter				2				
Do	Do	Thos. Noon & wi Paps	Cotter								
Do	Do	Danl. Noon & wi Paps	Piper								
Do	Do	Lau. Costello & wi Paps	Cotter				1				
Do	Do	Andw. Kenedy & wi Paps	Tenant								
Do	Culnecallagh	Da. Lyons & wi Paps	Tenant				1				
Do	Do	Red. Lyons & wi Paps	Tenant		2						
Do	Do	Wm. Banaghan & wi Paps	Tenant				1				
Do	Do	Dudy. Banaghan & wi Paps	Tenant		2						
Do	Do	Pat. Nerheny & wi Paps	Cotter		1						
Do	Do	Thady Hoan & wi Paps	Cotter		1						
Do	Do	Jas. Murry & wi Paps	Cotter		1						
Do	Do	Pa. Flanigan & wi Paps	Labourer		1						
Do	Do	Catha: Hanah Papt.	Cotter				1				
Do	Do	Jon. Carrol & wi Paps	Labourer		2						
Do	Do	Micl. Redy & wi Paps	Labourer		1						
Do	Cullenemona	Jon. Hanly & wi Paps	Tenant				1				
Do	Do	Michl. Nerheny & wi Paps	Tenant		2						
Do	Do	Loughn Walsh & wi Paps	Broguemaker		1		1				
Do	Sheeawne	Jas. Bermingham & wi Paps	Tenant				1				
Do	Do	Jon. Bermingham & wi Paps	Tenant								
Do	Do	Thos. Tonery & wi Paps	Tenant	1			1				2
Do	Do	Pa. Dempsy & wi Paps	Tenant	1			1				
Do	Do	Fr. Garvin & wi Paps	Tenant		4						
Do	Do	Pat. Cox & wi Paps	Cotter		4						
Do	Do	Bry. Tigue & wi Paps	Cotter		1						
Do	Cappogh	Fr. Spareman & wi Paps	Tenant		2		1				
[f.95]	Do	Pat. Kelly & wi Paps	Tenant		2		1				
Do	Do	Dary. Bones & wi Paps	Cotter		1						
Do	Do	Fr. Nolan & wi Paps	Tenant		1						
Do	Do	Fr. Hanly & wi Paps	Tenant								
Do	Do	Dan. Corvechir & wi Paps	Labourer		1						
Do	Do	Fr. Hanly & wi Paps	Constable								
Do	Do	Cun. Conolly & wi Paps	Broguemaker		2						
Do	Cullalusset	Pat. Fallan & wi Paps	Tenant		1				1		1
Do	Do	Thos. Fallan & wi Paps	Tenant		1						2
Do	Do	Jas. Fallan & wi Paps	Tenant		2						
Do	Do	Te. Kelly & wi Paps	Tenant		2						1
Do	Do	Fr. Hanly & wi Paps	Tenant		3						
Do	Do	Margaret Kelly Papt.	Cotter		2						
Do	Do	Pat. Bruthel & wi Paps	Labourer		2						
Do	Do	Dol. McSharny & wi Papt	Labourer		1		1				
Do	Ballichurry	Jos. Tems & wi Prot:	Tenant								

Com~Ros common Parish of	Place of Abode	Names and Religion	Proffession	Children under 14		Children above 14		Men Servts		Women Servts	
				Prot.	Paps.	Prot.	Paps.	Prot.	Paps.	Prot.	Paps.
Do	Do	Fr. Creevy & wi Paps	Tenant		2				1		1
Do	Do	James Connor Papt.	Tenant								
Do	Do	John Connor Papt.	Tenant								
Do	Do	Hugh Connor Papt.	Tenant								
Do	Do	Brian Connor Papt.	Tenant								
Do	Do	Mary Connor Papt.	Tenant								1
Do	Do	Micl. Mulvooly & wi Paps	Tenant				3				
Do	Do	Pat. Ternane & wi Paps	Tenant		2		1				2
Do	Do	Pat. Johnston & wi Paps	Tenant				4				
Do	Do	Thos. McGee & wi Paps	Tenant		2						1
Do	Do	Rich. Wallis & wi Paps	Tenant		2				1		
Do	Do	Jas. Brenan & wi Paps	Tenant		1						1
Do	Do	Wm. Gibbons & wi Paps	Tenant		1						
Do	Do	Jas. Mcglochlin & wi Paps	Tenant								
Do	Do	Pat. Brenan & wi Paps	Tenant		1		1				1
Do	Do	Bridget Hamlin Papt.	Cotter				1				
Do	Do	Cormick Doud & wi Paps	Tenant				4				
Do	Do	Jas. Mulvooly & wi Paps	Tenant		1				1		
Do	Do	Jas. Farrel & wi Paps	Cotter		1						
Do	Do	Ed. Killa & wi Paps	Tenant		1		1				1
Do	Do	Giles Connel Papt.	Cotter				2				
Do	Tumegranel	Bri. Conry & wi Paps	Cotter		2		1				
Do	Do	Pat. Flanigan & wi Paps	Cotter		3						
Do	Do	Pat. Coghlan & wife Papt.	Cotter				2				
Do	Do	Mary Brady Papt.	Cotter				4				
[f.96]Do	Do	Bri. Hanly & wi Paps	Cotter		1						
Do	Do	Jon. Hawkes & wi Prot	Farmer	1					4		2
Do	Do	Christ. Nort & wi Paps	Cotter		2						
Do	Do	Thos. Lussy & wi Paps	Herd		3		2		1		
Do	Do	Barw. Erwin & wi Paps	Cotter		2		1				
Do	Do	Mary Lyons Papt.	Cotter		2		2				
Do	Do	Jas. Farnel & wi Paps	Cotter								
Do	Do	Jon. Donnowil & wi Paps	Cotter		1						
Do	Do	Jon. Roarty & wi Paps	Herd				3				2
Do	Do	Bridget Stones Papt.	Cotter		2		2				
Do	Do	Kill Carty & wi Paps	Cotter		4		1				
Do	Do	Tha. Collins & wi Paps	Cotter		1		1				
Do	Do	De. McGuire & wi Paps	Cotter		2						
Do	Do	Jon. Lynch & wi Paps	Cotter								
Do	Do	Mi. McDermot & wi Paps	Smith		1		1				2
Do	Do	Hu. McDermot & wi Paps	Tenant				1		1		
Do	Do	Ed. McDermot & wi Paps	Smith		2						
Do	Bellaghnedan	De. Connor & wi Paps	Farmer		4		4		2		3
Do	Do	Thay. Connor & wi Paps	Cotter		3		2				
Do	Do	Bri. Hanly & wi Paps	Cotter		1						
Do	Do	Bri. Dowlan & wi Paps	Smith		2						
Do	Do	Jon. Plunket & wi Paps	Tenant								
Do	Do	Lu. Macher & wi Paps	Cotter						2		
Do	Do	Hu. Knowlan & wi Paps	Tenant		3						

Com~Ros common Parish of	Place of Abode	Names and Religion	Proffession	Children under 14		Children above 14		Men Servts		Women Servts	
				Prot.	Paps.	Prot.	Paps.	Prot.	Paps.	Prot.	Paps.
Do	Do	Bri. Conry & wi Paps	Tenant		1						
Do	Do	Pat. Hunt & wi Paps	Cotter		2						
Do	Do	Pat. McDermot & wi Paps	Tenant		3		2				
Do	Do	Jon. Connor & wi Paps	Cotter				1				
Do	Do	Wm. Hunt & wi Paps	Cotter								
Do	Do	Jas. Tonery & wi Paps	Broguemaker		2						
Do	Do	Pat. Fox & wi Paps	Cotter		1		1				
Do	Do	Pat. McGarry & wi Paps	Cotter		1						
Do	Do	Sarah Hanly papt.	Cotter				1				
Do	Do	Thos. Hanly & wi Paps	Cotter		2						
Do	Do	Jon. Quiveecher & wi Paps	Cottener								
Do	Do	Mart. Hunt & wi Paps	Cotter								
Do	Do	Honora Mealiff Papt.	Cotter				1				
Do	Do	Owen Hunt & wi Paps	Cotter		2						
Do	Do	Anne Hanly Papt.	Cotter				1				
Do	Do	Andw. Hunt & wi Paps	Cotter				1				
Do	Kilmacough	Ed. Coony & wi Paps	Farmer		1		2				1
[f.97]Do	Do	Thay: Corream & wi Paps	Cotter				3				
Do	Do	Ow. McDonnel & wi Paps	Cotter				1				
Do	Do	Mi. Hanly & wi Paps	Tenant				2				
Do	Do	Pat. Lenan & wi Paps	Tenant								1
Do	Do	Pat. Feeny & wi Paps	Tenant				2				1
Do	Do	Cha. McGlochlin & wi Paps	Tenant				4				
Do	Do	Cicely Hanly Papt	Farmer				1				
Do	Cortline	Martin Dillon & wi Paps	Farmer						2		1
Do	Do	Jas. Ganly & wi Paps	Cotter								
Do	Do	Walter Dillon Papt.	Farmer								
Do	Do	Pe. Flanigan & wi Paps	Tenant		1						
Do	Do	Mi. Kneelan & wi Paps	Cotter		2	1					
Do	Cooltacker	Catha. Ternan Papt.	Spinner								
Do	Do	Domi. Ternan & wi Paps	Tenant						1		1
Do	Do	Thos. Charleton & wi Paps	Tenant		1		1				
Do	Do	Eliz. Pate Papt.	Cotter		2		2				
Do	Do	Ow. Gibbons & wi Paps	Tenant		4						1
Do	Do	Ow. Mullaly & wi Paps	Cotter		1		2				
Do	Carrouard	Jon. Gibbons & wi Paps	Tenant				3		1		1
Do	Do	Nic. Gibbons & wi Paps	Tenant				4				
Do	Do	Mary Mugan Papt.	Spinner		1						
Do	Do	Ow. Hanly & wi Paps	Tenant		2						
Do	Do	Thos. Crarane & wi Paps	Tenant				2				
Do	Do	Jas. Crarane & wi Paps	Tenant		3						
Do	Do	Phe. McNeel & wi Paps	Labourer				1				
Do	Do	Fr. Goughan & wi Paps	Tenant		3						
Do	Do	Bridget Goughan Papt.	Spinner				1				
Do	Do	Jon. Dowd & wi Paps	Tenant		3						
Do	Do	De. McCormick Papt.	Feather monger		2						
Do	Do	Margaret Gill Papt.	Cotter				2				
Do	Do	Hu. Cormick & wi Paps	Tenant		1						
Do	Do	Eliz. Gibbons Papt.	Tenant		1						

Com~Ros common Parish of	Place of Abode	Names and Religion	Proffession	Children under 14		Children above 14		Men Servts		Women Servts	
				Prot.	Paps.	Prot.	Paps.	Prot.	Paps.	Prot.	Paps.
Do	Tumeever	Wm. Hussey & wi Paps	Tenant		3						
Do	Do	Da. Gibbons & wi Paps	Tenant		3						
Do	Do	Ed. Feeny & wi Paps	Tenant		2						
Do	Do	Cormick Hanly Papt.	Tenant		2		1				
Do	Do	Ed. Charleton & wi Paps	Tenant		1						
Do	Do	Br. Mungan Papt.	Tenant								
Do	Do	Chris. Parker & wi Paps	Tenant		2					1	
Do	Do	Fr. Parker & wi Paps	Tenant		1						1
Do	Do	Thos. Parker & wi Paps	Tenant		1				1		
[f.98]Do	Do	Pat. Branon & wi Paps	Tenant		3						1
Do	Do	Wm. Mungan & wi Paps	Tenant		3						
Do	Do	Jon. Branon & wi Paps	Tenant								
Do	Do	Mi. Connilan & wi Paps	Tenant		5						
Do	Do	Ter. Dempsy & wi Paps	Tenant								1
Do	Do	Ann Branon Papt.	Tenant				2				
Do	Do	Ann Doran Papt.	Tenant				3				
Do	Do	Dan. Murphy & wi Paps	Tenant		3						
Do	Do	Jon. Kilhooly & wi Paps	Tenant		2		2				
Do	Do	Con. Kery & wi Paps	Feather monger		1						
Do	Aughwerny	De. Hodd & wi Paps	Herd		2				1		
Do	Do	Pat. Graley & wi Paps	Cotter		2						
Do	Do	Bart. Murry & wi Paps	Cotter								
Do	Do	Thos. McDermot & wi Paps	Cotter								
Do	Do	Widow White Papt.	Cotter		1		2				
Do	Do	Mi. Cunn & wi Paps	Cotter								
Do	Do	Ter. Kelly & wi Paps	Cotter		2						
Do	Do	Own. Morris & wi Paps	Cotter		1						
Do	Do	Pat. Moony & wi Paps	Cotter		2						
Do	Do	Jon. Murphy & wi Paps	Cotter				1				
Do	Do	Do Junior & wi Paps	Cotter		2						
Do	Do	Jon. Cox & wi Paps	Tenant		2						
Do	Do	Bri. Kelly Papt.	Surgeon		1				1		1
Do	Do	Mi. Conry Papt.	Tenant		2		2				
Do	Do	Chris. Kelly & wi Paps	Taylor								
Do	Do	Cha. Erwin & wi Paps	Tenant						1		1
Do	Do	Tha. Carrol & wi Paps	Tenant		2		1		1		
Do	Do	Ed. Erwin & wi Paps	Tenant		3		1				
Do	Do	Mary Kine Papt.	Tenant								
Do	Do	Jon. Murry & wi Paps	Tenant		2		1				
Do	Do	Jon. Cuningham & wi Paps	Tenant		1		1				
Do	Cloonshee	Dud. Hanly & wi Paps	Farmer				1		1		1
Do	Do	Ed. Hanly & wi Paps	Tenant		3						
Do	Do	Jas. Moran & wi Paps	Labourer		1						
Do	Do	Ed. Gowran & wi Paps	Labourer								
Do	Do	Fr. Connor & wi Paps	Tenant		2						
Do	Do	Pat. Mally & wi Paps	Weaver								
Do	Do	Dan. Quin & wi Paps	Tenant		2						
Do	Do	Mi. Bochan & wi Paps	Labourer		1						
Do	Do	Cor. Hopkins & wi Paps	Labourer		2						

Com~Ros common Parish of	Place of Abode	Names and Religion	Proffession	Children under 14		Children above 14		Men Servts		Women Servts	
				Prot.	Paps.	Prot.	Paps.	Prot.	Paps.	Prot.	Paps.
Do	Do	Jon. Knowlan & wi Paps	Weaver								
[f.99] Do	Cloonicashel	Dary. Faghy & wi Paps	Tenant		2		1		1		1
Do	Do	Hu Connor & wi Paps	Cotter		1						
Do	Do	Wm. Flagharty & wi Paps	Labourer		1		1				
Do	Do	Jas. Petit & wi Paps	Labourer		1		1				
Do	Do	Lough. Noon & wi Paps	Labourer								
Do	Do	Wm. Noon & wi Paps	Tenant		1		1				
Do	Do	Pat. Noon & wi Paps	Tenant		1						
Do	Do	Jon. Martin & wi Paps	Tenant								
Do	Do	Pat. Hoan & wi Paps	Tenant		1						
Do	Do	Dan. Ward & wi Paps	Tenant		1						
Do	Do	Wm. Gavison & wi Paps	Tenant		1						
Do	Do	Lough. Neal & wi Paps	Labourer								
Do	Do	Ed. Hanly & wi Paps	Labourer		1						
Do	Do	Dan. Mally & wi Paps	Tenant		1						
Do	Do	Pet. Conaghton & wi Paps	Labourer								
Do	Do	Hu. Conaghton & wi Paps	Tenant		1		1				
Do	Do	Cun. McGlochlin & wi Paps	Tenant				1		1		1
Do	Do	Jon. Noon & wi Paps	Tenant								
Do	Do	Pat. Hanly & wi Paps	Tenant		1						
Do	Do	Fr. Hanly Papt.	Tenant		1						
Do	Carrumoneen	Mi. Nerheny Papt.	Tenant		1		2				
Do	Do	De. Branon & wi Paps	Tenant		2				1		
Do	Do	Ror. Nerheny & wi Paps	Tenant								
Do	Do	Bridt. Cunighton Papt.	Spinner		1						
Do	Do	Pat. McGan & wi Paps	Tenant		3						
Do	Do	Jon. Dolan & wi Paps	Tenant		2				1		
Do	Do	Ro. Farrel & wi Paps	Cotter		3						
Do	Do	Mat. Lynch & wi Paps	Tenant						1		1
Do	Do	Thos. Smith & wi Paps	Tenant		2						1
Do	Do	Pat. Cuff & wi Paps	Tenant		3						
Do	Do	Mi. Kelly & wi Paps	Cotter		3						
Do	Do	Mi. Birn & wi Paps	Tenant		4						
Do	Do	Do Loughan & wi Paps	Tailor		2						1
Do	Do	Do Smith & wi Paps	Tenant		2						
Do	Sheeawne 2d	Dar. Covechir & wi Paps	Labourer		1						
Do	Do	Fr. Hanly & wi Paps	Constable								
Do	Do	Cun. Conolly & wi Paps	Broguemaker		2						

NOTES

1.(*General Alphabetical Index*).

CLOONFINLOUGH, COUNTY ROSCOMMON

INTRODUCTION: *The parish of Cloonfinlough lies west of Cloontuskert, north of the parish of Kilgefin and south of Lissonuffy and is on the road from Strokestown to Roscommon. The parish was 7,814 statute acres in size.[1] The ruins of Ballynafad castle were still standing in 1837. A patent for a fair was issued in 1618, first to Charles O'Connor Roe and later to Nicholas Mahon.[2]*

The parish was united with that of Kilgefin and Cloontuskert from 1731, and the incumbent from 1742 was the Rev. Francis Bosquet (see Cloontuskert). The patron was the bishop.

OCCUPATIONS

Broguemaker	5	Groom	1	Servants, household	149
Carpenter	1	Herd	9	Shopkeeper	1
Constable	1	Horserider	1	Smith	4
Cooper	2	Jobber	1	Spinner	22
Cottier	63	Labourer	44	Tailor	3
Doctor	2	Merchant	2	Tenant	145
Esquire	2	Netmaker	1	Weaver	5
Farmer	8	Poundkeeper	1	Wheelwright	1
Gardener	1	Servant	1	Yarn merchant	2

Com~Ros common Parish of	Place of Abode	Names and Religion	Proffession	Children under 14 Prot.	Children under 14 Paps.	Children above 14 Prot.	Children above 14 Paps.	Men Servts Prot.	Men Servts Paps.	Women Servts Prot.	Women Servts Paps.
[f.99] Cloonfinlogh	Cloonslanner	Jas O' Connor & wi Paps	Mercht		1				1		2
Do	Do	Jon. Connor & wi Paps	Tenant		1		3				1
Do	Do	Jas. Owens & wi Paps	Broguemaker		1				1		
[f.100] Do.	Do	Jon. Connor & wi Paps	Weaver		3				4		2
Do	Do	Jas. Hussey & wi Paps	Constable		2						
Do	Do	Honor Forrostle Papt.	Cotter				2				
Do	Do	Pe. Castleton & wi Paps	Cotter		4						
Do	Do	Thos. Fitzgerald & wi Paps	Netmaker								
Do	Do	Mi. Forrestle Papt.	Tenant				3				
Do	Do	Pat. Kelly & wi Paps	Labourer		3						
Do	Do	Phe. Duffy & wi Paps	Herd				1				
Do	Do	Tha. Moran & wi Paps	Labourer		1						
Do	Do	Tig. Murphy & wi Paps	Broguemaker								
Do	Do	Jas. Murphy & wi Paps	Cotter		1						
Do	Do	Con. Oates & wi Paps	Labourer		2						
Do	Do	Mi. Ryan & wi Paps	Labourer		1						
Do	Do	Mi. McVagher & wi Paps	Labourer		2						
Do	Do	Oli. Walker & wi Paps	Labourer								
Do	Do	Ellen Ward Papt.	Cotter								
Do	Do	Pat. Connor & wi Paps	Labourer								
Do	Do	Jon. Kelly Papt.	Labourer								
Do	Do	Pat. Forrestle & wi Paps	Labourer		1						
Do	Cloonfinlogh	Wm. Lough & wi Paps	Tenant		1		2		1		
Do	Do	Pat. Brenan & wi Paps	Cotter								
Do	Do	Ed. Kenedy & wi Paps	Herd		3						
Do	Clooncaugh	Jas. Madden & wi Prot.	Farmer	5					2		2
Do	Do	Jas. Mugan & wi Paps	Cotter		3		2				
Do	Do	Mary Hobkins Papt.	Cotter				3				
Do	Do	Jon. Cuningham & wi Paps	Cotter		4		2		1		1
Do	Do	Phi. Mccormick & wi Paps	Cotter				4				
Do	Do	Cha. Feely & wi Paps	Cotter		3						1
Do	Do	Cath. Dempsy Papt.	Cotter				4				
Do	Do	James Kelly Papt.	Labourer								
Do	Do	Jas. Magan & wi Paps	Labourer		3						
Do	Do	Ma. Cunnaghton Papt.	Spinner				2				
Do	Do	Ulick Burke & wi Prot.	Horserider	1							
Do	Reaugh	Dar. Rourty & wi Paps	Tenant				4				1
Do	Do	John Reynolds & wi Paps	Tenant				2		1		
Do	Do	Dar.Croghan & wi Paps	Tenant		1				1		
Do	Do	Jas. Fox & wi Paps	Labourer		1						
Do	Do	De Mugan & wi Paps	Tenant		2						
Do	Do	Jas. Cuningham & wi Paps	Tenant		1		1				
Do	Do	Tha. Mey & wi Paps	Tenant								
Do	Do	Lu. Croghan & wi Paps	Tenant		1						
[f.101]	Do	Pat. Mey & wi Paps	Tenant		2						
Do	Aughlard	Hu. Kearin & wi Paps	Tenant								
Do	Do	Mi. Kearin & wi Paps	Tenant		1						
Do	Do	Jas. Vesey & wi Paps	Tailor				5		2		1
Do	Do	Dar. Loughan & wi Paps	Tenant		4						

Com~Ros common Parish of	Place of Abode	Names and Religion	Proffession	Children under 14		Children above 14		Men Servts		Women Servts	
				Prot.	Paps.	Prot.	Paps.	Prot.	Paps.	Prot.	Paps.
Do	Do	Own. Loughan & wi Paps	Tenant		2		3				
Do	Do	De. Treasey & wi Paps	Tenant		1				1		
Do	Do	Ed. Cuningham & wi Paps	Tenant		1		1				1
Do	Do	Jas. Carol & wi Paps	Tenant						1		2
Do	Do	Mur. Egan & wi Paps	Labourer		1						
Do	Clooncaugh 2d	Thos. Hinde & wi Paps	Farmer		5		1		2		2
Do	Do	Dar. Murry & wi Paps	Cotter		3						1
Do	Do	Jon. Harraghton & wi Paps	Cotter		2						
Do	Do	Ma. Elvers & wi Paps	Labourer								
Do	Do	Mi. Dempsy & wi Paps	Herd		1						
Do	Do	Do. Carly & wi Paps	Tenant		3		1				
Do	Do	Own. Treasey & wi Paps	Tenant		1						
Do	Do	De. Coleman & wi Paps	Tenant		2						
Do	Do	Mi. Mugan & wi Paps	Tenant		1						
Do	Do	Ann Carly Papt.	Spinner		3						
Do	Do	Wm. Reynolds & wi Paps	Tenant		1						
Do	Do	Con. Nerheny & wi Paps	Tenant		1		2		1		1
Do	Do	Own. Kilhooly & wi Paps	Tenant		1		1				
Do	Do	Mi. Connor & wi Paps	Smith		3		3				
Do	Do	Jas. Dempsy & wi Paps	Tenant		1				1		1
Do	Do	Jas. Shanacher & wi Paps	Cowper		1						
Do	Do	Pat. Shanacher Papt.	Cowper								
Do	Do	Joan Shanacher Papt.	Spinner								
Do	Do	Jon. Turner Prot & wi Papt.	Weaver	3							
Do	Do	Jas. Feeny & wi Paps	Tenant		1						
Do	Kilultough	Mar. Lachy & wi Paps	Herd		2						
Do	Do	Hu. Murry & wi Paps	Cotter		2						
Do	Do	Bry. Codkin & wi Paps	Cotter								1
Do	Do	Jo. Gibbons & wi Paps	Cotter		4		1				
Do	Do	Rich. Cox & wi Paps	Labourer		1						
Do	Do	Ed. Lyons & wi Paps	Weaver								
Do	Do	Ma. Trishan & wi Paps	Labourer		1						
Do	Do	Bridget Casserly Papt.	Spinner				1				
Do	Do	Miles Carrol & wi Paps	Labourer		3						
Do	Do	Ma. Cuningham & wi Paps	Broguemaker		2		2				
Do	Aghalurchy	Dan. Kelly & wi Paps	Herd		2						1
[f.102] Do.	Do	Pat. Codkin & wi Paps	Broguemaker		3						
Do	Do	Wm. Dillon & wi Paps	Cotter		2						
Do	Do	Fr. Connell & wi Paps	Cotter								
Do	Moher	Mal. Kelly & wi Paps	Tenant		4		2				2
Do	Do	Loug. Kelly & wi Paps	Tenant		5				1		1
Do	Do	Pat. Harrachton & wi Paps	Tenant		1		2				1
Do	Do	Da. Donogho Papt.	Tenant								
Do	Do	Thos. Donogho & wi Paps	Tenant		2						1
Do	Do	Da. Tigue & wi Paps	Tenant		2						1
Do	Do	Jas. Fanan & wi Paps	Labourer		2		2				
Do	Moher 2d	Pat. Hogan & wi Paps	Tenant				3		1		2
Do	Do	Widow Shiel Papt.	Cotter				3				
Do	Do	De. Smith & wi Paps	Cooper		5		1		2		

Com~Ros common Parish of	Place of Abode	Names and Religion	Proffession	Children under 14 Prot.	Children under 14 Paps.	Children above 14 Prot.	Children above 14 Paps.	Men Servts Prot.	Men Servts Paps.	Women Servts Prot.	Women Servts Paps.
Do	Do	Brid. Mahon Papt.	Spinner		1						
Do	Do	Denis Kelly Papt.	Labourer								
Do	Do	Jon. McCue & wi Paps	Tenant		2						1
Do	Do	Ed. Dogherty Papt.	Labourer				3				
Do	Do	Thos. Carol & wi Paps	Labourer		1						
Do	Do	Pat. Nerheny & wi Paps	Tenant		1				2		
Do	Do	Lough. Boulan & wi Paps	Tenant				2		1		2
Do	Do	Cha. Mulloy Papt.	Labourer								
Do	Do	John Mulloy Papt.	Labourer								
Do	Do	Nora Kinsalagh Papt.	Spinner		3						
Do	Do	Jas. Kinsalagh Papt.	Labourer		1						
Do	Derridaragh	Ed. Croghan Prot.& wi Papt.	Farmer	2		3			2		4
Do	Do	Pat. Connel & wi Paps	Cotter		3				1		1
Do	Do	Jas. Reynolds & wi Paps	Herd		4				1		
Do	Do	Ed. Ganon & wi Paps	Gardiner		1						
Do	Do	Jas. Cox & wi Paps	Groom		1				1		1
Do	Do	Hu. Ward & wi Paps	Cotter				1				
Do	Do	Will. Ward & wi Paps	Cotter		1						
Do	Do	De. Kerin & wi Paps	Cotter		3						
Do	Do	Wm. Collins & wi Paps	Cotter		4		1		1		
Do	Ballintample	Jon. Quin & wi Paps	Tenant		4						
Do	Do	Pat. Murray & wi Paps	Tenant		1		3				1
Do	Do	Jas. Donagher & wi Paps	Tenant		4		1		1		1
Do	Do	Mi. Conollan & wi Paps	Tenant								
Do	Do	Pat. Cladrane & wi Paps	Tenant		2						
Do	Do	Pat. Mulloly & wi Paps	Tenant		2		1				
Do	Do	Mart. Hely & wi Papt.	Labourer		1						
Do	Do	Ed. Kenedy & wi Papt	Tenant						1		
[f.103]	Do	Wm.Collins & wi Paps	Tenant		1						
Do	Do	Margt. Hanson Papt.	Cotter		1						
Do	Cloonreane	Hu. Deermot & wi Paps	Cotter		3						
Do	Do	Pat. Guin & wi Paps	Cotter		2						
Do	Do	Pe. Guin & wi Paps	Cotter		2				1		1
Do	Do	Conr. Prot. Tigue & wi Papt	Farmer		3		1		2		2
Do	Do	Jon. Leheny & wi Paps	Cotter								
Do	Do	Pat. Hedian & wi Paps	Cotter		3				1		
Do	Do	De. Covehir & wi Paps	Cotter								
Do	Do	Own. Mullooly & wi Paps	Cotter		1		2				
Do	Carruclogher	Chris. Devenish[3] Prot	Esqr.						2		2
Do	Do	Geo Devenish[4] Prot	Farmer								
Do	Do	Jane Devenish Papt	Farmer								
Do	Do	Jon. Burnet & wi Paps	Tenant		2				1		1
Do	Do	De. Birne & wi Paps	Cotter		2		1				
Do	Do	Ann Hanly Papt.	Cotter				2				
Do	Do	Hu: Manien & wi Paps	Cotter				3				
Do	Do	Pe. Dermot & wi Paps	Cotter								
Do	Do	Mi. Duawn & wi Paps	Cotter								
Do	Do	Tha. Hanly & wi Paps	Cotter		1		2				
Do	Do	Hu. Horoho Papt.	Cotter				2				

Com~Ros common Parish of	Place of Abode	Names and Religion	Proffession	Children under 14		Children above 14		Men Servts		Women Servts	
				Prot.	Paps.	Prot.	Paps.	Prot.	Paps.	Prot.	Paps.
Do	Carbohill	Dan. Hanly & wi Paps	Tenant		1		4				
Do	Do	Sarah Gilmarten Papt.	Cotter				3				
Do	Do	Jon. Hanly Papt.	Cotter		2						
Do	Ballinafad5	Own. Kilhooly & wi Paps	Herd		2		1		1		1
Do	Lacken	Barw. Carly & wi Paps	Mercht.		2				3		1
Do	Do	Cun. Connor Papt.	Weaver				2		1		
Do	Do	Dar. Nerheny & wi Paps	Tenant		5						
Do	Do	Jas. Kelly & wi Paps	Tenant		1						
Do	Do	De. Birn & wi Paps	yarn: mercht.								
Do	Do	Ni. Nerheny & wi Paps	Shopkeeper		1			1			1
Do	Do	Chas. McDonell & wi Paps	Tenant		3		3				
Do		Ma. Betaugh Papt.	Tenant				1				
Do	Do	Da. Murphy & wi Paps	Tenant				3				
Do	Do	Jas. Sheal & wi Paps	Doctor		4						
Do	Do	Wm. Magan & wi Paps	Tenant		1						
Do	Do	Own. Magan & wi Paps	Tenant		1						
Do	Do	Margt. Hoay Papt	Tenant				3				
Do	Do	Pa. Cunaghton & wi Paps	Labourer		4		1				
Do	Do	Pat. Wall & wi Paps	Weaver		3						
Do	Do	Fr. Thigh & wi Paps	Labourer		3						
[f.104]Do	Do	Hu. Mughan & wi Paps	Tenant		3						
Do	Do	Ed. Scot & wi Paps	Tenant		4						
Do	Do	Wi. Mullaly & wi Paps	Labourer		1						
Do	Do	Ja. Nerheny & wi Paps	Tenant								
Do	Do	Thos. Kelly Papt.	Yarn: mercht.								
Do	Do	Mic. Kelly Papt.	Tenant								
Do	Do	Ellen Kelly Papt.	Spinner								
Do	Do	Da. Murphy & wi Paps	Labourer		1						
Do	Do	Hu. Mulloly & wi Paps	Labourer		2						1
Do	Do	Bridgt. Egan Papt.	Tenant		2		2				
Do	Do	Æneas Neal Papt.	Pound: keeper6								
Do	Do	Margt. Jekins Papt.	Spinner								
Do	Do	Jon. McQuone & wi Paps	Tenant		2						
Do	Do	Mic. Carly Papt.	Tenant								
Do	Do	Ja. Carly Papt.	Tenant								
Do	Do	Ann Carly Papt.	Spinner								
Do	Do	Ann Donlan Papt.	Tenant				2				
Do	Cluniragh	Jon. Birn & wi Paps	Tenant		2				1		
Do	Do	Tha. Fallon & wi Paps	Tenant		1		1		1		1
Do	Do	Own. Caffry & wi Paps	Tenant		4		1		1		
Do	Do	Margt. Fanin Papt.	Tenant						1		
Do	Do	Con. Hicken & wi Paps	Tenant		1						
Do	Do	Margt. Flanigan Papt.	Spinner								
Do	Do	Ni. Lamb & wi Paps	Tenant						1		
Do	Do	Sarah Lamb Papt.	Tenant		2		1				
Do	Do	Mi. Mulloly & wi Paps	Tenant		1		3				
Do	Do	Fr. Mulloly & wi Paps	Tenant		1						
Do	Do	Da. Corrily & wi Paps	Tenant								1
Do	Do	Bar. Comb & wi Paps	Tenant		2						

Com~Ros common Parish of	Place of Abode	Names and Religion	Proffession	Children under 14 Prot.	Paps.	Children above 14 Prot.	Paps.	Men Servts Prot.	Paps.	Women Servts Prot.	Paps.
Do	Do	Jon. Connilan & wi Paps	Tenant		3						
Do	Do	Tha. Fallon & wi Paps	Broguemaker		2						
Do	Do	Cath. Oates Papt.	Spinner				1				
Do	Do	Margt. Cooke Papt.	Spinner		1						
Do	Do	Ouna Duffy Papt.	Spinner				1				
Do	Do	Do. Gilleran & wi Paps	Tenant		1						
Do	Do	Mi. Hester & wi Paps	Tenant		2		2				
Do	Do	Mi. Carlisk & wi Papt.	Tenant		2		1				
Do	Do	Mi. Connel & wi Paps	Tenant		1				1		1
Do	Do	Tha. Connel & wi Paps	Tenant		1				1		
Do	Do	Jon. Boin & wi Paps	Labourer		2						
Do	Do	Ouna Gublin Papt.	Spinner				1				
[f.105]Do.	Do.	Ouna Neal Papt.	Cotter								
Do	Do	Bridgt. Kelly Papt.	Spinner		1						
Do	Do	Pa. Corrily & wi Paps	Tenant								
Do	Clunilian	Wal. Plover & wi Paps	Tenant				3		2		1
Do	Do	Thos. Comin & wi Paps	Tenant		4						
Do	Do	Tha. Cockly & wi Paps	Labourer		2						
Do	Do	Tha. Branan & wi Paps	Tenant		2						
Do	Do	Dar. Banan & wi Paps	Smith		3						
Do	Do	Pat. Banan & wi Paps	Smith		4						1
Do	Do	Te. Duffy & wi Paps	Tenant		2						
Do	Do	Margt. Igo Papt.	Tenant				2				
Do	Do	Ro. Carlisk & wi Paps	Tenant								
Do	Do	Ma. Carlisk & wi Paps	Tenant								
Do	Do	Andw. Flyn & wi Paps	Tenant		2				1		1
Do	Do	Elinor Flyn Papt.	Spinner		1						
Do	Do	Lu. Duffy & wi Paps	Tenant						1		3
Do	Do	Elinor Duffy Papt.	Spinner								
Do	Do	Jon. Duffy & wi Paps	Tenant								
Do	Do	Con. Duffy & wi Paps	Tenant								
Do	Do	Pe. Nerheny & wi Paps	Tenant		4						
Do	Clare	Ed. Reidy & wi Paps	Labourer		1		1				1
Do	Do	Tha. Konough & wi Paps	Labourer		3		1				
Do	Do	Pa. Lyhany & wi Paps	Cotter		2						
Do	Do	Jon. Bruder & wi Paps	Cotter		2						
Do	Lesineniren	Jas. Farrel & wi Paps	Cotter		4						
Do	Do	Jas. Carly & wi Paps	Cotter				2				
Do	Do	Mi. Birn & wi Paps	Cotter		3						
Do	Do	Pat. Murry & wi Paps	Cotter		2		2				
Do	Do	Pa. Mulligan & wi Paps	Cotter		3						
Do	Do	Ro. Moor & wi Paps	Cotter								
Do	Do	Mary Ternan Papt.	Spinner		1						
Do	Cloonery	Thos. Kilhooly & wi Paps	Tenant		3		3		1		
Do	Do	Lu. Gilhuly & wi Paps	Tenant		2		1				
Do	Do	Own. Gilhuly & wi Paps	Tenant								1
Do	Do	Jon. Gilhuly Papt.	Tenant								
Do	Do	Mi. O'Donel & wi Paps	Labourer		2		1				
Do	Do	Pa. Crorane & wi Paps	Cotter				1				

Com~Ros common Parish of	Place of Abode	Names and Religion	Proffession	Children under 14		Children above 14		Men Servts		Women Servts	
				Prot.	Paps.	Prot.	Paps.	Prot.	Paps.	Prot.	Paps.
Do	Do	Christ. Breheny Papt.	Spinner								1
Do	Glanamiltogue	Te. Connor & wi Paps	Cotter		2						1
Do	Do	Mi. Taim & wi Paps	Cotter		2						
Do	Do	Jane Taim Papt.	Spinner								
[f.106]Do	Glanamiltogue	Da. Lyhany & wi Paps	Labourer		2		1				
Do	Do	Bridgt. Lyhany Papt.	Spinner				2				
Do	Do	Pa. Eustace & wi Paps	Labourer		1		1				
Do	Cloonfree[7]	Ba. Mahon[8] & Wi Prot.	Esqr.		4			1	3	1	5
Do	Do	Ri. Brice & wi Prot.	Servant		6				1		2
Do	Do	Jon. Bawning & wi Paps	Smith		2		2		1		
Do	Do	Cor. Nartin & wi Paps	Herd		1		4				1
Do	Do	Hu. Igo & wi Paps	Labourer		3						
Do	Do	Jas. Connor & wi Paps	Cotter				3				
Do	Do	Dar. Hanon & wi Paps	Cotter				1				
Do	Do	Conr. Flanigan & wi Paps	Cotter				3				
Do	Dougheln	Jon. Moran & wi Paps	Tailor		4						
Do	Do	Mors. Ward & wi Paps	Doctor		1						
Do	Do	Pe. Kenedy & wi Paps	Tenant		2		1				
Do	Do	De. Ward & wi Paps	Tenant		1						
Do	Do	Dori. McDermot Papt.	Tenant				2				
Do	Do	Bri. Feeny & wi Paps	Tenant		2		2				
Do	Do	Thos. Dolan & wi Paps	Tenant		2						
Do	Do	Da. Gavickan & wi Paps	Tenant		1						
Do	Do	Da. Murtough & wi Paps	Tenant		1		1				
Do	Do	Pa. Gavickan & wi Paps	Labourer		1						
Do	Do	Da. Samon & wi Paps	Tailor								
Do	Do	Ed. Tearnan & wi Paps	Tenant		1						1
Do	Do	Fr. Reynolds & wi Paps	Tenant		1		1		1		
Do	Do	Ow. Reynolds & wi Paps	Tenant		1						
Do	Do	Mar. Shanon & wi Paps	Tenant		1						
Do	Do	Tha. Cox & wi Paps	Tenant								
Do	Do	Thos. Connel & wi Paps	Tenant		2						
Do	Do	Pe. Mulveechil & wi Paps	Tenant		2						
Do	Do	Da. Mulledy & wi Paps	Tenant				1				
Do	Do	Jon. Mulledy Papt.	Labourer								
Do	Do	Hu. Whakaran Papt.	Labourer		2						
Do	Do	De. Murry & wi Paps	Tenant		2		1				
Do	Do	De. Heanly & wi Paps	Herd		2		1				
Do	Do	Jas. Murry & wi Paps	Tenant		1						
Do	Do	Ow. Grork & wi Paps	Tenant		1		2		1		
Do	Do	Ed. Grork & wi Paps	Tenant		1				1		
Do	Do	Ma. Fitzgerald Papt.	Spinner				2				
Do	Do	Ri. Johnston & wi Paps	Tenant						1		2
Do	Do	Bar. Fallon & wi Paps	Tenant		2						
Do	Do	Cicey. Pore Papt.	Tenant		3		3				
[f.107]Do.	Do	Jas. Hanly & wi Paps	Tenant								
Do	Do	Mort. Hanly Papt.	Jobber								
Do	Do	Jas. Kelly & wi Paps	Tenant				3				
Do	Culivacken	Ma. Hanly & wi Paps	Farmer		4				1		2

Com~Ros common Parish of	Place of Abode	Names and Religion	Proffession	Children under 14		Children above 14		Men Servts		Women Servts	
				Prot.	Paps.	Prot.	Paps.	Prot.	Paps.	Prot.	Paps.
Do	Do	Mary Dowlan Papt.	Farmer								
Do	Do	Ma. Manan & wi Paps	Tenant		2						
Do	Do	Hu. Neal & wi Paps	Carpenter		2		1				
Do	Do	Jas. Crean & wi Paps	Tenant		2						
Do	Do	Mi. Scanlan & wi Paps	Labourer		1						
Do	Do	Mi. Dockery & wi Paps	Tenant								
Do	Do	Lau. Scanlan & wi Paps	Tenant		2						1
Do	Do	Jas. Hopkin & wi Paps	Tenant		3		2				
Do	Do	Jon. Manan & wi Paps	Tenant				1				
Do	Do	Pa. Horth & wi Paps	Tenant		3						
Do	Do	Hu. Croghan & wi Paps	Tenant				2				
Do	Do	Fr. Croghan & wi Paps	wheelwright								
Do	Do	Lau. Dockery & wi Paps	Labourer		4						
Do	Do	Jon. Kelly & wi Paps	Tenant		2						
Do	Do	Mi. Geohagan & wi Paps	Cotter		2						
Do	Do	Lau. Murry & wi Paps	Tenant		1						
Do	Do	Tha. Gavachen & wi Paps	Tenant		5						
Do	Do	Fr. Murry & wi Paps	Cotter				1				
Do	Do	Pat. Dolan & wi Paps	Tenant		3						
Do	Do	Jon. McCabe & wi Paps	Cotter								
Do	Do	Pat. Keny & wi Paps	Tenant		2						
Do	Do	Mat. Mugan & wi Paps	Tenant		4						
Do	Do	Mu. Querelly & wi Paps	Cotter		1						
omitted in	Carrouard	Lu. McDermott & wi Paps	Tenant		3		1				1
Do	Do	Jon. Nerheny & wi Paps	Tenant								
Do	Do	Pat. Stone & wi Paps	Tenant		1						
Do	Do	Ed. Egan Papt.	Tenant		1		1				
Do	Do	De. Grimes & wi Paps	Cotter		1		1				
Do	Do	De. McNemara & wi Paps	Tenant		1						
omitted in	Tumeever	Dan Bones & wi Paps	Tenant		2						
Do	Do	Bri. Finaghty & wi Paps	Cotter				1				
Do	Do	Phe. Flyn & wi Paps	Cotter				1				
Do	Do	Jas. Rany & wi Paps	Tenant				1				
Do	Do	Lu. Lenahon Papt.	Labourer								
Do	Do	An. Madden & wi Paps	Tenant		2						
Do	Do	Jas. Homes & wi Paps	Tenant		1		2				

NOTES

1. 3,411 acres were detached and 352 acres was water (*General Alphabetical Index*).

2. *Report ... fairs and markets.*

3. Christopher Devenish of Carrowneclogher was born 2 December 1708, the son of William Devenish and Elizabeth Blackburn. He died unmarried (Burke *LGI* (1958)).

4. George Devenish was the brother of Christopher (Note 3).

5. Part of the Mahon estate (N.L.I., Pakenham Mahon Papers, MS 3119).

7. Poundkeepers held distrained cattle for the bailiff until a debt was paid or until they were sold (Neal Garnham, *The Courts, Crime and the Criminal Law of Ireland 1692-1760* (Dublin 1996), p.96)).

7. Described in 1777 as 'cold tillage and pasture [with] sundry tenants' (N.L.I., Clonbrock Papers, maps with lists of tenants' holdings 1777, MS 19,672/11).

8. Bartholomew Mahon was a son of Nicholas Mahon and Magdalene French, daughter of Arthur French of Movilla Castle, County Galway (Burke, *LGI* (1958)).

ROSCOMMON, COUNTY ROSCOMMON

INTRODUCTION: *The town of Roscommon is 15 miles west of Athlone in the barony of Ballintobber. In the eighteenth century it probably had one main street with several lanes branching off it. The land in the neighbourhood of the town was good, and grew agricultural produce for sale in the markets.[1] The parish covers 9,819 acres.*

The town was incorporated by James I, with a provost (sovereign), twelve free burgesses and a an unlimited number of freemen. The town and much of the local land had been granted to the earl of Essex in the sixteenth century. By the eighteenth century, the earls of Essex were not only absentees but also pocketed the income from market tolls and taxes, spending nothing to develop the town. At the beginning of the nineteenth century it was still dependent for water on a single well in the centre of the town which could fail in the summer.[2] It sent two members to parliament before the Act of Union. The gaol was in the centre of town and the administration of justice had a network of officers appointed through influence and preferment: the gaoler, the postman, the revenue officer, the turnkey, the constable, 3 bailiffs and a gauger.

A market was held in Roscommon every Saturday and in the early nineteenth-century sold frieze, woollen goods, flannel and linen. It also sold coarse brown pottery made from the clay on the banks of the Shannon.[3] A patent was issued to Lord Ranelagh in 1665 to hold a fair four times a year, in March, September and December and on Whit Monday.[4]

The parish was united to those of Kilbride and Kilteevan, and the patron was the bishop of Elphin. The rectory was impropriate in the earl of Essex. The incumbent in 1749 was the Rev. James Blair who had been collated vicar of Roscommon, Kilbride and Kilteevan in 1742 and installed as prebendary of Kilgoghlin in 1752. He signed the manuscript returns for his parishes.

OCCUPATIONS

Ale seller	16	Gardener	2	Sawyer	1
Apothecary	2	Gauger	1	Schoolmaster	2
Bailiff	3	Gentleman	1	Servants, household	382
Baker	2	Hatter	2	Sexton	1
Brewer	3	Hawker	2	Shepherd	10
Broguemaker	7	Herd	7	Shoemaker	6
Builder	1	Horse rider	1	Shopkeeper	5
Butcher	9	Innkeeper	1	Shovemaker	1
Buttonmaker	1	Joiner	1	Skinner	6
Carman	5	Labourer	141	Slater	1
Carpenter	3	Lodger	12	Smith	10
Clerk	1	Maltster	1	Sovereign	1
Constable	1	Mason	7	Tailor	12
Cooper	3	Miller	1	Thatcher	1
Cottier	24	Nailer	1	Tobacconist	1
Cutler	1	Pedlar	2	Turnkey	1
Distiller	2	Piper	2	Vicar	1
Farmer	7	Postman	1	Villager	122
Fiddler	1	Revenue officer	1	Weaver	24
Gaoler	1	Saddler	2	Widow	56
				Wigmaker	3

Com~Ros common Parish of	Place of Abode	Names and Religion	Proffession	Children under 14		Children above 14		Men Servts		Women Servts	
				Prot.	Paps.	Prot.	Paps.	Prot.	Paps.	Prot.	Paps.
[f.108] Roscomon	Ballymartin	Thos. Digby Prot	Gent.	5		2			4		5
	Do	Richd. Digby Prot	Lodger			2					
*	Do	Bryan Keogh Pap	Herd		3		1				
	Do	Honnor Higgins Pap	Widw.		1						
	Lisadurn	Jn. Mills Pap	Cotter		3			1			1
	Do	Teigue Graly Pap	Do				2				
	Do	Dan. Conry Pap	Do.		1						1
	Do	Pat. Conry Pap	Do.		2						
*	Do	Wm Grehane Pap	Lodger					1			
	Do	Thady O'Brien Pap	Cotter		3		2		1		
	Do	Den. Connellan Pap	Do		4						
‡	Do	Richd. Walker Prot.	Do		2		1				
	Ballygalda	Anne Mitchell Prot	Farmer	2		2			2		2
*	Do	Ed Ormsby Prot	Lodger								
	Do	Ed. Kempsy Pap	Herd		3						
	Do	Wm. Cassane Pap	Cotter		3		1				
	Do	Peter Mullally Pap	Do		3						
	Do	Laugh Naichton Pap	Do		3						
	Do	Michl. Morrisy Pap	Do		3						
	Do	Ed. Bolton Pap	Villager		3						
*	Do	Pat. Mullan Pap	Do								1
	Do	Jn. Berne Pap	Do		2						
	Do	Ed. Johnston Pap	Do		1			1			
*	Do	Geor. Johnston Pap	Lodger								
	Do	M. McNamara Pap	Villager		1		1				
	Do	Thos Murray Pap	Do		3						
	Do	Robt. Mills Pap	Do								
	Do	Pat Naichton Pap	Do		2	~~2~~	2				
	Do	Dan McNamara Pap	Do		2						
	Do	Bar. Naichton Pap	Do		2		2				
	Do	Ed. Nowlan Pap	Do		2						
	Do	An. Nowlan Pap	Do		1						
	Do	Dan. Glancy Pap	Do		1						
	Do	Manus Rigny Pap	Do		1						
	Do	Peter Loghan Pap	Do		1		1				
	Do	Dom. Moregan Pap	Do		1						
	Do	Wm. Murphy Pap	Do		2						
	Do	Jn. Qeeny Pap	Do		1						
*	Do	Roger Collony Pap	Do								1
	Do	Margt. Keeragan Pap	Widw.		1		2				
	Total Families	70 Prot 7 Papt 64		7	61	6	15		9		10
[f.109] Roscommon	Ballygalda	Jas. Mulvihill Pap	Herd		1			1			
	Do	Conr. Murray Pap	Weaver		2		2				
	Stonypark	Richd. Jones Prot	Farmer	1				1		2	2
	Do	Ed. Cannavan Pap	Broguemaker	2							
	Do	Michl. Haraghton Pap	Taylor				2				
	Do	Peter Giraghty Pap	Gardiner		4						

Com~Ros common Parish of	Place of Abode	Names and Religion	Proffession	Children under 14		Children above 14		Men Servts		Women Servts	
				Prot.	Paps.	Prot.	Paps.	Prot.	Paps.	Prot.	Paps.
	Do	Pat. Morris Pap	Cotter		1						
	Do	Michl. Kearny Pap	Do								
	Do	Owen Sweeny Pap	Do		1		2				
*	Do	Danl. Gurly Pap	Do		1		2				
	Do	Ter. Mullaghan Pap	Do		4		1				
*	Do	Bryan Murray Pap	Do				3				
	Do	Jn. Thresham Pap	Do		1						
	Do	Thos. Hughes Pap	Do		1		1				
*	Do	Jn. Kenny Pap	Do		1		3				
	Do	Ed. Feeny Pap	Do		2		1				
	Do	Thady Mannion Pap	Do								
‡	Do	Richd. Murphy Prot	Smith	1	1		1				
	Do	Jn. Fitzgerald Pap	Shepherd		2				2		1
	Do	Jas. Fitzgerald Pap	Tailor		1						
	Do	Jn. Gireghty Prot	Weaver		1		1				
	Do	Pat. Loghnan Pap	Piper		1						
	Do	Jas. Dolan Pap	Villager		1				1		
	Do	Mich. Loghnan Pap	Do		2				2		
	Do	Mich. Fannane Pap	Do		1						
	Do	Jas. Keran Pap	Do		1						
	Do	Thos. Regan Pap	Do		4		3				
	Do	Pet. Golrick Pap	Do		3						
	Do	Pet. Flaherty Pap	Do		1				1		1
	Torville	Ed. Noon Pap	Weaver		1				1		
	Do	Wm. Gillane Pap	Do				3				
	Do	Jn. Hannane Pap	Broguemaker								
	Do	John Cassidy Pap	Smith						2		
	Do	Ellinor Geoghegan Pap	Widw.		2						
	Do	Darby Scally Prot	Villager	3					1		1
	Do	Jn. Brennan Pap	Do		2		1				
*	Do	Pet. Glin Pap	Do		2				2		1
	Do	Darby Mannion Pap	Do		1		2				
	Do	Luke Fitzgerald Pap	Do								
	Do	Bryan Geoghegan	Do		2				2		1
	Total Families	70 Prot 6 Papt 70		5	50		28		16	2	7
[f.110] Roscomon	Torville	Wm. McLoughlin Pap	Cotter		2				1		
	Do	Thady Quin Pap	Do		1		3				
	Do	Jn. Kilduff Pap	Tailor		1						1
	Do	Mary Connolly Pap	Widow				1				
	Do	Jas. Gilligan Pap	Labour.						2		1
	Do	Mat. Gilligan Pap	Do		2				1		1
	Ardsollagh5	Jas. Owens Pap	Do		1						
	Do	Elinr. Croghan Pap	Widw								
	Sleevengee	Hugh Guffin Pap	Villager				2				
	Do	Connr. Tody Pap	Do		3						1
	Do	Henry Callane Pap	Do		5		2				
	Do	Frans. Callane Pap	Do						1		1
	Do	Frans Neilan Pap	Do		3						

Com~Ros common Parish of	Place of Abode	Names and Religion	Proffession	Children under 14		Children above 14		Men Servts		Women Servts	
				Prot.	Paps.	Prot.	Paps.	Prot.	Paps.	Prot.	Paps.
	Do	Jn. Spallan Pap	Do		1		4				
	Do	Mich. Nulan Pap	Do		1		4				
	Do	Jn. Callane Pap	Do		1						
	Do	Richd. Guff Pap	Do		1						
	Do	M. Neilan Pap	Do		1		2				
	Do	Dan Neilay Pap	Do				2				
	Do	M. Kelly Do			2		2				1
	Do	Michl. Haroghtan Pap	Do		3						
	Do	Darby Guihean Pap	Weaver								
*	Do	Law. Kelly Pap	Do				1				
	Do	Dor Cullane Pap	Widw.			+	1				
	Ballynagard	Thady Kirwan Pap	Villager		1		2				
*	Do	Terence Berne Pap	Do								
	Do	Mich. Berne Pap	Do								
	Do	Wm. Murphy Pap	Do		1		1				
	Do	Bryan Kelly Pap	Do		1		1				
	Do	Ed. Curly Pap	Do		1						
	Do	Char. Murray Pap	Do		2						1
	Do	Val. Lennan Pap	Do		2						
	Do	Wm. Finnane Pap	Do		1						
	Do	Ed. Lennan Pap	Do		1						
	Do	Roger Curly Pap	Do		2						
	Do	Jn. Conolly	Do		2						
	Do	Morgan Mannion Pap	Do				2				
*	Do	Jas. Killmurry Pap	Smith				2				
	Do	Mary Connolly Pap	Widw.				1				
	Do	Joan Mannin Pap	Do		1		1				
	Total Families	40 Prot – Pap 73			4		33		5		7
[f.111] Roscomon	Ballynagard	Roger Mullan Pap	Villager								
	Do	Thady Mullan Pap	Do								
	Do	Dens. Grealy Pap	Do				1				
	Do	Owen Grealy Pap	Do								
	Do	Conn. Minahan Pap	Do		1		1				
	Do	Thos. Mannin Pap	Do		3						
	Do	Ed. Kelly Pap	Do								
	Do	Ed. Horogho Pap	Do		2						
	Do	Thady Mannin Pap	Do		2		1				
	Do	Barth Daly Pap	Do		1						
	Do	Thady Egan Pap	Do		2						
	Do	Laugh. Bern Pap	Do				3				
	Aghamult	Jn. Blakeney Prot	Gauger[6]					1	2		2
	Do	Jn. Murry Pap	Labour.		2						
	Do	Anw. Connaughton Pap	Do		1						
	Do	Magt. Hologhan Pap	Do		4		1				
	Do	Wm. Lungen Pap	Do		1						
*	Do	Rogr. Moffit Pap	Do								
	Do	Luke Lyons Pap	Do		3		1				
	Do	Pet. O'Donnell Pap	Do		2						

Com~Ros common Parish of	Place of Abode	Names and Religion	Proffession	Children under 14		Children above 14		Men Servts		Women Servts	
				Prot.	Paps.	Prot.	Paps.	Prot.	Paps.	Prot.	Paps.
*	Abbytown	Jas. Blair Prot	Vicar					1	2	1	1
	Do	Hatton Blair Prot	Widow								
‡	Do	Arthr. Lovelace Prot	Farmer						3		2
	Do	George Harrison Prot	Weavr.	1							1
	Do	Jn. Harrison Prot	Skinner	2							
	Do	Jas. Harrison Prot	Do	1							1
	Do	Law. Armstrong Prot	Do	1							
‡	Do	Dens. Guff[7] Prot	Nailer						4		1
	Do	Jas. Gaffy Prot	Hatter	1							
	Do	Wm. Cavenagh Prot	Mason	2		2					
	Do	Mary Brandon Prot	Widw.	1		1					
	Do	Wm. Cuthbert Prot	Pedlar	1							
	Do	Jas. Morrison Prot	Brewer	2							
	Do	Neal McSwine Pap	Postman		3		2		1		1
	Do	Mich. Rush Pap	Labour.		1				1		
	Do	M. Higgins Pap	Do		3		1				
	Do	Jas. Nugent Pap	Do		2						
	Do	Thady Ward Pap	Mason		1						
	Do	Jn. Murray Pap	Cooper		2						
*	Do	Hugh Curly Pap	Labourer		1						
	Total	Families 40 Prot 25[?] Papt 51		12	87		11	2	13	1	9
[f.112] Roscommon	Abbytown	Roger Hanly Pap	Labourer		1						
	Do	Peter Scanlan Pap	Do		1						
	Do	Mat. Connor Pap	Do		3						
	Do	Ed. McDaniel Pap	Do		1						
	Do	Mary Dempsy Pap	Widw.	1							
	Do	Michl. Redian Pap	Labourer		1						
	Do	Pet. Guff Pap	Do		2						
	Do	Pet. Dempsy Pap	distiller		1						
	Do	Cath. Guff Pap	Widw.								
	Do	Jane Doolan Pap	Widw.		3						
	Do	Ellinor Kelly Pap	Widw.	2							
	Do	Jn. Burk Pap	Hatter		1						
	Do	Jas Rigny Pap	Weaver		3						
*	Do	Walter Cooney Pap	Labour.	~~3~~			4				
	Do	Mary Behin Pap	Widow				1				
	Do	Law. Farrell Pap	Labour		1						
	Roscommon	Richd. Bermingham[8] Prot	Sovereign	6				3	3	2	3
	Do	Stephen Roper Prot	Innkeeper	1		4			1		4
	Do	Thos. Guff Prot	Shop-keeper	2					1		2
‡	Do	Barth. Guff Prot	Do	1							1
	Do	Phil. Connor Prot	Do	1							1
	Do	Jn. Hanly Prot	Schoolmaster						1		1
	Do	Wm. Harrison Prot	Do	2					1		1
	Do	John White Prot	Shooemaker	3				5			1
	Do	Frank White Prot	Do					1			1
*	Do	John White Prot	Sexton								
	Do	Thos. Roper Prot	Ale seller	1		3					4

Com~Ros common Parish of	Place of Abode	Names and Religion	Proffession	Children under 14		Children above 14		Men Servts		Women Servts	
				Prot.	Paps.	Prot.	Paps.	Prot.	Paps.	Prot.	Paps.
	Do	Richd. Giraghty[9] Prot	Do						1		2
	Do	Mary Brennan Prot	Widw.						1		1
‡	Do	Robt. Delap Prot	aleseller	4							
	Do	Richd. Cuthbert Prot	Do	1		3					1
	Do	Edwd. Cook Prot	Carpenter								1
‡	Do	Darby Keeregan Prot	Maultster			1					
	Do	Pat. Tobin Prot	Labour.	1							
‡	Do	Francis Hawkins Prot	Cutler	1							
	Do	John Warren Prot	Weaver	5		1					1
	Do	Luke Kelly Prot	aleseller	1							
	Do	Cath. Slater Prot	Widw.		2						
	Do	Matt. Weston Prot	Cooper					1			
‡	Do	Thos. Bonsal Prot	Constable						1		1
	Total Families	40 Prot 26 Papt 30		32	18	15	5	10	10	2	23
[f.113] Roscomon	‡ Roscommon	Edwd. Murray Prot	Smith	2					1		1
	Do	Samuel Tailor Prot	Sadler			2		1			
‡	Do	Isaac Hopkins Prot	Gaoler			3			2		2
	Do	Mary Kelly Prot	Widow	1							
	Do	Nicolas Richards Prot	Wigmaker						2		
	Do	Simon Digby Prot	Revenue officer	3							1
	Do	Joseph Thames Prot	Butcher	1					1		1
	Do	Dan. Ganly Prot	Shoemaker	2		1					1
	Do	Bryan Kelly Prot	Farmer			3					1
	Do	Wm. Etheridge Prot	Shooemaker	1				1		1	
	Do	Edwyn Stonham Prot	Butcher	2				2	2	1	2
	Do	Chris. Studdart Prot	aleseller								1
	Do	Mary Pitts Prot	Widw.	1							
*	Do	Andw. Curly Prot	Shooemaker	2							
	Do	Harloe Phibbs Prot	Ale seller	2		1					
‡	Do	Robt Malone Prot	Do	1							2
	Do	Edwd Fitzgerald Pap	Tailor		2						
	Do	Keadog Gurmly Pap	Labourer		2						
	Do	Paul Greavy Pap	Do	0	2						
	Do	Michl. Kedian Pap	Labourer	0	1						
	Do	Wm. McDonagh Pap	Do	0	2						1
	Do	John. Dufferty Pap	Do								
	Do	Law. Walsh Pap	Carman						1		3
	Do	Thos. Longane Pap	Do		1				1		1
*	Do	Bryan Connor Pap	Do				1	1			
	Do	Pat. Cullane Pap	Labourer								1
	Do	Widw.r Barret Pap	Carpenter								
	Do	Hugh Hart Pap	Butchr.		2		1				
	Do	Jn. Kneelan Pap	Labourer		2						1
	Do	Hen. Komick Pap	Ale seller								
	Do	Geo. Brennan Pap	Carman		2						
	Do	Danl. Brennan Pap	Do		3						
	Do	Conr. Kelly Pap	Labourer		5		2				

Com~Roscommon Parish of	Place of Abode	Names and Religion	Proffession	Children under 14 Prot.	Paps.	Children above 14 Prot.	Paps.	Men Servts Prot.	Paps.	Women Servts Prot.	Paps.
	Do	Richd. Healy Pap	Do		1						
	Do	John Healy Pap	Do		1						
	Do	Fergus Farrall Pap	Do		2				1		
	Do	Mary Connor Pap	Widw.				1				
	Do	Pat. Kearegan Pap	Labourer		2						
	Do	Jane Bannan Pap	Widw.		1		1				
	Do	Jane Murray Pap	Widw.		2		1				
	Total Families	40 Prot 26 Pap 49		17	33	10	7	4	12	2	17
[f.114] Roscommon	Roscommon	Jn. Mulry Pap	Weaver		2						
	Do	Luke Conry Pap	Mason		2						
	Do	Richd. Neary Pap	Do		3						1
	Do	Danl. Fox Pap	Smith								2
	Do	Luke Gaffy Pap	Labour.		1		1				1
	Do	Ed. Conolly Pap	Do		1						
*	Do	Wm. Curly Pap	Do				1				1
	Do	Chas. Callery Pap	Do								1
*	Do	Richd. Keon Pap	Labour								
	Do	Dan. Murry Pap	Do		1						
	Do	Jas. McCaddan Pap	Do		2		1				2
	Do	Wm Crosby Pap	Brewer		3		1				
	Do	Wm Connane Pap	Labour.		3						1
	Do	Murt. McLaughlin Pap	Weaver		2				2		1
	Do	Murtgh. Crogan Pap	Weaver						4		3
	Do	Pat. Green Pap	Labour.		4						
	Do	Own. McDermot Pap	Butchr.		3						
	Do	Henry Donellan Pap	Labour.		3						
	Do	Farrall Gara Pap	Butchr.		1						1
	Do	Ed. McDermott Pap	Brewer		2						1
	Do	Anne Giraghty Pap	Widw.		2		1				
	Do	Hugh Connor Pap	Labour.		4						
	Do	Laugh. Croghan Pap	Labour.								
	Do	Wm. Feely Pap	Do		3						1
	Do	Ter. Connor Pap	Do								1
0	Do	Franc. Croghan Pap	Do		1		1				2
	Do	Mary Finnane Pap	Widw.		5		2				
	Do	Finn Finnane Pap	Labour.		2		1				
	Do	Pat. Keon Pap	Do		1						
	Do	Darby Croghan Pap	Weaver		1		3				
	Do	Ed. Kelly Pap	Labour.								
	Do	Jane Igoe Pap	Widw.		2		1				
	Do	Thos. Feely Pap	Labour		1		4				
	Do	Hugh Flanagan Pap	Do		3						
	Do	Jas. Dempsy Pap	Do		1						1
	Do	Ed. Keating Pap	Do		3			1			1
	Do	Hugh McNeal Pap	Do		2		1				
	Do	Conr. Navin Pap	Do		2		1				
*	Do	Bryan Curly Pap	Do				2				
	Do	Chars Teigne Pap	Do		1		1				
	Total Families	40 Prot Pap 74			66		22		7		21

Com~Ros common Parish of	Place of Abode	Names and Religion	Proffession	Children under 14 Prot.	Paps.	Children above 14 Prot.	Paps.	Men Servts Prot.	Paps.	Women Servts Prot.	Paps.
[f.115] Roscommon	Roscommon	Mary Gaynard Pap	Widw.		1						
	Do	Michl. Brenan Pap	Skinner		4						
	Do	Chars Keon Pap	Labour.								
	Do	Jas. Kearny Pap	Do		3			1			2
	Do	Connr Keon Pap	Do		1						1
	Do	Wm. Croghan Pap	Do		1		1				
	Do	Anne Slaney Pap	Widw.		2						
	Do	Pat. Dowd Pap	Skinner		3						1
	Do	Wm. Gavin Pap	Herd		3		1		1		
*	Do	Chas. Condy Pap	Mason		2		1				
	Do	Pat. Gallagher Pap	Labour.		2						
	Do	Mary Donnellan Pap	Widw.								
	Do	Ellin. Rourk Pap	Widw.								
	Do	Jas Galbraith Prot	Weaver	3							
	Do	Jas. Crofton[10] Prot	Builder	3							1
*	Do	Richd. Bonson Prot	Hawker	1							
	Do	Mich. Flaherty Prot	Weavr.	2							
	Do	Dennis Connor Pap	Labour.		3						
	Do	Mary Walsh Pap	Widw.				2				
	Do	Jas. Fox Pap	Labour.		2						
	Do	Darby Tonree Pap	Do		1		1				
	Do	Thady Coony Pap	Do		1						
	Do	Roger McDermott Pap	Do								
	Do	Wm. Killmartin Pap	Do								
	Do	Francs Moore Pap	Farmer		4						1
*	Do	Thady Igoe Pap	Sawyer				3				2
	Do	Mich. Keogh Pap	Wigmaker		3		1				
	Do	Jas. Millighan Pap	Labour		1						
	Do	Terence Hanly Pap	Do								
	Do	Pat. Gallagher Pap	Do		2						
	Do	Peter Hanly Pap	Taylor				2				
	Do	Michl. Dowlan Pap	Do								
	Do	Thos O'Donald Pap	Labour								
	Do	Danl. Guyan Pap	Do				1				
[erasure]	Do	Pat. Coony Pap	Do		2		2				
	Do	Thos. Hanly Pap	Do								
	Do	Andw. Finnaghty Pap	Do		1						
	Do	Wm. Tonree Pap	Do				2				
	Do	Thos. Joyce Pap	Do		2						
	Do	Jn. Coolan	Do		4						
	Total Families	40									
		Prot 7 Pap 66		9	47		17		2		8
[f.116] Roscommon	Roscommon	Dens. Killmartin Pap	Labour.		2						1
	Do	Cath. Lyons Pap	Widw.		1						
	Do	Lacky Kelly Pap	Carpenter						1		
	Do	Mat. Concannon Pap	Labourer								
	Do	Pat. Murry Pap	Do		1						
	Do	Hugh Kelly Pap	Wig-maker					1			

Com~Ros common Parish of	Place of Abode	Names and Religion	Proffession	Children under 14		Children above 14		Men Servts		Women Servts	
				Prot.	Paps.	Prot.	Paps.	Prot.	Paps.	Prot.	Paps.
	Do	Thady Murry Pap	Smith		3				1		4
	Do	Jn. Mullally Pap	Labour		1		2				
	Do	Jn. Hinde Pap	Aleseller								1
	Do	Mat. Cox Pap	Fidler		3		3				
	Do	Barw. Corryline Pap	Slater				3				
	Do	Frans. Connor Pap	Labour.								
	Do	Barw. Kelly Pap	Baker		1		2				
	Do	Mary Mogers Pap	Widw.		1		1				
	Do	Mary Murry Pap	Widw.				3				
	Do	Rose Gurmly Pap	Widw.				1				
	Do	Margt. Kelly Pap	Widw.								
	Do	Peter Kelly Pap	Smith		1						
	Do	Own. Greavy Pap	Labourer		1						
	Do	Jn. Hanly Pap	Tailor								1
	Do	Edwd. Ward Pap	Do	4	4						
	Do	Dom Clary Pap	Labour								1
	Do	Bryan Gorman Pap	Hawker						1		
	Do	Hugh Navin Pap	Broguemaker		3						1
	Do	Jn. Nealon Pap	Butchr.				1				2
	Do	Mat. Mullane Pap	Labourer				1				
	Do	Michl. Doolan Pap	Joyner		4				2		
	Do	Thos. Berne Pap	Labour.				2				
	Do	Phil. Bryan Pap	Weaver				3				1
	Do	Jn. Heavy Pap	Labour.				5				
	Do	Thos. Kilmurry Pap	Custom man[?]		3				2		1
	Do	Pat. Mullany Pap	Labour.		5		2				
	Do	Mary White Pap	Widw.								
	Do	Jas. Mullany Pap	Labour.		1		1				
	Do	Dens. Geraghty Pap	Labour.		2				1		1
	Do	Jane Kelly Pap	Widw.		1		1				
	Do	Hugh Brennan Pap	Broguemaker						1		
	Do	Dom. Brogan Pap	Thatcher				1				1
	Do	Mich. Kearny Pap	Labourer		2						2
	Do	Law. Brogan Pap	Weaver		4				3		1
	Total Families	40 Prot Pap 73.			44		32	1	12		18
[f.117] Roscommon	Roscommon	Anne Fox Pap	Widw.				1				
	Do	Jas. McCan Pap	Mason		1		1		2		1
	Do	Bryan Coyn Pap	Butchr.		2						
	Do	Bar. Kelly Pap	Labour.		2						
	Do	Mary Mulvihill Pap	Widw.		1		1				
	Do	Peter Duke Pap	Labour		2						
	Do	Peter Hanly Pap	Tailor		3				1		
	Do	Ter. Croghan Pap	Bailiff[11]		1		2				
	Do	Jn. Kearny Pap	Miller		4						
	Do	Michl. Flanegan Pap	Alesellr.								1
	Do	Owen Smith Pap	Butchr.		1		1				
	Do	Ed. Mullany Pap	Bailiff		2		1	1			

Com~Ros common Parish of	Place of Abode	Names and Religion	Proffession	Children under 14		Children above 14		Men Servts		Women Servts	
				Prot.	Paps.	Prot.	Paps.	Prot.	Paps.	Prot.	Paps.
	Do	David Stuart Pap	Turnkey		1		2				
*	Do	Franc. Mulvihill Pap	Tailor				1		2		1
	Do	[?] King Pap	Bailiff		3						1
	Do	Pat. Giraghty Pap	Aleseller			2					
	Do	Roger Farrell Pap	Apothecary			2					1
	Do	Dan. Maugher Pap	Weaver		1						1
	Do	Roger O'Connor[12] Pap	Shopkeeper		3		2		4	1	4
	Do	Michl. Murphy Pap	Ale seller		2						1
	Do	Darby Shaughnessy Do	Do				2				2
	Do	Anne Giraghty Pap	Widw.				1				1
*	Do	Willm. Higgins Pap	Apothecary				1				
	Do	Hugh Hanly[13] Pap	Distiller		4		1		5		3
	Do	- Blany Pap	Widw.		1		1				
	Do	Pat. Feigne Pap	Sadler		2			1			1
	Do	Michl. Lynch	Shopkeeper		1		1	1	2		4
	Do	Wm. Keenelly Pap	Shooemaker								
	Do	Mary Burk Pap	Widw.		2						
	Do	Owen Mullaly Pap	Butchr.		1						2
	Do	Darby Slaney Pap	Labour.		3						
	Do	Wind. Cooney Pap	Widw.		4						
	Do	Jon. Bardon Pap	Tobacconist	✝	1						
	Do	Ellnr. Croghan Pap	Widw.				1		1		1
	Do	Jas. Igoe Pap	Labour.								2
	Do	Wm. Giraghty Pap	Piper		3						1
	Do	Thos. Navin Pap	Broguemaker		2				1		1
	Do	Pat. Hurly Pap	Baker		2						2
	Do	Darby Slimon Pap	Clerk						1		1
	Do	Thos. Giraghty Pap	Labour.		1						1
Total Families		40 Prot – Pap 71		1	55		23	4	19	1	33
[f.118]	Roscommon	Anne Donian Pap	Widw.								
	Do	Bridgt. Flaherty Pap	Do				1				
	Do	Esmy Magara Pap	Do								
	Do	Elizth. McCabe Pap	Do								
	Do	Jane Cullane Pap	Do		2		2				
	Do	Honor Mulloy Pap	Do		✝		1				
	Do	Mary Mills Pap	Do				2				
	Do	Cath. Raghtooe Pap	Do		2						
	Do	Jas. Hanly Pap	Taylor		2						1
	Do	Thady Flaherty Pap	Weaver		3				1		
*	Do	Andw. Navin Pap	Gardiner						1		1
	Do	Thady McDermott Pap	Labourer				4				
	Do	Dan. Lennon Pap	Do		3						
	Do	Pat. McNamara Pap	Do				2				
	Do	Jno. McCabe Pap	Do				3				
‡	Killearny	Jonathan Robinson Prot	Farmer	10					2		2
	Do	Robt. Heanon Prot	Weaver	3					1		
	Do	Jas. Heanon Prot	Do	1							
	Do	Jn. Burk. Prot	Do			3		1			

Com~Ros common Parish of	Place of Abode	Names and Religion	Proffession	Children under 14		Children above 14		Men Servts		Women Servts	
				Prot.	Paps.	Prot.	Paps.	Prot.	Paps.	Prot.	Paps.
	Do	Jas. McDonald Prot	Do	2				2			
*	Do	Dens. Burne Pap	Labour.		2		1				
	Do	Pat. Lyhany Pap	Do		4						
	Do	Dens. Kelly Pap	Do								
	Do	Jon. Brennan Pap	Do		2						
	Do	Dens. Lyhany Pap	Do		4						
	Lisbride	Martin Cullane Pap	Shepherd		2		1		1		
	Do	Pat. Tully Pap	Labour		1						
	Creviquin	Laugh. Kilroy Pap	Do		3		1				1
	Do	Jn. Gannon Pap	Do		3						
	Do	Jas. Moran Pap	Do		5		1				
*	Acres	Own. McDermot Pap	Do		2		4				1
	Do	Thos. Tracy Pap	Horse rider		3						1
	Do	Anne Cusher Pap	Widw.				2				
	Ardsallagh	Jas. Gaffy Pap	Shepherd		2		2				2
	Carrowmore	Danl. Raghtikin Pap	Labourer		2						
	Do	Jn. Murphy Pap	Do		1						
	Do	Pat. Irwin Pap	Do		3						
	Do	Conr. Croghan Pap	Do		3						
	Do	Wm. Murphy Pap	Shepherd		1						
	Carrowroe	Michl. Bannan Pap	Labour.		3						1
	Families	70 Pr. 9 Pa. 60		16	58	3	27	3	5		9
[f.119] Roscommon	Carrowroe	Michl. Watts Pap	Villager		1						1
	Do	Miles. Hannon Pap	Do						1		2
	Do	Owen Hannon Pap	Do		4						1
	Do	Pat. Curly Pap	Do								
	Do	Wm. Horogho Pap	Do								
−	Do	Laugh Loose Pap	Do				3				
	Do	Bryan McDermot Pap	Do						1		2
	Do	Laugh. Curly Pap	Do				2				
	Do	Michl. Curly Pap	Do		1						
	Do	Edwd. Killeen Pap	Do		2		1				
	Do	Jn. Fox Pap	Do		2						
	Do	Edmd. Naughton Pap	Do		3						
	Do	Pat. Hannon Pap	Do		1						1
	Do	Peter Hannon Pap	Do								
	Do	Luke Curly Pap	Do		2						
	Do	Wm. Horogho Pap	Do								
	Do	Conr. McDermott Pap	Do		3		1				1
	Do	Frank Tully Pap	Do		5						
	Do	Darby Tully Pap	Do				2				
	Do	Thady Hannon Pap	Do		1				1		
	Do	Mary Watts Pap	Widw.		1				1		
	Do	Anne Hannon Pap	Do		1		2				
	Do	Michl. Hannan Pap	Broguemaker								
	Do	Laugh. Egan Pap	Pedlar		4						
	Do	Roger Noon Pap	Weaver		6						
	Do	Law. Curly Pap	Labour.		3						

Com~Ros common Parish of	Place of Abode	Names and Religion	Proffession	Children under 14 Prot.	Paps.	Children above 14 Prot.	Paps.	Men Servts Prot.	Paps.	Women Servts Prot.	Paps.
	Gallowstown	Chars. Finnane Pap	Villager		2		1		1		1
	Do	Pet. Corkran Pap	Do						1		1
	Do	Jn. Finnane Pap	Do		2						
	Do	Thos. Finnane Pap	Do		2						
	Do	Thady Killully Pap	Do		3				1		
	Do	Pat. Moran Pap	Do		2						
	Do	Domk. Dowd Pap	Do		3						
	Do	Dens. Lennan Pap	Do						3		1
	Do	Dens. Lyhany Pap	Do		3						
*	Do	Pat. Kilully Pap	Do				3				
	Do	Jn. McDermott Pap	Do		1		3				
	Do	Jn. Lyhany Pap	Do		3						
	Do	Michl. Lyhany Pap	Do		4						
	Do	Jas. Killmartin Pap	Do								
	Total Families	40									
		Prot. - Pap 77 -			65		18		10	~~10~~	11
[f.120] Roscommon	Gallowstown	Denis Lyon Pap	Smith		3						
	Do	Bridgt. Killmurry Pap	Widw.		1						
	Do	Pat. Oates Pap	Broguemaker		2				1		
	Do	Jams. Shrowan Pap	Skinnr.		2				1		
	Ballinvoher	Pat. Conway Pap	Farmer		3				1		1
	Do	Andw. Flin Pap	Herd		2				1		1
*	Do	Wm. Gowry Pap	Labour.				1				
	Do	Pat. Glin Pap	Do		3						
	Do	Jn. Correen Pap	Do		4						
	Do	Pat. McDonald Pap	Do		2						
	Ballindall	Chars. Rourk Pap	Shepherd		2		2				1
	Do	Owen Cavery Pap	Villager		2		1		1		
	Do	Michl. Lenaghan Pap	Do		2		2				1
	Do	Francs. Donnellan Pap	Herd		2		2				1
	Do	Jas. Murphy Pap	Shepherd				2				
	Do	Peter Kirwan Pap	Labour.		2				1		
	Do	Thos. Kirwan Pap	Do		1						
	Do	Michl. Murray Pap	Do				4				
	Do	Wm. Lenaghan Pap	Do				2				
	Do	Pat. Flanegan Pap	Do		3						
	Do	Danl. Horogho Pap	Do				1				
	Do	Murtogh Horogho Pap	Do		2						
	Amooe [?]	Wm. Mulloy Pap	Do		3		1				
	Do	Andw. Finegan Pap	Do						2		2
	Do	Laugh. Gilleran Pap	Do		1				1		2
	Do	Cormuck Gilleran Pap	Do		2		2				
	Do	Peter Gilleran Pap	Do		3						
	Do	Michl. Gilleran Pap	Do								
	Do	Michl. Finnegan Pap	Do								
	Do	Thos. Crosby Pap	Tailor		5		1		1		
	Do	Hugh Gilleran Pap	Smith		4				1		1
	Barts Cartron	Connor Rush Pap	Ale seller				1		1		1
	Coots Cartron	Cormuck Gowan Pap	Villager		2		1				

Com~Ros common Parish of	Place of Abode	Names and Religion	Proffession	Children under 14		Children above 14		Men Servts		Women Servts	
				Prot.	Paps.	Prot.	Paps.	Prot.	Paps.	Prot.	Paps.
	Do	Marcus Giblan Pap	Do								
	Do	Hugh McSharry Pap	Do		1						
	Do	Manus McSharry Pap	Do								
	Do	Michl. Grevy Pap	Do		1		1				
	Do	Luke Garvin Pap	Do				1				
	Do	Owen Farrell Pap	Do								
	Do	Darby Coony Pap	Smith		2						
	Total Families	40 Prot - Pap 78			62		25		12		11
[f.121] Roscommon * *	Coots Cartron	Owen McGlaw Pap	Villager								
	Do	Dennis Coony Pap	Lodger								
	Do	Ed. Coony Pap	Do								
	Derrycunny	John Mahon Pap	Do								1
	Do	Thady Hanly	Do		2						
	Do	Laugh. Murry Pap	Do		1		1				
	Do	Simon Navin Pap	Do				2				
	Do	Wm. Navin Pap	Do								
	Do	Pat. Garvin Pap	Do		2		1				
	Ballybride	Pat. Kirwan Pap	Shepherd		2		3				
	Do	Laugh. Naighton Pap	Cooper				2				
	Do	Thos. Hobay Pap	Labour.		2		3				
	Do	Andw. Kennedy Pap	Do		4						
	Do	Mat. Fleming Pap	Do				3				
	Do	Thos. Finnan Pap	Do				2				
	Do	Hugh Kennelly Pap	Do		3						
	Do	Peter Dermott Pap	Herd				5				
	Ardkeel	Darby Kennedy Pap	Shepherd				2		1		1
	Ballybohan	Wm. Murry Pap	Shepherd				2		1		1
	Do	Andw. Murry Pap	Do		1						
	Do	Comk. Keon Pap	Labour.		1		2				
	Do	Andw. Finnan Pap	Do		2		3				
‡	Do	Jn. Slater Prot.	Do		2						
	Total Families	23 Prot. 1 Pap 43			22		31		2		2

[verso f. 121]

A Return of the Inhabitants of the Parish of Roscommon in ye County of Roscommon & diocese of Elphin made to the Right Revd. The Lord Bishop - July 12th 1749

Families	Prot	72
	Pap:	471
	Total	548
Children under 14.	Prot,	79
	Pap,	672
		751
Children above 14 -	Prot	89
	Pap	192
		231
Men servants	Prot.	24
	Pap	134
		158
Women servants	Prot	8
	Pap	188
		196
Housekeepers	Prot	120
	Pap	884
		1104
Total of Inhabitants	Prot. -	270
	Pap -	2070
		2840

Jams. Blair, Vicar[14]. -

Note - they whose names are markd thus * have not wives & they whose names are markd thus ‡ are married to Papists.

NOTES

1. Lewis, 'Roscommon'.

2. *Report from Commissioners on Municipal Corporations in Ireland* HC 1835, xxvii, 415-6.

3. Lewis, 'Roscommon'.

4. *Report ... fairs and markets.*

5. A lease of Ardsalaugh, County Roscommon, granted by the Earl of Ranelagh in 1703 was assigned to Sir Edward Crofton on 13 June 1704 (N.L.I., Crofton Papers, MS 8828/8).

6. A customs official who measured casks and vessels containing liquids.

7. Paul Connell, Denis A. Cronin and Brian Ó Dálaigh (eds), *Irish Townlands*, (Dublin 1998) p.114, fn. 36.

8. Richard Bermingham was a commissioner for taking affidavits for the Four Courts in November 1745 (John Watson, *The Gentleman's and Citizens' Almanack* (Dublin 1748) (Hereafter cited as Watson, *Almanack*)).

9. A Richard Giraghty, merchant was in Roscommon town in the mid-seventeenth century (*Census of Ireland*).

10. John Crofton, a Roscommon ironmonger, was indicted for forging a will made by Sir Edward Crofton, which purported to leave estates to Sir Oliver Crofton. He appeared at the Roscommon assizes in 1746 represented by Sir Oliver Crofton who thus could not be called as a witness. John Crofton was found guilty and sentenced to transportation but the sentence was not carried out (See note 6 to Marcus Crofton of Mote, parish of Kilmeane; Crofton, *Memoirs*, p.114).

11. Bailiffs were responsible to sheriffs for serving warrants and collecting fines (Garnham, *Crime, the Courts*, p.96).

12. Roger O'Conor of Roscommon was a brother-in-law of Charles O'Conor of Belanagare. In 1748 he was a lay supporter of the Rev. William (alias Augustine) O'Kelly, prior of St Mary's, Roscommon to succeed Patrick French as bishop of Elphin (*Letters of Charles O'Conor*, p.29; Fenning, 'Diocese of Elphin', p.166)

13. Probably Hugh O'Hanly of Roscommon, also a lay supporter of the Rev. William O'Kelly in 1748 to succeed Patrick French as bishop of Elphin (Fenning, 'Diocese of Elphin', p.166).

14. James Blair (1707-1777) was born in Sligo and educated by his father. He was admitted to TCD in 1723 and graduated in 1727. He became vicar of Abbytown (part of Boyle) and prebendary of Kilgoghlin 1752-77 and vicar of Roscommon, Kilbride and Kilteevan 1742-77. He was one of the witnesses of Edward Synge's will in 1761 (Leslie, 'Elphin', p. 201).

KILTEEVAN, COUNTY ROSCOMMON

INTRODUCTION: *The parish of Kilteevan is in the barony of Ballintobber and is 2 miles south-east of Roscommon. The river Shannon and Lough Ree form its eastern boundary. It covers 8,411 statute acres.*[1] *Lewis says that there was a 'great deal' of bog.*[2] *The incumbent was the Rev. James Blair, who signed the return (see Roscommon) The patron was the bishop.*

OCCUPATIONS

Ale seller	1	Glover	1	Servants, household	64
Broguemaker	1	Hawker	1	Smith	3
Carpenter	1	Herd	1	Tailor	2
Constable	1	Labourer	25	Turner	1
Cooper	1	Lodger	2	Villager	38
Cottier	38	Mason	1	Weaver	5
Farmer	1	Miller	2	Widow	15
Gentleman	1	Potter	2	Woodranger	1

Com~Ros common Parish of	Place of Abode	Names and Religion	Proffession	Children under 14 Prot.	Children under 14 Paps.	Children above 14 Prot.	Children above 14 Paps.	Men Servts Prot.	Men Servts Paps.	Women Servts Prot.	Women Servts Paps.
[f. 22] Kilteevan	Cloonkeen	Jn Compton Pap	Herd		1				1		1
	Do	Pat. Geary Pap	Cotter		2		2				
	Do	Conr. Glavy Pap	Do		3						
	Do	Andw. Quin Pap	Do				1				
	Do	Paul Grinnan Pap	Do		2		2				
	Do	Michl. Geoghegan Pap	Do		1						
*	Do	Ed. Moony Pap	Do				3				
	Do	Bridgt. Brennan Pap	Widw.		2						
	Do	Mary Delamare Pap	Do								
	Do	Thos. Delamare Pap	Cotter		2						
	Do	Luke Killmartin Pap	Do		2						
	Do	Barthw. Killmartin Pap	Do		3						1
	Do	Pat. Feeny Pap	Do				1				
	Do	Matt. Rigby Pap	Do				3				
	Do	Thos Gibbons Pap	Do				1				
	Do	Thos. Finnane Pap	Do								
	Do	Robt. Hanly Pap	Do		1						
	Do	Laugh. Brennan Pap	Do				2				
	Anaghmona	Ed. Gowran Pap	Do		2		1				
	Do	Bryan Nolan Pap	Do		2						
	Do	Peter Hanly Pap	Do								
	Cloonmurly	Bry. Mulkeran Pap	Villager		~~2~~	~~2~~	2				
	Do	Jn. Hanly Pap	Do		2						
	Do	Bry. Kelly Pap	Do								
	Do	Laugh. More Pap	Do								
	Cloontimullan	Jas. Ward Do			1		4				
*	Do	Ferd. Gorrick Pap	Taylor				2				
	Do	Jn. Birt Pap	Villager				2				
*	Do	Wm. Birt Pap	Lodger								
*	Do	Wm. Fox Pap	Villager				4				
	Do	Bridget Wade Pap	Widw.				4				
	Do	Law. Finneran Pap	Miller				4				
	Do	Jn. Mooney Pap	Villager		2		2				
	Do	Bridgt. Bannan Pap	Widw.		1		1				
	Do	Thady Flin Pap	Villager								
*	Derrimacarbry	Michl. Hanly Pap	Do								1
	Do	Jn. Hanly Pap	Do		2						
	Do	Hugh Flin Pap	Do				3				
	Do	Nichs. Pettit Pap	Do								
	Do	Nichs. Pettit Pap	Do								1
	Families 40	Prot – Pap 72			31		44		1		4
[f.123] Kilteevan	Derrimacarbry[3]	Margt. White Pap	Widw.				2				
*	Do	Chris. Killen Pap	Weaver				3				
	Derrinturk	Hu. McGuire Pap	Villager				2				
*	Do	Thos. McGuire Pap	Do				2				
	Do	Hu. McGuire Pap	Do		1						
	Do	Ed. Hanly Pap	Do		1		2				
	Do	Frans. Hanly Pap	Do								

Com~Ros common Parish of	Place of Abode	Names and Religion	Proffession	Children under 14 Prot.	Children under 14 Paps.	Children above 14 Prot.	Children above 14 Paps.	Men Servts Prot.	Men Servts Paps.	Women Servts Prot.	Women Servts Paps.
	Do	Ed. Pettit Pap	Do		1						
	Ballinaboy	Ed. McGarry Pap	Hawker						1		2
	Do	Owen. McSweeny Pap	Villager		1		1				
	Do	Bryan Barran Pap	Do				1				
	Do	Pat. Noon Pap	Do		2						
	Do	Frans. Dolan Pap	Do		1		2				
	Aghadrishan	Thos. Kane Pap	Smith		1						
	Do	Thos. McGuire Pap	Villager		8						
	Do	Jn. Hanly Pap	Do		1						
	Do	Frans. Spallan Pap	Do		2		1				
	Do	Jn. Spallan Pap	Do								
*	Do	Danl. Hanly Pap	Do								1
	Do	Jn. Haly Pap	Do								
	Do	Jn. Tinsey Pap	Do		1		1				
	Do	Ed. Wheelan Pap	Do		3						
	Do	Law. Finneran Pap	Do		1						
	Do	Danl. Haly Pap	Do				1				
	Do	Pat. Haly Pap	Do								
	Do	Frans. Spallan Pap	Do								
	Do	Wm. Hanly Pap	Do		2						
	Do	Pat. Finneran Pap	Do								
	Do	Denny Brady Pap	Cotter		1		1				
	Do	Thos. Flin pap	Do		1		1				
	Killenboy	Thady Giblan Pap	Do				1				
	Do	Pat. Giblan Pap	Do				1				
	Do	Wm. Giblan Pap	Do								
	Do	Roger Carroll Pap	Do								
	Do	Owen Brennan Pap	Do				3				
	Do	Peter Garraghan Pap	Do								
	Do	Jn. Mulvikill Pap	Do				2				
‡	Kilteam	Ed. Mapother[4] Prot	Gent						2		3
	Do	Jn. Murray Pap	Cotter		3						
	Do	Roger Spallan Pap	Do		2		2				1
	Families 40	Prot 1 – Pap 75			33		28		3		7

[f. 123 and f. 124 bound in upside down]

[f.124] Kilteevan	Newtown	Jas. Burne Prot	Farmer	3					1	1	2
		John Nevill Prot	Weaver						1		1
*		Wm. Nevill Prot	Weaver								
		Roger Fallon Pap	Labour.		3		1				
*		Thos Farrel Pap	Do				1				
		Wm. Cunnane Pap	Do		1						
		Gilbt. Connaughton Pap	Do		1		1				
		Tim. Flin Pap	Do						1		
		Thady Gurrich Pap	Do		2		2				
		Cath. Smith Pap	Widw.				2				
		Jn. McGaw Prot	Weaver	5							
*		M. Cane Pap	Smith				3				
		Pat. Cane Pap	Do		2						
		Jn. Brandon Pap	Potter				2		1		1

Com~Ros common Parish of	Place of Abode	Names and Religion	Proffession	Children under 14 Prot.	Children under 14 Paps.	Children above 14 Prot.	Children above 14 Paps.	Men Servts Prot.	Men Servts Paps.	Women Servts Prot.	Women Servts Paps.
		Mat. Murray Pap	Do		3						
		Jas. Russel Pap	Ale seller		1		4				
		Terence Casey Pap	Glover		3		3				
	Cloncraff	Law. Brennan Pap	Labourer		3		2				1
		Owen Brennan Pap	Do		3		3				1
		Luke Brennan Pap	Do				2				
		Luke Brennan Pap	Do		1				3		1
		Peter Golrick Pap	Do				2		1		
		Jas.Fox Pap	Do				1		1		1
		Michl. Murphy Pap	Do		3						
*		Barthw. Brennan Pap	Weaver						3		1
		Mary Brennan Pap	Widw.		2				1		
	Cloncagh	Francs. Killeen Pap	Woodranger			3			1		2
		Ed. Killroe Pap	Turner						1		
		Mat. Weston Prot	Cooper					1			
	Cloonsellan	Hugh Finneran Pap	Miller		1				1		1
		Pat. Egan Pap	Carpenter		3		1				
		Jn. Egan Pap	Labourer		1						
		Owen Murray Pap	Do		1						
		Hugh Cox Pap	Do		2		1				
		Luke Scanlan Pap	Do		2						1
		Wm. Horogho Pap	Do		4						
*		Andw. Killcline Pap	Do		1		2		1		
		Mat. Lough Pap	Do		1						
		Jas. Mullane Pap	Do		2						
		Martin Lough Pap	Do								
Total Families 40		Prot 9 Pap 64		3	54		33	1	17	1	13
[f.125] Kilteevan	Cloonsellan	Michl. Mullane Pap	Lab .								
	Do	Jn. Killcline Pap	Do		1						
	Do	Dens. Gorrick Pap	Broguemaker		3						
	Do	Cicely Hanly Pap	Widw.				1				
	Do	Mary Fox. Pap	Widw.		3		1				
	Do	Mary Killcline Pap	Widw.		1		1				
	Do	Jn. Mullane Pap	Tailor		4						
	Do	Jas. Gowane Pap	Labourer		3		2				
	Kilteevan	Jas Farrell Pap	Cotter		1		1				
	Do	Owen Gannon Pap	Do		3		1				
*	Do	Pat. Mallan Pap	Do						2		1
*	Do	Bryan Hanly Pap	Do						1		2
*	Do	Martin Connor Pap	Do		1				1		2
	Do	Bridgt. Brennan Pap	Do		3						
*	Do	Luke White Pap	Do		2						1
	Do	Matt Pettit pap	do		3				1		1
	Do	Robert Pettit Pap	Do		3						
	Do	Wm. Tracy Pap	Do		2		3				
	Do	Wm. Craige Prot	Mason	1					3		
	Do	Brid. Brennan Pap	Widw.		3						
	Do	Brid. Egan Pap	Widw.				1				
	Do	Cath. Egan Pap	Lodger								

Com~Ros common Parish of	Place of Abode	Names and Religion	Proffession	Children under 14		Children above 14		Men Servts		Women Servts	
				Prot.	Paps.	Prot.	Paps.	Prot.	Paps.	Prot.	Paps.
	Do	Wm. Harraghan Pap	Constable		2		1				1
	Do	Margt. Regan Pap	Widw.		1		1				1
	Cloonmore	Jane Killin Pap	Widw.		3						
Ø	Do	Cath. McDermott Pap	Widw.		2						
		Total Families 26 Prot: 1 Pap 49		1	44		13		8		9

[verso f. 125]

A Return of the Inhabitants of the Parish of Kilteevan County of Roscommon & diocese of Elphin made to the Right Revd. yͤ Lord bishop July 12ᵗʰ 1749

Families	Prot -	7
	Pap -	139
		146
Housekeepers	Prot	11
	Pap:	251
		262
Children under 14,	Prot.	4
	Pap.	182
		186
Children above 14,	Prot	
	Pap	118
Men servants -	Prot	1
	Pap	29
		30
Women servants,	Prot	-
	Pap	33
		33
Total of Protestants		16
of Papists -		613
Total of Inhabitants		629

Jams Blair: Vicar -

Note, They whose names are markd thus * have not wives -
They whose names are markd thus Ø are women who keep Houses; whose Husbands are domestick Servts to Gentlemen.

NOTES

1. Less 959 acres of Lough Ree (*General Alphabetical Index*).

2. Lewis, 'Kilteevan'.

3. A Mahon property (N.L.I., Pakenham Mahon Papers, MS 3119).

4. A Thomas Mapother Esq and Richard Mapother gentleman, both Roman Catholics, were living at Kiltivuan in the mid-seventeenth century (*Census of Ireland*).

KILBRIDE, COUNTY ROSCOMMON

INTRODUCTION: *The parish of Kilbride is in the baronies of Roscommon and South Ballintober. It is 5 miles north of the town of Roscommon on the road to Strokestown. It covers 11,812 statute acres, but there was a large amount of bog In 1837 much of the land was under tillage.[1] There was a great deal of limestone. Four townlands were owned by the Hanley/Hanly family in 1641.[2] In 1749, fourteen Roman Catholic members of that family still remained in the parish.[3]*

The parish of Kilbride was held with those of Roscommon and Kilteevan. The incumbent in 1749 was the Rev. James Blair who signed the return (see Roscommon). The patron was the bishop.

OCCUPATIONS

Ale seller	1	Joiner	1	Servants, household	362
Broguemaker	4	Labourer	40	Shepherd	4
Cooper	4	Lodger	8	Shoemaker	1
Cottier	141	Mason	4	Smith	4
Esquire	2	Miller	7	Steward	1
Farmer	9	Pedlar	1	Tailor	3
Farrier	1	Piper	1	Villager	122
Gardener	1	Plasterer	1	Weaver	5
Gentleman	2	Ploughman	3	Widow	16
Groom	1	Saltmonger	1	Wool spinner	1
Herd	9	Servant	1		

Com~Ros common Parish of	Place of Abode	Names and Religion	Proffession	Children under 14		Children above 14		Men Servts		Women Servts	
				Prot.	Paps.	Prot.	Paps.	Prot.	Paps.	Prot.	Paps.
[f.126] Kilbride	Darham[4]	Edwyn Sandys Reynolds Prot.	Gent.	1		5		2	1	3	1
	Do	Paul Horogho Pap	Lab.		3		1				1
	Do	Richd. Connor Pap	Do			3					3
*	Do	Jn. Curly Pap:	Do		3		1				4
	Do	Jn. Curly Pap	Do						1		1
	Do	Roger Ganyard Pap	Do								
	Do	Michl. Graham Pap	Do		2						2
	Do	Henry Devany Pap	Farrier		1						1
	Do	Thos. Reynolds Pap	Joiner						2		1
	Do	Martin Hurly Pap	Mason		3				1		1
	Do	Jn. Kelly Pap	Do								
	Do	Bryan Tonaree Pap	Broguemaker		1						1
	Do	Martin Connaughton Pap	Piper								
	Do	Phelim Dolan Pap	Shepherd		2				1		1
*	Do	Wm. Ganyard Pap	Groom		4						4
	Do	Thady Hadiran Pap	Lab.				2				2
	Do	Hugh McSweeny Pap	Do				1				1
	Do	Michl. Lowry Pap	Do		3						3
	Do	Jn. Bryan Pap	Do		2						2
	Do	Pat. Green Pap	Do		4						4
	Do	Anne Hopkins Pap	Widw.		3						3
	Cloonara	Dennis Keogh Pap	Miller		3						3
*	Do	Morris Spallan Pap	Villager		2		2		1		1
	Do	Dom. Murray Pap	Do				1				1
	Do	Jn. Caffrey Pap	Do		3				1		1
	Do	Dens. Feeny Pap	Do	2	1			1			4
	Do	Jas. Feeny Pap	Do		2		1		1		1
	Do	Roger Teigue Pap	Do				1				1
	Do	Luke Feeny Pap	Do		2				2		4
	Do	Pat. Dowd Pap	Do		2				1		3
	Do	Frans. Hanly Pap	Do		3		1				1
	Do	Peter Dillon Pap	Do		2				1		3
*	Do	Chas. Kehum Pap	Do		2		3				5
	Do	Jn. Dillon Pap	Do		2				1		3
	Do	Law. Murry Pap	Do		1				1		1
	Cloonera	Owen Redian Pap	Villager		2						2
	Do	Hugh Burne Pap	Do		2		1				1
	Sallymount[5]	Dens. Sheean Pap	Do		1				1		2
	Do	Wm. Flin Pap	Do		2						1
	Do	Martin Burne Pap	Do		2				1		1
	Total Families 40 Prot 2 Paps 64			1	68	5	16	2	17	3	18
Kilbride [f.127]	Sallymount	Owen Redian Pap	Villager		3		1		1		1
	Do	Roger Flin Pap	Do		1				1		1
	Do	Thady Feeny Pap	Do		2						1
	Do	Gilbert Cain Pap	Do		3				1		
	Do	Frans. Lennon Pap	Do		2		1				1
	Do	Bryan Kilday Pap	Do		4		1		1		
	Do	Wm. Loughlin Pap	Do		2						1

Com~Ros common Parish of	Place of Abode	Names and Religion	Proffession	Children under 14 Prot.	Children under 14 Paps.	Children above 14 Prot.	Children above 14 Paps.	Men Servts Prot.	Men Servts Paps.	Women Servts Prot.	Women Servts Paps.
	Do	Thos. Kerry Pap	Do		2		1		1		
	Do	Jn. Conry Pap	Do		3						
	Do	Peter Tody Pap	Do		1		1		1		1
	Do	Ed. Farrell Pap	Do		2						1
	Do	Danl. Dun Pap	Do		3				1		
	Do	Margt. Feely Pap	Widw.		1				1		1
	Hollywell[6]	Barnaby Gunning[7] Prot	Esqr.		4		1	7	2	2	3
	Do	Pat. Connolly Pap	Mason		3						1
	Do	Hugh Connaughton Pap	Cotter		1						
	Do	Roger Feely Pap	Do								
*	Do	Pat. Judge Pap	Lodger								
	Do	Luke McLaughlin Pap	Labourer		1		1				
	Do	Bryan Clary Pap	Do								
	Do	Dens. Kearny Pap	Do		2						
	Do	Dens. Killmartin Pap	Do		1		3				
	Do	Jas. Kevin Pap	Do		1		1				
*	Do	Mur. Mannin Pap	Plowman								
	Do	Jn. Carthy Pap	Labourer		1				1		
	Do	Mat. Mullane Pap	Do		3						
	Do	Jn. Hanly Pap	Do		2						1
	Do	Robt. Raghtikin Pap	Do		3		1				
	Do	Mary Glin Pap	Widw.								
*	Do	Thady Kilmartin Pap	Cotter								2
*	Do	Owen Ternan Pap	Do								1
*	Do	Bryan Ternan Pap	Do								2
	Do	Wm. Lennon Pap	Do		3						
	Do	Roger Dermott Pap	Do		4		2				
	Do	Richd. Hedian Pap	Smith		3		2				
	Newtown	Thos. Raghtikin Pap	Villager								
	Do	Pat. Raghtikin Pap	Do		2		1				
	Do	D. Raghtikin Pap	Do		2				1		1
	Do	Richd. Kenny Pap	Do				2				1
	Do	Mat. Reynolds Pap	Weaver		3				4		
	Total Families 40	Pro 2 Pap 63		4	64	1	18	7	16	2	20
[f.128] Kilbride	Newtown	Owen Connaughton Pap	Villager		1		1		1		1
	Do	Wm. Rock Pap	Do		1						
	Do	Pet. Murphy Pap	Do				1				1
	Do	Rogr. Giraghty Pap	Do		1						
	Do	Charls. Durnan Pap	Do		1				1		1
*	Do	Pat Durnan Pap	Saltmonger								
	Do	Jn. Kelly Pap	Cotter		1				1		1
*	Do	Pat. Boyle Pap	Do								
	Do	Owen O'Neil Pap	Do		1						
	Do	Garret Hanly Pap	Do								
	Do	Hugh Horoho	Do				2		1		
	Do	Jn Kenny pap	Do		2						
	Do	Wm Coggin Pap	Cotter		2						
	Do	Andrew Desmond Pap	Do		1						
	Do	Andw. McDermott Pap	Villager		1				1		

Com~Ros common Parish of	Place of Abode	Names and Religion	Proffession	Children under 14 Prot.	Paps.	Children above 14 Prot.	Paps.	Men Servts Prot.	Paps.	Women Servts Prot.	Paps.
	Do	Pat. Poor Pap	Cotter		2				1		
	Do	Felim Allan Pap	Do								
	Do	Jas. Carly Pap	Do								
	Do	Jas. Dempsy Pap	Do		1						
*	Do	Jas. Hanly Pap	Do		2		3				
	Do	Red. Lynagh Pap	Do		1				1		1
	Do	Jn. Nugent Pap	Do		2		1				
	Do	Wm Dwyer Pap	Do								1
	Do	Alexr. Parker Pap	Do		3						
*	Do	Wm. Wheelan Pap	Do			2					
	Do	Jn. Wheelan Pap	Do								
	Do	Thos. Kelly Pap	Do		1						
	Do	Michl. Dwyer Pap	Cooper				1				
*	Do	Pat. Parker Pap	Plowman								
	Do	Ed. Cavicher Pap	Pedlar		2						
	Do	Jn. Conolly Pap	Tailor		3						
Ø Servants	Hollywell	Eliz.McDonnell Prot	Servant	3	3				1		1
	Do	Anne Sandford Prot	Lodger								
Ø	Do	Cicely Lennan Pap			2				1		
Ø	Do	Anne Farrell Pap					3				
Ø	Do	Elinor Nixon Prot					4				
	Do	Pat. Burke Pap	Miller		3						
	Do	Pat. Griffin Pap	Smith		2		1				
	Do	Darby Moran Pap	Wool spinner		3						
	Do	Thady Kelly Pap	Weaver		2		2		2		
Total Families 40		Prot 3 Paps 69		3	49[?]		21		11		6
[f.129] Kilbride	Hollywell	Ge.Hutchinson Prot	Plasterer	3							2
	Do	Anne Dogherty Pap	Widw.								
	Do	Geo Croghan. Pap	Villager		1		2		1		1
*	Do	Ge. Armstrong Prot	Do		2						
	Do	Rogr Farrell Pap	Labour		1						
	Do	Jn. Conry Pap	Do				2				
	Do	Jn. Farrell Pap	Do		3						
	Do	Bryan Kelly Pap	Do		3						
	Do	Pet. Kelly Pap	Do		3		2				1
*	Rocksboro'	James Irwin[8] Prot	Esqr.	4	4—			1	5	1	6
	Do	Cath. Hodson Prot	Widw.								
	Do	Jn. Timons Prot	Steward		6						
*	Do	Jas. Downes Prot	Shepherd								2
	Do	Frans. Downes Pap	Cotter		3						
	Do	Br. McManus Pap	Do		3				2		
	Do	Jas. Hicky Pap	Do		1						
	Do	Ed. Hicky Pap	Do		1						
	Do	Owen Keran Pap	Do		3						
	Do	Pat. Dolan Pap	Do		2						
	Do	Jn. Moran Pap	Do		1				1		1
	Do	Michl. Ford Pap	Do		1						1
	Do	Hugh Farrell Pap	Do				1				
	Do	Jn. Cooney Pap	Do		3						

Com~Ros common Parish of	Place of Abode	Names and Religion	Proffession	Children under 14		Children above 14		Men Servts		Women Servts	
				Prot.	Paps.	Prot.	Paps.	Prot.	Paps.	Prot.	Paps.
*	Do	Jn. Taaffe Pap	Do						1		2
	Do	Miles Murphy Pap	Do		2						
	Do	Thos. Farrell Pap	Do		5		1				
	Do	Peter Brehony Pap	Do		1						1
	Do	Corl Farrell Pap	Do		3						1
	Do	Jas Lions Pap	Do		2		2				
	Do	Mary Sharry Pap	Widw.		2						
	Do	Thos Hicky Pap	Labour.		3		1				
	Tully	Hugh Maddin[9] Prot	Gent.		4				2		2
	Do	Pat. Hanoe Pap	Herd		3						
	Do	Ed. Reynolds Pap	Cotter		4						
	Do	Pat. Egan Pap	Do		2		1				
	Do	Luke Gorrig Pap	Do		1						
	Carroward	Jn. Connellan Pap	Herd		1		2				
	Do	Jn. Lally Pap	Cotter		4						
	Do	Darby Murphy Pap	Do		4						
	Do	Mat. Hicky Pap	Do		3		2				
	Total Families 40	Prot 10 Pap 62		7	85[?]		16	1	12	1	20
	[f.130] Kilbride Drumduff	Charls. Croghan Pap	Farmer						2		4
	Do	Hen. Mapother Pap	Lodger		1						
	Do	Jn. Irwin Prot	Do						1		
	Do	Anne Mapother Pap	Do								
	Do	Roger Hanly Pap	Villager		1				1		1
	Do	Rose Piper Pap	Widw.		2						
	Do	Bryan Fleming Pap	Cotter		1						
	Do	Jas. Irwin Pap	Do		1						
	Do	Thos. Nelson Pap	Do		2						
*	Do	Gregory Muldoon Prot	Do	1		2					
	Do	Thos More Pap	Lodger		4						
*	Do	Pat. Croghan Prot	Villager	4							1
	Do	Henry Gibbons Pap	Cotter		2						1
	Do	Hugh Garvin Pap	Cotter		2		1				1
*	Do	Pat. Conolly Pap	Do				2				
	Do	Darby McGarry Pap	Do		2						
	Do	Jn. Igoe Pap	Do		2						
*	Do	Richd.Jones Pap	Lodger				1				
	Do	Peter Quin Pap	Cotter		2				1		1
	Do	Hugh Mcdanill Pap	Do								
	Do	Paul Flanegan Pap	Do		3						
	Do	Peter Murry Pap	Smith		2						1
	Do	Bryan Connor Pap	Weavr.		1						
	Cloonerk[10]	Thady Murray Pap	Herd		4				1		1
	Do	Hugh Dolan Pap	Cotter		2						
*	Do	Roger Connor Pap	Do		1		3				
	Do	Thos. Higgins Pap	Do		1		3				
	Do	Charls Raghtikin Pap	Do		2						
	Do	Bridgt Connor Pap	Widw.		1						
	Rathconnor	Owen Shiel Pap	Herd		5		3				
	Do	Woodhouse Mapother Pap	Cotter		1						1

Com~Ros common Parish of	Place of Abode	Names and Religion	Proffession	Children under 14		Children above 14		Men Servts		Women Servts	
				Prot.	Paps.	Prot.	Paps.	Prot.	Paps.	Prot.	Paps.
	Do	Jn. Irwin Pap	Do 2								
	Do	Barry Quin Pap	Do		1				1		
	Do	Ed. Kenry Pap	Do				1				1
	Do	Ferdinando Gravy Pap	Do		2		1				
	Do	Darby Cane Pap	Do		2						
	Do	Laugh. Murray Pap	Broguemaker		2						1
	Do	Pat. Groom Pap	Tailor		1						
	Do	Jn. Dolan Pap	Cotter		1						
	Do	Wm Quin Pap	Do								
Total Families 40		Prot 5 Paps 69		5	56		14		7		14
[f.131] * Kilbride	Tonregee	Luke Croghan Prot	Farmer	1		4			4		3
	Do	Hugh Dolan Pap	Cotter		1		1				
	Do	Jas. Dockrey Pap	Do		2		2				
	Do	Pet. Fannon Pap	Do		3		1				
	Do	Jn. Connor Pap	Do				1				
	Do	Roger Connor Pap	Do		1		1				
	Do	Danl. Moran Pap	Do		2						
	Do	Roger Killmartin Pap	Do		2						
	Do	Darby Noon Pap	Do				1				
	Do	Bryan Noon Pap	Do		3		1				1
	Do	Owen Feely Pap	Do		2		1				1
	Do	Roger Egan Pap	Do				1				
	Do	Michl. Duffey Pap	Do		2						
	Do	Thos. Dillon Pap	Do		1						
	Do	Jas. Killully Pap	Do		5		1		1		
	Do	Wm. Connolly Pap	Do		4		1				
	Do	Hugh Keogh Pap	Do		1		2				1
	Do	Frans. Kervan Pap	Do				1				
	Do	Patt. Cunnane Pap	Do		1		1				
*	Do	Wm. Navin Pap	Do		1		2				
*	Do	Connor Tully Pap	Do		1		2				
	Cloghbrack	Michl. Teigue Pap	Villager		3		1				2
	Do	Bryan Dolan Pap	Do				1		2		2
	Do	Pat. Kelly Pap	Do		2						
	Do	Wm. Groon Pap	Do		2						
	Do	Wm. Hubbon Pap	Do				2				
	Do	Peter Murray Pap	Do								
*	Do	Jn. Kelly Pap	Do		2		3				
	Do	Terence Finnane Pap	Do		2		1				
	Do	Bartholw. Early Pap	Do		2						1
	Do	Luke Quin Pap	Do				1				
	Do	Danl. Murray Pap	Do								
	Do	Chars. Feeny Pap	Do		1						
	Do	Andw. Collins Pap	Do		1						
	Do	George Grevy Pap	Do		2		2				
	Do	Wm. Carroll Pap	Do		3		1				
	Do	Jas. Fallon Pap	Do		2						
	Cogill	Peter Redian Pap	Herd		2						1
	Do	Jas. Redian Pap	Cotter		2						

Com~Ros common Parish of	Place of Abode	Names and Religion	Proffession	Children under 14 Prot.	Children under 14 Paps.	Children above 14 Prot.	Children above 14 Paps.	Men Servts Prot.	Men Servts Paps.	Women Servts Prot.	Women Servts Paps.
	Do	Andw. Cunnane Pap	Do		3						1
	Total Families 40	Prot.. Pap 77		1	61	4	32		7		13
Kilbride [f.132]	Mullymucks	Ed. Dolan Pap	Cotter				3				
	Do	Ed. Kelly Pap	Do		2				1		
	Do	Pat. Mountain Pap	Do		3						
	Do	Hugh Conlan Pap	Do								
	Do	Owen Conlan Pap	Do								1
	Do	Ed. Fannane Pap	Do		3						1
	Do	Ed. Connaughton Pap	Do		1						
	Do	Roger Doyle Pap	Do		5						
	Do	Danl. Kenian Pap	Do		4						
*	Do	Thady Croghan Pap	Do		1		2				
	Do	Morrice Croghan Pap	Do								
	Do	Thos. Connolly Pap	Do		1						
	Do	Thady Murray Pap	Do		2						
	Do	Richard Navin Pap	Do		2						
	Do	Owen McManus Pap	Do		3						
	Do	Law. Killully Pap	Do		1						
	Do	Richd. Pendergast Pap	Do		2		1				
*	Do	Danl. Manus Pap	Do				4				
	Do	Martin Cooge Pap	Do								1
	Do	Chars. Hallam Pap	Do				1				
	Do	Pat. Atkinson Pap	Do				2				
	Do	Andw. Judge Pap	Do								
	Do	Thady Martin Pap	Do		1						
	Do	Thady Curly Pap	Do		1						
	Do	Owen Martin Pap	Do		2						
	Do	Conr. Gireghty Pap	Herd		1				1		1
	Do	Pat. Hewston Pap	Tailor		1		1				
	Do	Jas. Rash Pap	Shepherd				1				
	Do	Henry Fallon Pap	Weavr								
‡	Lisgobban	Jas. Nevil Prot	Farmer	4					2		3
	Do	Wm. O'Brien Pap	Shooemaker		1						1
*	Do	Darby Farrell Pap	Smith				3				
	Do	Terence Connor Pap	Miller		6		1		1		
	Do	Darby Finigan Pap	Do		2						1
	Do	Thos. Wheelan Pap	Do		1						
	Do	Luke Hanly Pap	Do		2						
	Do	Jas. Cavany Pap	Do						1		2
	Do	Peter Oats Pap	Villager								1
	Do	Pat. Oats Pap	Do		3		3				
	Do	Jas. Kelly	Do		2						1
	Total Families 40	Prot 1 Paps 76		4	53		22		6		12
Kilbride [f.133]	Lisgobban	Hugh Kelly Pap	Cotter		1						1
	Do	Brian McDermott Pap	Do				2				1
*	Do	Jn. Fox Pap	Do				3				
	Do	Owen Fallon Pap	Do								1
	Do	Ed. Killmartin Pap	Do		1						

Com~Ros common Parish of	Place of Abode	Names and Religion	Proffession	Children under 14		Children above 14		Men Servts		Women Servts	
				Prot.	Paps.	Prot.	Paps.	Prot.	Paps.	Prot.	Paps.
	Do	Ed. Bourk Pap	Do		4						1
	Derrycumsy	Luke Nevil Pap	Farmer		1		1		1		2
	Do	Mary Connor Pap	Widw.				1				
	Do	Mary Moran Pap	Do				3				
	Do	Barthw. Kevan Pap	Villager		2				1		1
	Do	Laugh. Hanly Pap	Do				1		1		1
	Do	Luke Grevy Pap	Cotter		1		2				
	Carrowirin[11]	Luke Betegh Pap	Farmer		1		3		1		
	Do	Michl. Kilmartin Pap	Cotter						1		
	Do	Jn. Hanly Pap	Do		2						
	Do	Bryan Staunton Pap	Do		1						
	Do	Gerald McDermott Roe Pap	Do		1				1		1
	Do	Ed. Farrell Pap	Do								1
*	Do	Jas. Nolan Pap	Do		1		3				
	Do	Marcus More Pap	Do				1				
	Do	Thady Morris Pap	Do								
	Corboe[12]	Thos. Killsey Pap	Villager		3						
	Do	Michl. Sweeny Pap	Do		2						
	Do	Pat. Sweeny Pap	Do		3						
	Do	Miles Burne Pap	Do		2						
	Do	Terence McLaughlin Pap	Do			2					
	Do	Jn. Ruddy Pap	Do		1						
	Do	Thady Hanly Pap	Do		3						
	Do	Roger Connor Pap	Do		1						
	Do	Cormuck Garraghan Pap	Do								
	Do	Bryan Noon Pap	Do		1						
	Do	Mattw. Noon Pap	Do		1						
	Do	Thady Murry Pap	Broguemaker		3						
	Do	Jas. Howen Pap	Do		1		3				
	Do	Wm. Burne Pap	Weaver								1
	Do	Farrell Feeny Pap	Labour.		3		1				
*	Carrowbane	Richd. Farrall Pap	Farmer		2				1		3
	Do	Luke Noon Pap	Cotter								1
	Do	Owen Murray Pap	Do		2						
	Do	Ed. Murray Pap	Do				3				
	Total Families 40	Prot. – Pap 74			44		29		7		15
[f.134] Kilbride	Leitrim *	Ter. Curly Pap	Cotter				1				
	Do	Darby Daly Pap	Do		3		2				
	Do	Luke Cormuck Pap	Do		4						
	Do	P. Trindeloy Pap	Do		1						
	Do	Dens. Kelly Pap	Do		1						
	Do	Laugh. Smith Pap	Herd		4		2				1
	Do	Peter Daly Pap	Cotter		2		1				
	Do	Dens. Dockry Pap	Do		3				1		1
	Do	Jn. King Pap	Cooper		1						
	Cappagh	Dom. Garry Pap	Cotter				3				
	Do	Hugh Higgins Pap	Do		1						
*	Do	Ed. Cole Pap	Do				3				
	Correlfin	Thady Navin Pap	Do		2		1				

Com~Ros common Parish of	Place of Abode	Names and Religion	Proffession	Children under 14		Children above 14		Men Servts		Women Servts	
				Prot.	Paps.	Prot.	Paps.	Prot.	Paps.	Prot.	Paps.
	Do	Own. Garvy Pap	Do		3						
	Do	Mich. Clancy Pap	Do		2						
	Do	Rogr. Flin Pap	Do		1						
	Do	Jn. Navin Pap	Do		1						
	Do	Mark Lenny Pap	Do		1						
	Do	Peter Kelly Pap	Do		3		1				
	Cloonecumsy	Hugh Garragh Pap	Do		2						
	Do	Rogr. Covegan Pap	Do		2						
	Do	Jn. Duffy Pap	Do		4						
	Do	Jas. Curly Pap	Do		1		1				
	Do	Jas. Downes Pap	Do		1						
	Do	Jas Duffy Pap	Do		2						
	Do	Thady Flanegan Pap	Do		1		1				
*	Rin	Hugh Sweeny Pap	Farmer		2		2		1		1
	Do	H: Gilleran Pap	Cotter		1						
	Castlemyan	Thos. McDermott Pap	Farmer				2		5		6
		Thos Hevican Pap	Herd				2				
	Do	Mary Glin Pap	Widw.								1
	Do	Pat. Keany Pap	Shepherd				2		1		
	Do	Thos. Dwyer Pap	Gardiner		6						
	Do	Bar. Parker Pap	Plowhman						1		1
	Do	Jn. Fallon Pap	Herd		5						
	Do	Jas. Hanly Pap	Mason		5						
	Do	Michl. Dwyer Pap	Cooper								
	Do	Wm. Dwyer Pap	Do		1						
	Do	Wm. Keegan Pap	Labour.		1						1
	Do	Jn. Kelly Pap	Do								
	Total Families 40	Prot. Pap 77			64		24		9		12
Kilbride [f.135]	Castlemyan	Redd. Lynagh Pap	Labour.		1						
	Do	Garret Hanly Pap	Do		2		1				
	Do	Hu. Horogho Pap	Do								1
	Do	Jas. Dempsy Pap	Do		2						
	Do	An.McDermott Pap	Do		4						
	Do	Jas. Corly Pap	Do								
	Do	Jn. McDermott Pap	Do		1						
	Do	Jas Corly Pap	Do								
	Do	Jn. McDermott pap	Do		6						
	Do	[?] Allen Do									
	Cloneigh	Michl. Hanly Pap	Villager		3		2				
	Do	Andw. Hanly Pap	Do		1						
	Do	Rogr. Brennan Pap	Do		1		1				
*	Do	Hugh Hanly Pap	Do						1		1
	Do	Pet. Gavahan Pap	Do		2		4				
	Ballinderry	Christr. Fallon Pap	Farmer						3		3
*	Do	Jn. Bermingham Prot	Lodger								
	Do*	Dens. Keney Pap	Cotter		1		3		3		
	Do	Jn. Cunnane Pap	Do								
	Do	George Kennedy Pap	Do		1		2		4		2
	Do	Thady Farrell Pap	Do		1		1				

Com~Ros common Parish of	Place of Abode	Names and Religion	Proffession	Children under 14		Children above 14		Men Servts		Women Servts	
				Prot.	Paps.	Prot.	Paps.	Prot.	Paps.	Prot.	Paps.
	Do	Pat. Dolan Pap	Do		1		1	1			1
	Do	Chars Kenegan Pap	Do		2						
	Do	Thos. Loghanae Pap	Do		1		3				
	Do	Bridget Connane Pap	Widw.		2						
	Do	Michl. Groom Pap	Cotter				1				1
	Do	Pat. Dalany Pap	Do		2						
	Do	Darby Mara Pap	Do		1		1				
	Do	Michl. Keon Pap	Do				1				
	Do	Jn. Cunningham Pap	Do		2						
	Do	Dens. Higgins Pap	Do		2						
	Do	Win. Ranger Pap	Widw.		2						
	Do	Jas. Dear Pap	Cotter								
	Do	Jn. Cologhan Pap	Do		1						
	Do	Jn. Breheny Pap	Do				1				
	Do	Jn. Dungan Pap	Do				2				
	Do	Jn. Balf Pap	Do		1						
	Do	Pat. Dingan Pap	Do				1				
	Do	Chars. Duck Pap	Villager		2						
	Do	Dens. Duck Pap	Do		1						
	Tot Fams 40	Prot 1, Pap 74			45		25		12		8
[f.136] Kilbride	Ballinderry	Thos. Groom Pap	Villager				4				
	Do	Michl. Mulleedy Pap	Do		1		6				
	Do	Ed. Feenan Pap	Do				4				
	Do	Pat. Tadtin Pap	Do								
	Do	Darby Dempsy Pap	Do		4		2				
	Do	Bryan Reily Pap	Do		1						
	Do	Conr. Flin Pap	Do		1		3				
	Do	Thady Kelly Pap	Do		5		2				2
	Do	Mur. Conlan Pap	Do		2				1		1
	Do	Michl. Coil Pap	Do		3						
	Do	Pat. Malady Pap	Do		1						
	Do	Mat Cooney Pap	Do		2		2				
	Do	Pat. Pendergast Pap	Do		5						
	Do	Darby Tully Pap	Do		3						
*	Cloonbunny	Michl. Brogan Pap	Do		2				1		1
*	Do	Wm. Lane Pap	Do		2				1		1
	Do	Phil. Early Pap	Do		1				1		1
	Do	Andw. Tandeloge Pap	Do		2						
	Do	Bryan Hedian Pap	Do						1		1
	Castletara	Owen Loghnan Pap	Do		2		2				
	Do	Luke Brady Pap	Do		1		2				
	Do	Danl Slevan Pap	Do		2		2				
	Do	Jas. Brook Pap	Do				2				
	Do	Hugh Donegan Pap	Do		2						
	Do	Pat. Early Pap	Do		2		2				
	Do	Ed. Skally Pap	Do		2		2				
	Do	Bryan Conclee Pap	Do		2		2				
	Do	M. Mullane Pap	Do		1						1
	Do	Jas. Butler Pap	Do		1		1				1

Com~Ros common Parish of	Place of Abode	Names and Religion	Proffession	Children under 14		Children above 14		Men Servts		Women Servts	
				Prot.	Paps.	Prot.	Paps.	Prot.	Paps.	Prot.	Paps.
	Do	Hugh Cralan Pap	Do		2		4				
	Do	Pat. Doyle Pap	Do								
	Do	Jn. Connor Pap	Do		1		1		1		1
	Do	Matt. Hicky Pap	Do		3		2				
*	Do	Thos. Coine Pap	Ale seller		5		1		1		2
	Carrownlassane	Rich. Lamb Prot	Cotter								
	Do	Chars. Dunn Pap	Do				2				
	Do	Jas. McCabe Pap	Do		2						
	Do	Jn. Moran Pap	Do		2						
	Do	Jas. Dooner Pap	Do		1						
	Do	Ed. Cullane Pap	Do				3				
	Total Families 40	– Prot Pap 77			66		51		7		12
Kilbride [f.137]	Carrownlassane	Own. Killully pap	Villager		1		1		1		1
	Do	Mat. Cunniff pap	Do		1		3		1		1
	Do	Ar. McDavin pap	Do		1		3		1		1
	Do	M. Beaty pap	Do		1		2		2		2
	Do	Luke Moore pap	Do		3		1		1		1
	Do	Jas. Nevin pap	Cotter				4				
	Do	Mary Dwyer pap	Widw.				2				
	Do	Hugh Beaty pap	Cotter								
	Do	Hugh Doneghan pap	Do		2						
	Do	Own. Laly pap	Do		2		2				
	Do	Jas. Flanegan pap	Do		1		3				
	Do	Jn. Beaty pap	Do				1				1
	Do	Jn. Garnan pap	Do		1						
	Do	Peter Carly pap	Do								
	Do	Bart. Rush pap	Do		1		4				
	Do	M. Rush pap	Do		2						
	Do	Ed. Fannin pap	Do				2				
	Do	Wm. Flighan pap	Do		2						
	Do	Conr. Kelly pap	Do				3				
	Do	Pat. Corker pap	Do		2						
	Do	Philip Garran pap	Do		2						
	Do	Dens. Nugent pap	Do		2		2				
	Do	Thos. Kelly pap	Do		1		2				
	Do	M: Murray pap	Do		1		2				
	Do	Jas. Trindelogue pap									
	Do	Thos. Flighan pap	Do				3				
	Do	Pat. Flighan pap	Do		1						
	Do	Hugh Moran pap	Do		2						
	Do	Jas. Miles pap	Do				2				
	Do	Darby Carly pap	Do								
	Do	Bry. Moghan pap	Do		2						
	Do	Jn Connor pap	Do		1		2				
	Do	Thos. Walsh pap	Do		2				1		1
	Do	Jn. Corry pap	Do		2						
	Do	Farrell Chade pap	Do		2						
	Do	Jn. Nighton pap	Do		3						
	Firmore	Mulagh Cassidy pap	Villager		2				1		1

Com~Ros common Parish of	Place of Abode	Names and Religion	Proffession	Children under 14		Children above 14		Men Servts		Women Servts	
				Prot.	Paps.	Prot.	Paps.	Prot.	Paps.	Prot.	Paps.
*	Do	Jn. Croghan pap	Cotter								1
	Do	Bridgt. Leheny pap	Widw.		1		1				
	Do	Wm. Hargidan pap	Cotter		2		1				1
Total Families 40 – Prot Pap 78					46		36		8		11
Kilbride [f.138]	Firmore	Dens. Daly pap	Cotter		1		1				1
*	Do	Jas. Mulloy pap	Cotter						1		1
	Gubbylannon	Wm. Giraghty pap	Cotter		2				1		1
	Do	John Nevin pap	Cotter		3						1
	Do	Henry Davis pap	Cotter			2					
	Do	Owen Bush pap	Cotter		2		1				1
	Kinalty [Kilally]	Peter Murray pap	Cotter		1		1		1		
	Do	Thos. Brehony pap	Cotter		3		1				
	Do	Pet. Dun pap	Cotter		3						
	Do	Richd. Lyons pap	Cotter				4				
	Do	Wm. Fannon pap	Cotter		1						
	Do	M Cunniff pap	Cotter		1				1		
	Do	Mary Murray pap	Widw.				2				
Total Families 13 Prot. Pap: 25					17		12		4		5

[verso blank page]

A Return of the Inhabitants of Kilbride Parish in ye County of Roscommon and diocese of Elphin made to ye. Rt. Revd. the Ld. Bishop July 12th 1749

Families –	Prot	14
	Pap	519
		582
Children under 14 –	Prot	24
	Pap	651
		675
Child above 14 –	Prot	10
		326
		336
Men servants –	Prot.	10
		123
		133
Women servants –	Prot	6
	Pap	166
		172
Housekeepers –	Prot	24
	Pap.	885
		909
Total of Inhabitants –	Prot	74
	Pap	2151
		2225

Jams Blair Vicar -

Note, They whose names are markd. thus * have not wives

They whose names are marked thus ‡ are married to Papists

& They whose names are markd. thus Ø are women who keep houses whose Husbands are domestick servants to Gentlemen.

[f.138]   Union of Killenvoy

1749

	Prot:	Pap:
Wives of the Parish of Portron	2	20
Do. of the Parish of Killenvoy	15	136
Do. of the Parish of Killmean	19	91
Do of the Parish of St. John	11	193
	====	====

	Prot:	Pap:
Total of the Parish of Portron} Wives included	21	144
Total of Killenvoy Wives Included	73	734
Total of Killmean Wives Included	103	585
Total of St. Johns Wives Included	81	1010

NOTES

1. Lewis, 'Kilbride'.

2. Carrowkrin - Rory Ballow McTeige o Hanley; Cloonerk - Conner Oge mcFerdorgh Hanly and Hugh Carragh Hanly; Corbohil [Corboe] - Connor Oge McFerde Hanley; Lissgobban - Hubert mcffeoghy Hanly (*Books of Survey and Distribution*, Roscommon).

3. Cloonera - Frans Hanly, villager; Hollywell - Jn. Hanly, labourer; Newtown - James and Jas. Hanly, villagers; Drumduff - Roger Hanly, villager: Lisgobban - Luke Hanley, cottier; Derryminny - Laugh. Hanly villager; Carrowirin - Jn Hanly, cottier; Corboe - Thady Hanly, villager; Jas Hanly, mason; Castlemyan -Garret Hanly, labourer; Cloneigh - Michael, Andrew and Hugh Hanly, villagers (Census, ff 126, 127, 128, 130, 133, 134, 135).

4. Part of the estate of St. George Caulfield in 1802 (N.L.I., Longfield Maps, MS 21 F 23/25).

5. ibid.

6. ibid.

7. Barnaby Gunning was the third son of Bryan Gunning of Castle Coote. He married Ann Staunton of Galway and was an uncle of the Rev. Alexander Gunning of Elphin. He died c. 1792 (International Genealogical Index).

8. James Irwin of Rocksboro' was the son and heir of Christopher Irwin of Newtown, Co. Roscommon. Both he and John Irwin of Drumduff (see below) were probably members of the family who settled in Ballybride outside Roscommon and leased Abbey lands there (*King's Inns Admission Papers*; Burke, *LGI* (1958).

9. Hugh Maddin was born ca 1718 and in 1744 married Catherine Crogan born 1723 (N.L.I., Marriage Licence Bonds Diocese of Elphin, mic. p.1881).

10. Part of the estate of St. George Caulfeild in 1802 (N.L.I., Longfield Maps, MS 21 F 23/25)

11. Arable and pasture. Part of the estate of St. George Caulfeild in 1802 (N.L.I., Longfield Maps, MS 21 F 23/25)

12. Part of the estate of St. George Caulfeild in 1802 (N.L.I., Longfield Maps, MS 21 F 23/25)

KILLINVOY, COUNTY ROSCOMMON

INTRODUCTION: *The parish of Killenvoy is in the barony of Athlone. It is 10 miles north-north-west of Athlone, and covers 5,139 acres. Much of the land in the parish was judged in 1777 to be in 'good heart, fit for [stock] feeding or sheepwalk' and Corboly had a lake which 'abounds with pike and trout'.[1] There was an 'abundance of excellent limestone' and only a small quantity of bog.[2] A patent to hold a fair three times a year was granted in 1612 to Col. O'Kelly.[3] William Gacquin's analysis of a 1733 account book from the village of Knockcroghery shows that the inhabitants shopped locally but went to Athlone and Roscommon for cloth, seeds and nails.[4]*

In 1641, William McLaughlin and Terence Laughlin owned the townland of Corboly. In 1749 Teige McLaughlin, a member of the family was a labourer in the townland.[5] Three members of the Kelly family owned two townlands in 1641, and 22 members of the family were still in the parish in 1749.[6]

The census has Rev. John Vance living in the parish. The incumbent was the Rev. Richard Garrett, who held the parish with Kiltrustan, Kilmeane, and Bumlin (see Kiltrustan). The patron was the bishop. The rectory was impropriate.

OCCUPATIONS

Broguemaker	3	Labourer	133	Servants, household	211
Carpenter	1	Maltster	1	Shepherd	3
Constable	1	Mason	1	Smith	2
Cooper	1	Merchant	1	Tailor	3
Dog teacher	1	Miller	3	Weaver	7
Esquire	1	Parish minister	1	Wheelwright	2
Farmer	14	Pipemaker	1	Widow	9
Horserider	1	Piper	1	Wigmaker	1
Innholder	2	Potter	2		

Com~Ros common Parish of	Place of Abode	Names and Religion	Proffession	Children under 14 Prot.	Children under 14 Paps.	Children above 14 Prot.	Children above 14 Paps.	Men Servts Prot.	Men Servts Paps.	Women Servts Prot.	Women Servts Paps.
Portron	Portron	John Harward[7] Prot	Esqr.					1	4	1	4
		George Gardiner[8] Prot	Farmer	3		6			4	1	3
		John Vance[9] Prot	P.Minister					1			
		Francis Murry Pap:	Labr.		4		1				
		Teige Burn Pap:	Labr.		4						
		Michael Murry Pap:	Labr.		1						
		Fran. Hanly Pap:	Labr.		1		2				1
		Nicholas Cunnelly Pap:	Labr.						2		3
		Mathias Brenan Pap:	Labr.		2						
		Wm. Murry Pap:	Labr.		2						
		Mary Mitchell Pap:	Widdow		1				1		
		Pat. Knowlane Pap:	Labr.		3		2				
		James Roony Pap:	Labr.		5		1				1
		Michl Hanly Pap:	Labr		2		2				
		John Roony	Labr		2		3				1
		Mary Kelly Pap:	Widdow		3						
		Bryan Killeen Pap:	Labr.		3		1				
		Teige Connor Pap:	Labr.		3		1				
		Boetius Egan Pap:	Labr.		2		1		1		
		Andrew Trasy Pap:	Labr.		3						
		Denis Casy Pap:	Labr.				1				1
		Patrick Casy Pap:	Labr.		1				1		
		Teige Mulruny Pap:	Labr.						1		1
		John Murry Pap:	Sheepherd		2		2		1		1
		Thom. Casy Pap:	Turner		2						1
		James Farrell Pap:	Labr.				3				1
Total of Portron Parish		Prot: 3: Pap: 23:		3	48	6	20	2	15	2	18
[f.139] Parish of Killenvoy	Knockroghery	John Cruicer Prot:	Farmer	1		3		┼	1		1
		Barnaby FitzGerald Prot	Labr.	2	2			1		1	
		Luke Purcell Pap:	Labr.		2						
		Jno. Cunaghtan Pap:	Mason				2				
		Michl. Cladara Pap:	Labr.		4		2				
		Danl. Knavon Pap:	Labr.						1		1
		Mary Knavon Pap:	Widdow				3				
		Pat: Knavon Pap:	Labr.		2		1				1
		Hugh Kelly Pap:	Labr.		2				1		1
		Bryn. Cunaghtan Pap:	Labr.				2		1		1
		Domk. McLaughlin Pap:	Innholder				1		1		1
		Michl. Connor Pap:	Wiggmaker		1		3				1
		Danl. Fallon Pap:	Merchant							1	
		Darby Graly Pap:	Tailor		5		1				
[f.140] Killenvoy	Knockroghery	Thomas Buckley Prot:	Pipe-maker	4		1					
		Catherine Kelly Pap:	Widdow		3						3
		Peter Currelly Pap:	Miller		2						1
		Patrick Kelly Pap:	Labr.		4						
		John Dowell Pap:	Labr.								
		William Carns[10] Pap:	Potter	2							
		Teige Brackan Pap:	Potter		2				1		1
		Denis Dowda Pap:	Labr.		1						1
		Peter Kelly Pap:	Labr.		2						

Com~Ros common Parish of	Place of Abode	Names and Religion	Proffession	Children under 14		Children above 14		Men Servts		Women Servts	
				Prot.	Paps.	Prot.	Paps.	Prot.	Paps.	Prot.	Paps.
	Kellenrivagh	Phelim Chone Pap:	Labr.				5				
		John Nicholson Pap:	Weaver								1
		Marcus Bannan Pap:	Labr.		1						
		Laughn. Cunnaghan Pap:	Labr.								
		John Donleavy Pap:	Innholder								
		Peter Teige Pap:	Weaver				3				
		Michael Quegly Pap:	Tailor								
		Daniel Judge Pap:	Smith		1						
		Hanna Glinnan Pap:	Widdow				1				
		Patrick Connaghtan Pap:	Labr.		4						
		Owen Connaghtan Pap:	Labr.		1						
		John Banane Pap:	Maltster		3						
		Mathias Quegly Pap:	Labr.		1						1
		John Brennan Pap:	Labr.						1		
		William Brennan Pap:	Labr.		1		2				
		Martin McLaughlin Pap:	Labr.								
		John McLaughlin Pap:	Labr.		7		1				
		Bridget Kenny Pap:	Widdow		1		1				
		Hugh Martin Pap:	Labr.		3						
		Thomas Kelly Pap:	Labr.				1				
		Michael Gorrhy Pap:	Labr.				1				
		Patrick Lyster Pap:	Labr.		1						
		Michael Egan Pap:	Labr.				1				
		Patrick Egan Pap:	Labr.		1						
		Margt Brehony Pap:	Widdow		1				1		
		John Martin Pap:	Labr.		1				1		1
		Owen Cunnaghtan Pap:	Labr.		3						
		Phelim Murry Pap:	Labr.		2						2
		John Martin Pap:	Labr.		2						1
		John Daly Pap:	Labr.								
		Owen Daly Pap:	Labr.						1		1
		Peter Daly Pap:	Labr.		5						
[f.141] Killenvoy	Kellenrivagh Cloghorny	John Killmartin Pap:	Labr.		2						
		Cormick Leavy Pap:	Labr.		2						
		Edmund Mee Pap:	Shooemakr:		1		2				
		Daniel Mee Pap:	Labr.		1		2				
		Patrick Cundelan Pap:	Labr.						1		1
		Murtagh Dolan Pap:	Labr.		1						
		Phelim Egan Pap:	Constable		2		1				
		Patrick Cunsaly Pap:	Labr.		3						
		Denis Duff Pap:	Labr.				4				
	Scregg	John Condelloe Pap:	Labr.		1		1				2
		Murtagh McNeal Pap:	Labr.						1		1
		Patrick Egan Papt:	Labr.				4				
		Hugh Mannen Pap:	Miller		5		4		1		
		Martin Kelly Pap:	Labr.								
		Agustin Killeen Pap:	Labr.		2				1		
		Patrick Killeen Pap:	Labr.		1						
		Michael Martin Pap:	Labr.		1						
		Agustine Muldoon Pap:	Labr.						1		1
	Lissdallun	James Murry Pap:	Tailor		1		1				

Com~Ros common Parish of	Place of Abode	Names and Religion	Proffession	Children under 14 Prot.	Children under 14 Paps.	Children above 14 Prot.	Children above 14 Paps.	Men Servts Prot.	Men Servts Paps.	Women Servts Prot.	Women Servts Paps.
		Arthur Kelly Pap:	Dog teacher		3		1		1		
		Patrick Murry Pap:	Labr.		2						1
		Patrick Kelly Pap:	Wheelwrigt		2						
		Andrew Mannon Pap:	Labr.		1		3				
		John Currilly Pap:	Farmer				1		1		1
		Henry Burne Pap:	Sheepherd		1						
		James Brehony Pap:	Labr.		1		1				
		Teige Kelly Pap:	Labr.				2				
		Roger Cunnaghtan Pap:	Labr.		3						
		Teige Connell Pap:	Labr.		1						
		Daniel Moran Pap:	Labr.		3						
		Hugh McEntire[11] Prot:	Farmer						1		3
		Michl. Mulloghal Pap:	Broguemakr		1						
		James Grealy Pap:	Labr.		3						
		Faragh Torpy Pap:	Labr.				3				
		Bryan FitzMorris Pap:	Labr.				3				
		Hugh Gillmor Pap:	Labr.		1						
		John Gillmor Pap:	Labr.				3				
		Peter Bannan Pap:	Labr.								1
		Patrick Burk Pap:	Labr.		2						
		James Slime Pap:	Labr.		1						
		James Torpe Pap:	Labr.		2						
[f.142] Killenvoy	Lissdallun	Henry Campion Prot	Farmer			2			2		2
	Bannapreaghan	Mary Kelly Pap:	Widdow				3				2
		John Fallon Pap:	Labr.		3		2				
		John Kelly Pap:	Labr.		1				1		
		Bryan Conorane Pap:	Labr.				2				
		Ambrose Creahan Pap:	Labr.			1					1
	Corboly	Patrick Tully Pap:	Labr.		3						
		Michael Mulldoon Pap:	Labr.		1		2				
		Teige McLaughlin Pap:	Labr.		1						
		Darby Mullin Pap:	Labr.		2						
		James Mullin Pap:	Smith		1				1		1
		Thomas Dowd Pap:	Labr.		3		2				
		Laughlin Hughs Pap:	Labr.		1						
		Thomas Ward Pap:	Labr.		1		2				
		Joana Lyster Pap:	Widdow		2						
		Daniel Heavy Pap:	Labr.				3				
		Patrick Lunsk Pap:	Weavr.		1		4		1		
		Patrick Killmartin Pap:	Labr.				3				
		Owen Killduff Pap:	Horserider		1				1		
		John Kelly Pap:	Labr.		2						
		Michael Kelly Pap:	Piper		2						
		Bryan Duff Pap:	Labr.				1				
		Domnick Gahully Pap:	Labr.		2						
		Michael Higgins Pap:	Labr.		1						
		Patrick Quin Pap:	Labr.		1						
		Teige Mullin Pap:	Labr.		2		1				1
		Teige Mulvoly Pap:	Labr.		1				2		1
		Patrick McDaniel Pap:	Labr.						2		1
		Teige Kelly Pap:	Labr.		2		1				

Com~Ros common Parish of	Place of Abode	Names and Religion	Proffession	Children under 14		Children above 14		Men Servts		Women Servts	
				Prot.	Paps.	Prot.	Paps.	Prot.	Paps.	Prot.	Paps.
	Cornemant	Morris Cunnane Pap:	Labr.		1		2				
		Thomas Quegly Pap:	Labr.						1		1
		John Kelly Pap:	Weaver						1		
		Teige Ward Pap:	Labr.		4		2				
		Denis Connor Pap:	Farmer				2		1		1
		Roger Murry Pap:	Broguemakr.		2				1		1
		William Connor Pap:	Broguemakr.		1				1		2
		Patrick Lennon Pap:	Labr.		3		2		1		2
		Thomas Corckan Pap:	Labr.				2				
		James Ward Pap:	Weaver		2		2				
		Roger Bolan Pap:	Weaver		2				1		
		William Keelan	Weaver		4				1		
[f.143] Killenvoy	Cornemant Churchborough	Michael Keane	Cooper		2				1		
		Edmond Kelly[12] Prot:	Farmer	1					3		3
		James Thewless Prot:	Farmer			2	1		2		2
		Daniel Thewless Prot:	Labr.	1					2		2
	Knockbrack	Patrick Kelly Pap:	Labr.		1						
		Daniel Sweeny Pap:	Labr.				1				
		Patrick Kelly Pap:	Labr.		2						
		William Kelly Pap:	Labr.		1						
		Charles Kelly Pap:	Labr.								
		James Farrell Pap:	Labr.		1						
		Laughlin Kelly Pap:	Labr.						1		
		Owen Kenedy Pap:	Labr.		1				1		1
		William Thomson Pap:	Labr.		2				1		1
		Laughlin Bennet Pap:	Labr.		2						
		Michael Grady Pap:	Labr.		1		2				
	Keelogues	Bryan Kelly Pap:	Farmer				2				1
		Patrick Killmartin Pap:	Labr.		2			2			2
		James Lynane Pap:	Labr.								
	Lissgarrow	Peter Plunket Pap:	Farmer						4		1
		Patrick Murry Pap:	Labr.								3
	Galy[13]	John Alexander[14] Quakr.	Labr.			1					1
		Thomas Liggins Prot:	Farmer			3					
		George Alexander Prot	Wheelwright								
		James Burne[15] Quaker	Farmer			4			1		1
		John McLaughlin Quakr.	Labr.						1		1
		John Gilmor Prot:	Labr.	2							
		Daniel Quegly Pap:	Labr.		1				1		1
		Michl. Connell Pap:	Labr.		2						
		William Kenedy Pap:	Shepherd				5				
		John Burne[16] Quaker	Farmer	1					1	1	1
		Patrick Mungan Pap:	Miller				3			1	2
		Teige Kenny Pap:	Labr.		2						
		John Tennant[17] Prot	Carpenter			3					
	Mihane	George Crofton[18] Prot	Farmer					1		1	1
		Thomas Cunnaghtan Pap:	Labr.		2						1
Total of Killenvoy Parish		Prot: 18 Pap: 154		14	194	22	119	1	59	3	72

NOTES

1. N.L.I., Clonbrock Papers, MS 19,672/21, 23, 25, 54, 61.

2. Lewis, 'Killenvoy'.

3. *Report ... fairs and markets.*

4. William Gacquin has studied the parishes of Killenvoy and Portron and other parts of the diocese in the light of an account book from 1733-4, now held in the Argyll and Bute Council Archive. The account book links a household near Knockcroghery with traders in the townland. (William Gacquin, 'A household account from County Roscommon, 1733-4' in Cronin et al. (eds), *Irish Fairs and Markets*, pp. 99-123; Census, ff.139-140).

5. *Books of Survey and Distribution*, Roscommon; Census, f.142.

6. Keelogues - ffarriagh mchugh Kelly, Collo mcHugh Kelly and George Heines; Knockcroghery - John mcCollo Kelly (*Books of Survey and Distribution*, Roscommon; Census, ff. 139, 140, 141, 142, 143).

7. Probably Luke Dillon's agent between 1738 and 1761 (N.L.I., Ainsworth Report no.4, Dillon Papers).

8. George Gardiner sold ribtrees (Gacquin, op.cit., p. 114).

9. John Vance was a son of William Vance of Callow. He entered Trinity College Dublin in 1736 aged 16 and took BA in 1741 (*Alumni Dubliniensis*).

10. Gacquin, op.cit., p.114, fn. 37.

11. Will proved 1767 (N.L.I., Index to Diocesan Wills, Elphin. p. 1727)

12. In 1757, Edmond Kelly, a widower of Churchborough married Molly Con[d]ry, daughter of John Con[d]ry of Cloonhee, 'a beautiful young Lady, possessed of every good Qualification and six thousand pounds Fortune' (*Faulkner's Dublin Journal*, 6-9 June 1752).

13. A Dillon property with a 'farm in good heart fit for feeding or sheepwalk' and a good farm house (N.L.I., Ainsworth Report no. 4).

14. John Alexander, a Quaker of Gaily, was the father of Thomas Alexander who married in 1750 (Friends Historical Library, Register of Marriages, Moate Monthly Meeting).

15. James Burne of Galy leased 80 acres from Edward Crofton in 1735. He and his wife Judith had a son born in Galy in 1723 (N.L.I., Crofton Papers, MS 8828/8; Friends Historical Library, Moate Monthly Meeting Register of Births).

16. John Burne leased 30 acres from Sir Edward Crofton in 1735. John and Elizabeth Burne had a daughter in Galy in 1750 (N.L.I., Crofton Papers, MS 8828/8; Friends Historical Library, Moate Monthly Meeting Register of Births).

17. John Tennant was a ship's carpenter. He leased land from Sir Edward Crofton in 1735 (N.L.I., Crofton Papers, MS 8828/8).

18. George Crofton leased the cartron of Mihane in 1736 (N.L.I., Crofton Papers, MS 8828/8).

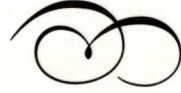

KILMEANE, COUNTY ROSCOMMON

INTRODUCTION: *The parish of Kilmeane is in the barony of Athlone, 3 miles south-south-east of Roscommon. The parish covered 8,966 statute acres.[1] The soil is light and there was a small quantity of bog. Limestone 'of very good quality' was used for building and for making mantelpieces.[2] The land was considered to be 'sound limestone ground fit for dairy, sheep walk and tillage.[3] In 1837 there was a small pottery in the parish using local clay and in 1749, a potter lived in Carrownamada.[4]*

The main Protestant landowner was Marcus Crofton of Mote. In 1641, five members of the Murry family had owned or part-owned four townlands. In 1749 there were seven members of the family still living in the parish.[5]

The incumbent in 1749 was probably the Rev. Joseph Vance (see Killenvoy). The patron was the bishop.

OCCUPATIONS

Aleseller	1	Herd	2	Shepherd	3
Butcher	1	Keeper	1	Smith	1
Carpenter	1	Labourer	87	Surveyor	1
Esquire	1	Maltster	1	Tailor	4
Farmer	9	Mason	3	Weaver	1
Garnor	1	Potter	1	Widow	2
Hatter	1	Servants, household	167		

Com~Ros common Parish of	Place of Abode	Names and Religion	Proffession	Children under 14		Children above 14		Men Servts		Women Servts	
				Prot.	Paps.	Prot.	Paps.	Prot.	Paps.	Prot.	Paps.
[f.144] Killmean	Mote	Marcus Crofton[6] Prot	Esqr	3				4	7	2	8
	Ballymurry[7]	John Hawkins Prot	Farmer	2							1
		Gershon Boate[8] Prot	Butcher	2							1
		Samuel Boate[9] Prot	Maltster								1
		Christopr. Dillon Prot	Farmer	1		1			1		1
		James Mears Pap:	Sheepherd		1		4				
		John Walsh[10] Prot	Farmer	1				2		1	1
		James Walsh Prot	Smith	3					1		1
		Terence Quin Pap:	Aleseller		3						2
		Bryan Quin Pap:	Labr:				1		1		2
	Boganfin	William Jackson[11] Prot	Farmer	4			1				
		Gilbert McHutson Prot	Weaver	2					1	1	1
		John Mullhollan Pap:	Labr:		1						
		Patrick Gatully Pap:	Labr:		1						1
		Roger Fallon Pap:	Labr:		2						1
		Martin Coghlan Pap:	Hatter		2						
		Michael Tormy Pap:	Labr:		2		2				
	Carrownamada	Patrick Keef Pap:	Labr:		2				2		1
		Robert Mason Prot	Keeper	1				2		2	
		Bryan Geige Pap:	Labr:		2				1		1
		John Linch Prot	Porter	3					1		1
		John Quin Pap:	Labr:		1		2				
		Nicholas Egan Pap:	Labr:		3				1		1
	Monymore	Denis Hannan Pap:	Labr:		2		2				1
		William Teige Pap:	Labr:		6		2				
		Daniel Sweeny Pap:	Labr:		2				1		
		Luke Ware Pap:	Labr:		1				1		1
		Thomas Kelly Pap:	Labr:				1				
		William Grork Pap:	Labr:						1		
		James Murry Pap:	Labr:		2		2				
		Patrick Murry Pap:	Labr:								1
		Michael Cunnigam Pap:	Labr:		2		2				
		William Egan Prot	Mason			2					
	Coolefobole	John Siggins Prot	Farmer	1				2	1		1
		Edmund Flood Prot	Labr:	2		1					
		Teige Neal Pap:	Labr:		2				1		
		James Petty Pap:	Labr:		3						
		Denis Conahlan Pap:	Labr:								1
		John McConnell Prot	Farmer	1		2				1	
		Michael Kelly Pap:	Labr:		1		1				2
		William Kearny Pap:	Labr:						1		2
[f.145]		Edward Creaghan Pro	Scholar								
	Ballinlugg[12]	Thomas Egan Pap:	Labr:						2		1
		John Feeane Pap:	Labr:								
		Luke Dillon Pap:	Labr:						2		
		Michael Feeane Pap:	Labr:		1						
		Hugh Connor Pap:	Labr:		1						
		Patrick Geenay Pap:	Labr:		2		2				
		Patrick Glinane Pap:	Labr:		1		2				

Com~Ros common Parish of	Place of Abode	Names and Religion	Proffession	Children under 14		Children above 14		Men Servts		Women Servts	
				Prot.	Paps.	Prot.	Paps.	Prot.	Paps.	Prot.	Paps.
		Michael Fallon Pap:	Labr:		2						
		Patrick Quegly Pap:	Labr:		1		1				
		Michael Feeny Pap:	Labr:		2				2		1
	Knockdumdonil	James Kilolhooly Pap:	Labr:		2						
		John Murry Pap:	Labr:		4						1
		Patrick Gorrick Pap:	Labr:		1		1		1		1
		Elinor Gorrick Pap:	Widdow				3				
		James Lough Pap:	Labr:		3				1		2
		Martin Mangan Pap:	Labr:		2						1
		Mathias Killroe Pap:	Labr:		2				2		1
		Owen Fallon Pap:	Labr:		1						2
		Hugh Higgin Pap:	Labr:		3		2				1
		William Galully Pap:	Labr:		2		2				
		Hugh Connaghtan Pap:	Labr:		2		1				2
		Hugh Murry Pap:	Taylor		2		4				1
		Mathias Cunaghtan	Labr:		3				1		2
	Cargeen	Oliver Train Prot	Herd	2		1			2		1
		John Finnegan Prot	Surveyr.	1					1		
		Thomas McDonnell Pap:	Labr:				2				
		Hemy Lennon Pap:	Labr:		3		1				
		Luke Pilleen Pap:	Labr:						2		1
	Correa	George Salt Prot	Carpenter	4					2		2
		Thomas Connor Pap:	Labr:		4				2		1
		Mathew Kennedy Pap:	Labr:				3				1
		Darby Cunnane Pap:	Labr:		5				1		1
		Luke Cunnane Pap:	Taylor		1		4		1		1
	Scrine	Patrick Currily Pap:	Labr:		1		3				
		Augustin Currily Pap:	Labr:		3				1		
		Denis Currily Pap:	Labr:		2		2				
		Redmond Glenan Pap:	Herd		2		2				
		Michael Diffily Pap:	Labr:		2						
		Edmond Currily Pap:	Labr:		2						
		Richard Cormuck Pap:	Labr:		1		2				
		Owen Carty Pap:	Labr:		4						1
[f.146] Killmean	Killcosh	Sarah Kean Pap:	Widdow				2		1		
		Teige Mullin Pap:	Labr: 3 1								
		Thomas Farrell Pap:	Labr:						1		2
		James Girraghty Pap:	Labr:		6		2				2
		Owen Mullin Pap:	Labr:		1				1		
		Patrick Fealem Pap:	Labr:		1		2		1		
		William Scally Pap:	Labr:				4				
		Patrick Gatully Pap:	Labr:		2						2
		Thomas Scally Pap:	Labr:		2				1		1
		Edmond Killduff Pap:	Labr:		2						
	Gortnabloisk	Patrick Kearny Pap:	Labr:		1				1		2
		Owen Daly Pap:	Labr:		1		1				
	Farbreagues	Edmond Campion Prot	Sheepherd	1					1		2
		Richard Farrell Pap:	Labr:				1				
		Michael Horton Pap:	Taylor		3						1

Com~Ros common Parish of	Place of Abode	Names and Religion	Proffession	Children under 14 Prot.	Paps.	Children above 14 Prot.	Paps.	Men Servts Prot.	Paps.	Women Servts Prot.	Paps.
		Hugh Murry Pap:	Taylor				2				
		John Murry Pap:	Garnor				3				
	Tullyroe	David Lyons Pap:	Labr:		3				1		1
		James Heas Pap:	Labr:		3						1
		William Carroll Pap:	Labr:		2				1		1
	Toghorfin	Denis Connor Prot	Farmer				2				
		Kean Higgins Prot	Farmer						2		2
		Edmond Connor Prot	Labr:	3					1		1
		James Gannan Pap:	Sheepherd								1
		Gilbert Lough Pap:	Mason		1		3		1		1
	Glanegon	Luke Higgins Pap:	Farmer		2		6		1		1
		William Grork Pap	Labr.		1						
	Ballenfoll	James Daly Pap	Labr.		2				1		1
		Andrew Daly Pap:	Labr:						2		1
		Michael Daly Pap:	Labr:		1						2
		Patrick Daly Pap:	Labr:		1				1		1
		Patrick Daly Pap:	Labr:		1		1				
		James Cassan Pap:	Labr:				2				2
		John Keef Pap:	Labr:				2				
	Knockmanagh	Teige Green Pap:	Labr:		1						
		Peter Green Pap:	Labr:		2		1				
		Denis Green Pap:	Labr:		2						
		Thomas Murray Pap:	Labr:				2				
		John Daly Pap:	Labr:		2						
Total of Killmean parish		Prot: 22 Pap: 99		37	154	7	93	11	63	7	85

NOTES

1. Less 964 acres of Lough Ree (*General Alphabetical Index*).

2. Lewis, 'Kilmean or Kilmain'.

3. N.L.I., Clonbrock Papers, MS 19,672/5.

4. John Linch (Census f. 144).

5. Rory Mc Donnell Murry in Ballinlugg; Manus Murrey, Thomas Murry in Correa; Cashell Murry and Kelly McCollo in Knockdumdaniel; Donnogh Oge Murry in Tullyroe (*Books of Survey and Distribution*, Roscommon; Census ff. 144, 145, 146).

6. Marcus Crofton was a son of Edward Lawder of Kilmore, County Roscommon. He married Katherine Crofton, sister of Sir Edward Crofton who died in 1745, and took the name Crofton. Sir Edward disapproved of his sister's marriage and left his estates to Oliver Crofton of Lissanarre, County Limerick. The will was never executed and the estates passed to Katherine Crofton. After a long legal dispute, including allegations of burglary of Sir Edward's papers and of forgery, the Court of Common Pleas granted Marcus Crofton the whole estate in 1751. During the late 1740s, Marcus Crofton placed advertisements in the *Dublin Courant* assuring the Crofton tenants they would be protected against Oliver Crofton (Crofton, *Memoirs*, p.112-114; *Dublin Courant*, 7-10 March 1746-7).

7. Ballymurry was leased in 1724 by Sir Edward Crofton and his son Edward to Henry Wilson, yeoman. It was described in 1777 as a 'farm well enclosed, large orchard. sound limestone ground fit for dairy. Sheep walk and tillage' (N.L.I., Crofton Papers, MS 8828/8; Clonbrock Papers, Maps with lists of tenants' holdings 1777, MS 19672/11).

8. Gershon Boate leased the mill, millhouse and all the tackle, water and watercourse on the lands of Galy, Killenvoy in 1735. He also leased 294 acres of land at Ballymurry and Carrigarrow in 1735. He sold meat in 1733 (N.L.I., Crofton Papers, c1693-1867, MS 8828/8); Gacquin, 'A household account', p. 116, fn. 54).

9. Samuel Boate leased part of the town and lands of Ballymurry and Monymore totalling 15 acres 1 April 1735 (N.L.I., Crofton Papers, MS 8828/8).

10. N.L.I., Clonbrock Papers, Maps with lists of tenants' holdings 1777, MS 19,672/11.

11. William Jackson was a tenant of the Clonbrock estate (ibid.).

12. The townlands of Ballinlugg, Knockdrumdonil and Correa were part of the estate of St. George Caulfeild (N.L.I., MS 21 F 23/4).

ST JOHN'S, COUNTY ROSCOMMON

INTRODUCTION: *The parish of St John's was in the barony of Athlone, 8 miles north-by-west from Athlone. It covers 11, 634 statute acres.[1] It is bounded by the parishes of Killinvoy, Rahara, Cam and Kiltoom. The eastern boundary is Lough Ree. Rindoon, that part of the parish that forms a peninsula into the lough developed as a Norman colony in the thirteenth-century. A castle was built near a safe harbour, and a town grew up around it. The walls of the town, which stretch from one side of the peninsula to the other still exist, but by the eighteenth-century the town had gone.[2] There is an early seventeenth-century windmill tower which is in ruins.[3]*

The incumbent was the Rev. James Henthorn who was installed in 1743.[4] The patron was the bishop.

OCCUPATIONS

Ale seller	2	Hatter	1	Spinster	2
Bailiff	1	Labourer	157	Tailor	3
Butcher	1	Merchant	2	Weaver	5
Carpenter	1	Miller	2	Wheelwright	1
Constable	1	Servants, household	130	Widow	19
Esquire	3	Shepherd	3	Yarnbuyer	1
Farmer	7	Smith	4		

Com~Ros common Parish of	Place of Abode	Names and Religion	Proffession	Children under 14		Children above 14		Men Servts		Women Servts	
				Prot.	Paps.	Prot.	Paps.	Prot.	Paps.	Prot.	Paps.
[f.147] St Johns[5]	Kellybrook	Denis Kelly Prot:	Esqr.	4		2		1	3		6
		Catherine Murphy Pap:	Widdow		1		1				
		Laughlin Girraghty Pap:	Labr.	2			1				
		James Quegly Pap:	Labr.		2		2				
		Thomas Mullin Pap:	Labr.		2		3				
		Robert Purcill Pap:	Labr.		1						
		Patrick Moran Pap:	Labr.				2				1
		Laughlin McGaih Pap:	Taylor		1						1
		Laurance Quegly Pap:	Smith		2						
		Edward Thewlis Pap:	Labr.		2						
		Honor Elmor Pap:	Widdow		3		2				
	Killeghan	Mable Kelly Pap:	Widdow		1		4		2		2
		Anthony Rork Pap:	Weaver				3				1
		John Nerheny Pap:	Labr.		2				1		1
		James Gaffy Pap:	Labr.		2		1		1		1
		Edmond Connor Pap:	Labr.		3						
		Edmond Horogho Pap:	Labr.				1				
		John Moran Pap:	Labr.				3				1
		Bryan Quegly Pap:	Labr.		2						
		Mary Brennan Pap:	Widdow		2		1				1
	Lowpark	Edward Stanley Prot	Farmer			3		1	2		2
		Patrick Diffily Pap:	Labr.		6		2				
		Owen Donnelly Pap:	Labr.		3		2				
		Laughlin Donnegan Pap:	Labr.				3				
		Andrew Brenan Pap:	Labr.				3				1
	Gort	Patrick Kelly Pap:	Farmer						3		3
		Roger Hannan Pap:	Miller		1						
		Luke Coyle Pap:	Labr.		1						
		Owen Quegly Pap:	Labr.								
		James Quegly Pap:	Labr.		1						
		Connor Quegly Pap:	Labr.		2						
		Columbus Gordon Pap:	Labr.		4						
		John Brennan Pap:	Labr.				3				
		Teige Brennan Pap:	Labr.		2						
		John Keelan Pap:	Taylor		1						
		Owen Connell Pap:	Labr.		1						
		Owen Horogho Pap:	Labr.		1						
		Martin Quegly Pap:	Labr.		1						
		Owen Ginane Pap:	Labr.		3						
		Edward Quegly Pap:	Labr.		1						
		Michael Dowlin Pap:	Labr.				2				
[f.148] St.John's	Gort	Patrick Lanooly Pap:	Labr.		1						
		Owen Ward Pap:	Labr.		1						
		Patrick Ailmor Pap:	Labr.		2		1				
		Michael Greevane Pap:	Labr.		3						
		Rose Fallon Pap:	Widdow				3				
		Rose Feehilly Pap:	Widdow				2				
		Patrick Condelan Pap:	Labr.		1						1

Com~Ros common Parish of	Place of Abode	Names and Religion	Proffession	Children under 14 Prot.	Paps.	Children above 14 Prot.	Paps.	Men Servts Prot.	Paps.	Women Servts Prot.	Paps.
	Carnagh	Morgan Orus Pap:	Labr.		1		3				
		Bryan Doonnagan Pap:	Labr.				2				
		Charles Quegly Pap:	Labr.		2		2				
		Thomas Quegly Pap:	Labr.				1				
		John Coyle Pap:	Smith		4						
		John Orus Pap:	Labr.		2						
		Teige Ailmer Pap:	Labr.		2						
		Marcus Conry Pap:	Labr.		4						
		Catherine Hannen Pap:	Widdow				2				
		John Coyle Pap:	Labr.								
		George Ward Pap:	Labr.		2						
		Roger Banane Pap:	Labr.		1		3				
		Daniel Quegly Pap:	Labr.		3						
		Walter Gaffny Pap:	Labr.		1						1
		Stephen Quegly Pap:	Labr.		1						
		Laurance Quegly Pap:	Labr.						1		
		Connor Kelly Pap:	Farmer		3		5		1		2
		Owen Rork Pap:	Weaver		2		2				
		Thomas Conry Pap:	Labr.		2		3				
		Thomas Keogh Pap:	Butcher		3		3				
		Michael Evans Pap:	Hatter					5			
		Patrick Connway Pap:	Mercht		1				1		1
		Catherine Kelly Pap:	Widdow		3						
		Hugh Dolan Pap:	Labr.		2						
		Bryan Gannon Pap:	Labr.		1						
		James Gannon	Labr.		1		1				
		Winifrid Kearny Pap:	Widdow		4		1				
		James Killooly Pap:	Labr.								1
		Roger Kelly Pap:	Labr.		1						
		John Lynon Pap:	Labr.		4						
		Thomas Lynon Pap:	Labr.				3				
		Francis Hannen Pap:	Labr.		1						
		Cormick Carty Pap:	Labr.		2						2
		William Carty Pap:	Labr.		1		1				
		Edward Croghan Prot:	Clerk								
[f.149] St.John's	Carrownamadra	Francis Burn Pap:	Labr.		3		2				
		Peter Fallon Pap:	Labr.		3		2				
		Daniel Burn Pap:	Labr.				5				
		Catherine Burn Pap:	Widdow				5				
		James Low Pap:	Sheepherd				6				
		Owen Seery Pap:	Labr.				5				
		Owen Diffilly Pap:	Labr.		3						
		Mable Russell Pap:	Widdow				4				
		James Stafford Pap:	Labr.				4				
		Michael Diffilly Pap:	Labr.						1		1
		Bryan McCuniff Pap:	Labr.		3						
		James Looby Pap:	Labr.		2						
		John Cunnigham Pap:	Labr.		3		2				
		James Egan Pap:	Labr.				4				

Com~Ros common Parish of	Place of Abode	Names and Religion	Proffession	Children under 14		Children above 14		Men Servts		Women Servts	
				Prot.	Paps.	Prot.	Paps.	Prot.	Paps.	Prot.	Paps.
		Luke Brennan Pap:	Labr.				3				
		Andrew Grady Pap:	Labr.				3				
		Ann Gready Pap:	Labr.				3				
		Peter Kenny Pap:	Labr.				4				
		Patrick Mannon Prot	Labr.		4				1		
		Edward White Pap:	Labr.		2						
		Timothy Gray Prot	Labr.								1
	Carrownure	William Naghlen Pap:	Farmer						1		1
		Domnick Donnelly Pap:	Yarn buyr.		2				1		1
		Henry Donnelly Pap:	Carpenter								1
		Peter Olus Pap:	Labr.								1
		Owen Mahon Pap:	Labr.		3						
		Daniel Banan Pap:	Labr.		1						
		James Brannan Pap:	Labr.		2						
		Peter Brannan Pap:	Labr.				2				
		Ignatius Donnellly	Prot Labr.	1							
		John Donnelly Pap:	Labr.		3						
		Daniel Healy Pap:	Labr.				2				
		Charles Grork Pap:	Labr.				2				
		John Donegan Pap:	Labr.		1						
		Teige Scally Pap:	Labr.		1						
		Patrick Seery Pap:	Labr.				2				
	St.John's	William Hodson[6]	Prot Esqr.	1		7		1	2		4
		Marcus Lynch Pap:	Labr.				4				
		John Kelly Pap:	Labr.		1						
		Darby Leery Pap:	Labr.				5				
[f.150] St.John's	Carnagh	William Farrell Pap:	Labr.				2				1
		William Giraghty Pap:	Labr.		2						
		Peter Hannen Pap:	Labr.		2						
		Thomas Hannen Pap:	Labr.		2				1		1
	Carrowpadan	William Naghton Pap:	Aleseller		3		1				1
		John Donegan Pap:	Labr.		1		3				
		Mary Moran Pap:	Widdow				2				1
		John Cuddy Pap:	Labr.		2				1		
		James Cuddy Pap:	Labr.						2		
		Connor Corneen Pap:	Labr.		1		1				
		John Kelly Prot	Labr.								1
		Benjamin Hall Pap:	Labr.								
		John Dolan Pap:	Smith		1				2		
		Ever Grimes Pap:	Labr.		3						
		Francis Cullen Pap:	Labr.		1						
		Charles Carty Pap:	Mercht.								1
		William Knowlan Pap:	Wheelright								
		Margaret Clusk Prot	Widdow			1					
	Killmore	Robert Waller[7] Prot	Esqr	6				5	5	6	6
		John Mee Pap:	Bailiff		3				1		1
		William Mee Pap:	Sheepherd						1		
		Patrick McGawly Pap:	Labr.		1		2				1
		Luke Cuddy Pap:	Labr.		1						

Com~Ros common Parish of	Place of Abode	Names and Religion	Proffession	Children under 14		Children above 14		Men Servts		Women Servts	
				Prot.	Paps.	Prot.	Paps.	Prot.	Paps.	Prot.	Paps.
	Carrownamada	Francis Arkins Pap:	Labr.		2		2				
		William Keenaghty Pap:	Labr.		1						
		Edmond Burk Pap:	Labr.		3						
		John Proctor Pap:	Labr.		3		1				
		Walter Burk Pap:	Labr.		1						
		Peter Nolan Pap:	Labr.		1		2				
		Thomas Lunny Pap:	Labr.		2		1				
		Francis Lamb Pap:	Labr.		1						
		John Dolan Pap:	Labr.		1		1				
		Bridget Burk Pap:	Spinner		5						
		Bridget McDonogh Prot	Spinner		4						
		Bryan Kelly Pap:	Labr.				2				
		Daniel Lough Pap:	Mason		3						
		Edward Stephens Pap:	Labr.		4						
		Catherine Green Pap:	Widdow		1						
		Denis Gray Prot	Farmer								1
		Gregory Scally Pap:	Labr.		3						
		Thomas Scally Pap:	Labr.		1						
[f.151] St.John's	St.John's	Patrick Kelly Pap:	Labr.		1						
		John Kelly Pap:	Labr.				3				
		Bryan Burne Pap:	Labr.				1				
		Ann Murry Pap:	Widdow				1				
	Knockony-conner	James Mitchel Prot	Constable			1					
		Robert Clerk Prot	Weaver	2							
		Benjamin Pordue Prot	Ale seller	1							1
		Patrick Ward Pap:	Smith	2		4					
		Patrick Fineran Pap:	Miller		3				3		2
		Bridget Donevan Pap:	Widdow				2				
		Edmund Olus Pap:	Labr.		1						
		Michael Quegly Pap:	Labr.		2				1		1
		Murtagh Hoar Pap:	Labr.		1		1				
		Bryan Knaven Pap:	Labr.				2		1		1
		Cathrine Banan Pap:	Widdow				2				
		Cormick Green Pap:	Labr.				1				
		Peter Seery Pap:	Labr.		1		1				
		Henry Grork Pap:	Labr.		2		1				
		Mary Kenny Pap:	Widdow				2				
		Patrick Keelty Pap:	Labr.		3				1		1
		Edmond Glennon Pap:	Labr.		2						
		Owen Linnane Pap:	Labr.		4						
		Cormick Ward Pap:	Labr.		2						
	Galybegg	John Naghlen Prot	Farmer	4		5		1	2		3
		Samuel Jackson Prot	Farmer			2					
		Edmund Gatully Pap:	Labr.		1						
		Edmond Laugh Pap:	Tailor		4						
		John Bryan Pap:	Weaver		3				1		
		Luke Fallon Pap:	Labr.		1						
		Laughlin Knavin Pap:	Labr.		3		1				

Com~Ros common Parish of	Place of Abode	Names and Religion	Proffession	Children under 14		Children above 14		Men Servts		Women Servts	
				Prot.	Paps.	Prot.	Paps.	Prot.	Paps.	Prot.	Paps.
		Patrick Twolan Pap:	Labr.		1						
		William Ward Pap:	Weaver		2		1				
		James Lynan Pap:	Labr.		1						
	Lissaniska	Daniel Cunnigam Pap:	Labr.				2				
		Henry Cunnigam Pap:	Labr.		2						
		James Brennan Pap:	Labr.		1		2				
		Michael Cunnigam Pap:	Labr.		1						
		William Cunnigam Pap:	Labr.		3						
		Henry Cunningham Pap:	Labr.		1						
		Murtagh Cunnigam Pap:	Labr.		2						
		Onor. Cunnigam Pap:	Widdow				3				3
[f.152] St.John's	Ballynasagarl	Patrick Egan Pap:	Labr.		1		2				
		Bryan Gormly Pap:	Labr.		2						
		Luke Cunnigam Pap:	Labr.		3						
		Bryan Cunnigam Pap:	Labr.		1		2				
		Patrick Walsh Pap:	Labr.						1		1
	LissPhelim	John Donnelly Pap:	Labr.		1		3				
		Owen Donnelly Pap:	Labr.		2						
		James Martin Pap:	Labr.		3						
		Edmond Shaglingly Pap:	Labr.						1		1
		James O Hara Pap:	Labr.		2						1
	Cargen	Bryan Quegly Pap:	Shepherd		3				1		
		James Brennan Pap:	Labr.		2						
		John Murphy Pap:	Labr.		2		1				
		Mary Brennan Pap:	Widdow								
Total of St Johns Parish Wives of the Parish of Portrun		Prot:15 Pap: 205		18	287	28	212	9	46	6	67

NOTES

1. Including 3,616 acres of Lough Ree and 38 acres of Lough Funshinagh (*General Alphabetical Index*).

2. Lewis, 'St. John's or Ivernoon'.

3. J.A. Claffey, 'Rindoon Windmill tower' in Harman Murtagh, (ed.) *Irish Midland Studies: Essays in commemoration of N.W. English* (Athlone 1980), p. 85.

4. James Henthorn was born in County Meath, a son of Isaac Henthorn, a farmer. He was educated by Mr Ross of Oldcastle and entered TCD in 1724 aged 18. He took BA in 1728. He was collated to the parish in 1745 (*Alumni Dubliniensis*; Leslie, 'Elphin', p.145).

5. A large section of the parish is the peninsula into Lough Ree which is the site of Rindoon (*Rinn Duin* 'the fort of the promontory') now marked on modern maps as Warren. In 1749 it would seem to have had no inhabitants. There is a pre-Norman fort next to a small and secure harbour, and an early Christian church site. The town around the castle was probably founded in or around the first third of the thirteenth century. A market cross, bawn and ditch were mentioned as being there in 1236. The town wall which spans the peninsula remains, together with the ruins of the castle and surrounding buildings. The site is said to be one of the most important complexes of medieval buildings in Ireland (John Bradley, 'Rindoon, Co. Roscommon: A Management Plan' (Heritage Council, Kilkenny, 1998)).

6. William Hodson (1731-1779) married Olivia, third daughter of the Rev. Edward Munns, vicar of Drumcliff. Hodson stood security to his brother Robert Hodson who had been a hearth-money collector in Loughrea, County Galway. Robert died in indebted to the Crown and his other security proved insolvent. William was sued for the balance, but successfully paid over time (Leslie, 'Elphin', pp.32, 131; N.A., P.R.O., CUST 1/33/20).

7. Robert Waller (1701-?) married Jane Ormsby. Bishop Synge described Kilmore as 'a vast open [sic] of a noble river, and fine trees can make it...The house is not good'. It was situated on the river Shannon which makes a long sweep around the north of the parish (*Synge Letters*, p.40; Burke *LGI* (1958)).

TISRARA, COUNTY ROSCOMMON

INTRODUCTION: *The parish of Tisrara is in the barony of Athlone on the river Suck and on the road from Roscommon to Ballinasloe. It covers 8,482 statute acres.[1] The soil was said to be light, and there was a 'great quantity' of bog. Limestone was quarried and used for stone gate piers and chimney pieces (there were 4 masons in the parish in 1749). Fairs were held at Mount Talbot.[2] Eight townlands were owned by the Kelly/mcKelly family in 1641, and thirty-one members of that family lived in the parish in 1749, two of whom were farmers.[3]*

The church of Ireland incumbent was the Rev. William Digby, who from 1718 held this parish together with Ahascragh, Rahara, Cam, Dysert, Kiltoom, and Taghboy. He lived in Cloondara in this parish.[4] The patron was the bishop. The rectory was impropriate.

OCCUPATIONS

Ale seller	3	Gardener	1	Priest	1
Beggar	1	Gentlewomen	3	Pumpmaker	6
Broguemaker	1	Glover	1	Servant	5
Butcher	4	Herd	2	Servants, household	126
Carman	3	Joiner	3	Shepherd	10
Carpenter	1	Labourer	86	Shoemaker	1
Cleric	1	Maltster	2	Smith	7
Constable	1	Mason	5	Stonecutter	1
Cooper	1	Merchant	1	Tailor	5
Cottier	1	Miller	1	Teacher	1
Cowherd	2	Nailor	3	Tenant	52
Esquire	1	Periwig maker	1	Weaver	12
Farmer	15	Piper	1	Widow	1
		Ploughman	1		

Com~Ros common Parish of	Place of Abode	Names and Religion	Proffession	Children under 14		Children above 14		Men Servts		Women Servts	
				Prot.	Paps.	Prot.	Paps.	Prot.	Paps.	Prot.	Paps.
[f.153] Taughsrara	Cloondara	Revd. William Digby[5]	Vicar			2		1	1	1	3
	Ditto	Widdow Bannon Pap			1		3				
	Ditto	Bryan Ceasey Ditto	Labr.		2						
	Ditto	Wm. Kelly Do	Ditto		1		1				
	Ditto	Widdow Lanis Do	Do				2				
	Ditto	Patk. Conboy Ditto	Do				1				
Mountalbott	~~~~~~~	Wm. Talbott[6] Esq	Protest	3				1	6	1	8
	Ditto	Miss Jane Rose Talbott	Ditto								
	Ditto	Miss Talbott	Do								
	Ditto	Miss Southwell	Do								
	Cloonedilern[?]	Benjamin Cuthburt Protest	Mason		2						
	Ditto	Simon Cuthburt Do	Periwig maker								
	Ditto	Widdow Conboy pap				1					
	Ditto	Thos. Conboy[7] papist	Gardinr		5						
	Ditto	Widdow Garman			1						
	Ditto	Patrk Birn Papt	Cowherd		2						1
	Ditto	John Conboy Do	Constable		4						
	Ditto	Patrk Bodkin Do			1						
	Ditto	James Field Do	Nailor		1						
	Ditto	James Walsh Do	Shoemaker		2		1				
	Ditto	Michl. Delany Do	Mason		2						
	Ditto	Patrick Kelly Do	Pumpmaker		4						
	Ditto	Widdow Pettit Do			1		1				
	Ditto	Peter white	Mason		2						
	Ditto	Domnick Convoy	Labr.		1						
	Ditto	Michl. Brenan Do			2		1				
	Ditto	Thom. Hoey Prost	weaver	2		3		3			
	Ditto	Denis Derham Pap	ale seler		1		1		1		2
	Ditto	Denis Lians Papt	Smith		1		4				
	Ditto	Widdow Egan Prost	Ale Seller		2				2		2
	Ditto	Hugh Keogh Papist	Ale seller		1				2		
	Ditto	John Kelly Papist	Mercht		2						
	Ditto	Wm. Turner Prost	Labr.	2							
	Ditto	Richd. Dillon Papist	Labr.						2		
	Ditto	Widdow Graddy papist			1						
	Ditto	Denis Kelly pumpmaker	Papist								
	Ditto	Andrew Tute papist	Butcher						3		
	Ditto	Danl. Ward papist	Joyner		1						1
	Ditto	Wm. Kelly papist	Labr.		2						
	Ditto	Wm. Kelly papist	Miller		1		1		2	1	1
	Ditto	Henry Lawler Do	Labr.							2	
	Ditto	James Lians	Labr.		2				1		
[verso f.153]		Forwd. Prot 7 Pap 44 Child under 14		9	~~	17	2		25	3	18
[f.154 Taughsrara	Cloon Loughnan	Danl. Ward papist	Joyner		1						1
	Ditto	Andrew Tute papist	Butcher				3				
	Ditto	Wm. Kelly papist	Labr.		2						
	Ditto	Henry Lawler papt.	Butcher				2				1

Com~Ros common Parish of	Place of Abode	Names and Religion	Proffession	Children under 14 Prot.	Children under 14 Paps.	Children above 14 Prot.	Children above 14 Paps.	Men Servts Prot.	Men Servts Paps.	Women Servts Prot.	Women Servts Paps.
	Ditto	James Lians papt.	Labr.		2						
	Ditto	Patk. Dowel Do	Taylor				3				
	Ditto	Widdow Box Do			1	1					
	Ditto	Widdow Walsh Do.			1						
	Ditto	Roger Killen Do	Labr.				3				
	Ditto	Pathk. Tooll[8] Do	Taylor		3						
	Ditto	Michl. Egan Ditto	Labr.		1		3				
	Do	Hugh Conner Do	Labr.								
	Ditto	Denis Ward Do	Joyner		1		3				
	Do	Bryan Girraghty Do	farmer				2		3		2
	Ditto	Frank Hanly priest[9]	Papt-						1		
	Ditto	Owen Daily papist	Labr.				1				
	Ditto	John Paine Protes	Nailor	3				1			
	Ditto	Widdow Bryan									
	Do	John Fallon Do	Labr.		3						1
	Do	Thoms Fallon Do	Labr.		1						
	Ditto	Luke Kelly Ditto	pumpmaker		1						
	Do	Thom. Cormick Do	Labr.				2				
	Ditto	Roger Kenedy Do					1				
	Ditto	Mathias Treassey			2		2				
	Ditto	Redmond Dillon Do					4				
Part of Cloon Loughnan	Ditto	William Greely Do	tenant		1						
Called Cartron Kelly	Ditto	Hugh Clogher	tenant		2						
	Ditto	Augustine Clogher			1						
	Ditto	John Dolan					2				
	Ditto	Patrk. Concannon			4						
Clooncagh	Ditto	Edwd. Giltenane	Servt.		6		2				
	Ditto	Roger Mullon	Servt.		2		3				
	Ditto	Bryan Mullon	Labr.		2		1				
	Ditto	Morgan Kenedy	Labr.		2		1				
Killne Grall	Do	Ambrose Madden	tenant				1				
	Ditto	Charles Madden	tent-		3		2				
	Ditto	Patk. Kelly	Weaver				2				
	Ditto	Martin Carty	Labr.		1						
	Ditto	Luke Carty			2						
	Ditto	Laurence Queeny	Glover		1		2	1	4		
				3	45	~~	46	1	6		5
[f.155] Taughsrara	Killne Grall	Bryan McDonnel	tent		1		2				
	Ditto	Thom. McKelly			1		2				
	Ditto	James Carty	tent		2						
	Ditto	Morgan Mulry	tent				1				
	Ditto	James White	Labr.		2						
	Ditto	Widdow Kelly	Widow								
	Ditto	Valentine Derivan	tent		1		2				
	Ditto	John Mulry	tent		2						
	Ditto	Widdow Glue			3		3̶				
	Ditto	Denis Dermott	Labr.		2						
	Ditto	Bryan Fitzmaurice	tent						1		1

Com~Ros common Parish of	Place of Abode	Names and Religion	Proffession	Children under 14 Prot.	Children under 14 Paps.	Children above 14 Prot.	Children above 14 Paps.	Men Servts Prot.	Men Servts Paps.	Women Servts Prot.	Women Servts Paps.
	Ditto	Mr Wm. Lenon Prot	farmer						1		1
	Ditto	John Meare papist	herd		1						
	Ditto	John Cuff papist	Labr.		1						
Lissmaho	Ditto	Darby Finan papt.	Shepherd		2						
	Ditto	Barth. Conolly Prot	Servt.	6							1
	Ditto	Wm. Mulry Papist	Smith		3		1				
	Ditto	Rogr. Kellaghan Do	weaver		1						
	Ditto	James Buttler	Labr.		1						
	Ditto	John Buttler	Labr.		3						
	Ditto	Widdow Kelly pap			1						
	Ditto	Michael Fallon pap	Labr.		1		2				
	Ditto	Widdow Mulry pap					1				1
	Ditto	Miles Queeny Do	Labr.				1				
	Ditto	Mark Madden Do	Labr.				1				
	Ditto	Patt. Courale pap	Labr.		2						
	Ditto	Widdow Goldrick Do					2				
	Ditto	Daughter Do			2						
Atty Knockan	Ditto	Mr Wm. Siggins Pros	farmer	4	1						1
	Ditto	Henry Sumers Pros	farmer	2			1				
	DI	John Jackson Pros	farmer	3		1	1				
	Ditto	Thos. Murry pap	Labr.				1				
	Ditto	Terence Killduff	Labr.		3						
	Ditto	Owen Curlly Pap	Labr.		3						
Cornepalace	Ditto	Toby Dillon pap	farmer		2						1
	Do	Mathias Giblan	Labr.		3						
	Do	Francis Mulry Do	Labr.								1
	Do	Hugh Kelly Do	Labr.		2						
	Do	Miles Lohan Do	Cooper		1						
Dubarn	Ditto	Francis Naven Do	Shepherd		2		1				
	Do	Peter Kelly Do	Labr.		4		2				
[f.156] Cornepalis		Patk Glenane pap	Labr.		1						
	Derrinlarg	Patk Moran papt	Labr.		1						
	Ditto	Owen Birn papist	Labr.		1						
	Ditto	Patk. Kelly Do	tent								1
	Ditto	John Lohan Do	Labr.		2						
	Ditto	Laughlin Kelly Do	tenant		1						
	Ditto	John Moran Ditto	tenant		3						
	Ditto	Widdow Moran Do			2		2				
	Ditto	Mulry papist	tent		1						
	Ditto	Roger Moran Do	tent				3				
	Ditto	Hugh Farrel Do	Piper				2				
	Ditto	Fargus Norton	teacher								
	Ditto	Edmd. Bryan papist	pumpmaker								
	Ditto	Danl. Mulry Ditto	Smith		3		3		1		1
	Ditto	Conner Glenane Do	Labr.		2						
	Ditto	Laughlin Boyle	Labr.		3		2				
	Ditto	Thos Cureale pap	Labr.								
	Ditto	Thady Conole pap	Labr.		3		2				
	Ditto	Thady Hannan Do	pumpmaker		2						

Com~Ros common Parish of	Place of Abode	Names and Religion	Proffession	Children under 14 Prot.	Children under 14 Paps.	Children above 14 Prot.	Children above 14 Paps.	Men Servts Prot.	Men Servts Paps.	Women Servts Prot.	Women Servts Paps.
	Ditto	Laughlin Glenane	Labr.		2						
	Ditto	Wm. Mulry papist	Labr.		1		1				
	Ditto	Thady McDonnel Do	Labr.								
	Ditto	Wm. Cureale papist	Shepherd		2						
	Ditto	John Queeny Do	taylor		1		2				
	Ditto	Patk. Connole Do	Labr.		1		1				
	Ditto	Miles Bryan papist	Labr.		3						
	Ditto	Widdow McDonnel			3						
	Line Mallow	Mr Jams Kelly papt	farmer				2		1		
	Ditto	Thom Hopkins Do	Stone Cutter		3		1				
	Ditto	Patk. Moran Do	Labr.		1						
	Cloony Shead	John Gallvan Do	tent					1			1
	Ditto	John Heavoghan Do	tenant				3				
	Ditto	Peter McDonnel	tent				3				
	Ditto	Luke Gallvan Do	tent				1				
	Ditto	Andrew Coony Ditto	tent		1		2				
	Ditto	Thady Galvan Do	tent				1				
	Do	James Kelly Do	tent		2						
	Ditto	Wm. Gregan Do			1						
	Ditto	Laurence Moran	tent		2		1				
	Ditto	Manus Downey	tent		2						
	Ditto	Laughlin Grork	tent			1					
					51		32		3		2
[f.157] Taughsrara	Lismak	Will Pin Prot	Nailor	2							
	Cloony Shead	James Gallvan pap	tent						1		
	Ditto	Hugh Fallon pap	tenant		1		1		1		
	Ditto	Patk. Hannan pap	Smith		3						
	Ditto	Widdow Healy pap					2				
	Ditto	Roger Healy pap	tenant		1		2				
	Ditto	Martin Heally pap	tent		1		1		1		1
	Ditto	Jam Gunay pap	tenant				3				
	Ditto	Patk. Gallvan pap	taylor		2						
	Ditto	Lau: Gately pap	tenant		1						
	Ditto	Darby Dolan Do	tent				3				
	Cooll Derry	Mr. Robt. Mitchel Pro	farmer						3	1	2
	Ditto	Darby Cuningham	Labr.		2						
	Ditto	Uulick Keive	Shepherd				2				
	Ditto	Wm. Mulry papist	Brogmaker				3				
	Ditto	Bryan Dolan pap	plowman		3		2				
	Ditto	Thady Kelly pap	Maltster		3						
	Ditto	Greghan Widdow pap					2				
	Ditto	James Greghan Labr.			1						
	Carregbegg	Widdow French pap	farmer		1				4		3
	Ditto	Darby Flyn pap	Servt.		1		1				
	Cloonyleg	Mr Danl. Ffallon pap	farmer		3				2		2
	Ditto	Francis Heally pap	tenant		2		2				
	Ditto	Lau: Clerk pap	tent		1						
	Ditto	Stephen Collon pap	tent		1						
	Ditto	John Lenon pap	tent		2						

Com~Ros common Parish of	Place of Abode	Names and Religion	Proffession	Children under 14		Children above 14		Men Servts		Women Servts	
				Prot.	Paps.	Prot.	Paps.	Prot.	Paps.	Prot.	Paps.
	Ditto	Peter Healy pap	tent		3						
	Ditto	Carbary Heally pap	tent								
	Ditto	Lau: Mullon pap	tent		3						
	Ditto	Conner Mannen	tent								
	Ditto	Laughlin Kelly pap	tent		4						
	Ditto	David Collins Prot	tent		2		2				
	Ditto	Charles Collins Prot	tent	3		1					
	Killvoney	Mr. Wm. Kelly pap	farmer		2		2				2
	Ditto	John McKelly pap	Weaver		2		2				
	Ditto	Luke Gately pap	Labr.		2						
	Ditto	John Gately [a[	Labr.		1						
	Ditto	Widdow Naven pap					3				
	Ditto	Andrew Heally pap	Labr.		3		1				
	Ditto	Andrew Burn pap	Smith		2		1				
	Forsonough	Laughlin Kelly pap	Servt.					1			
				3	55	1	36		12	1	10
	Ditto	Connor Curlly pap	Labr.		2						
[f.158] Taughsrara	Forsonough	John Fallon papist	Labr.		1		1				
	Ditto	Owen FitzMaurice	Labr.		2						
	Ditto	Wm. Kelly papist	Labr.		1						
	Ditto	Patk. Kelly Ditto	weaver				3				
	Ditto	Lau: McKelly Do	Labr.		2						
	Ditto	Widdow McKelly Do					1				
	Ditto	Thady Fallon Do	Labr.		1						
	Ditto	Jam. McKelly Do	Shepherd		1		2				
	Ditto	Henry O'Neal Do	Labr.		2						
	Ditto	Patk. Grork papist	Cotter		2		1				1
	Ditto	James Kean Ditto			2		1				
	Ditto	Danl. Kenny Ditto	Weaver		2		1				
	Ditto	Widdow Heally Do					1				
	Ditto	Bryan Heally Do	Labr.		1						
	Ditto	John O'Bryan Do	Labr.		2						
	Ditto	Denis McKelly	Shepherd		3						
	Ditto	Widdow Lenon Do			1		1				
	Ditto	Widdow McKelly					1				
	Ditto	Thom Garry Do	Labr.		1						
	Carunthleave	Thos. Connif papist	weaver		2						
	Ditto	Wm. Connif papist	weaver				2				
	Ditto	Mark Killmurry	Shepherd		2		1				
	Ditto	Thady McDonnel	herd		4		2		1		1
	Ditto	Owen Coyle papist	Labr.		1						
	Ditto	Roger Coyle Ditto	Labr.		3						
	Ditto	Owen Kilroy Dito	Labr.		3		1				
	Ditto	Darby Moran Do.	Smith		1		3				
	Lissne										
	Gobrough	Michl. Coyle Do	Carman				4				
	Ditto	Michl. Moran Do	Cowherd		2						
	Ditto	Owen Curlly Do	Carman		2						
	Ditto	Mathew Keigheran					2				
	Carunthleavy	Patk. Curly Do.	Carman		2						
	Caruard	Mr. Wm. Fallon Do	farmer		3		3		1		4

Com~Ros common Parish of	Place of Abode	Names and Religion	Proffession	Children under 14 Prot.	Children under 14 Paps.	Children above 14 Prot.	Children above 14 Paps.	Men Servts Prot.	Men Servts Paps.	Women Servts Prot.	Women Servts Paps.
	Ditto	Thady McDonnel Do	Labr.		3		1				
	Ditto	Jam Heath Do	Shepherd		4						
	Do	Thos. Heath Do	Shepherd		3						
	Ditto	Widdow Condilan Do			2						
	Ditto	Michl. Galvan Do	Labr.		3						
	Ditto	Roger Naughten Do	Labr.		3		1				
	Ditto	Patk. Killmurry Do	butcher				1				
	Ditto	John Carroll Ditto	weaver				1				
					69		35	2			6
[f.159] Taughsrara	Caruard	Wm. Connor papist	Labr.				3				
	Ditto	Edmond Gately Do	Labr.		1		2				
	Ditto	Patk. Heath Do	Labr.		2						
	Ditto	Patk. Molloghan Do	Maltster					2			
	Ditto	Augustine Mulry Do	pump Maker		2						
	Ditto	Patk. Bowe Do	weaver				2		1		
	Ditto	Andrew Ready Do	Mason				2				
	Ditto	Thady Egan Do	Shepherd		3						
	Ditto	Jam. Kenedy Do	Labr.		1						
	Ditto	Hugh Dolan Do	Carpenter		3		2				
	Ditto	Danl. Egan Do	tenant		3						
	Ditto	Matthew Moony Do	tent -								1
	Ditto	Jam. McGloghlin Do	tent -		4						
	Ditto	Wm. Kennedy Do	tenant		3						
Taghboy	Cloghan	Mr. Garrt. Bermingham	farmer				1	2			3
	Ditto	Thos. Geoghegan Do	Cabint maker					1			1
	Ditto	Jam. Cormick prot.	weaver	3				1			
	Ditto	Jam. Greenham pap	farmer					1			1
	Ditto	James Dillon pap	farmer								
	Ditto	Roger Hannan pap	Mason	2						1	
	Ditto	John Fallon pap	proctor		3						1
	Ditto	Denis Ward pap	Labr.		4						
	Ditto	Thos. White pap	begar								
	Ditto	Wm. Keigheran pap	Labr.		1						
	Ditto	Anthoney Stone Do	weaver		1						
	Ditto	Michl. Kelly pap	taylor								
	Ditto	Wm. Clogher pap	Labr.		1		2				
	Ditto	Roger Kelly pap	Labr.		2		1				
	Ditto	John Kelly pap	Labr.		1		2				
	Ditto	Danl. Killern pap					1				
	Ditto	Wm. Moore pap	Labr.				2				
	Ditto	Danl. Lennon pap	Labr.								1
	Ditto	Patk McDonnell	Smith		2		1				
	Ditto	Danl. Kenedy pap	Constable	1							
	Ditto	Widdow Rock pap									
	Ditto	John Kenedy pap	Labr.								
	James Town	Robt. Steell protes	tent	1	1	1					
	Ditto	Jam. Mulvihil pap	tent		2						
	Ditto	Morgan Mulvihil Do.	tent		2						
	Ditto	Michl. Moore pap	tent		2						
	Ditto	Owen Moore pap	tent								
				6	45	1	23	6	1	8	

NOTES

1. Including 135 acres of water (*General Alphabetical Index*).

2. Lewis, 'Tessaragh or Taughsrara'.

3. In Ally Knockan, Edmond mcTeige Kelly and Bryan Oge mcBryan; in Clooncagh and Killvoney, Bryan Oge mcBryan mcLaughlin Kelly; in Cloondara and Cornepalace, Donnogh mcBrien mcLaughln Kelly (*Book of Survey and Distribution*, Roscommon; Census, ff. 153, 154, 155, 156, 157, 158).

4. Census, f. 153.

5. William Digby was born at Mote, a son of bishop Simon Digby who was Bishop of Elphin from 1690-1720. He was educated by the Rev. Michael Griffin at Elphin and was admitted to TCD in 1712 aged 18. He graduated BA in 1716 (*Alumni Dubliniensis*).

6. Sir Harry Talbott Knt. lived at Cloondaratt in the mid-seventeenth century (*Census of Ireland*).

7. An Ed. Conboy died in 1759. His monument was erected by his father Thomas (Jim Higgins, *Tisrara Medieval Church, Carrowntemple, Four Roads, Co. Roscommon* (1995), p.134).

8. Patrick Tool died in November 1771, aged 63. His wife Anne Philips died in April 1779, aged 60. They were buried in the church at Carrowntemple (ibid, p.60).

9. Francis Hanly, pastor of Tisrara was also prebendary of Killyon. He died in April 1761 and was buried in the church at Carrowntemple where Francis Finglass erected a memorial (Fenning, 'Clergy Lists', pp.144, 145, fn.8; Higgins, *Tisrara* p.115).

TAGHBOY, COUNTY ROSCOMMON

AND

COUNTY GALWAY

INTRODUCTION: *The parish of Taghboy is partly in County Roscommon in the barony of Athlone and partly in County Galway in the barony of Killian. It is 3 miles east of Ballinamore.[1] 8,861 statute acres are in County Roscommon and 5,134 acres are in County Galway.[2] The soil was said to be light, with a lot of bog.[3] A fair was held at Ballyforan seven times a year.[4]*

The church of Ireland incumbent was the Rev. William Digby, who from 1718 held this parish together with Taughsrara, Rahara, Cam, Dysert, Kiltoom and Ahascragh[5] (see Tisrara). The patron was the bishop.

OCCUPATIONS

Aleseller	1	Gentleman	1	Shepherd	5
Carman	5	Gentleman farmer	1	Sievemaker	1
Carpenter	1	Labourer	47	Smith	3
Cooper	3	Merchant	1	Tailor	1
Esquire	2	Mower	1	Tenant	48
Farmer	4	Pumpmaker	1	Weaver	2
Feltmaker	1	Servant	3	Widow	1
Fowler	1	Servants, household	43		

Com~Ros common Parish of	Place of Abode	Names and Religion	Proffession	Children under 14		Children above 14		Men Servts		Women Servts	
				Prot.	Paps.	Prot.	Paps.	Prot.	Paps.	Prot.	Paps.
[f.160] Taughboy	Jam Town[6]	Luke Moore	tenant				1				
		Widdow Bourke					2				
	Ditto	Peter Clogher Do.	tenant								
	Mullough-ardogh	Mr. Edmd. Fallon	farmer		2		1				1
	Ditto	Bryan Kelly papist	Shepherd		3						
	Torpane	Widdow Crosby papt	farmer				3				
	Ditto	Simon Dolan pap			2						
	Ditto	Michl. Brisklane Do	Labr.		1						
	Ditto	Luke Brisklane Do	tent.		2						
	Ditto	Wm. Conncarty Do	tent								
	Ditto	Wm. Nowlan Do	Labr.				1				
	Ditto	Jam. Nowlan Do	Labr.		2						
	Ditto	Widdow Kelly Do					2				
	Ditto	Son in law pap			1						
	Ditto	Frans. Naghten pap	Labr.		1		3				
	Ditto	Thos. Flyn pap	Labr.				2				
	Ditto	John Farrel pap	tent.								
	Ditto	Lau: Gately pap	Smith		3						
	Ditto	John Naghton Do	Labr.								
	Ditto	Edmd. Naghton Do	Labr.								
	wheremore	Denis Naghton pap	tent.		3						
	Ditto	Danl. Naghton pap	tent.		3						
	Ditto	Wm. Naghton Do	farmer		2		2				
	Ditto	Michl. Kenedy Do									
	Ditto	Martin Kenedy									
	Ditto	Thady Crosby Do	tent.		1						
	Ditto	Conner More Do	tent.				6				
	Ditto	Law: Crosby pap	tent.		1						
	Ditto	Widdow Birn pap	~~~		3						
	Ditto	Laughlin Woods Do									
Taughboy	Ditto	Danl. Brenan	tent.				1				
	Ditto	Barth. Brennan	tent.		2						
	Ditto	John Fallon pap	weavr.				2				
	Ditto	Edwd. Casserly pap	Cooper				4				
	Ditto	Michael Kelly Do	Labr.		1						
	Ditto	Thady Heaveghan pap	tent.		2						
	Ditto	Hugh Dolan Do	tent.		2						
	Ditto	Garret Muvile Do	tent.		3		1				
	Ditto	Widdow Mulvile pap	tent.		3						
	Ditto	Garret Farrel Do	Cooper		2						
	Denis	P Bryan pap	weaver				2				
[f.161] Taughboy	Furea	Laughlin McDonnel pt	tent.				3				
	Ditto	Clogher Terrance Do	tent.		2						
	Ditto	Patk. Leavy papt	tenant		1						
	Ditto	Annaias McDonnel Do	labr.		1		1				
	Ditto	Widdow Nolan papt	tent		2		1				
	Ditto	Denis Naghten	tent								

Com~Ros common Parish of	Place of Abode	Names and Religion	Proffession	Children under 14		Children above 14		Men Servts		Women Servts	
				Prot.	Paps.	Prot.	Paps.	Prot.	Paps.	Prot.	Paps.
	Ditto	Patk. Mulvihil	tenant		3		1				
	Do	Roger Kelly	Carman				2				
	Ditto	Jam. Naghten	labr.		3						
	Ditto	Maurice Mentane	Labr.		2		3				
	Ditto	Danl. Kelly	Sheperd		2		3				
	Ditto	Dennis Gaffin pap	Carman		3						
	Ditto	James Fallon papt	Shepherd		2						
Ballynahaen	Ditto	Mr.Wm. Fallon Do Gent	~~~~~~		5		1				2
	Ditto	Lau: Leary Do pap	Labr.		4						
	Ditto	Widdow Gaufin pap									
	Ditto	John Finn Ditto	Labr.		1						
	Ditto	Jam. Monoughan pap	Carpenter		2						
	Ditto	Matthew Carregher	Labr.		1						
	Ditto	Michl. Gately papt	Labr.		2						
	Ditto	Law: Mullon papt	Labr.		2						
Cloonagh	Ditto	Mr.Patt.Fallon Do	Gent. farmer		5		1		2		4
	Ditto	Lau: Fallon papt	Labr.		2		1				
	Ditto	Danl. Fallon Ditto	Labr.		2						
	Ditto	Bryan Fallon Ditto	Labr.		3						
	Ditto	Jam. Mullon ~	Labr.		1						
	Ditto	Anthony Mulvee ~	Labr.		3		1				
	Ditto	Lau: Mulloghan Do	Labr.		2		1				
	Killenvoy	Denis Keigherin Do	tenant				1				
	Gorrynegron	Jam. Killroy Ditto	pump Maker		3						
	Ditto	Bryan Mullvoigh Do	tenant		3						
	Ditto	Bryan Gately Do	tenant		3						
	Ditto	Michael Gately ~	tenant		3						
	Ditto	Bryan Tyrroll Do	tenant		1						
	Ditto	Michl. Gately Do	tenant		3						
	Ditto	Widdow Gavan Ditto					2				
	Ditto	Jam. Gately Do	tent		4						
	Ditto	Michl. Moran Do	tent		2						
	Ditto	Roger McKelly ~	tenant		2						
	Ditto	Widdow Gately Do			1		1				
	Ditto	Hugh Fallon tenant			2		1				
	Toruck	Danl. Kelly Esq prot.		1		1		+	4		4
	Ditto	Michael Kenedy pap	Labr.				3				
	Ditto	Owen Currlly Do.	Labr.		2						
	Ditto	John Heavy papt	Labr.		2		1				
	Ditto	John Heally papt	fowler		2						
	Ditto	Will Farrel papist	Servant				1				
	Ditto	Halbert Farrel papt	Shepherd		1		2				
	Ditto	Wm. Kelly papist	Mower								
	Ditto	Anthony Brisklane	Carman		1		2				
	Ditto	Jam. Nowlan papt.	Carman		1						
	Ditto	Charles Dempsey	Carman		1		2				
	Ditto	Matthew Keigheran	Labr.		3		1				
	Ditto	Thom. Flyn papist	Seivemaker		1						
	Ditto	John Fallon papist	Labr.								

Com~Ros common Parish of	Place of Abode	Names and Religion	Proffession	Children under 14		Children above 14		Men Servts		Women Servts	
				Prot.	Paps.	Prot.	Paps.	Prot.	Paps.	Prot.	Paps.
	Ditto	John Busby papt	Cooper								
		Lau Moran Do	Labr.								
[f.162] Taughboy	Toruck	Michael Girraghty	Papt. Labr.		2						
		Patt. Madden papt.	Servant						1		1
	Carunderty	Jam. Kelly ~	Shepherd						2		
		John Fallon papist	Labr.		1						
	Ballyfuron	Hugh Kelly[7] Esqr.							3		3
	Ditto	Conner Kelly pap	Smith				1				1
	Ditto	Michl. Kelly Do	Merchant				1				1
	Ditto	Hugh Downey Do	Servant		2						
	Ditto	Jam. Cahane	Labr.								
	Ditto	Laughlin Cahane	Labr.		2		4				
	Ditto	Danl. Kelly	Labr.		2						
	Carventerof	Bryan Gately pap	Smith		3						
	Ditto	Wm. Kelly pap	Labr.		2						
	Ditto	Peter Dillon	Labr.		2						
	Ditto	Edmond Kelly	Labr.		2						
	Ditto	Wm. Meares Do	Labr.		3		2				
	Ditto	Dens Gately Do	Labr.		4						
	Ditto	Dens Gately	Labr.		3		2				
	Mucklon	Edwd. Glenon Do	Aleseller		2		1		1		2
	Ditto	Danl. Hanan pap	Labr.		2						
	Ditto	John Gaughfin Do	Labr.		2		1				
	Ditto	Roger Ward	Labr.		1		2				
	Ditto	Bryan Farrel	Labr.		2						
	Ditto	Manus Burn	Labr.								
	Ditto	John Nowlan Do	Labr.		2						
	Ditto	Jam. McGloghlin	Tenant		3						
	Tohercoll	Mark Connif pap	Tailor				2				
	Ditto	Teige Fallon pap	Tenant		3						
	Ditto	Lau: Menlane Do	Tenant		2						
	Ditto	Patk. Connole pap	Tenant		1						
	Ditto	Gilbt. Goose pap	Tenant		1						
	Ditto	James Gately Do	Tenant		4						
	Ditto	Denis Kelly pap	Tenant		2						
	Ditto	Bryan Gately	Tenant		1						
	Ditto	John Gately	Tenant		1						
	Do	Jn. Flanagan	Tenant		1						
		Danl. McCormick pap	Labr.		2		2				
		Michl. Kennedy Do	Tenant		3						
		Patt Cormick Do	Tenant		1						
		John Gavan Do	Labr.								
	Mucklon	Danl. Kelly[8] Esqr Prot	Esquire						1		1
		Mr Edwd. Rich pap	Farmer						2		2
		Patt Ward pap	Feltmaker		2				2		2
	Derefada	Thady McDermot	Tenant		1						
	Do	Wm. Codikin	Tenant		3						
		Luke Conner	Tenant		3						
		Danl. Norton	Tenant		2						

NOTES

1. Lewis, 'Taghboy or Taughboy'.

2. Including 129 acres of water in in County Roscommon and 104 acres of water in County Galway (*General Alphabetical Index*).

3. As note 1.

4. *Report ... fairs and markets.*

5. Leslie, 'Elphin', p.214.

6. Described by Daniel Beaufort as 'miserably small' (Beaufort, 'Journal', T.C.D., MS 4026/2 f.69).

7. Hugh Kelly, freeholder of Ballyfurin, was a tenant of Denis Kelly in 1768 (Dennis Kelly's tenants and friends, Freeholders of Co. Roscommon, 1768, N.L.I., MS 35,163)

8. Daniel Kelly was the eldest son of William Kelly of Mucklon. He had four brothers and three sisters: will of William Kelly, 12 July 1746 (P.B. Eustace (ed.), *Registry of Deeds, Dublin, Abstracts of Wills* (2 vols, Dublin, 1954-6), ii, 310. (Hereafter cited as *Abstracts of Wills*)).

DYSART, COUNTY ROSCOMMON

INTRODUCTION: *The parish of Dysart was 10 miles from Athlone in the barony of Athlone, on the road to Ballinamore. The parish covered 2,972 acres, of which much of the land was bog, with some limestone.[1] The enumerator did not include the wives of heads of households. The parish was described in the 1820s as 'a desert of wilderness ... a very poor district of country, a great portion of it being rocks ... several large villages but the inhabitants are very poor and the houses bad'.[2] Three townlands were held by the Fallon family in 1641.[3] In 1749, eight members of the Fallon family were living in the parish.[4]*

The incumbent was the Rev. William Digby who held the parish with Tisrara, Ahascragh, Cam, Kiltoom, and Taghboy (see Tisrara). The patron was the bishop. The tithes were impropriate in Lord Ranelagh.

OCCUPATIONS

Ale seller	1	Labourer	23	Shepherd	4
Carman	4	Mason	1	Tailor	2
Carpenter	1	Miller	2	Tenant	8
Farmer	4	Mower	1	Turner	1
Freeholder	4	Pumpmaker	1	Weaver	1
		Servants, household	4		

Com~Ros common Parish of	Place of Abode	Names and Religion	Proffession	Children under 14		Children above 14		Men Servts		Women Servts	
				Prot.	Paps.	Prot.	Paps.	Prot.	Paps.	Prot.	Paps.
[f.163]Disert	Killincirvane	Jam Durpe papist	farmer					1			1
	Ditto ~	Widdow Killmurry					2				
	Ditto ~	Patrick Fallon Do	Shepperd		3						
		Thom Lenon pap	Labourer		3						
		Thady McDonnel[5] pap	Labourer		4						
		Thos. McDonnel Ditto	Labourer		1						
		Patt. McDonnel Ditto	pump Maker		4						
		John Fallon papish	Labourer		4						
		Denis Norton papish	Labourer		2						
		Widdow Devire pap									
		Wm. Cusack Ditto	Miller		1						
		Danl. Kelly Ditto	Mason				2				
	Breadough	Connor Mcdonnel[6]	Labourer		2		1				
		Patk. Kenedy Ditto	Shepperd		2						
		Thady White pap ~	Labourer								
		Patt. White[7] pap	Ale Seller		2						
		Franc. White Ditto	Mower		2		3				
		Thom. Longwood Ditto	Labourer		1						
		Daniel Fallon Ditto	Labourer		2						
		Thady Mullon Ditto	Labourer		2						
		Michl. Dun Ditto	Miller		4		2				
		Martin mcDonnel Do	Labourer		3						
		John Cusack Ditto	Carpenter				3				
		Widdow McDonnel pap			3						
	Kilinirvan	Jam Dwire pap	farmer				1	1		ꝉ	1
		Widdow Kelly pap	farmer		2						
	Milltown Fallon	Mr. Jam Kelly pap	farmer								
		Darby Gately[8] pap	Labr.				3				
		Daniel Daw pap	Carman								
		John Menton Ditto	Carman		2						
		Jam. White Ditto	Labour				2				
		Peter White Ditto	Labour		1						
	Killinolough[9]	Edmd. Naghton pap	Shepherd		2						
		John Filane pap	Labourer				2				
		Thos. Fallon pap	Labr.								
		John Kelly Ditto	Labr.								
		Terence Dowel Do	Carman				3				
		Frans. Norton pap	Labour				2				
		Thos. Conniff pap	Weaver		3		3				
		Garrt. White pap	Carman		1						
		Patt. Monoughan	Labr.		1						
		Thady Heavoughan Do	Labr.		1						
		Hugh Tyrrol Do	Labr.		2		4				
		Widdow Fallon Do			3						
		Jam. Keneddy Do	Turner		2						
	fevagh[10]	John Kelly papt.	tenant		3						
		Thady Lenon Do	tenant		2						
		Wm Kelly Do	tenant		3						
		Laughlin Lenon Do	Do		2		1				

DYSART, COUNTY ROSCOMMON

Com~Ros common Parish of	Place of Abode	Names and Religion	Proffession	Children under 14		Children above 14		Men Servts		Women Servts	
				Prot.	Paps.	Prot.	Paps.	Prot.	Paps.	Prot.	Paps.
		Danl. Heavoghan	Shepherd		2		2				
		Widdow Kelly papist	freeholder		1		2				
		Patt. Keigheran Do.	tenant				2				
		Wm. Keigheran Do	tenant		4						
		Patt. Gately[11] pap	tenant		2						
		Thady Kelly[12] pap	freehold				2		0		0
		Martin Fallon pap	Taylor		1		2				
		Bryan Kelly D	Labr		2		1				
		John Fallon pap	Labr		4		2				
		Jam Fallon Do	freehold		2						
		Franc. Kelly Do	freehold				1				
		Charles Hardagon Do	tenant		3						
		John Moran Do	Taylor		3				0		0
				0	100		48		2		2

NOTES

1. Lewis, 'Dysert'.

2. Quoted from Ordnance Survey Name Books in *Dysart and its Christian Past* (Dysart Historical Society, 1994), p. 3.

3. Fevagh - Edmond mcRedmond O ffallon; Milltown Fallon - Jasper ffallon; Killinolough - Redmond mcRedmd ffalon (*Books of Survey and Distribution* Roscommon).

4. Killincirvane - Patrick Fallon, shepherd, and Patt. Fallon, pumpmaker; Breadough - Daniel Fallon, labourer; Killinolough - Thomas Fallon and Widdow Fallon, Martin and John Fallon, labourers; Fevagh - Jam. Fallon, freeholder (Census f.163).

5. Thady McDanell erected a monument in Dysert churchyard for himself and his wife Mary McAannell als Finaghty in February 1752 (*Dysert and its Christian Past*, p.13).

6. Con McDaniel erected a monument to his wife Mary Glynin who died in July 1767 (*Dysert and its Christian Past*, p. 23).

7. Patrick White and Loughlin Fallon erected a monument to John Fallon (possibly Loughlin Fallon's father) in Dysert Church in 1729 (*Dysert and its Christian Past*, p. 19).

8. A monument was erected in Dysert churchyard to Darby Gatley who died September 1749 and his wife Elizabeth Brook and their son William (*Dysert and its Christian Past*, p.18).

9. A townland of arable pasture and a meadow (N.L.I., Map of lands in the barony of Athlone, Ballintober, Ballymoe and Boyle, MS 21 F 23/21).

10. Part of the Sandford estate (N.L.I., Map of Ballyglass and Feevaghbeg, MS 21 F 23/11).

11. Patrick Gately erected a monument in August 1761 to Laughlin Gately who died in 1730 and Giles Gately als Kenedy (probably his wife) who died in November 1733 (*Dysert and its Christian Past*, p.19).

12. Thady Kelly erected a monument to his first wife Ann who died in 1740, intended also for his new wife Ann in May 1750 (*Dysert and its Christian Past* p.19)

RAHARA, COUNTY ROSCOMMON

INTRODUCTION: *The parish of Rahara is in the barony of Athlone. It covers 5,362 statute acres.[1] The land was said to be tolerably good with only a small portion of bog.[2] In 1641, seven members of the Kelly and Fallon families owned the bulk of the parish.[3] In 1749, six members of the Kelly family and five members of the Fallon family were still in the parish.[4]*

The incumbent in 1749 was the Rev. William Digby who held the parish with Tisrara, Ahascragh, Cam, Dysert, Kiltoom, and Taghboy (see Tisrara). The patron was the bishop.

OCCUPATIONS

Ale seller	1	Gardener	1	Pumpmaker	1
Beggar	4	Gentleman	3	Saddler	1
Clerk	1	Herd	1	Servant	2
Cottier	14	Labourer	32	Servbants, household	57
Dragoon	1	Miller	1	Shepherd	7
Esquire	1	Poor woman/widow	6	Smith	1
Farmer	3	Priest	1	Tenant	14
				Weaver	1

Com~Ros common Parish of	Place of Abode	Names and Religion	Proffession	Children under 14		Children above 14		Men Servts		Women Servts	
				Prot.	Paps.	Prot.	Paps.	Prot.	Paps.	Prot.	Paps.
[f.164]Rahara	Longfield	Jams Sprowle⁵ prot -	Gent ~			3		1	2	1	4
	Ditto	Jams Sprowle Esqr	Gent ~								
	Rahara	Mr Michl. Dalton papist	Gent ~				1		3		3
	Ditto	Wm. Lians papist	Smith		1		3				1
	Ditto	John Glyn pap	herd				1				
	Ditto	Michl. Gately pap	Labr~				4				
	Ditto	Darby Mulvil pap	Labr~		1						
	Ditto	Martin Curlly pap	Shepherd		3						
	Ditto	Widdow Gately pap	poor				4				
	Ditto	Michl. McDonnel	Servant		4						
	Ditto	Peter Kelly pap	Servant		3		2		1		1
	Ditto	Widdow Hanan pap	poor				3				
	Caruskeel	Roger Lians pap	tenant		1						1
	Ditto	Edward Girraghty pap	Labr~		3						1
		Patk. Kearney Do	Labr~		2						1
		Peter Murry pap	tenant		3						1
		Barth. Kelly pap	Shepherd		3				1		1
		Widdow Condon	poor								
	Ballough	Mr Wm. Dowlin pap	farmer		3				1		2
		Laughlin Dowlin pap	Shepherd		3		1		1		
		Simon Hindes pap	cotter		3						
		Widdow Griver pap	beggar				1				
		Roger Murry pap	Labourer		1						
		Widdow Cuningham pap	poor		1		2				
		Patt. Connole papst	Cotter								
		John Norton⁶ papist	priest		3		2		1		2
		Thom. Owles pap	cotter		2		3				
		Owen Killduff pap	cotter		3		1				
		Widdow Downy pap	poor		3		2				
		Laurence Girraghty Do	Labourer		2						
		Bryan feeny pap	Labr.		4						
		Widdow Watts pap	poor				2				
		Jam Daily pap	Labr.		5						
		Patk.Cuningham Do	Labr.								
		Wm. Dowlin pap	Labr.		1						
		Luke Glinane Do	Labr.		2		1				
		Fergus Kelly pap	Cotter		2						
		Danl. Gately pap	Cotter		4		1				
		Patt. Owles pap	Cotter		2						
		Edmond Cuningham	Cotter				3				
		John Higgins papist	Cotter		2						
		Garret FitzGerald pap	ale Seller		3		6				1
		Bryan Dogherty pap	Labr.		2						
		Wm. Cormick pap	Labr.		2						
		Widdow Corkan pap	begar				2				
		Luke FitzGerald Do	farmer				5				
		Thady Kerney pap	Labr.		2						
		James Furry pap	Shepherd		2						
		Denis Gorrick pap	Labr.		3						

Com~Ros common Parish of	Place of Abode	Names and Religion	Proffession	Children under 14 Prot.	Children under 14 Paps.	Children above 14 Prot.	Children above 14 Paps.	Men Servts Prot.	Men Servts Paps.	Women Servts Prot.	Women Servts Paps.
	Ardvone	Edmond Kenny Do	tenant		4				1		2
		Jam. Kenny pap	tenant		1				1		1
		Michael Kenny Do	tenant		3				1		1
	Barnacullin	Patt. Courale Do	tenant		1						
		Laughlin Conna Do	Labr.		3						
		Widdow Kenny Do	begar				1				
	CaruMonough	Charles Fallon Do	tenant		1		2				
		Thady Curreale Do	tenant		1		1		1		
		Laug. Cuningham Do	tenant		2		2		1		
		Rogr. farmer pap	Lyons		2		1		2		1
		Jam Fallon Do	tenant		4		2		1		3
		Lau: Flyn pap	Shepherd		4		3		1		1
		62 popish families			110	3	62	1	19	1	28
[f.165 Rahara	Lacken	Widdow Kelly pap	Cotter		1		1				
		Laurence Grork	Labourer		1		2				1
		Luke Delmare	Cotter		2		1				
		Martin Kive			1						
		Bryan Fallon	Labr.				4				
		Bryan Fineron	Labr.		2						
		Edmd. Fallon	Labr.								
		Jn. Condon pap	Weaver		4						
	Ganvins	Gilbert Kelly	Cotter		2						
		Laughlin Bryan	Labr		2		1				
		Patt. Fallon	Tenant						1		1
		Patt Coyl	Labr.		1		3				
		Wm. Murly pap	Labr.		2		1				
		Jam. Cuningham	Labr.				2				
	Killindeeny	Thad Muley pap	Labr.		3						
		Tho Muley Do	Labr.		2						
		Thady McDonel	Labourer				1				
		Edmd Moran	Labr.		3						
		Bryan Kelly	Labr.		1		1				
		Hugh Feeny	Labr.				2				
		Michl. Murry	Labr.		2		1				
	Rover Kelly	Thady Burn	Shepherd		3		6				
		John Conole	Cotter		2		1				
	Gort Ganny	Thom Conole	Sadler		2		1				
		Widdow Conole	Begar								
		Danl. Muley	Cotter				3				
	GortnaMonsogh	Ricd.fitzGerald	Gardiner				2				
		Widdow Girraghty					2				
		Wm. Smith Prot	Clerk	4							1
		Michl. Lawler	Labr.		1		1				
		Patt. Curlly	Miller				1		1		1
		Johnston Pro	Dragoon	2							
	Classlaher	Connor Muny	Shepherd				2				
		Thady Egan	tenant		3						1
		Patk. Egan	tenant				2				
		Mathew Raftry	pump Maker		1				1		

Com~Ros common Parish of	Place of Abode	Names and Religion	Proffession	Children under 14		Children above 14		Men Servts		Women Servts	
				Prot.	Paps.	Prot.	Paps.	Prot.	Paps.	Prot.	Paps.
		Bryan Egan	tenant	~	4	~	1	~	~	~	5
		finis	~	~	~		~				5
		35 papis famly		4	45		42	0	3		29
		2 protestant forwd		3	110		62		19		33
			Total	7	155		104	0	22		

[verso f.165]Mr Digby

NOTES

1. Including 161 acres of Lough Funshinagh (*General Alphabetical Index*).

2. Lewis, 'Raharrow or Rahara'.

3. Ballough - William Mc hugh Kelly; Barnacullen - Edmond mcRedmond O ffallon; Carokeel - Jasper mcRichard Fallon, Rory mcLoghlin ffallon; Gortnamonsogh - Bryan mcKedagh Kelly; Roven Kelly - Bryan o Kelly; Lacken – William Mc hugh Kelly (*Books of Survey and Distribution* Roscommon).

4. Census, f. 164, 165.

5. James Sprowle [Sprowell] of Longfield was a son of Joseph Sprowel, a gentleman. He was born in Roscommon and educated by a Dr Poole. He entered TCD in 1736, aged 17 and graduated BA in 1731 (*Alumni Dubliniensis*).

6. John Naughton was listed as Roman Catholic pastor of Rahara in 1739 and 1756. His five children were probably his orphaned nephews and nieces (Beirne, (ed.) *Diocese of Elphin*, p.124; Fenning, 'Clergy Lists', p.145).

ST. PETER'S, ATHLONE, COUNTY ROSCOMMON

INTRODUCTION: *Divided by the river Shannon, the parish of St. Peter's on the Connaught side of the town of Athlone was in the diocese of Elphin in the barony of Athlone. The military defences of the town were situated on this side, with the Castle and the advanced forts and redoubts defending the approach from Galway by way of Ballinasloe. A patent to hold a fair every Tuesday and Saturday was issued in 1606 and 1672 to the Corporation and to Lord Ranelagh.[1] In 1749, Athlone was owned by the trustees of the estate of Lord Ranelagh who had died in 1712. Ranelagh had set up a trust to fund Protestant schools there and in Roscommon. This was to be funded by the rents of the castle, manor, town and lands in the town. Bishop Edward Synge was a trustee and his trusteeship got him into considerable trouble.[2]*

The occupations within the town demonstrate its importance to its agricultural hinterland and to its commercial centre. Trades connected with the sale of cattle and the processing of skins include glovers, saddlers, shoemakers, skinners, tanners, smiths and a cutler. The tanning yards were in the north of the town on the bank of the Shannon. The town had long had a reputation for felt hats, and there were 10 hatters in the County Roscommon part of the town. There were also apothecaries, a watchmaker, and an upholder. As a post town, Athlone had a postmaster and was a centre for trading upriver from Limerick.

The parish had no Church of Ireland church and was grouped with the parish of St. Mary's, across the Shannon in County Westmeath. The two parishes were served by a single incumbent until the beginning of the nineteenth-century. During the eighteenth century, there were complaints by the vestry of St. Mary's about the shortage of pews because of the attendance of non-residents, whose tithes were impropriate to the earl of Ranelagh and who did not pay cess.[3] The census manuscript is signed by the Rev. Lewis Hawkes.[4]

OCCUPATIONS

Aleseller	12	Fisherman	1	Schoolmistress	1
Apothecary	3	Gauger	1	Schoolmaster	1
Baker	4	Gentleman	3	Servants	4
Beggar	1	Gentlewoman	1	Servants, household	201
Boarding school mistress	1	Glazier	1	Shoemaker	7
Broguemaker	5	Glover	6	Skinner	4
Butcher	11	Grocer	1	Smith	5
Carpenter	4	Hatter	10	Snuffmaker	1
Clothier	2	Huckster	12	Soapboiler	3
Cobbler	1	Husband(man)	1	Spinner	8
Comber	1	Innkeeper	8	Tanner	3
Cooper	2	Labourer	135	Tailor	8
Cottoner	1	Maltster	3	Thatcher	1
Cowboy	1	Miller	2	Tiller (?Tiler)	1
Cutler	1	Nailer	3	Tobacconist	2
Distiller	2	Pensioner	3	Upholder	1
Doctor	1	Postmaster	1	Watchmaker	1
Dyer	1	Parish Clerk	1	Weaver	9
Esquire	2	Shepherd	1	Widow	18
Farmer	2	Saddler	3	Wigmaker	4
				Yeoman	1

Com~Ros common Parish of	Place of Abode	Names and Religion	Proffession	Children under 14		Children above 14		Men Servts		Women Servts	
				Prot.	Paps.	Prot.	Paps.	Prot.	Paps.	Prot.	Paps.
[f.166] St. Peters	Athlone	Dens. Naughten papt	Sadler					1	3		3
		Dillon Naghtn papt	Mercht.		3				1		2
		James Mullegan[5] papt	Tanr.		1				1		1
		Edwd. Welsh Protest	Wigmakr.					2			1
		Andw. Burn papt	Mercht.				3	~~2~~	1		2
		James Fflood[6] Protest	Mercht.	4		3			1		1
		Margt. Lorcan papt	Inkeepr.		2		4		3		3
		Peter Burk papt	Mercht.								
		Thom. Groom Protest	Carpter.			2			1		1
		Willm. Sproule Prost	Soapboylr.			4					1
		Clemt. Moore papt	Taylor				1		2		
		Danl. Conner papt	Laborr.								
		Edmond Naughton papt	Servts				2				
		Jane Moore papt	Servt.		1						
		Honr. Mackin Do	Widow		1						
		John Chapman Protest	Weaver	1			1				1
		Mss. Longworth Protest	Spinster			2					
		Sauckville Kid Protest	Wigmker.	3					2		1
		Mr Bryn Shiele papt	Gent.		5				1		1
		John St.John Protest	Dyer	4							1
		Mrs Jane Potts	Gentn.	2		5			4		1
		Ed. Loftus Glass[7] Do	Esqr.	1		1		2		2	1
		Widdow. Hughes papt					1				
		Peter Doolan papt	Servt.		1						
		Mr Hen Fry[8] Protest	Mercht.	4		1		2		3	
		Willm. O Brian papt	Spiner				1				4
		Thos. Hall[9] Protest	Inkeepr.	2					3	2	1
		Simon Dowell papt	Mercht.		2		3				1
		Laurence Galvin Do	Sadler						1		
		Widdow Burns Do	Grocer				2				1
		James Moore[10] Do	Apothry						1		1
		Fergus Naghten Do	Mercht.		2		2		1		2
		Mat. McNamara Do	Apothry			1					2
		Peter Longworth Prot	Sadler								
		David Gibbons Protest	Inkeepr.	1		1			1	1	
		Jam. Geoghan papt	Mercht.		4				1		1
		Widdow Ffallon Do	Spinr.				3				1
		Laurence Conr. Do	Wigmr.		4				1		
		Robt. Colum Do	Baker		2						1
		John Plumr.[11] Protest	Esqr.	1		1		1	1		
	Page (1)	John Hamilton Protest	Gent.	2		2		1	1		1
[f.167] St Petrs	Athlone	Terence Dun Protest	Combr.[12]	1		1					
		Thom. Walton[13] Do	Shoemakr.								
		Bryn. Mackin papt.	Huckster		3						
		Mary Liney Protest	Baker	1		1					
		Bryn. Eagen papist	Labour.								1
		James Connelly Do.	Labour		2						
		James Hughes Prot.	Psh Clrk			1					

Com~Ros common Parish of	Place of Abode	Names and Religion	Proffession	Children under 14		Children above 14		Men Servts		Women Servts	
				Prot.	Paps.	Prot.	Paps.	Prot.	Paps.	Prot.	Paps.
		Mrs Nevil papt.	Widw.	2							
		Thady McDermot Do.	Broguem.							1	1
		Matthew Nugt. papt.	Miller	2			1		1	1	
		Willm. Hosbro Protest	Distiller	3		2		2			4
		Geo: Clark Do.	Baker	3		2					
		Michl. McLaughlin Do.	Shoemkr.	2			3			1	
		Geo: ffury Prost	Pensinr.	1							
		Widw Fineran papt.			2		2				
		Jonathan Nichlson Prost.	Taylor								
		Robt. Codnor[14] Prott.	Distiller	5		2					3
		Lacky Naghten papt.	Upholdr[15]				2				
		Willm. McKoan Prost.	Snuffmr.								
		Widow Neile Prot	Aleseller			2					1
		Willm. Wright Do.	Shoemr.	2			1				
		James Dillon papt.	Mercht.		2		1				
		Edwd Mobbet Prot	Watchmakr.	1							1
		John Naughten Do	Baker	1		3					
		Michl. Knavin papt.	Aleseller	2		1					2
		Thom. Bell[16] Protest	Doctor	1		6		2			1
		Hen Sproule Do	Post mr.			2					1
		Geo. Dunin papt.	Aleseller		2						2
		ffrancis McDonnell Prot.	Aleselr.	1							1
		Barthow. Bryn papt.	Wigmakr.		1						1
		Michl. Burns Do.	Innkeepr.		4				2		3
		Thady Meally Do.	Do.		2		1		2	0	1
		Nick. Shaughnussy Do	Do.		2		2				1
		James Grogan Do.	Hucksr.		3						1
		Jon. fflynn Do.	Smith		1						1
		Jon. Burnet Protest	Weavr.	2							
		Thady Moran papt.	Smith		2						
		John Joice papt.	Labr.		2						
		Peter Murry Do	Nailor		3						
		Willm. Kelly Do	Aleselr.		1						
	Page (2)	ffaragh Kelly Do.	Yeoman		3						
[f.168] St Petrs	Athlone	James Fury papist	Labourer	0	1						
		Elizth Carr Do.	Spinr.								
		Widow McNamara Do.	Do.								
		John Mackin Do.	Labourr.								
		Hugh Mackin Do.	Do.		2						
		Michl. Foulster Do.	Do.				1				
		John Burmingham Do.	Do.		2		1				
		Jon. ffeeny Do.	Do.				3				
		Patrick Cox Do.	Do.								
		Edmd. Dillon Do.	Do.		1		1				
		John Grey Protest.	Weaver								
		Allice Dillon papt.	Widow								
		John Higgins Do.	Labourr.		1		1				
		Dennis Kelly Do.	Do.		1		1				
		James Killelagh Do.	Do.								1

Com~Ros common Parish of	Place of Abode	Names and Religion	Proffession	Children under 14		Children above 14		Men Servts		Women Servts	
				Prot.	Paps.	Prot.	Paps.	Prot.	Paps.	Prot.	Paps.
		Bridgt. Bourk Do.	Spinr.								
		John Dunin Do.	Broguemr.		2						
		Winifred Duffy Do.	Huxster								
		John Lenon Protest.	S[?]herd	4		3		1			1
		Patrick Maley papt.	Labr.		2						
		Mary Malley Do.	Spinr.								
		Patrick Daugherty Do.	Labourr.								
		Thom. Doolan Do.	Cooper		2				1		
		Thom. Ellison Protest.	Butchr.	2		1					
		Rogr Conner papt.	Tobaconst		3						1
		Arthur Dunlap Prost.	Butchr.	2							1
		Elizth. Coughran papst	Widow		2						
		John Whiskin Protest	Schoolmr.	2							
		John Killdoyle papt.	Smith		1						
		Barnard Browne Prot	Hucksr.	3							
		John Stoneam Prost	Butchr.						1		1
		Maurice Humphry Do.	Hucksr.	2				1			
		Thomas Blyth Do.	Do.	2						1	
		Jon. Lorcan Do.	Shoemr.	2				1			1
		Jon. McGrath papt.	Miller				1				
		Jon. Goff Do.	Mason								1
		Willm. Ellison Protest.	Butchr.					1			
		Jon. Hanna[17] Do.	Taylor	4		4					
		Charls McDonald Do.	Weavr.	1		3				1	2
		Daniel McNamara Do.	Labr.								
	Page (3)	Patrick Heagan papt.	Do.	1							
[f.169] St Petrs	Athlone	Jon. Robinson Protes.	Thatcher	1							
		Simon Kelly papt.	Labr.					1			
		August. Burk Do	Cloather		~~2~~		2	1	1		
		Alexr. Montgomery Protes.	Coopr.								
		Thoms. Talbot Do	ffisher[18]								
		Valentine Parker Do.	Gaugr.								
		Edmd. Keogh papt.	Hucster								
		Michl. Kelley Do	Labour.		2						
		Jon. Delemere Do	Hatter								
		Hen. Heap Protes.	Weavr.	6		1					
		Terence Gallaghr papt.	Taylor		2				1		
		Matthew Hevran Prot.	Malster	2							
		Robt. Henderson Do.	Weavr.								
		Laughlin ffallon papt.	Hatter		3						
		David Mulhallon papt.	Cutler	2				1			
		Teige Corkran papt.	Tanr.		3						
		Thom. Murey Do	Labour.								
		Thom. Hartbourn Prots	Skinr.	2							
		Hugh Killen papt.	Hucksr.								
		Edmd Murphey Do	Butchr.								
		Nick. White Do	Aleselr.		1						1
		Willm Grinam Do	Labour.		2						
		Catherin Grinam Do	Spinr.		1						

Com~Roscommon Parish of	Place of Abode	Names and Religion	Proffession	Children under 14		Children above 14		Men Servts		Women Servts	
				Prot.	Paps.	Prot.	Paps.	Prot.	Paps.	Prot.	Paps.
		Geo. Gibbons Do	Taylor				2				
		James Barret Do	Broguemr.						2		1
		Jon. Hall Protes.	Hucksr.	2							
		Peter Coyle papt.	Butchr.		1						
		ffrank McNamara Do	Do.		2						
		Jon. Kelly Do	Labr.		1						
		Mary Monaghn. Do	Widow		1						
		John Eagen Do	Cloither		2						
		Daniel Lyons Do	Soapboylr.								
		Widdow Manin Do	Ale Seller				2		1		1
		Edmd. Malley Do	Hucksr.		5						1
		Jon. Donil Protes. Do.		3							
		Laur. Thewless Do	Servt.	2							
		James Begg papt.	Alekeepr.								
		John Malley Do	Soapboylr.								1
		Hen. Murrey Do	Nailer		4			1			2
		Hen. Warren Do	Glovr.		1				2		1
	pa: (4)	Thom. Lackey Protes.	Pensionr.								
[f.170] St Petrs	Athlone	Widdow Hawkins Prots			3						
		Miss ffrench papts	Schoolmistr.								
		Phillip Duffy Do.	Husband[19]								
		Thoms. Dillon Do.	Mercht.		4		·1		2		1
		Willm. Knouth Prots	Butchr.			3					
		Connor Horan papt	Labour.		2		1				
		James Glynn Do.	Do.								
		Mrs Ffallon[20] Do.	Boarding Schoolmstrs.				8				1
		ffrancis Mullegan Do.	Mercht.		1		4		1		1
		Jon. Bourk papt	Inkeepr.		3						1
		Jon. Naylor Do.	Labr.		1						1
		James Coffy Protest.	Butchr.								
		Garth. Coughlan papt	Taner		2		2				
		Widdow Brogan Do.					2				
		Arthur Ellison Prots.	Butchr.	2							
		Barthw. Deleny papt.	Glovr.								
		Widdow Burk Do.									
		Widdow Tulley Prot.	Weavr.	4							
		Thom. Kelly papt.	Labour.		1						
		Widw. Cain Do.									
		Willm. Ffineran Do.	Labour.		1						
		Dennis Naghten Do.	Broguem.		1						
		Teige Lenaghan Do.	Mercht.		1						
		Bryn. Warren Do.	Glovr.		1		1	1	2		1
		Jams. Connelly papt.	Tobconst.				1				
		Jon. Duin papt.	Labr.		2						
		Honr. Creegan papt.	Widw.		2						
		Marn. Healy pa	Labr.		1						
		Mary McGara papt	Widw.		1		2				
		Patk. Dunnin papt.	Labr.		1						

Com~Ros common Parish of	Place of Abode	Names and Religion	Proffession	Children under 14		Children above 14		Men Servts		Women Servts	
				Prot.	Paps.	Prot.	Paps.	Prot.	Paps.	Prot.	Paps.
		Anstas Ruth papt	Widw.								
		Nichls Tully papt.	Skinner								1
		Pat. Teige papt.	Labr.		2						
		Sarah Glinn papt.	Widw.								
		Jon. Thoman papt	Labr.		1						
		Jon. Duffy papt.	Labr.								
		Walter Kelly21 papt.	Apotecry		2						1
		Edmond Naghten papt	Gent.								
		Jon. Evans protest.	Scholmr.	1							
		Wm. Connor Protest.	Shomakr.	1	1						
[f.171] St Petrs	Pa (5)	Ed Seymore papt.	Labr.		2						
	Athlone	Wm. Coffy papist	Butchr.		1		2				
		Michl. Sloman papt.	Taylor		1						
		Justin Graham Protest	Cobler	2							
		Scisly Ward papt.	Widw.								
		Wind. Ward papt.	Widw.								
		Jon. Dolan papt.	Malster		3						1
		Bridgt. Costello papt.									
		Chrisr. McGinis papt.	Labr.								
		Jeofry Murphey papt.	Labr.								
		Edmd. Collins papt.	Weavr.		2		2				
		Tho. Deleny papt.	Skiner		3		1				
		Wm. Clark Protest	Shomr	3							1
		Wm. Lawson Protest.	Pensionr								
		Pat. Maley papt.	Labr.								
		Richd. Gibbons papt.	Labr.				1				
		Jonnack Gibbons papt.	Labr.								
		Ter. Fox papt.	Labr.		2		3				
		Tho. Malley papt.	Labr.		1						
		Jam. Lawler papt.	Labr.		2						
		Con. Mara papt.	Labr.		1						
		Conner Gaffy papt.	Labr.		1						1
		Petr. Keogh papt.	Taylor		5						1
		Edmd. Kelly papt.	Carpenr.				2				
		Peter Kelly papt.	Labr.		2						
		Jam. Mara papt.	Labr.		1						
		Bryn. Kelly papt.	Labr.								
		Jon. Jordan papt.	Huxster		1						
		Jon. Kennedy papt.	Labr.		3		1				
		Bryn. Kenedy Prott.	Nailer	1							
		Jon. Kelly papt.	Labr.								
		Jams. Mulldoon papt.	Aleseller						1		1
		Own. Mulldoon papt.	Alesell.				2		1		1
		Jams Doyle papt.	Labr.		1		2				
		Jon. Donnellan papt.	Labr.		1		1				
		Hugh Kelly papt.	Hatter				1				
		Rogr. Creamr. papt.	Cotner				3				1
		Jon. Shaw Protest.	Hatter	3							
		Richd. Burk papt.	Labr.								

Com~Ros common Parish of	Place of Abode	Names and Religion	Proffession	Children under 14 Prot.	Children under 14 Paps.	Children above 14 Prot.	Children above 14 Paps.	Men Servts Prot.	Men Servts Paps.	Women Servts Prot.	Women Servts Paps.
		Thad Cuncann. papt.	Labr.								
		Darby Manin papt.	Labr.								
	Page (6)	James Geraghty papt.	Labr.				1				
[f.172] St Petrs	Athlone	Hen. Fury papt.	Malster		4						
		Jon. Killkenny papt.	Cowboy								
		Widow Greghan pt			14						
	Gallowshill	Thos. Deleny papt.	Skinr.		4				2		1
		Thady Buckley papt.	Brogemar.		3		3				
		Hugh Warren papt.	Glovr.								
		Mic: Kegan papt.	Labr.								
		James Gowan papt.	Labr.								
		Willm. Burn papt.	Labr.		2						
		Widw. Curry papt.			1						
		Cormk. Duffy papt.	Labr.								
		Widw Grey Protest.		1		1					
		Danl. fflyn papt.	Labr.								
		Patrick Curley papt.	Begr.		2						
		Widw. Branan papt.									
		Widw ffallon papt.			2						
		Thomas Deane[22] Protest.			1						
		Denis ffeeny papt.			2						
		Thos. Costello papt.	Hatter		1						
		Matthew Brann. papt.	Labr.		4						
		Jon. ffallon papt.	Labr.								
		Thim. Conr. papt.	Labr.		1						
	Belagh	Lewis Doyle papt.	Labr.		3		3				
		Wm. Heifran Protest.	Hatter		3	1					
		Jon. Dolan papt.	Labr.								
		Danl. Dolan papt.	Labr.				4				
		Mark Hargadn. papt.	Labr.				1				
		Bryn. Maley papt.	Labr.								
		ffrank Bird papt.	Hatter		2				2		1
		Jam. Conner papt.	Shoemr.	2	1			1			1
		Wm. Ffallon papt.	Aleseller		2						1
		Wm. Maxwell Protest.	Weavr.								
		Nat. Nixon Protest	Hatter	3			1				
		Thos. Manin papt.	Smith		2		2				
		Con. Coughlan papt.	Labr.		1						
		Jon. Manin papt.	Labr.		2						
		Thos. Grey Protest.	Hatter	1		4			2		
		Charls McDermt papt.	Hatter		3						
		Patrick Frane papt.	Hatter		2						
		Joan Dolan papt.	Widw.								
	Page (7) Monksland	Willm. Talbot[23] Protest.	Inkepr.								
[f.173] St. Peter's	Monksland	James Deane Protest	Tiller	5							
		Laugh. Tully papt.	Glaizer				1	1			2
		Den. Cone papt.	Taylor				2	+			2

Com~Ros common Parish of	Place of Abode	Names and Religion	Proffession	Children under 14 Prot.	Children under 14 Paps.	Children above 14 Prot.	Children above 14 Paps.	Men Servts Prot.	Men Servts Paps.	Women Servts Prot.	Women Servts Paps.
		Peter Coniff papt.	Labr.		1						
		Peter Kelly papt.	Carpenr.		2						
		Cat. Dooling papt.	Widow		1						
		Thos. Griffin papt.	Labr.		4						
		Peter Coony papt.	Labr.		3						
		Bryn. Coony papt.	Labr.		3						
		Rose Cain papt.	Widow				1				
		James Kelly papt.	Labr.								
	Bigmeadw	Danl. Donin papt.	Labr.		2						
		Jaspr. Correlly papt.	Labr.		1						
		Hugh Correlly papt.	Labr.		2						
		Wm. Cassy papt.	Labr.		1						
		Jon. Murry papt.	Labr.		1						
		Hen Cosgrove papt.	Labr.		1						
	Bunariby	James Classy papt.	Labr.		1		2				
		Patrick Donen papt.	Labr.		1						
		Wm. Henry papt.	Labr.		1						
		Jon. Henry papt.	Labr.		1						
		–. Gillegan papt.	Labr.		2						
		Rose Donen papt.	Widow		1						
	Kellnamanagh	James Ward papt.	Labr.		4						
		James Kenelly papt.	Labr.		2						
		Hugh Macin papt.	Labr.		2						
		Bryn. Macin papt.	Labr.				3				
		Den. Macin papt.	Labr.		2		2				
		Darby Macin papt.	Labr.		4						
		Thady McLane papt.	Labr.		2		1				
		Pat. Naghton papt.	Labr.		2		3				
		Mary Henry papt.	Widow				2				
		Charls. Galvin papt.	Labr.		3		3				
		Joan Killen papt.	Widow				1				
		Den. Kelly papt.	Labr.		1		2̶				
	Rooscagh	Jon. Kenelly papt.	Labr.		1						
		Mic. Geracuse papt.	Smith		0		2		2		1
		Pat. Mulldoon papt.	Labr.								1
		Pat. Mulldoon papt.	Labr.								
		Richd. Mulldoon papt.	Labr.								
	Page (8)	Giles Kelly papt. L̶a̶b̶r̶.	Widwr.				1				
[f.174] St. Peter's	Rooscagh	Hugh Naghton papt.	Labr.				1				
		Andw. Bean papt.	Labr.		1						
		Patr. Martin papt.	Labr.		2						
		Patr. Watch papt.	Labr.				3				
		Laughn. Watch papt.	Labr.								
		Dan. Hanin papt.	Labr.				1				
		Jon. Shehine papt.	Labr.		1		2				1
		Mich. Shehine papt.	Labr.		1						1
		Jon. Correlly papt	Labr.				1				
		James Owers papt	Labr.		1						1
		John Dooling papt.	Labr.								

Com~Ros common Parish of	Place of Abode	Names and Religion	Proffession	Children under 14		Children above 14		Men Servts		Women Servts	
				Prot.	Paps.	Prot.	Paps.	Prot.	Paps.	Prot.	Paps.
		Coner Naghten papt.	Carpenr.		1						1
		Murtagh Correen papt.	Labr.								
		Den. Correen papt.	Labr.								
		Peter Pesly papt.	Labr.				1				
		Willm Geraghty papt.	Glover				1				1
		Jon Geraghty papt	Glovr.								
	Cloonown	Patr. Ffones papt.	Labr.				3				
		Bryn. Dunin papt.	Labr.		5						
		Bryn. Dunin papt.	Labr.		6						
		Willm. Sheen papt.	Labr.		2						
		Thos. Joice papt.	Labr.				1				
		Michl. Henry papt.	Labr.		1		1				
		Darby Kinoyster papt.	Labr.		2						
		Hugh Brenan papt.	Labr.		3						
		Danl. Gaffy papt.	Labr.		3						
		Danl. Curly papt.	Labr.		3		1				
		Thady Murry papt.	Labr.		2						
		Hubbert Burk papt.	Farmr		2		1		1		1
		Nably Dolan papt.	Widw.		1						
	Bealamully	Jams. Dowdel papt.	Farmr		4		1		1		1
		Ricd. Burk papt.	Aleseller				2		1		1
		Bryn. Kelly papt.	Labr.				2				
		Willm. Dolan papt.	Labr.		3		1				
		Andw. Freeman papt.	Labr.								
		Hugh Owls papt.	Labr.		2						
		Peter Rourk papt.	Labr.				1				
		Richd. Rourk papt.	Labr.		2						
	Page (9)	Jon. Kelly papt.	Labr.		3						
[f.175]		From page - 1		25	24	22	28	9	30	8	38
		From page - 2		30	35	23	13	4	5	3	26
		From page - 3		25	29	11	9	4	2	2	9
		From page - 4		20	31	1	7	3	8	0	7
	Totals	From page - 5		8	33	6	22	1	5	0	8
		From page - 6		10	31	0	22	0	2	0	7
		From page - 7		7	61	6	14	1	6	0	5
		From page - 8		5	52	0	24	0	3	0	4
		From page - 9		0	51	0	21	21	3	0	8
		Sums Total		130	338	69	163	43	64	13	112
		Sums Total of the abov Protestants 255									
		Papists 677									
		Those named as Parents Total [erased]									
		Gross Total of all [erased]									
	Rev. Lowy Hauke			5					1	3	1
		Protestant families 87									
		Papist families 281									
		Totall Number of Protestants 438									
		Totall Number of Papists 1239									
		Number in the whole Parish 1677									

NOTES

1. *Report... fairs and markets*

2. Marie-Louise Legg, 'Money and Reputations: the effects of the Banking Crises of 1755 and 1760', *Eighteenth-Century Ireland*, 11, (1996), pp 74-87.

3. Visitation of the Diocese of Meath about 1723 (N.L.I., MS 1619); Harman Murtagh, *Athlone: History and Settlement to 1800*, (Athlone 2000), pp. 39, 202.

4. Lewis Hawkes, son of John Hawkes and Catherine Goldsmith was tutored by Thomas Contarine. He was born in Co. Roscommon and admitted pensioner to TCD 1723 aged 18. He graduated BA 1728. He married Sarah, daughter of Dr. Thomas Bell (Census f.167; *Alumni Dubliniensis*; Leslie, 'Elphin' (Representative Church Body Library, MS 61/2/5 f.156); N.L.I., Genealogical Office MS 802/10).

5. James Mulligan leased land in Connaught Street, Athlone from Gustavus Hamilton for 31 years 18 May 1753 (N.L.I., Hastings-Potts Papers, MS 3150).

6. James Flood was a freeholder (Freeholders of Co. Roscommon, 1768, N.L.I., MS 35,163).

7. Loftus Glass was a freeholder. He was an executor of his brother Edward's will made 29 January 1749 and proved in 1750 (Freeholders of Co. Roscommon, 1768, N.L.I., MS 35,163; *Abstracts of Wills*, ii, 68).

8. Henry Fry, merchant witnessed the will of Edward Glass of Athlone, 29 January 1749 (*Abstracts of Wills*, ii, 68).

9. As well as being an innkeeper, Thomas Hall was a bailiff (Watson, *Almanack*).

10. Marriage articles dated 1747 between James Moore apothecary and Mary, elder daughter of Walter Kelly both of Athlone provide for Moore taking over Kelly's business (N.L.I., Ainsworth Report No 18, Brabazon Papers).

11. John Plummer was a freeholder (Freeholders of Co. Roscommon, 1768, N.L.I., MS 35,163).

12. A comber of wool prior to spinning.

13. Thomas Walton was a freeholder (Freeholders of Co. Roscommon 1768, N.L.I., MS 35,163)..

14. Robert Codner was a freeholder (Freeholders of Co. Roscommon 1768, N.L.I., MS 35,163)

15. Dealer or maker of furniture.

16. Thomas Bell was formerly an army surgeon. He died in Athlone on 29 December 1768 (Royal College of Physicians of Ireland, Fitzpatrick Archive).

17. Jon. Hannah was a freeholder (Freeholders of Co. Roscommon 1768, N.L.I., MS 35,163).

18. Possibly fishing for eels; there were a large number of eel weirs in the river Shannon north of Athlone (OS 6":1 mile map County Roscommon 1838, Sheet 52).

19. A cultivator of land.

20. Mrs Susanna Fallon was an Augustinian nun placed in Athlone by Bishop Patrick French in 1747 to provide education for the daughters of the Roman Catholic gentry (Fenning, 'Clergy Lists', p.145, fn.10).

21. See Note 10.

22. Thomas Deane was a freeholder (Freeholders of Co. Roscommon 1768, N.L.I., MS 35,163).

23. William Talbot was a freeholder (Freeholders of Co. Roscommon 1768, N.L.I., MS 35,163).

CAM, COUNTY ROSCOMMON

INTRODUCTION: *The parish of Cam is in the barony of Athlone. The parish covered 12,402 statute acres.*[1] *In 1837 Lewis says that the land was set to tillage, and there was some bog but no waste land.*[2] *Limestone was available for agricultural purposes.*

The parish had been united with Kiltoom from 1636. The church of Ireland incumbent was the Rev. William Digby who held the parish with those of Ahascragh, Cam, Dysert, Kiltoom, Rahara and Taghboy. (See Tisrara). There was no Protestant church in the parish, the medieval church having fallen into disrepair.[3]

A friar Fr. Patrick Conife lived at Trine.

OCCUPATIONS

Ale seller	3	Gentleman	3	Shepherd	11
Beggar	2	Hatter	2	Sheriff Bailiff	1
Carman	26	Herd	2	Smith	6
Constable	1	Labourer	122	Tailor	1
Cowboy	1	Maltster	1	Tealor (?tailor)	1
Dealer	1	Manager	2	Tenant	34
Farmer	12	Mason	1	Tiler	1
Feathermonger	2	Miller	2	Weaver	8
Friar	1	Pound keeper	1	Wigmaker	1
		Servants, household	58		

Com~Ros common Parish of	Place of Abode	Names and Religion	Proffession	Children under 14		Children above 14		Men Servts		Women Servts	
				Prot.	Paps.	Prot.	Paps.	Prot.	Paps.	Prot.	Paps.
Cam [f.176]	Grange	Thos. Lyster[4] Prot.	Gentl:	1					4		3
	Do	Jams. Glinan Pap:	Labr.		5						
	Do	Gill Glinan Pap:	Carman		1						
		Math. Dolan Pap:	Labr.		4						
	Do	Redmond Stanton Pa:	Labr.		3						
	Do	Own. Moran Pap:	Labr.		1						
	Do	Teady Moran Pap:	Labr.		1						
	Do	Patt. Birn Pap:	Labr.				3				
	Do	Richard Stanton Pap:	Smith		2		4				
	Do	Edmd. Kelley Pap	Labr.		1						
	Do	Edmond Concarly Pap	Carman		1		2				
	Do	Rogr. Fallon Pap	Carman		1		2				
	Do	Teady Hoverty Pap	Smith				2				
	Do	Martin McDanell Pap	Labr.		1						
	Do	Wm. Giraughty Pap	Sheperd				1				
	Do	Thos. McDanel Pap	Carman								
	Do	Luke McKelly Pap	Labr.		3						
	Do	Teady McConife Pap	Labr.		2						
		Andrew McConife Pap	Labr.		2						
		Jon. Murly Pap	Cowboy		2		2				
		Larnce Moran Pap	Labr.		3						
		Bryan Murly Pap	Tealor		2		1				
		Martin Cuniham Pap	Labr.		2		2				
		Widow Glinan Pap					2				
		Wm. Fihilly Pap	Labr.								
		Bryan Hay Pap	Labr.		2						
		Tady Fallon Pap	Labr.		3						
		Hugh Finilly Pap	Labr.		3						
		Edmd. Boughelly Pap	Labr.		1						
		Jno. Corkan Pap	Labr.								
		Michl. Fallon Pap	Carman		2						
		Martn. Cuniham Pap	Labr.								
		Martn. Keivill Pap	Labr.				3				
		Roger Gordon Pap	Smith		3		1				
		Danell Murly Pap	Labr.		1						
		Bryan Groork Pap	Herd				2				
		Jon. Higins Pap	Labr.		2		1				
		Widow Higins Pap			2						
[f.177]Cam	Lysterfield	Thos. Lyster[5] Prot.	Gent					2	3		3
	Do	Coll. Doran Pap	Millar		3				1		
	Do	Widow Galvin	Pap				4				
	Do	Dar. Fallon Pap	Labr.		3						
	Do	Own. Moran	Malster								
	Do	Matt. Moran Pap	Labr.		2						
	Do	Jno. Galvin Papist	Carmn.								
	Do	Michl. Gathely Pap	Labr.		4		1				
	Do	Patt Gathely Pap	Labr.		3						
	Do	Patt. Glinan Pap	Manager				4				
	Do	Danell Knough Pap	Labr.		1						

Com~Ros common Parish of	Place of Abode	Names and Religion	Proffession	Children under 14 Prot.	Paps.	Children above 14 Prot.	Paps.	Men Servts Prot.	Paps.	Women Servts Prot.	Paps.
	Do	Walter Doyle Papist	Labr.		1						
	Do	Teady Doyle	Labr.								
	Do	Edmd. Fallon Papist	Sheperd				3				
	Do	Petr. Gilligan Pap	Labr.		3		1				
	Do	Jn. Kelley Papist	Labr.				3				
	Do	Patt. Cormuck Pap	Labr.		1						
	Do	Teady Fallon Pap	Labr.				2				
	Do	Loughlin Cormuck Pap	Labr.		1		2				
	Do	Michale Terlls Pap	Labr.		1		1				
Do	Ballilion[6]	Roger Doyle Pap	Hatter				4				
		Jno. Moran Prots.	Constabl.			2					
		Thos. Edwards Prot:	Weaver	1							
Do		Loughn. McDanell Pap	Carman		2		3				
		Nichl. Dowlan Pap	Labr.		2						
		Edm. Stanton Pap	Sheephd				4				
		Jams. Timoughty Pap	Weaver		2		1				
		Will Burke Pap	feathermon.								
Do		Terence Clougher Pap	Do		1						
	Lissmoile	Hugh Kelly	Gent						1		1
		Own. Dowlan Pap	Labr.		1						
		Teady Glinan Pap	Labr.		1		2				
		Hugh McConife	Tailor								
	Corelea	Jno Manion Papist	Carman		3		2		1		1
		Ounah Crobbane Pap	Labr.		1		2				
		Wm. Broocks Pap	Labr.		1		2				
		Jno Concann Pap	Labr.		1						
		Patt. Giraughty Pap	Labr.		2						
		Laurence Milie Pap	Labr.		2		1				
[f.178]Cam	Corelea	Domni. Donnly Pap	Shephd.		1						
		Jno. Naughton Papist	Labr.		3		2				
		Patt. ffallon[7] Pap	Begger		2						
		Widw. Sumoughn	Pap		4						
	Cashvughbeg	Jno. Naughn Papist	Labr.		2						
		Augese Muldowney Pa	Labr.		1						
		Teady Naughn Papist	Labr.		2						
		Luke Dowell Papist	Labr.		1						
	Trine	Fr. Patrick Conife[8]	fryar						1		1
	Lisscom	Danll. Gaffie Pap	Carman				1				
		Wid. Manaughan Pap	Tenant				1				
		Mich: Gaffie Pap	Dealer		2						
	Carrick	Own. Monoughn Pap	Carman		3		2				
		Darby Monoughn Pap	Carmn		4		2				
		Lough. Coffie Pap	Carmn		1		2				
		Lough. Naughn Pap	Carmn				1				
		Dinis Menton Pap	Labr.						1		1
		Petr. Birne Pap	Shephd				3				
		Thos. Glinan Pap	Labr.				1				
		Jno. Naughn Pap	Labr.		2						
		Teady Gilligan Pap	Labr.		1						

Com~Ros common Parish of	Place of Abode	Names and Religion	Proffession	Children under 14 Prot.	Paps.	Children above 14 Prot.	Paps.	Men Servts Prot.	Paps.	Women Servts Prot.	Paps.
		Conor Coniffe Pap	Labr.								
	Ferenykelly	Bryan Hughs[9] Pap	farmer		2				1		1
		Terance Hughs Papist	farmer		2				1		1
		Antho. Hughs Pap	farmer		2				2		
		Wm. Killroy Pap	Labr.		1						
		Bryan Killroy Pap	Labr.		1						
	Lisfflin	Teady Fallon	Tenant						1		
		Edmd. Fallon Pap	Tenant		1						
		Teady Gilgan Pap	Tenant		1						
	Killerny	Bar. Kielty Pap	farmer		1				1		1
		Widw. Keough					3				
	Inchroe	Jno. Kelly Papist			4		1				
		Teady Kelly									
		Bar:Kelly Papist———			3						
		Jno. McGinn Pap			3						
[f.179] Cam	Ardmullen	Thos. Rork Papist	Weaver		4						
		Thos. Leoge	Labr.								
		Patt. Gilligan Pap	Shephd.		2						
		Own. Mutton Pap	Shephd.		1		2				
		Jms. Naughton Pap	Shepherd				4				
		Jno. Kelly Papist	Labr.		2						
	Corroughboy										
Pap 39		Thos Cormuck	Carman								
37		Anias McDanell Pap	Weaver				5				
81		Patt. Keavghrane Pap	Po: keepr		2						
157		Simon Lyster Pap	Labr.		2						
		Peter Kenny Pap	Labr.								
		Patt Coony Pap	Labr.		1						
		Peter Costolo Pap	Labr.		2						
		Roger Glin Papist	Carman				2				
		Widw. Fallon Paps					2				
		Do. son-in-law	Weaver								
		Hugh Higgins Paps	Weaver		1						
		Loughn. Murry Paps	Smith		1		3				
		Patt. Birn Pap	Labr.		2						
		Thos. Cooney Paps	Labr.		1						
		Thos. Crikole Paps	Labr.		2						
		Darby Crikole Paps	Labr.								
		Daniell Glinan Paps	Shephd		2						
		Jams. Dowle Paps	Carman		3						
		Jams. Coffie Paps	Tenant		2		2				
		Jno. Sheahine									
		Rogr. Rooney Pap	Labr.		1						
		Dens. Dorehy Pap	Labr.		2						
		Michl. Gunane	Sheriff Baliffs[10]		3						
		Jno. Gilligan Pap	Carman		1		3				
		Jno. Sumougn Pap	Labr.		2						
		Edmd. McDanell Pap	Labr.		4		2				
		Jams. Glinan Pap	Labr.		2						

Com~Ros common Parish of	Place of Abode	Names and Religion	Proffession	Children under 14 Prot.	Children under 14 Paps.	Children above 14 Prot.	Children above 14 Paps.	Men Servts Prot.	Men Servts Paps.	Women Servts Prot.	Women Servts Paps.
		Conor heavy Pap	Carman		2						
		Dins. Mary Paps	Labr.		2						
		Thos. Knough									
	Killcar	Laurce. Dolan Pap	Labr.		3						
		Mich. McConife Pap	Weaver		1		2				
		Anthy Dowlly Pap	Labr.		1						
[f.180]	Killcar	Teady Glinan Pap	Labr.		2						
Cam		Edmd. Cravan Pap	Labr.		73						
		Mathw. Cravan Pap	Carman				2				
		Petr. Cravan Pap	Labr.		3						
		Willm. Doony Pap	Carman		1		1				
		Lau: Dowlan Pap	Carman		3						
		Murta: McDonell Pap	Carman		2						
		Lougn. McDanll. Pap	Labr.		4						
	Cam	Connor Glinn Pap	Labr.		2		2				
		Edmd Dowlly Pap	Labr.				1				
		Jno Mully Pap	Shepherd		2						
		Bryan Gathely Pap	Carman								
		Danl. Finllon Pap	Labr.		4						
		Patt. Glinan Pap	Labr.		2						
		Dan. Leage Pap	tenant				1				
		Will. McConife Pap	Mason		+		2				
		Jno Murry Pap	Labr.		2						
		Mich: Craven Pap	Labr.								
		Tho. Kein Pap	Labr.		5						
		Loughn. Groark Pap	Labr.								
		Will. McDanell Pap	Tenant		4						
		Andw. Kerry Pap	Tenant		5						
		Do Brother Pap									
		Loughn. Curelly Pap	tenant		3						
		Jno. Gilligan Pap	tent		1						
		Mart. Dowlan Pap	Labr.								
		Dinus Dowlly	Labr.								
		Wm. Morvemough Pap	tent		3						
		Morgan Murly Pap	Labr.		1						
		Mart. Leoge Pap	tent		2						
		Wm. Greogan Pap	tent				3				
		Conr. Mary Pap	Labr.				2				
		Patt. Fenoughty Pap	tent		3						
		Mich: Dora Pap	Labr.		2						
		Thos. Dara Pap	Labr.		1						
		Jno. Glinan Pap	tent		5						
		Teady Glinan Pap	tent		3						
	Iskerbane[11]	Teady Dowllan Pap	tent		3		1				
		Thos. Dowllan Pap	tent								
[f.181]	Iskerbane	Bryan Keavghn. Pap	tent		+		2				
Cam		Patt. Gurhy Pap	tent		3						
		Roger Dowlan Pap	tent								
		Thos. Dillon Pap	Labr.		4						

Com~Ros common Parish of	Place of Abode	Names and Religion	Proffession	Children under 14 Prot.	Children under 14 Paps.	Children above 14 Prot.	Children above 14 Paps.	Men Servts Prot.	Men Servts Paps.	Women Servts Prot.	Women Servts Paps.
		Thos. Gurly Pap	Labr.		3						
		Peter Gren Pap	Labr.		2						
		Bryan Kelly Pap	tent		2		2				
Pap 39		Teady Kein Pap	Labr.		4						
39		Robet. Kelly Pap	Labr.		2						
102		Teady Kelly Pap	Labr.		1						
180		Patt. Kelly Pap	Labr.		2						
		Dan Kelly Pap	Labr.		1						
		Will Fallon Pap	Labr.		4						
		Jms. Doyle Pap	Labr.		2						
		Patt. Kelly Pap	Wig mr.		2						
		Jon. Fallon Pap	Ale seller				2				
	Coruntober	Mich: Keough Pap	farmer		3				1		1
		Jms. McDanell			3						
		Tige Gaffie Pap					1				
		Mich: Keine Pap	begr				3				
		Hugh Rush Pap	Ale seller				1				
		Jno. Dowllan Pap	Hatter		2						
		Hugh Dowlan Pap			1						
		~~Jno Edwards Prot~~	~~Weaver~~			~~2~~					
	Polleher	Dan. Dowlan Pap	Tent.				3				
		Mich: Dowlan Pap	tent		1						
		Geo: Morgan Pap	tent		1						
		Anthy. Morgan Pap	tent		2						
		Charls. Morgan Pap	tent		2						
		Thos. Morgan Pap	tent								
	Corrowduff	Edmd. Naughn. Pap	tent				2				
		Edmd. Beade Pap	farmr.		2						
		Bar. Glinan Pap	farmr.		2						
		Thos. Naughn	farmr.								
		Wm. Murry Pap	tent		3						
	Do	Michl. Tully Pap	Miller		1		4				
		Mark Glin Pap	tent		2		2				
	Coolgarry	Bryan Fallon Pap	farmr.		4		3		3		4
		Edmd. Banan Pap	Labr.		2						
		Hugh Keogh Pap	Labr.				3				
[f.182]	Coolgarry	Hugh Glinan Pap	Labr.		2						
Cam		Mich: Stanton Pap	Labr.		1						
		Danl. Glinan Pap	Labr.		1						
		Edmd. Crobane	Labr.		2						
		Widow Daw Pap			1		2				
		Lough: Gathely Pap	Labr.				2				
		Patt. Dowllan Pap	Labr.		1						
		Edmd. Dowllan Pap	Labr.		1						
		Patt. Dowllan Pap	Labr.		2		2				
		Conor Moran	Maneger						1		1
		Petr. Giraughty Pap	Sheepd						1		1

Com~Ros common Parish of	Place of Abode	Names and Religion	Proffession	Children under 14		Children above 14		Men Servts		Women Servts	
				Prot.	Paps.	Prot.	Paps.	Prot.	Paps.	Prot.	Paps.
Pap 40		Pat. Gathely Pap	Carman		2		2		1		1
39		Mancr. McDanll Pap	Labr.		1						
102		Andw. McDanll Pap	Labr.		3						
171		Jno McDanell Pap	Labr.		2						
		Teady Kelly Pap	Carman		1						
		Teady Kelly Pap	Smith		3		1				
	Do	Dins. Moran Pap	Tilor		1		2				
		Manas Galvan Pap	Labr.		3		1				
		Edmd. Gathely Pap	Labr.		2						
	Do	Conor Dorcha Pap	Labr.		2		1				
		Con. McDanll Pap	Herd		2		1				
		Dar. ffallon Pap					3				
		Matt. Manion Pap			3						
		Danl. Conole Pap	Carman				3				
		Hugh McDanl Pap	Smith		2		1				
		Mich: Gormle Pap			2		1				
		Connor Gathely Pap			1						
		Thos. Cunihan Pap			1						
		Lewis Mollangn Pap	Labr.		1		2				
		Michl. McDanll Pap	Labr.		3		1				
		Patt. Doyle Pap			1		1				
		Edmd. Gathely Pap			2						
		Rogr. Gathely Pap					3				
		Patt. Gathely Pap			1						
		Jms. Doyle Pap			1		4				
		Tiran Doyle									
		Rogr. Doyle			2						
		Rogr. Moran Pap					4				
		Mary ffallon Pap					2				
[f.183]	Coolgarry	Dom: Doyle Pap			2						
Cam		Jms. Gathely Pap			1						
		Jms. Gormalee Pap			1						
		Con. Mee Pap			3						
		Patt. Kelly Pap			4						
	Cornelee	Larm. Fallon Pap	farmer		1				3		2
		Bryan Doyle									
		Tirans. McDanll Pa			2						
		Bryan Mulloy Pap					1				
		Ed. Mulloy Pap			2						
Pap 38		Jms. Hanroughon Pap			2						
36		Widw. Stanton Pap					5				
91		Patt. Mullane Pap			1						
91		Wm. Gathely Pap			2						
105		Widw. Dowell Pap					3				
		Thos. Downy Pap					3				
		Luke Heally Pap			2						
		Terance Doyle Pap			2						
		Mar. Gathely Pap			2		2				
		Fargs. Gathely Pap			2						

Com~Ros common Parish of	Place of Abode	Names and Religion	Proffession	Children under 14		Children above 14		Men Servts		Women Servts	
				Prot.	Paps.	Prot.	Paps.	Prot.	Paps.	Prot.	Paps.
		Jams. ffallon Pap			2						
		Jno. Conole Pap			2		2				
		Jno. Killroy Pap			1						
		Mark. Killroy Pap			1						
		Tige Conole Pap					1				
		Con. Killbone Pap			2		2				
		Robt. Bleak Pap	Ale seller								
		Dar. Gathely Pap			2		1				
	Garinford	Bar. Kelly Pap	farmr.		1		1		2		2
		Con. Mulvil Pap	Labr.		3						
		Art. Mellaughn. Pap	Labr.		3						
		Matt. Concart Pap			3						
		Mark Flyn Pap			1						
		Thos. Cuniham Pap			1						
	Cornegee	Teady Kelly Pap	tent				4				
		Jno. ffallon	tent						1		
		Jno. Gathily Pap	tent				3				
	Do	Bryan Kelly Pap	farmr.		2						

Tot. Pro: families in this parish 4 Totall number of protestants 13

Tot Pap families in this Par: 304 Totall number of Papists <u>1325</u>

Tot number of Papists & Protestants 1338

NOTES

1. *General Alphabetical Index*

2. Lewis, 'Camma'.

3. William Gacquin, *Roscommon before the Famine: the parishes of Kiltoom and Cam, 1749-1845* (Blackrock, 1996), pp. 18-9.

4. Thomas Lyster was educated in Dublin by Dr Young and entered TCD in 1731, aged 17. He was born in Athleague, the son of Anthony Lyster (*Alumni Dubliniensis*).

5. Thomas Lyster was a son of Rev. James Lester and Joyce Lyster. Thomas married Mary, daughter of Boleyn Whitney (Crofton, *Memoirs*, p.167).

6. 'Arable pasture and meadow in which is a considerable quantity inclined to heath and liable to be overflown by the Lough'. Part of the estate of St. George Caulfield in 1802 (N.L.I., Survey of Aughagad and Buckfield, MS 21 F 23/7).

7. A William Fallon Esq lived at Cornle in the mid-seventeenth century (Census of Ireland).

8. Fr. Patrick Coniffe was probably an Augustinian friar from Dunmore (Fenning, 'Clergy Lists', p.145, fn.11).

9. See Gacquin 'A Household Account', p.115, fn. 43.

10. A bailiff working on the orders of a sheriff seizing goods to meet unpaid debts.

11. The townland of Iskerbane (or Eskerbane) has been analysed in detail by William Gacquin in Connell et al. (eds), <u>Irish Townlands</u>, pp. 141-163.

KILTOOM, COUNTY ROSCOMMON

INTRODUCTION: *The parish of Kiltoom is in the barony of Athlone, 5 miles north west from Athlone. It covers 13,246 statute acres.[1] The soil was said to be 'light and fertile' with only a 'moderate proportion' of bog.[2]*

The church of Ireland incumbent was the Rev. William Digby who held the parish together with those of Cam, Dysert, Rahara, Taghboy and Ahascragh (see Tisrara). The patron was the bishop.

OCCUPATIONS

Ale seller	2	Gentleman	1	Smith	1
Cottier	18	Hatter	7	Tinker	1
Dancer	1	Labourer	99	Weaver	4
		Miller	1		
Farmer	5	Servants, household	52	Widow	14
Freeholder	1	Shepherd	1	Wigmaker	1

Com~Ros common Parish of	Place of Abode	Names and Religion	Proffession	Children under 14 Prot.	Children under 14 Paps.	Children above 14 Prot.	Children above 14 Paps.	Men Servts Prot.	Men Servts Paps.	Women Servts Prot.	Women Servts Paps.
Kiltoom [f.184]	Bigg=Berries	Tady Hevin pa	Labr.		2						
		Edmd. Kellelea pa	Labr.		2		1				
		Mortgh. McGrinna pa	Labr.		1		~~1~~				
		Patr: McGrinns pa	Labr.		3		2				
	Little Berries	Jams. Connor pa:	Labr.		~~3~~		3		1		
		Robert Henry pa:	Labr.		2		1				
		Darby gill pap	Labr.		1		2				
		Jams. Malone pa:	Labr.		5						
		patr. Maden pa:	Dancer		1		2				1
		John Russell pap	Labr.		2		2				
		Dinnis Naugten pa:	Labr.		3		2				
		Darby Heneghan pa:	Labr.				2				
		Patr: Coniffe pap	Labr.		3		4				1
		Patr. Duffy pa:	Labr.		3						
		Nem. Long Prots:	Labr.	3							
		Dinnis Hennig pa:	Labr.		2						
		Pett. Naught pa:	Labr.		3						
		Mic: Naught pa:	Labr.		3		2				
		Tho: Duffy pa:	Labr.		2		2				
		James Duffy pa:	Labr.		3		3		1		1
		Nem. Coniff pa:	Labr.				1				
		Jno. Coniff pa:	Labr.								
	Boginfin	Cormc. Mealy pa:	Labr.		3						
		Cha: McDonald pa:	Labr.		2		3				
		Jno Healy pap	Labr.		3		1				
		Jno. Kerregan pa:	Labr.		2						
		Tully Galaghr pa:	Labr.		3		3				
		Tady Mealy pa:	Labr.						1		
		Wm. Kelly pap	Labr.		2		1				
		Hen: Hamilton p:	Labr.		4		1				
[f.185]	Beggantown	Patr. Lyons pa:	aleselr.				1				
		Tady Lyons pa:	farmr.		4						1
		Jeffy Lyons pa:	farmr.		4						
		Gat. Dillon pa:	Labr.		1						
		Patr. Brenon pa:	weaver		1		2				
		Cha: Mcgee pa:	Labr.		1						1
		Lough: Mulin pa:	Weaver		1						
		Davy Brenon pa:	Tinker		2		1				
		Suiy Davis pa:	Widw.		2						
		Elinr. Mury pa:	Widw.				2				
		Jno. Noon pa:	Labr.		1						
	Capalishine	Conr. Lurin pa:	Labr.		1		2				
		Margt Loorin pa:	~~Do~~				3				
		Jno. Tarp pa:	Labr.		1		3				
		Jno Galvin pa:	Labr.		2		1				
		mary Connr pa:	widow		1		1				
	Curramore	Mart. Feeny pa:	Do.		3						
		Tho. Feely pa:	Do.		1						
		Mich: Kearny pa:	Do.		2		1		1		1

— 244 —

Com~Ros common Parish of	Place of Abode	Names and Religion	Proffession	Children under 14		Children above 14		Men Servts		Women Servts	
				Prot.	Paps.	Prot.	Paps.	Prot.	Paps.	Prot.	Paps.
	attiogh	Hugh Falon pa:	Do.		3						
		Patt: Ward pa:	Do.		2						
		Roger Kelly pa:	Hatter		3						
		Jno McKina pa:	Do.				2				1
	Corrowmoragh	Bartle Long pa:	Do.		1						
		Nic: Conll pa:	Do.		2						
		Nm. Horny pa:	Do.				2				
		Tady Dalton pa:	Do.		3				1		
		Rich. Gormy pa:	Do.				1				
[f.186]		Conr. Garmly pa:	Labr.								
Kiltoom		Jams. Carroll pa:	Labr.			3					
		Cha: Gatley pa:	Labr.								
		Jams. Flyn pa:	Labr.		2		1		1		
		Jno Fallon papt.	Miller		1		3				
	Corrow Derry	Mattw. Hoey pa:	Do.				1[?]				
		Dan: Naughn Do	Do.		2						
		Jams: Coyle pap	Do.								1
		Jno. Martin pa:	Do.		1		2				1
	Part of Ardmuln	Jams. Keough Do.	Do.		1		1		1		
		Thos: Cassidy Do	Do.				1				
		Maur: Naughtn: Do	Do.		3						
		Hugh Glman Do	Do..		5						
		Jno Moran Do	Do..				2				
		Jams: Mulan Do	Do..								
		Bryan Fallon Do	Do..		1						
		Edw. Durnan pa:	Do.		4						
	Carrokeeny	Wm. Doran pa:	Do.				3				1
		Mic: Naughton pa:	Do.		2						1
		Dens. Rogers pa:	Do:wig:		1				1		
		Den: Gillance pa:	Do.		2						
		Jno. Feely pa:	Do.								
		Dan. Mullan pa:	Do.		3						
		Tho. Martin pa:	Do.				2				
		Laug. Martin Do	Do.		1						
		Jno. Naught. pa:	Do.		5						1
		Bryan Banon pa:	Do.		2						
		Jno. Mullon Do	Do.		1						
		Tho. Connow Do.	Do.								
		Jams. Martin Do.									
[f.187]	Mivanon 4 Qrs + severall sub: Denominations	Jams Campell prot:	freeholdr	3		5		1	2		2
Kiltoom		Jno. Knight Prot	farmr.		1		2				2
		Jno. Hamiln. Prot	farmr.		3				1		1
		Jno. Farrell prot	Cottr.		1		2				1
		Wm. Walsh papis	Shepd		3				1		
		Fran: Dowdrell pa:	Cottr.		1						
		Jams. Connor pap	Do.								
		Matt. Bryan Do	Do..		1						
		Tho. Mullan Do	Do..		3						

Com~Ros common Parish of	Place of Abode	Names and Religion	Proffession	Children under 14		Children above 14		Men Servts		Women Servts	
				Prot.	Paps.	Prot.	Paps.	Prot.	Paps.	Prot.	Paps.
		Bridt Powdrell Do:	widow				1				
		Sarah Feily Do	Do..				4				
		ann Walsh Do	Do..		3						
		Jams. Mannion Do:	Cottr.								
		Patrk. Eagan Do	Do..		1						
		Owen Cammough Do	Do..		1		2				
		Lough: Naught. Do	Do..		2						
		Jane Irwin Do	Do..								
		Jno. Fallon									
		Bry. Fallon									
		Thos. King									
		Mic. Heavin									
		Jams. Glinnan									
		Pett. Fallon									
		Lau:. McDonough									
		And. Donley Do:	Do.		2						1
	Kiltoom	Jno. Corkan Do:	Do.		1						1
		Rogr. Coggall Do:	Do.		3		1				
		Tha. Dooling Do:	Do.		3						1
		Hugh Govan Do:	Do.		2						2
f.188] Kiltoom	Lisbane	Bry. Judge pa:	Do.		2						2
		Tho. Meily Do.	Do.		3		1				
		Mic. Meare Do	Do.		2						
		Jno. Nooney Do	weaver								
		Mic. Fiemg Do	Labr.		1						
		Luke Mullen Do.			4						
		Mic. Gregan Do	Do.								
	Carnasee	Jas. Walsh pa:	Do.		1						1
		Bart. Walsh Do	Do.								
		Tady Feely Do	Do.		1		1		1		1
		Dan. Golagr. Do	Do.				1				
		Hugh Donly Do	Do.		1						
		Patt. Donly Do	Do.		1						
		Bryan Doyle Do	Do.				4				
		Dan. Shehn. Do	Do.		1						
		Own. Kelly Do	Do.								
		Dan. Mannn Do	Do.		2						
		Tho. Burn Do	Do.		1		1				
		Conr. Kelly Do	Do.		2						
		Mark Kelly Do	Do.								
		Conr. Fallon Do	Do.								
		Patt. Connell Do	Do.	+							
	Miltown pass	Pet. Flyn Pap	aleselr.		3		2				
		Jas. Stern prot.	farmr.	1		1					
		Rose Kelly pa:	widow				3				
		Edmd. Bates pa:	Smith				2				
		Wm. Butler pa:	Labr.		2		2				
		Jas. Mann pa:	Do.		2		2				1
		Bry. Lynch pa:	Do.		3						

Com~Ros common Parish of	Place of Abode	Names and Religion	Proffession	Children under 14		Children above 14		Men Servts		Women Servts	
				Prot.	Paps.	Prot.	Paps.	Prot.	Paps.	Prot.	Paps.
		Jon. Walsh pa:	Do.		1		1				
		Jas. Costlo pa:	widowr.				3				
[f.189] Kiltoom	Cornetatan	Mic: Mulchen pa:	Labr.		3						
		Hugh Fenr pa:	Labr.		2		1				
		Jno. Butler pa: pr.	Do. 1								
		Mic. Feenecan pa:	Do.								
		Bart. Hovin pa:	Do.								
		Richd. Feenecan pa:	Do.								
	Knocknenooll	Patr. Naught. pa:	Do.		2						
		Jas. Kenelly papis	Do.		3				1		
		Lough: Kenelly pap	Do.		2		1				
		Hugh Watch pap	Do.		1		1				
		Tho. Kelly Paps Do.	Weaver		3						
		Jas. Burn Paps.	Labr.				2				
		Geo. Morgan pa:	Do.		1						1
		Jno: Bates paps	Do.		2						
		Elinr. Walch Pap	Widow		1		1				
	Newpark	anth: Lyster[3] prot	Gent.	1		3			3		4

Totall protestants in the whole Parish 35

Totall Papists ———————————— 669

704

NOTES

1. Less 2,787 acres of Lough Ree and the river Shannon (*General Alphabetical Index*).

2. Lewis, 'Kiltoom or Kiltomb'.

3. Anthony Lyster of Newpark, Co. Roscommon was a son of John Lyster of Rocksavage and Elizabeth, daughter of Dixie Coddington. Anthony Lyster died in 1754 (Pedigree of Lyster, N.L.I., Genealogical Office MS 812/43).

AHASCRAGH, COUNTY GALWAY

INTRODUCTION: *Ahascragh is in the barony of Kilconnell. It is west of Athlone and north-west of Ballinasloe, and the towns of Ahascragh, Killglass and Ballybaun are on the road from Ballinasloe to Castlebar, Co. Mayo. The parish covers 17,342 statute acres.*[1] *Local limestone quarries would account for a stonecutter and a number of masons.*

The Church of Ireland incumbent in 1749 was the Rev. William Digby who held the parish together with those of Tisrara, Cam, Dysert, Kiltoom, Rahara and Taghboy (see Tisrara).

OCCUPATIONS

Aleseller	3	Doctor	1	Miller	1
Broguemaker	3	Esquire	1	Priest	1
Butcher	2	Farmer	3	Servants, household	68
Clothier	1	Gentleman	8	Shoemaker	1
Constable	1	Innkeeper	1	Skinner(?)	1
Cooper	1	Joiner	1	Smith	7
Cottier	2?	Journeyman	1	Stonecutter	1
Cottoner	1	Labourer	262	Tailor	4
Dancing master	1	Mason	4	Weaver	11
Distiller	1	Merchant	5	Wigmaker	1
				Yeoman	6

Galway Parish of	Place of Abode	Names and Religion	Proffession	Children under 14 Prot.	Children under 14 Paps.	Children above 14 Prot.	Children above 14 Paps.	Men Servts Prot.	Men Servts Paps.	Women Servts Prot.	Women Servts Paps.
[f.190]											
Ahascragh	Ahascragh	Pat Cosgrife papt.	Labourr.		4		2				
Ahascragh	Ahascragh	John Gatelly[2] papt.	Miller		2		3				
Ahascragh	Ahascragh	Arthur Murphy Prot.	Innkeeper	4					2		2
Ahascragh	Ahascragh	Tim. Goldin prot	mercht.						1		1
Ahascragh	Ahascragh	Thoms. Meeagh	Labourr.		4						
Ahascragh	Ahascragh	Michl. Gallagher papt.	Labourr.				1		1		
Ahascragh	Ahascragh	Thos. Carrel papt	Smith		2						
Ahascragh	Ahascragh	Michl. Coffy papt	butcher		2						
Ahascragh	Ahascragh	Jno. Donnelly papt.	Labourr.		3						
Ahascragh	Ahascragh	Jno. Henderson prot.	shoemaker	3							
Ahascragh	Ahascragh	Michl. Burk papt	yeoman		4						
Ahascragh	Ahascragh	ffrans. Kelly papt	aleseller		2						
Ahascragh	Ahascragh	Peter ffallon papt.	Labourr.		4						
Ahascragh	Ahascragh	ffrans. Stanley papt	mercht.		2						
Ahascragh	Ahascragh	Jno. Scott papt.	Labourr.		1		1				
Ahascragh	Ahascragh	Patt. Grealy papt.	Labourr.								
Ahascragh	Ahascragh	Bryn. Naughten papt	Butcher		5						
Ahascragh	Ahascragh	Thos. Grealy papt	Broguemakr.						1		
Ahascragh	Ahascragh	Charles Carrol prot.	Constable	1							
Ahascragh	Ahascragh	James Dillon papt.	mercht.		2						
Ahascragh	Ahascragh	Mark. Shaghnesy papt	mercht.								
Ahascragh	Ahascragh	Thos. Cosgry papt.	Labourr.		3						
Ahascragh	Port	Teig. Flanagan papt.	Labourr.		1[?]		3				
Ahascragh	Port	Jas. Lynch papt.	Labourr.		2						
Ahascragh	Port	Patk. Lynch papt.	Labourr.		1						
Ahascragh	Port	Wm. Kennedy papt.	Labourr.		1		3				
Ahascragh	Port	Jno. Cahane papt.	Labourr.		2						
Ahascragh	Kilglass	Edmd. Dally papt	Cotner								
Ahascragh	Kilglass	Domnick Madden papt.	Labourr.								
Ahascragh	Kilglass	Jas. Scott papt.	Labourr.		3						
Ahascragh	Kilglass	Geo: Crowe prot.	mercht.	1							
Ahascragh	Kilglass	Robt. Bigly prot.	Labourr.	2		3					
Ahascragh	Kilglass	Hugh Delany prot.	dancing mastr								
Ahascragh	Kilglass	Laughlen Madden papt	stonecutter								
Ahascragh	Kilglass	Teig Coffy			1		1				
Ahascragh	Kilglass	Patk. Grisset papt	weavr.		2						
Ahascragh	Kilglass	Patk. Hurrigon papt.	Labourr.		2						
Ahascragh	Kilglass	Gregory Keaghrone papt	broguemaker		4						
Ahascragh	Kilglass	Mark Lynch papt	labourr				1				
Ahascragh	Kilglass	Ricd. Grisset papt	Weaver		3						
Do	Do	Redmd. Finarty	Labr				2				
[f.191]											
Ahascragh	Kilglass	Pat. Nowland Pa	Labr		3						
Do	Do	Jn. Stanton Pa	Smith		2						
Do	Do	Pet. Stanton Pa	Smith		2						
Do	Do	Redmd. Stanton Pa.	Labr		2						
Do	Do	Mich. Fury Pa	mt.		4						
Do	Do	Connor Morrissee Pa	Labr		1						

Galway Parish of	Place of Abode	Names and Religion	Proffession	Children under 14		Children above 14		Men Servts		Women Servts	
				Prot.	Paps.	Prot.	Paps.	Prot.	Paps.	Prot.	Paps.
Do	Do	Mar. Flin Pa	Lr.								
Do	Do	Mi: Burn Pa.	Labr				3				
Do	Do	Ja. Joyce Pa	Labr		1						
Do	Do	Mi. Connor Pap	Labr				3				
Do	Do	Bri: Connor Pap	Labr		2						
Do	Do	Ed. Burn Pap	Labr		1						
Do	Do	Mar. Grady Pap	Labr		1						
Do	Do	Jn. Corroly Pap	Labr		3						
Do	Do	Ja. Condan Pap	Labr		1						
Do	Do	Pat. Gown Pap	Labr		2						
Do	Do	Rogr. Morrisee Pap	Labr		4						
Do	Do	Tha: Gerrarty Pap	Labr		1						
Do	Do	Jn. Grady Pap	Labr								
Do	Do	Mi: Lennan Pap	Labr		2						
Do	Banavane	Patt. Gerrarty Pap	Labr				4				
Do	Do	John Gerrarty Pap	Labr		2						
Do	Do	Nic. Gerarty Pap	Labr		3						
Do	Do	Ed. Brown Pap	Labr		2						
Do	Do	Hu: Lyon Pap	Labr		2				1		
Do	Do	Rogr. Wallace Pap	Labr		2						
Do	Do	Hu: Bleheen Pap	Labr		1						
Do	Gowla	Luke Noon Pap	Labr		1						
Do	Do	La. Noon Pap	Labr		1						
Do	Do	Pa. Raftry Pap	Labr		1						
Do	Do	Jes. Finarty Pap	Labr		3		1				
Do	Do	Jn. Maguire	Labr		4		2				
Do	Clogher	Thos. French Prot	Gentle				5		4		4
Do	Do	Lau: Coney Pap	Labr		3						
Do	Do	Thos. Quinn Pap	Labr		3						
Do	Do	Mi: Finarty Pap	Cr.		2						
Do	Do	Roger Lyon Pap	Labr		1						
Do	Do	Den. Lyon Pap	Labr		1						
Do	Do	Pat. Cooney Pap	Labr		2						
Do	Do	Mi. Finarty Pap	Labr								
Do	Do	An. Cooney Pap	Labr								
[f.192] Ahascrah	Clogher	Pe. Tully Pap	Labr		1						
	Do	Tho. Cahill Pap	Labr		4						
Do	Iskermon	Pat. Cahill Pap	Labr		2						
Do	Do	Den. Cahill Pap	Labr		4						
Do	Do	Pet. Finarty Pap	Labr		4						
Do	Do	Pet. Crahwell Pap	Labr		3						
Do	Do	M. Goal Pap	Labr		2						
Do	Do	Hu: Cahill Pap	Labr		2						
Do	Do	Wm. Kelly Pap	Labr		4				1		1
Do	Do	Jn. Johnings Pap	Labr		2						
Do	Do	Ge. Burn Pap	Labr		2						
Do	Do	Th. Finerty Pap	Labr		1						
Do	Do	Peter Gucce Pap	Gent		1						
Do	Lanortan	Fr. Costelo Pap	Labr		4						

Galway Parish of	Place of Abode	Names and Religion	Proffession	Children under 14		Children above 14		Men Servts		Women Servts	
				Prot.	Paps.	Prot.	Paps.	Prot.	Paps.	Prot.	Paps.
Do	Do	Pe: Hughs Pap	Labr		2						
Do	Do	Ri: Hughs Pap	Weaver				1				
Do	Do	Rob. Verden Pap	Labr				1				
Do	Do	Wm. Kelly Pap	Farmer		4						
Do	Do	Den. Costelo Pap	Farmer		2						
Do	Do	Ro. Raftry Pap	Labr				4				
Do	Do	Ro: Kelly Pap	Gent		2						1
Do	Do	Lau: Tully Pap	Doctr						1		1
Do	Do	Tei: Kelly Pap	Lar		1						
Do	Balliboggan	Wm. Hogarty Pap	Lapr		2						
Do	Do	Jn. Kelly Pap	Weaver		4						
Do	Do	Mar: Finarty Pap	Joyner		3						
Do	Do	Pat. Fin Pap	Labr						1		
Do	Do	Har. Gowran Pap	Labr								
Do	Do	Den. Lenon Pap	Labr		2						
Do	Do	Mi: Gowran Pap	Labr		4						
Do	Do	Jas. Kelly Pap	Labr		2						
Do	Do	Jas. McKelly Pap	Labr								
Do	Do	Ed. Moran Pap	Weaver		1						
Do	Do	Pat. Harman Pap	Labr		1						
Do	Do	Corm. Tully Pap	Labr		1						
Do	Do	Jas. Finarty Pap	Labr		1						
Do	Do	Owen Finarty	Labr				4				
Do	Do	Owen Finarty Jnr Pap	Labr		1		4				
Do	Do	Jas. Finarty Jnr Pap	Lr.		2						
Do	Do	Jn. Gowran Pap	Labr		3						
Do	Do	Mar. Finarty Pap	Lr.		1		2				
[f.193] Ahascra	Balliboggan	Jn. Slaman Pap	Lr.				1				
Do	Do	Luke Finerty Pap	Lr.				2				
Do	Do	Jn. Miscel Pap	Smith				2				1
Do	Lattoon	Danl. Caul Doyl Pap	Lr				1				
Do	Do	An. Rogerson Pap	Lr								
Do	Do	Mi: Grady Pap	Lr				2				
Do	Do	Par. Grady Pap	Lr				1				
Do	Do	Ed. Egan Pap	Lr		2						
Do	Do	Ch: Cugly Pap	Lr		3						
Do	Do	An: Egan Pap	Lr		3						
Do	Do	Pat: Tanclan Pap	Smith		4						
Do	Do	Hu: Loghan Pap	Lr		2						
Do	Do	Mi: Quin Pap	Taylor		2						
Do	Do	Hu: Manning Pap	Lr		3						
Do	Do	Wm. Johnings Pap	Lr		2						
Do	Do	Jas. Glin Pap	Lr								
Do	Do	Pat: Lough Pap	Lr		2						
Do	Do	Thos: Flin Pap	Lr		1						
Do	Do	Dnl Hary Pap	Mason				3				
Do	Do	Wm. Glin Pap	Lr								
Do	Do	Ow: Glin Pap	Cottier								
Do	Balibane	Jn. Horton Prot	Farmer	3							

Galway Parish of	Place of Abode	Names and Religion	Proffession	Children under 14		Children above 14		Men Servts		Women Servts	
				Prot.	Paps.	Prot.	Paps.	Prot.	Paps.	Prot.	Paps.
Do	Do	Jas: Daws Prot	Lr								
Do	Do	Sam: Johnston Prot	Weaver	2							
Do	Do	Jas Johnston Prot	Clothier	2							
Do	Do	Jas: Johnston Prot	Weaver	1							
Do	Do	Jam: Johnston Prot	Weaver			1					
Do	Do	Jas Downey Prot	Journeyman	2							
Do	Do	Lewis: Talbot Pa:	Aleseller		2				1		1
Do	Do	Jas. Maguire Pap	Lr		2						
Do	Do	Dar. Maguire Pa	Lr		1						
Do	Cloncannon	Far Kelly Pap	Gent		5		3		1		1
Do	Do	Lau: Mulvihill Pap	Lr		5		3				
Do	Do	Thos. Colrony Pap	Lr		2						
Do	Do	Ow: Lally Pap	Lr		2						
Do	Do	Jn. Brisland Pap	Lr		2						
Do	Do	Th: Brisland Pap	Lr		1						
Do	Do	Th: Hacket Pap	Lr		4						
Do	Do	Lau. Egan Pap	Lr		2						
Do	Do	Ow: Finarty Pap	Lr		1						
Do	Do	Bri: Finerty Pap	Lr		4						
[f.194] Ahascra	Cloncannon	Pe: Lenan Pap	Lr		4						
Do	Do	P. Naghton Pap	Lr								
Do	Do	Bar: Finerty Pap	Lr				2				
Do	Do	Brian Kelly Pap	Lr		1		4				
Do	Do	Hu: Moran Pap	Lr		5						
Do	Do	Ed. Costello Pap	Lr		1						
Do	Do	Dar: Hort Pap	Lr		1						
Do	Do	Pat. Killkelly Pap	Lr				3				
Do	Cornamucla	Jas. Gathla Pap	Lr		1				1		
Do	Do	Dan. Kenedy Pap	Lr		2						
Do	Do	Jam. Hogarty Pap	Wr		2						
Do	Do	Jn. Donelan Pap	Lr		1						
Do	Do	Own. Fury Pap	Lr		4						
Do	Do	Pet. Hartican Pap	Lr		3		2				
Do	Do	James Hughs Pap	Lr								
Do	Do	Frank Hugh Pap	Lr								
Do	Do	Dan. Noman Pap	Mason		2						
Do	Do	Pat. Grady Pap	Lr		4						
Do	Do	Pat. Donelan Pap	Lr		1						
Do	Do	Jn Kenedy Pap	Lr		3						
Do	Do	Lau. Grady Pap	Lr				5				
Do	Do	Pat. Lyon Pap	Lr				2				
Do	Do	Lou: Manning Pap	Skiner[?]				2				
Do	Do	Jn. Concannon Pap	Lr				2				
Do	Do	Connr. Hughs Pap	Lr				3				
Do	Do	Thos. Hartican Pap	Lr		3						
Do	Do	Ow: Moony Pap	Lr		2		2				
Do	Do	Th: Kenedy Pap	Lr		2						
Do	Do	Jn: Kilroe Pap	Lr								
Do	Do	Ph: Hughs Pap	Lr		2						

Galway Parish of	Place of Abode	Names and Religion	Proffession	Children under 14 Prot.	Paps.	Children above 14 Prot.	Paps.	Men Servts Prot.	Paps.	Women Servts Prot.	Paps.
Do	Do	Dn: Glin Pap	Lr		2		2				
Do	Do	Jas: Coleman Pap	Lr				2				
Do	Do	Mi: Coraly Pap	Lr		2						
Do	Do	Ro: Lenon Pap	Lr				4				
Do	Do	Lou: Clinton Pap	Mason		3						
Do	Do	Jas. Gattely Pap	Weaver								1
Do	Do	Rgr. Morgan Pap	Br.maker		2						
Do	Do	Th: Hart Pap	Lr		2						
Do	Do	Pa: Glin Pap	Lr		1						
Do	Clonskee	Edmond Fury Pap	Lr		2						
Do	Do	Ed: Maguire Pap	Lr		1						
[f.195] Ahascra	Clonskee	Jn. Concannon Pa	Yeomn.		4						
Do	Do	Jn. Roe Pro	Yeomn.	1		3			1		1
Do	Do	Tr. Concannon Pa	Lr		1						
Do	Do	Hu: Concannon Pa	Lr								
Do	Do	Wil: Kelly Pa	Lr								
Do	Do	Thos: Kelly Pa	Lr		2						
Do	Do	Hu: Rogerson Pa	Lr		2						
Do	Do	Jn. Kelly Pa	Lr				3				
Do	Do	Mi: Garvan Pa	Lr				2				
Do	Do	Hu: Morgan Pa	Priest								
Do	Do	Lu: Morgan[3] Pa	Lr		2						
Do	Do	Hu: Morgan Pa	Lr		4						
Do	Do	Dan. Connor Pa	Lr				3				
Do	Lisseacgan	Th: Dolan Pa	Lr		3						
Do	Do	Lau: Harney Pa	Lr		2						
Do	Do	Pat. Gredy Pa	Lr		1						
Do	Do	La: White Pa	Lr		4						
Do	Do	Jn. Rourty Pa	Lr		1						
Do	Do	Thos. White Pa	Lr		4						
Do	Do	Peter Hardican Pa	Lr		2						
Do	Do	Den. Hardican Pa	Lr		1						
Do	Toomrilan	Lu: Colan Pa	Lr		2						
Do	Do	Bri: Mulvihill Pa	Lr		1						
Do	Do	Jn. Connor Pa	Lr		1						
Do	Do	Dens. Connor Pa	Lr								
Do	Do	Peter Heylan Pa	Lr		1						
Do	Do	Den. Gerarty Pa	Taylor		2						
Do	Do	Ri. White Pa	Lr		1						
Do	Do	Tho. Creman Pa	Lr		3						
Do	Do	Rich. Kelly Pa	Distiller		1						
Do	Do	Dan. Kelly Pa	Lr								
Do	Castlegar	Ross Mahon[4] Esqr Pro				4		2	4	1	5
Do	Do	Ro. Kelly Pa	Smith		3		2				
Do	Do	Jn. Kelly Pa	Lr		2						
Do	Do	Brian Grady Pa	Lr		1						
Do	Do	Th. Connituny Pa	Lr		1						
Do	Do	Mi: Haly Pa	Lr		4						
Do	Do	Wm. Lyons Pa	Lr		4						

Galway Parish of	Place of Abode	Names and Religion	Proffession	Children under 14		Children above 14		Men Servts		Women Servts	
				Prot.	Paps.	Prot.	Paps.	Prot.	Paps.	Prot.	Paps.
Do	Do	Jn. Glin Pa	Lr		3						
Do	Do	Hen. Grady Pa	Lr		1						
Do	Do	M. Mulvihill Pa	Lr				3				
[verso f.195] Ahascra	Clonbanough	Fr. Daly Pa	yeomn				4	2			1
Do		Th: Manning Pa	yeomn		4			1			1
Do		Jn. Keugh Pa	Wgmakr.		3						
Do		Jn. Nogton Pa	Lr.		1						
Do		Br. Coroly Pa	Lr.		4						
Do		M. Coffy Pa	Lr.		1						
Do		Dar: Finarty Pa	Lr.		2						
Do		Lu: Keegan Pa	Lr.		1						
Do		Pa: Delany Pa	Lr.		3		1				
Do		Jn. Glin Pa	Lr.		4						
[f.196] Ahascra	Castlegar	Frank Gardner pa	Lr.								
Do	Do	Dens Costelo pa	Lr.				1				
Do	Do	Hu: Costelo pa	Lr.		2						
Do	Do	Mi: Kelly pa	Lr.		1						
Do	Irvillah	Connor Morgan pa	Lr.								
Do	Do	John Lennon pa	Lr.		2						
Do	Do	Mi: Lally pa	Lr.		2						
Do	Do	Ths. Nagton pa	Lr.		2		2				
Do	Do	Brian Kelly pa	Lr.		2						
Do	Do	Owen Kelly pa	Lr.				2				
Do	Do	Laugh Lally pa	Lr.		1		2				
Do	Do	Luke White pa	Lr.		2						
Do	Do	An: White pa	Lr.		1						
Do	Do	Ed. White pa	Lr.								
Do	Do	Ths. White pa	Lr.		2						
Do	Do	Thos. Kelly pa	Lr.		2						
Do	Do	Jn. Kelly pa	Lr.								
Do	Do	Wm. Lyons pa	Lr.				1				
Do	Do	Thos. Lyons pa	Lr.				3				
Do	Do	Jn. Grady pa	Lr.		4						
Do	Do	Jas. Colan pa	Lr.		2						
Do	Do	De. Kennedy pa	Lr.		2						
Do	Do	Thos. Kevney pa	Cooper		2		1				
Do	Do	Thos Connolan pa	Lr.								
Do	Do	Ed. Kelly pa	Lr.								
Do	Do	Peter Lynch pa	Lr.		2						
Do	Do	Jn. Cosgrave Pap	Lr.		2		2				
Do	Balliglass	Dn. Craghwell pa	Lr.		2						
Do	Do	Tady Coffie Pap	Lr.								
Do	Do	James Grehan pa	Lr.		2						
Do	Do	Den. Rovarty pa	Lr.				2				
Do	Do	Mar. Rovarty pa	Lr.		1						
Do	Do	Jn. Malone pa	Lr.		2						
Do	Do	Ed. Morrisey pap	Yeoman		1						
Do	Do	Wm. Cotsgrave pa	Lr.		4						

Galway Parish of	Place of Abode	Names and Religion	Proffession	Children under 14		Children above 14		Men Servts		Women Servts	
				Prot.	Paps.	Prot.	Paps.	Prot.	Paps.	Prot.	Paps.
Do	Do	Jn. Crahwell pa	Lr.								
Do	Do	Mi: Cussane pa	Lr.		1						
Do	Do	James Mahon[5] Pro	Gent						2		2
Do	Anahbeg	John Moor pa	Gent		3				3		3
Do	Do	Mark Grady pa	Lr.		2						
Do	Do	Jn. Carroll pa	Smith				2				
[f.197] Ahascra	Anahbeg	Pe. Colligan pa	Lr.		2		1				
Do	Do	Ni. Gerarty Pa	Lr.		4						
Do	Do	Jn. Daly Pa	Weaver		4						
Do	Do	Jn. Kelly Pa	Lr.								
Do	Do	Jn. Delany Pa	Lr.		1						
Do	Do	Hen: Lynch Pa	Lr.								
Do	Do	Jn. Mullan Pa	Lr.		2						
Do	Do	Dn. Kelly Pa	Taylor		2						
Do	Do	Mi: Kelly pa	Lr.		2						
Do	Do	Pa: Kerny pa	Lr.		1						
Do	Do	La: Costelo pap	Taylor								
Do	Do	Jn. Trustnane Pap	Lr.		2						
Do	Do	Fr. Coffy Pap	Lr.		2						
Do	Do	M. Kelly pa	Lr.								
Do	Do	Ja: Kelly Pap	Lr.								
Do	Do	Ed. Flinn pa	Lr.		3						
Do	Do	Wm. Maddin pa	Lr.								
Do	Do	Jn. Corroly pa	Lr.		1						
Do	Do	Pa: Colman pa	Lr.				1				
Do	Do	Wm. Haggarty pa	Lr.		2						
Do	Do	Pa: Hart pa	Lr.		4						
Do	Do	Wm. Reeve pa	Aleseller		1		1		1		1
Do	Do	Mi: Carroll pa	Lr.		2						
Do	Do	Pat. Carroll pa	Mason		1						
Do	Ballyerter	Pe: Dowdell pa	Lr.		3						
Do	Do	Bri: Doyle pa	Lr.		4						
Do	Do	Lo: Cormuck pa	Lr.								
Do	Do	P: Flin Pap	Lr.		3						
Do	Do	Ed. Trusnane pa	Lr.								
Do	Do	Bri: Cormack pa	Lr.		2						
Do	Do	An: Largan pa	Lr.		1						
Do	Do	Ed. Mulry pap	Gent		4				1		1
Do	Do	Da: Craffy pa	Lr.				2				
Do	Cregan	Bar. Kelly pa	Gent		6				3		2
Do	Do	Bri: Glin Pap	Lr.		3						
Do	Do	Lau: Cassey pa	Lr.		3						
Do	Do	Sim: Mulrian pa	Lr.		2		2				
Do	Do	Jn. Brudor pa	Lr.		2						
Do	Do	Jn. Downey pa	Lr.		2						
Do	Do	Jn. Hart. pa	Lr.		4						
Do	Do	Tho. Downey pa	Lr.		2						
Do	Do	Wm. Downey pa	Lr.				1				

NOTES

1. Less 59 statute acres of Cloonty Lough and other water (*General Alphabetical Index*).

2. John Gately of Ahascragh, County Galway, miller, was a witness of the will of William of Mucklon 12 July 1746 (*Abstracts of Wills,* ii, 10).

3. Fenning, 'Clergy Lists', p. 445.

4. Ross Mahon, eldest son of Bryan Mahon and Ellinor Gaynor married Jane Ussher. In 1747 Ross Mahon was granted a premium by the Dublin Society for draining 250 acres of bog with 2060 perches of drains. He was, with James Mahon, trustee and executor of the will of William Kelly of Mucklon, Taghboy, 12 July 1746. He died in 1757 (Watson *Almanack*; Abstracts of Wills, ii, 10; N.L.I., Genealogical Office MS 813/9).

5. Brother of Ross Mahon of Castlegar (Census f. 196) and trustee of the estate of William Kelly of Mucklon, Taghboy in 1746 (*Abstracts of Wills,* ii, 10).

KILLIAN, COUNTY GALWAY

INTRODUCTION: *The parish is in the barony of Killian. It is on the road from Roscommon to Mount-Bellew, 4 miles north east of Caltra. It covered 13,564 statute acres.*[1]

The incumbent was the Rev. William Glass, vicar from 1730 to 1799.[2] *It is not known where he lived. The patron was the bishop.*

OCCUPATIONS

Gentleman	2	Mason	1	Smith	1
Labourer	177	Servants, household	201		

Com~ Galway Parish of	Place of Abode	Names and Religion	Proffession	Children under 14		Children above 14		Men Servts		Women Servts	
[f.198] Killyon	Crogane	W. Kilroy Pap Lab.		2	pa						
Do -	Do -	Michl. Kilroy Pap	Lab.	1	pa					1	pa
Do -	Do -	Michl. Naghton Pap	Lab.	2	pa	1	pa			1	pa
Do -	Do -	Joseph Chevers Pap	Lab.	4	pa					1	pa
Do -	Do -	Roger Concars Pap	Lab.							1	pa
Do -	Do -	Hugh ffoaly Pap	Lab.	1	pa	1	pa			1	pa
Do -	Do -	Mark ffiny Pap	Lab.	2	1	1	pa			1	pa
Do -	Do -	Thos. Murry Pap	Lab.	1	pa	1	pa			1	pa
Do -	Do -	Wm. Kealy Pap	Lab.					1	pa	1	pa
Do -	Do -	Thos. ffeardan Pap	Lab.	2	pa	1	pa			1	pa
Do -	Do -	Patk. Kilroy Pap	Lab.	2	pa			1	pa		
Do -	Do -	Hugh McDonoll Pap	Lab.	3	pa			1	pa	1	pa
Do -	Do -	Danl. Cane Pap	Lab.	1	pa	1	pa				
Do -	Do -	Michl. Quin Pap	Lab.	1	pa	1	pa				
Do -	Do -	Jas. Dermot Pap	Lab.	2	pa	1	pa			1	pa
Do -	Do -	Thos. Quin Pap	Lab.	2	pa					1	pa
Do -	Do -	Jas. Kilcomor Pap	Lab.			1	pa	1	pa		
Do -	Do -	Jno. ffyn Pap	Lab.	1	pa	1	pa				
Do -	Do -	Teig. Loghan Pap	Lab.			1	pa			1	pa
Do -	Do -	Thos. Manin Pap	Lab.	2	pa	1	pa	1	pa		
Do -	Do -	Jas. Loghan Pen	Lab.	2	pa	1	pa	1	pa	1	pa
Do -	Do -	Patk. Connolly Pap	Lab.	1	pa					1	pa
Do -	Do -	Jno. Connolly Pap	Lab.	2	pa	1	pa			1	pa
Do -	Do -	Thos. Conolly Pap	Lab.	2	pa	1	pa				
Do -	Do -	Luke Connoly Pap	Lab.	1	pa	1	pa	1	pa	1	pa
Do -	Do -	Danl. ffeavy Pap	Lab.	1	pa	1	pa				
Do -	Do -	Jas. Martin Pap	Lab.	1	pa	1	pa				
Do -	Do -	Jno. Martin Pap	Lab.	2	pa	1	pa				
Do -	Do -	Wm ffeavy Pap	Lab.	2	pa			1	pa	1	pa
Com~	Do -	Darby Loghan Pap	Lab.	3	pa	1	pa				
Do -	Do -	Wm. Kolly Pap	Lab.	1	pa	1	pa	1	pa		
Do -	Do -	Owen ffeavy Pap	Lab.	3	pa			1	pa		
Do -	Do -	Laur Loghan Pap	Lab.	2	pa			1	pa	1	pa
Do -	Do -	Laur. Croghan Pap	Lab.	4	pa			1	pa		
Do -	Do -	Jno. Kellon Pap	Lab.	1	pa	1	pa	1	pa	1	pa
Do -	Do -	Peter Kilcomer Pap	Lab.	3	pa	1	pa				
Do -	Do -	Andrew Loghan Pap	Lab.	2	pa						
Do -	Do -	Jas. Manin Pap	Lab.	1	pa	1	pa				
Do -	Do -	Owen ffeavy Pap	Lab.					1	pa	1	pa
Do -	Do -	Laur. Loghan Pap	Lab.	1	pa	1	pa				
Do -	Do -	Wm. Croaghan Pap	Lab.	3	pa					1	pa
[f.199]	Ganavine	Michl. Chevers Gent Pap	Gent	3	pa			3	pa	3	pa
Do -	Do -	Jno. Chevers Pap	Gent			2	pa	2	pa	2	pa
Do -	Killyon	John Manin Pap	Lab.					1	pa	1	pa
Do -	Do -	Christr. Cary Pap	Lab.	1	pa	1	pa				
Do -	Do -	Edmd. Caragagh Pap	Lab.					1	pa	1	pa
Do -	Do -	Patk. Doyl Pap	Smith	2	pa	1	pa	1	pa		
Do -	Do -	Richd. Crosby Pap	Mason	2	pa			1	pa	1	pa

Com~ Galway Parish of	Place of Abode	Names and Religion	Proffession	Children under 14		Children above 14		Men Servts		Women Servts	
Do -	Do -	Michl. ffallon Pap				2	pa				
Do -	Do -	Jno. ffallon Pap	Lab.							1	pa
Do -	Do -	Laur. Lawler Pap	Lab.			2	pa	1	pa	1	pa
Do -	Do -	Martin Lawler Pap	Lab.	3	pa					1	pa
Do -	Do -	Robert Lawler Pap	Lab.							1	pa
Do -	Do -	Jas. Lawler Pap	Lab.					1	pa	1	pa
Do -	Do -	Edmd. Kilduff Pap	Lab.	2	pa	1	pa				
Do -	Do -	Pat. Kilduff Pap	Lab.			2	pa	1	pa	1	pa
Do -	Lisawrogy	Michl. fflyn Pap	Lab.	3	pa	1	pa	1	pa	1	pa
Do -	Do -	Jno. Loghan Pap	Lab.	2	pa	1	pa	1	pa	1	pa
Do -	Do -	Jas. Lynch Pap	Lab.	3	pa			1	pa	1	pa
Do -	Do -	Michl. Dermot Pap	Lab.	2	pa					1	pa
Do -	Do -	Jno. Wall Pap	Lab.	4	pa						
Do -	Do -	Wm. Kilcoman Pap	Lab.	2	pa	1	pa	1	pa		
Do -	Do -	Michl. Conolly Pap	Lab.	1	pa	1	pa			1	pa
Do -	Do -	Edmd. Kelly Pap	Lab.	2	pa	1	pa	1	pa	1	pa
Do -	Do -	Conor Loghan Pap	Lab.					1	pa		
Do -	Do -	Bartly Loghan Pap	Lab.	2	pa	1	pa	1	pa		
Do -	Do -	Denis Loghan Pap	Lab.			2	pa				
Do -	Do -	Michl. Loghan Pap	Lab.	1	pa	1	pa	1	pa	1	pa
Do -	Do -	Laur. Ganby Pap	Lab.	1	pa	1	pa				
Do -	Do -	Connor Loghan Pap	Lab.					1	pa	1	pa
Do -	Do -	Connor Cormuck Pap	Lab.					1	pa	1	pa
Do -	Do -	Denis Dolan Pap	Lab.	1	pa	1	pa	1	pa	1	pa
Do -	Do -	Thos. Loghan Pap	Lab.					1	pa	1	pa
Do -	Do -	Laur. Killoa Pap	Lab.	1	pa					1	pa
Do -	Do -	Martin ffeavy Pap	Lab.	2	pa						
Do -	Do -	ffrancis Dermot Pap	Lab.	2	pa	1	pa	1	pa	1	pa
Do -	Do -	Thos. Dowdall Pap	Lab.	2	pa			1	pa	1	pa
Do -	Do -	Thos. Wall Pap	Lab.	2	pa	1	pa	1	pa		
Do -	Crogane	Luke Loghan Pap	Lab.	2	pa	1	pa	1	pa	1	pa
Do -	Do -	Patk. Loghan Pap	Lab.	1	pa	1	pa				
Do -	Do -	Mathew Clark Pap	Lab.	3	pa	1	pa			1	pa
Do -	Do -	Edmd. Clark Pap	Laboror		1	1	pa	1	pa		
[f.200]Killyon	Cloonscarbry	John Kenedy Pap	Lab.	1	pa	2	pa			1	pap
Do. Parish	Do -	Michl. Coleman Pap	Lab.		2		1	1	pa		
Do -	Do -	John Loughan Pap	Lab.	1	pa	3	pa			1	pap
Do -Glin	Do -	Teig Glin Pap	Lab.	1	pa	1	pa	1	pa		
Do -	Do -	John Kelly Pap	Lab.	1	pa	1	pa				
Do -	Do -	Bryan Kilduff Pap	Lab.	2	pa	2	pa	1	pa	1	pa
Do -	Do -	Luke Groaghan Pap	Lab.	1	pa	1	pa				
Do -	Do -	Bryan Kilroy Pap	Lab.	1	pa	2	pa	1	pa	1	
Do -	Do -	Michl. Killen Pap	Lab.	1	pa	1	pa				
Do -	Do -	Danl. Kilcomon Pap	Lab.	1	pa	2	pa	1	pa	1	pa
Do -	Do -	Mathew Killea Pap	Lab.					1	pa	1	pa
Do -	Do -	Danl. Finey Pap	Lab.	1	pa	1	pa	1	pa	1	pa
Do -	Do -	Wm. Finey Pap	Lab.	1	pa	2	pa				
Do -	Do -	Darby Killea Pap	Lab.	1	pa	2	pa				
Do -	Do -	Patk. Neall Pap	Lab.	1	pa	1	pa	1	pa	1	pa

Com~ Galway Parish of	Place of Abode	Names and Religion	Proffession	Children under 14		Children above 14		Men Servts		Women Servts	
Do -	Do -	Andw. Killea Pap	Lab.							1	pa
Do -	Do -	Peter Killea Pap	Lab.	1	pa	2	pa	1	pa	1	pa
Do -	Do -	Willm. Killea Pap	Lab.							1	pa
Do -	Do -	Thos. Killea Pap	Lab.	1	pa	1	pa	1	pa	1	pa
Do -	Do -	Mark Killea Pap	Lab.							1	pa
Do -	Do -	Anthony Killea Pap	Lab.	1	pa	1	pa			1	pa
Do -	Do -	Math. Cuncars Pap	Lab.					1	pa		
Do -	Do -	Michl. Comon Pap	Lab.	1	pa	1	pa	1	pa		
Do -	Do -	Edmond Kilduff Pap	Lab.	1	pa	2	pa			1	pa
Do -	Do -	Luke Kelly Pap	Lab.	1	pa	1	pa				
Do - parish	Lyskyle	Martin Loghan Pap	Lab.	1	pa	1	pa	1	pa	1	pa
Do -	Do -	Hugh Loghan Pap	Lab.							1	pa
Do -	Do -	Michl. Loghan Pap	Lab.			1	pa			1	pa
Do -	Do -	Patk. Loghan Pap	Lab.								
Do -	Do -	Math. Higny Pap	Lab.			2	pa				
Do -	Do -	Edmd. Heavy Pap	Lab.			1	pa	1	pa	1	pa
Do -	Do -	Danl. ffinn Pap	Lab.					1	pa	1	pa
Do -	Do -	Hugh Crow Pap	Lab.	1	pa	2	pa				
Do -	Do -	Teig Crow Pap	Lab.					1	pa	1	pa
Do -	Do -	Domk. Loghan Pap	Lab.	1	pa	2	pa	1	pa	1	pa
Do -	Do -	Jno. Loghan Pap	Lab.								
Do -	Do -	Patk. Loghan Pap	Lab.	1	pa	1	pa	1	pa	1	pa
Do -	Do -	James Kenedy Pap	Lab.			1	pa			1	pa
Do -	Do -	Owen Donogho Pap	Lab.	1	pa	1	pa	1 pa			
Do -	Do -	Mathew ffarroll Pap	Lab.	1	pa	1	pa			1	pa
Do -	Do -	Michl. ffarroll Pap	Lab.	2	pa	1	pa			1	pa
[f.201]Killyon	Do -	Jno.Higny Pap	Lab.	1	pa	2	pa	1	pa	1	pa
Do -	Lyskyle	Connr. Kilcomon Pap								1	pa
Do -	Do -	Mathew Higny Pap	Lab.	1	pa	3	pa	1	pa		
Do -	Do -	Edmd. Shaghnesy Pap	Lab.	1	pa	2	pa			1	pa
Do -	Creeverae	Mark Butler Pap	Lab.	1	pa	1	pa	1	pa		
Do -	Do -	Wm. Butler Pap	Lab.	1	pa	2	pa			1	pa
Do -	Do -	Patk. Butler Pap	Lab.	1	pa	1	pa	1	pa	1	pa
Do -	Do -	Teig Kelly Pap	Lab.							1	pa
Do -	Do -	Patk. Duffy Pap	Lab.	1	pa	2	pa	1	pa		
Do -	Do -	Edmd. Kelly Pap	Lab.	1	pa	1	pa	1	pa		
Do -	Do -	Laughlin Magher Pap	Lab.	1	pa	3	pa				
Do -	Do -	Edmd Smyth Pap	Lab.	2	pa			1	pa	1	pa
Do -	Do -	John Hughs Pap	Lab.	1	pa	1	pa	1	pa	1	pa
Do -	Do -	Patk. Smyth Pap	Lab.	2	pa	1	pa				
Do -	Do -	Patk. Doyl Pap	Lab.	2	pa	1	pa	1	pa	1	pa
Do -	Do -	Peter. Loghan Pap	Lab.	2	pa			1	pa		
Do -	Do -	Teig Creaghan Pap	Lab.	4	pa			1	pa	1	pa
Do -	Do -	Michl. Gaffy Pap	Lab.	2	pa	3	pa				
Do -	Do -	John Quin Pap	Lab.							1	pa
Do -	Do -	Jno. Gaffy Pap	Lab.			1	pa				
Do -	Do -	Laughlin Connor Pap	Lab.	1	pa	1	pa	1	pa		
Do -	Do -	Charles O:Regan Pap	Lab.			2	pa	1	pa	1	pa
Do -	Do -	Patk. Egan Pap	Lab.			1	pa	1	pa	1	pa

Com~ Galway Parish of	Place of Abode	Names and Religion	Proffession	Children under 14		Children above 14		Men Servts		Women Servts	
Do -	Do -	Hugh Manon Pap	Lab.							1	pa
Do -	Do -	Michl. Kelly Pap	Lab.	2	pa						
Do -	Do -	Michl. fflanagan Pap	Lab.			3	pa	1	pa		
Do -	Do -	Jno. Madden Pap	Lab.	3	pa	1	pa	1	pa	1	pa
Do -	Do -	Richard Morary Pap	Lab.	2	pa	1	pa	1	pa	1	pa
Do -	Cloonsweeny	Owen ffahy Pap	Lab.	1	pa	1	pa	1	pa	1	pa
Do -	Do -	Nichs. ffahy Pap	Lab.	2	pa	1	pa				
Do -	Do -	Michl. Creaghan Pap	Lab.					1	pa	1	pa
Do -	Do -	Connor Creaghan Pap	Lab.	2	pa						
Do -	Do -	Patk. Manin Pap	Lab.	1	pa	1	pa	1	pa	1	pa
Do -	Do -	Michl. Kelly Pap	Lab.	2	pa	1	pa	1	pa	1	pa
Do -	Do -	Jno. Kelly Pap	Lab.	3	pa	1					
Do -	Ballynamore	Denis Kelly Pap	Lab.	2	pa	1	pa	1	pa	1	pa
Do -	Do -	Vallentin Hanly Pap	Lab.			2	pa	1	pa	1	pa
Do -	Do -	Bryan Hanly Pap	Lab.	1	pa	1	pa	1	pa	1	pa
Do -	Do -	ffrancis ffallon Pap	Lab.			2	pa				
Do -	Do -	Charles Tully Pap	Lab.							1	pa
[on separate sheet]Killyon	Ballynacorr	Dan. Connollan Pap	Lab.	3	pa	1	pa	1	pa		
Do -	Do -	Bartly Croaghan Pap	Lab.	3	pa					1	pa
Do -	Do -	Jno. Croaghan Pap	Lab.	3	pa	1	pa			1	p
Do -	Do -	Teig Connolly Pap	Lab.	4	pa	1	pa				
Do -	Do -	Owen Connolly Pap	Lab	2	pa			1	pa		
Do -	Do -	Martin ffinane Pap	Lab.	2	pa			1	pa	1	pa
Do -	Do -	John Dillon Pap	Lab.	2	pa			1	pa		
Do -	Do -	Michl. Kelly Pap	Lab.	4	pa	1	pa	1	pa		
Do -	Do -	Thos. Coleman Pap	Lab.	2	pa			1	pa	1	pa
Do -	Do -	Darby Loghan Pap	Lab.	1	pa					1	pa
Do ~	Do -	Denis Loghan Pap	Lab.	2	pa			1	pa	1	pa
Do -	Do -	Michl. Coleman Pap	Lab.	1	pa	1	pa	1	pa		
Do -	Do -	Wm. Coleman Pap	Lab.	2	pa	1	pa	1	pa		
Do -	Do -	Michl. Dowel Pap	Lab.	2	pa			1	pa		
Do -	Do -	Luke Dermot Pap	Lab.					1	pa	1	pa
Do -	Do -	Mark Quin Pap	Lab.	2	pa					1	pa
Do -	Do -	John Quin Pap	Lab.	3	pa	1	pa	1	pa		
Do -	Do -	Patk. Quin Pap	Lab.	3	pa	1	pa	1	pa		
Do -	Do -	Thos. Quin Pap	Lab.	2	pa	1	pa				
Do -	Do -	Patk. Murray Pap	Lab.	3	pa	1	pa	1	pa	1	pa

[on separate cover sheet]

To the Rt Rd Lord Bishop of Elphin
in Cavan Street
Dublin

[stamped]   FREE

NOTES

1. Less 14 acres of water (*General Alphabetical Index*).

2. William Glass was born in Athlone and educated by Mr. Thewles. He entered TCD in 1717 aged 18 and graduated BA in 1727. He was ordained in 1725. He married Margaret Thewles in 1726 (*Alumni Dubliniensis*; N.L.I., Leslie, 'Elphin', p. 83).

KILLOSOLAN or CASTLEBLAKENEY, COUNTY GALWAY

INTRODUCTION: *The parish of Killosolan is in the barony of Tiaquin. It is on the road from Ballinasloe to Tuam, County Galway. The parish covered 11,482 statute acres.*[1] *Lewis noted that there was pasture and arable land and some waste land and bog, with abundant limestone.*

The Church of Ireland incumbent was the Rev. William Tisdall, who was rector and vicar from 1743/4 to 1754.[2] *He held it with the parishes of Killeroran in the diocese of Elphin and Kilronan in the diocese of Ardagh. The patrons were the Crown and the bishop of Elphin alternately.*

OCCUPATIONS

Broguemaker	1	Innkeeper	1	Shoemaker	1
Carpenter	1	Labourer	118	Smith	1
Farmer	6	Merchant	3	Weaver	6
Gentleman	4	Servants, household	43	Wigmaker	1

Com~ Galway Parish of Killosolan	Place of Abode	Names and Religion	Proffession	Children under 14 Prot.	Children under 14 Paps.	Children above 14 Prot.	Children above 14 Paps.	Men Servts Prot.	Men Servts Paps.	Women Servts Prot.	Women Servts Paps.
[f.202] Castleblakeney	Castleblakeney	Php. Mcmanus Prot	Inkeepr	5					2		2
Castleblakeney	Castleblakeney	Hen. Johnston Prot	Weaver	1							1
Castleblakeney	Castleblakeney	Geo: Patty Prt.					2		1		1
Castleblakeney	Castleblakeney	Peter Whiskin Pr.	Weaver						1		1
Castleblakeney	Castleblakeney	Robt. Patty Pr.		1		1					1
Castleblakeney	Castleblakeney	John Price Pr.	Shoemr	2							1
Castleblakeney	Castleblakeney	Thos. Johnston Pr.	Weaver	5							1
Castleblakeney	Castleblakeney	Richd. Cook Pro	Carpinter	4							
Castleblakeney	Castleblakeney	Jn. Concannon Pr.		0					2		2
Castleblakeney	Castleblakeney	Rr. Dillon Pr.		0	2				1		1
Do	Gurteenmore	Thos. Hanly Pa	Farmer	‡	3				1		1
Do	Do	Robt. Verdon Pa	Farmer		1						
Do	Do	Gilbert Bercer pa	Farmer				1				
Do	Castleblakney	Hu: Macige pa	Lr		1						
Do	Do	Wm. Quin pa	Lr		1						
Do	Do	Lu: Finarty pa	Lr								
Do	Do	Teige Relley pa	Lr		3		1				
Do	Do	Bri: Magaver pa	Lr		3		1				
Do	Do	Hu: Keough pa	Lr		2						
Do	Do	Richd. Brenden pa	Lr		1						
Do	Do	Pa: Finegan pa	Lr		1		2				
Do	Do	Wm. Finegan pa	Lr		1						
Do	Do	Rob. Hare Pro	Farmer				2				
Do	Do	Robt. Dillen pro	Weaver		1						
Do	Do	Js. Fallon pa	Lr		1						
Do	Do	L: Mulln. pa	Lr		3		2				
Do	Do	Th: Manion pa	Lr		2		1				
Do	Do	Jn. Mule pa	Lr		1						
Do	Do	Jn. Butler pa	Lr		2		2		1		1
Do	Calbrahpally	Jas. Joyce pa	Mt.				2				
Do	Do	Jn. Handy pa	Mt.		1				1		1
Do	Do	An: Fallon pa	Lr		1		2				
Do	Do	Fr: Lynch pa	Lr		2		1				
Do	Do	Mar: Griffin pa	Weaver		2		2				
Do	Do	Tho: Burk pa	Lr		1						
Do	Do	Wm. Bredar pa	Lr		1						
Do	Do	Thos. Morresy pa	Lr		3		2				
Do	Do	Jn. Finane pa	Lr		1		1				
Do	Do	Jn. Kelly pa	Lr		2						
Do	Do	Mi: Noon pa	Lr		2						
Do	Do	Da: Nee pa	Lr		1						
[f.203] Castleblakeney	Calbrah	M: Royan pa	Lr		2		1				
Do	Do	Jn. Stanton pa	Lr		2						
Do	Do	Th: Hanly pa	Mt:		2						
Do	Do	Robt. Verden pa	Lr		1						
Do	Do	Pat. Courtney pa	Br:		2		2				
Do	Do	Dn. Hare pa	Lr		2		1				
Do	Do	Pat. Martin pa	Lr				2				

Com~ Galway Parish of	Place of Abode	Names and Religion	Proffession	Children under 14 Prot.	Paps.	Children above 14 Prot.	Paps.	Men Servts Prot.	Paps.	Women Servts Prot.	Paps.
Do	Do	Jn. Welsh pa	Lr								
Do	Do	Jn. Lace pa	Lr		3		1				
Do	Do	De. Martin pa	Lr		2						
Do	Do	Bar: Gavan pa	Lr		1						
Do	Do	Tho. Smyth pa	Weaver		3				1		
Do	Ticooly	An: McDonah pa	Lr		1						
Do	Do	Th: Finarty pa	Lr		2						
Do	Do	Ja.Galvan pa	Lr		3						
Do	Do	Wm. Galvan pa	Lr		2						
Do	Do	Br. Flanagan pa	Lr								
Do	Do	Ow: Coffy pa	Lr		2						
Do	Do	Pe: Galvan pa	Lr		1						
Do	Do	An. Collon pa	Lr		2						
Do	Do	Pe: Bodison pa	Lr		2		1				
Do	Do	Br. Noon pa	Lr		3						
Do	Do	L. Monkley pa	Lr		6						
Do	Do	Mile McGlaughlin pa	Lr		2						
Do	Do	Eavy Thompson pa	Lr		2						
Do	Do	Hu: Gill pa	Lr		3						
Do	Do	Jn. Gill pa	Lr		2						
Do	Do	Th: Kinselah pa	Lr		2						
Do	Do	Th: Brian pa	Lr		3		1				
Do	Do	Mi:Monahan pa	Lr		2						
		M: Monahan pa	Lr		2						
Do	Do	R: Coffeey pa	Lr		3						
Do	Do	Ma: Johnston pa	Lr		3						
Do	Do	Ja: Mannin pa	Lr		2		1				
Do	Do	Don: Lohan pa	Lr		3						
Do	Do	M: Verdon pa	Lr		2						
Do	Do	Ja: Diffy pa	Lr		3						
Do	Do	R: Conheeny pa	Lr		3						
Do	Do	Fer: Kelly pa	Gent		4		2		3		2
Do	Do	Jn. Crofton pro	wigmaker		1						
[f.204] Castleblakey	Kinclare	An. Fallen pa	Lr		4						
Do	Do	Jn. Shonesey pa	Lr		5						
Do	Do	Pa: Dillon pa	Lr		3						
Do	Do	Ri: Costely pa	Lr		2		1				
Do	Do	Ni: Garvin pa	Lr		2						
Do	Killasolan	Th: Dillon pa	Lr		3		1				
Do	Do	Thos: Clery pa	Lr		2		1				
Do	Do	Lo: Clery pa	Lr		1						
Do	Do	Pa: Conry pa	Lr		3						
Do	Do	Dar: Gredy pa	Lr								
Do	Do	Lu: Finerty pa	Lr		1						
Do	Do	Jn. Kilginan pa	Lr		2						
Do	Do	Pa: Corheeny pa	Lr		1						
Do	Do	Pa: Kelly pa	Lr		2						
Do	Do	Jas. Kelly pa	Lr		1						
Do	Do	Pa. Gerarty pa	Lr								

Com~ Galway Parish of	Place of Abode	Names and Religion	Proffession	Children under 14		Children above 14		Men Servts		Women Servts	
				Prot.	Paps.	Prot.	Paps.	Prot.	Paps.	Prot.	Paps.
Do	Do	Ja. Gerarty pa	Lr		1						
Do	Do	M. Corheeny pa	Lr		3		1				
Do	Do	M: Rush pa	Lr								
Do	Do	Da. Coffee pa	Lr		2						
Do	Do	Lu: Donahooe pa	Lr		2		1				
Do	Do	Pa. Quin pa	Lr		1						
Do	Do	Ni. Gerarty pa	Lr		3						
Do	Do	Ed. French pa	Gent				1		3		4
Do	Do	Hen: Dillon pa	Gent		4				3		1
[f.205] Castleblakny	Clogher	Jn. Tully pa	Farmer		1						1
Do	Do	Jn. Conry pa	Farmer		3						
Do	Do	Mi: Geraty pa	Lr		3						
Do	Do	Mi: Smith pa	Lr		3		1				
Do	Do	Ja. Rogerson pa	Lr		2		1				
Do	Do	Jn. Lohan pa	Lr		3						
Do	Do	Hu. Tully pa	Lr								
Do	Do	Mi. Gerity Jr. pa	Lr		1						
Do	Do	Wm. Contreny pa	Lr		5						
Do	Do	Corm. Tully pa	Lr		2						
Do	Do	Lu. Coffee pa	Lr		2						
Do	Do	Th. Follon pa	Lr		3						
Do	Do	Pet. Conway pa	Lr		2		1				
Do	Do	Hu. Tully pa	Lr		1						
Do	Do	Pat. Martin pa	Lr		2						
Do	Do	Pa. Verdin pa	Lr		1						
Do	Do	Pat. Ridson pa	Lr		2		1				
Do	Do	Ja. Regan pa	Lr		1		2				
Do	Do	Th: Flinn pa:	Lr		2						
Do	Do	Jn. Curly pa	Lr		3		1				
Do	Do	Wm. Curly pa	Smith		2						
Do	Do	Jn. Burk pa	Lr		1						
Do	Bredah	Ro: Noon pa	Lr		2						
Do	Do	Pat. Kelly pa	Lr		3		1				
Do	Do	Ni. Rogerson pa	Lr		2						
Do	Do	Pa. Melet pa	Lr		1						
Do	Do	De. Noon pa	Lr		1						
Do	Do	Jn. Luff pa	Lr		2						
Do	Lorgan	Farrell Ward pa	Lr		2		1				
Do	Do	D. Lohan pa	Lr		2						
Do	Do	Pat. Mannon pa	Lr		2						
Do	Do	Si. Reilly pa	Lr		2						
Do	Do	Ja. Brannan pa	Lr		1						
Do	Do	Bri.Burn pa	Lr		2						
Do	Do	Pa. Burn pa	Lr		1						
Do	Do	Mar. Farrel pa	Lr		1						
Do	Do	Ed. Tyrrell pa	Lr		3						
Do	Do	Ja. Conry pa	Lr		1						
Do	Do	Wm. Concannon pa	Gent		3				[?]2		1
Do	Kinclare	Lu: Carrick pa	Lr		3						
Do	Do	Th. Lau.Nane pa	Lr		3		1				

NOTES

1. (*General Alphabetical Index*).

2. There is some uncertainty as to which William Tisdall was the incumbent of Killasolan. The most likely is William who was born in Dublin, a son of the Rev. William Tisdall DD. His father was a friend of Jonathan Swift and shared Swift's controversial politics. Tisdall senior married Eleanor Morgan of Cottlestown, County Sligo. Their son William entered TCD in 1723 aged 17 and graduated BA in 1728. He married Lady Mary, daughter of Chambre Brabazon, Earl of Meath. Tisdall was presented rector and vicar of Castleblakeney by the Crown in 1743 (*Alumni Dubliniensis; Dictionary of National Biography*).

KILLERORAN, COUNTY GALWAY

INTRODUCTION: *The parish was in the barony of Killian. It is 3 miles north east of Ballinamore, on the road to Roscommon. It covers 12,595 statute acres. The river Shriven runs through part of the parish which has a great deal of bog.*[1]

The incumbent was the Rev. William Tisdall (see Killosolan). The patron was the bishop. The rectory was impropriate in the King family.[2]

OCCUPATIONS

Doctor	1	Labourer	62	Smith	1
Gentleman	3	Servants, household	26	Tanner	1

Com~ Galway Parish of	Place of Abode	Names and Religion	Proffession	Children under 14 Prot.	Paps.	Children above 14 Prot.	Paps.	Men Servts Prot.	Paps.	Women Servts Prot.	Paps.
[f.206] Kilroran	Gortacousane	Den: Mulry Pa:	Lr.				2				
Do	Do	Mar. Gattely Pa	Lr.		3						
Do	Do	Mau. Mulry Pa	Lr.								
Do	Do	Mar. Mullord Pa:	Lr.		1						
Do	Do	Pat. Brislane Pa:	Lr.		2						
Do	Do	Bri. Mulry Pa:	Lr.								
Do	Do	Jn. Kelly Pa:	Lr.								
Do	Do	Wm. Mullan Pa:	Lr.				2				
Do	Ballinlass	Wm. Kelly Pa	Gent.		7		2		2		3
Do	Do	Ma. Concannon pa	Smyth				2				
Do	Do	Con Carhane Pa:	Lr.		1						
Do	Do	Pat. Hone Pa:	Lr.		1						
Do	Do	An. Kinselah Pa:	Lr.		2						
Do	Do	Ed. Cholahan Pa:	Lr.		1		1				
Do	Do	Con. Maurice Pa:	Lr.		1		1				
Do	Do	Brian. Finarty Pa:	Lr.								
Do	Do	Bri. Cahill Pa:	Lr.		2						
Do	Do	Jn. Egan Pa:	Lr.		1						
Do	Do	Bar. Egan pa	Millar		1						
Do	Cloonibrig	Bri. Kenny Pa:	Lr.		1						
Do	Do	Pat. Kilcommon Pa:	Lr.		2						
Do	Do	Tei. Duffy Pa:	Lr.				1				
Do	Do	Lu. Kelly Pa:	Lr.								
Do	Do	Con. Locan Pa:	Lr.				1				
Do	Do	Mi. Kelly Pa:	Lr.		2						
Do	Do	De. Mannion Pa:	Lr.		2						
Do	Do	Mi. Ternan Pa:	Lr.				1				
Do	Do	Jn. Ternan Pa:	Lr.		1						
Do	Do	An. Kelly Pa:	Lr.		2						
Do	Cloonlion	Hugh Lochan Pa:	Lr.				1				
Do	Do	Lu. Hennan Pa:	Lr.		2						
Do	Do	Jn. Hena Pa:	Lr.				1				
Do	Do	Wm. Holahan Pa:	Lr.		2						
Do	Do	Thos. Fitzjames Pa:	Lr.		3						
Do	Do	Den. Feeny Pa:	Lr.								
Do	Do	H. Feeny Pa:	Lr.		3						
Do	Do	M. Chaherne Pa:	Lr.								
Do	Do	Con. Hanning Pa:	Lr.				2				
Do	Do	Mi. McDonah Pa:	Lr.								
Do	Do	Jn. Connor Pa:	Lr.		3		1				
Do	Do	Ma. Carthy Pa:	Lr.				1				
Do	Do	Pat. Noghton Pa:	Lr.		3						
[f.207] Kilroran	Clonlyon	Den. Farrell pa	Gent						4		3
Do	Tulla	R. Holohan pa	Tanner		3				1		1
Do	Do	Dan. Murry Pa:	Lr.						1		1
Do	Do	Wm.; Kenedy Pa:	Lr.		2		1				
Do	Do	Ed. Combes Pa:	Lr.		2						
Do	Do	Pat. Noon Pa:	Lr.		2		1				

Com~ Galway Parish of	Place of Abode	Names and Religion	Proffession	Children under 14 Prot.	Children under 14 Paps.	Children above 14 Prot.	Children above 14 Paps.	Men Servts Prot.	Men Servts Paps.	Women Servts Prot.	Women Servts Paps.
Do	Do	Jas. Healy Pa:	Lr.		1		1				
Do	Do	Jn. Heely Pa:	Lr.								
Do	Do	Hu. Healy Pa:	Lr.		2						
Do	Do	Lu. Lochan Pa:	Lr.		1						
Do	Do	Tei. Quin Pa:	Lr.		3		1				
Do	Do	An. Heavy Pa:	Lr.		1						
Do	Meeanah	Dnl. Meelah Pa:	Lr.		2						
Do	Do	Jas. Meelah Pa:	Lr.				1				
Do	Do	Lu. Healy Pa:	Lr.						1		1
Do	Do	Pat. Holahan Pa:	Lr.		2						
Do	Do	Wm. Harty Pa:	Lr.		1		1				
Do	Do	Lau. Carthy Pa:	Lr.		2						
Do	Do	And. Kelly Pa:	Lr.				1				
Do	Do	Ow. Flin Pa:	Lr.				1				
Do	Do	Mi. Flin Pa:	Lr.		3						
Do	Cornonant	Chr. Gillar Pa:	Lr.		1						
Do	Do	Ri. Leven Pa:	Lr.		2						
Do	Do	Pe. Blakeney Pa:	Lr.		1						
Do	Do	Tho. Hoan Pa:	Lr.		1		1				
Do	Do	Jn. Kevan pa	Gent						2		2
Do	Kilrahiscra	Ri. Burk pa	Doct		1				2		2

NOTES

1. Less 51 acres of water (*General Alphabetical Index*).

2. Lewis, 'Killararan or Kilronan'.

FUERTY, COUNTY ROSCOMMON

INTRODUCTION: *The parish of Fuerty was in the barony of Athlone. It is 3½ miles from Roscommon and is crossed by the river Suck. It covered 8,989 statute acres. There were quarries of limestone and gritstone. The gritstone quarry was said in 1814 to have excellent stone which was used for the grooves of the water wheel axle at the mill at Castlecoote.[1] The townland of Castlestrange was held by Harmon Strange in 1641, but there were no members of the family remaining in the parish in 1749.*

The rector was the Rev. John Hickes who held the living with that of Athleague, Kilbegnet and Dunamon. He lived in Castlestrange. The rectory was impropriate in the earl of Essex. The fee simple proprietors were the bishop of Elphin, Sir Charles Coote, Thomas Mitchel, John Mitchel and V. Waldron. The patron was the bishop.

OCCUPATIONS

Ale seller	2	Labourer	122	Sievemaker	1
Broguemaker	5	Maltster	1	Smith	5
Butcher	1	Mason	5	Tailor	4
Esquire	1	Miller	1	Tanner	1
Farmer	9	Sawyer	3	Turner	1
Gardener	3	Servants, household	105	Vicar	1
Gentleman farmer	1	Schoolmaster	1	Weaver	14
Joiner	3	Shepherd	9		

Com~Ros common Parish of	Place of Abode	Names and Religion	Proffession	Children under 14 Prot.	Children under 14 Paps.	Children above 14 Prot.	Children above 14 Paps.	Men Servts Prot.	Men Servts Paps.	Women Servts Prot.	Women Servts Paps.
[f.208] Fuerty	Castlestrange	Patrick									
		Margret Murhanoe Papt	Sheppard		2						
Do	Do	Michael									
		Mary Kenny Papt:	Labourer		3						
Do	Do	James									
		Nelly Kenny Papt:	Weaver		3						
Do	Do	Luke									
		Onnor Makelly Papt:	Butcher		3						
Do	Do	William									
		Dorothy Sheeny Paps:	Labourer		1						
Do	Do	Edmond									
		Burne Ellis Paps:	Labourer		1						
Do	Do	Loghlin									
		Margret Haraghtin Paps:	Labourer		1						
Do	Do	Mark									
		Bridget Naughtin Paps:	Labourer		1						
Do	Do	Connor									
		Bridget McGloo Paps:	Labourer		2						
Do	Do	James									
		bridget Nealon Paps:	Brogemaker		3						
Do	Do	Henry Prots									
		bridget Walker Paps	Joyner	2			3				
Do	Do	Thos.									
		bridget Noon Paps	Labourer		3		1				
Do	Do	Rojer									
		Anne Leanahon Paps	Mason		3		1				
Do	Do	Francis									
		Ellis Kelly Paps	Mason				2				
Do	Do	Anne Cranoge Widdow Paps					2				
Do	Do	James									
		Ellis Dooravon Pap	Mason								
Do	Do	John									
		Cathrine Meighan Paps	Aleseller		6		1				
Do	Do	Connor									
		Mary Neelan Paps	brogemaker				3				
Do	Do	James									
		bridget Kean Paps	Labourer		1						
Do	Do	Patrick									
		Cathrine Hannen Paps	Labourer		3						
Do	Do	Francis									
		Margret Haneen Paps	Labourer				1				
Do	Do	John									
		bridget McGloghlin Paps	Labourer		3						
Do	Do	Roger									
		Cathrin McLanny Paps	farmer		4						
Do	Do	Connor									
		Dorothy Kelly Paps	Labourer								
Do	Do	John Kelly Papt	Labourer								
Do	Do	Edmond									
		Joan Gilligan Paps	Labourer		2		1				
Do	Do	Edmond									
		Mary Nealan Paps	Labourer		3		1				
Do	Do	Theady									
		Mary Garner Paps	Mason				3				
Do	Do	Cornelius									
		Ellinor Cox Prot	Schoolmaster						1		1
Do	Do	John									
		Giles Cuddy Paps	Shepherd		1						
		Revd.John Hickes[2] & wife Prot	Vicar of Athleague	3		3		1	1	1	2

Com~Ros common Parish of	Place of Abode	Names and Religion	Proffession	Children under 14 Prot.	Children under 14 Paps.	Children above 14 Prot.	Children above 14 Paps.	Men Servts Prot.	Men Servts Paps.	Women Servts Prot.	Women Servts Paps.
	Tobervaddy	Lewis Ormsby³ Esqr Cathrine Prot							3	2	2
	Do	Richard Elizabeth Hogan Prots		2		1					
		John Sanders Prot Winnafrid Pap:	Gardiner				2				
[f.209]Fuerty	Buckfield⁴	William Reddish Kelly Paps	farmer		6		2		2		3
Do	Do	Rojer Mary Whoolahan Paps	Labourer		2		1				
Do	Tonilamony	Murtagh Mary Summahon Paps	Shepherd		4						
Do	Do	Michl Cathrine Cuddy Paps	Labourer		2						
Do	Do	Bryan Pap Elizabeth Conry Prot	Joyner								
Do	Ahagad	Michael bridget Higgins Paps	Labourer		1						
Do	Do	Hugh bridget Gaffy Paps	Labourer		3		3				
Do	Do	Theady Ellinor Gaffy Paps	Labourer		2		1				
Do	Do	William Winafrid Mee Paps	Labourer		1						
Do	Farnikelly	Edmond Margret Kenny Paps	Labourer								
Do	Do	Redmond Winnafrid Kenny Paps	Labourer		1		2				
Do	Do	Rojer Bridget McCormick Paps	Labourer		1						
Do	Do	James Onnor Lewis Paps	Labourer		1						
Do	Do	Patrick Mary Tummulty Paps	Labourer								
Do	Do	James Margret Kelly Paps	Labourer		2						
Do	Do	Michael Onnor Kean Paps	Labourer		2						
Do	Do	Charles Rose Lewis Paps	Labourer		1						
Do	Do	Andrew Mary Lary Paps	Shepherd		3						
Do	Clooniquin	Edward Rebecka Hodson Prots.	Farmer	3					2	1	3
Do	Do	Michael Margret Mulrain Paps	Ale seller		2						1
Do	Bracklon	Edmond Margret Fallon Paps	Labourer				3				
Do	Do	John Ellinor Lennon Paps	Labourer				2				
Do	Do	Eneas Cathrine Ruddy Paps	Labourer		1						
Do	Do	Patrick Burne Paps	Labourer								
Do	Do	William Winnafrid Naughtin Paps	Labourer		2					1	
Do	Do	Michael Bridget Gowran Paps	Labourer		2						
Do	Do	Cormick Onnor Giblon Paps	Labourer		3		1				
Do	Do	Michael Mary Croghan Paps	Labourer		1		1				

Com~Ros common Parish of	Place of Abode	Names and Religion	Proffession	Children under 14		Children above 14		Men Servts		Women Servts	
				Prot.	Paps.	Prot.	Paps.	Prot.	Paps.	Prot.	Paps.
Do	Do	Bryan									
		Anne McGuire Paps	Labourer		1		1				
Do	Do	Anne Finn Pap	Widdow				3				
Do	Boxford	Thos.									
		Allice Hodson Prots.		4					3		4
Do	Do	Michael									
		Anne Keegan Paps	Labourer		5		1				
Do	Rockfield	John									
		Cathrine Kennedy Paps	Labourer		3		2				
Do	Do	Farrell									
		Margret Kennedy Paps	Labourer		2		1		1		1
Do	Do	Sandy									
		Liddy Flynn Paps			4						
Do	Do	Patrick									
		Cunnaun Paps	Labourer				2				
Do	Do	Dennis									
		Mary Cunnaun Paps	Labourer		2						
Do	Do	Andrew Ruddy Paps	Labourer								
Do	Do	John Knavin Paps	Labourer								
Do	Do	Roger									
		Bridget Egan Paps	Labourer		2						
Do	Do	John									
		Margret Lamb Paps	Labourer		4						
[f.210]Fuerty	Lisgallin	Daniel									
		Mary Breghany Paps	Labourer		2						1
Do	Do	Wiliam									
		Bridget Breghany Paps	Labourer		1						
Do	Do	Cristopher									
		Cathrine Keerawon Paps	Labourer		2						
Do	Do	Andrew									
		Onnor Flanigan Paps	Labourer		1						
Do	Do	Theady									
		Nola Deary Paps	Labourer		3						
Do	Do	Michael									
		Sarah Lennon Paps	Labourer		2						
Do	Do	Theady McNeal Paps	Labourer								
Do	Do	Michael									
		Mary McNeal Paps	Labourer		2						
Do	Do	John									
		Mary Costello Paps	Labourer		1						
Do	Do	John									
		Mary Kilkooly Paps	Labourer		4						
Do	Do	James									
		Sarah Mannin Paps	Labourer		2						
Do	Do	Owen									
		Onnor Loo Paps	Labourer		1						
Do	Do	James									
		Rose Gannan Paps	Smith		2						
Do	Do	Edmond									
		Cicily Kelly Paps	Labourer		3						
Do	Do	Thos.									
		Bridget Carty Paps	Labourer								
Do	Do	John									
		Elinor Keerakun Paps	Labourer								
Do	Do	Patrick Hanimnay Paps	Labourer		1						
Do	Do	Theady									
		Ellinor Kelly Paps	Labourer		1						
Do	Do	Thos.									
		Mary Cusxcar Paps	Labourer		2						
Do	Do	Ann Finn Pap	Widdow				2				
Do	Do	Giles Headin Pap	Widdow			2					

Com~Ros common Parish of	Place of Abode	Names and Religion	Proffession	Children under 14 Prot.	Paps.	Children above 14 Prot.	Paps.	Men Servts Prot.	Paps.	Women Servts Prot.	Paps.
Do	Do	Mark									
		Cathrine Connelly Paps	Labourer								
Do	Do	Winnafrid Grady Pap	Widdow		1		1				
Do	Do	Hugh									
		Margret Healy Paps	Labourer				3				
Do	Do	Theady									
		Bridget Lennon Paps	Shepherd		2						
Do	Rockfield	Rojer									
		Rose Flanigan Paps	Labourer		4						
Do	Do	James									
		Cathrine Flynn Paps	Labourer		1						
Do	Do	Loghllin									
		Mary Gerughty Paps	Labourer		1						
Do	Do	Thos.									
		Mary Keerawon Paps	Miller[5]		2						
Do	Do	Anne Leanahon Pap	Widdow		1		1				
Do	Do	Deniss									
		Onnor Coghlan Paps			3		2	1			1
Do	Do	Deniss									
		Lettice Coghlan Prots									
Do	Do	Cristopher									
		Mary Anne Irwin[6] Paps			5			1	2		2
Do	Do	Charles									
		Rose Flanigan Paps			2				2		1
Do	Do	Richard									
		Mary Giblon Paps									
Do	Do	Martin									
		Winafrid Conway Paps	Labourer								
Do	Do	Wiliam									
		Mary Conolan Paps	Labourer		4						
Do	Do	Anthony									
		Sarah Rider Paps	Gardner		4						
Do	Do	John									
		Mary Hambleton Prots		4							
Do	Do	Edmond Eagan Pap			2		2				
Do	Do	Loghlin Donelan					2				
[f.211]Fuerty	Carrowstellan	Darby									
		Hannah Mannian Paps	Labourer		1				1		
Do	Do	Hugh									
		Onnor Mannian Paps	Labourer				2		1		
Do	Do	Patrick									
		Bridgett Kilroe Paps	Labourer		2				1		
Do	Do	Matthias									
		Mary Naghton Paps	Labourer		1		2				
Do	Do	Edwd									
		Margret Feehily Paps	Malster		2						
Do	Do	John									
		Mary Hargadon Paps	Shepherd				1				
Do	Do	Connor									
		Mary Hargadon Paps	Labourer								
Do	Ballinlegg	Jon.									
		Jane Stroaker Prots	Labourer	3							
Do	Do	Jon.									
		Sibby Cuddy Paps	Labourer		1						
Do	Do	Danl.									
		Onnor Healy Paps	Shepherd		1						
Do	Do	Edmd.									
		Mary Connor Paps	Labourer		2		1				
Do	Do	Thos.									
		Black Prot Cath. Pap	Labourer	3							

Com~Ros common Parish of	Place of Abode	Names and Religion	Proffession	Children under 14 Prot.	Children under 14 Paps.	Children above 14 Prot.	Children above 14 Paps.	Men Servts Prot.	Men Servts Paps.	Women Servts Prot.	Women Servts Paps.
Do	Do	Edmd. Margt Curry Paps	Labourer				1				
Do	Do	Roger Margt. Ruddane Paps	Labourer		2		1				
Do	Do	Jn. Cicily Kenny Paps	Labourer		2						
Do	Do	Thos Cormack Pap Cicily	Labourer		1						
Do	Ballinturly	Thos. Mitchell[7] Prot	Farmer						5		4
Do	Do	Pat. Margt. Clary Paps	Labourer								
Do	Do	Bryan Bridget Mee Paps	Labourer		4						
Do	Do	Martin Bridget Corly Paps	Labourer		3						
Do	Do	Connor Giles Feeny Paps	Labourer		3						
Do	Do	Onnor McConna Pap	Widdw		1						
Do	Do	Darby Jane Correen Paps	Labourer		3						
Do	Do	Patrick Mary Cranoge Paps	Shepherd						1		
Do	Do	Peter Mary McConna Paps	Labourer		8						
Do	Do	James Cath. Clancy Paps	Labourer				2				
Do	Do	Pat. Giles Clancy Paps	Labourer		1						
Do	Lisgallen	Owen Mary Kelly Paps	Labourer								
Do	Do	James Giles Goowaun Paps	Labourer		2						
Do	Do	John Mary Rush Paps	Labourer								1
Do	Do	Bartholomew Elizabeth Cowen Paps	Labourer		3						
Do	Do	Eulick Burke Paps.	Labourer								
Do	Do	John Mary Roork Paps	Broguemaker		1						
Do	Do	Denis Mary Finnan Paps	Labourer				3				
Do	Do	Robert Cathrine Devnish Paps	Labourer				2				
Do	Do	Ferns Bridget Kelly Paps	Labourer		3		2				
Do	Do	Murtagh Cathrine Bryan Paps	Labourer		2						
Do	Do	Thos. Mary Hines Paps	Labourer		2						
Do	Do	Luke Mary Gaffy Paps	Labourer		2						
Do	Do	James Cathrine Dempsy Paps	Labourer		2						
Do	Do	Cathrine Owens Paps. Widdow			3						
[f.212]Fuerty	Castlecoote	Thos. + Mary McGan Paps	Labourer		1		2				
Do	Do	James + Brigett McGan Paps	Labourer		2		1				
Do	Do	Cormack +									

Com~Ros common Parish of	Place of Abode	Names and Religion	Proffession	Children under 14		Children above 14		Men Servts		Women Servts	
				Prot.	Paps.	Prot.	Paps.	Prot.	Paps.	Prot.	Paps.
Do	Do	Margret Rogers Paps Owen +	Weaver	1							
Do	Do	Margt McConree Paps David +	Taylor	2							
Do	Do	Winny Glinane Paps Andw.	Labourer	1		1					
Do	Do	Mary Kilroe Paps Thos. +	Labourer	3		2					
Do	Do	Eliz. Cuddy Paps Peter +	Tanner	3		2					
Do	Do	Mary Dowd Paps Denis +	Labourer	3							
Do	Do	Ellinor Mcnama Paps James +	Labourer	2							
Do	Do	Sarah Dowd Paps Wm. +	Weaver	3							
Do	Do	Mary Dowd Paps Edmd. +	Labourer								
Do	Do	Sarah Moran Paps David +	Smith	3		4					
Do	Do	Elizth. Burke Paps David +	Weaver	2		2					
Do	Do	Cicily Cuddy Paps Geo. +	Labourer	1							
Do	Do	Sinny Pollard Paps Manus +	Labourer								
Do	Do	Mary Fallon Paps Wm. +	Labourer	1							
Do	Do	Catherine Kelly Paps Danl. +	Taylor	5		2					
Do	Creevmully	Mary Dowd Paps Jon. +	Labourer	1							
Do	Do	Mary Fallon Paps Danl. +	Labourer	5		1					
Do	Do	Margrett Giraghty Paps Simon +	Labourer	4							
Do	Do	Mary Cahill Paps Jon. +	Labourer	4		1					
Do	Do	Elizth. Neilan Paps Phelim +	Broguemaker	3		3					
Do	Do	Margt. Neilan Paps Patt. +	Labourer	1							
Do	Do	Margtt. Neilan Paps Wm.	Labourer	2							
Do	Do	Margtt Heath Paps James	Weaver	1							
Do	Do	Agnes Kine Paps Edwd.	Labourer			2					
Do	Do	Ann Kelly Paps Patrick	Taylor	2		1					
Do	Do	Bridgett Hart Paps Darby	Labourer	1							
Do	Do	Elizth. Horogho Paps David	Labourer	2							
Do	Do	Mary Heath Paps Michl. Pap	Sawyer	2		3					
Do	Do	Elizth. Connor Prot Thady	Joyner	2							
Do	Do	Mable Connor Paps John Kennucan Pap	Labourer								
Do	Do	Penelope Prot	Labourer	1							

Com~Ros common Parish of	Place of Abode	Names and Religion	Proffession	Children under 14		Children above 14		Men Servts		Women Servts	
				Prot.	Paps.	Prot.	Paps.	Prot.	Paps.	Prot.	Paps.
Do	Do	Danl. Onnor Duvine Paps	Sawyer		3		2				
Do	Do	Andw. Cath. Noon Paps	Labourer		2				1		
Do	Do	Jon. Noon Pap	Taylor								
Do	Do	Michl. Mary Keerucan Paps	Weaver		2		4				
Do	Do	Patrick Elizth Duvine Paps	Sawyer		3						1
Do	Do	James Mary Kilroe Paps	Labourer		1						
Do	Do	Bryan Ann Keggan Paps	Labourer		2						
[f.213]Fuerty	Creevmully	Jon. Mary Kilroe Paps	Labourer		2				1		
Do	Do	James Margt. Neilan Paps	Labourer		2				1		
Do	Do	Patrick Ellinor Murry Paps	Labourer		2						
Do	Do	Thos. Cath. Reggan Paps	Labourer		2		2				
Do	Do	Roger Marjery Noon Paps	Labourer		5						
Do	Do	Laughlin Cath. Knaven Paps	Labourer		1						
Do	Do	James Winnifred Knaven Paps	Labourer		1						
Do	Do	Edmd. Onnor Knaven Paps	Labourer		1						
Do	Do	Laughlin Margtt Knaven Paps	Labourer		1				1		
Do	Do	Wm. Sarah Neilan Paps	Labourer		2						
Do	Do	Owen Mary Kilduff Paps	Labourer								
Do	Do	Peter Margtt Mannian Paps	Labourer		1		3				
Do	Do	John Cath. Rouine Paps	Labourer		3		3				
Do	Do	Thos. Margtt. Ward Paps	Labourer		4		2				
Do	Do	Patrick Ann Goulane Paps	Labourer		3						
Do	Do	Darby Mary Noon Paps	Labourer				1		2		1
Do	Aghagad Begg[8]	Danl. Mary Fallon Paps	Labourer		2		2				
Do	Do	Darby Mary Ruddy Paps	Labourer		1				1		1
Do	Do	Wm. Mary Cravane Paps	Labourer		2				1		
Do	Do	Wm. Winnifred Mee Paps	Weaver		1				1		
Do	Castlecoote	Peter Murphy Prot Ann Pap	Smith	3		2					
Do	Do	John Bingham Prot Cath: Pap	Weaver	3			1				
Do	Do	Peter Elizth. Lavendar Prot	Turner	2		1					
Do	Do	Murtagh Neilan Prot Anne Pap	Labourer	3							

Com~Ros common Parish of	Place of Abode	Names and Religion	Proffession	Children under 14		Children above 14		Men Servts		Women Servts	
				Prot.	Paps.	Prot.	Paps.	Prot.	Paps.	Prot.	Paps.
Do	Do	Laurence / Mary Roirk Paps	Labourer				1				1
Do	Do	Jon. Kelly Pap.	Weaver								
Do	Muff	Thos. / Sarah Clarke Prots	Weaver	4				1	1		
Do	Castlecoote	James / Ann Burne Prots	Farmer								
Do	Ballnascarrow	Thos. / Ellinor Turner Prots	Weaver	4	[?]1	1			1		
Do	Do	Michl. / Dorothy Kean Paps	sievemaker		2						
Do	Coolmeen9	Allice Mitchell Prot widow		1		2		1	2		2
Do	Do	Jon. / Mary Gallagher Paps	Labourer		5				1		
Do	Do	Jon. / Margtt Feehily Paps	Labourer		3		1		1		
Do	Do	Thos. / Bridgett Kean Paps	Labourer		2						
Do	Gortmore	Bryan / Cath. Naghten Paps	Labourer		1						
Do	Do	Hugh / Nabby Killroe Paps	Labourer								
Do	Fuerty	George Lilly Prot / Mary Pap	Farmer		3	1	1		1		2
Do	Do	Danl. / Margtt Doolan Paps	Labourer		3						
Do	Do	James / Cath. Harkan Paps	Farmer		2				1		1
Do	Do	Thos. Kennedy Pap	Labourer		1		1				
[f.214]Fuerty	Lisneville	Peter / Mary Reeve Paps	Labourer		4						
Do	Do	John / Mary Walsh Paps	Labourer								
Do	Do	Andw. / Francess Connor Paps	Labourer		1						
Do	Do	Edmd / Mary Kennahane Paps	Labourer		1						
Do	Do	Edmd. / Mary Gallagher Paps	Labourer		1						
Do	Do	Michl. Cooney Paps	Labourer						1		
Do	Do	Roger / Joan Moore Paps	Labourer				1				
Do	Do	Terence / Mary Bryan Paps	Weaver				2				
Do	Do	Denis / Bridget Crosbie Paps	Labourer				2				
Do	Do	Luke / Mary Connelly Paps	Labourer		1						
Do	Do	Aneas / Ann Ward Paps	Labourer		2						
Do	Do	James / Mary Walsh Paps	Labourer				1				
Do	Do	Peter Croghan Pap	Labourer								
Do	Do	Michl. / Mary Mannian Paps	Labourer				1				
Do	Do	Danl. / Giles Neilan Paps	Labourer								
Do	Do	Cath. Cuddy Pap widdw.									
Do	Do	John / Mary Connaghan Paps	Labourer				2				
Do	Do	Bryan / Mary Lyons Paps	Labourer								

Com~Ros common Parish of	Place of Abode	Names and Religion	Proffession	Children under 14		Children above 14		Men Servts		Women Servts	
				Prot.	Paps.	Prot.	Paps.	Prot.	Paps.	Prot.	Paps.
Do	Do	Michl.									
		Rose Hanly Paps	Labourer								
Do	Do	Laurence									
		Margr Dauly Paps	Labourer						1		
Do	Do	James									
		Mary Dauly Paps	Labourer		1		1				
Do	Do	Thos.									
		Cath. Croghan Paps	Labourer								
Do	Ballintrughan	Michl.									
		Mary Keerucan Paps	Labourer		1						
Do	Do	Edmd.									
		Ann McDermott Paps	Labourer		1		1				
Do	Do	Patrick									
		Mary Gill Paps	Labourer		1						
Do	Do	Margtt Murry Paps Widdow					2				
Do	Do	Wm.									
		Onnor Whoody Paps	Broguemaker		2				2		
Do	Do	John									
		Giles Hanly Paps	Labourer		1						
Do	Do	Patrick									
		Bridget Donnelan Paps	Labourer								
Do	Do	Murtagh									
		Winnifred Cullagh Paps	Labourer								
Do	Moyliss	Thady									
		Sibby Murry Paps	Labourer		2						
Do	Do	Jon.									
		Mary Turner Paps	Weaver			1					
Do	Do	John									
		Grace Egan Paps	Labourer		1		2				
Do	Do	Peter Pap									
		Agnes Fury Prot.	Weaver			2	2				
Do	Do	Hugh									
		Giles Teige Paps	Labourer								
Do	Do	Laughlin Hannan Pap	Labourer				1				
Do	Do	Danl.									
		Mary Tummullty Paps	Smith		2						
Do	Do	Bryan									
		Mary Naghten Paps	Labourer								
Do	Do	Wm.									
		Ann Dolan Paps	Labourer		1						
Do	Do	Ann Gurrick Pap: widdw					2				
Do	Do	Thos.									
		Onnor Cunaghten Paps	Labourer		1						
[f.215]Fuerty	Moyliss	Constantine									
		Nell McGuire Paps	Labourer		1		3				
Do	Do	Denis									
		Ann Hines Paps	Labourer								
Do	Do	John									
		Ann Mannian Paps	Labourer		1						
Do	Do	James									
		Mary Egan Paps	Labourer		1						
Do	Do	Wm. Brannan Paps									
		Onnor	Labourer								
Do	Do	Hugh									
		Onnor Connaghten Paps	Labourer								
Do	Do	Laughlin									
		Joan Healy Paps	Labourer		4						
Do	Do	John									
		Nabby Curnely Paps	Labourer		1						

Com~Ros common Parish of	Place of Abode	Names and Religion	Proffession	Children under 14		Children above 14		Men Servts		Women Servts	
				Prot.	Paps.	Prot.	Paps.	Prot.	Paps.	Prot.	Paps.
Do	Do	Patrick Mary Koin Paps	Labourer		2						
Do	Do	Murtagh Sibby Diffily Paps	Labourer		2						
Do	Do	Patrick Onnor Tyrrell Paps	Labourer		3						
Do	Do	Patrick Mary Kenny Paps	Labourer		2						
Do	Do	Wm. Mary Mitchell Prot	Farmer						1		2
Do	Do	James Margtt Durnean Paps	Labourer		3						
Do	Do	Michl. Cath. Hussy Paps	Labourer		1						
Do	Do	Michl. Prot Mary Brehiny Pap	Labourer				3				
Do	Do	Owen Cath. Gowrane Paps	Labourer		2						
Do	Corrill	Patrick Joan Kegly Paps	Labourer				1				
Do	Do	Bridgett Corkeen Pap					2				
Do	Do	John Margtt Mulhvighill Paps	Labourer		1						
Do	Do	James Cath. Cavenagh Paps	Labourer		1						
Do	Do	Martyn Nell Lennon Paps	Labourer								
Do	Do	Hugh Lennon Paps	Labourer								
Do	Do	Luke Rose Mulhvighill Paps	Labourer		1						
Do	Do	John Mary Ruddane Paps	Labourer		1						
Do	Do	Peter Grace Gallagher Paps	Labourer								
Do	Do	Owen Cath. Gallagher Paps	Labourer								
Do	Do	Bryan Rose Boyle Paps	Labourer								
Do	Do	Jon. Rose McNally Paps	Mason		1						
Do	Do	Timothy Mary Giraghty Paps	Gardener				2				
Do	Do	Peter Mary Boyle Paps	Labourer				3		1		
Do	Do	James Bridgett McGloghlin Paps	Labourer				2				
Do	Do	Owen Cath. Crosbie Paps	Labourer								
Do	Do	Laughlin Cath. Connor Paps	Labourer								
Do	Do	James Ann Boyle Paps	Labourer								
Do	Do	Patrick Neal Pap	Labourer								
Do	Do	Thady Onnor Lyn Paps	Shepherd				3				
Do	Do	Th. Waldron Gent Prot	Gentleman Farmer					2	1		3
Do	Do	Robert Ormsby Prot	Farmer	4		1			2		
Do	Farfass	Winnifred Conry Paps	Smith		1						

NOTES

1. 'Fuerty' by the Rev James Crawford in W. Shaw Mason, *A statistical account, or parochial survey of Ireland drawn up from the communications of the clergy* (Dublin 1814-9), p. 402.

2. John Hickes was born near Elphin in Co. Roscommon, son of Richard Hickes *generosus*. He was educated by the Rev. Michael Griffin of Elphin. He entered Trinity College, Dublin in 1739 aged 17 and graduated BA in 1743, MA in 1747. He was collated in the parishes of Fuerty, Athleague, Kilbegnet and Dunamon in 1734. He signed the parliamentary return for his parishes in 1766. He died ca. 1780 (Leslie, Elphin, p. 91; *Alumni Dubliniensis*).

3. Lewis Ormsby was born about 1716, son of George of Ormsby of Belvoir, Co. Sligo and Jane Wynne of Hazlewood. He entered TCD in 1733 aged 17. In 1749 he married Catherine Donnelan, daughter of Nehemiah Donnellan, 'an accomplished young lady with a very large fortune'. They had a daughter in 1751 (*Alumni Dubliniensis*; *Dublin Courant*, 3-10 June 1749).

4. Mainly arable and pasture land with mountain and heathy bog, owned by the Caulfeild family (Survey of Aughagad and Buckfield 1803, N.L.I., MS 21 F 43/1).

5. The mill at Rockfield which ground flax and corn dated back to 1671. It was leased to a Denis Croghan in the early 1700s (*Cloverhill: A Social History*, (Oran Development Committee, 2000) pp. 90-1).

6. Christopher Irwin was a son of Edward Irwin of Rockfield and Mary Molady. He married the Hon. Mary Anne, daughter of Lord Riverstown (N.L.I., MS GO 806/7).

7. Thomas Mitchell established a linen factory near Fuerty in 1760 (Stephenson, *Reports and Observations*, p. 61).

8. Mainly arable and pasture owned by the Caulfeild family (Survey of Aughagad and Buckfield 1803, N.L.I., MS 21 F 43/1).

9. The half quarter of Coolemeen leased for three lives by Sir Edward Crofton to William Mitchell (N.L.I., Crofton Papers, MS 8828/8).

ATHLEAGUE, COUNTY ROSCOMMON AND COUNTY GALWAY

INTRODUCTION: *Athleague parish is partly in County Galway and partly in County Roscommon. It is in the baronies of Killian (County Galway) and Athlone (County Roscommon) and covers 13,011 statute acres on the river Suck.[1] The town of Athleague is 4¹/₂ miles south-east of Roscommon on a major road from Roscommon to Loughrea, Co. Galway.*

The parish had fairs twice a year. One at Athleague under a patent which was granted in 1634 to the Earl of Clanrickard, and the other at Mount Talbot in 1710 to Henry Talbot.[2] John Lyster, who died ca. 1754, owned the manor of Athleague, its fairs and markets and sixteen townlands in the barony of Athlone.[3] Masons in Scardane, Trumane, Blindwell, Corramore, and Lissnagirra underline Lewis's observation that the area possessed quantities of limestone and freestone.[4]

The incumbent was the Rev. John Hickes, who was appointed in 1734 and held the living with Fuerty, Kilbegnet and Dunamon (see Fuerty). He lived at Castlestrange, in the parish of Fuerty. The patron was the bishop. The rectory was impropriate in the estate of Lord Ranelagh.

OCCUPATIONS

Ale seller	5	Freeholder	1	Shepherd	9
Breechesmaker	1	Gardener	2	Shoemaker	2
Broguemaker	3	Herd	3	Shopkeeper	2
Butcher	3	Innkeeper	1	Sievemaker	1
Carpenter	4	Labourer	180	Smith	2
Constable	1	Maltster	1	Tailor	7
Cooper	1	Mason	6	Tobacco spinner	2
Esquire	1	Miller	1	Weaver	5
Farmer	12	Presser	1	Widow	3
Fisherman	1	Servants, household	54	Wigmaker	1
				Woodranger	1

Com~Ros common Parish of	Place of Abode	Names and Religion	Proffession	Children under 14 Prot.	Paps.	Children above 14 Prot.	Paps.	Men Servts Prot.	Paps.	Women Servts Prot.	Paps.
[f.216] Athleague	Lissnesellagh	Luke									
		Mary Malin Paps					3				
Do	Do	Terence									
		Cath. Fallon Paps	Labourer				1				
Do	Do	Laughlin									
		Onnor Groirk Paps	Labourer		1						
Do	Do	Patrick									
		Cath. Groirk Paps	Labourer				2				
Do	Do	Laughlin									
		Bridgett Conway Paps	Labourer		2						
Do	Do	Patrick									
		Cath. Donnely Paps	Labourer		1						
Do	Do	Edwd.									
		Mary Carty Paps	Labourer		2		2				
Do	Do	John									
		Giles Groirk Paps	Labourer				1				
Do	Do	Thos.									
		Bridgett Higgins Paps	Labourer		2						
Do	Do	Charles									
		Margtt Hanly Paps	Labourer		2						
Do	Do	Terence Donnely paps	Labourer		1						
Do	Do	Patrick									
		Cath. McFealim Paps	Labourer		1						
Do	Do	Murtagh									
		Nell Currely Paps	Labourer		1		1				
Do	Do	Thos.									
		Onnor Kevel Paps	Labourer								
Do	Do	John									
		Cicily Feeny Paps	Labourer				2				
Do	Do	Barth.									
		Onnor Keeghran Paps	Labourer				1				
Do	Do	Edwd.									
		Margt. Kelly Paps	Labourer								
Do	Lissnagirra	George									
		Margtt Black prot	Weaver	2		3					
Do	Do	Laughlin									
		Giles Knavin Paps	Labourer		2						
Do	Do	Patrick									
		Cath. Cuningham Paps	Labourer		3						
Do	Do	Anth.									
		Margtt. Pursel Paps	Labourer		3						
Do	Do	Connor									
		Bridget Kelly Paps	Labourer		1						
Do	Do	Connor the Elder									
		Mary Kelly Paps	Labourer				3				
Do	Do	Matth. Currely Paps	Mason		1		2				
Do	Do	Thady									
		Mary Currely Paps	Mason								
Do	Do	Daniel									
		Cath. Moran Paps	Labourer				1				
Do	Do	James Moran Paps	Labourer				1				
Do	Do	Saml. Campion prot	Labourer								
Do	Do	Abraham									
		Mary Campion prot	Ale seller	2							
Do	Kilmore	Charles									
		Ellinor Kean Paps	Labourer		2						
Do	Do	James									
		Bridget Peat Paps	Labourer		2						

Com~Ros common Parish of	Place of Abode	Names and Religion	Proffession	Children under 14		Children above 14		Men Servts		Women Servts	
				Prot.	Paps.	Prot.	Paps.	Prot.	Paps.	Prot.	Paps.
Do	Do	Luke									
		Margtt Peat Paps	Labourer		3						
Do	Do	Patrick									
		Mary Breaghan Paps	Labourer		1		2				
Do	Do	John Tressy Paps	Labourer		1						
Do	Do	Michl.									
		Dorothy Healy Paps	Labourer		4						
Do	Do	Charles Doyle Paps	Labourer								
Do	Do	James									
		Jane Fallon Paps	Labourer								
Do	Do	James Kelly Paps	Labourer				1				
Do	Do	Edwd									
		Nabby Hanly Paps	Labourer		1						
Do	Do	Hugh									
		Cath. Gublan Paps	Labourer		4		1				
Do	Do	Thady									
		Cath. Deal Paps	Labourer		3						
[f.217] Athleague	Kilmore	Laughlin									
		Mary Fallon Paps	Labourer		4						
Do	Lisscoffy	Danl. Hoey Paps	Labourer								
Do	Do	John									
		Margtt Hoey Paps	Labourer		1						
Do	Do	Denis									
		Grace Crosby Paps	Labourer		1						
Do	Do	Connor									
		Ann Fitzmorris Paps	Labourer		2						
Do	Do	Bryan Currely Pap	Labourer		2						
Do	Do	Wm.									
		Giles Girraghty Paps	Labourer		2						
Do	Do	Patrick									
		Mary Fitzmorris Paps	Labourer			1					
Do	Do	Barth.									
		Cicily Fitzmorris Paps	Labourer		1						
Do	Do	Danl.									
		Bridget Loghnane Paps	Labourer		2						
Do	Do	John									
		Una Murray Paps	Labourer		1						
Do	Do	John									
		Mary Fitzmorris Paps	Labourer		1						
Do	Do	Peter									
		Mary Kilcool Paps	Weaver		1						
Do	Do	Connor									
		Margt Giraghty Paps	Labourer		1						
Do	Do	Thady									
		Bridgett Conniff Paps	Labourer								
Do	Do	Patrick									
		Mary Knaven Paps	Labourer								
Do	Do	Nichs. French Farmer			3				1		2
~~Do~~	~~Athleague town~~	~~Mark Murry Pap~~									
Do	Athleague Town	Mark Murry Pap	Labourer								
Do	Do	John									
		Mary Devnish Pap	Shoemaker								
Do	Do	Edward									
		Cathrine Mee Pap	Wigmaker		4						
Do	Do	Francis									
		Bridget Jones Pap	Butcher		2		3				
Do	Do	Thos.		Tobacco-spinner							
		Ellinor Monaghan Pap									
Do	Do	Thos Burne prot	Presser			1					
Do	Do	James Bodkin Pap	Labourer				1				

Com~Ros common Parish of	Place of Abode	Names and Religion	Proffession	Children under 14 Prot.	Children under 14 Paps.	Children above 14 Prot.	Children above 14 Paps.	Men Servts Prot.	Men Servts Paps.	Women Servts Prot.	Women Servts Paps.
Do	Do	Dennis Fallon Pap	Tobacco-spinner		1						
Do	Do	Arthur Mary Corn Pap	Taylor		3						
Do	Do	Danl. Giles Lohan Pap	Labourer				1				
Do	Do	James Corr Pap	Butcher								
Do	Do	Peter Cathrine Corr Pap	Labourer				1				
Do	Do	James Nabby Johnston Pap	Ale seller		2						
Do	Do	Laughlin Bridget Crow Pap	Ale seller				1				
Do	Do	Tully Cathrine Daly Pap	Labourer				2				
Do	Do	Danl. Elizabeth Fallon Pap	Ale seller								
Do	Do	James Sibby Coghlan Pap	Labourer		1		2		1		
Do	Do	James Susanna Dobbins prot	Shopkeeper	4							1
Do	Do	Henry Jane Campion Prot	Labourer	4							
Do	Do	John Margret Lahy Pap	Malster				2				
Do	Do	Barth. Mary Bryan Pap	Miller		2		2		2		
Do	Do	Robert Ellenor Dobbins Prot	Labourer	4							
[f.218] Athleague	Athleague Town	Henry Sibby Gannan Pap	Smith		1						
Do	Do	Patrick Lennon Pap	Labourer		1						
Do	Do	Thos. Anne Healy Pap	Taylor		2						
Do	Do	Luke Joan Queeny Pap	Labourer				2				
Do	Do	Hugh Cathrin Rogers Pap	Broguemaker						2		
Do	Do	Michl. Queeny Pap	Labourer		1		1				
Do	Do	Thos. Mulhivighill Pap	Labourer		2						
Do	Do	Edward Prot Catherine Egan Pap	Constable				1				
Do	Do	John Bryan Pap	Butcher								
Do	Do	Luke Corr Pap	Farmer								1
Do	Do	Francis Taaffe Pap	Farmer						1		1
Do	Do	Robert Anne Dempsey Pap	inn keeper		1		1		2		2
Do	Do	Thos. Gerughty prot	farmer			1			1		1
Do	Do	Andrew Cathrine Connor Pap	Labourer		1						
Do	Cloonikelly	Patrick Margret Keeny Pap	labourer		2						
Do	Do	Michl. Mary Ginnane Pap	broguemaker		3						
Do	Do	Edmd. Cornmon Pap	shepherd								
Do	Do	Matthew Bridget Kenny Pap	labourer		2		3				
Do	Do	Patrick Margret Fin Pap	labourer		3						

Com~Ros common Parish of	Place of Abode	Names and Religion	Proffession	Children under 14		Children above 14		Men Servts		Women Servts	
				Prot.	Paps.	Prot.	Paps.	Prot.	Paps.	Prot.	Paps.
Do	Lisgamon	Matthew Onnor Carty Pap	labourer				1				
Do	Do	John Fallon Pap	labourer								
Do	Keenagh	James Onnor Campbell Pap	Ale seller		2						
Do	Do	Philip Jane Doyle Pap	Taylor		2						
Do	Do	Barth: Giles Corr Pap	labourer								
Do	Do	Owen Cathrine Kerin Pap	labourer				1				
Do	Do	Manus Ginnane Pap	labourer				1				
Do	Do	Thady Rose Kerin Pap	labourer								
Do	Do	Thos. Mary Hughes Pap	labourer		1						
Do	Do	Michl. Ellinor Lennon Pap	Broguemaker		3						
Do	Do	Thady Giles Muldoon Pap	labourer								
Do	Corbeg-hurlingah	Patrick Moran Pap	Breeches-maker				1				
Do	Do	Thady Bridget Moran Pap	labourer								
Do	Do	Roger McGloghlin Pap	labourer								
Do	Do	Hugh Mary Muldoon Pap	labourer				1				
Do	Do	Laughlin Winnafrid Moor Pap	Shepherd		2						
Do	Araghty	James Bridget Lohan Pap	labourer		1						
Do	Do	Daniel Onnor Lohan Pap	labourer		2						
Do	Do	James Margret McGloo Pap	labourer					2			
Do	Do	Geo: Jane Cuningham prot	Cooper			1		1	1		
Do	Do	Luke Hannan Pap	Woodranger								
Do	Do	Wm. Clogher Pap	labourer								
[f.219] Athleague	Araghty	Edward Onnor Moor Pap	Carpenter		1		2				
Do	Do	Andw. Ellinor Murry Pap	labourer		2						
Do	Do	Edwd. Giles Feeny Pap	labourer		2						
Do	Do	Thady Sarah Finnegan Pap	labourer				2				
Do	Do	Darby Onnor Bryan Pap	labourer		2						
Do	Do	Roger Girraghty Pap	labourer		1						
Do	Do	Owen Mary Finnehan Pap	labourer		1		1				
Do	Do	Wm. Neilan Pap	labourer								
Do	Do	Farrell Finnekan Pap	labourer								
Do	Do	Mark Ellinor Giraghty Pap	Taylor		3						2
Do	Do	Wm. Sarah Cuthbert Prot				3					
Do	Do	Thady Margret Donnely Pap	Smith		1		2				

Com~Ros common Parish of	Place of Abode	Names and Religion	Proffession	Children under 14 Prot.	Children under 14 Paps.	Children above 14 Prot.	Children above 14 Paps.	Men Servts Prot.	Men Servts Paps.	Women Servts Prot.	Women Servts Paps.
Do	Do	Peter									
		Margret Herrily Pap	labourer		3						
Do	Do	Andw Finneran Pap	labourer								
Do	Do	Matthias									
		Nabby Giraghty Pap	labourer		1		1				
Do	Do	Denis									
		Cathrine Gillane Pap	labourer		1		1				
Do	Do	John Gillivan Pap	Sievemaker								
Com Galway	Do Parish Cornecask	Bryan									
		Margret Finnegan Pap	Carpenter		2						
Do	Do	Henry									
		Anne Walker prot	Farmer	2	~~2~~	1			1		1
Do	Do	Wm.									
		Mary Clark prot	Farmer			2					
Do	Do	Pat. Kelly Pap	labourer		1						
Do	Culespudane	James									
		Cathrine Keagarty Pap	Shepherd		1		2				
Do	Do	Danl.									
		Mary Kenny Pap	labourer		4		2				
Do	Do	Allen									
		Winnafrid Doyle Pap	labourer		3						
Do	Corvoghlow	Patrick									
		Susanna Doyle Prot	Herdsman			2					
Do	Gorteenruckane	Jon									
		Sarah Kelly Pap	labourer								
Do	Do	Darby McNeal Pap	labourer		1		3				
Do	Do	Patrick									
		Ellinor Joyce Pap	labourer								
Do	Do	Jon.									
		Joan Connogher Pap	labourer				3				
Do	Do	Manus Rush Pap	labourer		3		1				
Do	Do	Bryan									
		Margret Connogher Pap	labourer		2						
Do	Do	Patrick									
		SibbyHannely Pap	labourer				2				
Do	Do	Joseph									
		Margret Strattan Pap	labourer		3						
Do	Do	Bryan									
		Cathrine Healy Pap	Herdsman				3				
Do	Do	Michl.									
		Sibby Rogers Pap	labourer				2				
		Wm Rogers Pap	labourer		3						
Do	Monastirhnaleer	Thady									
		Ellinor Kelly Pap	Herdsman				2				
Do	Do	Edwd									
		Elizabeth Kelly Pap	labourer								
Do	Clooancannon	John									
		Mary Finnegan Pap	Shepherd								
Do	Rookwood[5]	Bryan									
		Anne Moran Pap	Gardiner		4						
[f.220] Athleague	Corramore	John									
		Cathrine Keating Prot	Weaver	3							
Do	Do	James									
		Elizabeth Moran Pap	labourer		1						
Do	Do	Francis									
		Cathrine Moran Pap	labourer		2		3				
Do	Do	Michl. Mullan Pap	labourer		1						
Do	Do	John									
		Cathrine Mullan Pap	labourer		1						

Com~Ros common Parish of	Place of Abode	Names and Religion	Proffession	Children under 14		Children above 14		Men Servts		Women Servts	
				Prot.	Paps.	Prot.	Paps.	Prot.	Paps.	Prot.	Paps.
Do	Do	Hugh									
		Mary Feeny Pap	labourer								
Do	Do	Denis									
		Ellinor Mannian Pap	labourer		1						
Do	Do	Danl.									
		Anne Carty Pap	labourer				2				
Do	Do	Francis									
		Margret Moran Pap	labourer		2		3				
Do	Do	Patrick									
		Onnor Goghegan Pap			2		3				
Do	Do	Myles									
		Cathrine Queeny Pap	labourer		1						
Do	Do	John									
		Margret Hart Pap	labourer		3		2				
Do	Do	Ralph									
		Allice Walker prot							1		
Do	Do	John									
		Rose Connor Pap	Mason		2		2				
Do	Do	John									
		Onnor Giraghty Pap	labourer				2				
Do	Creggany	Michl.									
		Ellinor Tobin Pap	Fisherman								
Do	Do	Edmd									
		Mary Clary Pap	Weaver								
Do	Do	James Moran Pap	labourer		1		1				
Do	Boonacurry	Michl.									
		Dorothy Mills prot	Farmer	3		2					1
Do	Lisseenerin	Patrick									
		Cath. Plunkett prot	Freeholder	3							
Do	Do	Luke									
		Mary Currely Pap	labourer		2						
Do	Do	Martyn Naghten Pap	labourer		3						
Do	Glannenomer	Hugh Murry Pap	Shepherd				3				
Do	Carrowreevagh	Jas.									
		Cath. Finaghty Pap	Shepherd				2				
Do	Do	Denis									
		Rose Crubbane Pap	labourer				2				
Do	Do	Wm.									
		Onnor Crubbane Pap	labourer								
Do	Do	Thos. Burke Pap	labourer								
Do	Do	Laughlin									
		Frances Giraghty Pap	labourer		3						
Do	Do	Thos.									
		Nell McGau Pap	labourer		1						
Do	Do	Patrick									
		Cath. Connell Pap	labourer		1						
Do	Do	Domk. Egan Pap	labourer								
Do	Do	Bryan									
		Margtt Mulvighilh Pap	labourer		3		1				
Do	Do	Connor McGloo Pap	labourer		1		1				
Do	Do	Matthew									
		Mary Mulvighilh Pap	labourer		3						
Do	Do	Jon.									
		Margtt. Common Pap	labourer		1						
Do	Do	Hugh									
		Onnor McGloo Pap	labourer		1				1		
Do	Do	Thos. Mulvighilh Pap									
Do	Blindwell	Thos. Stroaker prot	labourer			2					
Do	Do	Patrick Burk Pap	Mason		2						1
Do	Knockadangan	Thos.									
		Winnefred Donnely Paps	Shepherd		4						

Com~Ros common Parish of	Place of Abode	Names and Religion	Proffession	Children under 14 Prot.	Children under 14 Paps.	Children above 14 Prot.	Children above 14 Paps.	Men Servts Prot.	Men Servts Paps.	Women Servts Prot.	Women Servts Paps.
Do	Do	Luke Winifred Giraghty Paps	labourer		1						
[f.221] Athleague	Pulbaun	Patrick Cath: Breaghan Paps	labourer		3						
Do	Do	Michl. Mary Kean Pap	labourer		2						
Do	Do	Hugh Kean Paps	labourer				2				
Do	Do	Peter Jane Diguenan Pap	Farmer		3						1
Do	Do	Laughlin Sarah Naghten Pap	labourer		1						
Do	Do	Michl. Mary Moran Pap	labourer		4						
Do	Do	Jon. Cath. Kean Pap	labourer		2		3				
Do	Do	Connor Nell McGloo Pap	labourer		5		1				
Do	Do	Wm. Glinnane Pap	labourer		4						
Do	Do	Patrick Durneen Pap	labourer				1				
Do	Do	Bryan Runey Pap	labourer		2						
Do	Do	James Clidrane Pap	labourer		3						
Do	Do	James Giraghty Pap	labourer								
Do	Do	Wm. Jane Ward Pap	Carpenter		2						
Do	Do	Richd. Cullane Pap	labourer		4						
Do	Do	Hugh Cath. Giraghty Pap	Taylor		1						
Do	Do	Patrick Onnor Jones Pap	labourer				1				
Do	Do	Bath. Eliz. Clinton Pap	Gardiner				1				
Do	Do	Pat. Frances Kelly Pap	labourer		1						
Do	Do	John Margtt. Ganly prot	Taylor								
Do	Do	David Ann Price prot	Shoemaker	4				1	3		1
Do	Do	Danl. Cath. Healy Pap	Weaver		2						
County Galway Parish Do	Mountalbott	Walter Mary Walsh Pap	Shopkeeper		4					1	1
Do	Do	Wm. Cathrine Rigney Pap			2g:c						
Do	Do	Martyn Mary Morrisy Pap	labourer		3		2				
Do	Do	Walter Ellinor Stephens Pap	labourer		2						
Do	Do	Denis Margret Keogh Pap	labourer		3		1				
Do	Do	Fran: Fallon Pap	Farmer								1
Do	Do	Laughlin Sibby Fallon Pap	labourer								
Do	Do	Darby Winnafrid McDermott Pap	labourer		2						
Do	Do	Edmd Margret Mannian Pap	labourer								
Do	Do	Connor Onnor Kelly Pap	Taylor				1				

Com~Ros common Parish of	Place of Abode	Names and Religion	Proffession	Children under 14		Children above 14		Men Servts		Women Servts	
				Prot.	Paps.	Prot.	Paps.	Prot.	Paps.	Prot.	Paps.
Do	Do	Henry Cathrine Kennedy Pap	labourer		3						
	Aghrane Cloonruff	John Kelly⁶ Esqr. Prot							4		4
		John Ellinor Killeen Pap	Shepherd		2						
		John Margret Fitzgerrald Pap	labourer				2				
[f.222] Athleague	Trumane⁷	Hugh Bridgett Corrily Pap	Mason		5						
Do	Do	Pat. Ann Shiell Pap	labourer		4						
Do	Do	Giles Madden Widdw. Pap			1						
Do	Do	Laughlin Cath. Murry Paps	labourer		2						
Do	Do	Bryan Onnor Feeny Paps	labourer		1						
Do	Do	Edmond Margtt Neal Pap s	labourer								
Do	Do	Bryan Mary Murry Pap s	labourer		4						
Do	Do	Pat. Ellinor Ruddy prot	labourer	3		1					
Do	Do	Laurence Cath. Keeve Paps	labourer		1						
Do	Do	Darby Margtt. Connell Paps	labourer				1				
Do	Do	Laurence Cath. Brehiny Paps	labourer		1						
Do	Do	Thos. Margtt Keggin Paps	labourer								
Do	Do	Una Kelly widdw. Paps	Widow				2				
Do	Do	Laurence Kelly Paps Mary prot	Carpenter	4	4						
Do	Lissnelanew	Farrogh Mable Kelly Paps	Farmer								
Do	Do	Edmd. Cath Connor Paps	labourer		2						
Do	Scardane	Wm. Cicily Keys Paps	Mason				3				
Do	Do	Wm. Onnor Murry Paps	labourer		1		1				
Do	Do	Thady Margtt Feeny Paps	labourer				1				
Do	Do	Thos. Mary Fitzmorris Paps	labourer		1						
Do	Do	Laurence Ann Daly Paps	labourer								
Do	Do	Giles Murry widow Pap					1				
Do	Do	Hugh Giles Queeny Paps	labourer				1				
Do	Rocksavage	Edmd. Sarah Bolton Paps	labourer		3						
Do	Do	Michl. Mary Murry Paps	Farmer		1						1
Do	Do	John Giles Scally Paps	labourer						1		
~~Do~~	[erasure]	[erasure]	~~labourer~~								
~~Do~~	~~Do~~	[erasure]									
Do	Currabegg	Thos. Onnor Cornell Paps	Shepherd								
Do	Do	John Anne Carty Paps	labourer		2						
Do	Keenagh	Oliver Elizabeth Kelly Paps	Farmer		1				2		3
Do	Do	Peter Ellinor McDonagh Paps	labourer		2						

NOTES

1. Including 148 acres of water (*General Alphabetical Index*).

2. *Report ... fairs and markets*.

3. *Abstracts of Wills,* ii, 178.

4. Lewis, 'Athleague'.

5 This townland was owned by the Mahon family. It consisted mostly of arable, meadow and pasture, the bottom subject to floods. Part of the bog had been drained and levelled and part was sandy mixt pasture (N.L.I., Pakenham-Mahon Accounts, MS 10,155/1).

6. Eight townlands were owned by members of the O Kelly family in 1641. John Kelly formerly lived at Clonline, County Galway, and inherited land at Aghrane from his cousin Denis Kelly of Dublin in 1734, and his eldest son Denis was Denis Kelly's godson. He was a son of John Kelly of Clonlyon in the same parish and Mary, daughter of Nicholas Mahon. In 1729 he married Honoria de Burgh (*Book of Survey and Distribution*, Roscommon; *Abstracts of Wills*, i, 654; N.L.I., Pedigree of the family of Kelly of Skreen, MS GO 809/14).

7. Trumane was leased by Sir Edward Crofton to a William Woolgar in 1709 (N.L.I., Crofton Papers, MS 8828/8).

KILBEGNET, COUNTY GALWAY

INTRODUCTION: *The parish of Kilbegnet is 6 miles south west of Roscommon in the barony of Ballymoe. There are 10,867 statute acres.*

The incumbent of the parish was the Rev John Hickes who held the living with Fuerty, Donamon and Athleague (see Fuerty). The patron was the bishop. The parish was impropriate.

OCCUPATIONS

Ale seller	1	Harper	1	Shepherd	2
Broguemaker	3	Horse rider	1	Shopkeeper	2
Butcher	1	Labourer	239	Smith	1
Farmer	9	Mason	1	Tanner	1
Flax dresser	1	Merchant	1	Weaver	6
Gardener	1	Miller	1	Widow	13
Glover	1	Servants, household	38	Wigmaker	1

Com~ Galway Parish of	Place of Abode	Names and Religion	Proffession	Children under 14 Prot.	Paps.	Children above 14 Prot.	Paps.	Men Servts Prot.	Paps.	Women Servts Prot.	Paps.
[f.223] Kilbegnett	Gorvogh	John									
		Margret Barret Paps	Labourer								
Do	Do	Godfrey									
		Onnor McDonnel	Labourer		3		1				
Do	Do	Patrick									
		Onnor Naugtin Paps	Labourer		1						
Do	Do	Patrick									
		Bridget Shivnan Paps	Labourer								
Do	Do	William									
		Ellinor Shivnan Paps	Labourer								
Do	Do	Michael									
		Rose Naughtin Paps	Labourer		2						
Do	Do	Fealem									
		Margret Wead Paps	Miller		3		2				
Do	Do	James									
		Elizabeth Brannon Paps	Weaver		4						
Do	Do	Margret Farrell widow Pap					1		1		1
Do	Do	Andrew Gorden Pap	farmer						1		
Do	Do	Connor									
		Onnor Curry Paps	Labourer			1					
Do	Loghoghgloss	John									
		Mary Dillon Paps	Labourer		2						
Do	Do	Rojer									
		Ellinor Garry Paps	Labourer		3		1				
Do	Do	Laurence									
		Cathrine Garry Paps	Labourer								
Do	Do	Cathrine Grary Widdow Pap					4				
Do	Do	Darby									
		Sarah Kean Paps	Labourer								
Do	Do	Martin Morgan Pap	Labourer		1						
Do	Do	John									
		Mary Royn Paps	Labourer		1						
Do	Do	Richard									
		Margret Mahon Paps	Labourer		2		2				
Do	Do	Martin									
		Mary Kean Paps	Labourer		1		1				
Do	Do	Theady									
		Cathrine Mahon Paps	Labourer		1						
Do	Do	James Cunningham Pap	Labourer				4				
Do	Do	William									
		Cathrine Giblon Paps	Shepherd		2		1		1		
Do	Do	James Conway Pap	mason								
Do	Furoo	James									
		Cathrine Lohan Paps	Labourer		4				1		
Do	Do	Thos.									
		Sarah Currily Paps	Shepherd		1				1		
Do	Do	William									
		Cathrine Moran Paps	Farmer		1				1		1
Do	Do	Edmond									
		Mary Kean Paps	Labourer								
Do	Do	Thos.									
		Onnor Naughtin Paps	Labourer		1						1
Do	Do	Cathrine									
		Cuddy Widdow Pap	Labourer					1			
Do	Do	James									
		Cathrine Kean Paps	Labourer		3						
Do	Do	Cathrine Mulvihill Widdow Pap				3					
Do	Rosmilan	James									
		Mary Barlow Prots	Farmer	6					2		3

Com~ Galway Parish of	Place of Abode	Names and Religion	Proffession	Children under 14		Children above 14		Men Servts		Women Servts	
				Prot.	Paps.	Prot.	Paps.	Prot.	Paps.	Prot.	Paps.
Do	Do	James Margret Whoolahon Paps	Labourer		2				1		1
Do	Do	Henry Onnor Crean Paps	Labourer		3		2				
Do	Do	Owen Mary Brogan Paps	Brogemaker		3						
Do	Do	Michael Bridget Gaffy Paps	Labourer		2						
Do	Do	Bryan Mary Whoolahan Paps	Labourer		1		1				
Do	Do	Barth Margret Kenny Paps	Labourer				4				
Do	Carthron	Michael Margret Conner Paps	Labourer		3						
Do	Do	James Mary Keagerty Paps	Labourer		3						
[f.224] Kilbegnett	Creggs	Loghlin bridget Kean Paps	Labourer		1		4				
Do	Do	John Dorothy Carraher Paps	Labourer		2		3				
Do	Do	Michael Bridget Goowaun Paps	Brogemaker		3		1				
Do	Do	Edmond Margret Walsh Paps	Labourer				1				
Do	Do	Patrick Mary Doyle Paps	Labourer				2				
Do	Do	David Burke Pap	farmer								
Do	Do	Edmond Margret Connollan Paps	flax dresser								
Do	Do	Michael Sibby Manton Paps	Labourer		2						
Do	Do	Eulick Ellinor Burke Paps	Labourer				3				
Do	Do	James Cathrine Keegan Paps	Labourer		1		2				
Do	Do	Walter Mary Lasy Paps	Wigmaker		4						
Do	Do	Bryan Margret Doyle Paps	Labourer		2		2				
Do	Do	Michael Cicily Keegan Paps	farmer								2
Do	Do	Patrick Onnor Goonan Paps	Labourer		2		2				
Do	Do	William Concannon Pap					1				
Do	Do	James Jane Fitzpatrick Paps	Labourer								
Do	Do	Francis Bryan Pap	Labourer		2						
Do	Do	James Winnafrid Hines Paps	Smith								
Do	Do	William Ellinor Hibron Prots	Labourer			2					
Do	Do	Bridget Walsh Widdow Pap					2				
Do	Do	Andrew Concannon Pap	Shop keeper								
Do	Do	James Winnifrid Rush Pap	Labourer								
Do	Do	James Kelly Pap Margret Prot	Labourer				2				
Do	Do	Peter Mary Fallan Paps	Labourer		3						
Do	Do	Luke Mary Kelly Paps	Labourer		3		6				

Com~ Galway Parish of	Place of Abode	Names and Religion	Proffession	Children under 14 Prot.	Children under 14 Paps.	Children above 14 Prot.	Children above 14 Paps.	Men Servts Prot.	Men Servts Paps.	Women Servts Prot.	Women Servts Paps.
Do	Do	Ferns									
		Sarah Brady Paps	Harper								
Do	Do	Mathew									
		Mary Lewis	Weaver	4		3					
Do	Do	Luke									
		Mary Concannon Paps	Shop keeper		5						
Do	Do	William									
		Bridget Sandford Paps	Labourer	1							
Do	Do	Daniel									
		Mary Keegan Paps	Labourer								
Do	Do	Daniel									
		Bridget Coghlan Paps	Ale seller								
Do	Do	John Ward Pap	Brogemaker		2						
Do	Do	Dennis									
		Elizabeth Groork Paps	Labourer		1						
Do	Do	Anthony									
		Mary Egan Paps	farmer		1		3				
Do	Do	Rose Quin Widdow Pap			2		3				
Do	Gorvogh	James Kelly Pap	Farmer						3		2
Do	Do	Edmond									
		Cathrine Melee Paps	Gardiner		1		2				
Do	Do	James									
		Mary Casy Paps	Tanner		3				1		
Do	Do	Patrick									
		Winnafrid Troy Paps	Labourer		2		2				
Do	Do	Thos.									
		Sarah McDermott Paps	Labourer								
Do	Do	Sarah Barret Widdow Pap					1				
[f.225] Kilbegnett	Corroghrevagh	Hugh									
		Margret Kean Paps	Labourer				3				
Do	Do	Brian									
		Ellinor Egan Paps	Labourer		1						
Do	Do	Bryan									
		Winnifred Kean Paps	Labourer		2						
Do	Do	Laughlin									
		Margret Conry Paps	Labourer		3						
Do	Do	William									
		Ellinor Conboy Paps	Labourer		1		4				
Do	Do	Michael									
		Ellinor Sweeny Paps	Labourer		1						
Do	Gortmore	John									
		Mary Keeghran Paps	Labourer		2						
Do	Do	Batholemew									
		Anne Maldoon Paps	Labourer		2						
Do	Do	Rojer									
		Margret Finnegan Paps	Labourer		1						
Do	Do	Bryan									
		Ellinor Bragan Paps	Labourer		2						
Do	Corlack	James									
		Mary Harrahy Paps	farmer		4						
Do	Do	Henry									
		Dorothy Wilson Prot	Weaver								
Do	Do	Edmond									
		Winnifred Brogan Paps	Labourer		2						
Do	Gortmorriss	Theady									
		Sarah Dolan Paps	Labourer		1						
Do	Do	John									
		Anne Burke Paps	Labourer		2		1				
Do	Do	Richard									
		Anne Burke Paps	farmer						1		

Com~ Galway Parish of	Place of Abode	Names and Religion	Proffession	Children under 14		Children above 14		Men Servts		Women Servts	
				Prot.	Paps.	Prot.	Paps.	Prot.	Paps.	Prot.	Paps.
Do	Do	Bryan Mary Conner Paps	Labourer		1						
Do	Moat	Andrew Mary Rayne Paps	Mercht.		2				1		1
Do	Do	Hugh Margret Rayne Paps	Labourer		2						1
Do	Do	Michael Mary Flynn Paps	Labourer		2		1				
Do	Do	Cathrine Birane Widdow Pap			3						
Do	Do	Patrick Cathrine Mulhane Paps	Labourer				1				
Do	Do	Michael Ellinor Cuningham Paps	Labourer		1						
Do	Do	Michael Anne Rayne Paps	Labourer		3						
Do	Do	Cicily Cunningham Widdow Pap			1		1				
Do	Do	Domnick Ellinor Conner Paps	Labourer		3						
Do	Do	Laurence Mary Mullane Paps	Labourer		1						
Do	Do	Thos. Catherine Mullane Paps	Labourer		1						
Do	Do	Darby Winnafrid Cormack Paps	Labourer				3				
Do	Do	Roger Joan Cormack Paps	Labourer								
Do	Do	Peter Ellinor Mee Paps	Labourer		1						
Do	Do	Michael Rose Cunningham Paps	Labourer		1						
Do	Do	John Bridget Bush Paps	Labourer		1						
Do	Do	John Catherine Crubbane Paps	Labourer		1		1				
Do	Do	James Cathrine Crubbane Paps	Labourer		2						
Do	Do	Mary Gilligan Widdow Pap					1				
Do	Do	Anthony Onnor Burke Paps	Labourer		2		1				
Do	Do	Michael Bridget Gavan Paps	Labourer								1
Do	Do	Darby Gavan Pap	Labourer								
Do	Do	James Gavan Pap	Labourer								
Do	Do	Robert Margret Merrick Paps	Labourer								
[f.226] Kilbegnett	Gortnalawn	Patrick Margret Cuddy Paps	Labourer		3						
Do	Do	Michael Burke Pap	Labourer								
Do	Do	James Mary Dogherty Paps	Labourer				2				
Do	Do	Robert Mary Delany Prot	Labourer	4							
Do	Do	Owin Winnafrid Carroll Paps	Labourer				1				
Do	Do	Thos. Bridget Elrum Prots	Weaver	2							
Do	Do	William Delany Prot	Labourer								
Do	Derryhuppo	Conner Bridget Tummulty Paps	Labourer		1						

Com~ Galway Parish of	Place of Abode	Names and Religion	Proffession	Children under 14 Prot.	Paps.	Children above 14 Prot.	Paps.	Men Servts Prot.	Paps.	Women Servts Prot.	Paps.
Do	Do	James / Margret Queeny Paps	Labourer		1		1				
Do	Do	Rojer / Sarah Moony Paps	Labourer		3						
Do	Do	Patrick / Cathrine Huestan Paps	Labourer		1		1				
Do	Do	Thos. / Cathrine Hannily Paps	Labourer		4						
Do	Do	Theady / Bridget Trummane Paps	Labourer		3						
Do	Do	Patrick Keegan Pap	Weaver				2				
Do	Do	Hugh / Margret Keegan Paps	Labourer								
Do	Aghalattive	Mark / Mary Connif Paps	Labourer		2						
Do	Do	Mark / Sarah Kiernan Paps	Weaver		1		1				
Do	Do	Patrick / Sarah Gavan Paps	Labourer		1						
Do	Do	Owen / Mary Ricon Paps	Labourer		1						
Do	Do	Patrick / Sarah Kiernan Paps	Labourer		1						
Do	Do	William / Bridget Raghtagon Paps	Labourer		1		2				
Do	Do	Laurence / Sarah Kiernan Paps	Labourer		1				1		
Do	Do	Daniel / Sarah Raghtigan Paps	Labourer		2		3				
Do	Do	Loghlin / Sarah Raghtigan Paps	Labourer		2		2				
Do	Do	Patrick / Margret Kiernan Paps	Labourer		1						
Do	Do	Peter / Mary Lyons Paps	Labourer		2						
Do	Do	William / Bridget Nary Paps	Labourer				2				
Do	Do	Edmond / Bridget Kelly Paps	Labourer		2		3				
Do	Do	Owen / Bridget Kelly Paps	Labourer		3		1		1		
Do	Do	William / Margret Connor Paps	Labourer		3						
Do	Do	James / Sarah Raghtagan Paps	Labourer		2		2				
Do	Do	Michael / Mary Raghtagan Paps	Labourer		1						
Do	Do	Patrick / Jane Hurly Paps	Labourer		2		1				
Do	Do	William / Margret Hurly Paps	Labourer		3		1				
Do	Do	Patrick / Winnafrid Connife Paps	Labourer		1		1				
Do	Guranmore	Michael / Winnafrid Egan Paps	Labourer		2						
Do	Do	James / Bridget Connelly Paps	Labourer		1						
Do	Do	Laughlin / Cathrine Crubbane Paps	Labourer				3				
Do	Do	Patrick / Margret Ruddighan Paps	Labourer		1						

Com~ Galway Parish of	Place of Abode	Names and Religion	Proffession	Children under 14 Prot.	Children under 14 Paps.	Children above 14 Prot.	Children above 14 Paps.	Men Servts Prot.	Men Servts Paps.	Women Servts Prot.	Women Servts Paps.
Do	Do	Bartholomew Cathrine Egan Paps	Labourer				1				
Do	Do	Thos. Mary Egan Paps	Labourer								
[f.227] Kilbegnett	Gorteenfadda	Richard Margret Giblan Paps	Labourer		2		1				
Do	Do	Theady Cathrine Doogan Paps	Labourer		2		1				
Do	Do	James Mary Tully Paps	Labourer		2						
Do	Creggans	Michael Sarah Kelly	Labourer		1		3				
Do	Do	John Bridget Delany Paps	Glover		2						
Do	Do	William Burne Pap	Labourer				2				
Do	Do	John Sarah Burne Paps	Labourer		4						
Do	Do	Patrick Cathrine Kneavin Paps	Labourer		4						
Do	Do	Bartle Bridget Burne Paps	Labourer		1						
Do	Do	Daniel Kelly Pap	Labourer		1						
Do	Do	Onner Paudeen Widdow Pap					1				
Do	Do	Patrick Winnafrid Keegan Paps	Labourer		1						
Do	Do	Bryan Cuddy Pap	Horse rider		2						
Do	Do	John Elizabeth Ratchfort Paps	Butcher		3						
Do	Do	Keadugh Sarah Burke Paps	Labourer				3				
Do	Do	Thomas Bridget Keegan Paps	Labourer		1						
Do	Do	Eulick Mable Burke Paps	Labourer								
Do	Do	Loghlinn Bridget Flanigan Paps	Labourer		1						
Do	Do	Thomas Winnifrid Kelly Paps	Labourer		1						
Do	Do	Francis Bridget Doud Paps	Labourer		1						
Do	Do	Edmond Ellinor Dogherty Paps	Labourer		2		2				
Do	Do	Daniel Ellinor Donnilly Paps	Weaver								
Do	Do	Michael Cathrine Flanigan Paps	Labourer				1				
Do	Do	James Cicily Carroll Paps	Labourer				1				
Do	Do	Elizabeth Barlow Widdow Pap					3				
Do	Do	James Cathrine Fallon Paps	Labourer		2						
Do	Do	Daniel Margret Lohan Paps	Labourer		2		1				
Do	Do	Owen Margret Feeny Paps	Labourer				1				
Do	Do	Andrew Elizabeth Carty Paps	Labourer		1		3				
Do	Gortnalowee	James Mary Boyle Paps	Labourer				6				

Com~ Galway Parish of	Place of Abode	Names and Religion	Proffession	Children under 14		Children above 14		Men Servts		Women Servts	
				Prot.	Paps.	Prot.	Paps.	Prot.	Paps.	Prot.	Paps.
Do	Do	Barthle									
		Cathrine Boyle Paps	Labourer				3				
Do	Do	Patrick									
		Mary Boyle Paps	Labourer		1				1		
Do	Do	William									
		Sarah Daly Paps	Labourer		1						
Do	Do	Bridget Hannily Widdow Pap			1						
Do	Do	Michael									
		Ellinor Dogherty Paps	Labourer								
Do	Do	Ellinor Flanigan Widdow Pap					2				
Do	Do	John Barret Pap	Labourer				1				
Do	Do	Daniel									
		Onnor Daly Paps	Labourer		2						
Do	Do	James Daly Pap	Labourer								
Do	Do	Martin									
		Mary Flanigan Paps	Labourer		2		2				
Do	Do	John									
		Winnafrid Kean Paps	Labourer		1		1				
[f.228] Kilbegnett	Buggaun	Domnick									
		Onnor Pitted Paps	Labourer		2						
Do	Do	Michael									
		Sarah Pitted Paps	Labourer		1						
Do	Do	Owen									
		Margret McDonald Paps	Labourer		2		1				
Do	Camderry	Darby									
		Mary Doude Paps	Labourer		2						
Do	Do	Thos.									
		Onnor Britton Paps	Labourer								
Do	Do	William									
		Mary Doude Paps	Labourer								
Do	Do	John									
		Cathrine Doude Paps	Labourer								
Do	Do	William									
		Onnor Clary Paps	Labourer		2						
Do	Do	John									
		Bridget Giblon Paps	Labourer		2						
Do	Do	James									
		Margret Keirny Paps	Labourer								
Do	Do	Mathew									
		Onnor Giblan Paps	Labourer		2						
Do	Do	Laurence Giblan Pap	Labourer								
Do	Do	Patrick									
		Jane Loaghan Paps	Labourer								
Do	Do	Patrick									
		Jane Cunningham Paps	Labourer								
Do	Do	John Logan Pap	Labourer		2						
Do	Leagh	James									
		Cathrine Holran Paps	Labourer		2						
Do	Do	Patrick									
		Mary Royen Paps	Labourer		2						
Do	Do	Thomas									
		Ellinor Gill Paps	Labourer		1						
Do	Do	Theady									
		Margret Giblan Paps	Labourer								
Do	Ballinahoune	William									
		Ellinor Canninoh Paps	Labourer		2						
Do	Do	Richard									
		Mary Giblan Paps	Labourer		3						
Do	Do	Michael									
		Cicily Giblan Paps	Labourer		1						

Com~ Galway Parish of	Place of Abode	Names and Religion	Proffession	Children under 14 Prot.	Children under 14 Paps.	Children above 14 Prot.	Children above 14 Paps.	Men Servts Prot.	Men Servts Paps.	Women Servts Prot.	Women Servts Paps.
Do	Do	Darby / Ellinor Morgan Paps	Labourer		2		1				
Do	Do	Patrick / Rose Grive Paps	Labourer		2		1				
Do	Do	Michael / Mary Muligan Paps	Labourer				1				
Do	Do	Thos / Margret Sirr Paps	Labourer				1				
Do	Do	Henry / Bridget Sirr Paps	Labourer								
Do	Do	Patrick McGuire Pap	Labourer								
Do	Do	James / Mary Skine Paps	Labourer		2						
Do	Do	Rodger / Mary Quinn Paps	Labourer		1						
Do	Gorteenfadda	Domnick / Mary Mee Paps	Labourer								
Do	Do	John / Winnafrid Halen Paps	Labourer								
Do	Do	Theady / Mary Brannon Paps	Labourer		1		2				
Do	Do	Bryan / Winnafrid Daly Paps	Labourer								
Do	Do	Rodger / Cathrine Fallon Paps	Labourer		1						
Do	Do	Thomas / Elizabeth Blee Paps	Labourer				1				
Do	Do	Patrick / Cathrine Hurly Paps	Labourer		1						
Do	Do	John Blee Pap	Labourer								
Do	Do	John / Cathrine Gane Paps	Labourer								
Do	Do	Darby / Bridget Hannen Paps	Labourer		2						
Do	Do	Owen / Sarah Giblan Paps	Labourer		2						
[f.229] Kilbegnettt	Gurrane	Edmond / Onnor Keggan Paps	Labourer		3						
Do	Do	Patrick / Onner Conney Paps	Labourer		2						
Do	Do	John / Cathrine Garvine Paps	Labourer								
Do	Do	Edmond Kelly Paps	Labourer		3		1				
Do	Do	Michael / Bridget Reney Paps	Labourer		2						
Do	Do	Theobald / Dorothy Kevey Paps	Labourer		3						
Do	Do	Richard / Margret Kevey Paps	Labourer		2		1				
Do	Do	Henry / Margret Lynen Paps	Labourer				2				
Do	Do	Theady / Margret Graney Paps	Labourer								
Do	Do	William / Cathrine Barlow Paps	Labourer		2		1				
Do	Do	Patrick / Onner Noon Paps	Labourer		2		2				
Do	Do	Peter / Onner Lyons Paps	Labourer		3		1				
Do	Do	Mathew / Margret Dair Paps	Labourer		3						

Com~ Galway Parish of	Place of Abode	Names and Religion	Proffession	Children under 14		Children above 14		Men Servts		Women Servts	
				Prot.	Paps.	Prot.	Paps.	Prot.	Paps.	Prot.	Paps.
Do	Do	Bridget McDonagh Widdow Pap			1						
Do	Do	Henry Burke Pap	Labourer		1		4				
Do	Do	Michael									
		Mary Burke Paps	Labourer		3						
Do	Do	Hebrum									
		Mary Daly Paps	Labourer								
Do	Do	Owen									
		Margret Reily Paps	Labourer				2				
Do	Do	Deniss									
		Mary Birne Paps	Labourer								
Do	Do	Michael									
		Margret Birne Paps	Labourer								
Do	Kilbegnett	James									
		Bridget Brehany Paps	Labourer		2		2		2		
Do	Do	Conner									
		Sarah Cunnane Paps	Labourer		1				1		
Do	Do	Matthew									
		Cathrine Ward Paps	Labourer		1		2				
Do	Do	Daniel									
		Cicily Kelly Paps	Labourer		2						
Do	Do	Peter Kenny Pap	Labourer		1		1				
Do	Do	Patrick									
		Mary Kenny Paps	Labourer				1				
Do	Do	Michael									
		Cicily Ward Paps	Labourer		2		1				
Do	Donamaddy	John									
		Cathrine Hagarty Paps	Labourer		5				1		1
Do	Do	Edmond									
		Bridget Murphy Paps	Labourer		3		1		1		1
Do	Do	Theady									
		Ellinor Cuddy Paps	Labourer				2				
Do	Do	James									
		Cicily Dermott Paps	Labourer				3				
Do	Do	Hugh									
		Bridget Kilroe Paps	Labourer				5				
Do	Do	Martin									
		Ellinor Dermott Paps	Labourer								
Do	Do	William									
		Ellinor Mee Paps	Labourer		1						
Do	Do	William Sharry Pap	Labourer								
Do	Do	Loghlin									
		Cathrine Scanlon Paps	Labourer		3		2				
Do	Derryhuppo	Laughlin									
		Margret Furmo Paps	Labourer								
Do	Do	Edmond									
		Mary Furmo Paps	Labourer								
Do	Do	Theady									
		Bridget Furmo Paps	Labourer		3						
Do	Do	Bryan									
		Margret Lennon Paps	Labourer				2				
Do	Do	Bryan									
		Elizabeth Tumulty Paps	Labourer		1						
[f.230]Kilbegnett	Derryhuppo	Hugh									
		Jane Johnston Paps	Labourer				2				
Do	Do	Conner									
		Margreet Queeny Paps	Labourer		[?]3						
Do	Do	Thomas									
		Mary McGuire Paps	Labourer		1						

[verso f.230 in E.S. writing]

Totals	Protestants	Papists
Fuerty	124	1236
Athleague	102	913
Kilbegnet	36	1054
	262	3203

NOTE

1. *General Alphabetical Index.*

ORAN, COUNTY ROSCOMMON

INTRODUCTION: *The parish of Oran is 5 miles north-west of Roscommon in the barony of Ballymoe. It covers 5,181 statute acres and is on the river Suck.[1] The land was good with no waste or bog. There were limestone quarries.[2]*

The parish was united 'from time immemorial' to the vicarage of Drimtemple'[3]. The incumbent in 1749 was the Rev. Thomas Contarine, vicar of Drimtemple from 1729 and prebendary of Oran from 1730.[4] Contarine, who was born in Chesterfield in 1694, was Oliver Goldsmith's uncle.[5] The rectory was impropriate in the earl of Essex. The patron was the bishop.

OCCUPATIONS

Agent	3	Farmer	3	Smith	2
Broguemaker	1	Labourer	55	Surveyor	1
Butcher	1	Maltster	1	Tailor	1
Carpenter	1	Mason	3	Weaver	3
Clerk	1	Miller	1		
Cooper	1	Servants, household	122	Wigmaker	1
Cowherd	3	Shepherd	5	Yeoman	32

Com~Ros common Parish of	Place of Abode	Names and Religion	Proffession	Children under 14		Children above 14		Men Servts		Women Servts	
				Prot.	Paps.	Prot.	Paps.	Prot.	Paps.	Prot.	Paps.
[f. 231] Oran	Oran	John Irwin pa	Farmer						3		4
		Bryan Flanigan W pa	Farmer	2					2		3
		Thos. Meares W pa	Mason	1			2		1		1
		Teige Coin W pa	Shepard	1							
		Thos. McDonagh w pa	Carpenter	2			1		1		1
		Luke Brisk w pa	Labr.	1							
		Martin Lorkan w pa	Shepard	3					1		1
		Thos. Lynagh w pa	Labr.	2			1				
		Bryan Lennon w pa	Butcher	2					1		
		James Farrel w pa	Shepeard	2							
		Peter Ward w pa	Labr.				3				
		Willm. Firnan w pa	Labr.	1			2				
	Creeve	Edmd. Gordon w pa	Smith	2					1		1
		Luke McDermott pa	Agent				3		1		2
		Miles Swiny w pa	Labr.	2							
		Roger Teige w pa	Surveyor				3				
		John Kelly w pa	Labr.	4							
	Runnibocan	Willm Kief w pa	Shepherd	5					1		
		Dan Swiny w pa	Labr.	2			1				
	Newtown	Edwd. Fallon pa	Farmer	1					3		4
		Patt. Duigonan w pa	Agent						1		2
		Ja. Teige pa	Mason				3				
		Richard Kane pa	Labr.				3				
		Michl. Dean w pa	Labr.	3							
		Willm. Burke w pa	Cowherd	1							
		John Heeny w pa	Labr.	2							
	Ranagh	Willm. Horagho pa	wigmaker						1		
		Will. Skally w pa	Labr.	2							
		Widow Judge pa					3				
		Willm. Ternan pa	Labr.				4				
		Teige Skally w pa	Smith	1					1		1
		John Grady w pa	Weaver	1			3		2		
		Owen Ward pa	Brougemaker	1			3		1		
		Walter Dillon w pa	Yeoman	3					1		1
		Garret Dillon pa	Yeoman						1		1
		Edwd. Stanton w pa	Yeoman	2					1		1
		Luke Dolby w pa	Yeoman	1					1		1
		Thos. Donellan w pa	Yeoman	2					1		1
		John Donellan w pa	Yeoman	3					1		1
		Willm. Stanton w pa	Yeoman	4					1		1
		Peter Grady pa	Yeoman	1			4		1		1
[f.232]Oran	Ranagh	Garret Grady w pa	Yeoman	2			2				
		Dan Farrel w pa	Labr.	3			3				
		Thos Cavenay w pa	Labr.	3							
		Bartho. White w pa	Taylor	2					2		1
		Hugh w pa	Labr.	3							
		Teige Keen w pa	Labr.	1							
		Martin Kenny w pa	Labr.	2			4				
		Pat. Fudagh pa	Labr.				4				

Com~Roscommon Parish of	Place of Abode	Names and Religion	Proffession	Children under 14 Prot.	Children under 14 Paps.	Children above 14 Prot.	Children above 14 Paps.	Men Servts Prot.	Men Servts Paps.	Women Servts Prot.	Women Servts Paps.
		Pat. White w pa	Labr.		2						
	Carranag-eelogue	Charles Hanly w pa	Yeoman		3				1		2
		Pat. Brennan pa	Yeoman		1		3		1		1
		Antho. Mulloy pa	Yeoman		1		2		1		1
		Charl. Kein w. pa	Yeoman		1		3		1		1
		Jas. Teige w. pa	Labr.		3						
		Mic. Ward w. pa	Labr.		2						
	Rah	Hugh Luoog w. pa	Yeoman		3				1		1
		Thos. Cooney w. pa	Weaver		4				1		
		George Dowd w. pa	Yeoman				2		1		1
		Thos. Mcsweeny w. pa	Yeoman		3		1		1		2
		Bryan McConnif w. pa	Labr.		2						
		Luke Hedian w. pa	Labr.		1						
		Patt. Kearny w. pa	Labr.		1						
		Matt. Conniff w. pa	Labr.								
		Laurence Coony w. pa	Labr		1						
		John Cooney w. pa	Labr.		3						
	Carragarra	Patt. Keavenny w. pa	Labr.		2						
		Pat. Finane w. pa	Labr.				3				
		Connor Connelly w. pa	Labr.		3						
		Willm. Flyn w. pa	Labr.		3						
		Peter Dunn w. pa	Yeoman		4						
		Owen Flyn w. pa	Yeoman		1		4		1		1
		Charles Connelly w. pa	Yeoman		3				1		1
		Patt. Finnerne w. pa	Yeoman		3				1		1
		John Flyn pa	Labr.		2						
		Mark Croghan w. pa	Labr.				3				
		Patt. Luoog w. pa	Labr.		5						
		Mic. White w. pa	Labr.		1						
		Patt. Minure w. pa	Labr.		3						
		John Minure w. pa	Labr.		2						
	Cloonecolgan	Dom. Higgins w. pa	Labr.		2						
		Connor Hagarty w. pa	Agent				1		1		2
[f.233] Oran	Cloonecalgan	Phelim Keegan w. pa	Labr.				3				
		Thos. Hegarty w. pa	Malster		2				2		1
		Jas. Dogherty w. pa	Labr.		4						
		Teige Higgins w. pa	Labr.				5				
	Ballydooly	Owen Finraghty w. pa	Yeoman		3				1		1
		Bryan Finraghty w. pa	Yeoman		1				1		1
		Gilbert Hanly w. pa	Yeoman		1				1		1
		Oliver Jones w. pa	Labr.		2						
		Widow Jones pa					2				
		Terence Farrel w. pa	Yeoman		3		2		1		1
		Luke Croghan w. pa	Labour		2						
		David Roch w. pa	Labr.		2						
		Richard Moore w. pro	Mason	1				1			1
		Willm. Abram w. pro	Yeoman	3							
		Jas. Harraghan w. pa	Cooper		4						
		Will Keatoo w. pa	Yeoman				3				

Com~Ros common Parish of	Place of Abode	Names and Religion	Proffession	Children under 14		Children above 14		Men Servts		Women Servts	
				Prot.	Paps.	Prot.	Paps.	Prot.	Paps.	Prot.	Paps.
		Denis Coghlan w. pro	Yeoman					1			1
		Robt. Saunders w. pa	Labr.	1							
	Emlaghmore	Thomas Contarine[6]	Clk			1		3	1	1	1
		Charles Connor w. pa	Labr.				3				
		Martin Mulligan w. pa	Labr.				1				
		Teige McNamara W. pa	Labr.				4				
		Peter Connor w. pa	Cowherd		4						
	Emlaughbegg	Thos. Farrel w. pa	Sheapherd		4						
		Widow Teige pa					2				
	Emlaghnagry	Dan. Brehanny w. pa	Cowherd				3				
Com. Gallway	Cloonconnoo	Frans. Farrel w. pa	Yeoman		2		3		1		1
		Luke Farrel pa	Yeoman		2				1		1
		Laurence Mee pa	Labr.				3				
		Mic. Kane w. pa	Labr.		1						
		Jas. Kane w. pa	Labr.		2		2				
		Thos. Kane w. pa	Labr.		1						
Co Roscomon Parish of Drimtemple	Toberumkee	Edmd Kenny w. pa	Yeoman		3				1		1
		Dan Kenny w. pa	Yeoman		2				1		1
		Carbry Kenny w. pa	Yeoman		2				1		1
		Bryan Flyn w. pa	Labr.		1		1				
		Mic. Hogan w. pa	Labr.				3				
		Patk Finnaran w. pa	Miller		2		3		1		2
		Dan Bohan w. pa	Labr.		2						
		Jas. Bone W pa	Weaver		1		2				
		Widow Flyn pa			2		2			1	1

[verso f.232]

The Parish of Oran Contains 18 Protestants 600 Papists Men, Women, Children & Servants Included -

NOTES

1. Including 11 acres of the river Suck (*General Alphabetical Index*).

2. Lewis, 'Oran'.

3. Ibid.

4. Leslie, 'Elphin' p. 200.

5. Patrick Murray, 'Goldsmith's ancestry: fact and tradition' in *Irish Midland Studies*, p.156.

6. Thomas Contarine was born in Chester, a son of Austin Contarine. He entered TCD in 1701 and took BA in 1706. He married an aunt of Oliver Goldsmith and his sister Jane married James Lawder of Lowfield, Kilmore (see Census f.38). He was rector of Kilmore from 1723 (*Alumni Dubliniensis*).

DRUMATEMPLE, COUNTY ROSCOMMON & COUNTY GALWAY

INTRODUCTION: *The parish of Drumatemple is partly in County Galway and partly in County Roscommon in the barony of Ballymoe. It is four miles from Castlerea on the road to Roscommon town. It contains 6,530 statute acres. The land use in 1837 was principally pasture and arable.*[1]

The parish was held with that of Oran. The incumbent was the Rev. Thomas Contarine, who held it from 1729 (see Oran).[2] *He lived in Emlaghmore, parish of Oran. The patron was the bishop.*

OCCUPATIONS

Bailiff	1	Labourer	75	Shopkeeper	1
Cowherd	8	Mason	1	Smith	1
Esquire	1	Music master	1	Tailor	3
Farmer	3	Servants, household	98	Weaver	4
Gentleman	3	Shepherd	5	Wigmaker	1
Groom	1	Shoemaker	1	Yeoman	27
Joiner	2				

Com~Ros common Parish of	Place of Abode	Names and Religion	Proffession	Children under 14 Prot.	Children under 14 Paps.	Children above 14 Prot.	Children above 14 Paps.	Men Servts Prot.	Men Servts Paps.	Women Servts Prot.	Women Servts Paps.
[f.234] Drimtemple	Toberumkee	Patt. Cugley w. pa	Labr.		3						
	Laraugh	Richard Teige pa	Farmer						3		2
		Bryan Hand w. pa	Shepherd				2		1		
		Jas. McDonnaugh w. pa	Labr.		3						
		Willm. Mulrey w. pa	Labr.		2						
		Thos. Lorkan w. pa	Labr.				2				
		Jas. Hand w. pa	Labr.		1		2				
		Matthias Lorkan w. pa	Tailor		2						
		Luke Padin w. pa	Labr.		2						
		Thady Lorkan w. pa	Labr.		1						
		David Fleming w. pa	Labr.		2						
		Mic. Javin w. pa	Labr.		2						
		Connor Hagg w. pa	pumpmaker		1		4				
		Peter Kelly w. pa	Labr.		2						
	Ballycahir	Thos. Smith w. pa	Labr.				2				
		Willm. Murphy w. pa	Labr.		2						
		Thos. Donore w. pa	Cowherd		3						
	Cloonedirha	Patt. Spallan pa	Yeoman				2		1		
		Roger Connor w. pa	Yeoman		3				1		
		Barth. Spallan w. pa	Yeoman				3				
		John Hanly w. pa	Yeoman		2		1				
		Jas. McNemara pa	Yeoman		1		2		1		
		Teige Connelly w. pa	Labr.		2						
		John Kenny w. pa	Labr.		4						
		Matt Conniff w. pa	Labr.		2						
		Patt. Flyn w. pa	Labr.		1		1				
		Andrew Nylan w. pa	Labr.		1		3				
	Dundermott	John Lea w. pro	Farmer	6		3			3		4
		John Gannon w. pa	Smith						1		1
		Teige Connor w. pa	Cowherd		3						
		Matt. Kareen w. pa	Labr.		2						
		Thos. Tracy w. pa			1						
		Erril Farrel pa	Cowherd		1		3				
		Thos. Cooney pa	Labr.		2						
		Andrew Tobin pa	Labr.		1		2				
		Mic. Hallinan w. pa	Labr.		4						
		John Rush w. pa	Labr.		2						
		Laughlin Kareen pa	Labr.		1		3				
		Thos. Cunane w. pa	Labr.		3						
	Drimtemple	Hugh McNamara pa	Labr.		1		2				
		Mic. Donagh w. pa	Labr.		2		1				
[f.235] Drimtemple	Drimtemple	Laughlin Boyd pa	Shepherd				4				
		Thoms. Dolan w. pa	Cowherd		1		2				
		George Boyd w. pa	Labr.		3						
		Bryan Carthy w. pa	Labr.								
		Dom. Kelly w. pa	Labr.		3						
		Owen McDonagh w. pa	Labr.				4				
		Hugh Conniff pa	Labr.		1		2				
		John Mooney w. pa	Labr.		2						
	Leabegg	John Irwin[3] w. pa	Gent.				4		2		3

Com~Ros common Parish of	Place of Abode	Names and Religion	Proffession	Children under 14		Children above 14		Men Servts		Women Servts	
				Prot.	Paps.	Prot.	Paps.	Prot.	Paps.	Prot.	Paps.
		Anthony Rush w. pa	Cowherd		3						
	Cloonagrasan	Edmd. Moran w. pa	Taylor		4				2		1
		Thos. Byrne pa	Yeoman				3		1		1
		Patt. Kane w. pa	Yeoman		2		3		1		1
		Cor. McDonagh w. pa	Yeoman		2				1		1
		Thos. Giraghty w. pa	Weaver		4				1		
		Laughlin Mollan w. pa	Yeoman		3				1		
		Peter Hunt w. pa	wigmaker		3				1		
		Laugh. Kareen w. pa	Labr.		4						
		Edmd. Muloy w. pa	Labr.		2						
		Bart. Egan w. pa	Labr.		3						
		Farrel Brin w. pa	Labr.		1		2				
		Widow Carney pa					3				
	Coristoonabeg	Owen Cormor pa	Farmer				4		2		3
		Bryan Hannon w. pa	Labr.		3						
		Mic. Carney w. pa	Labr.		2		2				
	Coristoonamore	Richard Kirwan pa	Gent						3		3
		John Bush w. pa	Shepherd		3						
		Martin Keelly w. pa	Labr.		1						
		Thos. Coffee w. pa	Labr.		2						
	Killar	Luke Connelly w. pa	Shepherd		1		3				
		Chris. Lynagh w. pa	Bailiff		4						
		Charles English pa	Labr.		3						
		Widow Connor pa	Labr.		2						1
		Laurence Farrel w. pa	Labr.				3				
		Nichos. Hoy pa	Groom		1						
		Mic. Hannolan w. pa	Mason		1		2				
	Shanco	Owen Conway w. pa	Labr.		2						
		Roger Brennan w. pro	Cowherd	3		3			1		1
	Raheverin	Christ. Kirwan w. pro	Labr.	2				2	1	1	2
		Patt. Connelly w. pa	Cowherd		3						
		Frans. Kiely w. pa	Yeoman		1		2		1		1
[f.236] Drimtemple	Carnan	Bartho.FitzGerald pa	Yeoman				1		1		
		Tho. FitzGerald w. pa	Labr.		1						
		Laurence Quinn w. pa	Labr.		1						
		Michl. Carroll w. pa	Labr.		2						
		John Nelly w. pa	Labr.		2						
		Patt. McNeal w. pa	Labr.		2						
		John Cunningham w. pa	Labr.		1						
		Manus Coyn w. pa	Labr.		3						
		Connor Coin w. pa	Labr.				3				
		John Concannon w. pa	Labr.		1						
		Thos. Kelly w. pa	Weaver						1		
		William Moore w. pa	Joyner				2				
		Dom Conner w. pa	Labr.		2						
		John Cane w. pa	Yeoman		2						
		Hugh Concannon w. pa	Yeoman		2						
		Willm. Concannon w. pa	Yeoman		1						
		John Concannon w. pa	Yeoman		1						
		Michl. Brehanny pa	Yeoman		1						
		Bryan Cane w. pa	Yeoman		1		1				

Com~Ros common Parish of	Place of Abode	Names and Religion	Proffession	Children under 14 Prot.	Paps.	Children above 14 Prot.	Paps.	Men Servts Prot.	Paps.	Women Servts Prot.	Paps.
		Thos. Cone w. pa	Yeoman		1						
		Andrew Ruddy w. pa	Yeoman		1				1		
		John Carrol w. pa	Yeoman								
[f.237] Drimtemple	Rahoverin	Willm. FitzGerald w. pa	Yeoman		6		3		1		1
Coun Gallway Drimtemple parish		Willm. Egan w. pa	Shepherd		2						
	Bellamon	Frans. Cuff[4] w. pro	Esq.	2		3		2	1		3
		Patt. Kenny w. pro	Labr.		1						1
		Peter Concannon pa	Shopkeeper						1		2
		Felix Kelly[5] w. pa	Musick master		2				3		2
		Gilbert Egan w. pa	Taylor	3					3		3
		Richd Dean w. pa	Weaver		2		3				
		Laurence Hedian w. pa	Labr.		1						
		Widow Kelly pa			2		3				
		Peter Murray pro	Joyner			1					2
		Pett. Heverin w. pa	Labr.		1		1				
		Darby Muldown w. pa	Labr.		1		1				
		Jas. Waldron pa	Shoemaker		1		3				
		Wat. Hanly w. pa	Labr.			1					
	Cloonee	Thos. Cuff w. pro	Gent	2					1		2
		Willm. Joyce w. pa	Yeoman		1						
		Roger Brennan w. pa	Yeoman		2						
		Jas Mullen w. pa	Yeoman		4						
		Jas White w. pa	Labr.		1						
		Roger Lennon w. pa	Labr.		4		3				
		Patt. White w. pa	Labr.		1						
		Patt. Kane pa	Cowherd				2				
		Thos. Flyn w. pa	Labr.		3		2				
Parish of Killcroan	Ballyglass	Teige Farrel w. pa	Labr.		2		2				
		Hubert Burk w. pa	Labr.		2						
		Hu. Burk w. pa	Labr.		3		2				
		Jas. Burk w. pa	Labr.		3						
		Edwd. Burk pa	Weaver		2						
		Roger Rush pa	Labr.				2				
		Connor Mulvihill w. pa	Labr.		2		2				
		Patt. Kelly pa	Labr.		1		3				
		Bryan Burk w. pa	Labr.		1		1				
		Lough. Coffee pa	Labr.		4						
		Luke Duffy w. pa	Labr.		3		1				
		Thos. Colleran pa	Labr.								
		Thos. Wade pa	Saltseller		1		1				
	Ballaghidageag	Thos. Kelly w. pro	Innkeeper	2					1		1
		Edmd. Connor pro	Yeoman			3			1		1
		Dan Egan w. pa	Yeoman		4				1		2
		Chars Kelly w. pa	Yeoman		3				2		1

[verso f 236]

The Parish of Drimtemple
Contains 26 Protestants 669 Papists
Men, Women, Children & Servants Included

NOTES

1. Lewis, 'Drumatemple'.

2. Leslie, 'Elphin', p. 200.

3. John Irwin, probably a son of Christopher Irwin of Leabegg was a lay supporter of the Rev. William O'Kelly, prior of St. Mary's Roscommon in 1748 to succeed Patrick French as bishop of Elphin (Burke, *LGI* (1958); Fenning, 'Diocese of Elphin', p.166).

4. Both Thomas Cuff of Bellamon and Francis Cuff of Cloonee were sons of Caulfield Cuff, a clergyman. They were born in County Roscommon and educated by Dr Blayer of Sligo. Thomas was admitted to TCD in 1731, aged 17, and Francis was admitted the same year aged 16 (*Alumni Dubliniensis*).

5. In February 1748/9, Felix Kelly asked the Board of Customs for leave to distil. Enquiries were instituted to discover whether Ballymoe [Bellamon], where he then lived, was a market town. In April the opinion was that Kelly would be a 'great injury to the Excise because Ballymoe's having a patent for a Markett under which he claims a Licence, will be a means of People's setting up Stills at many other places where there are old Patents for weekly markets which the present officers would be unable to visit. People will remove their stills from places where they might visit to these pretended Market Towns and quit Roscommon, Elphin, Castle Reagh &c the great market towns of that country *entirely* as they have already done *in part*'. Clearly Kelly gave up the distilling business (N.A., P.R.O., CUST 1/46 ff. 58, 112).

KILCROAN, COUNTY GALWAY

INTRODUCTION: *The parish of Kilcroan is 11 miles north-west of Roscommon in the barony of Ballymoe. It covers 3875 acres, and contained a large quantity of bog.*[1]

The parish was held with that of Dunamon from 1622. The Rev. John Hickes was the incumbent from 1741-1780.[2] *The tithes of the rectory were impropriate in Lord Ranelagh.*

OCCUPATIONS

Brewer	1	Gardener	1	Minor	1
Broguemaker	1	Gentleman	3	Pedlar	1
Butcher	2	Glover	1	Servants, household	58
Constable	1	Hackler	1	Smith	2
Cooper	2	Herd	3	Steward	1
Cowherd	4	Joiner	1	Tailor	2
Dealer	1	Labourer	58	Weaver	4
Farmer	2	Mason	1	Yeoman	3

Com~ Galway Parish of	Place of Abode	Names and Religion	Proffession	Children under 14 Prot.	Paps.	Children above 14 Prot.	Paps.	Men Servts Prot.	Paps.	Women Servts Prot.	Paps.
[f.238] Killcroan	Ballydaghery	Thos. Kereen pa	Yeoman		2		4		1	1	
		Luke Finegan w. pa	Yeoman		1				1	1	
		Luke Egan w. pa	Yeoman		4				1	1	
		Jas. Egan w. pa	Labourer		1				1	1	
		Thos.Simmons pa	Labourer								
		Darby Brennan w. pa	Labourer		2						
		Thos. Petit pa	Labourer				1				
		Widow Hurly pa					3				
		Edmd. Lynch w. pa	Labourer		3		2				
		Bryan Curly w. pa	Labourer		2		2				
		Pattk. mcOwen w. pa	Labourer		2		3				
		Owen Ward w. pa	Labourer								
		John Mee pa	Labourer				3				
		Darby Culliane w. pa	Labourer		2						
		Edwd. McOwen w. pa	Labourer		1						
		Thos. Kane w. pa	Labourer		1						
		Denis Royn w. pa	Labourer		1						
		Thos.Royn pa	Labourer								
		Roger Keaghry pa	Tailor		3						
		Owen Curly pa	Labourer								
	Turlagh	Coll Flyn prot w. pa	Gent	5				1	2	2	
		Thos. Common pa	Steward				3		1	2	
		Hubert Burk w. pa	Brewer		1		1				
		Thos. Burk w. pa	Labourer		2						
		Patt. Mullin w. pa	Labourer		3		1				
		Thos. Tully w. pa	Labourer		4		2				
		Gregory Muldown w. pa	Cowherd		2		1				
		Patt. Wallis w. pa	Labourer		4		1				
		Luke Brennan w. pa	Labourer		2						
		Patt. Royn w. pa	Labourer		4						
		Jas. Flyn w. pa	Labourer		3						
		Phelim o'Hara pa	Labourer								
		Peter Shiel w. pa	Labourer		3		1				
		Mic. Cormick w. pa	Labourer		4						
		Hugh Flyn w. pa	Smith		4				1		1
		Jas. Flyn w. pa	Labourer		3						
		Thos. Flyn w. pa	Constable								
		Mark Concannon w. pa	Weaver				4		1		
		Jas. Cooney w. pa	Labourer		2						
		John Kelly w. pa	Herd		3				1		
		Connor Egan pa	Herd		3				1		
[f.239] [20 entries crossed out]	Cregawon	Jas. Marnell w. pa	Gent		5		1		2		3
		David Tobin pa	Gent				2		2		3
		Edwd. Marnell pro	Minor						1		1
		Patt. Egan pa	Farmer				2		1		1
		Den. Saughnassy w. pa	Pedlar		2				1		

Com~ Galway Parish of	Place of Abode	Names and Religion	Proffession	Children under 14		Children above 14		Men Servts		Women Servts	
				Prot.	Paps.	Prot.	Paps.	Prot.	Paps.	Prot.	Paps.
		Thos.Quinn w. pa	Labourer		2						
		John Mulloony pa	Labourer								
		Roger Farrel w. pa	Labourer		1		2				
		Darby Finnegan pa	Labourer								
		Dom Kenny pa	Labourer								
		Cormick Lyre w. pa	Labourer		2						
		John Burk pa	Labourer								
		Jas Burk pa	Labourer								
		Bryan Low w. pa	Labourer		1						
		Barnaby Gray w. pro pa	Weaver		2						
		Thady Lennlon pa	Herd		3		1				
		Hugh Sheen w. pa	Weaver		1						
		Darby Shahill w. pa	Cowherd		4		1			1	
		Cormuck Royn pa	Labourer								
		Patt Shahill w. pa	Labourer		2						
		Miles Joyce w. pa	Labourer		2						
[verso f.239]											
		Parish of Killcroan Contains 13 protestants 449 Papists Men, Women, Children & Servants Included									
[f.240] Killcroan		Willm. Connor w. pa	Farmer						1		1
		Thos. Duneen w. pa	Labourer		1						
		Patk. Royn w. pa	Labourer		4						1
		Willm. Flyn w. pa	Labourer		3		1				
		Mich. Sharkey pa	Labourer				1				
		Owen Lahee w. pa	Butcher		2				1		1
		Thos. Connane pa	Cowherd				2		1		1
		Martin Kane w. pa	Dealer		3						
		Willm. Connolly w. pa	Labourer		3						
		Martin Flyn w. pa	Labourer		4						
		Joseph Michell pro w. pa			2		2				
		Laughlin Linnane pa	Labourer		3						
	Killsallagh	Edmd. Mulligan pa	Cowherd						1		1
		Natee Morgan w. pa	Cooper		3		1				
		Simon Mulligan w. pa	Labourer		3						
		Willm. Mulligan w. pa	Labourer		2		1				
		Willm. Flyn w. pa	Labourer		3		1				
Parish of Ballynakill	Glynisk	Martin Bodkin w. pa			4		2		2		3
		Bryan Connor w. pa	Smith		2		2				
		John Burk w. pa	Wigmaker		2						1
		John Trily w. pa	Mason		1		5		1		
		Patk. Sheel w. pa	Tailor		2		1				
		Laughlin Grourke w. pa	Butcher		4						1
		Thos. Cudely w. pa	Labourer		2						
		Thos. Mulloy w. pa	Hackler		3						
		Patt. Cane w. pa	Gardiner								
		Thos. Dillon pa	Carman				1				
		Thos. Cunniff pa	Cowherd						1		1

Com~ Galway Parish of	Place of Abode	Names and Religion	Proffession	Children under 14		Children above 14		Men Servts		Women Servts	
				Prot.	Paps.	Prot.	Paps.	Prot.	Paps.	Prot.	Paps.
		Peter Cuniff w. pa	Labourer		3						
		Owen Cunniff w. pa	Labourer		2						
		Nicholas Farrel pa	Cooper								
		Willm. Cudely w. pa	Weaver		2		2				
		Jas. Royan w. pa	Labourer		3						
		John Skahill w. pa	Broguemaker		3						
		John Conneelly w. pa	Glover		3				1		
		Michl. Conneelly w. pa	Labourer		1						
		Patt. Ward pa	Joiner				2				1
		Dan McGrourk w. pa	Labourer		1						
		Patt. Feylan pa	Labourer				1				
		Mic. Phillips w. pa	Labourer		2						
		Thos. Burke pa	Labourer				2				

NOTES

1. Lewis, 'Kilcroan'.
2. Leslie, 'Elphin', p. 136.

BALLYNAKILL, COUNTY ROSCOMMON & COUNTY GALWAY

INTRODUCTION: *The parish of Ballynakill is divided into three parts, one in County Roscommon, one in County Galway and one in County Sligo. It was in the baronies of Ballymoe (Roscommon), Killian (Galway) and Tirerill (Sligo). The section in County Roscommon in the barony of Ballymoe was on the border of County Galway, that in County Galway in the Barony of Killian adjoined it 6 miles from Roscommon near the road from Roscommon to Dunmore. The detached part in County Sligo was about 40 miles north-east of the County Roscommon section (see separate entry). Lewis describes the Galway/Roscommon part of the parish as having 3000 acres of arable land and 20,000 acres of mountain pasture, waste and bog.[1] The largest centre of population in 1749 was at Glynisk (Glinsk), County Galway.*

The Church of Ireland incumbent was the Rev. John Holmes, who held the parish with that of Ballysumaghan, County Sligo from 1729.[2] It is not known where he lived. The patron was the bishop. The living was impropriate in the first Earl of Ranelagh.

OCCUPATIONS

Agent	1	Gentleman	2	Servants, household	76
Baronet, a minor	1	Herd	3	Shepherd	1
Broguemaker	2	Labourers	84	Thatcher	1
Butcher	1	Lady	1	Weaver	1
Carman	2	Mason	1	Widow	2
Cowherd	4	Merchant	1	Yeoman	7
Farmer	7	Miller	2		

Com~ Galway Parish of	Place of Abode	Names and Religion	Proffession	Children under 14 Prot.	Children under 14 Paps.	Children above 14 Prot.	Children above 14 Paps.	Men Servts Prot.	Men Servts Paps.	Women Servts Prot.	Women Servts Paps.
[f.241] Ballynakill	Glynisk³	sr.Ulick Burk⁴ pa	Bart. a Minor								
		Cicely Burk widow pa	Lady		3		2		4		6
	Ballinavohir	Laughlin Kane w. pa	Labr.		2						
		Willm. Fineren w. pa	Miler		3						
		Patt. Fineran pa	Miller								
		Thos. Connell w. pa	Labr.		3						
		Roger Conneely pa	Labr.				2				
		Edmd. Connor w. pa	Labr.		3						
		Edmd. Kane w. pa	Labr.				2				
		Owen Kane w. pa	Labr.		2						
		Mic. Lenane w. pa	Labr.		1						
		Patt. Reily w. pa	Labr.		3						
		Thady Mee w. pa	Mert.		1		3				
		Edw. Morgan pa	Labr.								
		Willm. Shonry pa	Labr.				1				
		Roger Shonry w. pa	Labr.		1						
		Farrell Rush w. pa	Labr.				2				
		Thady Egan w. pa	Labr.		3						
		Darby Egan w. pa	Labr.		2						
		Jas. Mullen w. pa	Labr.		1						
		Eneas McDonnel pa	Tatcher								
		Thos. Bennett pa	Weaver				3				
		John Kelly w. pa	Cowherd		4						
		Patt. Waldron w. pa	Cowherd		4						
		Thos. Kelly pa	Labr.								
	Newtown	John Burke pro	Gent			2			2		2
		Michl. Keogh pa	Cowherd		2		3				
		Jas. Cooney w. pa	Labr.		2		1				
		John Kelly w. pa	Labr.		3						
		Connor Logan w. pa	Labr.		4						
	Cam[?]	Thos. Royn w. pa	Labr.		2		1				
County Roscomon	Corbally	Willm. Egan w. pa	Farmer		3				1		1
		Patt. Healy w. pa	Farmer		2		1				1
		Michl. Luog pa	Farmer		4				1		
		Jas. Mihan w. pa	Labr.		1				1		
		Thady Fallon pa	Labr.		3		3		1		1
		William Brogan pa	Labr.				2				
		Patt. Dunn w. pa	Agent		1		2				
	Emlaghglassan	Willm. Mulrennan pa	Labr.								
		Anthony Kelly pa	Labr.		1		3			1	
[f.242]	Ballynakill	Leamore Frans. Teige w. pa	Labr.		4				1		1
		Thos. Graly pa	Labr.		1		2				
		Darby Moran w. pa	Farmer		5		1		1		2
		Cormick Royn Carman					2				
	Emlaghglassan	Dens. McNamara w. pa	Cowherd		1		3				
		John Dunn w. pa	Labr.						1		
		Jas. Farrel pa	Labr.		1						

Com~ Galway Parish of	Place of Abode	Names and Religion	Proffession	Children under 14		Children above 14		Men Servts		Women Servts	
				Prot.	Paps.	Prot.	Paps.	Prot.	Paps.	Prot.	Paps.
	Leamore	Bryan Fox w. pa	Herd		3		1		1		1
		Edmd. Connor w. pa	Labr.		4		1		1		
Com Gallway	Issey[?]	Robt. Plunket w. pa	Farmer		3		1		2		2
		Robert Kennedy w. pa	Farmer		3						1
		Phil King w. pa	Labr.		2		1				
		John Connor w. pa	Herd		1				1		
		Will. Fether w. pa	Herd		1				1		
		Patt. McGlaghlin w. pa	Labr.		2						
		Will Lally w. pa	Broguemaker		3						
		Thos. Kane w. pa	Labr.		4						
	Ardagh	Red Carrol w. pa	Gent		3		2		3		4
		Mic. Killfoil w. pa	Labr.		1		2				1
		Cormick o'Hara w. pa	Labr.		1		2				
		John Killfoil jnr w. pa	Labr.		2		3		1		1
		Will Mee w. pa	Labr.		2		3				
		Jas. Grourk w. pa	Labr.		2		1				
		Luke Conniff Sen. w. pa	Labr.		2						
		David Kerry w. pa	Labr.		2						
		Jas. Kerry w. pa	Labr.		2						
		Bryan Mihan pa	Labr.		2		3				
	Lishnageeragh	Owen Keargen pa	Shepherd						1		1
		Mich. Blygh w. pa	Labr.		2		1				
		Rogr. Blygh w. pa	Labr.		4		2				
	Keelogues	Margarett Burk pa	Widow				5		3		3
		Walt. Burke pa	Farmer						2		2
		Connor Regan pa	Labr. .		1		4				
		Thady Egan w. pa	Labr.		2		1				
		Simon Flyn w. pa	Labr.		2						
		Jas Cahan w. pa	Labr.				2				
		John Mee pa	Labr.		1		3				
		Owen Mee pa	Labr.				4				
		Laurence Quin w. pa	Labr.		3		1				
		Owen Keerin pa	Labr.						1		1
		Farrel Daquin w. pa	Labr.		1		2				

[verso 242]
Parish of
Ballynakill contains 3 Protestants
635 Papists Men Women &
Children & Servants Included

[f.243] Ballynakill	Keelogues	Michael Igoe w. pa	Labr.		2						
		Peter Igoe w. pa	Labr.		3		1				
		Dan McCown w. pa	Labr.		2		2				
		Henry Royn w. pa	Labr.				3				
		Dan Royn pa	Labr.				3				
		Jas. Mulligan w. pa	Labr.		1		3				
		Jas. Morrine w. pa	Labr.		3		2				
		Patt. Muldoon w. pa	Labr.		1		3				
		Thady Cahan w. pa	Labr.		4		1				
		Bryan Cahan w. pa	Labr.		1		3				
		Will Cahan w. pa	Labr.		2		1				

Com~ Galway Parish of	Place of Abode	Names and Religion	Proffession	Children under 14		Children above 14		Men Servts		Women Servts	
				Prot.	Paps.	Prot.	Paps.	Prot.	Paps.	Prot.	Paps.
		Dan Saughlan pa	Labr.								1
		Thos. Dowd pa	Labr.				2		1		1
		Connor Tiernan w. pa	Labr.		1		3		1		1
		Cormick Tiernan pa	Labr.								
		Jas. Waldron pa	Labr.				2				
		Patt. Cahan w. pa	Labr.		4		3				
		Darby Cahan w. pa	Labr.		2		1				
		Patt. Crubane pa	Labr.		2		3				
Coun Gallway Parish of Dunamon	Carranaglough	John Cahan w. pa	Yeoman		1						1
		Henry Cahan w. pa	Yeoman		2						1
		Jas. Regan w. pa	Yeoman		2						
		Philip Regan pa	Yeoman				2				1
		Roger Regan w. pa	Yeoman		2				2		1
		Thos. Egan w. pa	Broguemaker				3				
		Denis Ward w. pa	Yeoman		3						1
		Connor Ward pa	Yeoman				1		1		1
		Bryan Hurly w. pa	Labourer		2		1				
		Hugh Ward w. pa	Labourer		3						
		Thos. Lennon w. pa	Labourer		3						
		Jas. Codengan w. pa	Labourer		2						
		Catherine Conry pa	Widow		1						
		Jas. Calliane w. pa	Labourer		1						
		Thady Culliane w. pa	Labourer		2						
		John Fetherston w. pa	Labourer		2						
		Edmd. Naughton w. pa	Labourer		1						
		Martin Naughton w. pa	Labourer		1						
		Thos. Heally w. pa	Labourer		4						
		Matthew Farrel w. pa	Labourer		2						
		Patt. Cullane w. pa	Labourer		4						

NOTES

1. Lewis, 'Ballynakill'.

2. John Holmes was collated vicar of Ballynakill and Ballysumaghan in 1729. He had been vicar of Boyle, 1701-16, and Kilmactranny from 1722.. He was either the John Holmes who entered TCD in 1732 and graduated BA 1736, or John Holmes, born Dublin and son of Thomas, *generosus* who was taught by Dr McMullen and entered TCD in 1739 (Leslie, 'Elphin', pp. 104, 108).

3. Glynisk (Glinsk) was a place of refuge for Roman Catholic bishops of Elphin in the eighteenth century (Fenning, 'Diocese of Elphin', p.166; Beirne, (ed.), *Diocese of Elphin*, p.116).

4. Ulick Burke was son of Sir Henry Burke of Glinsk. Burke's *Peerage* says that he succeeded his father in 1756. In view of the entry here one must assume that in their terms 'succeed' meant at the age of 21. It is therefore probable that Cicely Burk below was his mother. Ulick Burke married Elizabeth O'Carroll of Ardagh, County Galway. He was a lay supporter of the Rev William O'Kelly, prior of St. Mary's Roscommon in 1748 to succeed Patrick French as bishop of Elphin (Burke, *Peerage of the British Empire* (London 1860), 'Burke of Glinsk'; Fenning, 'Diocese of Elphin', p.166).

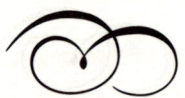

DUNAMON, COUNTY GALWAY

INTRODUCTION: *The parish of Dunamon is 4 miles from Roscommon, on the river Suck betwen Castlerea and Athleague in the barony of Ballymoe. The parish covers 4,655 statute acres including 37 acres of the river Suck and 82 acres of other water.[1] There were quarries, used for building stone.[2]*

It is unclear whether there was a church in the parish. Lewis refers to the church in Oran, the next parish, having been blown down and that the Caulfield family chapel was used by the Dunamon parishioners, but this may have been later in the century.

The parish of Dunamon was held with that of Athleague, Fuerty, Kilcroan, and Kilbegnet from 1666. The incumbent in 1749 was the Rev. John Hickes who was vicar from 1741 (see Fuerty). The patron was the bishop.

OCCUPATIONS

Attorney General	1	Miller	1	Smith	1
Cowherd	1	Park keeper	1	Tinker	1
Farmer	1	Plasterer	1	Weaver	3
Gardener	1	Servants Household	25	Wheelwright	1
Herd	2	Shepherd	1	Yeoman	6
Labourer	29	Shoemaker	1		

Com~ Galway Parish of	Place of Abode	Names and Religion	Proffession	Children under 14		Children above 14		Men Servts		Women Servts	
				Prot.	Paps.	Prot.	Paps.	Prot.	Paps.	Prot.	Paps.
[f.244] Dunnamon	Carranaglough	Jas. Ward w. pa	Labr.								2
		Walter Coorely w. pa	Labr.		3						
		Eleanor Naughton pa	Widow				2				
		Bryan Connor pa	Labr.								1
	Shanvalladin	Edm. Grady w pro	Weaver		6						
		John Cahan w. pa	Labr.		2						
		Andrew Feelan w. pa	Labr.		3						
		Stephen Crean w. pa	Labr.		3		1				1
		John Cloon w. pa	Labr.		1						
	Carrowkeel	Will Corly w. pa	Yeoman		1		3				
		Patt. Curley w. pa	Yeoman		5						
		Patt. Gallagher w. pa	Yeoman		2				1		
		Thos. Royn w. pa	Yeoman		2		2				
		Denis Mee w. pa	Yeoman		2		3				
		John Read w. pa	Wheelwright						1		
		John Brennan w. pa	Labr.		2				1		
		Thos. Grady pa	Weaver						1		1
		John Kenny w. pa	Labr.		3						
		John McGann w. pa	Labr.		4		2				
		Patt. McGann pa w. pro	Yeoman		5						
	Corneveigh	Thady Me w. pa	Herd		3				1		1
		Andrew Donnelly w. pa	Gardiner				1				
		Mary Head pa	Widow				2				
		Thos. Hurly w. pa	Labr.		3						
		Bartm. Gawran w. pa	Labr.		1		2				
		John Donnelly w. pa	Labr.				2				
		Dunamon Robert Killy w. pro	park keeper	1					1		1
		Hugh Teige w. pa	Farmer		2		3		2		1
		Hugh Royn w. pa	Labr.		1						
		John Connelly w. pa	Cowherd		2						
Coun. Roscommon	Dunnamon	St.George Caulfield[3] pro	Att Gen					4		4	
		John. Stuart w. pro	Shoemaker	5							
		Will Smith pro	Tinker	2							
		Peter Traynor w. pro	Plaisterer	4							
		Matthew Mahon w. pa	Smith		1		4				
		Will Lavin w. pa	Labr.		2						
	Cargeens	Edm. Cadangan w. pa	Labr.		4						
		Cormick Murray w. pa	Labr.				4				
		John Knavin w. pa	Labr.		2		3				
		Michl. Dowd w. pa	Weaver		4		2				
		John Finane w. pa	Labr.		1		1				

[verso f. 244]
Parish of
Dunnamon
Contains 28 Protestants 358 Papists
　　　Men, Women & Children and
　　　Servants Included
　　　Total of Protestants in the foregoing five Parishes 88
　　　Total of Papists in Said ~~Said~~ five Parishes 2705

Com~ Galway Parish of	Place of Abode	Names and Religion	Proffession	Children under 14 Prot.	Children under 14 Paps.	Children above 14 Prot.	Children above 14 Paps.	Men Servts Prot.	Men Servts Paps.	Women Servts Prot.	Women Servts Paps.
[f.245] Dunnamon	Cargeens	Richard Tracy w. pa	Miller		3		2		1		1
		Morgan Condellan pa	Labr.		2						
	Ballynapheren	Thos. Hort w. pa	Labr.		3		2				
		Owen Hort w. pa	Labr.		2		1				
		John Connor w. pa	Labr.		3						
		Peter Mulry w. pa	Labr.		1		1				
		Laurence Fane w. pa	Labr.		2		1				
		Teige Loogh pa	Labr.				4				
		Owen Loogh w. pa	Labr.		3						
		Luke Jones w. pa	Shepherd		4						
		Dom Clery pa	Labr.		2						
	Emlaghroin	Hugh McRourk pa	Labr.		3		1				
		Patt. Keatoo w. pa	Herd		3		2				
		Widow Teige pa					4				

[12 pages blank]

NOTES

1. *General Alphabetical Index.*

2. Lewis, 'Dunamon'.

3. St George Caulfeild was the fourth son of Mr Justice Caulfeild and Lettice, a daughter of Sir Arthur Gore of Newtown, Co. Mayo. The Caulfeild family had been in Dunamon for at least three generations. Caulfeild was called to the Middle Temple in 1716 to the King's Inns 1723. He was appointed counsel to the Revenue Board in 1734, solicitor general in 1739, attorney general in 1741 and chief justice of the Kings Bench in 1751. He had houses in Dublin in Bride Street and Aungier Street. He became MP for Tulsk in 1727 until 1760, when he resigned possibly because he had been attacked by a mob in Dublin the previous year. He was also assaulted by a former bailiff in Dunamon in 1770 (F. Elrington Ball, *The Judges in Ireland* (2 vols, London, 1926), ii, 193-4, 208-9).

[opposite f.246]

Abstract of the Number of Souls in

the Union of Kilkevin otherwise Castleregh

	Protestants
In Kilkevin	251
Baslick	18
Balintobber	69
Total of Prots.	338

	Papists
in Kilkevin	2114
Baslick	1500
Balintobber	869
Total of Papts	4483

KILKEEVAN, COUNTY ROSCOMMON

INTRODUCTION: *The parish of Kilkeevan is 13 miles north-west of Roscommon. Lewis said that some of the land was of good quality, though much was bog. There was very good limestone. There is a measure of coal deposited in a strip running north east of Castlerea which would account for the large number of welders in Kilkeevin and adjoining parishes of Baslick and Ballintober. Beaufort visited the area in 1787 and described the colliery, and its relation with an ironworks in the locality. He said that preparations had been made to work the iron, but it had not begun yet.[1] There was another pocket of welders in the parish of Termonbarry in the east where there is a further deposit of coal bordering the river Shannon and facing the main Irish coalfield of Arigna in County Leitrim across the river.[2]*

The major town, Castlerea, was a post town which had fairs four times a year, originally granted to Matthew Simpson and Henry Sandford in 1701. It also had a regular Saturday market.[3] Castlerea was said to have particularly good spring water, and had a brewery and a distillery.

The O'Conor family owned eleven townlands in the parish in 1641.[4] In 1749 eleven members of the family remained. The O'Conor Don moved from Belanagare to Clonalis in the early nineteenth-century.[5]

The incumbent was the Rev. Nathaniel Barton (c.1710-1771) who was prebendary of Ballintobber. The patron was the bishop. The rectory was impropriate in the Earl of Essex.

OCCUPATIONS

Ale draper	5	Flax dresser	1	Postboy	1
Apothecary	1	Forgeman	1	Priest	1
Beggar	2	Fowler	1	Reed maker	1
Blacksmith	5	Gauger	1	Saddler	1
Breeches maker	1	Gentleman	2	Sawyer	1
Broguemaker	4	Glover	4	Servants, household	338
Butcher	6	Hatter	3	Shepherd	3
Cadger	4	Henwife	1	Shoemaker	3
Carman	1	Herd	27	Skinner	1
Carpenter	3	Horse rider	1	Slater	1
Chandler	1	Labourer	64	Smith	3
Clerk	1	Land Sergeant	1	Spinster	11
Clothier	1	Maid	1	Stranger	1
Cobbler	1	Mantua maker	1	Subagr.[?]	1
Constable	1	Mason	5	Tailor	6
Cooper	3	Maltster	1	Tanner	1
Cottier	109	Merchant	7	Tobacco spinner	1
Dealer	9	Miller	2	Turner	2
Distiller	1	Minister (CofI)	1	Weaver	26
Esquire	1	Peruke maker	3	Welder	114
Farmer	12	Poor man	1	Yarn buyer	1
				Yarn jobber	1

Com~Ros common Parish of	Place of Abode	Names and Religion	Proffession	Children under 14		Children above 14		Men Servts		Women Servts	
				Prot.	Paps.	Prot.	Paps.	Prot.	Paps.	Prot.	Paps.
[f.246] Killkeevin	Knockro als Castlereagh	Edmd									
		Sarah Gallagher Pas	Labr.				1				
		Mary Bluett Pas	Widdow	1			1				
		Theobald Bluett Pas	Labr. Wm.								
		Elizabth Cooney Pas	Weaver	1			1		1		
		Ellinr. Long Pa	Widdow								
		Willm. Makins Pro	Carpenter	3							2
		John									
		Bridgett Mulry Pas	Brogemaker	3			1				
		Mary Kearny Pa	Widdow	2							
		Barthw.									
		Bridget Callaghan Pas	Yarn jober	1			2				
		Cormk. Callagher Pa	Labr.								
		Margrett Danugher									
		Catharin Kelly Pas	Widdows	3							
		James									
		Anne Caughlen Pas	Tanner[6]	1					1		
		Michl.									
		Giles Carroll Pas	Ale Draper	1							1
		Edwd									
		Margaret Murphy Pas	Labr.	1			2				
		Luke									
		Bridgett Carroll Pas	Labr.	2							
		Hugh									
		Jane Clark Pro:	Weaver	1				1	1		
		Jane Lord Pro	Widdow								
		Magnus									
		Judith Drury Pa	Labr.	+[?]			1				
		Loughlen									
		Anne Flanery Pas	Smith	2			2				
		Jno									
		Mary Kearny Pas	Labr.				1				
		Terence									
		Cathrin Carroll Pas	Mazon	1							
		Henry									
		Dorothy Reynolds Pas	Labr.				2				1
Prots 3		Owen									
		Catharin McDonogh Pa	Labr.								
6		Rogr									
		Mary McDonogh Pas	Labr.	1							
5		Thos.									
		Catharin McDonogh Pas	Labr.	2							
13		Honora Murphy	Widdow	2							
27		Hugh									
		Eliz. Teige Pas	Labr.	5							
_____		Mary Burke Pas	Widdow								
		Robert	Peruke Maker								
		Margaret Stephens Pas		+[?]				1			
Pasts 9		Bryan									
		Mary Bryan Pas	Taylor	1							
6		Ellinor Carroll Pa	Widdow				1				
17		Oliver									
		Bridgett Lord Protest	Labr.								
35		Ellinor Fowler Pro Widdow				1					
55		James									
		Elizabeth Lynch Pa	Distiller				1		1		1
_____		Jane Abott Protest.	Widdow	2	1						
120		Patrick									
_____		Catharin Walsh Pa	Weaver	1			1				
		Patt. Morron Pas	Black Smith						1		

Com~Ros common Parish of	Place of Abode	Names and Religion	Proffession	Children under 14		Children above 14		Men Servts		Women Servts	
				Prot.	Paps.	Prot.	Paps.	Prot.	Paps.	Prot.	Paps.
		William Jane Dinson Protes	Shoemaker	3	3				1			1
		Ephram Jane & Isabell Grinly Prot	Weaver			1					
		Peter Mary Kearney Pa	Smith	2						1		1
[f.247] Killkeevin	Knockro als Castlereagh	Edwd Ellinor Killkeney Pas	Weaver		2		1				
		Mary Hinds Pa	Widdow								
		Jams. Catharin Reynolds Pas	Dealer								
		Anne Reynolds Pas	Widdow				1				
		Mary Eccles Pas	Widdow								
		Owen Catharin Finane Pas	Hatter				2		2		
		Conn Sarah O'Harra Pas	Taner		1		1				
		Henry West Prot	Chandler								1
		Danl. Catharin Kenedy Pas	Butcher		2		2				
		Mary Carty Pa	Widdow		3						
		Jno Rosamunda Laurence Pas	Labr.				2				
		Honora Irwin Pa	ale drapr.		1		3				1
		Thos. Anne Dillon Pas	Labr.		1						
		Martn. Catharin Jourdon Pas	Labr.		1						
		Barthw. Sarah McDonell Pas	Cadger								
		Thady Margaret Flyn Pas	Mercht.		1		2		2		2
		Frans. Elizabth. Conally Pas	Mazon		4				1		
		Loughlen Mable Keely Pas	Cooper		5		1				
		Nichs. Mary Cowen Pro:	Britches maker	2	2				1		1
		Susana Killernagh Pas	Widdow	1		1	1				
		Joanna Williams Pro	Widdow								
		Honora May Pas	Mantua maker	1							
		Gregory Ferrall Pa Catharin Protest.	Ale draper				1				
		John Minshal Prot	Shoe maker								
		Judith McKeone	Widdow		3		2				
		Terce. Magrath Pro Mary Pas	Ale draper		2				1		1
		Arthr. Brooke Pro	a poor man			2	2				
		Martn. Anne Flangan Pro	Dealer	4		1	1		2	1	1
		Alexr. Mcdonell Pas	Mercht.		2		1				
		Mathw. Jane Ferrall Pro:	Dealer	2							
		Michl. Anne Simson Pas	Labr.		1						
		Anne Simson Pas	Widdow				1				
		Michl. Honora Kelly Pas	Parish clerk	1							
		Chr.r Fitzgerald Bridgett Pas	Labr.		1		1				

Com~Ros common Parish of	Place of Abode	Names and Religion	Proffession	Children under 14		Children above 14		Men Servts		Women Servts	
				Prot.	Paps.	Prot.	Paps.	Prot.	Paps.	Prot.	Paps.
[f.248] Kilkeevin	Knockro als Castlereagh	Thos. Cathrine Minshal Pro:	Constable	4		1					
		Bridgett Mary Rorke Pas	Spinsters		1						
		Dennis Flanagan Pas	Labr.								
		Catharine Flanagan Pa	Widdw.		1						
		Anne Clark Pro	Widdow			1					
		Honora Flanagan Pa	Widow				2				
		Dens. Margrett Hanly Pas	Glover		3						
		Thady Honora Hanly Pas	Ale drapr.		1						
		Robert Hanly Pa	Glover		-						
		Bryan Jane Conway Pas	Weaver		1				5		
		Jno. Copely Protes	Weaver								
		Richd. Copely Pro	Clothier								
		Bryan Sweeny Pa	Weavr.								
		Sarah Sweeny Pa									
		Michl. Honora Kelly Pas	Glover		2		2				
		James Kennedy Pat									
		Michl. Margaret Phelan Pas	Weaver		1		1				
		Pattk. Sarah Connor Pas	Labr.				4				2
		Jane Brenon Jane Ditto Pas	Widdow		3						
		Mary Connor Pas	Spinster		4						
		Michl. Elizth Silk Pas	Miller[7]						3		1
		Bryan Anne Dermott Pas	Herd		3				1		
		Bryan Ellinor Druch Pas	Labr.				1				
		Hugh Mary Flanagan Pas	Saweyer		2						
		Mary Corkran Pas	Widdow		3		1	1			
		Michl. Honora Culla Pas	Labr.				1				
		Margaret Cassy Pas	Widdow				1				
		Mary Culla Sarah Ruddy Pas	Spinsters								
		Thoms Catharin Lovelace Pas	Labr.		1						
		Catharin Mary Judge Pas	Spinsters		1						
		Bridget Seery Honora Seery Pas	Spinsters		1		1				
		Jeromiah Boyle Pa	Stranger								
		James Mary Giblane Pas	Malster		3		5				
		Mary McDonell Pa	Widdow				3				
		Catharin Colgan	Widdow				1				
		Patk. Margaret Fallon Pas	Labr.		2		1				
		Loughline Catharin Binns Pas	Labr.		3		2				
		Alice Bryode Pa	Widdow								
		Hugh Mary Connor Pas	Labr.		4						

Com~Roscommon Parish of	Place of Abode	Names and Religion	Proffession	Children under 14		Children above 14		Men Servts		Women Servts	
				Prot.	Paps.	Prot.	Paps.	Prot.	Paps.	Prot.	Paps.
		Danl. Cecilia Doyle Pas	Beggars								
		Ellinr. Bluett Pa	Widdow								
		John Anne Kenedy Pas	Weaver		2				2		1
		Jno Mary Guinn Pro	Weavr.	3							1
		Patk. Mary Kelly Pas	Skiner								
		Matthew Alice Hanly Pas	Weaver								
[f.249] Killkeevin	Knockroe als Castlerea	Owen Margaret Sharkey Pas	Cadger		1						1
		Thos. Susanna McManion Protes	Weavr.	2				1			
		Laur. Catharin Gubilane Pas	Labr.		2						1
		James Mary Connor Pas	Butcher		2		1				1
		Roger Margrett Kane Pas	Taylor		2		2	1	1		1
		Denis Honnor Connor Pas	Cobler								
		Edmd. Dillon Pa	Mercht.								
		Wm. Jane Harra Pas	Weaver		2				1		1
		Thos. Honora Mylan Pas	Cadger		3						1
		Patk. Kelly Pro	Glover								
		Winifrida Clark Pa	Widdow				2				
		Elizabth. Maxwell Pa	Widdow				2				
		Sarah Flaherty Pa	Widdow								
		David Burke Pa Anne Protest	Carpenr.	3		1					
		John Elizbth Finn Pas	Hatter		1						
		Rosamund Dowell Pa	Widdow		1		2				
		Edwd Margrett Makins Prots	Turner	4				2	1		
		Danl. Bridgett Flaharty Pas	Mercht.						1		1
		Redmd. Mary Donagher Pas	Taylor		2						
		Mary Stuart Prot:	Widdow								
		John Teige Pa Catharin Prot.	Peruke maker	4						1	1
		Owen Margaret Ganon Pas	Slater		2						
		Jane Thomson Pro	Widdow								
Pro.		Thos. Violetta Mears Prots	Weaver	1		4		1	3		
1		Richd. Cecilia Flyn Pas	Hatter		1		1		1		
5		Patk. Margarett Naughton Pas	Butcher								
5		Sarah Dillon Pa	Widdow				1				
		Hugh Connor Pa Anne Pro	Butcher		2						

Com~Ros common Parish of	Place of Abode	Names and Religion	Proffession	Children under 14		Children above 14		Men Servts		Women Servts	
				Prot.	Paps.	Prot.	Paps.	Prot.	Paps.	Prot.	Paps.
14		Wm. Margaret Kavanagh Pas	Mazon		1						
12		Mary McDonogh Pa	Widdow								
___		Robt.Dean Pro Elizabeth Dean Pa	Reed maker								
37		Edmd Mary Costello Pas	Labr.		1						
		Man. Sarah Gublan Pas	Labr.		1						
		Catharin Walch Pa	Widdow								
Paps 8		Margaret Costello Pa	Maid								
8		Thos. Mary Farry Pas	Weaver		2						
28		Terence Margrett Sweeny Pas	Peruke maker		1						
53		James Honora Dower Pas	Labr.								
		Bridgt. Dower Pa	Widdow								
___		Jams. Catharin Gormon Pas	Labr.		1						
___		Frans. Comins Pro	Dealer								
[f.250] Killkeevin	Knockro als Castlerea	John Murphy Pro	Butcher	1	4		4		1		1
		James Ellinor Magrath Protets	Mercht.				2		1		3
		Hugh Magrath Pro	Dealer								
		Roger Hanmore Pa Mary Protestant	Mercht.		1		1		1		1
		Owen Olivia Young Pro:	Gent	3				2	2	1	3
		Bridgett Young Pro	Widdow		1						
		Hugh Alice Mullin Pas	Cotter		2		1				
		Frans. Dorothy Kelly Prott	Mercht.			1			1		1
		John Bridgett Ferrall Pas	Labr.		1						
		Catharine Morriss Pa	Widdow		1	1					
		Hugh Smith Pas Elizabeth Prot	Sadler	1		5					3
		Nichs. Mary Walker Protest	Apothecary	5		1			1		1
		Thos. Rosamunda White Pro:	Shoemaker			1		1	1		1
		Hugh Judith Satchell Pro	Carpenter	1		2					1
		George Anne Haggerty[8] Pro	Gaugr.	2		0	1				2
		Robert Sandford[9] Pro	Esqr.			2		9		4	3
		Nath. Bridget Barton[10] Pro	Minister	2					3		3
	Ardass	Thomas Satchell Pro:	Welder						1		1
		Ralph Anne Satchell[11] Pro:	Welder	1		1			1		1
		Ralph Elizabth. Satchell Pro	Welder	1							1
		Wm. Mary Rock Pas	Labr.		1		3				
		Cormk. Bridgett Lavin Pas	Herd		1		2				
Prots 5	Tarmonmore	Conner Bryan Pa	Welder				2				1

Com~Ros common Parish of	Place of Abode	Names and Religion	Proffession	Children under 14		Children above 14		Men Servts		Women Servts	
				Prot.	Paps.	Prot.	Paps.	Prot.	Paps.	Prot.	Paps.
12		Patk. Catharine Bryan Pas	Welder		1						
14		Richard Sarah Mulvy Pas	Cooper				3				
17		Roger Mary Kelly Pas	Labr.				2				
27		Thos. Bridgett Dillon Pas	Farmer		2				2		3
———		Gerald Ellinor Dillon Pas	Herd				2		1		
75		Wm. Winifrida Daviss Pas	Labr.				2				
		Richd. Cecila Train Pas	Welder		1		1				
Paps 36		Rogr. Catharine Train Pas	Welder		2		1				
18		Bryan Ellinor Bryode Pas	Mazon				2				
32		Bryan Eliz. Flanagan Pas	Weaver		1				1		
		Robert Fitzgerald Mary Pas	Welder								1
124		Edmd. Ellinor Concanon Pas	Welder		2		1				
46		Hugh Mary Kelly Pas	Labr.		2						1
———		Patk. Giles Hevighan Pas	Welder		1						1
150		Patt. Winifrida Waldron Pas	Labr.		1						
	Knockmurray	James Mary Connor Pas	Mason		2		1		1		
		James Anne Morris Pas	Welder		2		1				
[f.251] Killkeevin	Knockmurray	John Ellinr. Conry Pas	Welder				1		1		1
	Cloonree	John Elizabeth Conry Pas	Welder		2						
		Richd. Eliz. Parks[12] Pro	Farmer	3		1			1		1
		Domk. Ellinor Kane Pas	Welder		5		1				3
		Danl. Honora Black Pas	Cotter		2		5				
		Thos. Winifrida Gormon Pas	Cotter		2		1				
		Domk. Gormon Pas	Herd				1				1
		Mich. Mary Kinin Pas	Cotter		1		2				
		Darby Honora Grivy Pas	Cotter				2				
		Michl. Anne Dermott Pas	Cotter		1		1				
		James Sarah Bevin Pas	Cotter				1			1	
		John Brenon Pro Bridgett Pas	Weaver				2				
	Taughill	Domk. Sarah Flyn Pas	Cotter		2		2				
		John Mary Flyn Pas	Cotter		1						

Com~Ros common Parish of	Place of Abode	Names and Religion	Proffession	Children under 14 Prot.	Paps.	Children above 14 Prot.	Paps.	Men Servts Prot.	Paps.	Women Servts Prot.	Paps.
		Darby Mary Beirn Pas	Cotter		3		1				
	Cloonlative	Darby Mary Finane Pas	Turner		1						
		Jane Kelly Pa	Widdow						1		1
	Trien13	David Catharin Gownan Pas	Cotter		1						1
		Edmd. Hevighan Pa	Cotter								1
		John Jane Killroy Pas	Cotter		1		1				
		Thady Bridgett Gowna Pas	Cotter				1				1
Prots 1											
3		James Mary Killkeney Pas	Cotter		1		1				
4		Thomas Rosamunda Codikin Pas	Cotter				1				
		Rogr Mary Dinigan Pas	Cotter		1						1
_____		Thos. Bridgett Kane Pas	Cotter		1		1				
8		Roger Catharin Flyn Pas	Cotter		1		2				
_____	Cregamean	Terce Elizabth Connor Pas	Herd		1		2				
		Denis Catharin McDonogh Pas	Cotter		3						1
		Hugh Bridgett Gavy Pas	Cotter		1						
		David Bridgett Gownan Pas	Weaver								
Papts 15	Anughvaghery	Wm. Mary Gready Pas	Welder		2		1				
3		Wm. Catharin Malley Pas	Welder		1						
42		Darby Catharin Mally Pas	Welder		1		1				
43		James Rosamunda Gownan Pas	Welder		1		2				
73		Richd. Catharin Gownan Pas	Cotter		1		-				
_____		John Catharin Ferrall Pas	Weldr.		2		3				
176		Patk. Catharin Ferrall Pas	Welder		1		1				
	Anughgila	Jno. Catharin Gready Pas	Herd				2				
	Cloonerafield	Richd. Mary Gibbons Pas	Herd		1						1
	Brenabegg	Wm. Giles Broader Pas	Herd		2		3				
[f.252] Kilkeevan	Mungagh14	Michl. Bridgett Blee Pas	Welder		3						1
		Domk. Bridget Rogers Pas	Welder		2				1		1
		Margtt Blee Pas	Widdow				1		1		
		Thoms. Margaret Rogers Pas	Welder		2						
		Conr. Bridgett Flanery Pas Domk.	Weaver								

Com~Ros common Parish of	Place of Abode	Names and Religion	Proffession	Children under 14		Children above 14		Men Servts		Women Servts	
				Prot.	Paps.	Prot.	Paps.	Prot.	Paps.	Prot.	Paps.
	Beagh	Mary Mulany Pas John	Labr.		1						
		Elinor Flyn Pas Danl.	Welder		1		1				1
		Honora Gill Pas Thos.	Welder				2				
		Bridgett Gill Pas Dav.	Welder		1						
		Bridget Bryode Pas Connor	Welder		1						
		Catharine Morriss Pas John	Weaver		1				1		
	Emlagh15	Margret Flyn Pas Conr.	Welder								
		Mary Flanagan Pas Willm.	Welder						1		
		Catharine Quin Pas	Welder				2				1
		Bridgtt Royen Pa Danl.	Widdow				1		1		
		Cecila Gownan Pas Danl.	Welder				2				
		Mary Morriss Pas Darby	Welder		1		1				
		Cecila Connor Pas Danl.	Welder				2				
		Mary Morriss Pas Darby	Welder		1		1				
		Mary Connor Pas Augustine	Labr.								
		Bridgett Morriss Pas Phill.	Labr.								
	Lisboy	Mary Cahill Pas Luke	Weldr.		2						
		Catharine Keaveny Pas Thos.	Welder		1				1		1
		Catherine Egan Pas Michl.	Welder		3				1		
		Catharine Croghon Pas Owen	Welder						1		1
		Bridgett Hester Pas Owen	Welder		2						1
		Catherine Igen Pas Owen	Welder								
		Giles Hester Pas	Cotter		1						
	Cashill	John Mulvihil	Labr.		1						
		John Mcdonogh Cecila his mother Pas Edmd.	Farmr.						2		1
		Bridgett Formo Pas John	Cotter		2						
		Cecila Killbride Pas Wm.	Cotter		1		1				
Paps. 11		Honora Killbride Pas Edmd.	Cotter		1						
11		Margaret Grorke Pas	Cotter				2				1
19		Thady Forma Pa Owen	Welder								
40	Arm	Ellinr. McDonnell Pas Waltr.	Welder		2		1				
76		Honora McDonell Pa Own.	Welder		2						
___		Mary Mcdonell Pas			2						
157											

Com~Ros common Parish of	Place of Abode	Names and Religion	Proffession	Children under 14 Prot.	Children under 14 Paps.	Children above 14 Prot.	Children above 14 Paps.	Men Servts Prot.	Men Servts Paps.	Women Servts Prot.	Women Servts Paps.
	Rathledge	John									
_____		Elinor McDermott Pas	Herd		1		2		1		
		James									
		Rosamunda Beirn Pas	Labr.		2						1
_____		Bryan									
		Mary Mara Pas	Labr.		2						1
		John									
[f.253]		Mary Hartt Pas	Labr.		2		3				
Killkevin											
	[10 lines erased]										
Ditto	Cloonda-harabegg	James									
		Bridgett Beirn Pas	Herd	~~2~~	2				1		1
		Wm.									
		Mary Kane Pas	Cotters		1		2				
		Pattk.									
		Anne Quin Pas	Cotter		1						
		Patk.									
		Margaret Johnens Pas	Cotter				2				1
		David									
		Anne Keavy Pas	Welder		2				1		
		Frans.									
		Mary Jurdon Pas	Brogemaker				1		1		
	Cloonda-haramore	Ens.									
		Winifrida Smith Pas	Herd		1						
		Wm.									
		Mary Kyne Pas	Cotter		2		1				
		John									
		Catharine Glyn Pas	Welder		1		3				1
		John									
		Bridgett Kine Pas	Welder		1		2				
		Thos.									
		Mary Sharkey Pas	Cotter		2		1				
		Murt.									
		Mary Flanery Pas	Welder				1				
		Thos.									
		Judith Morriss Pas	Welder		2				1		1
		Wm. Gunan Pa	Welder		1						1
	Clooncouse	Eliz. Blee Pas	Widdow				4		1		
		Domk. Mulrenin[16] Pa	Paris priest								
		Mary Sarah Blee Pas	Welder				1		1	0	1
		Darby									
		Mary Blee Pas	Welder		5		1				1
		Patk.									
Pas 15		Catharine Blee Pas	Welder		3						1
	Caugher	Michl.									
12		Mary Flyn Pas	Farmer		2				2		2
		John									
34		Margaret Kearny Pas	Cotter		2		1				
		Michl.									
40		Jane Bryan Pas	Cotter		3						1
		Danl.									
56		Giles Bryan Pas	Cotter		1						
		Edmd.									
	Cloontrask	Catharine Finane Pas	Cotter				1				
_____		Danl.									
157		Bridget McConaly Pas	Welder		3		2				
		James									
		Jane Cassey Pas	Cotter		1		1				

Com~Ros common Parish of	Place of Abode	Names and Religion	Proffession	Children under 14		Children above 14		Men Servts		Women Servts	
				Prot.	Paps.	Prot.	Paps.	Prot.	Paps.	Prot.	Paps.
	Cregisten	John Catharine Kyne Pas	Cotter				2				
		Jams Mary Fahy Pas	Smith		4				1		1
		Sarah Blee Pas	Widdow				5				
		Wm. Judith Egan Pas	Cotter				3				
[f.254] Killkevin	Drimdulan	Roger Ellinor Flyn Pas	Farmer		2				2		1
		Thos. Giles Lynch Pas	Cotter		4		1				
		Wm. Elinor Tully Pas	Cotter		2						
	Cloonselliff	Maths. Elinor Cornwal Prots	Weaver	3	3̶				1		
		Patrick Pa Jane Kelly Protes	Taylor		1						
		John Pro Elinor Maculroy Pas	Welder	3	3̶						
		Adam Catharine Maculroy Protest.	Forgeman								
		James Kane Pas	Welder								
		Mary Royen Pas	Widdow								
		Martin Cecilia Kearny Pas	Welder		3						
		Barthw. Catharin Culla Pas	Welder		1						
		Bridget Keane Pa:	Widdow				1				
		Catharin Egan Pas	Widdow				2				
	Cloonkeen[17]	Roger Rosamunda McNeal Pas	Labr.		1						
		Patrick Hanna Coffy Pas	Welder		3						1
		Patk. Elinor Page Pas	Welder		1		1		1		
		Cormk. Elinor McDermot Pas	Welder		2		1		1		
		James Kyne Pa	Labr.		1		1				
		Winifred Manion Pa	Widdow		2		2				
		John Honora Carroll Pas	Welder		1		1				
		Loughlin Honora Carroll Pas	Welder		2		1		1		
		Bridget Flanagan Pa	Widdow		1		1				
Pros 6		Roger Margaret Smith Pas	Welder		1		2				
6		Thos. Bridget Burke Pas	Welder		1						
___		Thos. Honora Manion Pas	Welder		2						
12		Patt. Sarah Kearny Pas	Labr.		2		1				
Paps 6		Thos. Mary Carroll Pas	Welder		1						
6		Bryan Margaret Flyn Pas	Labr.		1		1				
6		Terce Cecilia Flyn Pas	Welder				3				1
22		Charles Carroll Pa	Labr.								
48		Terce Bridgett Sweeny Pas	Welder		2						1

Com~Ros common Parish of	Place of Abode	Names and Religion	Proffession	Children under 14		Children above 14		Men Servts		Women Servts	
				Prot.	Paps.	Prot.	Paps.	Prot.	Paps.	Prot.	Paps.
62		Mary McDermot Pa Myles	Widdow		1		2				
———		Mary McSwine Pas	Labr.		2						
144		Catherine McSwine Pa	Widdow		2						
———		Farrell McLaughlen Pas Frans.	Welder								1
		Honora Caughlen Pas	Welder		2						
		Loughn. Caughlan Pa James	Taylor		1						1
		Mary Killbride Pas James	Labr.		1						
		Mary Crogan Pas Peter	Labr.		1		1				
		Honor Croghon Pas	Labr.		1						
[f.255] Killkeeven	Drimlogh	Thady									
		Anne Carty Pas James	Herd		2		2				1
		Sarah Rush Pas Frans.	Cotter		1		3				
		Mary Rush Pas	Cotter		1						1
	Cregalahan	Mary Kinnay Pa Edmd.	Widdow				1		1		
		Bridgt. Flanagan Pas Terce.	Cotter		2						
		Mary Flanagan Pas Patk.	Cotter		1						1
		Honora Gorman Pas Bryn.	Cotter		2		2				
		Winifrida Carroll Pas Morgan	Miller		1		1				
		Honora Grorke Pas Jas	Cotter				2				
		Ellinor Augustine Pas Jon.	Dealer		1						
		Catharine Barrett Pas	Butcher				1		1		
	Cloonalis	Edmd. Flanagan Pas Cormk.	Postboy								
		Bridgett Dermott Pas Rogr.	Cotter		2						1
		Elinor Finane Pas Owen	Taylor		1		1				
		Winifrida Teige Pas Danl.	Cotter		1		2				
		Ellinor Connor Pas Patk.	Cotter								
		Bridgett Teige Pas Peter	Cotter		1						
		Bridgett Flanagan Pas Michl.	Cotter		1		2				
		Mary Cornwal Prot Danl.	Fowler	1	+					1	+
	Cloonaff	Margaret O'Connor[18] Pas Con.	Gent		3		3		2		4
		Honora Flanagan Pas Darby	Welder								1
		Sarah Finane Pas Jas.	Welder		1						
		Margaret Gready Pas	Welder		1		2				

Com~Roscommon Parish of	Place of Abode	Names and Religion	Proffession	Children under 14		Children above 14		Men Servts		Women Servts	
				Prot.	Paps.	Prot.	Paps.	Prot.	Paps.	Prot.	Paps.
Prots 1		Conr. Mary Croghon Pas	Welder		2		2				
		Anne Flanagan Pa	Widdow		2		2				
		Bryan Rosamund Concannon Pas	Welder		2		1				
2		Thos. Mary Finane Pas	Cotter		2		2				
4		John Catharine Stretch Pas	Welder		1						1
____		Lau: Catherine Kearney Pas	Welder		1		3				
7		Henry Stretch Prot Mary Pa	Welder	1	+	2	2̶		1		
		John Mary Killroy Pas	Welder		1		2				
Paps 12		John Dorothy Gregan Pas	Welder		1						1
6		John Greghan Pas	Cotter				1				
42	Longford	Richd. Hooke Pas Anne Prot	Herd		1		2		1		1
37		Roger Margaret Murry Pas	Shepard								
72		Morgan Mary Flyn Pas	Cotter				1				
____		Wm. Mary Murry Pas	Labr.		1		1				
169		Anthony Mary Connor Pas	Labr.		1						
		Jas. Cathrine Cox Pas	Blacksmith				2				
		Domk. Margaret Tuffy Pas	Labr.				1				
[f.256] Killkeevin	Longford	Thos. Mary Satchell Prots	Su cagt [?]			2			1		1
		Thos. Catharin Fagan Pas	Tobaco spiner		1				1		
		Domk Horo Mary Pas	Weaver		1		2				
		Cormk. Mary Beirne Pas	Labr.		1		1				
	Harristown	Denis Mary Grogan Pas	Herd		1		4				
		Patk. Bridgett Manion Pas	Labr.		1						
	Moore	John Kenin Pa Ellinor Pro:	Welder		1		2		1		1
		Thady Bridgt. Kinin Pas	Welder		1				1		1
		Richd. Cruse Pro: Bridget Pa	Flax Dresser	1		2					
		Owen Margaret McDermot Pas	Labr.		1		2				
		Dorothy Eccles Prot.	Widdow			2					
	Tarmonbegg	Laur. Mary Cotton Pro:	Farmer	4		2			1		2
		Loughlen Catharine Gara Pas	Labr.		1						
		Edwd Margaret Madden[19] Prot	Farmer	1					2		2
		Darby Elizabeth King Pas	Herd		1		1				

Com~Ros common Parish of	Place of Abode	Names and Religion	Proffession	Children under 14		Children above 14		Men Servts		Women Servts	
				Prot.	Paps.	Prot.	Paps.	Prot.	Paps.	Prot.	Paps.
		Terce.									
		Bridgett Kelly Pas	Labr.		1						
		Patrick									
		Dorothy Horro Pas	Weaver				2	1			
		James									
		Bridget Loughlen Pas	Welder		1		2				
		Hugh									
		Catharin Finane Pas	Welder		1		1				
		John Fahy Pa	Dealer								1
		Thos.									
		Bridget Kierlly Pas	Labr.		1		2				
		Thos.									
		Honora Gormon Pas	Labr.		2						
		Hugh									
		Catharin Reily Pas	Welder				2				
		James									
		Anne Kinney Pas	Labr.								
		Ellinr. Magrath Pa	Widdow				1				
	Clooncaugh	Margt. Blee Pa	Widdow		1		3	1			2
	Clooncran	Thos.									
		Margaret Flyn Pas	Farmer					1			1
		Roger									
		Honora Flyn Pas	Farmer		1						1
		John									
		Ellinor Cristle Pas	Horse Rider		2		1				
	Taughnuse	Hugh									
		Mary Gallagher Pas	Herd	+	1		3	1			
		Cormk.									
		Bridgett Flanagan Pas	Cotter		2						
	Clooncill	John									
		Mary Brenan20	Land Serjant	1		2			2		1
		Domk.									
		Bridget Flanagan Pas	Cotter				1		1		1
	Taughnara	John									
		Cecilia Flyn Pas	Herd		2		2		1		
		Thady Killfeder Pa	Cotter		1		3				1
		Dudly									
		Catherin Mulrenin Pas	Cotter		3				1		
	Cloontarnse	John									
		Honora Greeny Pas	Cotter		2		1		1		
	Killmore	James									
		Margaret Mulrenin Pas	Herd		2		1				1
[f.257] Kilkeevin	Carumore	Michl.									
		Mary Broader Pas	Herd		3		2		1		1
		Laur.									
		Catharin Keaveny Pas	Cotter		2						
		Jas.									
		Mary Finane Pas	Cotter		2		1				
		Pattk.									
		Margt. Lenon Pas	Cotter		1		1				
		Michl.									
		Catharine Blee Pas	Cotter		1						1
		Darby									
		Giles Blee Pas	Sheperd				1		1		
	Carukeel	Thos. Whitehead Pro:									
		Mary Pa	Welder				2		1		
		Frans.									
		Catharin Murry Pas	Cotter				2				
		Luke									
		Mary Hobbon Pas	Brogemaker		1		2				

Com~Roscommon Parish of	Place of Abode	Names and Religion	Proffession	Children under 14		Children above 14		Men Servts		Women Servts	
				Prot.	Paps.	Prot.	Paps.	Prot.	Paps.	Prot.	Paps.
	Ballindrimly21	Charles Ellinor Reynolds Pas	Weaver		1		2				
		John Mary Downs Pas									1
		James Quinn Pa	Cotter				3				1
		James Judith Doude Pas	Cotter				2				
		Patrick Mary Murry Pas	Cotter		1		1				
		Darby Bridgett Murry Pas	Cotter				2				
		Luke Anne Beirn Pas	Cotter		1						1
		James Mary Drury Pas	Cotter		1						
		Owen Catharin Drury Pas	Cotter		1		1				
		James Dollon Pa	Weavr.				3				
		John Jane Doghorty Pas	Cotter		2						
		Michl. Mary Morron Pas	Blacksmith		1		3				
		Henery Bridgett Grorke Pas	Cotter		2						
		Wm. Hanna Flinn Pas	Cotter		2		1				
		Willm. Rosamunda Helbert Pas	Cotter		2		2				
Prot 1		Michl. Catharin Kelly Pas	Cotter		1						
2		Wm. Mary Kelly Pas	Cotter				2				
2		Patk. Mary Kelly Pas	Cotter								
———		Bryan Jane Lavin Pas	Cotter		2						
5		Martin Anne Cassey Pas	Cotter		2						
		James Honora Kelly Pas	Cotter		2		1				
Pas 7		Edmd. Elizabeth Kyne Pas	Cotter		1		1				
3		Andw. Bridgett Drury Pas	Cotter		1						
41		Peter Anne Hanly Pas	Cotter				4				
42		Bryan Jane Dogherty Pas	Cotter		2						
74	Pt. Of Arm	James Walker Pro Anne Pa	Farmr.	2		1					2
		John Anne Cunally Pas	Cotter		2		1				
127		Luke Catharine Quinn Pas	Cotter		2		1				
		Mark Margaret Mooney Pas	Cotter		3						
		John Catharin Mooney Pas	Cotter								
[f.258] Killkeeven	Cloonforest	Thos. Margett Gallagher Pas	Herd		3		2		1		

Com~Ros common Parish of	Place of Abode	Names and Religion	Proffession	Children under 14		Children above 14		Men Servts		Women Servts	
				Prot.	Paps.	Prot.	Paps.	Prot.	Paps.	Prot.	Paps.
		James Gallagher Pa ⎫	Herd								
		Andw. Gallagher Pa ⎭	Herd								
		Danl.									
		Margaret Greeny Pas	Cotter	3		3			1		
		Bryan									
	Cloonican	Rosamunda Greeny Pas	Cotter	2		1					1
		John									
		Cecilia Burke Pas	Cotter	2					1		
		Patrick									
		Mary Burke Pas	Herd	1		1			1		
		Patrick									
		Cecilia Ternan Pas	Cooper	2		3					1
		Luke									
		Catharin Waldron Pas	Cotter	1		2			1		
		Laurce.									
		Mary Treacy Pas	Cotter	1		2					1
	Derrine	Petr.									
		Anne Hartt Pas	Welder	2					1		
	Cloonsuck	Loughlen									
		Winifrida Flanagan Pas	Cotter	3		1					
		Thady Flanagan Pa	Cotter			3					
		Loughlen									
		Bridgett Flanagan Pas	Herd	3		5					
	Corriduane	Conr.									
		Ellinor Hevighan Pas	Blacksmith			3					
		Thos.									
		Bridgett Boyhane Pas	Cotter	1		2					
		Terce									
		Margaret Rogers Pas	Welder			2					1
		Bryan									
		Catharine Rogers Pas	Welder								1
		Mark									
		Judith Keaveny Pas	Welder	1		3		1		✝	
		Laurce. Flyn Pa									
		Mary Pro.	Welder								1
		Thos.									
		Mary Flyn Pas	Welder								1
		Danl.									
		Catharin Flyn Pas	Welder	2							1
		John									
Prots 1		Mary Killerna Pas	Brogemaker	2		1		1		✝	
		Darby									
		Winifrida Rogers Pas	Carman	1		3					
		John									
		Bridgett Naughten Pas	Welder	2		1		1		✝	1
		Patk.									
		Mary Conaghton Pas	Welder	1		4					1
		Loughlen									
		Bridgett Teige Pas	Welder			3					1
		John									
		Rosamunda Gill Pas	Welder	1		2		1		✝	
		Loughl.									
		Mary Gileran Pas	Welder	2		1					1
		Denis									
		Margaret Conally Pas	Welder			4					
		Patrick									
Pas 12		Bridgett Coine Pas	Dealer	1							
		John									
12		Giles Gill Pas	Herd			2					
		David									
		Mary Kelly Pas	Cotter	2							

Com~Ros common Parish of	Place of Abode	Names and Religion	Proffession	Children under 14		Children above 14		Men Servts		Women Servts	
				Prot.	Paps.	Prot.	Paps.	Prot.	Paps.	Prot.	Paps.
58		Catharin Mana Pa	Spinster Pa								
47		Darby									
74		Bridget Clogher Pas	Cadger		1						
	Frankfort otherwis Mulladoe	Patk									
263		Winifrida Glinn Pas	Shepherd		1		2		1	~~1~~	
		Owen									
		Bridgett Cunelane Pas	Cotter		1						
		Anne Quinn Pa	Widdow				2				
		Ellinr									
		Bridget Helfort Pas			2						
		Jas.									
		Mary Carty Pas	Herd		3				1	~~1~~	
[f.259] Kilkeevin	Lisslody	Thos.									
		Anne Walker Pros:	Farmer	1				1		1	3
		Ellinr. Rorke Pa	Widdow						3		
		Michl.									
		Margret Gownan Pas	Cotter		1		3		~~1~~		
		Patrick									
		Mary Cormack Pas	Cotter				1				
		Thady									
		Hanna Dollen Pas	Cotter				1				
		Darby									
		Catharine Manion Pas	Cotter				1		~~1~~		
	Cregancorr	Bridget Connor Pa	Widdow				2		~~2~~		
		Edmond									
		Mary Keveny Pas	Welder				4		~~2~~		
		Margtt Gownan Pa	Widow		1		1		~~2~~		
		Thomas									
	Lisslody	Mary Common Pas	Welder		1		2		~~2~~		
		Edmd.									
		Giles Common Pas	Welder				1		1		
		Cormk.									
	Clooncouse	Honora Comon Pas	Cotter						1		
		Patrick									
		Anne Sweeny Pas	Welder				1		1		
		Patk.									
		Mary Kennay Pas	Welder				2				
	Balenepark	Catherin Gallagher	Widdow		1		3				
		Wm.									
		Catharin Gubilan Pas	Welder		1						
		Darby									
		Margaret Winn Pas	Welder		1						
		Mary Bryan Pa	Widdow				1				
		Thady									
		Catharin Wynn Pas	Weldr.				2		1		
		John									
		Anne Killkeny Pas	Weldr.				2				
Prots 1		John									
		Bridgett Beirn Pas	Blacksmith		1						
1		Michl									
		Catharin Mooney Pas	Weldr.		1		2				
1		Honora Carny Pa	Widdow		2				1		
2		Catharin Moony Pa	Widdow								
		Jas									
		Bridgett Garra Pas	Welder								
5		Dens. Kyne Pa	Weldr.				2				
Papsts 4		Michl.									
		Mary Tully Pas	Welder								

Com~Ros common Parish of	Place of Abode	Names and Religion	Proffession	Children under 14		Children above 14		Men Servts		Women Servts	
				Prot.	Paps.	Prot.	Paps.	Prot.	Paps.	Prot.	Paps.
8	Cloonwindin	Michl.									
		Mary Kelly Pas	Yarn buyer		1						1
31		Thos. Simpson Pa	Herd		3				1		1
		Winifrida Simpson Pa	Widow								
11		Thos.									
		Eliz. Bermingham Paps	Welder						1		
76		Thady									
		Mary Connor Paps	Welder		2				1		1
		Dermot									
100		Elinr. Moran Paps	Cottier		1						
		Jas.									
31		Judith Mylan Paps	Cottier		3						
		John									
		Bridgett Coffy Paps	Cottier		3						
138	Cloone-chambers	Mary Kelly Paps	Henwife								
		George									
		Susanna Walker Prots	Farmer						1		2
		Thos.									
		Catharin Fahy Paps	Cottier								
		Edward									
		Giles Flanaghan Paps	Dealer								

[f.260]	Protests	Pg 1	27
		2	37
		3	6
		4	37
		5	75
		6	8
		9	12
		10	2
		11	29
		12	5
		13	11
		14	5
	Totl. of Prots.		241

Pg 1.	120
2.	117
3.	140
4.	108
5.	156
6.	176
7.	157
8.	157
9.	144
10.	169
11.	162
12.	167
13.	203
14.	138
Totl. of Papsts.	2114

NOTES

1. Beaufort, 'Journal' (T.C.D., MS 4026, 2 f.64).

2. OS Geological Map of Ireland 1:750,000 (3rd edition 1962).

3. *Report ... fairs and markets.*

4. The townlands of Anughvaghery, Carukeel, Carumore, Clooneran, Cloonforest [Clonfower?], Cloonsellif [Clonsellagh], Cregalahan [Creaghleagh], Knockmurry, Knockro, Rathledge [Rathlegg]. Taughnara [Taghnarrow] (*Books of Survey and Distribution* Roscommon).

5. Lewis, 'Belanagare'.

6. A tannery still existed in the town in the early nineteenth century, dependent on the river and on bark brought from Dublin (Weld, *Roscommon*, p.471).

7. There were two mills in Castlerea, a corn mill and a tuck mill. They were owned by the Sandford family in 1717 (N.L.I., Pakenham Mahon Papers, MS 2597).

8. Charles, son of George and Ellen Hagarty was baptised on 18 September 1748 (R.C.B., Register of marriages, baptisms and burials in the parishes of Kilkevin, Baslick and Ballintober 1748-1825, MS P.528).

9. Robert Sandford entered TCD in 1739, but there is no record of his having taken a degree. He became MP for Athy in 1753 and 1761 and was Governor of Galway (*Alumni Dubliniensis*).

10. Nathaniel Barton was a son of John Barton dean of Ardagh, and was born in Co. Meath in about 1718. He entered TCD in 1726/27 aged 16 and took BA in 1731. He became prebendary of Ballintobber from 1741-1761 and of Tibohine from 1761-1770. He married Bridget Young, daughter of Owen Young of Castlerea. He witnessed Bishop Synge's will in 1761. John, son of the Rev Nathaniel Barton was baptised 30 April 1748. Another child, Rachel was baptised 21 October 1750 (*Alumni Dubliniensis*; Leslie, Elphin, p. 38, N.A., P.R.O., MS PROB 11/894/563 f. 255; RCB Register of marriages, baptisms and burials in the parishes of Kilkevin, Baslick and Ballintober 1748-1825, MS P.528).

11. Margaret, daughter of Ralph and Elizabeth Satchell, was baptised 6 April 1749 (R.C.B., Register of marriages, baptisms and burials in the parishes of Kilkevin, Baslick and Ballintober 1748-1825 MS P.528).

12. Agnes, daughter of Richard and Elizabeth Parks, was baptised 3 March 1749 (R.C.B., Register of marriages, baptisms and burials in the parishes of Kilkevin, Baslick and Ballintober 1748-1825, MS P.528).

13. Less than a quarter of the townland was arable fit for tillage. There was a wood with bottom land subject to floods and much bog and mountain land and green pasture with rushy bottom (N.L.I., Map of Clonrogh Treen and Emlagh 1762, MS 16 M 14/35).

14. The townlands of Mungagh, Cloondaharamore, Clondaharabeg and Creagamean were owned by the see of Elphin (N.L.I., MS 16 I 13).

15. Emlagh townland had arable land, commonly under tillage, and pasture covered with boggall bushes and bog, impassable in winter. It was owned by the Mahon family (N.L.I., MS 16 M 14/35).

16. Dominick Mulrenan was listed as a parish priest in 1748. He was a supporter of the Rev. William (alias Augustine) O'Kelly, prior of St Mary's, Roscommon in 1748 to succeed Patrick French as bishop of Elphin (Fenning 'Diocese of Elphin', p.166; Beirne, (ed.) *Diocese of Elphin*, p.122).

17. Cloonkeen was owned by the see of Elphin (N.L.I., MS 16 I 13).

18. Daniel O'Conor was a son of Andrew O'Conor of Clonalis and Honora Dowell of Mantua, Co. Roscommon. He served in the French army. He was a lay supporter of the Rev. William (alias Augustine) O'Kelly, prior of St. Mary's, Roscommon in 1748 to succeed Patrick French as bishop of Elphin. He died in 1795 (Burke, *LGI* (1958); Fenning 'Diocese of Elphin', p.166).

19. Mary, daughter of Edward and Frances Madden was baptised on 6 February 1749 (R.C.B., Register of marriages, baptisms and burials in the parishes of Kilkevin, Baslick and Ballintober 1748-1825, MS P.528).

20. Thomas, son John and Elizabeth Brannan was baptised 6 April 1749 (R.C.B., Register of marriages, baptisms and burials in the parishes of Kilkevin, Baslick and Ballintober 1748-1825, MS P.528).

21. Ballindrimly townland was owned by the see of Elphin (National Archives of Ireland (henceforth N.A.I.) MS M545e)

BASLICK, COUNTY ROSCOMMON

INTRODUCTION: *The parish of Baslick (Baisleac-mor) was in the barony of Castlereagh. It is 5 miles north-east of the town of Castlerea, on the road to Elphin. It had 15,395 statute acres.[1] In 1837, Lewis said that there was little woodland in the parish, except in the demesnes, and that the land was largely arable. There were quarries of limestone, used mainly for constructing boundaries.[2]*

The main commercial centre was Castleplunket on the road from Strokestown to Castlerea. Fairs were held there three times a year.[3]

The Church of Ireland incumbent was the Rev. Nathaniel Barton, who held Baslick with Ballintobber and Kilkeevan (see Kilkeevin.) The patron was the bishop. The rectory was impropriate in the earl of Essex.

OCCUPATIONS

Bailiff	1	Farmer	10	Shepherd	10
Beggar	10	Herd	8	Smith	4
Broguemaker	1	Innkeeper	1	Tailor	1
Butcher	1	Labourer	12	Weaver	2
Carpenter	3	Maltster	1	Welder	108
Cooper	1	Mason	1	Widow	5
Cottier	124	Merchant	4	Yeoman	4
Dealer	1	Servants, household	140		

Com~Ros com Parish of	Place of Abode	Names and Religion	Proffession	Children under 14		Children above 14		Men Servts		Women Servts	
				Prot.	Paps.	Prot.	Paps.	Prot.	Paps.	Prot.	Paps.
[f.261]Baslick	Castleteehin	Phelim Dollon Pas									
		Honora	Sheperd		5		1		1		1
		Frans.Carroll Pas									
		Ellizab.	Cottier		1						1
		Mathw.Mulrenin Pas									
		Mary	Cottier		1						
		Patk. Rogers Pas									
		Mary	Cottier		1		1				1
		Robert									
		Catharin Rogers Pas	Cottier				1				
		Edmd.Dillon Pas									
		Mary	Cottier				1				
		John Finraghty Pas									
		Ellinor	Herd		1		1				
		Willm. Turner Protests									
		Bridgett	Weaver	3		2					
		Edmd Prendergast Pas									
		Mary	Cottier		3		1				
	Rafowdagh	Nichs.Scott Pas									
		Mary	Sheperd				1				
		Edmd Kelly Pas									
		Bridgett	Cottier		1						
		Chars Digenane Pas									
		Bridgett	Cottier		2		1				
		Luke Scally Pas									
		Margaret	Cottier		2		1				
	Gortneselagh	Bryan Rogers Pas									
		Margt.	Sheperd		5						
		Thos Treacy Pas.									
		Jane	Cottier		3		1				
		Eneas Maconelly and his mother	Cottier								
		Hugh Beirn Pas									
		Catharin	Cottier		2						
	Rathmoyle	Charles Dillon Pas									
		Mary	Farmr.		1				1		1
		Arthur Irwin Pas									
		Mable	Farmer		2				1		1
		Terce Dermott Pas									
		Moare	Cotter				2				
		John Brislane Pas									
		Mary	Cottier		1						
		Barthw. Dermott Pas									
		Mary	Cottier		1						
		Conner Conelane Pas									
		Mary	Cottier		1						
		John Fallon Pas									
		Bridget	Cottier		1						
9		Brits. Egane Pas									
		Allice	Cottier		2				1		1
7		Edmd Rock Pas									
		Catharin	Cottier		3						
21		John Gormly Pas									
		Sarah	Cottier		3						
54		John Gormly Pas									
79		Sarah	Cottier		3						
	Ballen-dullughans	Frans.Ferrall Pas									
———		Allice	Welder				2		1		1
Pas 150		Thos.Ganly Pas									
		Sister	Cotter								

Com~Ros common Parish of	Place of Abode	Names and Religion	Proffession	Children under 14 Prot.	Children under 14 Paps.	Children above 14 Prot.	Children above 14 Paps.	Men Servts Prot.	Men Servts Paps.	Women Servts Prot.	Women Servts Paps.
Prots 7	Rushine	Loughlen Gunn Pas									
		One Bror. 1 Sister	Herd								
		Michl. McGarry Pas									
		Mary	Sheeperd		4		1				
		Danl. Connor Pas									
		Juliana	Farmer				1		2		2
		Edmd. Loughlen Pas									
		Catharin	Cottier		1		1				
		Patk. Murray Pas									
		Winifrida	Sheeperd				3				
		Patk. Callery Pas									
		Sarah	Cottier		2						
		Loughlen Igoe Pas									
		Margaret	-		1						
		Bryan O'Harra Pas									
		Mary	-		1		1				
		Wm.									
[f.262]Baslick	Carugary	Mary Ganly Pas	-								
		Denis Shinane Pas									
		Margaret	Welder		1						
		Peter Connor Pas									
		Allice	-								
		John Parker Pas									
		Jane	-		1						
		Darby Mulany Pas									
		Mary	-		1		1				
		Loughne Dempsy Pas									
		Honora	-		1		1				
		Conr. Ternan Pas									
		Margaret	-		1		3				
		James Brenon Pas									
		Margaret	-		2		1				
		Andw. Mullane Pas									
		Mary	-		2		2				
		Peter Giraghty Pas									
		Mary	-		2						
		Thoms. Wallish Pas									
		Allice	-		2		2				
		Thos. Conughane Pas									
		Catharin	-		2		1				
		James Mulloy Pa	Carpenr.		2		1		2		
		Martn. Concanin Pas									
		Sarah	Welder		1		2				
		Bridgt. Hinigan pa	Widdow				2				
		James Keigher Pas & his Mother	Cotter				2				
		John Skinner Pas									
		Mary	-				2				
	Ballaghba	Charles O'Connor[4] Pas	Farmer		1		2		1		2
		Patk. Conry Pas									
		Margt.	Cotter		1						
		Edmd. Conry Pas									
		Bridgt.	-		2						
		Domk. Nicholson Pas									
		Honora	-		1		1				
		Patrick Gunn Pas									
		Anne	-		2						
		Michl. Flyn Pas									
		Bridgett	-		3						
		Patk. Killglass Pas									
		Margt.	-		2						
		Edmd. McGuire Pas									
		Anne	-								

Com~Ros common Parish of	Place of Abode	Names and Religion	Proffession	Children under 14		Children above 14		Men Servts		Women Servts	
				Prot.	Paps.	Prot.	Paps.	Prot.	Paps.	Prot.	Paps.
		Danl. Raghticane Pas									
		Margaret	-								
		Denis Filane Pas	-		2		1				
	Baslick	Edmd. Winston Pas	Farmer		3		2		3		2
		Darby Connor Pas									
		Margaret	Herd		3				1		1
		Patk. Lavin Pas									
		Catharin	Cotter				1				
		Redagh Sharry Pas									
		Mary	-		2						
		James Lavin Pas									
		Mary	-		2						
		Patrick Kinnin Pas									
		Margaret	-		3						
		Conr. Goulruck Pas									
		Mary	-		3		1				
		Patk. Naughten Pas									
		Sarah	Shepard		1						
		Loughlen Frain Pas									
		Margaret	Welder		1		3				
		Peter Egan Pas									
		Catharine	Welder								
		Patk. Frain	-		1		1				
		Wm. Mally Pas									
		Alice Smith			3						1
[3 lines erased] [f.263]Baslick	Tuberelvy	Hugh Flyn Pas									
		Mary	Cotter		1						
		Own. Dermott Pas									
		Catharin	-		3						
		Thos. Scott Pas									
		Margaret	-		5		1				
		Widow Rogers Pa					3				
		Hugh Mcguire Cotter			2		2				
		Robt. Milon									
		Mary Pas	-				1				
	Dillonsgrove	Patrick Moore									
		Mary	Shepard		4				1		1
		Luke Dermott									
		Winifrida	Cotter		3		1				
		Hugh Dermott									
		Mary	A Herd		1						
		Richard Colema Pas									
		Catharine	Cotter		2						
		Laurce Parker	Bailiff		2						
	Rardeevin	Michl. Moore Pas									
		Mary	Shepard		2				1		1
		John Cooke Pas									
		Anne	Cotter		2						
		Jams. Conma Pas									
		Sarah	-		4		1				
		Bryan Hester Pas									
		Catharin	-		4						
		Patk. Flyn Pas									
		Ellinor	-		3		1				
		Patk. Connelly Pas									
		Ellinor	-		2		2				
		Thos. Dillon Pas									
		Honora	-		3						
		Thady Spillane Pas									
		Honora	-								

Com~Ros common Parish of	Place of Abode	Names and Religion	Proffession	Children under 14		Children above 14		Men Servts		Women Servts	
				Prot.	Paps.	Prot.	Paps.	Prot.	Paps.	Prot.	Paps.
	Carugarry	Patk. Dillon Pas / Clare	-		2		2				
		Thady Giblane Pas / Mary	-		2						
		Patk. Gill Pas / Margaret	Welder		1						
		Murtagh Blee Pas / Mary	Mercht.		3				1		1
		Thady Moron Pas / Elizabth.	Welder		1		2				
		Conn Ternan Pas / Mary	-				1				
		Owen Carny Pas / Ellinor	-		2						
		James Comins Pas / Ellinr.	-		2						
		Michl. Hedian Pas / Ellinr.	-				1				
		Terce. Mulkeran Pas	-		2		3				
		Frans. Murphy Pas	-		1		3				
		Wm. Phynane Pas / Honora	-				2				
		James Phynane Pas / Ellinor	-		2						
4		Michael Phynane Pas / Anne	-				2				
4		John Phynane Pas / Margaret	-		2						
80		Luke McQueenay Pas / Mary	-		2		2				
70		Thady Egan Pas / Honora	-								
77		Patk. Connor Pas / Catharin	-		1						
		Danl. Magovrane Pas / Bridget	-		1						
——		Patrick Fanaghly Pas / Bridgett	-								
185		Laur. Treacy Pas / Mary	-		1						
		Laur. Mulloy Pas / Allice	-		2				1		1
[f.264]Baslick	Castleplunket	John Fehaly Pa: / Eliz. Pa	Mercht.				3				1
		Robt. Stanly Pa / Elinor Pa	Carpentr.		4						
		Kelly Teige Pa / Margt. Pa	Smith		3		2				
		Peter Conry Pa / Mary Pa	Beggar		3		2				
		Cormck Morris Pa / Bridgt. Pa	Yeoman		7				2		
		Hugh Grogan Pa / Mary Pa	Malster						1	+	1
		Michael Connor Pa / Bridget Pa	Beggar				3				
		Bryan Cummin Pa / Margt. Pa	Beggar		2						
		Patck. Moony Pa / Cathe. Pa	Labourr.		1						

Com~Ros common Parish of	Place of Abode	Names and Religion	Proffession	Children under 14		Children above 14		Men Servts		Women Servts	
				Prot.	Paps.	Prot.	Paps.	Prot.	Paps.	Prot.	Paps.
		Loghn. Durr	Labourr.		1						
		Margt. Pa									
		Loughlin Shinanan Pa	Beggar		4						
		Winifrida Pa									
		Wm. Brennan	Yeoman		3		1				
		Anne Pa									
		Dennis McNamara Pa	Labourr.		2						
		Honora Pa									
		Edmund Flanagn. Pas									
		Joanna	Butcher		3						
		Dennis Flanagn. Pas									
		Mary	Innkeeper				1				
		John Murray Pas									
		Katharin	Labourer		3		2				
		Roger Flanagan Pas									
		Katherine	Beggrs.		4		1				
6		Terce. O'Neil Pas									
		Mary	Dealer		3		4				
6		Mary Burgh Pa	Widow		2		2				
25		Robert. Ormsby Pas									
		Anne	Labourr.		2						
58		John Nary Pas									
		Katharin	Welder		2				1	+	2
53		John Hanly Pas									
		Bridget	Welder		4		1				
———		Jas Hunt Pas									
		Rosamunda	Welder		2				1	+	1
Paps 148		Luke Wallish Paps									
		Mary	Yeoman		3				1	+	1
		Patk. Brennan Pa									
		Judith	Welder				3				
		Edmd. Gaghron Pa									
		Kathn.	Labourr.								
		Francs. Drury Pap									
		Mary	Broguemaker								
[f.265]Baslick	Castleplunket	Michl. Drury Pa									
		Bridget	Taylour		2						1
		Thos. Dolan Papt	Labourer				3				
		Edmund Brennan Papt									
		Judith	Cooper								1
		John Burgh Papt									
		Margt.	Beggar								
		Martin Hamel Papt									
		Winifrida	Labourer		4						
		Patrick Beirn Papt									
		Rosama.	Labourer								
		Danl. Finn Papt									
		Mary	Carpenter		2		2				
		Dennis Conane Papt									
		Sarah	Labourer								
		Walter Prendergt. Papt									
		Mary	Welder							1	1
		John Prendergst. Papt									
		Naply	Beggar					1			
		Wm. Finane Papt									
		Dorothy	Cottier		3						
		Robt. Hougdin Papt									
		Mary	Cottier		1						
		Danl. Glynn Papt									
		Sarah	Cottier								

Com~Ros common Parish of	Place of Abode	Names and Religion	Proffession	Children under 14		Children above 14		Men Servts		Women Servts	
				Prot.	Paps.	Prot.	Paps.	Prot.	Paps.	Prot.	Paps.
	Lissalvey	Loughlin Bryan Papt Katharin	Welder		3		1				
		Michl. Kenny Papt Elizth	Cottier								
		Andreas Mugan Mary	Cottier								
		James Mugan Pat	Welder				2				
		Thos. Kenny Papt Bridget	-								
		Thos. Mugan Papt Katha	-				3				
		Miles Mugan Papt Margt.	-		3						
		Wm. Mugan Papt Joanna	-								
		Loughlin Kelly Papt Rosama.	-		2		3				
		Bridget Connor Papt Widow			2						1
		Andreas Maddin Papt Bridget	Labourr.		3				1		1
		John Madden Papt Mary	Welder		3						1
		Patrick Madden Pat Bridget	-		3				1	+	1
		Owen Madden Pa Winifrid	Labourer						1		1
		Stephen Groark Papt Anne	Welder		1				1		1
		Danl. Fenraghty Papt Giles	-		2						1
		Patrick Horoghy Papt Mary	Farmer				3				1
		Thos. Conry Pat Bridgt.	Beggar		2		1				
		Michl. Mulledy Pat Sarah	Farmer		2		2				1
		Thos. Mulledy Pas Bridgt Dto	Welder		1				1		1
		Patrick Loughlin Paps Winifrida	Beggar		2						
		James Varin Papt Elinor	Welder		2				1		1
		Owen Kean Papt Mary	-		8						
		Hugh Roger Papt Honora	-		5						
		Owen Gileran Papt	-		5						
		Gilbert Kryne Papt Margt.	-				1				
		Thady Kryne Papt Mary			4						
[f.266]Baslick	Lissaloy	Matthew Kryne Papt Mary	Welder		2						
		James Kryne Papt Margart.	-		2						
		Willm. Kenny Papt Margt.	-		5		2				
		Richd. Haneen Papt Mary	-		2		3				

Com~Ros common Parish of	Place of Abode	Names and Religion	Proffession	Children under 14		Children above 14		Men Servts		Women Servts	
				Prot.	Paps.	Prot.	Paps.	Prot.	Paps.	Prot.	Paps.
		Dennis Heavighan Papt									
		Anne	-								
		Michael Lavin Papt									
		Mary	-		2		1				
		Patt. Early Papt									
		Margt.	-		3		1				
		David Glinn									
		Catharin	-		1						
		Darby Kelly Pa	-		2						
		Thos. Beaty	-								
		James Loughlen Pa									
		Winifrida	-		4		2				
		Thos. Feenaghty Pa									
		Mary	-								
		Wm. Kynney Pa									
		Sarah	-							1	1
		Redmond Jonons Pa									
		Anne			3						
		Thady Halinan Pas									
		Sarah	-							1	1
		Patt. Rorke Pas									
		Mary	-		1					1	1
		Hugh Concanon Pa									
		Hugh Teige Pas									
		Winifrida	-		1						
		Danl. Hanly									
		Elizabth.	-				2				
		James Flyn Pas									
		Mary	Smith		2						
		Hugh Smith Pas									
		Mary			3		1				
		Patk. Keane Pas									
		Bridgett	Welder		3						
		Danl. Keane Pas									
		Bridgett	-		3						
		Patk. Keane Pas									
		Bridgett	-		3						
		Ter. Mulrenin Pas									
		Winifrida	-		3						
		James Conilan Pas									
		Winifrida	-		3		1				
		Wm. Bolane Pas									
		Giles	-								
		Peter Dolon Pa	-				1				
		Wm. Bolone Pas									
		Jane	-								
5		Patk Dollen Pas									
		Mary	-		1						
5		Jams. Dollen Pas									
		Margar.	-		1						
5		John Digenan Pas									
		Margaret	-		3		1				
62		Arthur Hogan Pas	-				2				
74		Michl. Shinane									
		Ellinor	Cottier		1						
		John Kelly									
———		Mary	Ditto		2						
Pas 171		Thady Kinney Pa			1		5				
		Ands Lynsk Pas									
		Elizabth.			3		2				
		Michl. Manion Pas									
		Catharin					1		1		1

Com~Ros common Parish of	Place of Abode	Names and Religion	Proffession	Children under 14		Children above 14		Men Servts		Women Servts	
				Prot.	Paps.	Prot.	Paps.	Prot.	Paps.	Prot.	Paps.
[f.267]Baslick	Lisaloy	Darby Gorman Pas Mary	Mercht.		3		2		1		1
		John Hinigane Pas Giles	Welder		3				1		1
		Thoms. Higginan Pa	-								
		Patt. Kinigane Pas Honora	-								1
		Michl Balfe Pas Catharin	Farmer		3				1		2
		Bryn Dermott Pas Anne	Shepard		1						
		Thos. Fryers Pas Jane	Cotter		5						
		Bryan Roger Pas Margt.	Shepard		4		3		1		
		Richd. Killduff Pas Margaret	Cotter		3						
		Myles Larken Pas Giles	Ditto		3		1				
		Petr. Clark Pas Mary	Ditto		1						
		James Lynsk Pas Anne	-		1						
		Patk. Dermott Pas	-		2						
		Patk. Dermott Pas Giles	-		2						
		Richd. Giraghan Pas Ellinor	Smith		2				1		
		Thady Horroghy Pas Sarah	Cotter		3						
		Michael Dillon Pas Bridgett	-		2						
		Patrick Lally Pas Winifrida	-		4		1				
		Thady Cunane Pas Margaret	-		2						
		Bryan Murtagh Pas Catharine	-		2						
		Domk. Trustin Pas Anne	-		2						
		Thady Grealy Pas Bridgett	-		3						
		Luke Quinn Pas Mary	-		3						
		Andw. Quin Pas Mary	-		3						
		Michl. Murtagh Pas Margaret	-		3						
		Phellem Lenon Pas Mary	-		2						
		Barthw. Connor Pas Mary	-		3						
		John Jonens Pas Winifrida	-				2		2		
		James Flyn	-				2		2		
5		Jams. Gavaghan Pas	Weaver		2						
5		John Connor Pas Mary	Cotter				1		1		
19	Pargaruff	Jn. Casidy Pas Mary	Welder		4						
88		James Cassidy Pas Bridgett			3						

Com~Ros common Parish of	Place of Abode	Names and Religion	Proffession	Children under 14		Children above 14		Men Servts		Women Servts	
				Prot.	Paps.	Prot.	Paps.	Prot.	Paps.	Prot.	Paps.
72		Edmd. Padden Pas									
		Giles			1		1		+		
———	Lissinivicane	Roger Cahill Pas									
		Bridgett	Cotter		1		1		+		
Pas 189		Darby King Pas									
		Elizabth.	-		3		1		+		
		Laur. Flyn Pas									
		Giles	-		3		1		+		
		John Beirn Pas									
		Catharin	-		4		1		+		
		Bridgett Beirn	Widdow		2		2		2		
[f.268]Baslick	Ballyglass	Terce. McDermott[5] Pas									
		Bridgett	Farmer		1		1		4		4
		Loughlen Coyne Pas									
		Rosamund	Herd		1		2				
		Thos Fox Pas									
		Mary	-		2		1		1		1
		Patt. Kinney Pas									
		Catharin	Welder		1						
		Loughlen Duffy Pas									
		Anne	-				1				1
		Roger McConmane Pas									
		Bridgett	-		2		1				
		Patt. Scally Pas									
		Bridgett	-		2						
		Hugh Hughs Pas									
		Margaret	Cotter								
		Darby Dorr Pas									
		Mary	Welder		2						
		John Hobbane Pas									
		Mary	-		2						
		Patk. Fox his Brors and sisters No 4 Pas	Welder				4		1		1
		Hugh Fox Pas									
		Ellinor	-		3		1		1		
		Carbry Fox Pas									
		Jane	-		4				1		
		Thady Fox Pas									
		Winifrida									
		John Egan Pas			2						1
		Gill Conellane Pas									
		Margaret	Cotter		1		2				
		Bryan Colgan Pas									
		Mary	-		1		1				
		Owen King Pas									
		Sarah	-		1		2				
		Michl. Drury Pas									
		Bridgett	Herd				3				
		Hugh Hobane Pas									
		Bridgett	Cotter		1						
		Thos. Hobane Pas									
		Anne	-		1						
		Owen Haughton Pas									
		Mary	-		1						
		Roger Murry Pas									
		Cathrin	-		2						
		Terce. Mungane Pas									
		Mary	-								
		Thoms Drury Pas									
		Cathrin	-		1						

Com~Ros common Parish of	Place of Abode	Names and Religion	Proffession	Children under 14 Prot.	Paps.	Children above 14 Prot.	Paps.	Men Servts Prot.	Paps.	Women Servts Prot.	Paps.
		John Drury Pas / Ellinor	-		1						
		Denis Dorr Pas / Margaret	-				1				
		John Dorr Pas / Bridgett	-		2						
		Bryan Dermott Pas / Margaret	Mercht.		2		1				
9		Winifrida Cole	Widdow		1		2				
		Terce Flanigan Pas / Margaret	Welder		3				1		1
9		John Hobane Pas / Jane	Cotter				1				
49		Patk. Flanagan Pas / Bridgett	-		1						
76		Timothy Owen Pas / Sarah			2						
175		Connor Dermott Pas / Bridgett	Mazon				1				
		Edmd. Roncanon Pas / Mary	Cotter		2		3				
	Gortnereask	Terce. Mullren Pas / Mary	-		2		2				
		Denis Ferrall Pas / Mary			2		2				
[f.269]Baslick	Glanvella	Walter Balfe Pas / Anne	Welder						1		1
		Farrell Coghlane Pas / Mabley	-								1
		Wm. Hourghane Pas / Bridgett	Cotter		1						
		James Crushim Pas / Judith	-		1						
		John Shinane Pas / Honora	-		5						
		Hugh Gillerane Pas / Ellinor	-								
		Danl. Egan Pas / Bridgett	-		1						
		Dens. Shinane Pas / Bridgett	-		1						
		Peter Bolane Pas / Ellinor	-		2						
		Morris Shinane Pas / Mary									
	Drissughane	Michl. Cassidy Pas / Honora	Welder		2				1		
		Gregory Cassidy Pas / Mary	-		2				1		
		Patrick Foord Pas / Sarah	-						1		1
		Isaac Plunkett Pas / Anne	-		2						
		Phillip Smith Pas / Giles	-								1
		John Smyth Pas / Catharine							1		1
		Edmd. Owens Pas / Bridgett			2						
	Emlagh	John Irwin Prots. / Mary	Farmer	3		5	5[5?]		1		2

Com~Ros common Parish of	Place of Abode	Names and Religion	Proffession	Children under 14 Prot.	Paps.	Children above 14 Prot.	Paps.	Men Servts Prot.	Paps.	Women Servts Prot.	Paps.
		John Egan Pas									
		Margaret	Cotter		2		3		‡[1?]		1
		Redmd. Dillon Pas									
		Bridgett	-		4						
		Darby Morron Pas									
		Cathrin	-		2						
		James Garra Pas									
		Mary	-				5				
		James Calaghan Pas									
		Mary	-				3				
		Owen Duidy Pas									
		Herd			2				1		1
		Peter Egan Pas									
		Anne	Cotters			1					
		Hugh Egan Pas									
		Giles	-		2						
		James Brenon Pas									
		Margaret			2				1		1
9											
8											
11		Total of Inhabitts in									
34[?]		the Parish of Baslick									
Pas 113	Protests	18									
Prots 11	Paps pg 1	171[?]									
	pg 2	169									
	pg 3	185									
	pg 4	148									
	pg 5	180									
	pg 6	171									
	pg 7	189									
	pg 8	175									
	pg 9	113									
		1500									

NOTES

1. *General Alphabetical Index*

2. Lewis, 'Baslick'.

3. *Report ... fairs and markets*.

4. Charles O'Connor of Ballaghba was a lay supporter of the Rev. William (alias Augustine) O'Kelly, prior of St. Mary's Roscommon in 1748 to succeed Patrick French as bishop of Elphin (Fenning, 'Diocese of Elphin', p.166).

5. Terence McDermott of Ballyglass was a lay supporter of the Rev. William (alias Augustine) O'Kelly, prior of St. Mary's Roscommon in 1748 to succeed Patrick French as bishop of Elphin (Fenning, 'Diocese of Elphin', p.166).

BALLINTOBER, COUNTY ROSCOMMON

INTRODUCTION: *The parish of Ballintober is in the barony of Castlereagh. It is 4 miles south east by south of the town of Castlerea. It had 6,351 statute acres.[1] In 1837 the village of Ballintober consisted entirely of cabins. The land was mainly bog, with a quarry of limestone in the nineteenth century.[2]*

In 1749, some of the occupations were proto-industrial due to the local coal (see Kilkeevan). The townland of Bracklon was composed almost entirely of welders, and there were other groups of welders at Cloonikerny, Cloonagh and Carureagh. A patent to hold a fair was issued in 1618 to Sir H. O'Connor Don.[3] Lewis wrote of Ballintober having a large fair for horses, but it had formerly been for the sale of yarn.

The incumbent was the Rev. Nathaniel Barton, who held Ballintobber with Baslick and Kilkeevan. (See Kilkeevan). The patron was the bishop.

OCCUPATIONS

Ale draper	1	Flax dresser	1	Shoemaker	2
Beggar	1	Gardener	1	Skinner	1
Broguemaker	1	Gentleman	1	Slater	2
Butcher	1	Herd	12	Smith	3
Cadger	1	Merchant	2	Steward	1
Cooper	1	Miller	1	Tailor	1
Cottier	95	Peddler	1	Tobacco spinner	1
Esquire	2	Priest	1	Weaver	6
Farmer	1	Servants, household	121	Welder	39
Farrier	1	Shepherd	6	Widow	16

Com~Roscom Parish of	Place of Abode	Names and Religion	Proffession	Children under 14 Prot.	Children under 14 Paps.	Children above 14 Prot.	Children above 14 Paps.	Men Servts Prot.	Men Servts Paps.	Women Servts Prot.	Women Servts Paps.
[f.268A] Ballintober	Bracklon	Patt Digenan Pas Mary	Welder		2						1
		John Digenan Pas Catharin	Welder				2				
		Markes Conelane Pas Margaret	Welder		1						1
		Domk Rourty Pas Margaret	Welder				1		1		
		Domk. Murry Pas Catherine	Welder		1		1				
		Frans. Duyer Pas Catherin	Welder		2		1		1		
		Neal Dogherty Pas Catharin	Welder		1						1
		Markus Rourty Pas Ellinor	Welder		1		1				1
		Thomas Lyons Pas Sarah	Welder		1		2		1		
		Bryan Conelane Pas Catharin	Welder		1		1				1
		Thomas Flyn Pas Bridget	Weaver		1		2		1		
		John Morron Pas Catharin	Welder		1		2				
		Roger Horroghy Pas Catharin	Herd				3				
		Thomas Gill Pas Margaret	Welder		1		1				
		Michl. Dollen Pas Cathrin	Welder		2						1
		Thos. Manion Pas Catharin	Welder		1		1				1
		Martn. Kearin Pas	Smith								1
		Edmd. Rush Pas Catharin	Weaver		1		2				
		Patk. Manion Pas Winifrida	Welder		1		3				
		Michael Raghtican Pas Catherine	Cottier		1		2				
		Patt. Flyn Pas Honora	Welder		1						
	Balymageihert	Thos. Concanon Pas Catherin	Cottier		2		1				
	Timanagh	Patrick Currishen Pas Mary	Slater				2				
		Jas. Hevighane Pas Honora	Cottier		1		2				
		Loughlen Royen Pas Mary	Cottier				3				
		Connor Cryne Pas Margaret	Cottier		2						
		John Egan Pas Honora	Cottier		2						
		Laur Bradikin Pas Mary	Herd		1		3				
		Patrick Larken Pas Mary	Cottier		1		1				
		Edmd. Flyn Pas Honora	Shepherd		1		2		1		
		Darby Connor Pa	Gent						1		1

Com~Ros common Parish of	Place of Abode	Names and Religion	Proffession	Children under 14		Children above 14		Men Servts		Women Servts	
				Prot.	Paps.	Prot.	Paps.	Prot.	Paps.	Prot.	Paps.
Prots 3	Rathnesoliagh	Thoms. Concanon Pa	Smith				3				
1		John MaGarry Pas									
—		Bridget	Herd				1				
4		John Mulrenin Pas	Cottier								1
Papts 16		Richd. Flanagan Pas									
9		Cathren	Cottier				3				
48		Thomas Moore Pa	Shepherd		1						1
		Mary Irwin Pro	Widdow			3			2		2
33	Cleboy	James Furry Pas									
71		Mary	Herd		2		2				1
—		Mary Roddy Pa	Widdow								
177	Lekerue	Cormk. McDonogh[4] Pa	Parish Priest						1		2
[f.269A Ballintober	Cloonikerny	Andw Keaveny Pas									
		Cathrin	Welder		3		1		1		2
		Patk. Killbride Pa	Welder		3						1
		Terce. Cooney Pas	Welder								1
		Mary Connor Pa	Widdow		2		1		1		
		Michl. Keaveny Pas									
		Cathrin	Welder						1		1
		James Kelly Pas									
		Mary	Herd				2				
	Rossmeen	Edmd. Ruane Pas									
		Rosamunda	Herd		1		1		1		
		Peter Fitzsymons Pas									
		Catharin	Shepherd		1		2				1
		Catharine Conry Pa	Widdow				1				
	Ballentober	Edwd Connor Pas									
		Jane	Mercht.		3				1		1
		Jas. Dermot Pas									
		Eliz.	Ale draper				3				
		Luke Horran Pas									
		Cathrin	Farrier				1				
		Patk. Hannen Pas									
		Margaret	Cottier				1				
		Patrick Dury Pa	Black Smith				4				1
		Charles Reily Pas									
		Eliz.	Butcher		1		2				
Prots 1	Ballyfinigan	Christopher Phare Pro									
		Elizabeth Pa:	Skinner	2				1	1		
4		Patrick McDonogh Pas									
		Mary	Welder		1		2				
7		Wm. Compton Pro									
		Cecilia	Farmer	3		1			1		2
7		Henery Higgins Papt	Herd				2				2
—		Loughlen Higins Pas									
19		Bridgett	Cottier						1		1
Paps 14		Michl. Beasly Pas									
		Margaret	Cottier		3		2				
9		John Dermott Pas									
		Anne Pro	Tobacco spinner		2						
	Snipehill	John Phare Pro									
34		Mary	Herd	2		3					
		Murtagh Royen Pas									
35		Cathrin	Cottier	2	2						
61		Patk. Donelane Pas									
—		Catharin	Cottier	3	3						
154		Owen Royen Pas	Cottier	1	1						

Com~Ros common Parish of	Place of Abode	Names and Religion	Proffession	Children under 14 Prot.	Paps.	Children above 14 Prot.	Paps.	Men Servts Prot.	Paps.	Women Servts Prot.	Paps.
		John Rogers Pas / Bridget	Cottier	~~3~~	2		1				
		John Killbride Pas / Mary	Flax dresser		1						
		Patk. Rogers Pas / Margaret	Cottier		2						
		John Healy Pas / Bridget	Cottier		1						
		Winifrida Connelly Pa	Widdow		1		2				
		John Collens Pas / Bridget	Cottier				1				
		Giles Connelly Pa	Widdow				1				
		John Kearny Pas / Sarah	Cottier								
		Terence Poile Pas	Cottier								
		James Kelly Pas	Cottier				~~2~~		1		1
	Rathmeige	Patrk McManus Pas / Catharin	Weaver				2				
		Loughlen fflanagan Pas / Margaret	Welder		1						
		John Whitehead Prot									1
		Loughlin Frain Pas / Catherine	Cottier		1		2				
[f.270]	Cloonagh	Frans Glancy⁵ Pro / Mary	Welder	3		1		1			1
		Robt. Blackburn Pro	Shoemaker	1		2					1
		Patrick Ferrall Pas / Bridget	Cottier		4		5				
		Roger Gormly Pas / Bridget	Cottier			3					
		Patk. Connelly Pas / Margaret	Cottier		1						
		James Dillon Pas / Margaret	Cottier		2						1
		Patrick Ferrall Pas / Cathrin	Cottier				1				1
		Mary Mooney Pa	Widdow		1						
		Michl. Burn Pas / Margaret	Cottier		1		1				
		Michl. Corkran Pas / Bridget	Cottier		3		1				
		Thomas Teige Pas / Anne	Cottier		1		1		1		
		Richd. Dillon Pas / Bridget	Cottier		3						
		Judith Ferrall Pa	Widdow				3				
		Owen Clark Pas / Judith	Cottier		1		1				1
		Patk. Ganly Pas / Honora	Cottier		1		1				
		Patt. Hartt Pas / Mary	Cottier		3		2				
		Charles Hallinan Pas / Ellinor			2			1		~~+~~	
		Henery Loyde Pa	Cottier		2						1
		Patk. Tracey Pas / Catharin	Miller		2				1		1
Prots 1		James McGarry Pas / Mary	Cottier		2		1				
6		Mary Garry Pa	Widdow		1						
17		Dens. Cullan Pas / Eliz.	Cottier		2						1
14											

Com~Ros common Parish of	Place of Abode	Names and Religion	Proffession	Children under 14		Children above 14		Men Servts		Women Servts	
				Prot.	Paps.	Prot.	Paps.	Prot.	Paps.	Prot.	Paps.
Paps 13											
7		Mark Lyons Pa	Begr.		2						
27		John Tyrrell Pas									
6[?]		Anne	Mercht.		2				1		2
51		John Poile Pas									
65		Margaret	Cottier		2						1
____		James Poile Pas	Cottier								1
164		Richd. Dunn Pro									
		Margaret	Shoemaker	2				1		1	
		Markus Fallon Pas									
		Honora	Cottier		1						
		Denis Kelly Pas									
		Margaret	Cottier		1		2				
		Owen Ternan Pas									
		Ellinor	Cottier		1						
		Markus Murry Pas									
		Margaret	Cottier		2						
		Patrick Manion Pas									
		Mary	Cooper		2		1		1		
		Edmd. Egan Pas									
		Mary	Welder		2				1		1
		James Quin Pas									
		Margaret	Cottier				2				
		John Quin Pas									
		Mary	Cottier								
		Thady Kelly Pas									
		Jane	Welder		2		2				
		Dens. Ganly Pas									
		Bridget	Cadger		2						
		Danl. Kelly Pas									
		Catharin	Welder								
		Margaret Kelly Pro	Widdow				2				
		Sarah Morron Pas	Widdow				1				
[f.271]	Cloonagh	James Noon Pas									
		Margaret	Weaver		1				1		
		Thady Flanagan Pas									
		Bridget	Cottier				2				
		James Timothy Pas									
		Margaret	Welder		1		1				1
		Patrick Timothy Pas									
		Bridget	Welder		1		2				
		John Kane Pas									
		Bridget	Cottier		1						1
		Patrick Kane Pas									
		Catharine	Welder		2		1				
		Luke Ternan Pas									
		Honora	Welder		1		3				
		Thady Kane Pas									
		Anne	Welder				1				1
		Edwd Concanon Pas									
		Sarah	Welder				1				1
		Andw. Fferrall Pas									
		Margaret	Cottier		1		3				
		John Croghon Pas									
		Mary	Cottier		3						1
		Michl. Millan Pas									
		Bridget	Welder								
		Hugh Conelly Pas									
		Bridget	Taylor		1						

Com~Ros common Parish of	Place of Abode	Names and Religion	Proffession	Children under 14		Children above 14		Men Servts		Women Servts	
				Prot.	Paps.	Prot.	Paps.	Prot.	Paps.	Prot.	Paps.
		Oliver Slanly Pas									
		Giles	Weaver		2		2		1		
		Martn. Connor Pas									
		Mary	Welder		2				2		1
	Willsgrove	Godfrey Wills Pro[6]									
		Sarah[7] Sarah the Elder[8] Pro	Esqr.	7[9]			1	2	4	2	2
	Bowagh	Phillip Carty Pas									
		Catharin	Shepherd		1				1		1
		Catharin Carty Pa	Widdow				1				
		Thomas Blee Pas									
		Bridget	Shepherd		3				1		1
		John Hinde Pro									
		Eliz.	Herd			2		2			1
	Knocklaght	Mathias Connor Pas									
		Judith	Cottier		2						
		Wm. Egan Pas									
		Mary	Cottier		1						
Prots 2		Danl. Hallinan Pas									
4		Mary	Welder		4				1		1
3		Maths. Hanon Pas									
5		Honora	Cottier		2						
20		Patk. Connor Pas									
Paps16		Catharin	Cottier		1		1				
12		Edmd. Cunane Pas									
29		Mary	Cottier		3						
55		Thady Flanagan Pas									
71		Mary	Cottier		2						
183		Hugh Fineran Pas									
		Mary	Cottier		1						1
		Patrick Dugan Pas									
		Catharin	Cottier		3						
		Catharin Blee Pa	Widdow		2		1				
		Danl. Bradikin Pa	Shepherd		2		2				
		Bryan Sharkey Pas									
		Catharin	Cottier				2				
		Andw. Beirn Pas									
		Mary	Cottier		3				1		1
		Henery Higgins Pas									
		Margaret	Cottier		2						
		Catharin Kerine Pa	Widdow				3				
		Terce. Cunigham Pas									
		Bridget	Cottier		2						1
		James Connor Pas									
		Mary	Cottier		2						
		Patrick Connor Pa:	Cottier								1
		Richd. Madden									
		Mary Pas	Slater		2						
		Bryan Corkran									
		Mary Pa:	Cottier		1		2				
[f.272] Ballintober	Knocklaght	Chas Corkran Pas									
		Mary	Cottier		2						1
		Myles Corkran Pas									
		Catharin	Cottier		2		1				
		Andw. Bradikin Pas									
		Mary	Cottier				1				
		Edmd. Murly Pas									
		Bridget	Cottier				1				
		John Murly Pas									
		Ellinor	Cottier		1						
		Margaret Ferrall	Cottier				3				

Com~Ros common Parish of	Place of Abode	Names and Religion	Proffession	Children under 14 Prot.	Children under 14 Paps.	Children above 14 Prot.	Children above 14 Paps.	Men Servts Prot.	Men Servts Paps.	Women Servts Prot.	Women Servts Paps.
	Carubane	Patrick Lenon Pas / Honora	Cottier		1		3				
		Darby Keaveny Pas / Jane	Herd								
		Loughlen Rogers Pas / Catharin	Cottier				2				
		Willm. Ducey Pas / Giles	Cottier		2						1
	Carureagh	John Langdale Pro / Ellinor Pas		1		3			1		1
		John Corkran Pro / Mary	Welder			2	2				1
		Peter Plunket Pas / Margaret	Welder	1							1
		Bryan Gubilane Pas / Ellinor	Welder		2						1
		Owen Egan Pas / Catharin	Welder		2				1		
		Danl. Keogh Pas / Bridget	Brogemaker		2						
		Bryan Gowran Pas / Cathrine	Cottier		2		1				
		James Plunket Pas / Mary	Cottier		1		2				
		John Kane Pas / Margaret	Cottier		1						1
		Thady Kyne Pas / Catharin	Weaver		2						
		John Rogers Pas / Mary	Herd		1		1				
	Tourenagh	John Cunigham Pas / Margaret	Cottier		2						
		Patk. McNeal Pas / Catharin	Cottier		3						
		John Connelly Pas / Bridget	Cottier		2		1				
		Connor Coyne Pas / Honora	Cottier				2				
		Manus Coyne Pas / Catharin	Cottier		3						
		Edmd Donelly Pas / Margaret	Cottier		1		2				
		James Gowran Pas / Mary	Cottier		1						1
		Michl. Shaughnesy Pas / Mary	Cottier		1		3				
		John Loughlen Pas / Bridget	Cottier		1		1				
Prots 1		Wm. Lenughane Pas / Margaret	Cottier		2		1				
3		Patrick Coyne Pas / Bridget	Cottier		2		3				
2		Cormk. McLoughlen Pas / Bridget	Cottier		2		1				
6		Michl. Mooney Pas / Catharin	Cottier		3						
12		Sarah Kerney Pa	Widdow				2				
Paps 10	Innfield	Edmd. Kelly Prots / Anne	Esqr.					1	2		2
4											
38											
50											
71											
173											

Com~Ros common Parish of	Place of Abode	Names and Religion	Proffession	Children under 14 Prot.	Children under 14 Paps.	Children above 14 Prot.	Children above 14 Paps.	Men Servts Prot.	Men Servts Paps.	Women Servts Prot.	Women Servts Paps.
[f.273]	The rest of Innfield	James Ward Pas Honora	Cottier		1		2				
		James Conelane Pas Mary	Cottier		1		2				
		Owen Burrane Pas Margaret	Peddler		1						
		Michael Sweeny Pa	Cottier		2		2				
		Edmd. Caffry Pas Anne	Steward				3				1
		Hugh Blee Pas Margaret	Gardnr.				3				
		John Blee Pas Mary	Cottier		1						
		Andw. Cunelane Pas Bridget	Cottier		1						
		Domk. Rogers Pas Mary	Herd		1		2				
		Clare Kelly Pa:	Widdow				2				

Papsts 1
10
3
11
25

Prots Pg 1. 4
2. 19
3. 14
4. 20
5. 12
Totl. Of Prots 69

Paps pg 1. 177
2 154
3 164
4 183
5 173
6 25
Totl of Paps. 869
Tot of Paps 876

[3 blank pages]

[verso last page]

Union of Kilkevin otherwise Castlereagh
Protestants 338
Papists 446[?]3

NOTES

1. *General Alphabetical Index.*

2. Lewis, 'Ballintober'.

3. *Report ... fairs and markets.*

4. Cormik McDonnagh was the Roman Catholic parish priest of Ballintober in the State of Popery report in 1731. He held it with Ogula (Beirne, (ed.) *Diocese of Elphin*, p.109).

5. Fras. Glancy, freeholder was a supporter of Godfrey Wills in 1768 (N.L.I., Freeholders of Roscommon, MS 35,163).

6. Godfrey Wills, who died 13 January 1781, was a son of James Wills and Sarah Curtis. Wills was a student at the Middle Temple in 1723, and admitted to the King's Inns in 1731. Godfrey Wills inherited land from his father who had died in 1731. Their marriage settlement included real estate from his uncle Caspar Wills and further property on Caspar Wills's death in 1742. He married Sarah Montgomery, daughter of Alexander Montgomery of Ballyleck, County Monaghan in 1731. They had eight children. Godfrey Wills was an intimate friend of Edward Synge, advising him on the repair of the cathedral at Elphin in 1760 and acting as executor and trustee of Edward Synge's will. It is possible that he was related to Synge by marriage, as Synge married Jane Curtis of Roscrea, co. Tipperary (N.L.I., Wills Papers, MS 3203).

7. Sarah Wills died 10 January 1766 (N.L.I., Wills Papers, MS 3203).

8. Sarah Wills, née Cole was the widow of Caspar Wills of Willsgrove (Will of Casper Wills, 3 January 1742, N.L.I., Wills Papers, MS 3203).

9. Elizabeth (Betty) Wills, daughter of Godfrey Wills married Thomas Mitchell of Castle Strange, Co. Roscommon. (Bernard Burke, <u>Landed Gentry of Ireland</u> (London 1912)).

CLOONYGORMICAN COUNTY ROSCOMMON

INTRODUCTION: *The parish of Cloonygormican is in the barony of Ballymoe. It is 5¹/₄ miles north-north-west from Roscommon on the road to Castlerea. It had 8543 statute acres, of which 45 acres was water.[1] It was principally pasture but there was some bog which was used for fuel for the inhabitants.[2] In 1837, Lewis noted that there was good limestone, but the quarries were not worked. In 1749, however, there were masons in the parish.*

The Church of Ireland incumbent was the Rev. Oliver Cary, prebendary of Kilcooley. The parish was held with those of Shankill, Kilcooley, Kilmacumsy, Kilcorkey, Killuken and Kilmctranny (see Shankill.) The patron was the bishop. The rectory was impropriate in the Earl of Essex and Lord De Ros. The church at Cloonygormican, 'a plain edifice', was built by Charles Hawkes of Briarfield as a chapel of ease in about 1720.[3]

OCCUPATIONS

Aleseller	1	Mason	2	Spinster	1
Constable	1	Merchant	1	Tailor	4
Cottier	17	Miller	1	Tenant	17
Esquire	1	Pumpmaker	2	Weaver	6
Farmer	8	Servant	8	Wheelwright	1
Herd	11	Servants, household	360	Wigmaker	3
Labourer	186	Smith	5		

Com~Ros com Parish of	Place of Abode	Names and Religion	Proffession	Children under 14		Children above 14		Men Servts		Women Servts	
				Prot.	Paps.	Prot.	Paps.	Prot.	Paps.	Prot.	Paps.
[f.274] Cloonygormican	Bryanfield	Chas Hawkes[4] & wife Prot	Esqr.					2		1	2
	Carrowbane	Domk. Mahon & wife Pap	Servt.	1	3				1		1
		Patk. Kielty & wife Pap	Labr.		4						
		Jas. Mulraney & wife Pap	Labr.		2				1		1
		Patk. Clayton & wife Pap	Servt.		2		2		1		
		Domk. Kielty & wife Pap	Servt.		2		2				1
		Thos. Laget Prot & wife Pap	Constable		1				2		1
		Stephen Plunket & wife Pap	Cottier		2				1		1
	Farraragh	Patk. Brady & wife Pap	Labr.		1		1				1
		Darby Lamb & wife Pap	Labr.		2				1		1
		Dennis Coen & wife Pap	Labr.		2				1		1
		Michl. Tenane & wife Pap	Labr.		1						1
		Michl. Lavin & wife Pap	Labr.		1		1		1		1
		Edwd. Lavin & wife Pap	Labr.		3		1				1
		Thady Lavin & wife Pap	Labr.		2				1		1
		Geo. Flanigan & wife Pap	Labr.		2						1
		Bryan Lavin & wife Pap	Herd		2				1		1
		Patk. Rogers & wife Pap	Labr.		2		1				1
		John Casserly & wife Pap	Labr.		2		1				1
		Thos. Conelly & wife Pap	Labr.		2		1		1		2
		John Faghy & wife Pap	Mercht.		3						1
		Owen Hester & wife Pap	Labr.		1						1
		Fergus Carolly & wife Pap	Labr.		3						1
		Conner Kenny & wife Pap	Weaver				1				
		John O Hara & wife Pap	Labr.		2				1		1
		Patk. Corkran & wife Pap	Labr.		3						1
		Luke Corkran & wife Pap	Labr.		1						1
		John Laurence & wife Prot	Labr.	3					1		1
		Michl. Kinnade & wife Pap	Labr.		3		1				1
		Dan. Shivnan & wife Pap	Labr.		2		4				1
		Hugh Geolyn & wife Pap	Labr.		1				1		1
		Mary Davies Widow	Farmer		2		2		2		3
	Highlake[5]	Jas. Colwell & wife Pap	Labr.		3						1
		Patk. Hedeen & wife Pap	Labr.		1				1		2
		Patk. Wynne Pa	Cottier				4				
		Owen Cormack & wife Pap	Smith		3				1		1
		Will. Commons & wife Pap	Labr.		4						1
		Ferral Noon & wife Pap	Labr.		3				1		1
		John Coyle & wife Pap	Labr.		3		1				1
[f.275] Cloony-gormecan	Highlake	Sarah Common Widow Pap	Cotter		2		1				1
		Patk. Laughlin & wife Pap	Labr.		4				1		1
		Patk. Cooney & wife Pap	Labr.		3				1		
		Bryan Cooney & wife Pap	Labr.		2		1				
		Myles Gayner & wife Pap	Labr.		3						
		Willm. Ward & wife Pap	Labr.		1		2				
		Anthony Henegan Pap	Labr.		1						2
		Willm. Coen & wife Pap	Labr.		1		4				

Com~Ros common Parish of	Place of Abode	Names and Religion	Proffession	Children under 14		Children above 14		Men Servts		Women Servts	
				Prot.	Paps.	Prot.	Paps.	Prot.	Paps.	Prot.	Paps.
		John Maxwell & wife Pap	Labr.		3						1
		Bryan Wynne & wife Pap	Labr.				2		1		
		Chas. Riley Pap	Smith						1		1
		Willm. Hobbin & wife Pap	Labr.								
		Martin Hobbin & wife Pap	Labr.		1		2		1		
		Bryan Hanley & wife Pap	Labr.		5						1
		Jas. Mahon & wife Pap	Labr.		4						1
		Thos. Fury & wife Pap	Labr.				3				
		Peter Fury & wife Pap	Labr.		1						1
		John McDermott[6] & wife Pap	Farmer		7		1		5		8
		Maggy Irwin Pap	Spinr.								
		Owen Gowren & wife Pap	Labr.		3						1
		Thady Eagan & wife Pap	Weaver		3				1		1
		John Finaghty & wife Pap	Labr.			2					
		Thos. Finaghty & wife Pap	Labr.		1				1		1
		Roger Carolly Pap	Labr.								
		John Dooney Pap	Labr.								
		Jas. Kelly & wife Pap	Wigmaker						1		1
	Ballymackeriley	Jas Fineraghty & wife Pap	Tent.		2				1		2
		Fran. Burk Pap	Labr.				2				
		Ferrall Hester & wife Pap	Labr.				3				1
		John Naghton & wife Pap	Labr.		1		1		1		1
		Jas. Finraghty & wife Pap	Labr.				2				1
		Elinor Ferral widow Pap	Cottier		1				1		2
		Bryan Kelly & wife Pap	Labr.				3		1		1
		John Cooney & wife Pap	Labr.			2					
		Garrett Ferrall & wife Pap	Labr.		2				1		1
		Andw. Rowan & wife Pap	Labr.				3		1		
		John Moran & wife Pap	Labr.		3						
		Peter Mullady & wife Pap	Labr.		2		1				1
		Patk. Conry & wife Pap	Farmer						3		2
		John Haley & wife Pap	Labr.		2				1		1
[f.276] Cloony-gormican	Ballymackeriley	Peter Foley & wife Pap	Weaver						1		1
		Hugh Finraghty & wife Pap	Labr.		2				1		1
		Andw. McDermott Prot & wife Pa Farmer		2		1			2		2
		Thady Fanikin & wife Pap	Taylor		2				1		1
		Chris. Boylan & wife Pap	Labr.		2						1
	Skehingan	Festus Flynn[7] & 2 Sisters Pap	Farmer						4		4
		Patk. Fetherston & wife Pap	Labr.		3						1
		Patk. Dwire & wife Pap	Labr.								
		Willm. Grindeloge & wife Pap	Labr.		1		3		1		1
		Jas. Ribbin & wife Pap	Labr.		1						
		Jas. Heanerey & wife Pap	Herd		1						2
		Watt Heanerey & wife Pap	Labr.		1				2		1
		Sarah Laughlen widow Pap	Cotter				1				
		Bryan Conner & wife Pap	Labr.				1				1
		Geo. Walder & wife Pap	Labr.		1		3				

Com~Ros common Parish of	Place of Abode	Names and Religion	Proffession	Children under 14		Children above 14		Men Servts		Women Servts	
				Prot.	Paps.	Prot.	Paps.	Prot.	Paps.	Prot.	Paps.
		Willm. Faghey & wife Pap	Servt.		2				2		1
		Chas Kennedy & wife Pap	Servt.		5						1
		Michl. Henry & wife Pap	Servt.		2				2		1
		John Kean & wife Pap	Pumpmaker						1		1
		Ferral Kean & wife Pap	Labr.	1		2					
		Thos. Gannon & wife Pap	Smith		1				1		1
		Owen Conner Pap	Labr.								
		Dan. Conner & wife Pap	Labr.				4		1		1
		Con. McDermott & wife Pap	Wigmaker		1				1		1
		Jas. Burk & wife Pap	Labr.		1						1
		Matt. Gannan Pap	Labr.								
		Luke Coyn & wife Pap	Labr.		1				1		1
		John Dooley & wife Pap	Tent.						1		1
		Alexr. Ferrall Prot & wife Pap	Mason	2					1		1
		Laughlin Skally & wife Pap	Labr.		2		2				
		Patk. Mulkerin & wife Pap	Labr.		2				1		
		Laur. Duffy & wife Pap	Labr.		1						
		Jas. Bannagher & wife Pap	Labr.								1
		Owen Kennedy & wife Pap	Labr.						1		
		Chas. Nally & wife Pap	Labr.		1						1
		Cormk. Capall & wife Pap	Labr.		1		1				1
		Patk. Mulchean & wife Pap	Labr.		2				1		1
		Patk. Kilgan & wife Pap	Labr.						1		1
		Thos. Dillon & wife Pap	Labr.		1				1		1
[f.276[A]]	Ballinturley	Edwd Hobbin & wife Pap	Tent.		2				1		1
		Thos. Hobbin & wife Pap	Tent.						1		1
		Jas. Hobbin & wife Pap	Tent.		1				1		1
		Dennis Cronan & wife Pap	Herd		1		1		1		1
		Peter Durr & wife Pap	Labr.				2				
		Michl. Connelan & wife Pap	Labr.		1		4				
		Patk. Ferrall & wife Pap	Labr.		2						1
		Domk. Dillon & wife Pap	Labr.		1				1		1
		Thos. Ferrall & wife Pap	Labr.		2						1
		Thos. Coyn & wife Pap	Lab:		1						
		Danl. Brenan & wife Pap	Labr.		2				1		1
		Elinor Ford widow Pap	Cottier		1		1				
		Den. Kallaghar & wife Pap	Labr.		1				1		
		Edwd. Conelly & wife Pap	Labr.		3						1
		Thady Higgins & wife Pap	Labr.			3					1
		Hugh Gadien & wife Pap	Tent.		2				1		1
		Manus Gadian & wife Pap	Tent.						1		1
		Martin Coyn & wife Pap	Labr.		3						1
		Dennis Kenny & wife Pap	Labr.		3						
		John Kallaghan & wife Pap	Labr.		1				1		1
		Patk. Kean & wife Pap	Labr.		1		2				
		Jos. Kennedy & wife Pap	Labr.		4				1		
		John Gevlyn & wife Pap	Aleseller						1		1
	Carrowduff[8]	John Griffin Pa & wife Prot	Tent.						2		2
		John Wilson & wife Prot	Tent.	3					4		1

Com~Ros common Parish of	Place of Abode	Names and Religion	Proffession	Children under 14		Children above 14		Men Servts		Women Servts	
				Prot.	Paps.	Prot.	Paps.	Prot.	Paps.	Prot.	Paps.
		Patk. Keechran Pro:	Tent.								
		Wm. Keechran Prot & wife Pa	Tent.		2				1		1
		Thos. Keechran Prot & wife Pa	Tent.	1					1		1
		Thady Rogers & wife Pap	Tent.		3				1		
		Myles McDermott & wife Pap	Labr.		3		2				
		Bryan Finerty & wife Pap	Labr.		3						
		Anthony Green & wife Pap	Labr.		2				1		
		Thos. Adair & wife Pap	Labr.		4						1
		Willm. Adair & wife Pap	Labr.		1				1		
		Richd. Lyons & wife Pap	Labr.		1						1
		Bryan Kelaghan & wife Pap	Labr.		2						1
		Patk. Kelaghan & wife Pap	Labr.								1
		Michl. Kelly & wife Pap	Labr.		3		1				
		Bryan Quigley & wife Pap	Labr.		1						2
		Roger Henagan & wife Pap	Labr.		3		2				
[f.278] Cloony-gormican	Carrowduff	Roger Carolly & wife Pap	Labr.		1		3				
		Edwd. Croghan & wife Pap	Labr.		2						1
	Raconilly	Geo. Waldron & wife Pap	Taylor		4						1
		Cormk. Crean & wife Pap	Labr.		3						
		Patk. mcDermott & wife Pap	Herd				2				
		Thos. McAndrew & wife Pap	Labr.		3						1
		John. Naghton & wife Pap	Labr.		1		2				
		Michl. Coyn & wife Pap	Labr.		2						1
		Owen Quigley & wife Pap	Labr.		1		2				
		Henry Kelly & wife Pap	Labr.		3						1
		Loughlan Kelly & wife Pap									
		Owen Cullen & wife Pap	Labr.								1
		Thos. McDermott & wife Pap	Labr.		3		1				
		Michl. Whyte & wife Pap	Labr.		3						1
		Thos. Whyte & wife Pap	Labr.								
		Margt. Conry widow Pap	Cottier		1		1				
		Peter Lough & wife Pap	Labr.		1		1				
		Patk. Kelly & wife Pap	Labr.				1				
		Dennis Conelly & wife Pap	Labr.		1		1				
		Edwd. Haydon & wife Pap	Labr.		2				1		1
		Jos. McDermott & wife Pap	Tent.				3		2		3
		Willm. Gormley & wife Pap	Tent.		3				1		2
		Edwd. Cowan & wife Pap	Tent.		3		1				
		Owen Hughes & wife Pap	Labr.				4		1		
		Willm. Naghton & wife Pap	Labr.		3						
		Patk. Carroll & wife Pap	Labr.		2		3				
	Killtultoge	Michl. Adair & wife Pap	Labr.		3		2		1		1
		Peter Kean & wife Pap	Labr.		2						
		Thos. Mccormk. & wife Pap	Labr.		2				1		1
		John Finan & wife Pap	Labr.		2				1		1
		Edwd Doherty & wife Pap	Labr.		2						
		Peter Conner & wife Pap	Labr.		2						
		Luke Adair & wife Pap	Labr.		3						

Com~Ros common Parish of	Place of Abode	Names and Religion	Proffession	Children under 14 Prot.	Paps.	Children above 14 Prot.	Paps.	Men Servts Prot.	Paps.	Women Servts Prot.	Paps.
		Ellen Mitchell widow Pap	Cottier		1		1				
		Willm. Grindeloge & wife Pap	Labr.						3		1
		Bryan Adair Pap	Labr.					3		1	
		Patk. Cavenagh & wife Pap	Labr.		3		1				1
		Jas. Donnellan & wife Pap	Labr.		2				1		1
[f.279] Cloony-gormican	Runnymead	Bryan Fallon & wife Pap	Farmer						6		10
		Bryan Higgins & wife Pap	Servt.		2				1		1
		Michl. Ward & wife Pap	Servt.						1		1
		Owen Carrick & wife Pap	Labr.		3						1
		John Monaghan & wife Pap	Labr.		3		1				
		Hugh Hanley & wife Pap	Labr.		3				1		1
		Bryan Gurrick & wife Pap	Labr.		4				1		
		Dennis Ferrall & wife Pap	Herd		4				1		1
		Jas. Traccy & wife Pap	Labr.				2		2		1
		Willm. Bryan & wife Pap	Labr.		4		2				1
		Jane Bryans widow Pap	Cottier		3				1		
		Patk. Drennen & wife Pap	Labr.		2				1		1
		Widow Gord Pap	Cottier		4						1
		John Farriley & wife Pap	Wheelright		2				1		1
		Patk. Murray & wife Pap	Labr.		3				1		1
		Jon. Dogherty & wife Pap	Labr.		3		3				1
		Anthony Mason & wife Pap	Smith								1
		Patk. Beasly & wife Pap	Labr.		2						2
		Patk. Carroll & wife Pap	Lab:		5						
	Ballyglass	John Fallon & wife Pap	Farmer		2				2		5
		Edwd Looagh & wife Pap	Herd		3				1		1
		Loughlin Ward & wife Pap	Labr.				1		2		2
		Patk. Ferrall & Mor & sisr. Pap	Labr.								1
		Dennis Ward & wife Pap	Labr.		3		1				
		Patk. Ward & wife Pap	Labr.		3						
		Peter Conry & wife Pap	Labr.		3						1
		Fran. Carroll widow Pap	Cottier				4				
		Laughlin Fagan & wife Pap	Mason		3				1		1
		Darby McDermott & wife Pap	Labr.		3						1
		Thos. Killcarly & wife Pap	Weaver		3		1				1
		Thady Mannin & wife Pap	Smith		1				1		1
		John Ferrall & wife Pap	Labr.		3						
		Fran. Glass & wife Pap	Lab:		4						
[f.280] Cloony-gormegan	Grange	Sus. Ormsby widow Prot	Farmer			2		1	2		2
		Tiege Cronan & wife Pap	Cottier		4						
		Patk. Hurley & wife Pap	Taylor		2						1
		Cormk. Duffy & wife Pap	Labr.		1						
		Neal Laughlin & wife Pap	Labr.		2				1		1
		John Laughlin & wife Pap	Labr.		3				1		1
		Bryan Daly & wife Pap	Labr.		5		1				
		Thady Hughes & wife Pap	Herd		2						1
		Richd. Joycer & wife Pap	Labr.		2						

Com~Ros common Parish of	Place of Abode	Names and Religion	Proffession	Children under 14 Prot.	Children under 14 Paps.	Children above 14 Prot.	Children above 14 Paps.	Men Servts Prot.	Men Servts Paps.	Women Servts Prot.	Women Servts Paps.
		Edwd. Dalton & wife Pap	Labr.		1		1				
		Fran. Neal & wife Pap	Cottier		2				1		1
		Willm. Carragher & wife Pap	Labr.						1		1
		Andw. Dalton & wife Pap	Taylor		3						1
		John Nish & wife Pap	Weaver		4						1
		Thos. Conaghten & wife Pap	Labr.		3						
		Michl. Neal & wife Pap	Weaver								1
		John Burk. & wife Pap	Labr.		3						
		John Carroll & wife Pap	Labr.		6				1		
		Michl. Lenagon & wife Pap	Labr.		4						
		Luke Barley & wife Pap	Labr.		2						1
		Conner O Hara & wife Pap	Labr.		1						
		Mary Nevin widow Pap	Cottier		3						
		John Kelly & wife Pap	Cottier		6		2				
		Thady Brenan & wife Pap	Labr.		4		3				
		Patk. Walsh & wife Pap	Pumpmaker		2						1
		Allice Lewis widow Pap	Cottier		1		2				
		Lau: Finarghty & wife Pap	Labr.		2		2				
		Michl. Finan & wife Pap	Labr.		2				1		
		Conner Brenan & wife Pap	Labr.		4						
		Willm. Whyte & wife Pap	Labr.		1		1		1		1
		Andw. McDermott & wife Pap	Labr.		3						
		Darby Moran & wife Pap	Labr.		3						
		Patk. Garner & wife Pap	Labr.		3		3				
		Hugh Corahan & wife Pap	Miller		5				1		1
		Dennis Kenny & wife Pap	Labr.		2						1
		Darby Finy & wife Pap	Labr.		2		2				
		Cath. Grogan widow Pap	Cottier				1				
		Lau: Scanlan & wife Pap	Herd		3						1
		Thos. Maley & wife Pap	Herd		2				1		1
		Phil. Common & wife Pap	Herd		1		2				
		Edwd. Golrick Pap	Labr.		2						1
[f.281]	Clooneetagan	Patk. Rayney & wife Pap	Herd		1		1				1
		Phil. Dowd & wife Pap	Labr.		1						
		Jas. Scanlon & wife Pap	Labr.						1		
		Luke Connery & wife Pap	Labr.		1		1				
		Andw. Garvin & wife Pap	Labr.		2						1
	Gubeglannow	Thos. Walsh & wife Pap	Tent.		2		1				2
		Ter. Connor & wife Pap	Wigmaker		3				1		1

[verso f. 281]

In the Parish	Pro: Men	Pro Wo:	Pa: Men	Pa Wo:
of Cloonegormegan	10	5	253	260

Pro. Children 15 under 14	Pa: Children 486 under 14
Pro: Children 3 above 14	Pa Children 161 above 14
Pro: Men Sts 3	Pa: Men Sts 142
Pro:Women Sts 1	Pa: Women Sts 215
All Prots 37	Tot: Paps.1517

NOTES

1. *General Alphabetical Index* .

2. Lewis, 'Ardclare or Clonigormican'.

3. Ibid.

4. Charles Hawkes of Briarfield married first, Ellen Loftus and second in 1748, Margaret Kirkpatrick. He had two daughters, Sarah and Susanna. He died ca. 1753 (N.L.I, Pedigree of the Hawkes family, MS GO 802/10).

5. Highlake townland was arable and pastureland with about 3 acres of moorland. There was a large proportion of cut and red bog (N.L.I., Longfield Maps, MS 21 F 23/33).

6. John McDermott of Highlake was a lay supporter of the Rev. William (alias Augustine) O'Kelly, prior of St. Mary's, Roscommon in 1748 to succeed Patrick French as bishop of Elphin (Fenning, 'Diocese of Elphin', p.166).

7. Festus O'Flyn of Skehine was a lay supporter of the Rev. William (alias Augustine) O'Kelly, prior of St. Mary's, Roscommon in 1748 to succeed his uncle, Patrick French as bishop of Elphin (Fenning, 'Diocese of Elphin', p.166).

8. Carrowduff townland had arable and pasture land, but the pasture was flooded part of the year. In the south of the townland there was wet bottom pasture with 'veins of marl'. There was some green pasturable cut bog (N.L.I., Map of lands in the barony of Athlone, Ballintober, Ballymoe and Boyle, MS 12 F 43(31)).

KILCOOLEY, COUNTY ROSCOMMON

INTRODUCTION: *The parish of Kilcooley is in the barony of Roscommon, 4 miles south west of Strokestown. Lewis said that the land was good grazing land, with little bog, and with good quality limestone which was quarried both for agriculture and for building.*[1]

The townland of Clooneagh was owned by the Connor family in 1641, and Mark Conner, a tenant was there in 1749.[2]

The parish of Kilcooley was joined with that of Killuken, Kilmacumsy, Shankill and Kilmactranny. The rectory of Kilcooley was part of the prebend of Kilcooley. The tithes were paid to the incumbent who was the Rev. Oliver Cary (see Shankill). The patron was the bishop.

OCCUPATIONS

Aleseller	2	Farmer	3	Labourer	110
Constable	1	Herd	1	Servants, household	104
				Spinster	1
Cottier	13	Innkeeper	1	Tenant	3
Esquire	1	Joiner	1	Weaver	2

Com~Ros common Parish of	Place of Abode	Names and Religion	Proffession	Children under 14		Children above 14		Men Servts		Women Servts	
				Prot.	Paps.	Prot.	Paps.	Prot.	Paps.	Prot.	Paps.
[f.282] Killcooley	Ballybrehan	Michl. Contrine & wife Pap	Constable		5		1				1
		Edwd. Tiernan & wife Pap	Lab:		1		2				2
		Willm. Rainy & wife Pap	Aleseller		3				1		1
		Margt. Finaghty Pap	Cottier		3						
		Chas. Tiernan & wife Pap	Lab:		2						1
		Roger Mulrany & wife Pap	Lab:		2		2				
		Winifrid Conner widow Pap	Cottier		3				1		1
		John Skally & wife Pap	Lab:		3						
		Pattk. Meahan & wife Pap	Lab:		1		2				
	Carkar	Terence Ferrall & wife Pap	Farmer		4				1		2
		Andw. Kelly & wife Pap	Tent.				2				
		Michl. Lenagan & wife Pap	Lab:		3				1		
		Michl. Keherny & wife Pap	Lab:				1				1
		Bryan Burn & wife Pap	Lab:		4				1		1
		John Tiernan & wife Pap	Lab:		3				1		
		Luke Macnive & wife Pap	Lab:		2						1
	Correagh	Conner Burk & wife Pap	Lab:		2		4				
		Cath. Conry widow Pap	Cottier				2				
		Patk. Conry & wife Pap	Lab:		2				1		
		Laughlin Bern & wife Pap	Lab:		2		2				
		Tim. Mulraney & wife Pap	Lab:		3		1				1
	Monyboy	Patk. Banaghan & wife Pap	Lab:				5				
		Ferral Broder & wife Pap	Lab:				2				
		Jos. Ash & wife Pap	Lab:		4						1
		Mary Brenan widow Pap	Cottier		1		1				
		Dens. Kerrawn & wife Pap	Lab:				2				
		Kedagh Morris & wife Pap	Lab:		4		1				1
	Killcooley	Jos. Conner & wife Pap	Tenter		4				1		1
		Marie McDermott widow Pap	Cottier		2						
		Tim. Flanigan & wife Pap	Lab:		2		1				
		Den. Lenard & wife Pap	Lab:				5				
		Martin Brenan & wife Pap	Lab:		1		5				
		John Haley & wife Pap	Lab:		3		2				
		Chas. McDermott & wife Pap	Lab:		3						1
		Tim. McDermott & wife Pap	Lab:		3		1				
		Peter McDermott & wife Pap	Lab:		2		2				
		Hon. Moran widow Pap	Cottier		2		1				
[f283] Killcooley	Cloonkillaron	Walter Rayney & wife Pap	Lab:		3				1		1
		John Collery & wife Pap	Lab:		3						
		Jos. Raghtagan & wife Pap	Lab:				5				
		Richd. Hansen & wife Pap	Lab:		4						1
		Patk. Burke & wife Pap	Lab:		2						1
		Widow Conner Pap	Cottier		2		2				1
	Carrygurrow	John Conner & wife Pap	Farmer		2				2		2
		Conner Croghan & wife Pap	Lab:		3						
		Roger Conner & wife Pap	Lab:		1						
		Roger Hanley & wife Pap	Lab:		2						
		Patk. Duffy & wife Pap	Lab:		2						1

Com~Ros common Parish of	Place of Abode	Names and Religion	Proffession	Children under 14		Children above 14		Men Servts		Women Servts	
				Prot.	Paps.	Prot.	Paps.	Prot.	Paps.	Prot.	Paps.
		Roger Duffy & wife Pap	Lab:		3						
		Michl. Madden & wife Pap	Lab:		2						
		Chas. Conner & wife Pap	Lab:		1		1				
		Bart. Call & wife Pap	Lab:				3				
		Margt. Chambers widow Pap	Cottier				2				
	Nadneveagh	Michl. Bolton & wife Pap	Lab:		2		2				
		Owen Hunt & wife Pap	Lab:		1		3				
		Willm. Brenan & wife Pap	Lab:		3						1
		Jas. Brenan & wife Pap	Lab:		2						1
	Clooneagh	Mark Conner & wife Pap	Tent.		2		3		1		1
		Stephen Kean & wife Pap	Lab:		3				1		
	Cloonekillen	Jas. Flanigan & wife Pap	Lab:		3						1
		Edwd Burn & wife Pap	Lab:		2						
		Loughlin Burn & wife Pap	Lab:		3				1		
		Willm. Fitzgerald & wife Pap	Lab:		3		1				1
		Margt. Conner widow Pap	Cottier		1		2				
		Mary Flanigan widow Pap	Cottier				4				
		Thady Higgins & wife Pap	Lab:		2						1
		John Dolan & wife Pap	Lab:				2				
		Patk. Higgins & wife Pap	Lab:		3						1
		Patk. Raghty & wife Pap	Lab:		2		4				
		Ter. McLaughlin & wife Pap	Lab:		1						
		Patk. McLaughlin & wife Pap	Lab:		3				1		1
		Patk. Shannan & wife Pap	Lab:		3				1		1
		Thady Bryan & wife Pap	Lab:		2		1				
[f.284] Killcooley	Clooncurr	Darby Haydyan & wife Pap	Lab:				4				
		Owen Brenan Pap	Lab:				4				1
		Thos. Rush & wife Pap	Lab:		2		4				
		Widow Dolan Pap	Cottier		1		4				
		Widow Conner Pap	Cottier		2						3
	Derrykirken	Peter McDermott & wife Pap	Lab:		3				1		
		Andw. McCulan & wife Pap	Lab:		1						
		Ferral Tiernan Pap	Lab:		2						1
		Peter Gaghran & wife Pap	Lab:		1		1				
		Bryan Coyn Pap	Lab:		1						1
		Mattw. Crean & wife Pap	Lab:		2		1				
	Ballybroghten	Michl. Carney & wife Pap	Lab:		1		2				
		Bryan Bern & wife Pap	Lab:		2						1
		Andw. Kelly & wife Pap	Lab:		2		1				
		John Tiernan & wife Pap	Lab:		1						1
		Luke Mcnive & wife Pap	Lab:		2						
		Peter Kean & wife Pap	Lab:		3						1
		Sarah Croghan widow Pap	Cottier				2				
		Jas Beatagh & wife Pap	Aleseller		1		2		1		1
		Michl. Smith & wife Pap	Lab:		3		1				1
	Carrowkeely	John McDermott & wife Pap	Lab:		2		1				
		Patk. Branely & wife Pap	Lab:				2				
		Conner Rorke & wife Pap	Lab:		3						1
	Liscorky	John Clabey Pap	Lab:				2				

Com~Ros common Parish of	Place of Abode	Names and Religion	Proffession	Children under 14 Prot.	Paps.	Children above 14 Prot.	Paps.	Men Servts Prot.	Paps.	Women Servts Prot.	Paps.
		Hu: Shanaghy & wife Pap	Lab:		2				1		1
		Widow Shanaghy Pap			3				1		
		Bart Cunningham & wife Pap	Lab:				1				
		Thady Muldowny & wife Pap	Lab:		2		1				
		Jas. Muldowny & wife Pap	Lab:		1						
		Thos. Flynn & wife Pap	Lab:		4						1
		Michl. Rainy & wife Pap	Lab:		3						
		Henry Stanley & wife Pap	Lab:						1		1
		John Riley & wife Pap	Lab:		2		1				
		Willm. Anderson & wife Prot	Weaver	1				1			1
		Peter Chevers & wife Pap	Lab:		1		2				
		John Glynn & Mor Pap	Lab:				2				
		John Parker & wife Pap	Lab:		2				1		1
[f.285] Killcooley	Ardkenagh	Michl. Plunkett Pap	Farmer		1				2		2
		John Clark & wife Pap	Lab:		3						
		Dennis Carty & wife Pap	Herd		3		1				
		Thos. Grady Pap	Lab:						1		2
		Michl. Hughes & wife Pap	Lab:		2		1				
		Owen Bowey & wife Pap	Lab:		3						
		Nichl. Lennan & wife Pap	Lab:		2		1				
		Thos. Oates & wife Pap	Lab:		1		3				
		John Dillon & wife Pap	Lab:		2		1				
		Den. McCulan & wife Pap	Lab:				2				
		Lau. Kearen & wife Pap	Lab:		6		1				
		John Kean & wife Pap	Lab:		3						1
		Roger Killgay & wife Pap	Lab:		3		2		1		
	Cloonekillaron	Andw. Conner[3] & wife Pap	Lab:		1				1		
		Patk. McGeraghty & wife Pap	Lab:		2						
		Thos. Conner & wife Pap	Lab:		2						1
		John Tige & wife Pap	Lab:		3						1
		Bart. Tige & wife Pap	Lab:		2						
		Amb. McCarolly & wife Pap	Lab:		4						1
		Michl. Gormly & wife Pap	Lab:		3						
		Bryan Gormly & wife Pap	Lab:				1				
	Tulsk	Mary Purcell widow Pap	Innkeeper				2		1		2
		Stephen Plunkett & wife Pap	Lab:		2				1		1
		Henry Stanley & wife Pap	Joyner				3		1		1
		John Conway & wife Pap	Weaver		2				1		
		Edwd. Mallay Pap	Lab:		1						1
		David Mallay & wife Pap	Lab:		2						
		Jas Shanaghan & wife Pap	Lab:		1						
	Carrigens	Igna: Kelly[4] & wife Prot	Esqr.	3					5		5
		Miss Naghten Prot	Spinsr.								

[f. 285]

In the Parish of Killcooley

Pro. Men	Pro: Wo:	Pa: Men	Pa Wo	
2	3	124	131	
Pro: Children			Pa: Childre	259
under 14	4		under 14	
Pro: Children			Pa: Children	
above 14	0		above 14	138
Pro: Men Sts	1		Pa: Men Sts	36
Pro: Wo: Sts	0		Pa Wo: Sts	67
	———			———
Tot. Pros	10		Tot Paps	755

NOTES

1. Lewis, 'Kilcooley'.

2. Callogh mcRory Duff Connor, Connor mcShaen and Carbery mcTeige Boy Connor (*Books of Survey and Distribution*, Roscommon).

3. A John Connor was living in Clounakilly in the mid-seventeenth century (*Census of Ireland*).

4. Ignatius Kelly was son and heir of Edmund Kelly of Castle Ruby, Co. Roscommon. He was admitted to Gray's Inn in 1725 and to the Middle Temple in the same year. He was admitted to the King's Inns in 1726, and Edward Synge called him 'Sheriff' Kelly. He leased 'rich feeding bullock and sheep ground' at Ballybeg, Ugula from the Clonbrock estate. He married Catherine Kelly in 1746 (*Alumni Dubliniensis; Synge Letters,* p.237; Maps with lists of tenants' holdings, 1777, (N.L.I., Clonbrock Papers, MS 19,672/37); N.L.I., Marriage Licence Bonds Diocese of Elphin, mic. p.1881).

KILLUKIN, COUNTY ROSCOMMON
(BARONY OF BOYLE)

INTRODUCTION: *The parish of Killukin is divided into two parts, the first in the barony of Boyle just south of Carrick-on Shannon and the second in the barony of Roscommon, some 7 miles to the south-west. This part, in the barony of Boyle, was bounded by the parishes of Tumna, Ardcarn, Killummod and Estersnow and bordered the river Shannon. The land was hilly with marshy edges on the river. It covers 5670 statute acres.[1] The land was used mainly for grazing dairy cattle. Weaving was the chief skilled occupation, and continued into the nineteenth-century. Labourers had only seasonal employment.[2]*

The incumbent was the Rev. Arthur Mahon, Archdeacon of Elphin, who held the parish with Kilcolagh, Eastersnow, Creeve and Tomna.[3] The patron was the bishop.

OCCUPATIONS

Aleseller	1	Labourer	110	Servant	5
Cottier	9	Merchant	2	Servants, household	130
Farmer	2	Piper	1	Tailor	1
Herd	3	Pumpmaker	1	Tenant	4
				Weaver	6

Com~Ros comon Parish of	Place of Abode	Names and Religion	Proffession	Children under 14		Children above 14		Men Servts		Women Servts	
				Prot.	Paps.	Prot.	Paps.	Prot.	Paps.	Prot.	Paps.
[f.286]Killukin	Doon	Mary Cooper widow Prot	Farmer	5					1		2
		Patk. Meahan & wife Pap	Servant		2				1		2
		John Bern & wife Pap	Herd		1						
		Fran. Bern & wife Pap	Labourer		2						1
		Thady Durneen & wife Pap	Pumpmaker		3				1		
		Thos. Griskin & wife Pap	Labourer		3						
		John Kennedy & wife Pap			1						1
		Sus. Cummin widow Pap	Cottier		1		4				
		Michl. Burk & wife Pap	Labourer		4				1		
	Rathmore	John Flanigan Pap	Labourer		1		3				1
		Geo. Coyl & wife Pap	Labourer		3						
		Michl. Brenan & wife Pap	Mercht.		4				1		2
		Patk. Rowen & wife Pap	Labourer		1						1
		Willm. Higgins & wife Pap	Labourer		3		1		1		
		John O Hara & wife Pap	Labourer		2						
		Patk. Smith & wife Pap	Labourer		3						1
		Domk. Brenan & wife Pap	Labourer		1		3				
		Cormk. Macnamara & wife Pap	Labourer				2				
		Hugh Caveney & wife Pap	Labourer		4						1
		Jas. Croghan & wife Pap	Labourer		2						
		John Trindeloge & wife Pap	Labourer		3						1
		Lau: Cronan & wife Pap	Labourer		2				1		
		Conr. Bolan & wife Pap	Labourer		3						
		Martin Conner & wife Pap	Labourer		3						1
		Terence Duffy Pap	Labourer		2						
		Widow Cronan Pap	Cottier		2				1		
		Dennis Duffy & wife Pap	Labourer		3				1		
		John Durcan & wife Pap	Tailor		2				1		1
		Patk. Reynolds & wife Pap	Labourer		2						
		Patk. Flynn & wife Pap	Labourer		1		2				
		Patk. Croghan & wife Pap	Labourer		3						1
		Jas. Walsh & wife Pap	Labourer		2						1
		Jas. Walsh & wife Pap	Labourer		1						1
		Edwd Garner Prot	Cottier						1		1
		Fran. Dignan & wife Pap	Labourer		1						
		Dennis Leonard & wife Pap	Labourer		3						
		Michl. Conner & wife Pap	Labourer		3		1				1
		Luke Ambroge & wife Pap	Labourer		2				1		1
		Owen Carney & wife Pap	Labourer		3				1		
		Laughlin Coragh & wife Pap	Labourer		1						1
[f.287]Killukin	Rathmore	John Carney & wife Pap	Labourer		2		2				
		Mattw. King & wife Pap	Labourer		3						
		Michl. Kean & wife Pap	Labourer		2						1
		Andw. Cronan & wife Pap	Labourer		2		1				
		Terence Bolan & wife Pap	Labourer		3		1				
		Patk. Cornyn & wife Pap	Labourer		2		2				
		David Jordan Pap	Servt.						3		1
	Cloonebern	Patk. Brenan & wife Pap	Labourer		1		1				
		Danl. McNamara & wife Pap	Labourer		2				1		1

Com~Ros common Parish of	Place of Abode	Names and Religion	Proffession	Children under 14		Children above 14		Men Servts		Women Servts	
				Prot.	Paps.	Prot.	Paps.	Prot.	Paps.	Prot.	Paps.
		Owen Finan & wife Pap	Labourer		2						1
		Laugh. Mulvihily & wife Pap	Labourer		3						
		Thady Casserly & wife Pap	Labourer								1
		Edwd. Walsh & wife Pap	Labourer				4				
		Chas. Hopkins & wife Pap	Labourer		1		4				1
		Thady Geowan & wife Pap	Labourer		1				1		1
		Maurice Fox & Mor Pap	Labourer								
	Falsk	Edwd. Doyle Pap & wife Prot	Farmer	2				1		2	0
		Laughlin Cronan & wife Pap	Labourer		4				2		2
		Laughlin Geraghty & wife Pap	Herd		3						1
		Thady Geraghty & wife Pap	Labourer		1						
		Thady Bern & wife Pap	Labourer				5				
	Anaghmore	Jas. McCormuck & wife Pap	Servt.		2		2				
	Bunymuck	Laur. Laughlin & wife Pap	Labourer		1		2				
		Thady Halen & wife Pap	Labourer		1		1		1		1
		Domk. Mannin & wife Pap	Labourer				2				1
	Cloonsreen	Owen Bolan & wife Pap	Labourer		1		5				
		Thady Murray & wife Pap	Labourer		3				1		1
		Jas. Lane & wife Pap	Labourer		1						1
		Danl. Murray & wife Pap	Labourer		2						1
		John Hanning & wife Pap	Aleseller				2		1		1
		Jas. Flanigan & wife Pap	Labourer		2				1		1
		John Eagan & wife Pap	Labourer		2		1				
	Carrownvalley	Thos. Kelly & wife Pap	Labourer		5						1
		Michl. Fetherston Pap	Servt.								
		John Cormuck Pap	Servt.								1
[f.288]Killukin	Anaghbeg	John Duffy & wife Pap	Tent.				2		1		1
		Laughlin Haydon & wife Pap	Weaver		3				1		1
		Nich. Haydon & wife Pap	Weaver		4				1		1
		Patk. Haydon & wife Pap	Weaver		4		1				1
		Jas. Haydon & wife Pap	Weaver		3		2				
		Luke Haydon & wife Pap	Weaver		3						1
		Owen Duffy & Mor & Sis Pap	Tent.						1		1
		Michl. Conner & wife Pap	Lab:				1				1
		Jas. Kiggan & wife Pap	Lab:		3						
		Owen Kennedy & wife Pap	Lab:		2		1				
		Stephen Helwood & wife Pap	Lab:		1		2				
		Michl. Duffy & wife Pap	Lab:		2				1		1
	Ballyglass	Mattw. Golrick & wife Pap	Lab:		2						1
		Luke Conelly Pap	Lab:						1		1
		Darby Cross & wife Pap	Lab:				3				
		Dennis Hester & wife Pap	Lab:		1		1				
		Matt: Hopkins & wife Pap	Lab:		1		3				
		Thos. Tiernan & wife Pap	Lab:		1				1		1
		John Walsh & wife Pap	Lab:		2		2		1		
		Peter Cranoge & wife Pap	Lab:		2						1
		Roger Haraghton & wife Pap	Lab:		3						1
		John Malone & wife Pap	Lab:		3		2				
		Pattk. Malone & wife Pap	Lab:		2						

Com~Ros common Parish of	Place of Abode	Names and Religion	Proffession	Children under 14		Children above 14		Men Servts		Women Servts	
				Prot.	Paps.	Prot.	Paps.	Prot.	Paps.	Prot.	Paps.
	Derryfattan	Owen Malone & wife Pap	Lab:		1				1		1
		Edwd. Johnnings & wife Pap	Lab:		2		1				
		Hugh Rorke & wife Pap	Lab:		3				1		
		Ambrose Heverin & wife Pap	Lab:		2				1		1
		Richd. Kennedy & wife Pap	Lab:		2		2				1
	Ardaghcullen	Thos. Rogers & wife Pap	Cottier		3		2				1
		Patk. Conway & wife Pap	Lab:		3				1		1
		Andw. Conner & wife Pap	Lab:		3						1
		Bryan Brenan & wife Pap	Lab:		1		1				
		Willm. Brehony & wife Pap	Lab:				3				
		Patk. Brenan & wife Pap	Lab:		1		3				1
		John Judge & wife Pap	Lab:		4						1
[f.289] Killukin	Killukin	John Walsh & wife Pap	Lab:		2		1				1
		Roger Haraghty & wife Pap	Lab:		2		1		1		1
		Danl. McNamara & wife Pap	Lab:		1		4				
		Owen Finan & wife Pap	Lab:		1		1				
		Cormk. Nally & wife Pap	Tent.		2				1		1
		Darby Nally & wife Pap	Cottier		2						1
		Bart. Nally & wife Pap	Cottier		3						1
		Bryan Nally & wife Pap	Cottier		3				1		1
		Owen Nally & wife Pap	Cottier		1		3				
		John Taylor & wife Pap	Weaver		1		4				1
		Bryan Conelly & wife Pap	Lab:		2						1
		John Dempsy & wife Pap	Lab:		1						
		Michl. McDermott & wife Pap	Lab:		2		1		1		1
	Cloonmurry	Luke Fadin & wife Pap	Lab:				2				
		Owen Fadin & wife Pap	Lab:		2		1				1
		Laughlin Teige & wife Pap	Lab:		3		1				
		Bryan Fadin & wife Pap	Lab:		2		1				
		Hugh Caulfield & wife Pap	Lab:		3						1
		Edwd Jones & wife Pap	Lab:		1		1				
	Ballydaly	Jas. Cuddy & wife Pap	Lab:		2						1
		Dennis Burn & wife Pap	Lab:		4						1
		Barry Hanley & wife Pap	Tent.		3				1		1
		Mary Conelly widow Pap	Cottier		2		1				
		Michl. Naghten & wife Pap	Lab:		4						1
		Murtagh Cullen & wife Pap	Lab:		1		2				
		Bryan Morris & wife Pap	Lab:		3						1
		John Morris & wife Pap	Herd		1				1		1
	Clasheganny	Danl. Rorke & wife Pap	Lab:		3		1				
		Thady Haley & wife Pap	Lab:		2		1				
		Michl. Scanlan & wife Pap	Piper		2						1
		Edwd. Scanlan & wife Pap	Lab:		1		1				
		Edwd. Barrett & wife Pap	Lab:		4						1
		Owen Hughes & wife Pap	Lab:		3				1		1
		Michl. Padin & wife Pap	Lab:		3						
		Edwd. Geraghty & Mor. Pap	Lab:						1		1

[verso f. 289]
In the Parish
of Killukin

Pro: Men 1	Pro: Women 2	Pa: Men: 141	Pa: Wo: 138
Pro: Children under 14	7	Pa: Children Under 14	274
Pro: children Above 14	0	Pa: Children Above 14	110
Pro: Men Sts.	1	Pa: Men Sts	44
Pro: Wo: Sts.	2	Pa: Wo: Sts	82
Tot: Pro.	13	Tot: Paps	789

NOTES

1. Lewis, 'Killuken'.

2. 'Killuken', by Rev. Oliver Cary in Shaw Mason, *A Statistical Account...* p. 404.

3. The Rev. Arthur Mahon was born about 1715. He was collated Archdeacon of Elphin, rector of Killukin, vicar of Kilolagh, Eastersnow, Creeve and Tomna in 1743. He became prebendary of Howth in 1750, precentor of Connor in 1752 (Leslie, 'Elphin', pp 32, 216).

TIBOHINE, COUNTY ROSCOMMON

INTRODUCTION: *Tibohine is in the barony of Roscommon on the river Gara or Lung and between Boyle and Ballaghadireen. It covers 44,092 statute acres.[1] The main centres of population were French Park and Loughglinn.[2] A market was held at French Park every Thursday and there were fairs there three times a year.[3] A patent was issued to Lord Dillon in 1633 to hold a fair in Loughglinn four times a year. Lewis said the land was for the most part isolated hills and ridges, surrounded by bogs. There were a number of turloughs. Nevertheless, the quality of cultivable land and bog was good.[4] The enumerator does not seem to have covered the islands in Lough Glynn and Lough Errit.*

The McDermot family owned three townlands in 1641, and sixteen members of the family were living in the parish in 1749.[5]

In the early 1740s, the parish church of Tibohine was in ruins and inconvenient and it was ordered to be removed to a more convenient piece of ground. This was granted by Arthur French to the patron, bishop Edward Synge. Synge caused a new church to be built by act of Council 14 February 1742. In 1747 the wall of the churchyard was still incomplete and furnishings were missing.[6] The incumbent was the Rev. Westenra Crumpe, who had been collated prebendary and vicar of Tibohine in 1731.[7]

OCCUPATIONS

Barber	1	Friar	1	Priest	1
Beggar	2	Gentleman	13	Pumpmaker	2
Broguemaker	3	Glazier	1	Schoolmistress	1
Carman	7	Horserider	1	Sergeant	7
Carpenter	2	Innkeeper	7	Servants, household	293
Clerk	1	Jobber	1	Shepherd	1
Clothier	2	Joiner	3	Smith	13
Cobbler	1	Labourer	423	Superannuated	1
Cooper	3	Mason	6	Tailor	8
Cordwainer	2	Merchant	4	Tenant	92
Cottier	7	Miller	6	Weaver	22
Esquire	1	Nailer	2	Wheelwright	1
Farmer	52	Physician	1	Widow	31

Com~Ros common Parish of	Place of Abode	Names and Religion	Proffession	Children under 14		Children above 14		Men Servts		Women Servts	
				Prot.	Paps.	Prot.	Paps.	Prot.	Paps.	Prot.	Paps.
[f.290] Tibohine	French Park	Arthur French8 and Lady Prot	Esqr			4	0	10	6	5	5
		Jane Anderson widow Prot	School-mistress		0	3	0	0	0	0	0
		T. Hand & wife Pap	Smith	0	2	0	0	0	5	0	2
		M. Welsh widow Pap	0	0	0	0	0	0	0	0	0
		Anthony & El. Warren Prot	Inn-keeper	3	0	0	0	2	0	0	2
		Henry Jones & M. Jones Prot	cordwinder	2	0	0	2	0	0	0	0
		J. Brockhurst Pre	cordwinder	0							
		D. Thompson & wife} Prot	Weave	3							
		And. Timane & wife Pa	Labr.	0	3						
		J. McCowan & wife Pa	Labr.	0	1						
		W. Griffin & wife Pa	Labr.	0	0	0	1				
		T. Burk Pa	Weaver		2		1				
		J. Petty & wife Pa	Labr.								
		J. Griffin & wife Prot	Weaver	1	0	1		2		1	
		J. Armstrong & wife Prot	Weaver	1				3			
		A. Warren & wife Prot	Glazier	3					1		1
		M. Kilgarive & wife Pa	Labr.		4				2		
		E. McGary & wife Pa	Labr.		3						
		T. Conigan & wife Pa	Labr.		1		2				
		O. Carty & wife Pa	Labr.		7						
		F. Doud & wife Pa	Labr.		2						
		T. Butler & wife Pa	Labr.		3						
		J. McDonagh & wife Pa	Carpenter		5				1		1
		B. Kenny & wife Pa	Labr.								2
		A. Mcdermot & wife Pa	Labr.		2		1				
		J. Malarky & wife Pa	Labr.		1						
		T. Keeneen & wife Pa	Labr.		1						
		W. Laurence & Wife Prot	Joyner	4				3	2		1
		H. Prichard Prot	Clerk								
		F. McCoy & wife Pa	Weaver		2						
		E. Kenny & wife Pa	Serjeant		1				2		3
	Turlogh	W. Gaffy & wife Pa	Mason		5		2				1
		K. Lavin & wife Pa	Labr.				3				
		J. Connoly & wife Prot	Mason								
		M. McDermot & wife Pa	Labr.		2						
		G. Gara & wife Pa	Mason		1		5				
		A. Gara & wife Pa	Physician		1		1				
		J. Mulany & wife Pa	Labr.		4		3				
		J. Scally & wife Pa	Cooper		3						
		A. Callaghan & wife Pa	Labr.				4				
[f.291] Tibohin	Turlogh	M. Conigan & wife Pa	Labr.				4				
		J. Cassedy & wife Pa	Labr.				4				
		E. Flanigan & wife Pa	horserider		2		2				
	Rakery	J. Kimmil Prot & wife Pa	Farmer			3			2		1
		J. Timane & wife Pa	Labr.		2						
		L. Kilcree & wife Pa	Labr.		1						
		T. Rautery & wife Pa	Labr.		2						

Com~Ros common Parish of	Place of Abode	Names and Religion	Proffession	Children under 14		Children above 14		Men Servts		Women Servts	
				Prot.	Paps.	Prot.	Paps.	Prot.	Paps.	Prot.	Paps.
		J. Carty & wife Pa	Labr.								
		J. Casey & wife Pa	Labr.		4						
		J. Callaghan & wife Pa	Farmer		5						
	Ratra	J. Coona & wife Pa	Labr.		2		2				
		E. Durneen Pa	Labr.						2		
		W. Sheridon Pa	Labr.								
		J. Dowdekan & wife Pa	Labr.		3						
		P. Fennaty & wife Pa	Labr.		3						
	Ochorin	T. Dillon & wife Pa	Gent.				5		1		1
		L. Dillon & wife Pa	Gent.		2				2		1
		J. Dillon & wife Pa	Gent.		3						
		L. Callely & wife Pa	Farmer		2		2				
		J. Kean & wife Pa	Farmer		1						
		L. Kean & wife Pa	Labr.								
		G. Callaghan & wife Pa	Labr.								
		O. Gallagher & wife Pa	Farmer		1		2				
		J. Carrol & wife Pa	Labr.								
		M. Higgins & wife Pa	Miller		3		4				
		J. Mcdermot & wife Pa	Farmer				3				1
		R. McDermot & wife Pa	Labr.		1						
		C. McDermot & wife Pa	Labr.				3				
		J. Gallagher & wife Pa	Labr.				3				
	Caranruddy	T. Kirk & wife Pa	Labr.		3		1				
		L. Kirk & wife Pa	Labr								
		E. Ternan & wife Pa	Labr.		1						
		D. Sheean & wife Pa	Labr.		1		1				
		T. Briegh & wife Pa	Labr.				2				
		J. Green & wife Pa	Joyner		2				1		1
		M. Kenny Pa	Widow		2						
		J. Killeen & wife Pa	Labr.		3						
		C. Swiney & wife Pa	Labr.		4						
		P. Kenny & wife Pa	Serjeant		1						
		O. Dyer & wife Pa	Labr.		2		2				
[f.292] Tibohin	Mullin	J. Barlow Prot & wife Pa	Gent.			4		1	3		3
		J. Corkran & wife Pa	Labr.		2		2				
	Cooldavin	J. McDonagh & wife Pa	Miller								2
		M. Mcdermot & wife Pa	Labr.		2						
		L. Irwin & wife Pa	Labr.		2						
		F. Swiney & wife Pa	Labr.		2						
	Aghalour	J. Greewy & wife Pa	Farmer		2		1				
		Mart. Roon & wife Pa	Labr.		2		1				
		J. Gallogher & wife Pa	Labr.		2						
		J. Scally & wife Pa	Farmer		2		1				
		P. Greewy & wife Pa	Labr.		4		2				
		J. Carty & wife Pa	Labr.		3		1				
		E. Carty & wife Pa	Labr.		1						
		M. Hewet Pa	Widow		3						
		E. McDertegal & wife Pa	Labr.								
		W. Cahil & wife Pa	Labr.		1						1

Com~Ros common Parish of	Place of Abode	Names and Religion	Proffession	Children under 14 Prot.	Children under 14 Paps.	Children above 14 Prot.	Children above 14 Paps.	Men Servts Prot.	Men Servts Paps.	Women Servts Prot.	Women Servts Paps.
		L. Hart & wife Pa	Labr.				4				
		B. Hart & wife Pa	Labr.				1				
		J. Harraughton & wife Pa	Labr.				3				
		O. Igo & wife Pa	Labr.		2		1				
		P. Keavny & wife Pa	Labr.								
		R. Jennings & wife Pa	Labr.		2		2				
		M. Gordon & wife Pa	Farmer				4				
		J. Gordon & wife Pa	Farmer		2						
		W. Cahil & wife Pa	Farmer				4				
		J. Noon & wife Pa	Farmer								
		B. Sharry & wife Pa	Farmer		3		1				
		J. Sharry & wife Pa	Labr.								
		M. Farrel Pa	Widow				1				
	Cloonard	James Walker Prot	Gen			3					
		J. Greewy & wife Pa	Labr.		2						
		D. Bow & wife Pa	Labr.		3						
		H. Finan & wife Pa	Labr.		3		2				
		J. Carrol & wife Pa	Labr.		4		2				
		P. Cahil Pa	Labr.		2		3				
	Cloonfinglas	G. Ingram & wife Prot	Weaver	3	3	3	0		3		1
		B. Sharry & wife Pa	Labr.		3						
		A. Wally & wife Pa	Labr.		1						
	Carokeel	J. Whitehead & wife Prot	tenant	2		2					
		P. McDermot Roe & wife Pa	Labr.		3		3				
[f.293] Tibohin	Carokeel	O. Kilbride & wife Pa	Labr.								
		O. Mcala & wife Pa	Labr.		1		3				
		R. Connor & wife Pa	Labr.		3						
		J. Corker & wife Pa	Labr.		3						
	Edon[11]	P. Morris & wife Pa	Farmer		2				2		
		T. Morris & wife Pa	super-annuated								
		D. Morris & wife Pa	Farmer		3						
		C. Corkran & wife Pa	Cooper		2						
		O. Mcdermot & wife Pa	Labr.		2		1				
		D. Morrisy & wife Pa	Labr.		1						
		W. Berne & wife Pa	Mason		1		4				
		T. McDermot roe & wife Pa	Carrman		3		1				
		J. Malroony & wife Pa	Labr.		1						
		B. Wally & wife Pa	Labr.		1		2				
		M. Malrenan & wife Pa	Carrman				2		1		
		M. Malrenan & wife Pa	Carrman		1						
	Cloonarra[12]	J. Keeneen & wife Pa	Tenant.		2		2				
		M. Teague Pa	Widow		2						
		O. McDermot Gal & wife Pa	Tenant.		1						
		M. Keeneen Pa	Widow		1						
		M. Macadruy & wife Pa	Tenant.				5				
		J. Gormly & wife Pa	Nailer				1				
		D. Brenan & wife Pa	Tenant.		2		2				
		J. MacDermot Gal & wife Pa	Tenant.		2						
		J. MacDermot Gal & wife Pa	Tenant.		2		1				

Com~Ros common Parish of	Place of Abode	Names and Religion	Proffession	Children under 14		Children above 14		Men Servts		Women Servts	
				Prot.	Paps.	Prot.	Paps.	Prot.	Paps.	Prot.	Paps.
		H. Sharry & wife Pa	Labr.		1						
		D. Hanly & wife Pa	Tenant.								
		C. Haughton & wife Prot	Cottier	1							
		C. Gormon Pa	Cottier		1						
		P. Keeneen Pa	Cottier		1						
		E. Morrisy & wife Pa	Mercht.		2						
		E. Gormon Pa	Widow				1				
		P. Gormon & wife Pa	Cottier		2						
		R. Parks & wife Prot	Gent.				2				
		B. Smiley & wife Prot	Nailer	4					2		1
		W. Guest & wife Prot	Weaver	2					1		3
		M. Macadruy Pa	Widow				1				
	Taunirover	L. Teague & wife Pa	Tenant.				2		1		1
	Kilgarive	L. MacDermot gal & wife Pa	Serjeant		2		4				
	Lisananny	D. Hurly & wife Pa	Tenant				3		1		1
[f.294] Tibohin	Lisananny	Connor Egan & wife Pa	Tenant.				1			0	1
		H. Egan & wife Pa	Tenant.		2						1
	Tullynashoge	Dan. Flanigan & wife Pa	Labr.		3		1				
		W. Walder & wife Pa	Pumpmaker		2						
		P. Flanigan & wife Pa	Labr.		3		1				
		H. Gyles Pa	Widow								
		K. Flanigan Pa	Widow								
		L. Flanigan & wife Pa	Labr.		3		2				
		M. Flanigan & wife Pa	Labr.				1				
		J. Lowry & wife Pa	Labr.		2						
		P. Dillon & wife Pa	Labr.		1						
		H. Flanigan & wife Pa	Smith		3						
		J. Morrely & wife Pa	Labr.				1				
		P. Duffy & wife Pa	Labr.		2		1				
		H. Frean & wife Pa	Labr.								
		J. Welsh & wife Pa	Labr.		1						
		P. Nolan & wife Pa	Labr.								
		B. Lowry & wife Pa	Labr.		3						
		J. Crowly & wife Pa	Weaver		3						
		M. Lowry & wife Pa	Labr.				2				
		T. Crowly & wife Pa	Labr.				1				
		D. Muloy & wife Pa	Tailer		1						
		C. Flanigan & wife Pa	Labr.		1						
		J. Waldrum & wife Pa	Labr.								
		M. Flanigan & wife Pa	Labr.		2						
		J. Lowry & wife Pa	Labr.		1						
		J. Casey & wife Pa	Labr.								
	Cloondart[13]	J. Wyer & wife Pa	Labr.		1		1				
		J. Wyer & wife Pa	Labr.		3						
		P.Reynolds & wife Pa	Miller[14]		2		1				
	Cornehulty	J. Hynds Pa	Labr.				2				
		D. Murphy & wife Pa	Labr.				2				
	Derrinomekan	T. Flyn & wife Pa	Tenant.								
		H. Woods & wife Prot	Tenant.	1							

Com~Ros common Parish of	Place of Abode	Names and Religion	Proffession	Children under 14		Children above 14		Men Servts		Women Servts	
				Prot.	Paps.	Prot.	Paps.	Prot.	Paps.	Prot.	Paps.
	Gortiganny	G. Tyler Prot	Gent.			2			1		1
		B. Flanigan & wife Pa	Labr.		2		1				
		P. Flanigan & wife Pa	Weaver				2				
		P. Feeny & wife Pa	Labr.								
		F. Lowry & wife Pa	Labr.				1				
		C. Dyer & wife Pa	Labr.		4		1				
[f.295] Tibohin	Gortiganny	O. Flanigan & wife Pa	Labr.		1						
		M. Flanigan & wife Pa	Labr.		1						
		C. Flanigan & wife Pa	Labr.		1						
		O. Duffy & wife Pa	Labr.		1		2				
	Carabehy[15]	J. Reny & wife Pa	Labr.		2						
		G.Dillon & wife Pa	Tailer		1		3				
		R. Dyer & wife Pa	Labr.		3						
	Cooligary	D. Connor & wife Pa	Barber		1						
		F. Loughlin & wife Pa	Tenant.		3		2				
		Da. Haniman Pa	Labr.				3				
		B. Danahoo & wife Pa	Tenant.		1		2				
		G. Carty & wife Pa	Tenant.		2		2				
		M. Grourk Pa	Widow		3		1				
		J. Gallagher & wife Pa	Smith				3				
		O. Kearny & wife Pa	Labr.				3				
		P. Gallogher & wife Pa	Labr.		4						
		J. Treagh & Mother Pa	Taylor		2						
		E. Dalton & wife Pa	Tenant				2				
		L. Flyn & wife Pa	Tenant		2		1				
		P. Coffy & wife Pa	Labr.				2				
	Loughglin	J. Abbit & wife Prot	Inn-keeper	3					1		2
		J. Hanimna & wife Pa	Labr.		2						
		Juggy Tully & sister Pa	Widows								
		T. Carty & wife Pa	Tenant		3		4				
		P. Davis & wife Pa	Inn-keeper				2		2		1
		B. Connolly & wife Pa	Labr.		2						
	Legatinty	D. Crean & wife Pa	Broguemaker		3		1				
		T. Rutledge & wife Pa	Inn-keeper				2				
		D. Berreen & wife Pa	Smith		2						
		P. Petyn & wife Pa	Labr.								
		E. Connor & wife Pa	Labr.								
		L. Malkeeren & wife Pa	Labr.								
		P. Berreen & wife Pa	Labr.								
		M. Malrony & wife Pa	Weaver		1						
		F. Connor & wife Pa	Tenant.		1		1				
		J.Loughlin & wife Pa	Labr.				1				
		T. Kelly & wife Pa	Tenant.		4						
		H. Moolack & wife Pa	Labr.		1						
		J. Cottely & wife Pa	Labr.		2						
		J. Mylan & wife Pa	Labr.								
[f.296] Tibohin	Legatinty	E. Hannelly & wife Pa	Labr.				2				
		M. Lowry & wife Pa	Labr.		1						
	Cloonshanvil[16]	Edmd. Nary & wife Pa	Innkeeper		1				1		1

Com~Ros common Parish of	Place of Abode	Names and Religion	Proffession	Children under 14 Prot.	Children under 14 Paps.	Children above 14 Prot.	Children above 14 Paps.	Men Servts Prot.	Men Servts Paps.	Women Servts Prot.	Women Servts Paps.
		J. Bruen & wife Pa	Labr.		3						
		D. Costelly & wife Pa	Labr.		3						
		M. Green & wife Pa	Miller		4						
		R. Mulkeeran & wife Pa	Labr.								
		D. Mylan & wife Pa	Labr.		2						
		J. Mylan & wife Pa	Labr.								
	Curska	B. Corkran & wife Pa	Labr.		4				1		
		E. Rogers & wife Pa	Labr.		4				1		
		D. Crean & wife Pa	Broguemaker		3		1				
		F. Rutlidge & wife Pa	Innkeeper				2				
		D. Berreen & wife Pa	Smith		2						
		P. Peter & wife Pa	Labr.								
		E. Connor & wife Pa	Labr.								
		L. Malheeren & wife Pa	Labr.								
		P. Berreen & wife Pa	Labr.								
		J. Connor & wife Pa	Labr.		1						
		A. Rogers Pa	Labr.				1				
		J. Flanigan Pa	Labr.								
		O. Dowd & wife Pa	Labr.		1		2				
		M. Tully & wife Pa	Labr.								
		J. Morris & wife Pa	Labr.		3		1				
		P. Moran & wife Pa	Labr.		2				1		
		P. Macadruy & wife Pa	Labr.		2				1		
		M. Smyth & wife Pa	Labr.		1		2		1		
		B. Morry & wife Pa	Labr.		2		2	.			
		D. Macala Pa	Widow		4						
		C. Higgins & wife Pa	Labr.		2				1		1
		P. Dowd & wife Pa	Labr.		5						
		O. Lavin Pa	Widow				1		1		
		Carogarive F. Kelly & wife Pa	Tenant.						1		1
		P. Corkran & wife Pa	Smith		2		3				
		M Lynsk & wife Pa	Labr.		1						
		D. Downachan & wife Pa	Labr.		1						1
		J. Gormly & wife Pa	Taylor		3		2				
		P. Quin & wife Pa	Pumpmaker				3				
		P. Ternan & wife Pa	Labr.		2		3				
		O. Casey & wife Pa	Labr.		2						
[f.297] Tibohin	Carogarive	C. Higgins & wife Pa	Labr.		1		3				
		J. Sharkety & wife Pa	Tenant.		3						
		C. Grourk & wife Pa	Labr.								
		M. McDonagh & wife Pa	Mercht.		1		1				
		M Higgins & wife Pa	Serjeant		1		2				
		P. Bruen & wife Pa	Labr.		1						
		J. Keewar & wife Pa	Weaver		1		3				
		H. Rogers & wife Pa	Labr.		2						
		L. Dillon & wife Pa	Labr.		2						
		T. Downachan & wife Pa	Labr.		2		3				
	Errit[17]	D. Lyons & wife Pa	Labr.				1				
		B. Lynsk & wife Pa	Labr.		1						

Com~Ros common Parish of	Place of Abode	Names and Religion	Proffession	Children under 14 Prot.	Children under 14 Paps.	Children above 14 Prot.	Children above 14 Paps.	Men Servts Prot.	Men Servts Paps.	Women Servts Prot.	Women Servts Paps.
		H. Mooney & wife Pa	Labr.				1				
		P. Egan & wife Pa	Labr.				1		1		
		L. Wyer & wife Pa	Labr.		2						
		A. Flanigan & wife Pa	Labr.		3						
		H. Dunlevy & wife Pa	Labr.		4						
		W. Frane & wife Pa	Labr.		3						
		M. Connor Pa	Widow				2				
		M. Flanigan & wife Pa	Labr.		2		1				
		J. Sullivan & wife Pa	Labr.		1						
		P. Mahon & wife Pa	Labr.		4						
		D. Croly & wife Pa	Labr.		2						
	Caronhard[18]	L.Tyler & wife Prot	Gent.						1		1
		M. Kenelly & wife Pa	Labr.		1		2				
		B. Kenelly & wife Pa	Labr.		4		1				
		J. Cassedy & wife Pa	Labr.		2						
	Lisergool	L. Pliben & wife Pa	Labr.				3				
		R. Mulooly & wife Pa	Labr.		2						
		M. Kerreen Pa	Widow		4						
		T. Feely & wife Pa	Labr.		2		2				
		D. Dillon & wife Pa	Serjeant		3		1				
		P. Frean & wife Pa	Labr.								
		A. Duffy Pa	Friar						2		2
		B. Malooly Pa	Widow		2						
	Balimagarra	J. Horan & wife Pa	Weaver								
		E. Kelly Pa	Widow				2				
	Kilteboe	G. Dillon & wife Pa	Mercht.		2						
		D. Scire & wife Pa	Labr.		1						
		W. Huetson Prot & wife Pa	Carpenter								
[f.298] Tibohin	Kilteboe	D. Dyer & wife Pa	Farmer		2						
		P. Dyer & wife Pa	Labr.		3						
		W. Berne & wife Pa	Labr.								
		R. Grourk & wife Pa	Labr.								
		F. Monaghan & wife Pa	Labr.		2						
		W. Kelly Pa	Labr.		1						
	Cahir	F. Elwood & wife Prot	Gent.	4					2		2
		C. Brady & wife Pa	Farmer		3		2				
		L. Grogan & wife Pa	Cooper				1				
		B. Duffy & wife Pa	Labr.		3						
		E. Lockart Pa	Widow								
	Errit	W. Barlow & wife Prot	Gent.	2					1		1
		J. Heydon & mother Prot	Farmer			2					
		M. Heydon widow Prot	Widow	3							1
		J. Egan & wife Pa	Labr.		2		2				
		W. Costello Pa	Labr.		2		2				
	Balliglass	P. Esther & wife Pa	Weaver		2		1				
		C. Cugly Pa	Widow		1						
		T. Kelly & wife Pa	Labr.		3		1				
		J. Page & wife Pa	Clothier		3		1				
		B. Monaun & wife Pa	Labr.		5						

Com~Ros common Parish of	Place of Abode	Names and Religion	Proffession	Children under 14		Children above 14		Men Servts		Women Servts	
				Prot.	Paps.	Prot.	Paps.	Prot.	Paps.	Prot.	Paps.
		T. Killeen & wife Pa	Smith		2						
		B. Killeen & wife Pa	Labr.								
		J. Costello & wife Pa	Weaver		2						
		J. Monaun Pa	Widow		2		1				
		W. Killeen & wife Pa	Weaver		3		2				
		J. Jennings Pa	Beggar								
		D. Giblane & wife Pa	Labr.				1				
		P. Giblane & wife Pa	Labr.		1						
		C. Giblane & wife Pa	Labr.		2						
		B. Lyons & wife Pa	Labr.		2		2				
		P. Shalloway & wife Pa	Labr.		3						
		F. Giblane & wife Pa	Labr.								
		T. Monaun & wife Pa	Weaver				2				
		P. Monaun & wife Pa	Labr.		1		1				
		J. Conry & wife Pa	Labr.		3						
		O. Giblane & wife Pa	Labr.		3						
	Clontorwart[21]	J. Dillon & wife Pa	Gent.		4				1		1
		J.Caran & wife Pa	Labr.								
		O. McAnulty & wife Pa	Labr.		2						
[f.299] Tibohin	Clontorwart	J. Fitzpatrick & wife Pa	Smith						1		1
		F. Allis Pa	Labr.		1						
		R. Dillon & wife Pa	Tenant.								
		J. Brady & wife Pa	Weaver		1		1				
		B. Conry & wife Pa	Labr.		4						
	Derreen	J. Dillon & wife Pa	Farmer		1						1
		M. Dillon & wife Pa	Farmer		4					1	1
		W. Caran & wife Pa	Farmer		5					1	
		T. Corby & wife Pa	Labr.								
	Caronokneran	M. Regan & wife Pa	Farmer		2						
		E. Timulty Pa	P. priest								1
		M. Regan & wife Pa	Farmer		3						
		T. Regan & wife Pa	Labr.		1						1
		E. Regan & wife Pa	Farmer		3						1
		P. Mulligan & wife Pa	Labr.		1		3				
		F. Flyn & wife Pa	Labr.		3						
		W. Swiney & wife Pa	Labr.		2						
		M. Cox & wife Pa	Labr.		3						
		J. Conolly & wife Pa	Labr.		3						
		O. Casserly & wife Pa	Labr.							1	
	Curroghsallow	E. McGra & wife Pa	Labr.		1	0	1				
		C. Moylan & wife Pa	Labr.		1						
		O. Swiney & wife Pa	Labr.								1
		J. Duffy & wife Pa	Labr.		1						
		M. Grady & wife Pa	Labr.		1						
		D. Mylan Pa	Labr.				2				
		T. Grady & w Pa	Labr.		1						
		J. Moran & wife Pa	Labr.		1						
		L. Flyn & wife Pa	Labr.								
		R. Moran & wife Pa	Labr.		1						

Com~Ros common Parish of	Place of Abode	Names and Religion	Proffession	Children under 14		Children above 14		Men Servts		Women Servts	
				Prot.	Paps.	Prot.	Paps.	Prot.	Paps.	Prot.	Paps.
		M. Fin & wife Pa	Labr.								
		P. Higgins & wife Pa	Labr.				1				
		O. Dogharty Pa	Tenant.								
		P. Moran & wife Pa	Labr.		1						
		Creevy W. Walder & wife Pa	Labr.		1				1		1
		T. Fitzpatrick & wife Pa	Smith					2			
		M. Corrogan & wife Pa	Labr.								
		J. Currogan & wife Pa	Labr.		1						
		M. Corrogan & wife Pa	Labr.		2			1		1	
		D. Regan & wife Pa	Labr.		4						
[f.300] Tibohin	Creevy	T. Corragan & wife Pa	Tent		1						1
		A. Ruddy & wife Pa	Labr.		1						
		E. Corrogan & wife Pa	Tennt.		2					1	
		T. Ruddy & wife Pa	Tennt.		3						1
		Fr. Barrot & wife Pa	Labr.		2						
		P. Quin & wife Pa	Labr.		1						
		J. McDonagh & wife Pa	Labr.								
		O. Kenelly & wife Pa	Labr.								
		D. Cafferty & wife Pa	Labr.		2						1
		A. Manulty & wife Pa	Labr.		1						
		J. Flanery & wife Pa	Weaver		2				1		1
		F. Costello & wife Pa	Labr.		1						
		F. Gollagher & wife Pa	Labr.		1						
		H. Corrogan & wife Pa	Tennt.		1		1		1		1
		D. Cafferty & wife Pa	Tennt.		3						1
		J. Macanulty Pa	Labr.		1						
	Erizan	J.Fitzgerald & wife Pa	Farmer				1		1		1
		J. Harraughton Pa	Widow								
		C. Gormly & wife Pa	Cobler		2		2				
		P. Teague & wife Pa	Labr.		2		1				
		A. Kelly & wife Pa	Labr.		4						
		P. Fitzpatrick & wife Pa	Smith				1				
		J. Flanigan Pa	Labr.		3						
	Cloonaraget	P. McCafry & wife Pa	Labr.				2				
		P. McCafry & wife Pa	Labr.		1						
		J. Mccafry & wife Pa	Tent		1		1		1		1
		J. Cafrick & wife Pa	Tent		2		2		1		1
		P. Kenny & wife Pa	Tent		3						1
		T. Fitzgerald & wife Pa	Tent						1		1
		P. Duffy & wife Pa	Labr.		1						
		D. Raughtery & wife Pa	Labr.								
		J. Duffy & wife Pa	Labr.		2						
	Taunadrisoge	D. Tarpy & wife Pa	Tent		1				2		2
		T. Caulfield & wife Pa	Labr.		4						
		J. Walder & wife Pa	Labr.								
		J. Moran Pa	Labr.								1
		J. Frane & wife Pa	Labr.		5						
		P. Frane & wife Pa	Tent						1		
		P. Moran & wife Pa	Tent		1				1		1

Com~Ros common Parish of	Place of Abode	Names and Religion	Proffession	Children under 14		Children above 14		Men Servts		Women Servts	
				Prot.	Paps.	Prot.	Paps.	Prot.	Paps.	Prot.	Paps.
	Curraghsalla	W. Moran Pa	Tent		1		1	1			1
[f.301] Tibohin		Ed. McGra & wife Pa	Tent		1		1	1			1
		C.Moylin & wife Pa	Labr.		1						
		O. Swiney & wife Pa	Tent		1						1
		J. Duffy & wife Pa	Labr.		1						
		M. Grady & wife Pa	Labr.		1						
		D. Moylan Pa	Labr.				2				
		J. Grady & wife Pa	Labr.		1						
		J. Moran & wife Pa	Labr.		1						
		L. Flyn & wife Pa	Labr.								
		R. Moran & wife Pa	Tent		1		+ [?]		1		1
	Lisadely	T. Fitzgerald & wife Pa	Mercht.						2		1
		B. Kelly & wife Pa	Labr.		3						
		D. Harraughton & wife Pa	Labr.				4				
		L. Plunket & wife Pa	Labr.		4						
		C. Skeneen & wife Pa	Miller				1				
		H. Carrol Pa	Labr.		2		2				
		O. Kine & wife Pa	Labr.		3						
		B. Conry Pa	Widow		1		1				
	Cloonicaly	E. Gormly & wife Pa	Labr.		1						
		T. Lynch & wife Pa	Labr.				2				
		J. Greenan & wife Pa	Labr.		2		1				
		J. Greenan & wife Pa	Labr.								
		L. Dunlevy & wife Pa	Broguemaker		2						
		L. Dunlevy & wife Pa	Labr.								
		J. Greenan & wife Pa	Tent		2				1		1
		C. Duffy & wife Pa	Labr.				1				
		J. Duffy & wife Pa	Labr.				1				
		T. Donnelly & wife Pa	Tent		2		1				1
		P. Morrely & wife Pa	Labr.		2						
		C. Duffy & wife Pa	Labr.		2		1				
		M. Rush & wife Pa	Labr.		5						
		T. Shrehan & wife Pa	Labr.				2				
	Kiltemane	R. Delamere & wife Pa	Tent				2				
		L. Dalton & wife Pa	Labr.								
		A. Loughlin & wife Pa	Labr.		3						
		T. Corrogan & wife Pa	Labr.								
	Tullileag	W. Rogers & wife Pa	Labr.				2				
	Kiltebranly	J. Dogharty & wife Pa	Labr.		1						
		J. Macanallen & wife Pa	Tent		2		2	1			1
		A. Frean & wife Pa	Labr.		1		1				
[f.302] Tibohin	Kiltebranly	J. Higgins & wife Pa	Labr.		2						
		E. Blewet & wife Pa	Labr.		1						
		P. Noon & wife Pa	Labr.		3						1
		E. Lally & wife Pa	Labr.		1						
		K. Macanallen Pa	Widow		2		1	1			1
		E. Higgins & wife Pa	Farmer		2		1	1			1
		D. Higgins & wife Pa	Farmer		1		1	1			1
		P. Fitzpatrick & wife Pa	Smith				2				1

Com~Ros common Parish of	Place of Abode	Names and Religion	Proffession	Children under 14		Children above 14		Men Servts		Women Servts	
				Prot.	Paps.	Prot.	Paps.	Prot.	Paps.	Prot.	Paps.
	Aghadriston	Wm. Grourk & wife Pa	Tent		4		3				
		B. Dolan & wife Pa	Tent		4				1		1
	Clooncagh	B. Moran & wife Pa	Tent		2		1		1		
		A. Gordon & wife Pa	Tent		1				1		
		J. Regan & wife Pa	Labr.				3				
		J. Collins & wife Pa	Labr.		3						
		P. Collins & wife Pa	Labr.		3						
		C. Collins & wife Pa	Labr.								
		J. Harraughton & wife Pa	Labr.								
		Pat. Collins & wife Pa	Labr.		1						
		Ph. Collins & wife Pa	Labr.		1						
		J. Horan Pa	Widow		2						
	Caracummeen	L. Kelly & wife Pa	Tent		1		1				
		T. Prendergast & wife Pa	Labr.		1						
		W. Prendergast & wife Pa	Labr.		2						
		M. Costelloe & wife Pa	Labr.				2				
		J. Costelloe & wife Pa	Labr.		1						
	Drummot	Ro. Whitehead & wife Pa	Tent		2						1
		Ri. Whitehead & wife Pa	Tent				2				
		R. McDermot & wife Pa	Tent		2		2				1
		H. Caran & wife Pa	Labr.		1		1				
		O. Mahon & wife Pa	Labr.		1		2				
		D. Connor & wife Pa	Labr.		1						
		P. Walder & wife Pa	Labr.		1						
		R. Lowry & wife Pa	Labr.		1		2				
	Aghaderry	P. Moran & wife Pa	Tent		3				1		1
		J. Moran & wife Pa	Labr.		4						
		L. Scally & wife Pa	Labr.								
		E. Grourk Pa	Beggar								
		P. Crawford & wife Pa	Labr.		1						
		R. Nolan & wife Pa	Labr.		1						
		G. Tregh & wife Pa	Labr.		1						
[f.303] Tibohin	Aghaderry	P. Scally & wife Pa	Wheelwright		1						
		P. Scally & wife Pa	Labr.		2		2				
		P. Cottelly Pa	Miller		2				1		1
	Fiegh	P. Connor & wife Pa	Innkeeper		1		1		1		1
		M. Brenan & wife Pa	Labr.				1				
		D. Moran & wife Pa	Tent		3				1		1
		J. Mary & wife Pa	Labr.		1						
		Peter Dolan & wife Pa	Tent						2		2
		D. Flanigan & wife Pa	Labr.								1
		J. Mary & wife Pa	Tent						2		1
		L. Mary & wife Pa	Labr.		1						
		J. Dolan & wife Pa	Tent		1				1		1
		D. Scally & wife Pa	Tent						2		3
		M. Coyne & wife Pa	Tent		2				1		
		T. King & wife Pa	Tent		1				1		
		D. Macanulty & wife Pa	Labr.								
		J. McNeal & wife Pa	Labr.				1				

Com~Ros common Parish of	Place of Abode	Names and Religion	Proffession	Children under 14 Prot.	Children under 14 Paps.	Children above 14 Prot.	Children above 14 Paps.	Men Servts Prot.	Men Servts Paps.	Women Servts Prot.	Women Servts Paps.
		L. Dillon & w Pa	Clothier		1				1		1
		P. Moran & wife Pa	Labr.								
		D. Dolan & wife Pa	Tent		2				1		
		T. Murray & wife Pre	Labr.								
	Cartoun	D. Dowdekan & wife Pa	Labr.		2						
		O. Keenarn & wife Pa	Tent		1		1				1
		D. Carty & wife Pa	Tent		1		2				1
		J. Digenan & wife Pa	Labr.		3						
		C. Kelly Pa	Widow				1				
		J. Carty & wife Pa	Labr.		1						
		C. Carty & wife Pa	Tent				2				
		J. Mallowly & wife Pa	Labr.		3						
	Edon	M. Mulrenan & wife Pa	Carrman				4		1		1
		M. Malrenan & wife Pa	Carrman		1						
		B. Wally & wife Pa	Farmer		2				1		1
		J. Malroony-fin & wife Pa	Labr.		2						1
		L. Carrol & wife Pa	Carrman					1	1		1
		T. McDermot roe & wife Pa	Carrman		7				1		1
		R. Moran & wife Pa	Labr.		3				1		
	Curriturpane	R. Savage[22] & wife Pr.	Gent.	1				2	2		2
		P. Mulroonyfin & wife Pa	Labr.		2		1				
		T. Timane	Labr.		1						
		C. Sampy & wife Pre	Weaver	2							
[f.304] Tibohin	Barnecaly	D. Hopkins & wife Pa	Labr.		3		4				
		J. Moran Pa	Labr.		2		2				
		O. Keeneen & wife Pa	Labr.				1		1		1
		C. McDermot & wife Pa	Labr.				2				
	Moyne	R. Winston & wife Pa	Farmer		2				1		1
		M. Grogan & wife Pa	Labr.		1						
		J. Greewy & wife Pa	Labr.		1						
		D. Moran & wife Pa	Smith		1				2		2
		O. Digenan & wife Pa	Labr.				3				
		E. Greewy & wife Pa	Labr.				1				
		M. Gormly & wife Pa	Labr.		2						
		M. Ward & wife Pa	Labr.		1						
	Corroghoghil	E. Madden & wife Pa	Tent		2		2				2
		D. Regan & wife Pa	Tent		3		2				
		P. Mcanulty & wife Pa	Tent		1						1
		W. Regan & wife Pa	Tent		4		2				
		O. Regan & wife Pa	Tent		3		1				
		J. Keanry & wife Pa	Tent		2						
		C. Casserly & wife Pa	Labr.		2						
		D. Macanulty & wife Pa	Labr.		2						
		P. Macanulty & wife Pa	Tent				1				
		W. Regan & wife Pa	Labr.		1						
		M. Walsh & wife Pa	Tent		1						1
		J. Macanulty & wife Pa	Tent		1				2		
		J. Dogharty & wife Pa	Tent		3		2				
		A. Regan & wife Pa	Labr.								

Com~Ros common Parish of	Place of Abode	Names and Religion	Proffession	Children under 14		Children above 14		Men Servts		Women Servts	
				Prot.	Paps.	Prot.	Paps.	Prot.	Paps.	Prot.	Paps.
		N. Regan Labr.									
		D. O'Donnel & wife Pa	Tent		1						
		Hugh Flyn Pa	Labr.								
		D. Casserly & wife Pa	Labr.		1						
		L. McShane & wife Pa	Labr.								
		M. O'Donnel & wife Pa	Labr.								
		J. O'Donnel & wife Pa	Labr.		1						
		J. Burk & wife Pa	Labr.		1						
		J. McNemarra & wife Pa	Labr.		1						
		J. Dogharty & wife Pa	Labr.		1						
		O. Regan & wife Pa	Labr.		1						
		J. Regan & wife Pa	Labr.		1						
		P. Flanigan & wife Pa	Labr.		1						
		P. Murrin & wife Pa	Labr.		1						
[f.305] Tibohin	Corroghoghil	C. Oran & wife Pa	Labr.		1						
		H. Gravethy & wife Pa	Labr.								
	Clegarna	W. Davis & wife Pre	Gent.	3					1		3
		B. Loo & wife Pa	Weaver		3						1
		M. Carty & wife Pa	Labr.								1
		J. Conigan & wife Pa	Labr.		2						
		H. McDermotroe	Weaver								
		O. Kincreag & wife Pa	Labr.		3						
		H. Conellan & wife Pa	Labr.				1				
		H. Rogers & wife Pa	Labr.		1						
	Kilruddan	O. Seire & wife Pa	Labr.		3						
		C. Greenan & wife Pa	Labr.		1						
		M. Burn & wife Pa	Labr.		2						
		O. Regan & wife Pa	Labr.		2						
		P. Macanulty & wife Pa	Labr.		1						
		M. Burn & wife Pa	Labr.		1						
		M. Casserly & wife Pa	Labr.		2						
		L. Regan & wife Pa	Labr.		1						
		P. Burn & wife Pa	Labr.		1						
	Tenecreevy	P. MacDermot & wife Pa	Labr.		1		1				
		E. Fanning & wife Pa	Labr.		1		2				
		E. Giblane Pa	Labr.				5				
		E. Conighan & wife Pa	Labr.		4						
		P. Egan & wife Pa	Labr.		4		1				
		E. Mahon & wife Pa	Labr.		1		1				
		T. Mahon & wife Pa	Labr.		2		3				
		J. Giblane & wife Pa	Labr.		2		3				
		M. Lowry Pa	Labr.		1		3				
		T. Kelly Pa	Jobber		2		1				
		M. Fanning Pa	Widow				3				
	Ballinfull	J. Giblane & wife Pa	farmer		1		4				
		A. Gihin & wife Pa	Cobler		1						
		M. Lavin & wife Pa	Labr.		1						
		D. Giblane & wife Pa	Labr.		2						
		P. Conigan & wife Pa	Labr.		1						

Com~Ros common Parish of	Place of Abode	Names and Religion	Proffession	Children under 14 Prot.	Children under 14 Paps.	Children above 14 Prot.	Children above 14 Paps.	Men Servts Prot.	Men Servts Paps.	Women Servts Prot.	Women Servts Paps.
		C. Carty & wife Pa	Labr.								
		W. Giblane Pa	farmer		1		1				
		B. Conigan Pa	farmer		2		2				
		T. Lynch & wife Pa	Labr.		2						
		M. Carty Pa	farmer		2						
[f.306] Tibohin	Ballinfull	J. Quin Pa	Farmer		2		1				
		J. Bolton & wife Pa	Farmer		1						
		P. Connor & wife Pa	Labr.		1						
	Tibohin	P. Kearney & wife Pa	Labr.				2				
		P. Kean & wife Pa	Farmer		2						
		J. Callaghan & wife Pa	Farmer		2		2				
		C. McDermot & wife Pa	Farmer		1		2				
		J. Callaghan & wife Pa	Tailer		1						
		P. Callaghan & wife Pa	Labr.				5				
		J. Kearney & wife Pa	Labr.		1		1				
		D. Callaghan & wife Pa	Farmer		1		3				
		J. Callaghan Pa	Labr.		1		3				
		D.Dolan & wife Pa	Labr.		2						
		M. Timane & wife Pa	Labr.				3				
		T.Timane & w. Pa	Labr.								
	Lisahark	P. Callaghan & wife Pa	Farmer								
		E. Callaghan & wife Pa	Farmer		2		4				
		M. Callaghan Pa	Widow		2						
		M. Gara & wife Pa	Mason		1		1				
		O. Higgins & wife Pa	Tailer		1		1				
		T. Callaghan Pa	Labr.		1		1				
		M. Lavin & wife Pa	Labr.				2				
		O. Keeneen & wife Pa	Farmer		1						
		J. Keeneen Pa	Weaver								
		M. Brenan Pa	Farmer		1		3				
		P. Lavin Pa	Farmer				4				
	Cloonfad	E. Corkran & wife Pa	Farmer		2		1				
		J. Kean & wife Pa	Farmer		2						
		C. Flyn & wife Pa	Farmer		2		3				
		M. Kenny & wife Pa	Labr.		2						
		C. Callaghan & wife Pa	Labr.		1						
		J. Greewachan & wife Pa	Labr.		1						
		P. Macdruy & wife Pa	Labr.		2						
		P. Sharkety & wife Pa	Farmer		2		1				
		M. McDonagh & wife Pa	Smith		2						
	Mullinashe	J. Macala & wife Pa	Labr.		2						
		R. Higgins & wife Pa	Labr.				1				
		P. MacDermotroe & wife Pa	Labr.				2				
		F. Bokin & wife Pa	Labr.		2						
		H. Grourk & wife Pa	Labr.		2						
[f.307] Tibohin	Grallagh	K. Egan Pa	Widow						1		1
		H. Macala & wife Pa	Labr.				2				1
	Letrym	D. MacGary & wife Pa	Labr.		2		1				
		C. Kennedy & wife Pa	Farmer		2		1				

0 Com~Ros common Parish of	Place of Abode	Names and Religion	Proffession	Children under 14		Children above 14		Men Servts		Women Servts	
				Prot.	Paps.	Prot.	Paps.	Prot.	Paps.	Prot.	Paps.
		B. Brislane & wife Pa	Labr.				2				
		C. MacDermot & wife Pa	Mason		3						
		F.Gara & wife Pa	Farmer		2						
		J. MacGary Pa	Tailer								
	Lisdoo	O. Lynch & wife Pa	Labr.		3						1
		M. Sheridon & wife Pa	Labr.		2						
		J. Callery & wife Pa	Labr.		2						
		J. Lowry & wife Pa	Labr.		1		1				
		A. Beran & wife Pa	Labr.		2						
	Balliglass	J. Sharry & wife Pa	Labr.		2						
		T. Sharry & wife Pa	Labr.		2		2				
		M. Dolan Pa	Widow		1		2				1
		M. Mallowly & wife Pa	Labr.		2		1				
		T. Mallowly & wife Pa	Labr.		2						
	Bockil	B. Moffit & wife Pa	Farmer				1		1		1
		B. Moffit & wife Pa	Tailer		3						
		J. Greevy & wife Pa	Labr.		2						
		J. Greevy & wife Pa	Labr.		3						
		M. Lavin & wife Pa	Tent		1						
		O. Lavin & wife Pa	Tent		3						
		T. Lavin & wife Pa	Tent		2						
		C. Moffit & wife Pa	Labr.								
	Listrumneal	C. Rogers & wife Pa	Farmer		2		2		1		
		J. Rogers & wife Pa	Tent								
	Driney	M. Lynch & wife Pa	Tent						1		1
	Clonmullen	J. Grourk & wife Pa	Cottier		2		1				
		M. Carty & wife Pa	Labr.		2						
	Clonbounogh	P. Malveely & wife Pa	Cottier		2						
	Drumenagh	M. Grourk & wife Pa	Labr.				2				
		C. Flanigan Pa	Labr.		1						
	Cleragh	W. Costello & wife Pa	Serjeant				3				
	Bryanmore	C. Flanigan & wife Pa	Serjeant		2						
	Raheely	N. Abbit & wife Prot	Cottier								
		C. Sharkety & wife Pa	Labr.		2						
		T. Coona & wife Pa	Labr.				1				
		P. Gihin Pa	Shepherd		1		3				
[f.308] Tibohin	Rahealy	J. Donahoo & wife Pa	Labr.								
		M. MacGary & wife Pa	Joyner		3						
		D. Lowry & wife Pa	Labr.								
		J. MacGary & wife Pa	Labr.		1		3				

[on paper pasted to verso f.308]

Total men & women   1669   Do: Pre: 114   Do Pa: 1555

Total children   1525   Do: Pre under 48   Do: Pa: 961

                             14

                        Do: Do: above 26   Do: Do: 490

Total men, women & Chiln: 3194   Do: Pre: 188   Do: Pa: 3006

NOTES

1. Including 867 acres of water (*General Alphabetical Index*).

2. Lewis, 'Taughboyne or Artagh also called Tibohine'.

3. *Report ... fairs and markets.*

4. N.L.I., Survey of estate of Paul Davis, 1788, MS 21 F 45, ff. 81, 83, 89, 92.

5. Turlogh and Cormack McDermot owned Caracumeen, Carogarive and Errit (*Books of Survey and Distribution*, Roscommon).

6. Leslie, 'Elphin', R.C.B., 61/2/5; *Synge Letters* p. 30.

7. Westenra Crumpe, son of the Rev. Richard Crumpe. Admitted to TCD in 1705, he graduated BA in 1709. He became chaplain to Brigadier General Jacob Orr's Troop in 1717. He married first, Susan Sherigly of Swords in 1714 and, second, Martha Campbell who predeceased him in 1755. He died in 1761 (*Synge Letters* p.30).

8. Arthur French was born in Liverpool in 1690, the eldest son of John French and Anne Gore. He was educated by Mr Wigmore of Dungar (French Park) and entered TCD in 1708 aged 18 but did not take a degree. He married Jane Perceval in 1722 and had four sons and one daughter. (George, one of his sons died in a duel with Sir Edward Crofton). He was MP for Tulsk from 1713-15 and again 1721-27 and MP for Boyle 1727-60. He became High Sheriff of County Roscommon in 1720 and 1722; Governor of the Dublin Workhouse 1732-60, Commissioner of the Tillage Act 1735, 1739-60. In 1735 he made an allegation of breach of privilege against Gerald Dillon of Skekin, County Roscommon who had ordered holes to be dug on his estate. He was one of the founder members of the Dublin Society in 1733. His father John built French Park in the 1720s. Arthur French died in 1761 (*History of the Irish Parliament; Alumni Dubliniensis*; Burke, *Peerage* (1912)).

9. James Armstrong of French Park was a freeholder supporting John French in 1768 (N.L.I., Freeholders of County Roscommon, 1768, MS 35,152).

10. A Theobald Dillon Esq was living in Loghlin in the mid-seventeenth century (*Census of Ireland*).

11. Arable and pasture, but the bottom pasture 'subject to flood'. Moory pasture, improvable mountain and cut bog (N.L.I., Map of lands in baronies of Frenchpark, Moycarn, Roscommon MS 21 F 45/89).

12. Part of the see of Elphin (N.A., MS 545e).

13. Arable and pasture, red bog 'most of which pasturable', dry pasturable mountain and bog (N.L.I, Map of Tully and Cloondart parish of Tibohine surveyed in 1770, MS 21 F 45/98).

14. The mill was on a fork in the river (N.L.I., Maps of lands on Boyle, Castlerea and Frenchpark MS 21 F 45/98).

15. Arable and pasture, heathy, 'morassy and boggy pasture and corragh mixt'. Improvable dry mountain (N.L.I., Map of lands in baronies of Frenchpark, Moycarn, Roscommon MS 21 F 45/98).

16. There was a pattern on St Dominic's day (4 August) which gathered here. This was probably the reason for the inn (Beirne, (ed.), *Diocese of Elphin* p. 108.

17. Arable and pasture, improvable bog. Some morassy deep pasture. 'Improvable mountain enclosed' (N.L.I., Map of lands in baronies of Frenchpark, Moycarn, Roscommon MS 21 F 45/80).

18. Arable and pasture land, with a turlough. The red bogs were said to be grassy and pasturable. There was a lough within the bounds of the townland. Survey of French Park (N.L.I., MS Map of lands in baronies of Frenchpark, Moycarn, Roscommon 1716-1838 MS 21 F 45/79).

19. Probably Andrew Duffy OP. (Fenning, 'Clergy Lists', p.146, fn 12).

20. William Barlow married Bridget Dillon in 1748 (N.L.I., Marriage Licence Bonds Diocese of Elphin mic. p.1881).

21. Arable and pastureland with 'about ten acres of coarse bottom pasture, part deep and morassy'. There was a 'deep overflown marsh'. The islands of Curragh and Sally were partly pasturable (N.L.I., Map of lands in baronies of Frenchpark, Moycarn, Roscommon 1716-1838, MS 21 F 45/79).

22. Robert Savage, freeholder of French Park supported John French in 1768 (N.L.I., Freeholders of County Roscommon, MS 35,152).

KILLUKIN, COUNTY ROSCOMMON
(BARONY OF ROSCOMMON)

INTRODUCTION: *The parish of Killukin is divided into two parts, the first part in the barony of Boyle just south of Carrick-on Shannon (see separate entry) and the second in the barony of Roscommon, some 7 miles to the south-west. This part was bounded by the parishes of Kilcooley, Ogulla, Kiltristan, Cloonfinlogh and Kilbride. It covers 2,883 statute acres.[1] It had grazing farms, lakes and much bog. There was a quantity of limestone. A patent for a fair to be held in Crogan twice a year was issued to William O'Malley in 1617.[2]*

The incumbent was the Rev. Arthur Mahon who held the parish with Tumna, Kilcolagh, and Estersnow (see Killukin, Boyle). The patron was the bishop.

OCCUPATIONS

Apothecary	1	Farmer	42	Merchant	1
Broguemaker	2	Gentleman	1	Priest	1
Butcher	1	Glazier	1	Servant	2
Carman	3	Glover	1	Servants, household	113
Chandler	1	Hatter	2	Smith	5
Cooper	1	Joiner	2	Tailor	2
Cottier	74	Labourer	2	Weaver	12
				Widow	14

Com~Ros common Parish of	Place of Abode	Names and Religion	Proffession	Children under 14 Prot.	Paps.	Children above 14 Prot.	Paps.	Men Servts Prot.	Paps.	Women Servts Prot.	Paps.
[f.309] Killukin	Taulagh	J.R. Rutlege Pr	Farmer	4							1
Killukin	Taulagh	M. Rutledge Pr	Widow								1
Killukin	Drimercash	M. Forester[3] P	priest								
Killukin	Knockdalton	B.M. Lavin P	Farmer		2						1
Killukin	Knockdalton	M. Lavin P	Widow				2				1
Killukin	Knockdalton	D.M. Feehely P	Farmer		2						1
Killukin	Knockdalton	B.E. Lavin P	Farmer		4						1
Killukin	Knockdalton	M. Salmon P	Widow		4						1
Killukin	Knockdalton	J.M. Lavin P	Farmer		5						1
Killukin	Knockdalton	E.M. Grevy P	Farmer		3						1
Killukin	Knockdalton	D. M.Bryan P	Farmer		2						1
Killukin	Mullimore	N.M. Farly P	Butcher		3						1
Killukin	Ditto	E.M. Lahy P	Farmer		4						
Killukin	Ditto	T.M. Lahy P	Farmer		1						
Killukin	Ditto	An.M. Hopkins P	Farmer				2				
Killukin	Ditto	M:E. Hopkins P	Farmer		1						
Killukin	Ditto	O.M. Lavin P	Farmer		2						1
Killukin	Ditto	D.M. Hilford P	Farmer		2						
Killukin	Ditto	M. Lavin P	Widow				1				
Killukin	Ditto	D.M. Dan P	Smith		6				1		
Killukin	Ditto	John E. Doneher P	Farmer		1		2				1
Killukin	Ditto	J.B. Mehen P	Farmer		1						1
Killukin	Ditto	M. Horan P	Widow				1				1
Killukin	Ditto	J.H. Winter P	Farmer		3						
Killukin	Ditto	P.E. Ford P	Cottier		1						
Killukin	Ditto	J.M. Loghran P	Cottier		2						
Killukin	Ditto	J. B. Salmon P	Farmer		3						
Killukin	Ditto	O:M:. Kelly P	Cottier		3						
Killukin	Killukin	J. E. Laird Pr	Farmer				1		1		1
Killukin	Killukin	G.E. Laird Pr	Farmer		2				1		2
Killukin	Killukin	M.L. Oats P	Cottier		4						
Killukin	Killukin	J.E. Becket P	Cottier		2						1
Killukin	Cordrehid	M. M Golrich P	Cottier		3				1		1
Killukin	Cordrehid	P.M. Lavin P	Cottier								
Killukin	Cordrehid	C. E. Regan P	Cottier								
Killukin	Cordrehid	C. M. Lavin P	Cottier								
Killukin	Mullowginnan	M. C. Ford P	Cottier		2				1		
Killukin	Mullowginnan	P. Glyn P	Cottier		2		1				
Killukin	Mullowginnan	L. H.Becket P	Cottier		4						
Killukin	Carronaff	G. M. Flyin P	Smith		3		2				
Killukin	Corronell	C.M. Keon P	Farmer		3				1		1
[f.310] Killukin	Carronaff	E.M. Common P	Smith								
Killukin	ditto	J.F. Cary Pr	Apothecary	1		3			1		1
Do	ditto	W.E. Adams Pr	Weaver					1		1	
Do	Cortoles	L.E. Clifford Pr	Chandler	3					1		1
Do	Ditto	P.M. Stanton P	B maker		3		1				
Do	Ditto	B.A. McSharry P	Weaver		2				1		1
Do	Ditto	P.M. Suffolk[?] P	Smith		2		1				1

Com~Ros common Parish of	Place of Abode	Names and Religion	Proffession	Children under 14 Prot.	Paps.	Children above 14 Prot.	Paps.	Men Servts Prot.	Paps.	Women Servts Prot.	Paps.
Do	Ditto	C.M.Nash P	Cottier		1		4				
Do	Ditto	J.M Tansy P	Labourer		1						
Do	Ditto	J. E.Ealy Pr	Weaver	2					1		
Do	Ditto	G. S. Henderson Pr	Weaver	3				3	2		1
Do	Ditto	F. E. Digenan Pr	Gentleman			1					
Do	Ditto	R. E. Walsh Pr	Taylor	2				2			
Do	Ditto	J. Luttrell Pr	Widow	1	1				1		1
Do	Ditto	J.M. Gallaher Pr	Farmer	1		4					1
Do	Ditto	C. Mulheran P	Widow		3				3		1
Do	Ditto	J. A McDonagh Pr	Labourer	2							
Do	Ditto	G. B.Low P	Weaver		2						1
Do	Ditto	R. M.Johnson Pr	Sadler	2							
Do	Ditto	H. S. Gillaspy Pr	Weaver	2							
Do	Ditto	H. E. Luttrell	Weaver		1	3					1
Do	Ditto	J. E. Harrison Pr	Glover	2							
Do	Ditto	W. E. Harrison Pr	Weaver	2				1			1
Do	Ditto	E. Clindillon Pr	Widow								
Do	Ditto	W. M. Low P	Cottier		2						
Do	Ditto	L. P. Stanton P	B:maker		1						
Do	Drissoge	C. M.Hely P	Farmer		1		1				1
Do	Ditto	Z. M. Williams Pr	Glazer	5[?]							
Do	Ditto	L.M. Conellan P	Cottier		2		2				
Do	Ditto	G. M. Byrn P	Cottier		2		2				
Do	Ditto	M. M. Lavin P	Cottier		3						
Ditto	Scregg	D. M.Padin P	Cottier		3				1		2
Do	Ditto	O. M.Fox P	Servant		2						
Do	Ditto	D. M.Dans P	Cottier		1						
Do	Killaquin	T. R. Throp Pr	Weaver	4					1		
Do	Ditto	O.M. Regan	Cottier				2				
Do	Mount Thady	J. M. Pendargress P	Cottier		1						
Do	Ditto	O. E. Lavin P	Servant		4						
Do	Ditto	L. M. Taaf P	Cottier		1		1				
Do	Ditto	J. E.Fahy P	Cottier		2						1
Do	Ditto	F. M.Priest P	Cottier		1		2				
[f.311] Killukin	Croghan	J. Lloyd Pr	Spinster		5[?]		3	2	2		3
Killukin	Croghan	W.M. Goodfellow Pr	Weaver	1			1				
Killukin	Croghan	J. E.Donellan P	Farmer				2		2		2
Killukin	Croghan	J.C. Donelan P	Farmer		3				2		3
Killukin	Croghan	P. M.Donellan P	Merchant						1		1
Killukin	Croghan	E. N.Coghran P	Cottier		2		2				
Killukin	Croghan	G. Hammel P	Widow		3						
Killukin	Croghan	W. M.Rogers P	Cottier		3		1				
Killukin	Croghan	J. C. Dillon P	Cottier		2						
Killukin	Croghan	C. Tanist P	Cottier		2		2				
Killukin	Croghan	J.J. McSharry P	Cottier		5[?]						
Killukin	Croghan	P. M.Conellan P	Cottier		5[?]						
Killukin	Lignashamur	J. C.Doyle P	Cottier		2						
Killukin	Lignashamur	M. M.Dowd P	Cottier				1				
Killukin	Lignashamur	R. M. Burne P	Cottier				4				

Com~Ros common Parish of	Place of Abode	Names and Religion	Proffession	Children under 14		Children above 14		Men Servts		Women Servts	
				Prot.	Paps.	Prot.	Paps.	Prot.	Paps.	Prot.	Paps.
Killukin	Lignashamur	C.C. Horan P	Cottier		3		2				
Killukin	Lignashamur	P. A.Bryn P	Cottier				5[?]				
Killukin	Ardmore[4]	D. M Dyar P	Cottier		4						
Killukin	Cashelhallin[?]	D. M. Connellan P	Cottier		2						
Killukin	Ardmore	M. M. Mulkeran P	Cottier		2		3				
Killukin	Ardmore	O. M.Regan P	Cottier				3				
Killukin	Ardmore	M. C. Regan P	Cottier		1						
Killukin	Ardmore	L. A. Gibbins P	Cottier				2				
Killukin	Ardmore	R. M. Fallon P	Cottier								
Killukin	Enagh	P.M. McDermot P	Cottier				1		1		1
Killukin	Enagh	W.B. Feehely P	Cottier		1		2				
Killukin	Enagh	M. J. Triston P	Widow		4		3				
Killukin	Enagh	J. C Triston P									
Killukin	Enagh	J.J. Campbell Pr	Weaver	2		3		1			
Killukin	Enagh	P. A.Cooper Pr	Farmer	4						1	
Killukin	Tully	T. G. Cown P	Cottier		2		1				
Killukin	Tully	J.C. Fury P	Cottier		1						
Killukin	Tully	T.M. McDermot P	Cottier		2						
Killukin	Tully	J. C.Ledan P	Cottier		1						
Killukin	Tully	E. A. Higgins P	Taylor		2						
Killukin	Tully	H.S. Mcnamarra P	Cottier		4						
Killukin	Tully	F. A. Monehan P	Cottier		2						
Killukin	Tully	C. E.Judge P	Cottier				4				
Killukin	Boher	E. McNeal P	Widow				2				
Killukin	Boher	M.O. McGragh P	Cottier		2						
Killukin	Boher	J. Lavin P	Cottier		2		4				
[f.312] Killukin	Boher	D.McNamarra	Cottier		2						
Killukin	Boher	G. Blunket P	Farmer		4		3		1		2
Killukin	Boher	R. McNeal P	Cottier		1						
Killukin	Boher	J. M.Blunket P	Cottier		1						
Killukin	Boher	J. M. McNeal P	Cottier		2						
Killukin	Killigarry	E. Tulloge P	Widow				3		1		3
Killukin	Killigarry	R.C. McGrevy P	Smith								
Killukin	Killigarry	J. O.Spallen P	Cottier		1						
Killukin	Killigarry	M. B. Cox P	Cottier								
Killukin	Killigarry	J. A. Dolan P	Cottier		1				1		
Killukin	Killigarry	J. C. McGrevy P	Cottier								1
Killukin	Killigarry	C.H. McDermot P	Cottier		2						
Killukin	Killigarry	D.M. Lahy P	Cottier						1		1
Killukin	Killigarry	M. C. Glyn P	Cottier		2						
Killukin	Killigarry	H. Regan P	Widow		2						
Killukin	Torymartin	B.F. Conelly P	Farmer		2		2				
Killukin	Torymartin	D.M. Coveny P	Farmer		1						
Killukin	Torymartin	H. B. Naghten P	Farmer								1
Killukin	Torymartin	D. M. Caslan P	Joyner		1		4				
Killukin	Torymartin	T. M.Lavin P	Joyner		3		2		1		2
Killukin	Torymartin	L. Leland Pr	Hatter			2					
Killukin	Knockananima	H.M.Warren P	Hatter		2						
Killukin	Torymartin	D. A. Henry P	Cottier		4						

Com~Ros common Parish of	Place of Abode	Names and Religion	Proffession	Children under 14 Prot.	Children under 14 Paps.	Children above 14 Prot.	Children above 14 Paps.	Men Servts Prot.	Men Servts Paps.	Women Servts Prot.	Women Servts Paps.
Killukin	Cashel	M.M. Ford P	Cottier		2						
Killukin	Cashel	M. M.McGowan P	Cottier		2						
Killukin	Knockanum	J.M. Gilmer Pr	Farmer	2					1		1
Killukin	Knockanum	T.M. Lahy P	Farmer		4		1				
Killukin	Knockanum	J.G. Conaghton P	Weaver		5[?]				1		
Killukin	Drumlion	T. S. Fahy P	Cottier		4						1
Killukin	Drumlion	E. M.Hely P	Cottier		4		1				
Killukin	Drumlion	L. M.Kelly P	Cottier								
Killukin	Drumlion	T. M.Kelly P	Carman		3						
Killukin	Drumlion	O. M.Glyn P	Cottier		1[?]		1				
Killukin	Drumlion	D. M.Dermot P	Cottier		3		1				
Killukin	Drumlion	C. E. Dermot P	Cottier		3						
Killukin	Drimernod	J.M. Ford P	Farmer		2		2				
Killukin	Drimernod	E. M.Golrick P	Farmer		3		2				
Killukin	Drimernod	T.M. Forester P	Farmer		2						1
Killukin	Drimernod	M. Dermot P	Widow		3		1				1
Killukin	Drimernod	T. M. Sarce Pr	Cooper	3		4					1
Killukin [f.313]	Drimernod	E. M. Rutlege Pr	Farmer	2							
Killukin	Mount Thady	M. F. Greghan P	Cottier		1		2				
Killukin	Ballinkilleen	E. M.Baden P	Farmer		3		2				1
Killukin		B. E. Baden P	Carman		4				1		1
Killukin		Th. M.Conry P	Carman		4				1		1
Killukin		L.M. Conry P	Farmer		2						1
Killukin		Jam. M. Walker P	Farmer		3						1
Killukin		Cor. M. Irons P	Farmer		4						
Killukin		O. M. Irons P	Farmer		2		2				
Killukin		C. E.Higgins P	Farmer		1						
Killukin		M. F. Power P	Farmer		2						1

NOTES

1. Lewis, 'Killuken'.

2. *Report ... fairs and markets*.

3. Matthias Forester, curate, died 1779 (Beirne, (ed.), *Diocese of Elphin*, p. 123).

4. Arable and pasture land with turloughs and land subject in winter 'to be overflown'. Poor boggy pasture with many old turf holes. Exact Maps of Part of the Estate of the Right Honourable Lord Kingston copied from maps of 1724 (N.L.I., MS 21 F 13/8).

TUMNA, COUNTY ROSCOMMON

INTRODUCTION: *The parish of Tumna is in the barony of Boyle, 1½ miles west of Carrick-on -Shannon. The parish covers 9,188 statute acres.[1] The land was said to be good with much limestone and freestone.[2] There was a fair once a year at Coote Hall.[3] The Coote Hall estate was on the eastern side of Upper Oakport Lough. In the eighteenth-century the area had the reputation of being a haven for 'a lawless race... many of the misdemeanours which disgraced the county had been traced... to people from this quarter, and criminals flying from others parts had here found a ready and secure asylum ...'.[4]*

In 1641, two members of the Dermot/mcDermot family owned two townlands in the parish, and there were six members of the family there in 1749. The St George family owned most of the parish in the eighteenth-century.[5]

The incumbent was the Rev. Arthur Mahon who held the parish with Killukin, Kilcolagh, and Estersnow (see Killukin, Boyle). The patron was the bishop.

OCCUPATIONS

Carman	1	Gentleman	3	Priest	1
Clerk	1	Glover	1	Schoolmaster	1
Cooper	1	Herd	1	Servant	8
Cottier	16	Labourer	27	Servants,household	97
Dealer	1	Miller	1	Smith	3
Farmer	62	Pedlar	1	Tailor	4
Gardener	1	Piper	1	Weaver	5

Com~Ros common Parish of	Place of Abode	Names and Religion	Proffession	Children under 14		Children above 14		Men Servts		Women Servts	
				Prot.	Paps.	Prot.	Paps.	Prot.	Paps.	Prot.	Paps.
[f.314]Tomna	Gortgrassagh	I. M. Coriam P	Servant				3				
Tomna	Gortgrassagh	J. E. Kilboy P	Weaver		3		1				
	Ditt	B.C. Cane P	Servant		1		1				
	Ditt	D.J. Bohan	Cottier		2		2				
	Ditt	J.E. Coriam P	Servant		2						
	Ditt	M. Mcdonagh P	Widow		1		1				1
	Ditt	O. Gageen P	Cottier		3		1				
	Ditt	M. McParten P	Cooper		1		1				
	Clongoonagh	J. Powel Pr	Servant			3	3[?]		1	1	1
	Dit	J. M.Hill P	Cottier		3		1				
	Dit	W. C. Conry P	Dealer		1						
	Dit	D.M. McDaniel P	Miller		4		2				
	Dit	B.M. Hely P	Cottier		1						
	Dit	O.M. Grevy P	Cottier		4				1		1
	Dit	J. Priest P	Cottier		4						1
	Dit	C. J.Murry P	Cottier				1				
		J.C.Murry P	Cottier		3						
	Dit	J.E. Eccles Pr	Gentleman	4		1					
	Kelticuneen	E. Gilmer Pr	Widow	1		2		1		1	
	D	L.E. Hog P	Glover		2			+̶			+̶
	D	James Mehen P	Cottier		2						
	D	B. M.Cullen P	Weaver								
	D	J.A. Thomson Pr	Weaver	2				1			
	D	J. E. Fanin Pr	Smith	3							
	D	M. Leland Pr	Widow			2					
	D	A. M.Hoy Pr	Clerk	5[?]		1					
	Ardcouhil	J. M. Thomson Pr	Farmer	3							
	D	M. Thomson Pr	Widow			1					
	D	R. M. Rogers Pr	Weaver	1		1					
	D	J.C. McGowen	Cottier		3						
	Ironheragh [?]	I.Gilmer Pr	Farmer			2					1
	D	D.M. Gilmer Pr							1	2	
	D	J.M. Gilmer Pr	Farmer	3				1		1	
	Meery	G.I. Jones Pr	Farmer	4					1		1
	D	T. M.Lloyd Pr	Farmer	4		1			2		2
	D	J.A. Cox Pr	Cottier	3		2					
	D	J.M. Bealon P	Cottier		2						
	D	B.M. Lavin P	Cottier		3						
	D	P.E. Monneen P	Cottier		2						
	D	C.M. Moneen P	Cottier		1						
	D	C.M.Rork P	Cottier								
[f.315] Tomna	Shanwallybane	H. M.Regan P	Farmer		3						
Tomna	Shanwallybane	C.B. Regan P	Farmer		2						
Tomna	Shanwallybane	B.E. Regan P	Farmer		1						
Tomna	Drummore	S. Farrell P	Farmer		3						1
Tomna	Drummore	T. M.Banone P	Farmer		3						
Tomna	Drummore	T.C. McDermot P	Farmer		2						
Tomna	Meeorane	J.M. Mullone P	Farmer		2						
Tomna	Meeorane	P. U.Hely P	Farmer		2						

Com~Ros common Parish of	Place of Abode	Names and Religion	Proffession	Children under 14		Children above 14		Men Servts		Women Servts	
				Prot.	Paps.	Prot.	Paps.	Prot.	Paps.	Prot.	Paps.
Tomna	Meeorane	L. M. Mullone P	Farmer		2						
Tomna	Meeorane	L.E. Mullone P	Farmer		2						
Tomna	Meeorane	T. M.Mahon P	Farmer		1						
Tomna	Meeorane	T.M. McTernan P	Labourer		2		2				
Tomna	Meeorane	E. M.Jordan P	Labourer		1						
Tomna	Meeorane	E. M. Brennan P	Farmer		2						
Tomna	Meeorane	T. E.Jordan P	Farmer		2						
Tomna	Meeorane	W.M. Farrell	Farmer		1						
Tomna	Meeorane	M.C. Cormick	Farmer		2						
Tomna	Meeorane	D.H.Reynolds	Farmer		2						
Tomna	Meeorane	M.M. Reynolds P	Farmer		2						
Tomna	Lustea	J.E. McGuire P	Farmer		4				2		1
Tomna	Lustea	B.M.Heslan P	Servant		2						
Tomna	Lustea	A.C. Ferrall P	Farmer		2						
Tomna	Lustea	B.E. Callary P	Farmer		1						
Tomna	Lustea	D.E. Regan P	Labourer		1						
Tomna	Lustea	C.M. Flyn P	Schoolmastr		1						
Tomna	Lustea	J.E. Costello P	Labourer		2						
Tomna	Braclone	E. C. Ternan P	Farmer		2						
Tomna		E.E. Muldoony P	Farmer		2						
Tomna		M.C. Parlan P	Farmer		1						
Tomna	Annaghmonahan[6]	P.E. Davis P	Farmer		1						
Tomna	Annaghmonahan	M.M. McRan P	Farmer								
Tomna	Annaghmonahan	W.J. Moore Pr	Farmer								
Tomna	Annaghmonahan	G.E. Linsk P	Farmer								
Tomna	Drimtreemanane	F.M Walpole P	Farmer		2						
Tomna	Drimtreemanane	O. Mcdermot P	Farmer								
Tomna	Drumbalon	B. M.Farrell P	Farmer		2						
Tomna	Drumbalon	J. Burk P	Farmer		1						
Tomna	Gobbertasnan	B. Hely P	Servant				1				
Tomna	Gobbertasnan	C. Grant P	Widow				1				
Tomna	Gobbertasnan	R.M.. McDermot Roe	Labourer		4						
Tomna	Gortgrassagh	C. Eccles Pr	Widow	3		1			2		2
[f.316] Tomna	Coot Hall[7]	G. Carthy P	Taylor								
	Coot Hall	H.E. Sharcot P	Piper		6						
	Coot Hall	W.E. [blank] P	Pedlar		2						
	Coot Hall	M. M.Kenedy P	Tailor		3		3				
	Coot Hall	J.M. Feely Pr	Farmer	1		1			1		1
	Coot Hall	R.C Lonogan P	Gardiner				5[?]				
	Knocknashana	H.C. Bell P	Weaver		1		2				
	Knocknashana	O.E. McGlaughlin P	Labourer		2						
	Knocknashana	P.W. Morahen P	Herdsman		1						1
	Knocknashana	P. Keeltehan P	Labourer		1		2		1		
	Knocknashana	H. M. Gray Pr	Farmer	2	+	1	2̶		2		2
	Knocknashana	W. H. Wynn Pr	Gentleman								
	Knocknashana	M. Gray Pr	Farmer		1				1		1
	Derrynaseer	J.A. Keveny P	Labourer				3				
	Osna	W.M. Phibbs Pr	Farmer	4		1			2		3
	Osna	H.A. Mullen P	Labourer		1						

Com~Ros common Parish of	Place of Abode	Names and Religion	Proffession	Children under 14 Prot.	Children under 14 Paps.	Children above 14 Prot.	Children above 14 Paps.	Men Servts Prot.	Men Servts Paps.	Women Servts Prot.	Women Servts Paps.
	Osna	J. C.Lavin P	Labourer		2						
	Osna	T.G. Shannon P	Labourer		2						
	Cloonbrislane	P.M. Gowane P	Labourer			~~1~~ 3	~~3~~ 1		1.p:		
	Kilmacuril	G.I.McCulla Pr				1		1 ~~2~~	1.p:		1.p:
	Kilmaculril	P.M. Lyons P		3	~~3~~						
	Laughill	F.K. McCulla Pr		3:							1
	Drimsallagh	J. E.Wood Pr		4					1	1	1
	Drimsallagh	J. E.Lyons P			1						
	Drimsallagh	E. Flanagan P			3						
	Drimsallagh	M.E. McHugh P			2		2				
	Drimsallagh	J.C. McCahil P			3		2				
	Cloheen	A.M. Regan P			4		1				
	Cloheen	C. M. Bealon			1				1		1
	Cloheen	N. A. Horan P			2						
	Cloheen	M. C.Mulvy P			3						
	Cloheen	P.S. Cammedin			3						
	Cloheen	D.E. Byrn P			2						
	Cloheen	E. H.Stanton P			2				1		
	Annagh	E.H. Mulloy P			2						
	Annagh	P.C. McDermot P			2						
	Annagh	J.N. McGrevy P			2		2				
	Annagh	Terce. McDermot P									
	Annagh	Ed.M. Reynolds P			2						
	Annagh	M. Linsk P			1		1				
	Annagh	T.M. Judge P									
[f.317]parish of Tomna	Cloheen	P.P. Feheely P									
Tomna	Cloheen	P.S. McGrevy									
Tomna	Cloheen	L.M. Campbell			1				1		
Tomna	Cloheen	J.M. McManus P									
Tomna	Osna	H. M. Cockran P	Labourer		1						
Tomna	Husetown	C. M.Mulloy[8] Pr	Gentleman	3		2			2	1	3
Tomna	Husetown	D.M. Boyd Pr	Labourer	4							1
Tomna	Husetown	P. M.Dolan P	Labourer		1						
Tomna	Husetown	G.I McGowuran P	Labourer		2						
Tomna	Husetown	O.M. McCabe P	Labourer						1		
Tomna	Husetown	M.D. Flanagan P	Labourer		2						
Tomna	Husetown	I.L. Farrell P	Labourer		1						
Tomna	Garroloher	G.C. Priest P	Labourer		3						
Tomna	Garroloher	P. I.Brin P	Labourer		2						
Tomna	Garroloher	A.C Mcdonnel P	Smith		2						
Tomna	Garroloher	D.M. Morohan P	Labourer								
Tomna	Garroloher	P.C. Dolan P	Taylor		2				2		
Tomna	Imalagh	G. E.White P	Labourer		1						
Tomna	Derrinasugh	F.C. McDermot P	Labourer		3						
Tomna	Derrinasugh	G.A. Reynolds P	Labourer								
Tomna	Mogh	D.B. McLaughlin P	Labourer		2						
Tomna	Mogh	P.C. Reynolds P	Carman		1						
Tomna	Mogh	J. E.Bealan P	Farmer		1						
Tomna	Mogh	M. Bealan P	Widow		2				1		

Com~Ros common Parish of	Place of Abode	Names and Religion	Proffession	Children under 14		Children above 14		Men Servts		Women Servts	
				Prot.	Paps.	Prot.	Paps.	Prot.	Paps.	Prot.	Paps.
Tomna	Mogh	P.E. Bealan P	Farmer		2						1
Tomna	Mogh	R. Dolan P	Priest						1		2
Tomna	Gortlech	W. C. Slattery P	Farmer								1
Tomna	Gortlech	T.M. Slattery P	Farmer		1						
Tomna	Gortlech	M.M. Linsk P	Farmer		3		3				
Tomna	Clonacose	F. Byrn P	Farmer		2						
Tomna	Clonacose	D.M. Byrne P			3						
Tomna	Clonacose	I.J. Cormick P	Farmer				2				
Tomna	Clonacose	L.G. Linsh P	Smith				4				
Tomna	Driminirlow	J.M. Kilboy P	Labourer		2						
Tomna	Driminirlow	J.M.Murray P	Servant		2						
Tomna	Shanwallybone	C. C. Cormick P	Farmer		2						
Tomna	Shanwallybone	E. B. Farrill P			1						
Tomna	Shanwallybone	C.M. McCue P	Farmer		1		2				
Tomna	Shanwallybone	J. A.Callary P	Farmer		1						
Tomna	Shanwallybone	P.A Cormick P	Farmer		1						
Tomna	Shanwallybone	B. M.Callary P	Farmer		2						
[f.318] Tomna	Meery	M. Borlan P	Widow		1		1				
	Ditto	W.P McGowan	Taylor				1				
	Clonmane	J. B. Whitlam Pr	Farmer			5[?]			2		2
	Tomna	J. H. Madden P	Servant		3				1		1
	Clonsheevan	L.M. Walpole P	Farmer		2		2			1	
	D	L.M. Conellan P	Farmer		2		2				
	D	I.M. Moran P	Farmer		3				1		1
	D	R.M. Moran P	Farmer		3		1				
	Tullyleige	W. A Cooper Pr	Farmer	2							1
	D	J. Rutlege Pr	Farmer	1						1	
	D	P. E. Egan P	Farmer		2		3				
	D	I. M.Conry P	Farmer		2						1
	D	C. M.Fehy P	Farmer		2		1				

NOTES

1. Including 730 acres of the river Boyle, 163 acres of the river Shannon and 77 acres of small loughs (*General Alphabetical Index*).

2. Lewis, 'Tumna, or Toemonia'.

3. *Report ... fairs and markets*.

4. Weld, *Roscommon*, p.249.

5. A Charles Cahell Dermot owned the townland of Drumharlow and Cahell mcDermot owned Meery (*Books of Survey and Distribution*, Roscommon).

6. Anoughmonaghan townland was 19a 0r 32p of which 5a 3r 9p were arable and pasture (N.L.I., Survey of Boyle and Rockingham estates, MS 3105).

7. Described in 1832 as a village with 'wretched cabins' (Weld, *Roscommon* p. 259).

8. Charles Mulloy, son of Charles was born in Hughstown and educated by Dr Maurice Neligan of Longford. He was admitted to Trinity College in 1735 aged 17 (*Alumni Dubliniensis*).

KILCOLAGH, COUNTY ROSCOMMON

INTRODUCTION: *The parish of Kilcolagh was in the barony of Boyle. It was divided into two parts. The major part bordered the parishes of Tibohine, Kilnamanagh, Estersnow, Kilmacumsy, Shankill and Kilcorkey. The detached and smaller part was bordered by Estersnow, Killummod, Creeve and Kilmacumsy. The census entries probably reflect that division, the larger part being entered in the parish of Estersnow. Together they covered 3,097 statute acres. In 1837, one-tenth of the parish was bog and the rest arable or pasture land.[1]*

The incumbent was the Rev. Arthur Mahon who held the parish with Killukin, Tumna and Estersnow (see Killukin, Boyle).

OCCUPATIONS

Cottier	27	Servants, household	24	Victualler	1
Farmer	17	Tailor	2	Weaver	4
Herd	7				

Com~Ros common Parish of	Place of Abode	Names and Religion	Proffession	Children under 14 Prot.	Children under 14 Paps.	Children above 14 Prot.	Children above 14 Paps.	Men Servts Prot.	Men Servts Paps.	Women Servts Prot.	Women Servts Paps.
[f.319]Killcola	Knock Hall	P.M. Common P	Cottier		2		2				
		W.E.Carny P	Cottier		2						
		J.F. Dockry P	Cottier								
		J.M. Brennan P	Cottier								
		P.E. Byrn P	Cottier		1						
		D.C. Byrn P	Cottier		2		1				

[The rest of the parish of Kilcola is at f.323]

[1 blank page]

NOTE

1. Lewis, 'Kilcola'.

ESTERSNOW, COUNTY ROSCOMMON

INTRODUCTION: *Estersnow parish is in the barony of Boyle, 3½ miles from the town of Boyle. The land borders the Cavetown loughs, and in the townland of Cavetown there are a number of caves. The parish covered 3199 statute acres, and the soil was suitable for tillage. About a tenth of the land was bog. There were quarries of good limestone.*[1] *In 1641, twelve townlands in the parish were held by the McDermott family.*[2] *In 1749, five members of the family were still in the parish.*[3]

The incumbent of the parish was the Rev. Arthur Mahon, archdeacon of Elphin who held the parish with Killukin, Kilcolagh, and Tumna (see Killukin, Boyle). The rectory was impropriate in the Crofton family.

OCCUPATIONS

Broguemaker	1	Herd	6	Servants, household	29
Carpenter	1	Innkeeper	1	Shepherd	4
Cooper	1	Jobber	1	Smith	3
Cottier	42	Labourer	9	Weaver	5
Farmer	41	Miller	1	Widow	1
Gardener	1	Priest	1		

Com~Ros common Parish of	Place of Abode	Names and Religion	Proffession	Children under 14 Prot.	Children under 14 Paps.	Children above 14 Prot.	Children above 14 Paps.	Men Servts Prot.	Men Servts Paps.	Women Servts Prot.	Women Servts Paps.
[f.320] Estersnow	Estersnow	John Tymon Paps.	Cooper		2						
		Peter Shinnan Paps.	Cotter		3						
		John Raney Paps.	Shepherd		6				1	1	
		James Connor Paps.	Weaver		3		2				
		Charles Connellan Paps.	Laborer		2						
		Phelim Dougherty Paps.	Labr.		1		2				
Parish Estersnow	Fass	John Flanigan Paps.	Sheepherd				1				
		Thady Kelley Paps.	Labr.		2						
		Timothy Oats Paps.	Cotter		2						
		James Breheny Paps.	Cotter								
	Ardkorkey	John Conry Paps.	Sheepherd								
		Bryan Bern Paps.	Cotter		2		2				
		Patrick Carrill Paps.	Cotter								
		James Pettit Paps.	Cotter		1						
	Cavetown	Wm. Hogan Prot	Gardener	3							
		James Fulton Prot	Cotter	4							
		Thady Glynn Paps.	Smith				1				
		Owen Eagen Paps.	Indkeeper		3						
	Tullaboy	Barthow. Freeman Paps.	Sheephd.	3		5					
		Peter Glynn Paps.	Smith		2						
		Bryan Dermottro Paps.	Cotter		0		3				
		Michel Carty Paps.	Cotter		1		4				
		Bryan Healy Paps.	Cotter								
	Clogher	John Kingston Prot	Farmer	4							
		Denis Rork Paps.	Cotter								
		James Bern Paps.	Cotter		3						
		Connor Bern Paps.	Cotter								
	Tullavahan	Patrick Bern Paps.	Cotter		2						
		Peter Keelty Paps.	Cotter		2						
		Christophr.Blunden Paps.	Farmer		4				1		1
		Michl. McManus Paps.	Farmer		2						1
		Andrew Manus Paps.	Farmer		1						
		Edmd. Sharkot Paps.	Farmer		3		2				
		John Sharkot Paps.	Farmer		2						
		James Reagon Paps.	Farmer		4		1				
		Francis Reagon Paps.	Farmer		1						
		Hugh Dermott Paps.	Farmer		3						
Parish of Estersnow	Ardkeena[4]	Thomas. Lockard Prot	ffarmer	1						1	
		Daniel Reavenscroft Prot	Weaver	2							
		Charles Reagon Paps.	herd		4						
		Wm. Keating Paps.	Labrour		1						
[f.321] Estersnow	Carrowngaple	John Higgan Paps.	Herd		1						
		Widow Kinney Paps.			3						
		Patrick Kinney Paps.	Cotter		1						
		Patrick Noon Paps.	Weaver				3				
		Dennis Maguire Paps.	Cotter				3				

Com~Ros common Parish of	Place of Abode	Names and Religion	Proffession	Children under 14		Children above 14		Men Servts		Women Servts	
				Prot.	Paps.	Prot.	Paps.	Prot.	Paps.	Prot.	Paps.
	Ballinboher	Thomas Brennan Paps.	ffarmer				3				
		Michl. Brennan Paps.	ffarmer		3						
		Cormack Brennan Paps.	ffarmer		2						
		Widow Kinney Paps.					3				
		Darby McAran Paps.	Farmer		3				1		1
	Cornafeigh	Henry Cregg Paps.	Farmer		2		2		2		1
		Domnick Cregg Paps.	Farmer		4		1		1		
		Darby Cregg Paps.	Farmer		3				1		1
		Bartholw. Cregg Paps.	Farmer						1		1
		Widow Cregg Paps.	Widow				3				
	Finisklin	Laughlin Cregg Paps.	Farmer		2		1				
		Anthony Bern Paps.	Farmer		2		1				
		Thomas Cregg Paps.	Farmer				1				
		Edmond Cregg Paps.	Farmer		1		1				1
		Roger Cregg Paps.	Farmer				3				
		Thady Reagon Paps.	Cottier		1						
		Widow Cregg Paps.					3				
[f.322] Estersnow	Ardkeena	David Goodfellow Presbeter	Weaver			4			1		
		Thoms Glaughlin Paps.	Labr.		1		1				
	Knockroe[5]	James Boyce Prot	Farmer	4		0		1		1	1
		Charles Dodd Prot	Farmer	2					2		2
		Frans. Graham Prot	Farmer	2							
		John Healey Paps.	Cotter		3						
		Connor Connel Paps.	herd		1		2				
		Dennis Bride Paps.	Labr.		1						
		Neal Kennedy Paps.	weaver		1		1				
		Patrick Mulkiran Paps.	Labr.				2				
Parish of Estersnow	Glorey	Myles Brenan Paps.	Priest								
		Charles Moris Prot	Jober	1							
		Patrick Reagon Paps.	Cotter		3						
		Bryan Reagon Paps.	Cotter		2						
		Frans. Bern Paps.	Cotter		2						
		Kead. Brenan Paps.	Cotter		3		3				
		Florance Carty Paps.	Farmer		2						
		Michel. Hister Paps.	Farmer				2				
		Bryan Gallaughr. Paps.	Farmer		2						
	Trinegry	Thomas Boyce Prot	Farmer	5		1					
		Patrick Conry Paps.	Cotter		3						
		Roger Corker Paps.	Cotter								1
	Cloonsaghn	Samuel Kiel Prot	herd	3		2					
	Harkhill	John Fox Paps.	Farmer		4		2		1		1
		Bryan Narey Paps.	Farmer		1		1				
		James Hedian Paps.	Farmer		2		2				
		James Leanaghan Paps.	Farmer		2						
		Patrick Bern Paps.	Farmer		1						
		Connor Kelly Paps.	Farmer								1
		Patrick Kennedy Paps.	Farmer								
		Thady Cary Paps.	Farmer		4						

Com~Ros common Parish of	Place of Abode	Names and Religion	Proffession	Children under 14		Children above 14		Men Servts		Women Servts	
				Prot.	Paps.	Prot.	Paps.	Prot.	Paps.	Prot.	Paps.
		Owen Dermott Paps.	Farmer		1		2				
		Charles Dwyer Paps.	Labr.		1		1				
	Trinemarly	Matthew Bern Paps.	Labr.		1						
		Bryan Ruddy Paps.	Cotter		3						
		Laughlin Bern Paps.	Cotter		2						
		Bryan Bern Paps.	Cotter		1		1				
		Andrew Bern Paps.	Cotter				1				
		Owin Ruddy Paps.	Cotter				1				
		Patrick Keany Paps.	Cotter		4						
		John Gibbins Paps.	Cotter		2						
[f.323 Killcola]	Dooneen	Daniel Bern Paps	Herd		3				1		
		Thady Bern Paps	Cotter		1						
		Patrick Bern Paps	Cotter		2				1		
		Thomas Bern Paps	Cotter		3		2				
		Thomas Bern Paps	Farmer								
		Patrick Bern Paps	Farmer		3				2		2
		Widow Bern Paps					4				
		Widow Bern 2d Paps					2				
		Henry Bern Paps	Cotter		2						
		Widow Bern 3d Paps					3				
		Widow Mylet Paps					2				
		Widow Macorm Pap					1				
		Widow Dermott Paps					1				
		Bryan Cormack Paps	Cotter		3						
		Bartholow. Dowd Pap	Cotter		4						
		Edmond Dowd Pap	Cotter								
		Luke Keon Paps	Taylor		2						
		Michl. Connor Paps	Farmer				1		1		1
		Henry Cain Paps	Farmer		3		2				
		Patrick Cain Paps	Farmer		4						
		John Cain	Farmer		1						
		Hugh McNamorrow	Herd		4						
		Charles Moran Paps	Cotter		2		2				
		Barthow. Dillon Paps	Cotter		3						
		Bryan Flanigan Paps	Cotter		2						
		Mark Dugan Pap	Weaver								
	Knockglass	Peter Dermott Prot	Farmer	3					1		2
		James Dermott Paps	Farmer				4				
		Felix Dermott Paps			1		2				
		Patrick Dockry Paps	Cotter				1				
		John Cooney Paps	Cotter		1						
		Domnick Brenan Pap	Taylor		2						
		James Keherny Pap	Cotter		1						
		Thady Keherny Paps	Cotter								
		Barthow. Kelly Paps	Cotter				1				
		Edmond Morishro Paps	Cotter				2				
		Patrick Bern Paps	Weaver		1						
		Owen Gray Paps	Herd		1						
		Thady Macalley Paps	Herd		2						

Com~Ros common Parish of	Place of Abode	Names and Religion	Proffession	Children under 14 Prot.	Paps.	Children above 14 Prot.	Paps.	Men Servts Prot.	Paps.	Women Servts Prot.	Paps.
		Patrick Early Paps	Cotter		2						
		Francis Common Paps	Cotter		2						
[f.324] Estersnow	Graney	Thomas Irwin Prot	Farmer	5				1			2
		Charles Dermott	Carpentr				3				
		Matthew Noon Paps	Cotter		3						
	Camlin	John Irwin Prot	Farmer	1				2		3	
		Darby Crine Paps	Smith		2						
		Laughlin Druey Paps	Cotter		1						
		Peter Poor Paps	Cotter		2						
		Luke Sharkot Paps	Cotter		2		3				
		Miles Tanesty Paps	Cotter		2						
		Farrell Gowran Paps	Miller		1						
		Roger Druey Paps	Cotter		1						
		Martin Ruddy Paps	Cotter		1						
		Domnick Kelly Paps	Cotter		1						
	Harkfree	Miles Walsh Paps	herd		1						
		Patrick Ruddy	Cotter				2				
		Domnick Dermott Pap	Cotter								
	Carageen	Michl. Reiley Paps	Herd		1		2				
		Barthlow. Brenen Paps	Broagmakr.		2						
Parish of Killcola	Killcola	Luke Cunoghan Paps	Cotter		2						
		Owen Golrick Paps	Cotters		3						
		Patrick Muldowny Pa	Weaver								
	Ratallin	Henry Dulin Paps	Cotter				2				
		Laughlon Cryne Paps	Herd		3				1		1
		Michl. Diffley Paps	Cotter		3						
		Hugh Bern Paps	Cotter		2		2				
		Thomas Triston Paps	Cotter		2						
		Widow Rudican Pap			1		2				
	Lickane	Cormack Dermott Paps	Farmr.				2				
		Patrick Nelley Paps	Farmer		3						
		Patrick Dolan Paps	Farmer		1						
		Michl. Donagher Paps	Farmr.		1						
		Michl. Dolan Paps	Farmr.		1						
		Myles Bern Paps	Weaver		2						
	Rinneboll &c	Bryan Dermott Paps									
		Michl. Duffey Paps	Victuler		2						
		John Mullvola Paps	Herd		3						
		John Narey Paps	Herd		2						
	Dooneen	Francis Duignan Pap	Farmr.		6		3		2		1
		Connor Oats Paps	Farmer		1		3				
		John Bern Paps	Farmer								
		Patrick Dowd Paps	Farmer		1						

NOTES

1. Lewis, 'Eastersnow'.

2. Owen McDermott held Ardkeena, Graney and Knockroe; Hugh Dermott, Camlin; Terence McDermott held Carageen, Fass, Glorey, and Trinenegree; Bryan McDermott held Clogher, Tullaboy and Tullavahan (*Books of Survey and Distribution*, Roscommon).

3. Tullaboy: Bryan Dermottroe, cottier; Tullavahan: Hugh Dermott, farmer; Harkhill: Owen Dermott farmer; Graney: Charles Dermott, carpenter; Harkfree: Dominick Dermott cottier (Census ff 320, 322, 323).

4. Owned by the King family of Boyle (N.L.I., Lord Lorton Estate lease book, MS 3105).

5. Ibid.

CREEVE, COUNTY ROSCOMMON

INTRODUCTION: *Creeve parish was in the baronies of Frenchpark and Roscommon, three miles north from Elphin on the road to Boyle. It had 4,573 statute acres, including 3,828 of Corbally Lough and three acres of other water.*[1] *The land is limestone and limestone gravel, with little bog.*[2]

The incumbent of Creeve was the Rev. Arthur Mahon, Archdeacon of Elphin (see Killukin, Boyle). The patron was the bishop.

OCCUPATIONS

Cottier	36	Herd	4	Weaver	2
Dealer	1	Joiner	1	Widow	5
Farmer	12	Servants, household	16		

Com~Ros common Parish of	Place of Abode	Names and Religion	Proffession	Children under 14 Prot.	Children under 14 Paps.	Children above 14 Prot.	Children above 14 Paps.	Men Servts Prot.	Men Servts Paps.	Women Servts Prot.	Women Servts Paps.
[f.325] Creeve	Martry	I.E. Byrn P			1		2				
		P.M. Harinton P	Farmer		2		2				
		G. M.Higgins P	Farmer		2						
		M. Byrn P	Widow		2		1				
	Lenigin	E. Mconry P	Farmer		2		2		2		2
		T.E. Shaw P	Cottier				2				
		C.S. Sharcot P	Cottier		2		1				
		B.M. McCue P	Cottier		1		1				
	Attingrenbeg	P.E. Horan P	Cottier		1						
		B.M Horan P	Cottier		1		1				
		J.M. Horan P	Cottier		1						
		B.M Huddingan P	Cottier		1						
		R. M.Butler P	Cottier				3				
		G.M. Linigan P	Cottier		1						
		J. M.Dolan P	Cottier		1						
		E. Dolan P	Widow				2				
	Rardinghra	A. M. Higgins P	Farmer		2						
		P. M. Collins P	Cottier		2		1				
		M.M. Oats P	Cottier		1		2				
		L.E. McCormick P	Cottier		2						
		O.M. McCormick P	Cottier		1						
		M. Mahon P	Widow		1				1		
		P. M.Butler P	Cottier		1		2				
		J. F.Carty P	Cottier								
	Ballyshearone	T. E.Keran P	Cottier		1						
		T. M. Doonan P	Cottier				1				
		M. Tristan P	Widow				1				
		M. Kitigan P	Widow				1				
		J.E. Conaghton P	Cottier		1						
		M. M. Forester P	Farmer		1						1
		J.E. Delap Pr	Dealer	1					1		
	Ballywellahan	L.M. Gormly P	Farmer						1		1
		J.E. Higgins P	Farmer		2						1
	Linnabull	W.M. Lambert Pr	Farmer	2		1					1
		M.E. Hangly P	Farmer		2		1				
		G.M. Finaron P	Farmer		1		2				
		H.M Brennon P	Farmer		1		1				
	Attin	G.C. Conry P	Cottier		1		1				
	Balliwelahan	M.M. Conry P	Cottier		1						
	Creevelan	D.M. McGarry P	Cottier		1		1				
		T.M. Sharcot P	Weaver				1				
[f.326] Creeve	Maludeen	B.M. Finlahin P	Cottier		2		1				
		E.F. Carny P	Cottier		1		2				
		M.M. Malrenan P	Herd				2				
		M. E.Costella P	Weaver		1						
	Laghhorris	T. M. Flanagan P	Cottier				3				1
		L. E. Conellan P	Cottier		1		2				
		P.E. Feehely P	Cottier		3						
		P.M. Horan P	Cottier		1						

Com~Ros common Parish of	Place of Abode	Names and Religion	Proffession	Children under 14		Children above 14		Men Servts		Women Servts	
				Prot.	Paps.	Prot.	Paps.	Prot.	Paps.	Prot.	Paps.
		T.M. Feehely P	Cottier		4						
		J. E. Fallehan P	Cottier				3				
	Eriblagh	I. M.Teige P	Joiner		1						
		P. M.Makin P	Herd		1						
	Corbally[3]	M.M. Clark P	Herd		1						
		G.E. Mulkeran P	Herd				2				
	Creeve	G. M.Hinds P	Farmer		3				1		1
		M.M. Linighan P	Cottier								1
	Correnamady	B. E. Neeleny P	Cottier		2						
		P.E. Minevan P	Cottier		2						
		T.M. Guire P	Cottier		3						1
		P.E. Monohan P	Cottier		2						
		E.M. Lenon P	Cottier		1						

[verso in Edward Synge's hand]

Archdeacon's Parishes

NOTES

1. *General Alphabetical Index*.

2. Lewis, 'Creeve'.

3. Lease by Edward Crofton to Patrick Kelly of 5 acres of Corbally 30 May 1735. Another to Chidley Crofton of the half Quarter of Corbally, 16 March 1749 (N.L.I., Crofton Papers, MS 8828/8).

ARDCARN, COUNTY ROSCOMMON

INTRODUCTION: *Ardcarn is in the barony of Boyle and surrounds Lough Key to the north, south and east. The eastern edge of the parish is defined by the river Shannon.[1] The parish of 19,962 statute acres lies east-south-east of Boyle on the road to Carrick-on-Shannon. On the edge of Lough Key there was a segment of the parish of Kilbryan within the parish.*

Arthur Young was told that the sheep-walks in the plains of Boyle excelled those of the Curragh in Kildare and that Ardcarn had the leading sheep and wool market in Connaught. The small number of shepherds in the parish might be explained by Young's comment that the country was enclosed by stone walls, so that one shepherd was kept for each flock.[2] Two masons, one at Ahrefican and one at Creevah, underline Lewis's comment that the limestone and freestone in the parish 'is of the best description for architectural purposes'.[3] There were four millers, and with the number of flaxdressers, weavers and tailors it is possible that at least two of these mills were for fulling and tucking in the processing of cloth.

The Rev. William French, Prebendary of Kilgoghlin was the incumbent of Ardcarn in 1743. He lived in the parish in Cloonybrian.

OCCUPATIONS

Cleric	1	Hatter	1	Servant, household	221
Cooper	1	Herd	5	Sexton	1
Cottier	155	Joiner	1	Shepherd	2
Dealer	1	Labourer	111	Shoemaker	1
Farmer	28	Mason	2	Smith	3
Fisherman	1	Merchant	1	Tailor	3
Flaxdresser	2	Miller	4	Tenant	1
Gardener	3	Pumpmaker	1	Weaver	7
Gentlemen	2	Servant	19		

Com~Ros common Parish of	Place of Abode	Names and Religion	Proffession	Children under 14 Prot.	Children under 14 Paps.	Children above 14 Prot.	Children above 14 Paps.	Men Servts Prot.	Men Servts Paps.	Women Servts Prot.	Women Servts Paps.
[f.327]Ardcarn	Knockdonel	Cormick Ciseny & wife Pa:	Servt.				1				
		Jon. Judge & wife Pa:	Labr.		2						
	Tiernemunter	Den. Kelly & wife Pa:	Cotier				4				
		Will. Burk Pa:	Do						1		
		Connor Fanan & wife Pa:	Do								
	Drumcuny	Jas. Dermott & wife Pa:	Labr.		2						
		Jas. Jordan & wife Pa:	Do		2		1				
		Morgan Cavenish & wife Pa:	Cooper		4						
		Edmd. Mulone & wife Pa:	Labr.		3						
		Peter Mulone & wife Pa:	Do		1						
		Thos Reynolds & wife Pa:	Do		2						
	Drumbrick	Myles Heanry & wife Pa:	Do		1		4				
		Ed Heanry & wife Pa:	Do		1						
		Hugh Owens & wife Pa:	Do		4		1				
		Bryan Murry & wife Pa:	Do		2						
		Owen Conolly & wife Pa:	Do				2				
		Roger Kilbee & wife Pa:	Do		2						
		Lurence Conolly & wife Pa:	Do								
		Mick Thorp & wife Pa	Do		1						
		Andrew Kilbee & wife Pa:	Do		1						
	Derygree	Jon. Means & wife Pro:	Farmer	4					1		1
		Jas. Means & wife Pro:	Do	2							
		Arth. Thos. Means Pro:	Do						1		1
		Will. Renick & wife Pro:	Weaver	2							
		Roger Regen & wife Pa:	Labr.								
	Killeen	Tady Moran & wife Pa:	Do		1						
		Pat. Morahan & wife Pa:	Do		4						
		Fran. Regan Pa:	Do		4						
		Patt. Flanigan Pa:	Do				4				
		Jas. Linsk & wife Pa:	Do		2						
	Clignah	Ed. Roningan & wife Pa:	Cotier		2						
		Patt. Carigan & wife Pa:	Hatter		3		1				1
		Anthony Ternan & wife Pa:	Labr.								1
		Jas. Rynolds & wife Pa:	Do		2						
		Myles McDonah & wife Pa:	Cotier		3						
		Tady McLoughlin & wife Pa:	Labr.		1						1
		Patt. McLaughlin & wife Pa:	Do		2						
		Jon. McManus & wife Pa:	Do		1		2				
		Jon. Bruen & wife Pa:	Cotier		3						
		Mary Collins Widow Pa:	Do								
[f.328]Ardcarn	Clignah	George Fanan & wife Pa:	Smith				1				
	Sliveformagh	Thos. Moran & wife Pa:	Cotier		4		2				
		Chas. Mulloy & wife Pa:	Do		3						
		Dan. McLaughlin & wife Pa:	Do				2		1		
		Fran. Moran Pa: Wife Pro:	Do		2						
		Neal Bradley & wife Pa:	Do		3						
		Roger Kelly & wife Pa:	Do		2						1
		Jon. Lehenny & wife Pa:	Do		1						
		Cornel Cube & wife Pa:	Do		2						1

Com~Ros common Parish of	Place of Abode	Names and Religion	Proffession	Children under 14		Children above 14		Men Servts		Women Servts	
				Prot.	Paps.	Prot.	Paps.	Prot.	Paps.	Prot.	Paps.
		Mary Mulloy Widdow Pa:	Do		1		4				
		Stephen Fanneen & wife Pa:	Do		1						
		Danl. McMurry & wife Pa:	Do		3						
		Ferdinand McLaughlin & wife Pa:	Do								
		Patt. Killeen & wife Pa:	Do		4						
		Jas. McNiff & wife Pa:	Do				1				
	Cleen	Jas. Carroll & wife Pro:	Tenant	2						1	
		Wil. Carrol & wife Pro:	Do	2							
		Patt. Linsk & wife Pa:	Herd		3				2		
		Tady Breen & wife Pa:	Smith		1		1				
		Tady Mulkeran & wife Pa:	Miller		1						
		Will. Killroy & wife Pa:	Labr.				3				
		Moor Long Widow Pa:	Cotier				2				
		Ed. Mcgreevy & wife Pa:	Labr.				3				
		Laughlin Morahan & wife Pa:	Do		1						
		Dennis Carty & wife Pa:	Do		1						
		Florence Carty & wife Pa:	Do		1						
		Darby Curty & wife Pa:	Do				1				
		Andrew McCormack & wife Pa:	Do		1						
		Mary McDermott Widow Pa:	Cotier		1		1				
[f.329] Cleen		Philip McDermott Pro: wife Pa:	Do		2						
		Philip Ryley & wife Pa:	Do		2				1		1
		Barth. Dignan & wife Pa:	Do		2						
		Will. Bennian & wife Pro:	Weaver	1							
		Jon. Bridge & Mor Pro:	Tent								
		Geo. Bridge Pro: wife Pa:	Do	2							1
		Ed. Murray & wife Pa:	Cotier				1				
		Rogr. Kenedy & wife Pa:	Do		2		2				
		Hugh McRann & wife Pa:	Do								
		Bryan Mully & wife Pa:	Do		1						1
		Eliner Ryly Widow Pa	Do				1				
		Will. Laughlin Pa & wife Pro:	Farmer				2		3		1
	Fanah[?]	Will. Donnelly & wife Pa:	Labr.								
		Will. Hurt & wife Pa:	Do								
		Jon. McDonah Pa:	Do		1		2				1
		Conor Bohan & wife Pa:	Do				3				
		Jon. Dermotroe & wife Pa:	Do		2						
		Tige Laughlin & wife Pa:	Do						1		1
	Oxhill	Jas. Peyton Pro:	Farmer	3				1	1		3
		Jon. Peyton Pro:	Gent					1			
		Philip McDermottroe & wife Pro:	Shoemakr	1		2					
		Jon. Glinn & wife Pro:	Cotier	2							
		Jas. Guilim & wife Pa:	Taylor		1				1		1
		Patt. Curley & wife Pa:	Labr.		4						1
		Will: Freeman Pro: wife Pa:	Servt	3							
		Chas. Glinn & wife Pa:	Joiner		3						1

Com~Ros common Parish of	Place of Abode	Names and Religion	Proffession	Children under 14		Children above 14		Men Servts		Women Servts	
				Prot.	Paps.	Prot.	Paps.	Prot.	Paps.	Prot.	Paps.
	Crusna	Dom. Carty & wife Pa:	Dealer		3				2		1
		Hugh Kenedy & wife Pa:	Cotier		3						
		Tim. Mccormack & wife Pa:	Do		2						
		Dan. Moran & wife Pro:	Farmer	4					3		3
		Patt. Moran & wife Pa:	Cotier		1						
		Ter. Murray & wife Pa:	Do								
		Jon. Bushell & wife Pa:	Herd		2						2
		Tady Connellan & wife Pa:	Labr.		1						
		Mary Grier widow Pro:	Cotier	2							
		Jane Murray widow Pa:			2						
		Hugh McDermott & wife Pa:	Do		2						
		Michl. McDermott & wife Pa:	Do		3						
		Peter McDermott & wife Pa:	Do		3						
		Jas. Mcdermott Pa	Do		1		1				
		Barth. Dignan & wife Pa:	Do				4				
	Ahernagulta	Ed. Kilmartin & wife Pa:	Do				3				
		Hugh Smith & wife Pa:	Do		2						
		Ter. Ternan & wife Pa:	Do				3				
		Hugh Kilmartin & wife Pa:	Do		2						
		Patt. Dignan Pa:	Do				3				
		Mary Dignan Widow Pa:	Do				2				
		Peter Brennan & wife Pa:	Do				1				
		Jon. Readen & wife Pa:	Do		2		1				
		Hen. Butler & wife Pa:	Do		2						
		Jane Magueran Widdow Pa:	Do				2				
[f.330]Ardcarn	Cloonbiker	Patt. Kilmartin Pa:	Cotier				3				
		Mary Roger Widow Pa	Do				2				1
		Tige Boy & wife Pa:	Do		2						
		Hugh Kireen & wife Pa:	Weaver				1				1
		Patt. Kireen & wife Pa:	Cotier				2				1
		Darby Conellan & wife Pa:	Do		2						
		Patt. Cullin & wife Pa:	Do		2		2				1
		Owen Smallen & wife Pa:	Do		2						
		Owen Leadon & wife Pa:	Do		1						1
		Pat. Murray & wife Pa:	Do		2						
		Fran. Leadin & Sister Pa:	Do								1
		Thos. Connor & wife Pa:	Do		1						1
		Richd. Gaffney & wife Pa:	Do		1						
		Owen Culln & wife Pa:	Do		2						
		Jeffry Cullin Pa:	Do								
		Margt.Ford widow Pa:	Do				3				1
		Owen Cullen & wife Pa:	Do				2				
		Jon. Kilger & Mor. Pa:	Do								
		Phelim Gaffney Pa:	Do						1		
		Michl. Bartley & wife Pa:	Do								1
		Michl. Vernon & wife Pa:	Do		2						1
		Tady Lyons & wife Pa:	Farmer		4		1		2		2
		Patt. Cullen & wife Pa:	Cotier		2		1				1
		Owen Murray & wife Pa:	Do		1						

Com~Ros common Parish of	Place of Abode	Names and Religion	Proffession	Children under 14 Prot.	Children under 14 Paps.	Children above 14 Prot.	Children above 14 Paps.	Men Servts Prot.	Men Servts Paps.	Women Servts Prot.	Women Servts Paps.
		Fran. Williams & wife Pa:	Do						1		1
		Bryn Higgins & Mor. Pa:	Do								
		Thos. White & wife Pa:	Do		1						
		Ferd. Kelly & wife Pa:	Do		2				1		1
		Bryan Loughlin & wife Pa:	Do		3						1
		Patt. Loughlin & wife Pa:	Do		2						1
		Michl. Fryer & wife Pa:	Do		3						1
		Hugh Rouen & wife Pa:	Do		1						1
		Thady Mulimore & wife Pa:	Do								
		Thady Berne & wife Pa:	Do		2						1
		Owen Conlish & wife Pa:	Do		1						
		Chas. Rowen & wife Pa:	Do		2						1
		Bryan Gilan & wife Pa:	Do		1						
		Farrell McDermot & wife Pa:	Do		2						1
		Thady Ford & wife Pa:	Do		2		1				
		Loughlin Kineen & wife Pa:	Do		3						1
[f.331]Ardcarn	Cloonbiker	Giles Horan Widow Pa:	Cotier		3				1		
		Ed. Glinn & wife Pa:	Do		2						1
		Dom. Nully & wife Pa:	Do		2						1
		Moris Killen & wife Pa:	Do		1						
		Phil. Mcdermotroe & wife Pa:	Do		2						1
		Patt. Killen & wife Pa:	Do		2						
		Patt. McSarah & wife Pa:	Do		2						
		Jas. Cogin & wife Pa:	Do		1		2				
		Patt. McDonah & wife Pa:	Do								1
		Martin McDonah & wife Pa:	Do		3						1
		Owen Tanesty & wife Pa:	Do		1						
		Patt. Mulkerin & wife Pa:	Miller		3		1				
		Barth. Mullermoe & wife Pa:	Cotier		2		3				1
		Connor Mullamoe & wife Pa:	Do				3				
		Thos. Wallace & wife Pa:	Do		1						
		Patt. Conolly & wife Pa:	Do		2						
		Michl. Noon & wife Pa:	Do		2						
		Danl. Mcmanus & wife Pa:	Do		1						1
		Ter. Bolan & sister Pa:	Do								
		Gilbt Mullamoe & wife Pa:	Do		3						1
		Owen Conner & wife Pa:	Do		1						
		Hugh Sharry & wife Pa:	Do		3						
		Patt. Connellon & wife Pa:	Do		2						1
		Jas. Cormick & wife Pa:	Do								1
		Jon. Cormick & wife Pa:	Do		3						
		Thos. Conellan & wife Pa:	Do		3						
		Chas Gillin & wife Pa:	Do		3		1				1
		Jon. Nally & wife Pa:	Do		1						
		Jon. Coggin & wife Pa:	Do				2				1
		Tige Nally & wife Pa:	Do		1						
		Will. Partlan & wife Pa:	Do		2						1
		Jas. Partlan & wife Pa:	Do		2						1
		Michl. Gaffny & wife Pa:	Do		1						

Com~Ros common Parish of	Place of Abode	Names and Religion	Proffession	Children under 14		Children above 14		Men Servts		Women Servts	
				Prot.	Paps.	Prot.	Paps.	Prot.	Paps.	Prot.	Paps.
	Ahrefinican	Arch. Frazier & wife Pro:	Farmer	3					1		1
		Jas. Frazer & wife Pro:	Do	2					1		1
		Hu. Magrah & wife Pa	Labr.		4						
		And. Magrah & wife Pa:	Do		1						
		Thos. Flinn & wife Pa:	Do		2						
		Conner Leaden & wife Pa:	Do		3						
		Mary Frazer widdow Pro:	Cotier								1
[f.332]Ardcarn	Ahrefinican	Darby Conelan & wife Pa:	Do								
		Owen Cokeran & wife Pa:	Do		1						
		And. Kilboy & wife Pa:	Do								
		Joseph McNeal & wife Pa:	Do				1				
		Bryan Fryar & wife Pa:	Do		2						
		Hugh Guilehan & wife Pa:	Do								
		Tim. Cryne & wife Pa:	Farmer		2				1		1
		Denn. Cryne & wife Pa:	Do		1				1		1
		Patt. Cryne & wife Pa:	Do		1						1
		Tady Rorke & wife Pa:	Labr.		3						
		Chas. McDermott & wife Pa:	Taylor		3						1
		Patt. Conolly & wife Pa:	Mason				3				
		Jas. Rittle & wife Pro:	Weaver	1		2			1		1
		Will. Thompson & wife Pro:	Labr.	1		3			1		1
		Patt. Conellan & wife Pa:	Farmer				2				
	Kilfaghna	Jon. Stanley & wife Pro:	Do	5				1			2
		Myles Ternan & wife Pa:	Labr.		3						
		Will Leandon & wife Pa:	Do		1						
		Thos. Mcdermotroe & wife Pa:	Do		2						
		Con. McDermotroe & wife Pa:	Do		1						
		Bryan Brenan & wife Pa:	Do		2						
		Den. Magrivee & wife Pa:	Do		1						
		Bryan Croney & wife Pa:	Do		2						
		Chas. Fryer & wife Pa:	Do		2						
		Peter LinsK & wife Pa:	Do		1						
	Drumcormack	Hanah Stanly widdow Pro:	Farmer	2		1			1		1
		Tady Linsk & wife Pa:	Cotier		1						
		Jon. Linsk & wife Pa:	Do								1
		Michl. Coonan & wife Pa:	Do		2		1				
		Martin Shanon & wife Pa:	Labr.		2						
		Patt. Shivnan & wife Pa:	Do		2						
		Anth. Carty & wife Pa:	Do		1						1
	Tullineshinahin	Owen Casy & wife Pro:	Farmr	2					1		1
		Ter.LKinsk & wife Pa:	Labr.		1						
		Margt. Mcnamara Pa:	Cotier								
	Errosuch[4]	Danl. Kingston & wife Pa:	Farmer	4				1	1		3
		Patt. Gallagher & wife Pa:	Labr.				3				
		Michl. Stuart & wife Pa:	Do		4						
		Patt. Linsk & wife Pa:	Pumpmaker		2						
		Jas. Carty & wife Pa:	Labr.		1		3				
[f.333]Ardcarn	Errosuch	And. Curley & wife Pa:	Cotier				1				
		Owen McDermott & wife Pa:	Do				1				

Com~Ros common Parish of	Place of Abode	Names and Religion	Proffession	Children under 14		Children above 14		Men Servts		Women Servts	
				Prot.	Paps.	Prot.	Paps.	Prot.	Paps.	Prot.	Paps.
	Creevah	Jon. Mills & wife Pro:	Farmer	1		1					1
		Barth. Berne & wife Pa:	Mason		1				1		1
		Greg. Hughes & Pro:	Flaxdresser	1							1
		Jas. Ingg Pro: wife Pa:	Do	1							
		Michl. Conellon & wife Pa:	Labr.		1						
		Rogr. McCatenah & wife Pa:	Do		1						
		Kath. Moran widdow Pa:	Cotier		1						
		Ter. McDermott & wife Pa:	Labr.		3				1		1
	Knockvicar5	John Carty & wife Pa:	Herd		1		1				2
		Tim. Dunn & wife Pa:	Gardnr.				2				
		Jon. Callely & wife Pa:	Fisherman		2		1				
	Luarton	Jas. Moran & wife Pa:	Labr.		1						
		Simon Lenahan & wife Pa:	Do				2				1
		Jon. McDrue & wife Pa:	Do		1		2				1
		Rose Higgins Pa	Cotier								
		Patt. Higgins & wife Pa:	Labr.		2		2				
		Dan. Skully & wife Pa:	Do								
		Thos. Skully & wife Pa:	Do								
		Michl. Skully & wife Pa:	Do		2						
		Dan. McNiff & wife Pa:	Do		1						
		Thos. Burne & mother Pa	Do								
		Winifred Burne widdow Pa	Cotier		2		1				
		Will Lenahan & wife Pa:	Labr.		1						
		Jas. Caulfield & wife Pa:	Weaver				4				
	Oxhill in Ardcarn	Thos Hall & wife Pro:	Farmr			2		1			
		Fran. Linsk & wife Pa:	Labr.		2		2				
	Ardcarn	Conr. Ridican & wife Pa:	Shepard		2		2				
		Cormack McDrue & wife Pa:	Labr.		1						
		Ed. Coyne Pa	Farmer						1		1
		Tim. Mcdermott & wife Pa:	Labr.		2						1
		Patt. McDermott & wife Pa:	Do		2						
		Michl. Plunket6 & wife Pa:	mercht						3		3
		Math. Tanesty & wife Pa:	Labr.		3						
		Ed. Glinn Pa	Do						1		1
	Derryskinin	Ambrose Linsk & wife Pa:	Do		3						
		Michl. Morahan Pa	Do				1				1
		Jon. Bingham Pro: wife Pa	Sexton	1					1		
[f.334]Ardcarn	Grevirk	Jon. Nesbitt & wife Pro:	Farmr		3	3		1	1		2
		Jas. Delancey & wife Pa:	Labr.		1		4				
		Will Gordon & Mother Pa	Do		1						
		Bryan Kilgen & wife Pa:	Do								
	Rockingham7	Owen Rick & sister Pa	Shepard		2						
		Patt. Keveny & Mother Pa	Herd								2
		Darby Keveny & wife Pa:	Servt		4				1		2
		Will. Miller Pro: wife Pa:	Gardnr			1					1
		Jas. Brady & wife Pa:	Labr.		1						

Com~Ros common Parish of	Place of Abode	Names and Religion	Proffession	Children under 14		Children above 14		Men Servts		Women Servts	
				Prot.	Paps.	Prot.	Paps.	Prot.	Paps.	Prot.	Paps.
		Bridget Brady widow Pa	Cotier				1				
		Mary Lenahan widow Pa	Do				3				
		Darby Moran & wife Pa:	Servt						1		1
	Carowgashel	Jas. Phibbs & wife Pa:	Do		1						2
		Cormack Berny & wife Pa:	Labr.				2				
		Bryan McDermott & wife Pa:	Do								
		Ed. McDermot & wife Pa:	Do		2						
	Carowmore	R. Barlow & wife Pro:	Farmr.	4					1	1	2
		Alex. Gilmer & wife Pro:	Do	4					1	1	
		H. Gilmer & Pro:	Do	2		1			1		
		Chas. Recroft & wife Pro:	Do			4					
		Thos. Recroft Pro: & wife Pa:	Do	2							
	Rusheen[8]	Jon. King & wife Pro:	Weaver	1				1	1		1
		Jon. Little & wife Pro:	Do	3					1		1
	Ardcash	Jas. Coyne & wife Pa:	Farmr.		3				2		3
		Will. Cumin & wife Pro:	Labr.	4							
		Garet Pettit & wife Pa:	Do		2		1				
		Jane Taylor widow Pro:	Cotier			1					
	Eastersnow	Jon. Timon & wife Pa:	Do				2				1
		Will. Glinn & wife Pa:	Do		1						
		Peter Sheenan & wife Pa:	Do		2						
		Mary Glinn Pa:	Do				1				
		Ed. Moran Pa:	Miller						1		
		Rogr. McNevin Pa	Labr.								
	Wrenn	Dom. Cormack & wife Pa:	Cotier		1		4				
		Mich. Clery & wife Pa:	Do								
	Ardgower	Chas. Hart & wife Pa:	Farmr.				1		1		2
		Jas. Gowran & wife Pa:	Miller	6							
		Sisly McDonah widow Pa	Cotier	2			1				
		Ed. Sharcott & sister Pa:	Do	1							
		Cormack Mullony & wife Pa:	Do						1		1
[f.335]Ardcarn	Ardgower	Peter Kevin & wife Pa:	Labr.	1							1
		Bridget Farrell widow Pa	Cotier	1			2	1			
		Bryan Goonin & wife Pa:	Taylor	1							1
	Holymount	Joly Dodd Pro: wife Pa:	Gent					1	1	1	2
		Michl. Glinn & wife Pa:	Servt	1							1
		Jon. Crosswell & wife Pa:	Gardnr	1							1
		Patt. Linsk & wife Pa:	Labr.	2							1
		Bryan Neal & wife Pa:	Do	1					1		
		Larine Heny & wife Pa:	Do	2			3				
		Owen Parttan & wife Pa:	Do	1							
		Tady Mulkran & wife Pa:	Do	1			3				
		Peter. McDermot & wife Pa:	Do	3					1		
		Patt. Cullen & wife Pa:	Do	1							
		Richd. Pendergast & wife Pa:	Servt				4		1		
		Tady Tanesty & wife Pa:	Labr.	3							
		Jas. Kean & wife Pa:	Do								1
		Fran. Collins & wife Pa:	Do	1					1		1

Com~Ros common Parish of	Place of Abode	Names and Religion	Proffession	Children under 14		Children above 14		Men Servts		Women Servts	
				Prot.	Paps.	Prot.	Paps.	Prot.	Paps.	Prot.	Paps.
	Cootehall	Chas. Brehany Pa	Servt		4						1
	Oakport	Dom. Morahan & wife Pa:	Do		2		1				1
		Luke Woolahan & wife Pa:	Labr.		4		1				1
		Patt. Costelo & wife Pa:	Do		2						
		Darby Flanigan & wife Pa:	Do				1				
		Luke Dowel & wife Pa:	Do		1						
		Jon. Broder & wife Pro:	Smith						1		
		Owen Murray & wife Pa:	Labr.								1
		Mary Skully Pa	Servt				1				
	Cullmore	Michl. Keelty & wife Pa:	Do		1		2				
		Michl. Forester & wife Pa:	Do		1						1
		Tim. Mcdermott & wife Pa:	Do		5		1				
		Jon. Ryley & wife Pa:	Do		2				1		1
		Michl. Regan & wife Pa:	Do		2		2				1
		Thos. Laughlin Pa	Do								
		Peter Parttan Pa	Do								
		Jas. Killeen Pa:	Do								
	Derreen	Michl. Dermott & wife Pa:	Do								1
		Michl. Dermott & wife Pa:	Do		2						
	Cloonibryan	Will. Rowen & wife Pa:	Herd				2				1
		Michl. Flanigan & wife Pa:	Labr.		2						1
		Dorothy Connor Pa:	Cotier		1						
		Marg. Win Pa	Do		1		1				
[f.336]Ardcarn	Cloonibryan	Jon. Bernard & wife Pa:	Do								
		Will. French[9] & wife Pro:	Parson	4		1		4	2	2	5

[on separate paper glued to sheet]

Papists —————— 1412
Protests ————— 0184

Inhabitants   1601

[f.337]

A

Return of the Parish

of

Boyle

NOTES

1. *General Alphabetical Index.*

2. Young, *Tour in Ireland*, i, 216-7.

3. Lewis, 'Ardcarne'.

4. Arable and pasture, with cut bog as waste, owned by the King family (N.L.I., Lord Lorton Estate lease book, MS 3105).

5. The bridge at Knockvicar was built in 1727 by John French, Edward Drury, Owen Lloyd, Charles Mulloy and James Seily, undertakers (Weld, *Roscommon* p.246).

6. A signatory of an address by the Catholic Committee to George III in 1761 (*Letters of Charles O'Conor*, p. 94).

7. On the shore of Lough Key and the site of the house built by the first Lord Lorton in 1810. The demesne in the eighteenth century covered 2668 acres, Irish plantation measure (Bence-Jones, *Guide*, 'Rockingham'; N.L.I., Lord Lorton Estate lease book, MS 3105).

8. Arable and pasture, with coarse deep pasture and green cut bog, owned by the King family (N.L.I., Lord Lorton Estate lease book, MS 3105).

9. The Rev. William French (1704-?) was born at Frenchpark. He was Prebendary of Kilgoglin in the diocese of Elphin from 1731 to 1752 and Precentor of Elphin 1752. He married Arabella Frances Marsh and was one of the witnesses of Edward Synge's will in 1761 (Burke's *Landed Gentry of Ireland* (London 1916); Leslie, 'Elphin', p.88; N.A., P.R.O., MS PROB11/894/563).

BOYLE, COUNTY ROSCOMMON

INTRODUCTION: *The parish of Boyle in the barony of Boyle is 20 miles south-south-east of Sligo and is divided by the river Boyle which flows from Lough Gara into Lough Key. The parish was 20,736 statute acres in size.[1] It was incorporated as a borough in 1613. The King family which owned the town was granted the right to hold a market eight times a year.[2] The town was incorporated in 1614 by James I. The Corporation had a burgomaster, 12 free burgesses and a commonalty of unspecified number of people. These are not identified in the census text.[3]*

The King family who owned the whole town were descended from Sir John King, an Englishman from Staffordshire who, in 1603, was granted a joint lease of Boyle Abbey and lands with Sir John Bingley.[4] By 1618, he was granted an outright grant of the Abbey and 4,127 acres of land. The first King house in Boyle was built in the mid-17th century and the first Lord Kingston arranged for his younger brother, Sir Robert King, to receive lands outside Boyle, which became the Rockingham estate where he built a house in 1673.[5]

The Boyle census entries, together with King estate papers in the National Library, provide evidence that some of the merchants and skilled tradesmen there rented farming land which would provide a second income. At least a dozen Boyle householders had land in the townparks Leases were granted to Protestant, Roman Catholic and Presbyterians alike. The Boyle census occupations, together with King estate papers, provide evidence of a mixed economy which would have enabled many to survive.[6]

The parish of Boyle was held with Kilbryan, Shancough, Kilmactranny, Aghanagh, Kilmacallan, Tawnagh and Drumcolumb from 1666. The incumbent in 1749 was the Rev. Robert Phipps who had been appointed in 1732 and was also vicar of Kilbryan.[7] In 1766 the church was described as being in ruins for 'some ages'. It was also more than an Irish mile from the town, which was inconvenient for the parishioners.[8] The patron was the bishop.

OCCUPATIONS

Apothecary	1	Gentleman	9	Servant	1
Baker	4	Glazier	1	Servants, household	344
Beggar	7	Glover	2	Sexton	1
Boatman	1	Grazier	1	Shearman	1
Brasier	1	Herd	11	Shoemaker	7
Butcher	8	Innkeeper	7	Shopkeeper	5
Carman	3	Labourer	197	Skinner	1
Carpenter	8	M.D. [medical doctor]	1	Smith	7
Clerk	1	Maltster	1	Staymaker	1
Cooper	3	Mason	11	Stonecutter	2
Cottoner	1	Merchant	3	Tailor	14
Currier	1	Miller	3	Tanner	3
Dealer	4	Park keeper	1	Thatcher	1
Distiller	1	Peddler	4	Tobacco spinner	1
Driver	1	Plasterer	1	Weaver	25
Esquire	1	Poor man	1	Wheelwright	1
Farmer	57	Priest	1	Widow	4
Fisherman	1	Pumpmaker	16	Wigmaker	5
Gamekeeper	1	Reedmaker	1	Woolcomber	1
Gardener	1	Saddler	3	Writing Master	1
Gauger	1	Saltman	1	Yarn Merchant	1

Com~Ros common Parish of	Place of Abode	Names and Religion	Proffession	Children under 14		Children above 14		Men Servts		Women Servts	
				Prot.	Paps.	Prot.	Paps.	Prot.	Paps.	Prot.	Paps.
Boyle [f.337]	Boyle	Lord Kingsborough[9] Pr						17	14	2	7
		Thos. Rowlatt[10], wife Pr	Gent.	4					1		1
		Kingoon Dodd & Wife Pr	Gent.	3					2		2
		Mattw. Mcdermotroe[11]									
& W P	M.D:			2			1		2		
		Edwd. Feel & Wife Pr	Apothecary	3	1				1		2
		Jon. Corristone[12] P Wife Pr	Innkeepr	4	2				3	2	1
		Widdow Lynch Pr				1					2
		Thos. Adamson & W Pr	Innkeepr			1		1	1		1
		George West & Wife Pr	Mercht	3				1	1		2
		Luke Matimo & W P	Shoopkr.		1			1			1
		Widdow Fant P					2				1
		Patt. Dougherty & W P	Shoopkr.								1
		Bart. Ganly & W Pr	Innkeepr.	1		2		1			1
		Widdow West Pr	Widow			1					
		Patt. Moran & W P	Carrman		3						1
		Widdow West[13] Pr	Innkpr.			2		1	1		2
		John West & Wife Pr	Tanner	2					1		1
		H. Mullany & Wife P	Taylor		5			1	1		1
		Widdw. Dennery					1				
		Jas. Corkran & W P	Baker		5				1		1
		Patt. Moore P Wife R	Wiggmr.	1							
		Wm. Holeran & Wife P	Carrman		2					1	
		Henry Armstrong & W Pr	Weaver			1					1
		John Mason & Wife Pr	Shoemakr								
		Wm. Corckean & Wife P	Labour.		3		1				
		Henry West & Wife Pr	Carpenr.	2		1					
		Jas. Heydon P Wife Pr	Baker	1							
		John Neely & Wife P	Labour.		2						
		Lawce. Kinselagh & Wife P	Labour.		2						
		Willm. Feneron & Wife P	Labour.		1						
		Patt. Higgins & Wife P	Labour.		2						
		Darby Cooney & Wife P	Labour.				2				
		Patt. Redican & Wife P	Pumpmar.		4				1		
		Widdow Nagle P			2						
		Garrett Nangle & Wife P	Dealer		2						
		Jams. Keaveny & Wife P	Labr.		1						
		Micl. Connor & Wife P	Carpenr.		1	1					
		Widdw. Connor P									
		Jams. Conyngham & W P	Tayr.								
		Hugh Higgins P & Wife Pr	Weavr.	3							
		Edwd. Cavanagh & Wife P	Mason		2						
[f.338]	Boyle	Moses Bruen[14] & Wife Pr	Mercht.	6		1		1	2	2	3
		John Knott[15] Pr	Do			1			1		1
		Dennis Fagan & Wife P	Grasier		3		1		1		2
		Richd. McKensie[16] & W Pr	Innkeepr.	1					1		1
		Jn. Smyth[17] & Wife Pr	Gent.	3		1				1	
		Widdw. Murry Pr									1
		John Knott & wife Pr	Gent			1			2		2

Com~Ros common Parish of	Place of Abode	Names and Religion	Proffession	Children under 14 Prot.	Paps.	Children above 14 Prot.	Paps.	Men Servts Prot.	Paps.	Women Servts Prot.	Paps.
		Patt. Coghlan & Wife P	Baker		2			1			
		Bryan Murry & W P	Shoopkr.				2				
		Wm. Loyd Wife Pr	Smyth		1		2			1	1
		Robt. Brennan[18] Pr	Wiggmar.			1					
		John Corker & Wife Pr	Smyth	4				1			1
		Widdw. Connolly Pr			3		1				
		Edwd. Drury & Wife Pr	Esqr.	7				1		1	
		Widdw. Hickey Pr		1		1		1			1
		Tady McDermott & W P	Sadler		1						
		Thos. Talbot & Wife Pr	Butcher	2		1					1
		Humpy. Bell & W Pr	Shoemr.					1			2
		Philip Tweed[19] & W Pr	Glover			3		2			
		Widdw. Sparks Pr		1		1					
		Wm. Young & Wife Pr	Brasier								1
		Widws. Glen & Perdue Pr		1							
		Chas. McManus & W P	Shoemr.					3			1
		Nichs. Henry Pr	poor old m.								
		Matt. Thomas Pr	reduced mn.	8							
		Bryan Sharcot & W P	Stonecur[20].		2						
		Thos. Farrel & W Pr	Sadler	2		2					1
		Darby Coony & W: P	Labour.		4						
		Josph. Hemsworth & W Pr	Shoemr.	2							
		Dennis Heney & W P	Labour.		2						
		Matt. Lynch P	Do		3						
		Widdw. McCormick P									
		Robt. Simpson[21] & W Pr	Distiller	1		1			1		2
		John Hogg & W Pr	Labour.	1							1
		Lawce. Kevin & W P	Do		1				1		1
		John Healy & W P	Carman		4						
		Rogr. McTanish & W P	Labour.		2						
		Rogr. Spellan & W Pr	Miller[22]				3		1		
		Widdow Philpot Pr	Widow	1							
		Ricd. Farrell[23] & W P	Innkeepr.		4			6	4		3
[f.339] Boyle	Boyle	Jas. Galaugher & W P	Pumpmr.		1						
		Danl. Higgins & W Pr	Smyth	4					2	1	
		Richd. Corkran & W P	Cooper[24]								1
		Owen Gaulagher & W P	Labour.		1						
		Richd. Brehony & W P	Do		1						
		Chas. Caulior & W P	Do		1						
		Patt. Mulvoge & W P	Drivr.	1			1				
		Oliver West & Wife R	Carpenr.	1		1					
		John Gray & Wife P	Do		2						1
		Danl. Gaullagher & W P	Labour.				1				
		John Freeman & W Pr	Servt.	3		2					
		Patt. Higgins & W R	Pumpmr.	2					1		
		John Mattimoe & W P	Do		3						
		Kennedy Ó Bryan & W Pr	Taylor	3							
		Owen Levy & W P	Pumpmr.		3		2				
		Cormk. Brennan Pr W P	Do	4		2					

Com~Ros common Parish of	Place of Abode	Names and Religion	Proffession	Children under 14		Children above 14		Men Servts		Women Servts	
				Prot.	Paps.	Prot.	Paps.	Prot.	Paps.	Prot.	Paps.
		Danl. Moore & Wife P	Wheelwrt.		1						
		Rogr. Scanlon & Wife P	Pumpmr.		5		1				
		Jams. Deaghen & Wife P	Pumpmr.		4						
		Widw. Mulvoge P		1	3		2				
		Neile Deaghan & W P	Do				1				
		Michl McGarvy & W P	Do				2		2		
		Thos. Welsh & W P	Do		2						
		Will. Welsh & W P	Do		1						
		Bryan Bradly & W P	Labour.		1						1
		Murtaugh Scanlon & W P	Pumpmr.								
		Patt. Flaherty & W P	Labour.		1						
		Martin Regan & W Pr	Gardiner	2							
		Edmd. McPadin & W P	Labour.		1						
		Patt. Mcteige & W P	Do		2		1				
		Laughn. Oates & Wife P	Thatcher[25]		2						
		Bryan Regan & Wife P	Labour.				1				
		Bryan Henery & Wife P	Do								
		Bryan McDermott & W Pr	Weaver	1		2					
		Terence McDermott & W P	Beggar		3		2				
		Farrel McManus & W P	Labourer		1		1				
		Patt. Oates & W P	Pumpmr.		3		1				
		Widdw. Gliman					1				
		John Gibbons & Wife Pr	Weaver	3		2		1	1		1
		John Rorke & Wife P	Do.		1						
[f.340] Boyle	Boyle	Patt. Egan & Wife P	Sadler				1				
		Mark Druhy & Wife P	Labour.		3						
		Patt. Brannan & W P	Plaisterer		2						
		Widdw. Dogherty P			1		1				
		Jas. Feneron & Wife P	Malster		1						
		Jas. Mullany & Wife P	Labour.		1						
		Wm. Mullany & Wife P	Do		1						
		Conr. Druhy & Wife P	Tanner								1
		Darby Sharcott & W P	Pedler								1
		Edwd. Druhy & W P	Do								
		Patt. Redican & W P	Weaver								
		Thos. Cannavan & W P	Cooper		3						
		Phelim Rogan & W P	Labour.								
		Danl. Dougherty P	Do								
		Widw. Little R				5					
		Widdow Kelly P					1				
		Thos. Feneron P	Labour.		2						1
		John Smyth & W P	Tanner		4				1		1
		Olivr. Russel[26] & Wife R	Wigmakr.		2	3			1		1
		Widdw. Knott R				1					
		John Kennedy & W P	Labour.		2						
		Jasp. Smyth & Wife R	Dealer	3		1				1	1
		Widdw. Dowdal P	Shoopkr				4				2
		Widdw. McGawran[27] P	Do				1				1
		John. Mcdermott & W P	Weaver		2						2

Com~Ros common Parish of	Place of Abode	Names and Religion	Proffession	Children under 14		Children above 14		Men Servts		Women Servts	
				Prot.	Paps.	Prot.	Paps.	Prot.	Paps.	Prot.	Paps.
[f.341] Boyle	Boyle	Cooly Johnson & Wife R	Wigmakr.	5		1					
		Edwd. Bruen & Wife R	Currier	2		3					
		Dennis Concagh P	Butcher		2						
		Patt. Fehely & Wife Pr	Writg. Masr.	3					3		
		Jas. O.Daniel & W P	Taylor		1			1	1		
		Widw. Lee & son R	Sheerman			1					
		John Rowlat & Wife R	Wigmakr.	3		2		1			
		John Flannary & W P	reduc'd				2				
		Patt. Knevin & W P	Fisher		1						
		Thos. Lynch P	Gent.		2				1		1
		Jas. Brennan & W P	Butcher		1		3				
		Tady Galaugher & W P	Clk		2						1
		Patt. Glyman & W P	Taylor		2			1	2		
		Jams Kirk & W P	Staymakr		2						
		John Curry & W P	Labour.		4						
		John Doyle P	Weaver		1						
		Geo. Cowan P wife R	Reedmr.		2				1		
		Anty. Deale & W Pr	Carpenr.	2							
		Widw. Radican P			1		2				
		John Murry & Wife R	Weaver			4			1		1
		Thady Mealy & W P	Glover		4						
		Patt. Sturry & Wife Pr	Taylor								
		John Sturry & W P	Do		1						
		Jas. Murray & W P	Weaver		2		1				
		Hugh Connaghton P & wife Pr	Carpenr.	3		2					
		Patt. Mullany & W P	Shoemr.		4						
		Hugh Mcdermott & W P	Butcher		1						
		Peter Adair & W P	Cottoner		2						
		Hugh McNelly & W P	Butcher	1	3	1				1	
		Thos. Kelly P	Shoemar.								
		Widw. Coane P									
		John Drury & W P	Tobacco spr		1						1
		Widw. Haggison P				1					
		Frans. Ryan R	Taylor						2		
		Philip Dunbar & Wife Pr	Pedler	3							
		Bryan Mulvihal[28] P & wife Pro	Stonecr.	2							2
		Gill. Connaghton & W P	Carpenr.		3						1
		Peter Heavy & W P	Butcher				1				
		Geor. Dorrington R & wife P	Taylor			2					
		Gregory Farrel P	Labour.								
		Widw. Brennan P									
		Robt. Garner & Wife Pr	Gauger								2
		Thos. Webbster & Wife R	Innkeer.			1					1
		Sam. White & Wife R	Shoemar.			4					
		Thos. Pitcher & Wife R	Glazier	1							
		Chs. Gormely & W P	Labour.				3				
		Patt. McGowan & W P	Weaver								
		Thos. Brennan & W P	Labour.		1						
		Widw. Michan P									1

Com~Ros common Parish of	Place of Abode	Names and Religion	Proffession	Children under 14		Children above 14		Men Servts		Women Servts	
				Prot.	Paps.	Prot.	Paps.	Prot.	Paps.	Prot.	Paps.
[f.342] Boyle	Boyle	John Carr R	Woolcomr								
		Terce. McDermotroe & W P	Cooper		2		3	1			
		Domk. McQuon & W P	Dealer		1						
		Widw. Narry P			1		1				
		Henry Brady & W P	Labour.		2						
		Stephn. Casey & Wife R	Skinner						1		
		John Swiny & W P	Weaver					1	2		
		Jas. Swiny & W P	Labour.		2						
		Jas. Murray & W P	Weaver		1						
		Hugh Cullen & W P	Labour.								
		Jas. McManus & W P	Do		2				1		
		Hugh Corkran & W P	Butcher		1						
		Thos. Ford & W P	Mason		1		1				
		Miles Ford & W P	Do								2
		Michl. McDermot & W P	Taylor		1						
		Wm. McManus & W P	Butcher		1						
		John Roberts & Wife R	Weaver	4		2			1		
		Danl. Murry & W P	Labour.		1						
		Andw. Gunogly & W P	Carpenr.		2		1				
		Thos. Connellan & W P	Labour.		1		1				
		Andw. Higgin & W P	Taylor				1				1
		Connor Cryne R	Beggar								
		Cormk. McManus & W P	Labour.								1
		Thos. Corkran & W P	Weaver		2						
		John Kirvan & W P	Labour.								1
		Rogr. Spellan & W P	Miller								1
		Thos. White & Wife R	Weaver	5		1					
		John Flannery & W P	Do		4						
		Cormk. Mullany & W P	Saltman		1						
		Bryan Rork & W P	Mason		1						
		Michl. Reily & W P	Labour.		1						
		Widw. Farrell P	Beggar								
		Patt. Concagh P	Beggar								
		John Flyn & Wife P	Mason						1		1
		Andw. Beirn[29] Popish	Priest						1		
		Bryan Dolan & W P	Mason								
		John Grey & Wife P	Labour.		3						
		Patt. McDruy & W P	Do		1						
		Jas. Kelly & Wife P	Taylor				1				
		Peter Nary & Wife P	Labour.								
		Domk. Corkran & W P	Weaver		2		1	2			
		Hugh Concagh & W P	Do		1						
		Henry McManus & W P	Labour.						1		
		August. Corkran & W P	Do		1						
		Terce. McHugh & W P	Do		1						
		Widw. McGowan P					1				
[f.343] Boyle		Widw. McGowan P					1				
		Thos. Goulding & W P	Labour.		2						
		Darby Spellan & W P	Miller		1						

Com~Ros common Parish of	Place of Abode	Names and Religion	Proffession	Children under 14		Children above 14		Men Servts		Women Servts	
				Prot.	Paps.	Prot.	Paps.	Prot.	Paps.	Prot.	Paps.
		Patt. Keating & W P	Labour.								
		Bryan Daly Pr	Sexton								
		Michl. O'Hara & W P	Labour.		2						
		Miles Clerk & W P	Pedlar		1						
		Edwd. Lennon P	Mason								
		Bart. McDruy P	Labour.		3						
		Widw. Williams P			3		1				
		Will. Hixon & Wife Pr	Weaver	4				4			1
		Jas. Irwin & Wife R									
		Davd. Irwin & Wife R	Beaker [Baker]	2							1
		Robt. Nelly & Wife R	Labour.	10							
		Hugh Hogg & Wife R	Park keer.	1		2		1		1	
		John McWilliam & Wife Pr	Boatman	5					1		1
		Thos. Deane & Wife R	Weaver	2					2		
	Killmacroy	John Johnson30 & Wife Pr	Farmer					1		2	
		John Johnson31 & Wife R	Do	6							
		Wm. Johnson & Wife R	Do			3					
		Henry Tingle & W P	Labour.		4						
		John Corrinan & W P	Pumpmr.								
		John Quinn32 & W R	Weaver	4							
		John Bradly33 & W R	Farmer	1				1		1	
		Patt. Bradly & W R	Do	4							
		Michl. Heraghty & W P	Labour.		1						
		Bryn. Killtughan & W P	Do		1						
		Hugh Maginnis & W P	Weaver						4		1
		John Casey & W P	Labour.		1						
		Neile McNulty & W P	Do		1						
		Wm. Hare & Wife R	Farmer	4							1
		John Kelly & W P	Smyth						1		
		Darby Mcdonagh & W P	Beggr.								
	Curnecarta	John Hogan & W P	Farmr.		3						
		Widw. Mcdermot P									1
		Bryan Conncah & W P	Labour.		2						
		Wm. Johnson34 & Wife R	Farmer			2					1
		Thos Fry35 & Wife R	Labour.	2					1		1
		Wm. Nary R & Wife P	Do								
		Matt. Keaveny & W P	Farmer								1
		Darby Connell & W P	Weaver		3		2				
[f.344]Boyle	Aughagorula	Richd. Sparks36 Pr	Woodrangr.	3		2					
		John Bartley & W P	Herd		2		1			1	
		John Moran & W P	Labour.		1		1				
		Patt. Moran & W P	Do		1						
		Andw. Bartly P	Do		1						
	Aughcar	Hugh McDermott P	Do								
		Peter. Mcdermott & W P	Do		1						
		Widw. Keaveny P			2		1				
		John Fogarty P Wife R	Mason			2				1	2
		John Keaveny & W P	Labour.								
	Drimdoe37	John Lilly & Wife Pr	Gent.	4						4	4

Com~Ros common Parish of	Place of Abode	Names and Religion	Proffession	Children under 14		Children above 14		Men Servts		Women Servts	
				Prot.	Paps.	Prot.	Paps.	Prot.	Paps.	Prot.	Paps.
		Darby McDonaugh & W P	Labour.		2				1		
		Jas. Keaveny & W P	Do		3		1				
		Andw. Donagho & W P	Do		3						
		Owen Nichols & W P	Do				3				
	Tintagh	Jas. Costello & W P	Farmer		1						
		Peter Nicholson & W P	Labour.		3						
		Jas. Dungan & W P	Do								2
		Hugh Mcdermott & W P	Do		1				1		
		John Hart & W P	Do		2						
		Rogr. Slane & W P	Smyth		2		1				
		Owen Regan & W P	Yarn Mt.		2						
	Killtinighan	Jams Sheerin & W P	Labour.		1		1		1		1
		Owen Finan & W P	Do		2						
		Thos. Sheerin & W P	Do		2		2				
		Laughn. McHugh & W P	Do				1				
		Luke Sheerin & W P	Do		2		1		1		1
		John Myhan & W P	Do		2						
		Widw. Burk P	Do		2		1				
		Tady Mcganny & W P	Do		1						
		Carbry McGann & W P	Do								
	Cashill	Michl. Birne & W P	Do		2						
		Patt. Trevor & W P	Do		2						
		Patt. Flannigan & W P	Do		2						
	Macmoyne[38]	Hugh Corkran & W P	Herd		2		1				1
		Widw. Casey P					3				
		Michl. McNiff & W P	Do		2						
	Ballymore[39]	John Sharcot & W P	Labour.				4				
		Chas. Noone & W P	Shepherd		4				1		
		John McLaughlin & W P	Do		3						
[f.345] Boyle	Leam[40]	John Connaghten & W P	Labour.		3						
		Patt. Connaghten & W P	Do		1						
	Legnagun	John Sharcott & W P	Farmer		2		1				
		Owen Crogan[41] Pr	Gent.			1			1		2
		Luke Crogan Pr Wife P	Labour.		4		1				
		Patt McDrury & W P	Do		2		1				
	Grangebegg[42]	Manus Lavin & W P	Pumpmr.		4		1				2
		Hugh Cox & W P	Taylor		2						
		Owen Handbury & W P	Labour.		2		3				
		Timothy Dowd & W P	Labour.		3						
		Miles Brenan P	Labour.				3				
		Micl. Cregg & W P	Labour.		1						
	Ballinroe	Thady McManus & W P	Farmer		3		1				
		Thady Quinn & W P	Labour.		2						
		Wm. White & Wife P	Do		1						
		Dudy. McDermott & W P	Do		2						
	Tawnacarrow	Hugh McDermott & W P	Farmer								1
		Owen Mcgan & W P	Labour.		2						
		Jams. Noon & W P	Do		1		1				
		Edmd. Keaveny & W P	Do		2		2				

Com~Ros common Parish of	Place of Abode	Names and Religion	Proffession	Children under 14		Children above 14		Men Servts		Women Servts	
				Prot.	Paps.	Prot.	Paps.	Prot.	Paps.	Prot.	Paps.
		Jas. Cox & W P	Do		2		2				
		Jas. White & Wife P	Do		2						
		Patt. Dyer & W P	Do		3		1				
		Patt. Ginnan & W P	Do		2						
	Taghwinnagh	John Tyler & Wife R Farmer		2							
		Hugh Gormly & W P	Labour.								
		Wm. Druhey & W P	Do				2				
	Killtabrannuck	Dudly Mullany P	Do				2				
		Jas. McHugh P	Farmer								1
		Widw. Higgins P	Widow		1		2				
	Curnaglick	Matt Casey & W P	Labour.		2		4				
		John Tivenine & W P	Do		2		2				
		Lauce. McKenna & W P	Do		2						1
		Domk. Keaveny & W P	Do		1						1
		Thos. Flannigan & W P	Do		1						
		Thos. Fury & Wife P	Do		3		1				
		Andw. Quin & Wife P	Do		2						
		John Keen & Wife P	Do		1						
	Cornamilta	Danl. McDaniel & W P	Herd		1		2				2
		Owen Mcdermotroe & W P	Mason				2				
		Luke Mally & W P	Labour.		1						
[f.346] Boyle	Carranalbanagh	Farrel Grey & W P	Farmer		2		1				
		Thos. Fallon & W P	Do		4						
		Widw. Fallon P			3						
		Dennis Beirn & W P	Do		2						
		Darby Teige & W P	Do		2						
		Wm. Teige & W P	Do		3						
		John Feneron & W P	Do		2						
		John Brennan R	Do					1			1
		Owen McConcagh & W P	Labour.		3		1				
		Dennis McCabe & W P	Do		2						
	Ballaghbuy	Thady McGlin & W P	Smyth		2						
		Kedagh Philips & W P	Labour.		3		1				
		Thady Mullany & W P	begr		3		2				
		Mattw. Biern & W P	Labour.				1				
	Doon[43]	Hugh Gormley & W P	Farmer		2		2				
		Peter Williamoe & W P	Do		2						1
		Cormk. Healy & W P	Do		3		1				
		Murtagh Corkran & W P	Do		2		1				1
		Michl. Lavin & W P	Do		3		1				
		Matt. Gallaugher P	Do				2				
		Thos. Higgins & W P	Do				4				
		Michl. Mattimoe & W P	Do		3						
		Domk. Keilty & W P	Do		1		1				
		Thos. Higgins & W P	Do		3						
		Owen Luagh & W P	Do		3						
		Rogr. Gaullagher & W P	Do		3						
		Farrt. Keilty & W P	Labour.		1		1				
		Thady Mullowly & W P	Do		2						

Com~Ros common Parish of	Place of Abode	Names and Religion	Proffession	Children under 14		Children above 14		Men Servts		Women Servts	
				Prot.	Paps.	Prot.	Paps.	Prot.	Paps.	Prot.	Paps.
		Jon. Keilty & W P	Do								
		Chars. Parlan & W P	Do	2							
		Jas. Mattimoe & W P	Farmer	2							1
		John Flannigan & W P	Labour.								
		Hugh Killalea & W P	Do	2							
		Rogr. Killalea & W P	Do	2							1
		Patt. Killalea & W P	Do	1							
		Peter Tivenin & W P	Farmer	2							1
		Bryan Deevin & W P	Do	6			6				
		Wm. Sheerin & W P	Labour.	1							
		Bart. Sheerin & W P	Do	3							
		Jas. Tanisty & W P	Do								
[f.347] Boyle	Doon	Thos. Gormly & W P	Farmer	1			1				
		Widw. Healy P					2				
		Patt. Willimo & W P	Labour.	2			1				
		Widw. McGlin P					2				
		Barty Mullowly & W P	Do	1			2				
		Widw. Horan P	Do				1				
		John Healy & W P	Do	2							
	Sheegory	Dudly Gaullagher & W P	Farmer	2			2		1		
		Morgan Duffy & W P	Do	1					1		1
		Luke Lavin & W P	Do	1			1				1
		Patt. Lavin & W P	Do	2			2				
		Owen Gallagher & W P	Do	1			1		1		
		Jas. Horish & W P	Do	2							
		Patt. Horish & W P	Labour.	1			1				
		Chas. Killalea & W P	Do				4				
		Hugh Ward & W P	Farmer	1					1		
		Patt. Welsh & W P	Do				2				1
		Mar. Welsh & W P	Do	1					1		
	Tawnnatasky	Jas. Ward & W P	Labour.	3							
		Pat. Knevin P	Labour.				3				
		John Welsh P	beggar				1				
		Widw. Sadler R	Widow	4							
		Peter Keavny & W P	Labour.	2							1
	Ballinfall	Lan Holms & Wife Pr	Gent.	2		1		2			5
		Lawce. Hagan & W P	Labour.	2			2				1
		Owen Mullany P	Do								1
		John Mullany & W P	Do	1							
		Bryan Cunningham & W P	Do								
	Knockabro[44]	Wm. Alexander & Wife R	Farmer	4					1		
		John Alexander R	Do	1		5			1		
		Wm. Moore & Wife R	Do	1		3					
		John Lytell & Wife R	Do	2							
		Michl. Sheerin & W P	Do	1			4			1	2
		Farrel Grey R Wife P	Labour.	1							
		John Greagan & W P	Do								
		Owen Ternan & W P	Do				1				
	Knockado	Robt. Knott & Wife R	Gent.	1		3			4		4

Com~Ros common Parish of	Place of Abode	Names and Religion	Proffession	Children under 14		Children above 14		Men Servts		Women Servts	
				Prot.	Paps.	Prot.	Paps.	Prot.	Paps.	Prot.	Paps.
		John Spellon & W P	Labour.		4						
		Giles Spellon & W P	Do				2				
		John Burk & W P	Do		1		1				
[f.348] Boyle	Knockado	Patt. Hawks & W P	Do		5						3
		Hugh Muillany & W P	Labour.		2		4				
		Dennis Blaney & W P	Do		4						2
		Laugn. Sharcott & W P	Do		1		1				
		Darby McNally & W P	Do		3				1		1
		Wm. Burnet & W P	Do		1				2		
		Connr. Luby & W P	Do		3		2				1
		Rogr. Dyer & W P	Do		3				1		2
	Grangemore	Michl. McDermotroe & W P	Do		1		1				
		Laugn. Brenan P	Do		2		2				
		Thos. Cregg & W P	Do		1						
		Hugh Handbury & W P	Do								
	Knockrush	Chas. Kenny & W P	Do		2						
		Wm. Moran & W P	Taylor		2						
		Owen Sharcot & W P	Labour.		1		2				
		Widw. Higgins P									1
		Thos. Cullin & W P	Shepherd		5		2				
		John Brennan & W P	Labour.		2						
		Patt. Sharcot & W P	Do		3						
		Domk. McDermot & W P	Do								
		John Spelman & W P	Do		3						
		Peter Rogers & W P	Dealer		1		1				
		Luke Bardin & W P	Smyth								
		Thady Tague & W P	Labour.				2				
		Andw. Tague & W P	Do		1						
		Owen Brennan & W P	Do		1						
		Jas. Quinn & W P	Do		3						
		Patt. Brannan Pr Wife P	Do		5						
		John Kennedy & W P	Do		2						
		Michl. Kennedy & W P	Do		1						
		Mattw. Lawhey & W P	Do		2		2				
	Ballytrassna	Edd McGowran & Wife Pr	Do	1		1					
		Hugh Flyn & W P	Mason						1		
		Jefsn Bird & Wife Pr	Maltster	3							
		Wm. Brennan & W P	Herd		1						
		Patt. McGlin & W P	Labour.		1						
		Patt. Mullready & W P	Do		1						
	Littleknockdo	Widw. Knott R				3			2		2
	Grallagh	Chas. Flynn & W P	Farmr.				1				
		Chas Flynn ju. & W P	Do		1						
[f.349] Boyle	Grallagh	Micl. Flyn & W P	Do		2						
		John Mullany & W P	Do		1		2				
		Anw. Mullohy & W P	Do		2		1				
	Lugnamuddy	Robt. Bell & W P	Labour.						2		1
		Rogr. McGowan & W P	Mason		1		2		1		
		Miles Higgins & W P	Herd		1		1				

Com~Ros common Parish of	Place of Abode	Names and Religion	Proffession	Children under 14		Children above 14		Men Servts		Women Servts	
				Prot.	Paps.	Prot.	Paps.	Prot.	Paps.	Prot.	Paps.
	Carromore	Bryan Reynolds P Wife Pr	Do		7						
	Aughagrange	Edwd. Power & W P	Do				1				
	Erris	Nichs Fennel & W P	Gamekeepr.		2						1
		Jas. Deane & Wife Pr	Weaver			1			1		
		Bar. Moran & W P	Herd		2						
		Bryan Connor & W P	Labour.		2						
		Wm. Connolly & W P	Do								1
		Michl. Coleman & W P	Herd		4						1
		Rogr. Rock & W P	Do		2						
		Ths. Brennan P	Labour.		3						
		Jas. Daly & W P	Do		2						

[f.350]

Brought from				Heads of families				[Children under 14]		[Children above 14]		[Men Servants]		[Women Servants]	
				Protestants		Papists									
				Men	Women	Men	Women	[Prot.]	[Paps.]	[Prot.]	[Paps.]	[Prot.]	[Paps.]	[Prot.]	[Paps.]
		No. 1		10	17	23	23	27	43	10	6	23	29	5	31
		2		21	24	13	15	44	28	16	7	18	14	7	23
		3		9	8	29	31	25	43	9	17	1	6	1	4
		4		7	9	27	30	16	41	17	13	3	9	1	13
		5		13	13	21	23	14	30	14	11	2	5	1	9
		6		3	2	35	35	9	31	3	7	3	7		7
		7		18	16	20	21	45	28	7	4	7	9	4	9
		8		2	2	35	37	7	56	4	22		11		11
		9		2	1	38	36	2	63	1	34		1		10
		10		1		38	38		80		25	1			6
		11		7	6	29	30	16	32	12	36		13	1	17
		12		3	3	35	36	4	64	4	20		6		12
		13		1	2	16	15		31	1	7		4		4
		Total		97	103	359	370	209	570	98	209	58	114	20	156

[R: Reformed religion.]

[verso of f.351]

A Return of the Inhabitants of Boyle parish by which it appears that there are one hundred and seven Protestant families Containing Five hundred and Eighty five souls and Three hundred and Seventy Eight popish Families Containing one thousand Seven hundred and seventy Eight souls In all two thousand three hundred and sixty three in said parish - 2363.

[M]em: Eleven protestant men have no wives and six have popish wives, Fourteen papists have no Wives and seven have protestants

NOTES

1. *General Alphabetical Index.*

2. *Report ... fairs and markets.*

3. *History of the Irish Parliament*, ii, 319-320.

4. King-Harman, *The Kings of King House*, p. 13.

5. Ibid, p.14.

6. N.L.I., MS 21 F 17.

7. Robert Phipps was the son of Matthew Phipps, a gentleman. He was born near Sligo and entered TCD in 1721/2 aged 18, graduating BA in 1730. He married a Miss Mercer of Dublin. He lived at Cooper's Hill, parish of Drumcolumb (f. 376) (*Alumni Dubliniensis*; Leslie, 'Elphin', p.110).

8. Leslie, 'Elphin', p.110a.

9. Robert King was born in 1724 and was created Baron Kingsborough in 1748. He was MP for Boyle, the family borough 1743-1748. He had a reputation as a rake, having run away with a Miss Johnston aged 16 in 1747. They were apprehended by her father who threatened to shoot him if he did not marry her. His servants rescued him from this predicament. He was said to have borrowed £40,000 from Mitchell's Bank in Dublin. He was a prominent freemason, lived at Boyle Abbey and died in 1755. He mortgaged his estates in Co. Roscommon and Co.Sligo, and this mortgage was continued by his successors, Sir Edward King and Henry King. After a dispute in 1762 the estate was divided, two-thirds to them and the other third sold to Lawrence Dundas to pay debts (*History of the Irish Parliament*; Lady Llanover (ed.), *The Autobiography and Correspondence of Mary Granville, Mrs Delany* (6 vols, London, 1861), ii, 482; P.R.O.N.I., Zetland Papers T 3418/29).

10. The will of Thomas Rowlatt of Boyle was proved in 1751 (N.L.I., Index to Diocesan Wills, Elphin, mic. p.1727).

11. Matthew Mcdermotroe rented 5 acres from the King estate (N.L.I., MS 21 F 17)

12. Jon Corristone rented 12 acres from the King estate (N.L.I., MS 21 F 17).

13. Widow West rented 1 acre from the King estate (ibid).

14. See John Johnston jnr. Note 27.

15. John Knott rented a town park from the King estate in 1724 (N.L.I., Ainsworth Report No 105, King Papers).

16. The will of Richard McKenzie of Boyle was proved in 1774 and the will of Isabella McKenzie of Boyle in 1794 (N.L.I., Index to Diocesan Wills, Elphin, mic. p. 1727).

17. James Smith rented a town park from the King estate in 1724 (N.L.I., Ainsworth Report No 105, King Papers).

18. Robert Brenan of Boyle, freeholder, was sworn at Roscommon in 1769 (N.L.I., Freeholders of Co. Roscommon, MS 35,163).

19. Philip Tweed, freeholder, was sworn at Roscommon in 1769 (ibid).

20. There was a quarry 'for the use of the farm' in the townland of Grange (N.L.I., MS 3105).

21. Robert Simpson rented 11 acres from the King estate in 1765 (N.L.I., MS 21 F 17).

22. The mills and 10 acres of land were part of the King estate at Boyle (N.L.I., MS 3105).

23. Richard Farrall rented 7 acres from the King estate (N.L.I., MS 21 F 17).

24. Coopers made butter casks and firkins for beer (Weld, *Roscommon*, pp. 204-7).

25. In the 1830s, Boyle had a large number of thatched cabins (Weld, *Roscommon,* p.189).

26. Oliver Russell of Boyle freeholder was sworn at Roscommon in 1769 (N.L.I., MS 35,163).

27. Widow McGawran rented 4 acres from the King estate (N.L.I., MS 21 F 17).

28. Edward Synge consulted Bryan Mulvihil, a stonecutter, about repairing a marble cistern from his parlour in Dublin. Mulvihil advised that it would be best to have it polished in Dublin (*Synge Letters*, p.101).

29. Andrew O'Beirn was listed as pastor of Boyle in 1739 and 1756. He was also prebendary of Ardagh. His will was dated 1773 (Beirne (ed.), *Diocese of Elphin* p.119; Fenning, 'Clergy Lists' p. 146, fn. 18).

30. John Johnston leased 48 acres Irish plantation measure in 1727 for three lives from Sir Thomas Dundas (N.L.I., MS 2786).

31. John Johnston jnr. leased 34a 0r 20p in 1734 for three lives from Sir Thomas Dundas (N.L.I., MS 2786).

32. John Quinn leased 37a 2r 26p in 1748 for three lives from Sir Thomas Dundas (N.L.I., MS 2786).

33. John Bradley leased 5 acres in 1727 from Dundas (N.L.I., MS 2786).

34. William Johnston leased 53 acres in 1727 for three lives from Dundas (N.L.I., MS 2786).

35. Thomas Fry farmed 50 acres at Cumecarta (N.L.I., MS 21 F 17).

36. Richard Sparks, freeholder was sworn at Roscommon in 1769 (N.L.I., MS 35,163).

37. The townland of Drimdoe consisted of 269a 1r 0p of arable, pasture bog and mountain (N.L.I., MS 3105).

38. There was a 'sand park' here (N.L.I., MS 21 F 17).

39. Townland owned by Edward Synge, bishop of Elphin (N.L.I., MS 16, I 13).

40. The townland of Leam consisted of 102a 2r 26p of arable and pastureland and 83a 3r 4p of bog and waste (N.L.I., MS 3105).

41. Owen Crogan, hearth money collector was stationed in the Rathmullan Walk. When it was suggested that another officer exchange with him, this was refused, 'Boyle being a Walk of greater consequence and Crogan being an experienced officer (N.A., P.R.O., MS CUST 1/42/4).

42. Grangebegg and Grangemor townlands were named for the out-farms of Boyle Abbey where grain was stored. The name also occurs in the parishes of Ahamlish, Cam and Kilbride (Beirne, (ed.) *Diocese of Elphin*, p.146).

43. The 761 acres of the townland of Doon consisted of arable, pasture, cut bog, moor, and waste which was partly rocky mountainside. It was owned by the King family (N.L.I., MS 3105).

44. The north division arable and pasture with two acres broken boggy pasture and five acres moory (N.L.I., MS 21 F 17).

KILNAMANAGH, COUNTY ROSCOMMON

INTRODUCTION: *The parish of Kilnamanagh in the barony of Boyle is 5 miles south west of Boyle. It covered 7,621 statute acres.*[1] *Lewis says that the land was principally under tillage, but included extensive bogs and marshes. Limestone was plentiful.*[2]

The incumbent was the Rev. Henry Cunningham who had been collated in 1744.[3] *The patron was the bishop of Elphin. The rectory was impropriate.*

OCCUPATIONS

Beggar	1	Farmer	7	Servant	4
Clockmaker	1	Innkeeper	1	Servants, household	41
Cottier	70	Miller	1	Shepherd	1

Com~Ros common Parish of	Place of Abode	Names and Religion	Proffession	Children under 14 Prot.	Children under 14 Paps.	Children above 14 Prot.	Children above 14 Paps.	Men Servts Prot.	Men Servts Paps.	Women Servts Prot.	Women Servts Paps.
[f.352] Kilnamanagh	Slieveroe	Loughlin Lavin Chiles Pa	Cottier	0	1	0	1				
		Cormuck Lavin Catherine Pa	Cottier		1				1		1
		Redmond Farrel Pa Catherine	Cottier		3		2				1
		Roger McDermot Pa Mary	Cottier		4						
	Cloomaguinen	Hugh McDonnough Pa	Cottier								
		Bartho. Donnough Pa Margaret	Miller		2						
		Mary Elwood Pa	Widow		1						
		Honour Coony Pa	Widow				1				
	Callow[4]	Joseph Isdell Pre = Sarah	Farmer	1		1			1		3
		Catharine McDermot Pa	Widow		4				2		1
		Patrick Ward Pa Sicily	Cottier		3						
		Bartholw Conigan Pa Mary	Cottier		2						
		Margaret McDermot Pa	Widow		2		1		2		2
	Runimullen	Luke Coyle Pa Ann	Cottier		2						
		Laurence Sheenane Pa Mary	Cottier		4		1				
		Luke Conigan Pa Mary	Cottier		5						
		Michael Hughs Pa Honour	Cottier		4						
		Willm Mullanny Pa Honour	Cottier		2						
		Cormuck Cuffe Pa Honour	Cottier		1		3				
		Amby Maddin Pa Mary	Cottier		2		2				
		Connor Flanigan Pa	Cottier								1
	Barnobuy	James Flanigan Pa Catherine			6						
		Peter Brenan Pa Catherine	Cottier				1				2
		Edwd. Flanigan Pa Mary	Cottier				1				
		Jonn Rogers Pa Ann	Cottier		3		2				
		Brian Connahan Pa Mary	Cottier		1		2				
		Rich. Journee Pa Bridget	Cottier		2						
		Timothy Hopkin Pa Honour	Cottier								
		Dennis Gallahar Pa	Beggar								
	Runabehee	Edwd. Madden Pa Mary	Cottier		2		1				
		Brian Dempsy Pa Sarah	Cottier				1				
		Connor Bokeen Pa Mary	Cottier		1						

Com~Ros common Parish of	Place of Abode	Names and Religion	Proffession	Children under 14 Prot.	Paps.	Children above 14 Prot.	Paps.	Men Servts Prot.	Paps.	Women Servts Prot.	Paps.
	Clooneen	Connor Coyne Pa Winifred	Cottier				3				1
		Fynne Coyne Pa Bridget	Cottier				1				
		Patrick McDermot Pa Mary	Cottier		2		1				
	Ballinvoher	Darby Greevy Pa Margaret	Cottier		3		2				2
		Richard Lenon Pa Honour	Cottier		3						
		Brian Regon Pa Winifred	Cottier								
	Killnamanagh	Patrick Sheenane Pa Mary	Cottier				4		1		
		James Brenan Pa Mary	Cottier		1						
[f.353]	Carrowreagh	Hen. Griffin Pre= Diana	Servts	1		1	+		2		1
		Edmd. Bourke Pa	Sert		5		3		1		1
	Cloonycarrow5	Thos. Griffin Pre= Margaret Pa	Do	2							
		Donnold Renolds Pa Honour	Cottier		5						
		Guild Keeneene Pa Honour	Cottier		1						
		John Nary Pa Mary	Cottier		2						
		Tiege Noon Pa Winifred	Cottier		1						
		Francis Mulready Pa Margaret	Cottier		2		1				
		Catharine McDermot a widow Pa Siby McDermot	widow Pa		1		1				
	Bridogue	Edwd. McDermot Pa	Innkeeper								2
		John Greehan Pa	Cottier								
		Margaret Kegan Pa									
	Carrowreagh	James Bern Pa Bridget	Cottier		3						
		Mary Hopkins Pa widow			1						
		Owen Magrath Pa Margaret	Cottier		2						
		Thomas Dowd Pa Sarah	Farmer		2						
		Andrew Hopkin Pa Honour	Cottier								
		Terence Mullanny Pa Ann	Cottier		2						
		Sicily Miller Pa Widow			1						
		Margaret Guihan Pa Widow			1						
		Hen. Conigan Pa Honour	Cottier								
		John Sharedy Pa	Cottier		3						
		Owen McGrevy Pa Mary	Cottier								
	Kingsland6	Miles McDonnough Pa Elizabeth Pre	Sert	1					2		2
		Tully Dooly Pa Margaret	Cottier		4				1		

Com~Ros common Parish of	Place of Abode	Names and Religion	Proffession	Children under 14		Children above 14		Men Servts		Women Servts	
				Prot.	Paps.	Prot.	Paps.	Prot.	Paps.	Prot.	Paps.
		Michael Bern Pa Margaret	Cottier				1				
		Darby Bern Pa Ann	Cottier		2						
	Derrycough	Edwd. Guihin Pa Margaret	Shepherd		1		1				
	Tournagee	John Dodd Pre Mary Pa	Farmer	2		1	0				3
		John Warren Pre Elizabeth	Farmer	2							
		Wm. Millet Pa Eleanor	Cottier		3						
		Paul Bern Pa Sarah	Cottier		1		2				
		Loughlin Dournan Pa Honour	Cottier		2		1				
	Carrowkeel	Stephen Sparks Pa Margaret	Cottier		4						
		Patrick Bern Pa Alice	Cottier		2						
	Ardmoyle	Henry Tyler[7] Pre Mary	Farmer	4							1
		Roger Mullowly Pa Mary	Cottier		2		1				
		James Kelly Pa Margaret	Cottier		1		1				
[f.354] Kilnamanagh	Ardmoyle	Dennis Conellan Pa Mary	Cottier		1						
		Michael Kelly Pa Bridget	Do				2				
		Owen Brenan Pa Winifred	Do		3						
	Runiradane[8]	Loughlin McTaunish Pa Sarah	Do		3						
	Tullahan	John Loyd Pre Deborah	Farmer	2		3					1
		John Irwin Pre Honour	Clockmaker	3							1
		Cormuck Bern Pa Margaret	Cottier		4						
		Michael Cox Pa Margaret	Do		2		1				
		Luke Bern Pa Margaret	Do		4						
		Thady Concreigh Pa Siby	Do								
		Andrew Durneen Pa Honour	Do		3						
	CloonMcmileen	Charles Dowd Pa Judith	Farmer		3			1			1
		Teig Noon Pa Mary	Cottier		2						
	Toneroe[9]	Patrick Concreigh Pa Sarah	Do		2						
		Brian Brennan Pa Catharine	Do		2						
		James Pendergrass Pa Sarah	Do		1						
		Andrew Sarcady Pa Sarah	Do		3						
		Thady Flanigan Pa Catharine	Do		1						

[on piece of paper attached to form]

Parish of Killnamanagh

Total Men & women 218		Do Reform'd <u>15</u>		Do Pa: <u>203</u>
Do. Children 224		Do Do Under } 18		Do Do 155
		Do Do Above 14} 6		Do <u>45</u>
		Total Children Pre 24		Do Pa 200
	_____	<u>Do Men & Women Do 15</u>		M & W Do <u>203</u>
Total	[erased]	Total Pre: 39		Do Pa 403

NOTES

1. Less 36 acres of Loughanlea and the Lung river (*General Alphabetical Index*).

2. Lewis, 'Kilnamanagh of Killenamanagh'.

3. Henry Cunningham was born in County Donegal, a son of the Rev. William Cunningham. He went to Bishop Hodson's School, Elphin where he was taught by Samuel Griffin. He entered TCD in 1710, aged 18, and graduated BA in 1714 and MA in 1719. Henry Cunningham became Archdeacon of Elphin in 1756 (*Alumni Dubliniensis*; Leslie, Elphin p.187).

4. Part of the estate of Thomas Harris in 1747 (N.A.I, .MS 320).

5. Ibid.

6. The townland of Kingsland belonged to the Kings of Boyle. It was of poor quality, consisting almost entirely of 'wet curragh' (N.L.I., MS 3105).

7. Henry Tyler leased 23a 8r 0p from Sir Thomas Dundas in 1746. Tyler died in 1782 (N.L.I., MS 2786).

8. The townland of Runiradane [Runnerredane] consisted of 55 acres of arable and pasture, 12 acres of red and cut bog and 7 acres of bog and curragh, owned by the King family (N.L.I., MS 3105).

9. Owned by the King family (N.L.I., MS 3105).

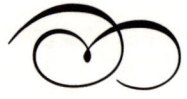

KILBRYAN, COUNTY ROSCOMMON

INTRODUCTION: *The parish of Kilbryan is in the barony of Boyle, 2 miles south east of Boyle. Most of Lough Key is within the parish, but the islands on Lough Key were not included by the enumerator of the census.*

The parish was held with those of Boyle, Shancough, Kilmactranny, Aghanagh, Kilmacallan, Tawnagh and Drumcolumb. The incumbent was Robert Phipps (see Boyle). The patron was the bishop. The rectory was impropriate in the Crofton family.

OCCUPATIONS

Cottier	60
Farmer	9
Servants, household	12
Weaver	1

Com~Ros common Parish of	Place of Abode	Names and Religion	Proffession	Children under 14		Children above 14		Men Servts		Women Servts	
				Prot.	Paps.	Prot.	Paps.	Prot.	Paps.	Prot.	Paps.
[f.355] Killbrine	Carrowstuckeen	Ralph Onion Pre: Elizabeth Pa:	Cottier			2					
		David Lightel Pre: Mary	Cottier	1							
		Thos. Graham Pre: Margaret	Do	1		1					
		Willm. Graham Pre:	Do								1
		Marcus Kelly Pa Mary	Do		2		2				
		Will. Rock Pa Winifrid	Do				1				
		Cormuck Lancy Pa Sarah	Do		1		2				
	Pullowen	Willm. Cummin Pa Sarah	Do				1				
		Richd. Grimes Pre Margaret	Do			2					
		Patrick Rock Pa Mary	Do		2		2				
	Radiveen	Owen Glyn Pa Catharine	Do		1		1				
		Tho. Dowlan Pa Gyles	Do				1				
		Brian Mcdermot Pa Winifred	Farmer								
		Edwd. Mcdermot Pa Margaret	Farmer				1				
	Killbrine	Owen Durneen Pa Catharine	Cottier				2				
		Carbery Bern Pa Elizabeth	Do				2				
		Laurence Rock Pa Mary	Do								
		Timothy McDermot Pa	Farmer						1		1
		Thady McDermot Pa Margaret	Do						1		1
		Owen McDermot Pa Mary	Cottier								
	Ahanasourn[1]	John Costello Pre Mary	Farmer								1
		John Garner Pre Bridget	Do	6		2					
		Brian Kelly Pre Mary	Do	4		2					
		Patrick McDonough Pre Dorothy	Do	2							
		Dominick Fehy Pa Mary	Cottier		3		1				
		Michael Naughton Pa Elizabeth	Do		3						
		Pat. Conclagh Pa Catharine	Do		3						
		Loughlin Kelly Pa Honour	Do		1		3				
		Patt. Conbane Pa Mary	Do		2						
		Ferdinando Lyons Pa Catharine	Do		1						
		Tho. Powell Pa Alice	Do				4				

Com~Ros common Parish of	Place of Abode	Names and Religion	Proffession	Children under 14 Prot.	Children under 14 Paps.	Children above 14 Prot.	Children above 14 Paps.	Men Servts Prot.	Men Servts Paps.	Women Servts Prot.	Women Servts Paps.
		Andrew Sheereene Pa Honour	Do		1						
		Gilbert Killane Pa Bridget	Do		3						
		Mark Skiventon Pa Sarah	Do								
		Peter Coleman Pa Mary	Do								
		John Brehenny Pa Mable	Do		3						
		Pat. Brehenny Pa Margaret	Do								
		Cormuck McGawran Pa Mary	Do		4		2				
		John Killkenny Pa Margaret	Do		1						
		Dudley Sweeny Pa Jane	Do				1				
[f.356]Do	Do	James Mcgrath Pa Honour	Cottier		1						
		Owen Corolly Pa Catharine	Do								
		Owen Conellan Pa Winifred	Do		3						
		Pat. Mcdermot Pa Alice	Do								
	Smutterna[2]	James Kerin Pa Catharine	Do		4		1				
		James Connel Pa Honour	Do		1						
		Owen Mcdermot Pa Mary	Do		2						
		Thady Connel Pa Rose	Do								
		James McLoughlin Pa Catharine	Do		1						
		Mary Mulloy Pa	Do		3						
		Brian Haly Pa Sarah	Do		3						
		Patrick Mcgary Pa Juggy	Do		1						
		Owen McLoughlin Pa	Do				2				
		James Bruin Pa Bridget	Do		4		1				
		George Carnell Pa Margareth	Do		3						
		Dennis Murphy Pa Mary	Do								
		Robert Hamilton Pre Mary	Do	2							
		Patrick Dohorty Pa Mary	Weaver								
		Mary Doyle widow Pa			2						2
		Fardy McLoughlin Pa Catharine	Cottier		4						
		Redmond Murphy Pa Mary	Do		3						
		Hugh Murphy Pa Sarah	Do		1						

Com~Ros common Parish of	Place of Abode	Names and Religion	Proffession	Children under 14		Children above 14		Men Servts		Women Servts	
				Prot.	Paps.	Prot.	Paps.	Prot.	Paps.	Prot.	Paps.
	Killisteen	John McCalagh Pa Catharine	Do								
		Owen Cuilish Pa Winifred	Do		4						
		Owen McConnolly Pa Winifred	Do		2						
		Terence Mcgrath Pa Rose	Do		2						
		Samuel Adams Pre Esther	Farmer						1		1
		John Callary Pa Catharine	Cottier								1
		Dennis Dunn Pa Honour	Do				2				
		Cormuck Carty Pa	Do		2		2				1
		John Bourk	Do								

[verso] Mr Cunningham Parish of Killbrine

[on paper attached to f.356]

Parish of Killbrine

Total men & women	147	Do Reform'd	<u>20</u> Do		Pa:	<u>127</u>
Do Children	136	Do Do Under 14}	16 Do		Pa	77
		Do Do Above	<u>9</u> Do		Do	<u>34</u>
		Total children Re:	25 Do		Pa:	111
			Do		Pa:	127

Total	283	Total Reform'd	45 Do		Pa:	238

[verso f.357] Shancoe

N.B. Every man named in the following tables is to be understood to have a wife except where Wr Denotes Widower.

NOTES

1. Lease from Edward Crofton to William Fitzgerald the land of Aghnasorn. 1 April 1735 (N.L.I., Crofton Papers MS 8828(8)).

2. The townland of Smutterna, measured for the 1851 census consisted of 363a 0r 6p. In the eighteenth century it had 28a 5r 0p of arable and pasture land and the rest was classed as waste (*General Alphabetical Index*; N.L.I., Lord Lorton Estate lease books, MS 3105).

SHANCOUGH, COUNTY SLIGO

INTRODUCTION: *The parish is in the barony of Tirerrill, 9 miles north by east from Boyle, on the borders of co. Leitrim. The parish covered 5,441acres, and the land was thought to be good, though much of it was mountain and bog. There was much limestone, and iron ore was thought to exist in the mountains.[1] The occupations of those living in the parish were entirely agricultural, and there were no gentry.*

The parish of Shancough was held with those of Boyle, Kilbryan, Kilmactranny, Aghanagh, Kilmacallan, Tawnagh and Drumcolumb from 1666. The incumbent in 1749 was the Rev. Robert Phipps (see Boyle).

OCCUPATIONS

Beggar	4	Farmer	35	Servants, household	50
Cottier	2	Herd	1	Labourer	23
Cowboy	3				

Com~Sligoe Parish of	Place of Abode	Names and Religion	Proffession	Children under 14		Children above 14		Men Servts		Women Servts	
				Prot.	Paps.	Prot.	Paps.	Prot.	Paps.	Prot.	Paps.
[f.357] Shancoe	Garvogue	Lough: Brehn Pa:	farmr							2	1
		Lau. Connilan Pa	farmr		4						
		Alex. Valentine Pa	Labourer		2						
		Ow. Mulkerran Pa	Labr.		2						
		Mary Mathew ww Pa	beggar								
	Cabragh2	Mich. Mullany Pa	Farmr		3		1				1
		Pat. Mullanny Pa	labr.								
		Hugh Conilan Pa	labr.		2						
		Pat. Connilan Pa	labr.		5		1				
		Logh. Conilan Pa	labr.		4						
		Mich. Kerin Pa	farmr				2				
		Phelim Waters Pa	labr.						1		
	Shancoe	Miles Higgins Pa	farmr		3						1
		Jn. Ternan Pa	farmr		1				1		
		Jn. Horoghy Pa	labr.								
		Jn. Waters Pa	labr.								
		Ch. Long Pa	labr.								
		Pat. Fallon Pa	farmr		1						1
	Ballintruffy	Jas. O'Bryan Pa	farmr		3		2				1
		Robt. Booley Pa	labr.		1		2		1		1
		Patt. Gouly Pa	farmr		3		1				
		Cormuck Lavin Pa	farmr		1				1		
		Bryn. Quigly Pa	labr.		2						1
		Honr. McGrevy widw Pa	begar		2						
		Jon. Horisk Pa	farmr		1		2				1
		Bryan McGrah Pa	farmr				1		2		1
		Phillip McGuir Pa	farmr		2				1		
		Thos. Milligin Pa	labr.		1						1
		Edmond Canahan Pa	Cowboy						1		
	Knockagaher	Hugh Brenon Pa	labr.				2			1	
		Patt. Phillips Pa	Cottr.		5		1				1,
		Jon. Rankin Pa	Labr.				3		1		
		Lodiwick Smith Pro	Farmr	3		1					1,
		Ter. Cauly Pa	Herd		2		1				
		Jon Fillpott Prott	farmr			1				1,	
		Patt. Murphy Pa	farmr		3		1				
		Bryn. McDrue Pa	Labr.		1						1,
		Mary Grourk widw. Pa	begar		2						
		Robt. Armstrong	Pro farmr	3		1			1		1
		Darby Coony Pa	Labr.		2		1				
		Thady Mullany Labr.					2				
		6 - 74		6	58	3	23		12	2	14

Shancoe

N.B. Every man named in the
following tables is to be understood
to have a wife except where Wr
Denotes Widower

Com~Sligoe / Parish of	Place of Abode	Names and Religion	Proffession	Children under 14		Children above 14		Men Servts		Women Servts	
				Prot.	Paps.	Prot.	Paps.	Prot.	Paps.	Prot.	Paps.
[f.358] Shanquogh	Glaikagh	Peter Horan Pa	farmr		2		1		1		1
		Georg ffarra Pa	farmr								1
		Niclass Duffy Pa	Labr.		3				1		
		Elinor Dowdle Pa	Widw.		2		1				
		Jon. Barry Pro	farmr	3		1					1
		Redmond Burk Pa	Labr.		1						1
		Patt. Sleaveen Pa	farmr		3				1		
		Deniss O Fagin Pa	Cowboy		5		2				1
	Drumlish	Bryan McGuir Pa	farmr		1				1		1
		Robt. Paterson Pro	farmr	3		2			1		1
		Patt. Foord Pa	farmr		2						
		Rogr. Foord Pa	farmr				2		1		
		Andrew Egg Pa	Labr.				4				1
		Jon. Coan Pa	farmr		5		2		1		
		Bryan Bircen Pa	Cowboy		6		1				
	Keaulgaru	Ben Green Prott	farmr			3			1		1
		Deniss Fagan Pa	begar		3		1				
		Jon. Roonian Pa	farmr				3				1
		Jon. Rusel Pa	Labr.		6		2				1
		Faril Doud Pa	Labr.				1				
		James Mophitt Pa	farmr		1				1		
	Qurafad	Peter Milligin Pa	Labr.		3		1				
		Manuss Hiens Pa	farmr		1						1
		Morgon Farill Pa	farmr		3				1		1
		Jon. Murray widw. Pa	Cottr.		2		1				1
		Patt. Murray Pa	farmr		4		1				1
	Mullaughkirk	Jon. Cox Pa	farmr		1						
		Robt. Hix Prott	farmr	3		1					1
		Jon. Lederdeal Pro:	farmr	1		1			1		1
		8 - 46		10	54	8	23		11		18

[verso]

Shaquogh

NOTES

1. Lewis, 'Shancoe or Shancough'.

2. Thirty five acres of ' very compact farm [the south east] is very fertile and well adapted for fattening cows). It was let in 1746 for three lives (N.L.I., MS 2786).

AGHANAGH, COUNTY SLIGO

INTRODUCTION: *Aghanagh is in the barony of Tirrerill. It covers 8,838 statute acres, stretching up the west coast of Lough Arrow.[1] It is bounded to the south by the range of the Curlew mountains and to the west by the Bricklieve mountains.*

The physical geography of the parish consists of mountain and bog, with quarries of marble-like limestone which was 'much used for building',[2] hence no doubt the presence of a mason. The other occupations were almost entirely agricultural, with farmers, herdsmen, shepherds and labourers predominating.

From 1666 the parishes of Boyle, Kilbryan, Shancough, Kilmactranny, Kilmacallan, Tawnagh and Drumcolumb were held together. The incumbent in 1749 was the Rev. Robert Phipps, who had been appointed in 1732 (see Boyle). The patron was the bishop.

OCCUPATIONS

Broguemaker	1	Herd	7	Shepherd	5
Cooper	1	Labourer	65	Smith	1
Cottier	19	Mason	1	Surgeon	1
Cowboy	1	Miller	1	Tailor	2
Cowherd	1	Servant	1	Widow	1
Doctor	1	Servant, household	72	Wigmaker	1
Farmer	18				

Com~Sligoe Parish of Aughana	Place of Abode	Names and Religion	Proffession	Children under 14 Prot.	Paps.	Children above 14 Prot.	Paps.	Men Servts Prot.	Paps.	Women Servts Prot.	Paps.
[f.359] Aughana	~~Holybrook~~	~~Coln. John Foliot Pr~~									
	holybrook	Coln John Foliot[3] pt						3	2	1	1
		James Griffiths prot	out servt	1							
		Robt. Duke prot	farmr.	5				1			1
	Coraducy	George Gaison prot	Labour.	2							
		Bryn. Folan papist	Labour.		2						
		Peter Mulany pap	farmr.		3						1
		Mich. Madn. papist	farmr.		1						
		Thady Noon pap	farmr.								1
		Thady Mcdermott pap	farmr.		1						
		Conr. Mulany pap	farmr.		1		1				
		Jas. Cullac pap	herd				1				
		Bridget Cuncky widow pap									
		Robt. Brenon prot	farmr.							1	
		Patt. Lavin pap	farmr.		4						1
		Patt. Sheradan pap	farmr.		1						
		ffrances Sheradon pap									
		John Lavin pap	Labour.								
		Margret McPhadn. widw.									
	Caricknahoran	Patt. Phey pap	herd		1		4				
		Thady McCormk pap	herd				2				
		Bryn. Madn. papt	herd		2						
		Rogr. McDermotro pap	sheperd		3				1		
		ffrancis Lyons pap	sheperd						4		1
		Mary Heraughty pap widw			4						
	Bunadolan	James Coleman papt	farmr.		3						
		Donel McGinane papt	farmr.		1						
		Anthony Mulany papt	farmr.		2						1
		Loughln Healy papt	farmr.								1
		Dudly McDermotro papt	farmr.		2						
		John Brennan papt	herd		1						
	Balymulan	Jerm. Duignan[4] pap	Doct in Phisk		1				3		3
		John Keviny pap	Labour.		2						
		Micl. Lang pap	Labour.		1						
		Rogr. Keviny pap	Labour.		2						
	Lecarow	Willm Hogg pap	herd		4						1
		Peter. Partlan pap	Tealor		4		2				
	Coolalongfal	Bryn. Kecey pap	Coter		2				1		
		Winy Quel papt	widw		4						
		Mathw. Ruttledge pap	Coter		1						
		Charles Nicholson pa	Coter		2						
		Murtaugh Spaln pa	Coter		1						
				9	51	8	56	10	4	11	13
[f.360] Aughana	Oughtanboy	John Ganly pap	Coter								
		Hugh Ganly pap	Coter		1						
		Darby Ganly pap	Coter		1						
		John Kilolan pap	Coter		1						1
		Barth.Ganly pap	Labour.		2						

Com~Sligoe / Parish of	Place of Abode	Names and Religion	Proffession	Children under 14		Children above 14		Men Servts		Women Servts	
				Prot.	Paps.	Prot.	Paps.	Prot.	Paps.	Prot.	Paps.
	Cartron	Edmond Morphy pap	Labour.								
		Peter Phaighn pap	Labour.		1						1
		Patt. Quinane pap	Labour.		1				1		
		Philip Lillias prot	farmr.	3					1		1
		Childly Forrest prot	farmr.	1		1					
		Patt McGarry pap	Labour.						1		1
	Balnafad	Robert Ruttledge pap	Labour.		1						
		Dudly McDermotro pap	Coter		2						
		Conr. McGarry pap	Tailor		1		2				
		Jean Norry widw. prot		1							
		Honr. Higins widw pap			2						
	Aughanaugh	Catrine Hogg wd. pap					3		1		
		Bryan Mulany pap	Labour.		1						
		Bridgt. Mullany Wd pap			2		4				
		Mary Brotter pap			2						
		John Moor papist	miller		2				1		
		Hugh Casey papist			1						
		Jas Killpick prot	Labour.		1				1		1
		Neal Higgins papt	Labour.		2		4				
		Francs. Lyance pap	herd								1
		Roger McDermottro	sheperd		2				1		
		Green Jacson prot	Labour.						1		1
	Killsheehre	Mary Mcgarry pa			4		2				
		Rogr. Mullany pap	Labour.		1						2
		Elizabeth Denoughr wd pa			4		2				
		Thad. Denoher pa	Labour.		1						1
		Peter Denoher pa	Labour.								
		John Reily pap	Labour.		1						1
		Margrett Hamilton pap wid			1				1		
		John Griffith prot	Labour.		3						
		Bryn. McGloughln pa	Mason						1		
		Patt. Greahan pap	Labour.		1						
		Micl. Welsh pap	Labour.								1
		Thos. Cromy pap	Labour.				1				
		Peter Morow pap	Labour.		2		2				
		Catrine Quin wd. pa			3						
				11	68	5	48	1	20	10	12
[f.361] Aughna	Cullsheahern	Willm. Cleary papist	Labour.		2						
		Thady Mullany pa	Cowboy								1
		Willm. Griffith prot	Labour.	1							
		Thos. Shanon pap	Labour.		3		1				
		Patt. Cleary papist	sheperd		2						
		Patt. Moriss papt	Labour.		2						
	Lillibrook	Ritchd. Lillies pro	farmr.					1	1	1	1
		ffrances Mehan pa	Labour.		2						
	Drumdony	Faril Gallahr pa	Labour.		1		1				
		Rogr. McDermotro pa	Labour.		1		1				
		Miles Candon pap	Labour.		1		2				
	Carrowkeel5	Bartholy Cromy pa	Labour.		1				1		

Com~Sligoe Parish of	Place of Abode	Names and Religion	Proffession	Children under 14 Prot.	Paps.	Children above 14 Prot.	Paps.	Men Servts Prot.	Paps.	Women Servts Prot.	Paps.
		Mary wid McDonaugh pa			2		2				
		Micl Kelly pap	Labour.		2						
		Martin Madn. pap	Labour.		2						
		Thos. Welch papist	Labour.								
		Catrine widw. Ganly pa			4						
		Martin Dinougher pap	Labour.		1						1
		Johnathon Speed prot	Labour.		4		1				
		Thos. Welch wid pa	Labour.		1						
		John Welch pap	Labour.				1				1
		James Welch pap La	bour.		5		1				
		Ann widw. Healy pa			1		1				
		Rogr. Gillgin papt	Labour.		1		1				1
		Bartholy Cromy pa	Labour.						1		
		Peter Healy papist	Labour.		2		1				
		Hugh Healy papist	Labour.		3						
		Jas. McSheen papist	Labour.		2		1				
	Cloughage	Edmond Rowlatt prot	Wiggmaker	2							
		Mathew Rowlett prot	farmr.			2		1			
		Pat. Rankin pap	Labour.			1					
		Thos. Morris widw. pa	Labour.			1					1
		Hugh Kelly papist	Labour.		3						
		Henry Wallis pa	Labour.		3						
		Gilbert Wallis prot	Labour.								
		Peter Glinn pap	Cowherd		3						
		Conn Gormley pap	Labour.								
		Micl. McGenane pap	Labour.								
		John Conor pap	Labour.		2						
		Moriss Shanon pa	Labour.		2						1
		Edmond Shann. wdr. pa	Labour.								
12 - 65				3	62	4	15	2	3	1	7
[f.362]	Cloughoge	John Lynch papist	Labour.		1						
		Mary widw Welch pa			1		2				
		Edmond Lynch pa	Labour.		1						
		Bridget widw. Fineran pa					1				
		Edmond Kilgan pa	Labour.		2						
		Henry Crofton pa	Smith		3				1		
	Aughanaugh	Patt. Welch papist	Brogemakr.		1						
		Charly Beley papist	Labour.		2		1				
		Will. Scanlan papist	Labour.		2		1				
		Danl. Lyons papist widwr.	Labour				2				
		Timothy Killoron pa	Labour.		2		1				
		John Brady papist	Cooper		1						
		John Conaughton pa	Labour.		1						1
		James Glymond pa	Surgon		3						1
	Trinescrabba	Jon. Lavin pa:	shepherd		4				1		
		29		24		8		1	1		2

1. Including 1,091 acres of Lough Arrow (*General Alphabetical Index*).

2. Lewis, 'Aughanagh'.

3. The ffolliotts were granted the estate, c 1659. At the time of the Census the house was still a castle. The child under 14 who appears in the Census is possibly Mary Folliot who married John Harloe. She inherited the estate and John Harloe demolished the castle in about 1756 and built the present house. John Folliot enlisted as a lieutenant in Major General Bowles's Regiment of Horse in 1709; he was promoted captain in 1714, major in Lord Cathcart's Regiment of Foot in 1729, and lieutenant-colonel in 1737. Made colonel in the 18th Regiment or Royal Irish Col Folliot's on 22 June 1743 and took command 23 December 1747 (N.A., P.R.O., WO64/10/15; WO 64/9/172); 'Hollybrook', Bence-Jones, *Guide*, p. 154).

4. Jeremiah Duignan (or Duigenan) of Balymulan, Aghanagh was used, with varying success, by Charles O'Conor in the treatment of his son Denis. The will of Jerome O'Duigenan of Ballymullany, Sligo was proved in 1769 (*Letters of Charles O'Conor*, pp 43, 50; N.L.I., Index to Diocesan Wills, Elphin, mic. p.1727).

5. Owned by the King family (N.L.I., MS 3105).

KILMACALLAN, COUNTY SLIGO

INTRODUCTION: *Kilmacallan is in the barony of Tirerrill, 5 miles south-east of Collooney. It covers 9,928 statute acres.[1] The land was said to be 'wet and spongy', set chiefly to tillage.[2] There was a fair at Castlebaldwin four times a year.[3]*

The parish of Kilmacallan was in part owned by members of the MacDonnogh family in the early seventeenth-century. There were a number of McDonoghs in the parish in 1749.[4]

The parish was held with that of Boyle, Kilbryan, Shancough, Kilmactranny, Aghanagh, Tawnagh and Drumcolumb from 1666. The incumbent in 1749 was the Rev. Robert Phipps who held it from 1745 (see Boyle). The patron was the bishop.

OCCUPATIONS

Beggar	5	Gardener	1	Servants, household	138
Broguemaker	1	Hatter	2	Sexton	1
Clerk	1	Herd	2	Shoemaker	1
Cooper	1	Innkeeper	1	Smith	3
Cottier	3	Labourer	138	Tailor	4
Cowboy	1	Merchant	1	Tanner	1
Esquire	1	Miller	2	Weaver	2
Farmer	69	Pedlar	1	Wigmaker	1
Friar	1				

Com~Sligo Parish of	Place of Abode	Names and Religion	Proffession	Children under 14		Children above 14		Men Servts		Women Servts	
				Prot.	Paps.	Prot.	Paps.	Prot.	Paps.	Prot.	Paps.
~~Kilmacalane~~ [f.363] Kilmacalane	Castlbaldwin	Hugh Dougan prot	Sexton	4		2					
		Domnick Dolan	shewmaker		3						
		Thos. Leland protest	Hatter								1
		Micl. Leland prot	Hatter			1					
		Willm. Cregg prot	miller	4		3			1		
		John Ternan prot	wigmaker								
		Bryn Hign papist	herd		4				1		1
		ffrancis Garmily pa	labr.		2						
		John Horaughty pa	labr.								
		Jas. Conr. Widr: pap	labr.		1		1				
		Loughlin Rennosl pa	farmr.						3		2
		Danl. McMurrin pa	labr.		3						1
		Elizbeth Young pa					1				
		Ritchd. Welch prot	labr.								
		Patt. Killgarn pa	Smiths								1
		Bryan Brehon pa	talor						1		
		John furbank prot	labr.			2				1	
		Bryan Heraughty pa	labr.		2		3				
		John Healy pa	labr.		3		2				
		Peter Hanly pa	labr.				2				
		George. Renalls pa	labr.								3
	Ballinvernun	Patt. Welch pa	labr.		1		1				
		Willm. Keaviny prot	labr.				3				
		Rev'd George Weir prot	clerk	3		1			4		
		Patt. McDermot prot	farmr.	1							1
	Slieveagh	Chas Nicholson pro	farmr.	4					2		2
		Michl. Mctims pa	Taylor						2		1
		John Summers pa	labr.		3						
		Manus Killgen pa	labr.		1				1		
		Richard Hawkins pa	labr.		1						
		Jean Berward pa					3				
	Ballyrush	Jon Connell pa	labr.		3						
		Mark Keane pa	labr.		3		3				
		Jon. Killhuly pa	labr.		2						
	Heapstown	Robt. Killpick prot	in ceepr.	2		1			1		
		Chars. Phey pa	labr.		1						
		Willm. Gaffiny pa	labr.		3		1				
		faraugh Maddin pa	labr.		2		1				
		Micl. Edian pa	labr.		1						1
		Dudly McDonaugh pa	mercht.		2				2		1
		Edmond Brennon pa	Labr.		5						1
60 shoud be 54		22 60		18	46	10	21		18	1	16
[verso] KillmcCollon Parish [f.364] Killmcalon	Heapstown	Willm. McDonaugh pa	Labr.		1						
		Mary Finneen pa			3						
		Martin Carty pa	Labr.		2						

Com~Sligo / Parish of	Place of Abode	Names and Religion	Proffession	Children under 14 Prot.	Children under 14 Paps.	Children above 14 Prot.	Children above 14 Paps.	Men Servts Prot.	Men Servts Paps.	Women Servts Prot.	Women Servts Paps.
		Owen Carty pa	Labr.				4				
		Chas. O'Hara pa	Labr.		3						
		Micl. Conily pa	Tealor						2		
		Thady Mcdonagh pa	Labr.		1						
		John Caril pa	Labr.		2						
		Conr. Flinn pa	Labr.		3		3				
		Owen Coningham pa	Labr.		1		1				
		Bryan Coningham pa	Labr.		4		1				
		Patt. flinn pa	Labr.		2						
	Anaugh	Danl. Gray pa	farmr.				2				1
		Thady Higgns pa	Labr.				1				
		Martin Coan pa	Labr.				1			1	
	Doon Sheheen	Patt. Kerin prot	farmr.								
		John Kerin pa	Labr.		5				1		
		James Kerin pa	Labr.		5						
		Darby Tahany pa	Labr.		2						
		John Banahan pa	Labr.		2						
	Carrownagelty	Edward Cleary pa	Labr.						1		1
		Loughlin Carty pa	Labr.		3		1				
		John Garvin pa	farmr.		1				1		1
	Drumaclull	~~Henry~~Ed. McGuir pa	Labr.		1		2				
		Rogr. Milligan pa	Labr.		1		2				
		Danl. Cauly pa	Labr.				2				
		Jas. McGolrick	Labr.				3				
	Drumlaughn	frances Irwin Pro	farmr.	2					1		1
		Michl Houereen pa	Labr.		2						
		Roger Golrick pa	Labr.								
		Edmond Callery pa	Labr.		2		1				
		phelim Callery pa	Labr.		2		1				
		Patt. Burk pap	Labr.		3						1
	Doonguillah	Jas. Donogher pa	Labr		1						
		Patt Donogher pa	farmr.		3						1
		Patt. ffrench pa	farmr				2		1		1
		Catrine widw. Conilan pa									
		Hugh Brehon pa	Labr.								
		Owen Brehon pa	Labr		6						
		Ed: Conilan pa	Labr		3						
		Mathew Brehon pa	Labr		3						
79 shou'd be 76 for all are supposed to be married except those yt. have ww. affixed		6[?] 79		2	67		47		7	1	7
[f.365] Killmcolon	Corlesheen	Michl Keown pa	Labr.		1						
	foxhill	Patt. Nangle pa	Labr.		1						1
		Jas. Nangle pa	Labr.								
	Carrowreah	Terance Cally pa	Labr.		2		1				
		Edmund Comisky pa	Labr.		1		3				
		Deniss Cally pa	Labr.		1		4				
		Terance Tilin pa	Labr.		4						
		Mathew Quinane pa	Labr.		2		2				

Com~Sligo Parish of	Place of Abode	Names and Religion	Proffession	Children under 14 Prot.	Paps.	Children above 14 Prot.	Paps.	Men Servts Prot.	Paps.	Women Servts Prot.	Paps.
		Patt. Camisky pa	Labr.		1						
		Thos Grevy pa	Labr.		1						
		John Tige pa	Brogmakr.		1		1				
		Ed. Doyle pa	Labr.								
		Catrine widw. Doyle pa							1		
	Ardaugh	Jas. Dodd prot	farmr.			4		1	3		6
		Willm Lawson prot	Labr.	2		4					
		Danl Healy pa	Labr.		4		1				
		Jas. Conor pa	Labr.		4						
		Jas Kerin pa	Labr.		4						
		John McCauley pa	Labr.		4						
		Thady Quinane pa	Labr.		1						
		Rob. Moor prot	Labr.								
		John Moor prot	Taner			1̶			1		1
		Patt Cally pa	Labr.		4						
		Chas. Dier pa	Labr.		2		1				
		Luke Kerin pa	Labr.		1						
		Darby Conor pa	Labr.		1						
		Jas. Conon pa	Labr.		3						
		Thady Killerne pa	Labr.		1						
		Darby Hart pa	Labr.		2						
		Hugh Golrick pa	Labr.		1						
	Ballinascark	Jon. Tige pa	Labr.		2						
		Jean widw. prot		1		1					
		William East prot	Labr.	3	0	2					
		James Haniway									
		Terance Callery pa	Labr.		4						
		Chas. fflinn pa	Smith		3						
		Thady fflin pa	Labr.		1						
		Dominick Brehn pa	Labr.		2						
		Domnik Brennan pa									
		Moriss Sheeghan pa									
		Micl. Hoy pa	Labr.		1						
76 for 71 this Error is evident from ye no of Columns		Paul Grennan pa	miller		1						
		11 76		6	61	12	13	1	5		8
[verso] Kilmacallane parish											
[f.366] Kilmacalane	Ballinscarra	Paul Grinan pa	labr.								
		Martin Grinan pa	labr.		2						
		Logh Quin pa	weavr.		3						
	Rosses	Patt. Doodican pa	farmr.				1				2
		Andw. Doodican pa	farmr.		5						1
		P. Connooghan pa	friar						1		1
		Ow. Banaghan pa	farmr.		4				1		
		Den. Conooghan pa	labr.								
		Fran. Long pa	farmr.				4				
		Wm. Fury pa	farmr.		1				1		1
		Jas. Nangle pa	farmr.				2				1
		Paul Lynsk pa	farmr.		3		2				
		Jn. Tigue pa	labr.		1						

Com~Sligo Parish of	Place of Abode	Names and Religion	Proffession	Children under 14		Children above 14		Men Servts		Women Servts	
				Prot.	Paps.	Prot.	Paps.	Prot.	Paps.	Prot.	Paps.
		Jn. Fineran pa	labr.		2						
		Bry. Nangle pa	labr.								
		Wm. Dowd pa	labr.		2						
		Jas. O'Hara pa	labr.								
		Mary Coghlan ww pa	Cottier		1						
		Godfrey Long pa	farmr.		2						
		Jas. Allen pa pa	labr.								
	Tonnagh	Brabry Finn pa	Pedlar		4				1		1
		Mich. Finn pa	labr.								
		Ow. Keerigan pa	farmr.						1		
		Patt. Brennan pa	farmr.								2
		Jn. McHugh pa	labr.		3						
		Wm. Finane pa	farmr.		1						1
		Andw. Donoghoo prot	farmr.	2							
		Richd. Donoghoo prot	farmr.	1		2					
		Ch. Brennan pa	labr.								
	Cloghfin⁵	Andw. Mulvanny pa	labr.								
		Mark Neelany pa	labr.								
		Eliz. Maxwell ww. prot	farmr.	3					1		
		Ann Maxwell ww. prot	farmr.			2					
		Geo. Maxwell prot	Smith								
		Hugh Connilan pa	farmr.		3				2		1
		Patt. Mulvany pa	farmr.		3						1
		Patt. Flin pa	farmr.		2				1		1
		Mary Connor w. pa	beggar		1						
		Giles Ledan widw. pa	farmr.		2		1				
		Den. Carril pa	farmr.				2				
		10 63		**6**	**45**	**4**	**12**		**9**		**13**
[f.367] Kilmacalane	Baladerouth	Luke Devitt widr. prot	farmr.			2			1		1
		ffarrel Finn pa	labr.								1
		Maud Cran widw. pa	farmr.				3				
		Conr. Cran pa	farmr.		3						
		Mich. Hoey pa	farmr.		3						
		Edmd. Finn pa	farmr.		2						
		Petr. Finn pa	farmr.		1						
		Jn. Higgins wr. pa	farmr.				2				
		Pat. Connilan pa	labr.		1						
		Js. Higgins pa	labr.		4						
		Jn. Walsh pa	labr.		2		2				
		Pat. McHugh pa	farmr.		2		2				
		Tha. Higgins pa	labr.		1						
		Bry. Lynsk pa	farmr.		2		3				
		Barth Lynsk pa	labr.				2				
		Rogr. McCormick pa	labr.		1						
		Sarah McCormick wdw. pa	farmr.		2		3				
		Jn. Walsh pa	farmr.		1						
		Ter. Kerin pa	labr.								
	Knockroe	Thos. Collis prot	farmr.			3			2		1
		Pat. Tigue pa	farmr.		1						

Com~Sligo Parish of	Place of Abode	Names and Religion	Proffession	Children under 14 Prot.	Children under 14 Paps.	Children above 14 Prot.	Children above 14 Paps.	Men Servts Prot.	Men Servts Paps.	Women Servts Prot.	Women Servts Paps.
		Dom. Greevy pa	farmr.								
		Rogr. O'Hara pa	farmr.		2		2				
		Bry. Conilan pa	farmr.		2						
		Tha. Matimo pa	farmr.				3				
		Ow. Egan pa	farmr.								1
		Th. McAuly pa	labr.		1		3				
		Roger Egan pa	farmr.		2				1		2
		Tha. Flyn pa	cowboy								
	Tanzyfort	Willm. Cooper prot	Esqr.			5		1	3	1	3
		Wm. Coghran prot	Gardinr.	2		2		1			
		Ed. Williams prot	labr.			1					1
		Sarah Hart pa	cottier				3				
		Bry. Quin pa	labr.		1						
		Patt. Meeghan pa	labr.		1						
		Conr. Meeghan pa	labr.		2						
		Mich. Meeghan pa	labr.		1						
	Lisbanagher	Luke Devanny pa	farmr.		3						
		Patt. Devanny pa	farmr.		1						
		Ter. Devany widr. pa	farmr.		4						
		Willm. Jones prot	farmr.	3						1	
		12 67		5	46	2	28	2	7	1	8
[f.368] Kilmacalane Killmacalane	Lisbanagher	Win Kane w. pa	Cottier		1						
		Peter Galda pa	labr.		1						1
	Caranspirawn	Jas. Middleton prot	farmr.					2		1	2
		Jn. Lawson prot	farmr.	3		1					
		Jn. Brislan pa	beggar		1						
		Jn. Scanlan pa	labr.								
		Th. Middleton prot	cooper	2							
		Andw. Brennan pa	labr.				2				
		Mary Lawson ww. prot	farmr.			3					
		Alexr. Irwin prot	farmr.				6		1	1	
		Gerard Irwin prot	farmr.	1		2		1	1		
		Thos. Kimmitt pa	labr.		3						
		El. Healy w pa	beggar								
	Knockanarrow	Patt. McDonagh pa	farmr.		5						1
		Pat. Connilan pa	farmr.		2						
		Pat. Hart widr. pa	farmr.				1		1		
		Pat. Brehon pa	farmr.				1				
		Bry. Mulvanny pa	farmr.		1		1				
		Js. Mulvanny pa	labr.								
		Richd. Hart pa	farmr.								
		Conr. Flyn pa	weaver								
		Mich. Kenny pa	farmr.		4		1				
		Ter. Mcdonogh pa	farmr.		3		3				
		Pat. Geelan pa	labr.		1						
		Simon Smith pa	labr.		3						
		Jn. Corkran pa	labr.								
		Bry. Mcdonagh pa	labr.								1
		Joan Giblan widw. pa	beggar								

Com~Sligo / Parish of	Place of Abode	Names and Religion	Proffession	Children under 14		Children above 14		Men Servts		Women Servts	
				Prot.	Paps.	Prot.	Paps.	Prot.	Paps.	Prot.	Paps.
	Lissicone	Sarah Folliott widw. prot	farmr.						2	3	1
		Jn. Candon pa	labr.		2						
		Mich. Candon pa	labr.				3				
		Jas. Walsh pa	labr.				1				1
	Cultilogh	Pat. Connor pa	herd		2		2				
		Jas. Connilan pa	labr.		3				1		
		Jn. Contilon pa	labr.		4						
		Wm. Connilan pa	labr.		2						
		Fra. Flyn pa	labr.		2						
		Darby Kilcleen pa	labr.		4						
		Mary Fox widw. pa	beggar								
		12 62		6	43	12	15	3	6	5	7
[f.369] Kilmacalane	Cleevery	Jn. Taylor prot	farmr.	1		3			1		2
		Miles Sheen pa	labr.		1						1
		Jn. Bradin pa	labr.				1				
		Jane Taylor prot	farmr.			1			1		
		Hugh McDruy pa	labr.		2						
		Tha. Carty wr. pa	labr.								
		Ow. Keeltaghan pa	labr.		2	1					
		Pat. Healy pa	labr.				2				
		3 11		1	5	4	4		2		3

[verso f.369] Kilmacalane

NOTES

1. Less 244 acres of Lough Arrow and various small loughs (*General Alphabetical Index*).

2. Lewis, 'Kilmacallane or Kilmacallen'.

3. James M'Parlan, *Statistical Survey of the County of Sligo* (Dublin 1802), pp 27-8. (Henceforth M'Parlan, *Statistical Survey*).

4. Dudley McDonaugh merchant, William and Thady McDonaugh, labourers of Heapstown. Patt, Terence and Bryan McDonagh farmers of Knockanarrow (W.G., Wood-Martin, *History of Sligo* (3 vols, (Dublin, 1889), ii, 165 (henceforth Wood-Martin, *Sligo*); Census, ff 363, 364, 368).

5. Townland owned by the Coopers of Markree. It consisted of arable and moory and rushy pasture land (N.L.I., Survey of lands owned by the Rt. Hon Joshua Cooper, 1788, MS 21 F 2/58).

TAWNAGH, COUNTY SLIGO

INTRODUCTION: *The parish of Tawnagh in the barony of Tirerrell is 9 miles north west from Boyle, on the road to Sligo. It is situated on the river Unshion which flows out of Lough Arrow. Lewis said it had a good deep soil and a small quantity of bog.[1] It covers 3,234 statute acres.[2]*

The parish was united with that of Kilmacallan after 1641, and was held with Boyle, Kilbryan, Shancough, Kilmactranny, Aghanagh, and Drumcolumb from 1666. The incumbent from 1745 was the Rev. Robert Phipps (see Boyle).

OCCUPATIONS

Ale seller	1	Farmer	20	Maltster	1
Beggar	6	Gentleman	2	Plowman	3
Broguemaker	2	Herd	3	Servants, household	48
				Shoemaker	1
Cottier	5	Labourer	41	Smith	1

Com~Sligoe / Parish of	Place of Abode	Names and Religion	Proffession	Children under 14		Children above 14		Men Servts		Women Servts	
				Prot.	Paps.	Prot.	Paps.	Prot.	Paps.	Prot.	Paps.
[f.370]Taunagh	Cams	Margt. Dodd widw. pro	farmr.			1		2			3
		Terence Donnel pa	labr.								
		Logh. Brehon prot	plowman	2					1		
		Laur. Bireen pa	labr.		1				1		1
		Rob. Connolly pa	labr.		4		1		1		
		Ths. Long pa	labr.		1						
	Ardlee	Wm. Chambers pa	farmr.		1				1		
		Pat. McAuly pa	farmr.		1		1		1		
		Denis Laydon pa	farmr.		1						
		Margt. McDruhy ww. pa	beggar								
		Fran. McDruhy widw. pa	labr.				1				
		Dom. Mcgarry pa	farmr.		2						
		John Fallon pa	labr.								
		Edmd. Connolly pa	farmr.		1						1
		Jas. McDonogh pa	farmr.				1				1
		Mich. Comisky pa	farmr.		2						1
		Ow. Birreen pa	farmr.		3		1				
		Jn. Guane pa	labr.		1		1				
		Connr. Corkran pa	farmr.		3		1				1
		Owen Flin pa	Smith		1						
		Tha. Scanlan pa	labr.		2				1		
		Jon. Scanlan pa	labr.		1						
		Margt. Barret ww. pa	cottier		1						
		Matt. Barret pa	labr.								
		Patt. Kerin pa	labr.		2						
		Cath. Kilcleen ww. pa	beggar								
		Jn.Killooly pa	labr.		3						
		Barth. Guane wr. pa	labr.				1				
		Petr. Guane pa	labr.		4						
	Emlagh	Jas. Nangle pa	farmr.						1		1
		Ow. Caleary pa	farmr.				1				
		Jn. Ternan widr. pa	labr.				1				
		Jn. McGarry pa	labr.		2						
		Patt. Tawny pa	labr.								
		Margt. Birreen widw pa	beggar								
		Patt. Caleary pa	labr.		3						
		Tha. McAuly pa	farmr.		3		1				
		May Tawny widw. pa	cottier		1						
		Martin Feeny pa	brogue mr.		3						
	Carneha	Ricd. Phibbs widr. prot	Gent	3		4		4	2		4
		Jn. Scanlan pa	plowman								
4 - 68		5 - 69		5	45	5	11	4	9		13
[f.371]Taunagh	Carneha	Manus Brady pa	labr.								
		Felim Brennan pa	labr.		2						
		Danl. McLowny pa	labr.				1				
		Peter Gilmor pa	maltster		1						
		Bryan McDonogh pa	Cottier				1				
	Carrowkeel	Hugh Cone pa	herd		3				1		1
		Thos. Gibbon prot	labr.	5		1				1	

Com~Sligoe / Parish of	Place of Abode	Names and Religion	Proffession	Children under 14		Children above 14		Men Servts		Women Servts	
				Prot.	Paps.	Prot.	Paps.	Prot.	Paps.	Prot.	Paps.
		Edmd. Rowlett prot	aleseller	4		2					
		El. Rowlatt ww. prot	farmr.			1			2		
	Behy	Jas. Dorcan pa	shoemr.		3				1		1
		Cha. Duke prot	farmr.						2		1
		Patt. Long pa	labr.		1		2				
		Pat. Gilmor pa	labr.		4						
		Wm. Boyce prot	herd	3							
		Laur. Bolton pa	labr.								
	Oagham	Alexr. Middleton pa	labr.		4		2				
		Miles Coyle pa	farmr.		2						
		Wm. Connel widr. pa	farmr.				2				
		Edmd. Lavin pa	labr.		1		1				
		Jn. Davey pa	farmr.				1				
		Farrel Guinan pa	labr.		1						
		Patt. Feeny pa	Brogmr.		1						
		Bryn. Guinane pa	labr.		2						
		Jas. Gilmr. pa	labr.								
		Laur. Gilmor pa	labr.		1						
		Jas. Dyer pa	labr.				3				
		Mart. O'Hara pa	cottier		2						
		Laur. McDonogh pa	farmr.				1				1
		Matt. Lavin wr. pa					1				
		Own. Feeny pa	labr.		2						
		Jon. Tawny pa	labr.		4						
	Whitehill	Morgan White prot	Gent				2		2	1	1
		Hugh Banahan pa	plowmn		3		2				1
		Fra. Kerin pa	labr.		4						
		Cormick Kelly pa	labr.		3						1
		Dor. O'Neil widw prot	cottier	2		2					
		Patt. Calery pa	labr.				2				
		Ow. Healy pa	labr.		2		2		1		
		Murtagh Kerin pa	labr.		3		2				
12 - 61		11 63		14	49	7	23		9	2	7
Taunagh	Cloonimeen-eghane	Jn. Farrel widr prot	farmr.			1			1		
		Hu. Higgins pa	labr.		3						
		Bridg. Higgins w pa	beggar				1				
		Jn. Devanny pa	labr.				1				
	Munnila	Phil Grehin pa	herd		2						
		Honr. Birreen wid. pa	beggar		1						
		Mary Gowry wid. pa	beggar		1	1	2		1		
shoud be 1–10		1 12			7	2	4		2		

[verso] Taunagh

NOTES

1. Lewis, 'Taunagh'.

2. Including 15 acres of Loughymeenaghan (*General Alphabetical Index*).

KILLADOON, COUNTY SLIGO

INTRODUCTION: *Killadoon is on Lough Arrow, 7½ miles north-north-west of Boyle. The parish covered 6,364 statute acres, the majority of which was wet, spongy land, a large quantity of bog and some limestone.*[1]

In the fifteenth-century, the family of Macdonogh, lords of Corran and Tererril founded a convent in the parish; two members of the family, a shepherd and a labourer, were in the parish in 1749.[2]

The incumbent in 1749 is not known. By the nineteenth-century the parish was held with that of Kilmctranny. The rectory was impropriate.

OCCUPATIONS

Beggar	1	Labourer	91	Smith	1
Cripple	1	Miller	1	Tealer	1
Farmer	2	Servants, household	45	Weaver	2
Herd	5	Shepherd	3		

Com~Sligoe Parish of	Place of Abode	Names and Religion	Proffession	Children under 14 Prot.	Paps.	Children above 14 Prot.	Paps.	Men Servts Prot.	Paps.	Women Servts Prot.	Paps.
[f.373] Killidoon	Killidoon	Jas Conilan papist	Labour.		2						
		Domnick Conilan pa	Labour.						1		
		Loughlin Conilan pa	Labour.								
		John Conilan pa	Labour.		1						1
		Jas. Mophitt pa	weaver		5		1		2		2
		John Murrin pa	Labour.		2						
		Owen Cranah pa	Labr.								
	Cornamukala	Patt. Higin pa	Labr.		2						
		Micl. Killernah pa	Labr.		1		1				
		Patt. Laughna pa	Labr.		1						
	Barnadarah	Owen Gaffiny pa	Labr.				1				
		Patt. Coan pa	Labr.		2						
		Owen McDonaugh pa	Labr.				2				
		John Coan pa	Labr.		4						
	Barroe	John King prot	Labr.	5	2	2					
		Peter Conilan pa	Labr.		2						1
		Lareman Simon pa	Labr.						1		1
		Henry Dier pa	Labr.		1		1				
		Luke Killcleen pa	Labr.		1		1				
		Bryn. Parlon pa	Labr.		3		1				
	Moor	Micl. Keny pa	Labr.		1						
		Paul Heney pa	Labr.								1
		Willm. Noon pa	Labr.			1					
		Murtaugh Heny pa	Labr.						1		1
	Kingsburoh	Jas. Brehon pa	Labr.						1		2
	Lahardon	Peter Deir pa	Labr.		4		1				
	Caroclauan	Jas. Crafort pro	Labr.	1							
		John Knox pro	Labr.	1							
		John Atchison pro	Labr.					1		1	
		Alexandr. Knocks pro	Labr.	1							
		Willm. Allinnan pa	Labr.		1						
		Bryn Varny pa	Labr.				1				
	Carromore	John Ormsby pro	Labr.	3							
		Martin Higgins pa	Labr.								1
		Patt. Kelly pa	herd		1		2				
		Patt. Carrane pa	herd		3						
		Willm. McDonaugh pa	sheperd		2						
		Patt. Hargadon pa	herd		2		1				
		Martin Conneel pa	Labr.								
		Luke Lavin pa	sheperd		3						
		Danl. McCormuck pa	Labr.		2						
		12 - 70		11	46	2	16	1	6	1	10
[f.374] Killadoon	Balraughbo	Rogr. Killerna pa	Labr.				2				
		John. Killerna pa	Labr.				1				
		Patt. Conaughton pa	Labr.		1						
		Danl. Kilerna pa	Labr.								1
		Ed. Mcanalta pa	Labr.								
		Mary Conaughrevy pa	criple								

Com~Sligoe Parish of	Place of Abode	Names and Religion	Proffession	Children under 14		Children above 14		Men Servts		Women Servts	
				Prot.	Paps.	Prot.	Paps.	Prot.	Paps.	Prot.	Paps.
		Catrine widw. Clery pa					1				
		Murthaugh Nangle pa	Labr.		1						
		John Hart pa	Labr.		2		1				
		Micl. Morphy pa	Labr.								
		Laughlin Heraghty pa	Labr.								
		Conor Looby pa	Labr.								
		Willm. Reany pa	beggr.								
		Roger McGuan pa	Labr.				1				
		Chas. Leadon pa	Labr.								
		Patt. Horan pa	Labr.		1						
		Ballioly Kerin pa	Labr.								
		Jas. Higgins pa	Labr.								1
	Runatruhan	Patt. Flinn pa	smith		1						1
		Denis. Heany pa	Labr.		2						
		Roger McDermotro pa	farmr.								1
		Domnik Tinneen pa	Labr.		2		1				1
		Ambrose Lavin pa	Labr.		1		2				
		Laurance Banaha pa	Labr.								
		Bryn. Nangle pa	Labr.								
		Bryn. Higgins pa	Labr.								
		Jon. Noon pa	Labr.								
		Thos. Noon pa	Labr.								
	Tully	Honr. widw: Conor pa									
	Cornamukolah	John Costilo pa	herd		3						
		Andrew Long pa	Labr.		1		2				
		Mich. Killerna pa	Labr.		2		1				
		Patt. Higgins pa	Labr.		4						
	Corlasheen	Owen Carty pa	Labr.								
		John Blaik prot	Labr.	2		2					
		John Cryn pa	Labr.		1						
		Mark Conilan pa	Labr.		1						
		Redmond Rork pa	Labr.		4						
		Ed. Rork pa	Labr.								
		Murthaugh Conilan pa	Labr.		4						
		Domnick Long pa	Labr.		1				1		1
No of Pa. 78. as there are 2 single women		2 - 80		2	32	2	12		1		6
[f.375] Killadoon	Carrowna-dargny	Jas. Carrane pa	herd		2		2				
		Eliz.wid. Healy pa					2				1
	Umercroe	Patt. ffarill pa	Labr.				4				
		Bartholy Muny prot	Labr.	1							
		Danl. McCormick pa	Labr.		2		1				
		Martin Luneen pa	Labr.		2						
		Patt. Healy pa	Labr.								
		Mary widw. Carran pa			1		1				
		Domnick Killeen pa	Labr.		3						
		Frances Mullany pa	Labr.		2		3				
		Bryn Mullany pa	Labr.								

Com~Sligoe Parish of	Place of Abode	Names and Religion	Proffession	Children under 14		Children above 14		Men Servts		Women Servts	
				Prot.	Paps.	Prot.	Paps.	Prot.	Paps.	Prot.	Paps.
		Bryan Rourk pa	Labr.								
		Darby Conilan pa	Labr.								
		Thos. Conilan pa	Labr.								
	Tapp	Thady Tyman pa	miller		2				1		1
		Laurance Cleary Labr.									
		Thady ffinitan pa	Labr.								1
		Patt. Higgins pa	Labr.		2						1
		Jas. Doodican pa	Labr.		5						1
		Hugh Galaugher pa	sheperd						4		1
	Knocadalton	Hugh Gallaher pa	Labr.		1						
		Conor Noon pa	Tealer		3				1		
		James Gallahr pa	Labr.				1				
		John Galaher pa	Labr.		2		1				
		Margret widw. Kealahan pa			1						
		Loughlin doodican pa	Labr.				1				1
		Cha. Gormly pa	weaver		1				2		1
		Jas. Conmy pa	Labr.		1						
		Hugh Gallaher pa	Labr.		1						
		Sarrah widw. Gallahr pa					1				
		Danl. Kavenah pa	Labr.		1		1				
		ffrancis Conmy pa	Farmer		1		5		1		3
shoud be 2 -58		2 - 61		1	33		23		9		11

[verso]Killidoon parish

NOTES

1. Lewis, 'Killadoon'.

2. Ibid; Census, f. 373.

DRUMCOLUMB, COUNTY SLIGO

INTRODUCTION: *The parish of Drumcolumb is 10 miles from Boyle, on the road to Sligo. It covered 4,528 statute acres, including 2,822 detached portions and 17 acres of water.[1] Lewis believed that the soil was generally good, but there was much marsh and bog.[2]*

The incumbent was the Rev. Robert Phipps, who lived in the parish at Cooper's Hill. He held the parish with those of Boyle, Kilbryan, Shancough, Kilmactranny, Aghanagh, Kilmacallan and Tawnagh (see Boyle). The patron was the bishop.

OCCUPATIONS

Aleseller	3	Farmer	64	Peddler	1
Basketmaker	1	Gentleman	1	Schoolmaster	1
Beggar	6	Herd	8	Servants, household	94
Broguemaker	1	Labourer	50	Shepherd	1
Carpenter	2	Mason	1	Smith	1
Cleric	1	Merchant	1	Tailor	1
Cottier	5	Miller	2	Weaver	2
Cowboy	1				

Com~Sligoe Parish of	Place of Abode	Names and Religion	Proffession	Children under 14 Prot.	Paps.	Children above 14 Prot.	Paps.	Men Servts Prot.	Paps.	Women Servts Prot.	Paps.
Drumcolumb [f.376]	Coopers Hill[3]	Robt. Phibbs prot	Clerk	7				1	1	2	2
		Paul McCormick prot	par. Clerk	4		5					1
		Wm. Allen prot:	labourer	2					1		1
		Dan. Teigue pa:	labourer	6							
		Jas. Banaghan pa:	labr.						1		1
		Conr. Greevy pap:	labr.								
		Bry. Milligan pa:	Labr.		1		4				
	Knocbreeni[4]	Wm Morris McCormick prot	Labr.		3		1				
		Danl. Mcnalo pa	Labr.								
		ffrancis Bern pa	Labr.		2						
		Eliz. Lynsk pap:	Labr.								
		Bartholy Mulkerin pa	Labr.		4						
		John Mulkerin pap	Labr.		2						
	Cullidion	Deniss Brehon pa	Labr.		3						
		Rogr. McAneelany pa	Labr.		1		3				
		Patt. Mcaneelany pa	Labr.		1						1
	Glanacaka	Jas. Doalan pap	Labr.		2						
		Jas. Coan papist	Labr.								
		Patt. Healy pap	Labr.		2						
	Drumcollam	Jas. Mallin protest	Herd		2						1
		Mathew Gillmer pa	Labr.		1						
	Aughoo	Laranus Bryan pa	Herd		2						
	Coolboy	Mark Mattimoe pa	farmer						1		2
		Barth. Kilcleen pa	farmer		1						
		James Mattimoe pa	farmer		2				1		
		Patt. Dowd pap	Herd		3						
		Jn. Murray widr pa	farmer		2		1				
		Mary Calery widw pa	Beggar								
		Jas. Burke widr pa	Labr.				1				
		Pat. McGuane pa	farmer		1						
		Laur. Mattimoe pa	farmer		3						
		Laughlin Mattimoe pa	farmer				1				
		Patt. Mattimoe pa	farmer				2				
		Maurice Mattimoe pa	farmer				1				
		Thady Lavin pa	farmer				2				
		Hugh Connilan pa	farmer		1						
		Hugh Brennan pa	farmer								1
		Mich. Brennan pa	farmer								2
		Mich. Brennan pa	farmer		3		1				
		Hon. Kilcleen widw pa	beggar		2		1				
	8 - 68			15	50	5	18	1	5	2	12
[f.377] Drumcollumb	Brickliffe	Wm. Dyer papist	farmer				4				1
		Hugh Gara pap	farmer		4			1			
		James Dyer pa	farmer				4				1
		Patt. McBryan pa	farmer		3		1				
		David Walsh pa	farmer		1						
		Patt. Mattimoe pa	farmer				5				
		Jas. McDonogh pa	farmer		1						1
		Jn. Sheerin pa	labourer								

Com~Sligoe Parish of	Place of Abode	Names and Religion	Proffession	Children under 14		Children above 14		Men Servts		Women Servts	
				Prot.	Paps.	Prot.	Paps.	Prot.	Paps.	Prot.	Paps.
		Patt. Paul pa	farmer						1		1
		Bridget Mcdonogh w. pa	beggar		1						
		Thady Keltighan pa	farmer				1		4		3
		Farrel McDonogh pa	labourer				3				
		Win. McDonogh ww. pa	farmer				1				2
		Mich. Keeltighan pa	labourer								
		Jas. McGuane pap	labourer		1		1				
	Coolskeagh	Paul Brett pa	farmer						1		1
		Luke Quilea pa	Herd				1				
		John Quilea pa	labourer		2						
		Barth. Horan pa	labourer								1
	Castle Douglass	John Johnston prot.	farmer	5		4				1	
		Jn. Buchanan prot	farmer	2		1		1			
		Wm. Taylor prot:	Weaver	2							1
		John. Johnston prot:	farmer	2							1
		Geo. Buchanan pr:	farmer	4							
		Jn. Anderson prot:	farmer	2							1
		Tim. McHugh pa	farmer		2						
		Jn. Connolly pa	labourer								
		Miles Sheridan pap	farmer		3				1		
		Dan. Finane pap	labourer.		1						
		Cath. Quigly widw. pa	Beggar		1						
		Cath. Guigheen pa	farmer		1						1
		Ths. Dyer papist	labourer		1						
		Mich. Higgin pap	labourer		3						
	Ardcomber[5]	Thos. Christian prot:	ale seller		1				1		
		Patt. Christian prot:	Carpentr		2						
		Ch. Phibbs prot:	farmer		3		1		1		1
		Hugh Hart pa	farmer			2		3			1
		Jn. Ternan pap	labourer		1		1				
		Cath. Golding widw pa	farmer				2				1
	Knockraver	Thady Horan pa	Carpenter		4		4				
		Wm. Johnston prot	farmer	1		3			1		1
shoud be 20 59		22 - 58		24	32	9	31	2	10	1	18
[verso] Drumcollum Parish											
[f.378]	Knockraver	Barth. McDonogh pa	farmer		1						
Drumcolumb		Humphrey Keeler pro	farmer	4							1
		Jn. Clarke prot	farmer	1							
		Mary McKimur prot	farmer	3		3					
		Dom. Nylan pa	Mason				6		1		1
		Jas. Madden pa	farmer				1		1		1
		Jn. Williams prot	Labr.			3					
		Peter Tigue pa	Labr.								1
	Trinemac- murtagh	Patt. Lavin pa	Shepherd		4				1		
		Jn. Mccormick pa	Labr.		2						1
	Kiltilogh	Jn. Banaghan pa	herd		3		1				1
		Patt. Connor pa	Labr.		2		2				
		Jas. Connilan pa	Labr.		3				1		
		Jn. Connilan pa	Labr.		4						

Com~Sligoe Parish of	Place of Abode	Names and Religion	Proffession	Children under 14		Children above 14		Men Servts		Women Servts	
				Prot.	Paps.	Prot.	Paps.	Prot.	Paps.	Prot.	Paps.
	Lisconney	Wm. Connilan pa	farmer		2			1			1
		Darby Kilcleen pa	aleseller		4						
		John Mortimer pr	Gent					1		1	
		Thos. Leviston pro	parish schoolmasr.	1		2					
	Coolback	Patt. Bolan pap	herd		1						
		Roger Waters wir. pa	Labr.		2		3				
		Pat. Mulleena pa:	miller[6]		4		2				
		Th. Bolan papist	Labr.						1		
		Jn. Carrol pa:	Pedlar		1						
		Laugh. Mccormick	Labr.		1						
		Ch. McHugh pa	Labr.		1						1
		Neal Gallagher pa	Labr.		1						
		Barth. Hoorisk pa	Smith				1				1
		Jas. Brennan pa	Labr.								1
		Bryan Mcdonogh pa	miller		3				1		1
		Wm. McHugh pa	farmer				1				
		Peter Lynch pa	aleseller		2		1				
		Thos. Lynch pa	Labr.		3						
		Owen Nangle wr. pa							1		
		Matt. Anderson pro	farmer	4		2			1		1
		Jn. Morrison prot	farmer			4					
		Js. Logheed prot	farmer	3		4					
		Owen Hart pap	Herd		3		1				
		Hon. Hart widw. pa	Cottier				1				
		Dan. Greaghan pa	Cottier		2						
		Bridgt. Gibbon ww. pa	Cottier		1						
		Thady Groghan pa	herd		4		1		1		
		17——61		16	55	18	21	1	10	1	12
[f.379] Drumcollum	Toomelidane	J. McShanley pa	Taylor		1				1		1
		Lau. McAuly pa	farmer		2		1				
		Jn. McHugh pa	Basket-maker		1						
		Bry. McSteen pa	farmr		4		1				
		Wm. McAuly pa	farmer		2		2				
		Luke McAuly pa	farmer		2						
		Mich. McAuly pa	Labourr.								
		Owen Long pa	farmer		4		1				
		Jn. Kinane pa	Labr.								
		Bridgt. Kearin ww. pa	farmer				2				
		Darby McAuly pa	farmer		2		1				
		Tho. Carabry pa	farmer		2		1				
		Jas Geehin pap	weaver		2				1		
		Farrel McAuly pa	Labr.		2		2				
		Farrel Gallagher pa	Labr.		2						
		Tho. McAuly pap:	farmer		2				1		
		Margt. Kerin widw. pa	Beggar								
		Patt. Kerin pap:	brogue-maker		2						1

Com~Sligoe / Parish of	Place of Abode	Names and Religion	Proffession	Children under 14		Children above 14		Men Servts		Women Servts	
				Prot.	Paps.	Prot.	Paps.	Prot.	Paps.	Prot.	Paps.
	Rusheen[7]	Cath. Kerin widw. pa	beggar		3						
		Henry Carter pro	farmer			1			3		1
		Bry. Goologh pa	Labr.		3						
		Pat. Dyer pap:	Labr.		3						
		Mary Nilany ww. pa	cottier				1				
		Carbry Healy widr. pa	cowboy		2		2				
		Bridt.Killooly widw. pa	cottier				2				
		Ths. Boyd widr. pro:	farmer	2		1					
		Geo. Buchanan pro	farmr			2			1		
		Geo Collis prot:	farmr	6					2		2
		Jn. Carter prot:	farmr	3					2		2
		Owen Banaghan pa	Labr.		2						
		Jn. Lee protesta:	farmr	1		1					
		Thos. Lee protes:	farmr	2					1		
		Ralph Lee pro:	farmr	1					11		7
shoud be 15		17 ———— 44		15	43	5	16		23		14

[verso] Drumcollum parish

NOTES

1. *General Alphabetical Index.*

2. Lewis, 'Drumcolumb'.

3. Cooper's Hill was owned by the Coopers of Markree, Co. Sligo. (This branch of the Cooper family later took the name of O'Hara). A large part of it was arable and pasture 'good for tillage meadow or fattening'. There was also 'mangled bog... good for turff and when the turff is cutt off it will make meadow by reclaiming' (N.L.I., MS 21 F 2/12).

4. The townlands of Knockbrinagher, Bricklee, Coolskeagh, Cashelduglass, Knockraver, Tryan McMuray, Killilogh, Lisconney and Coolbrack were leased in the mid-eighteenth century by the Cooper family to the O'Haras (N.L.I., MS 20,397).

5. The townland of Ardcomer consisted of 104 acres of arable pasture and bog, owned by the King family of Boyle (N.L.I., MS 3105).

6. The Stafford Survey had a 'good corn mill and tuck mill' at Lisconny (J. McTernan, *In Sligo Long Ago* (Sligo, 1998) p.352 (henceforth McTernan, *In Sligo*).

7. Rusheen was owned by the Cooper family of Markree, Co. Sligo. The land was arable and pasture, 'good for tillage or fattening light cows', some of it was bog and moorland which could be reclaimed with limestone gravel and draining and 'claying'. Some of the bog was 'very mangled' and good for turf only (N.L.I., Survey of lands owned by the Rt. Hon Joshua Cooper 1788. MS 21 F 2/9).

BALLYNAKILL, COUNTY SLIGO

INTRODUCTION: *The detached part of the parish of Ballynakill in the barony of Tirerrill was about 40 miles from the section in County Galway and County Roscommon, and 9 miles south-east from Sligo on the road to Ballyfarnon. Lewis says that in the County Sligo section the land was good, with a large extent of bog and limestone.*

The Church of Ireland inhabitants of the parish attended the church of Ballysumaghan. The incumbent was the Rev. John Holmes, who held the parish with that of Ballysumaghan, County Sligo from 1729 (see Ballynakill, County Galway/County Roscommon). It is not known where he lived. The patron was the bishop. The living was impropriate in the Earl of Ranelagh.

OCCUPATIONS

Beggar	4	Farmer	25	Priest	1
Cottier	7	Herd	6	Servants, household	52
Cowboy	2	Labourer	8		
Distiller	1	Miller	1	Tinker	1

Com~Sligoe Parish of	Place of Abode	Names and Religion	Proffession	Children under 14 Prot.	Paps.	Children above 14 Prot.	Paps.	Men Servts Prot.	Paps.	Women Servts Prot.	Paps.
[f.380] Ballynakill	Carrowkeel	Archd.Walker pro									
		Ter.Ternan pa	farmr.		1						
		Jn McDonogh pa	labr.								
		Jon. Campbell pro	Tinker						1		1
		Ben Whitesides pro	farmr.	3		1					
		Arthr. Whitesides pro	farmr.	1		2					
		Wm. Whitesides pro	farmr.	1							1
		Ja. McDonogh pa	farmr.		3						
		Jn. Allen pa	labr.		3						
		Bry. McGan pa	herd		2						
	Soohy	Martin Long pa	farmr.		1				1		1
		Mary widw. Long pa	Cotr.				1				
		Bridgt. widw. Long pa	begar				1				
		Willm. Farsuny pa	farmr.		2						
		Thady Farsuny pa	farmr.		2						
		Willm. Conily pa	farmr.		1						
		Mary widw. Conily pa	Cotr.								
		Jon. Knephin pa	herd		2						
	Coola	Jan. Tonrah pa	farmr.		1						
		Margrett widw McGary	begar								
		Philip North pa	farmr.		2		1				
		Conr. Fursany pa	farmr.		2						
		Thady mcCormick pa	farmr.		3		1				
		Jas. Carrill pa	farmr.		1		1				
		Tho. Boyd prot.	farmr.	2							
	Cloonaugh	Micl. Murphy pa	farmr.		2						
		Bridgt. Murphy pa	begar		1						
	Canalough	Gillbert McCloaghry pro	farmr.	3					3	1	
		Edwd. Willson pro	distiller	3		1					
		Patt. Hartt pa	herd		3						1
		Mary Brenn. Widw. pa	begar		2						
	Drumadralane	Patt. Cleary pa	herd		3						1
		Patt. Cooney pa	Cotr.		2		1				1
	Glen[1]	Roger Gouan pa	farmr.		3		2		1		
		Patt. Gouan pa	farmr.		2		1				1
		Deniss Burk pa	farmr.		3		2		1		
		phelim Cox pa	farmr.		1		3				1
		Bryan Keney	farmr.		4		1		1		
	Carrick	John Drue pa	herd		3		1		1		1
		Owen McCard pa	labr.		3						1
		Patt. Carty pa	labr.		2		2		1		
		16–60		13	59	6	18		9	2	18
[f.381] Ballynakill	Rockbrook	Willm. Phibbs[2] prott	farmr.	3		3		3	4	2	6
		Bryan Dauan pa	miller[3]		3				1		
		Patt. Killoran pa	Cowboy		2		2				1
		Mathew McCaw pa	labr.		2						1
	Cultidion	Rogr. Concelany pa	Cowboy		1		1				
		Catrine Concelany pa widw.	Cotr.		3		1				
	Ballinakill	Henry Burriss prot	farmr.	4		1			2	1	

Com~Sligoe Parish of	Place of Abode	Names and Religion	Proffession	Children under 14		Children above 14		Men Servts		Women Servts	
				Prot.	Paps.	Prot.	Paps.	Prot.	Paps.	Prot.	Paps.
	Knockbranah	Jon. Guerd pa	herd		1		3				1
		Danl. Nalty pa	Cotr.				2				
		Patt. Cally pa	Cotr.		1				1		
		Bartholy Mulkeran pa	farmr.		2		2				
	Mullaughmore	Hugh McTahany pa	farmr.		4		1		1	1	1
		Bryan Duffy pa	Cotr.		2		2		1		
	Rossmore	Deniss Foley pa	labr.		1				2		1
		Jas. Phegny papt	Priest								
		Ja. Boyd prot	labr.			2					
	Clooneen[4]	Jon. Kely pa	labr.		3		1				1
		8———26		7	25	6	15		12	3	12
		The above No shoud be 6									

NOTES

1. Townland owned by the King family (N.L.I., Map 16 F 9)

2. William Phibbs married Mary Harloe, daughter of John Harloe of Rathmullen, County Donegal. They had 21 children (*Alumni Dubliniensis*).

3. The Strafford Survey noted that there was a 'small Irish mill' at Rockbrook (McTernan, *In Sligo*, p.352).

4. Townland belonging to the Wynne estate. Consisted of arable and pasture, 95s 2r 10p 'good for tillage and fattening'and 'mangled turff bog, 52a 2r 36p, good for turff only' (N.L.I., MS 750/26).

KILMACTRANNY, COUNTY SLIGO

INTRODUCTION: *Kilmactranny is in the barony of Tirerrill, 6 miles north of Boyle. The parish covers 13,447 statute acres.[1] The soil was said to be 'light', but limestone was abundant, and there was iron ore and coal was found in the Geevagh mountains.[2]*

The parish of Kilmactranny was held with those of Aghanagh and Boyle from 1666. The incumbent in 1749 was the Rev. Robert Phipps, who had been collated in 1732 (see Boyle). The patron was the bishop.

OCCUPATIONS

Beggar	5	Herd	1	Priest	1
Broguemaker	2	Labourer	161	Schoolmaster	1
				Servants, household	90
Cooper	2	Merchant	1	Smith	1
Farmer	34	Peddler	1	Weaver	3

Com~Sligoe Parish of	Place of Abode	Names and Religion	Proffession	Children under 14		Children above 14		Men Servts		Women Servts	
				Prot.	Paps.	Prot.	Paps.	Prot.	Paps.	Prot.	Paps.
[f.382] Killmctranny	Caricknagruss	Alis wd. Mullan pa	labr.				1				
		Elinor wd. Mullany pa					1				1
		Bryn. McDonagh pa					3				
		Loughlin Flinn pa	labr.								
		Owen Conlian pa	labr.								
		Owen Conbane pa	labr.		1				1		2
		Mathw. Gaffiny pa	labr.		2						
		Manuss Conbane pa	labr.								
		Patt. Mullany pa	labr.		1						
		Hugh Conbane pa	labr.								
		Catrine wd. Gloughlin pa									
	Carginboye	Thos Noon papist	Labr.								
		John Phelan pa	labr.								
		Hugh Rork prot	farmr.	4					1		2
		Conr. Quinane pa	labr.		1						
		Andris Conilan pa	labr.		1						
	Creevaugh	Owen Lavin pa	labr.				1				
		Thos. Lavin pa	labr.								
		Cormuck Lavin pa	labr.		2						1
		Patt. Sheerin pa	labr.								
		Catrine Lavin pa									1
		Owen Lavin pa	labr.		1						1
		Thos. Lavin pa	labr.		1						
		Thos Conilan pa	labr.		2						
	Culoughtra	Robt. Lougna pa	farmr.		3						1
		Thos. Martin prot									1
		Thos. Martin prot.	farmr.						1		1
		Patt. McDonaugh pa	labr.		3						1
		Henry McDermott pa	labr.		1						
		Keadaugh McDonah pa	labr.		2						
		John McDonough pa	labr.		1						
		Peter Crannah pa	labr.		2						
		Owen Mcdonough pa	labr.		2						
		Willm. McDonough pa	labr.		2						
		Peter McDermott pa	labr.				2				
		Patt. Mcdonough pa	Scoolmasr.		1						
	Muterre	Peter Conilan pa	labr.		1						
		Thos. Conilan pa	labr.								
		Chas. Mullany pa	labr.		2		1				
		Derby Conilan pa	labr.		1						
		Mary Conilan pa									
	6 - 73	6 - 76		4	33		9		3		12
[f.383]	Muterre	Peter Conilan pa	farmr.				1		1		1
	Drumore	Thady Leadon pa	labr.		1						
		John Conaton pa	labr.		1						
		Patt. Healy pa	labr.		1						1
		Patt. Conilan pa	labr.								
		Hugh Conilan pa	labr.								
		Luke Noon pa	labr.		3						

Com~Sligoe / Parish of	Place of Abode	Names and Religion	Proffession	Children under 14		Children above 14		Men Servts		Women Servts	
				Prot.	Paps.	Prot.	Paps.	Prot.	Paps.	Prot.	Paps.
	Maherlack	Bartholy Gaffiny pa	labr.		1						
		Murhaugh Creen pa	labr.				1				
		Thos. Simon pa	labr.		3		1				1
		Patt.fFoord pa	labr.								
		Bryn. Conilan pa	weaver				1				
	Sraduff	Bryn Leadn pa	labr.								
		Loughlin Mcdonough pa	labr.		1						
		John Clery pa	labr.		1						
		Thady Mclahn pa	labr.		1						1
		Deness Clery pa	labr.								
		Terance McManuss pa	labr.								
		Deniss fflin pa	labr.		1						
		Pat. Mccormik pa	labr.						1		
		John McGauron pa	labr.		2						
		Thos. Malimo pa	labr.		3						
		Chars. Fflin pa	labr.								
		Thos. Early pa	labr.		2						
		Petr. Conor pa	labr.						1		1
		Chas Connor pa	labr.		1						
		Micl. Connor pa	labr.		2				1		1
		Sarah widw. Connor pa					1				
		Hugh Mullany pa	labr.		3		1				
		Chas. Mullany pa	labr.		1		2				
		Eneis Curraran pa	Brogmakr.								
	Tullinuer	Conor McManuss pa	labr.		3		1		1		1
		Sarrah widw. McManuss pa			2		1				
		Martin McAnelta pa	weavr.		1						
		Mary O' Brennan pa	labr.		1						
		Mary widw. Conaughten pa				2					
		Chas. Gallaugher pa	farmr.		1		2		1		1
		Owen mcmanuss pa	Herd								
		Deniss Long pa	labr.		1						
		Hana widw. Davy pa			1		1				
		Willm. Gallaughr pa	farmr.		2				1		2
78 as there are 4 widows		82			40		15		7		10
[f.384] Killmctranny	Anaughloy	Peter McCormick pa	Labourr.		2						
		Jas. Buttler pa	labr.				1				
		John Killgarv pa	labr.		4		2		1		
		Jas. ffinaran pa	labr.		1						
		Robt. Waugh pa	labr.				2				
		John Hartt prot.	farmr.								2
		Robt. Buttler pa	labr.		1						
		Richd. murrin pa	labr.		2						
		Micl. murrin pa	labr.								2
		Patt. Buttler pa	labr.		1						
	Ballinlegg³	Terance Kelly pa	labr.		2		2				
		John Bern pa	labr.		2						1
		Micl. Mullany pa	labr.		2						
		Thady Mulany pa	labr.				1				

Com~Sligoe Parish of	Place of Abode	Names and Religion	Proffession	Children under 14		Children above 14		Men Servts		Women Servts	
				Prot.	Paps.	Prot.	Paps.	Prot.	Paps.	Prot.	Paps.
		Luke Conor pa	labr.		1		3				
		Terance Mullany pa	labr.								
		Micl. Kelly pa	Brogemak.						1		1
	Anaughguan Ballinlegg	Jas: Conilan pa	labr		2				1		1
		Micl Hall pa	labr		3		2				
		Chas. McDermott pa	labr.		3		2				
		Bryn. McDermott pa	labr.		1		1				
		Jas. Vallinline pa	labr.		3		1				
	Ballinary	Rogr. Quinane pa	labr.		5						
		Patt. Quinane pa	labr.		5						
		Edmond Quinane pa	labr.		5						
		Margret wd. ffaril pa					1				
	Ballinlegg	Mich. Hall papist	labr.		3		2				
	Derelea	Nichols Hartt prot	farmr.			3			1		1
		Patt. Rolle pa	labr.				2				
	Drumsoughla	Meriteth Thom prot	farmr.	3					2	1	1
		John Keraughly pa	labr.		2		1				
		Domnick Conilan pa	labr.		1						
	Aurigna	John Thomson pro	farmr.	2					1		1
		Artr Brown pro	labr.								1
		Patt McAnegy pa	labr.		3		1				
		Patt. McDonough pa	labr.				3				
		Jas. McManuss pa	labr.								1
		Charly Nangel pa	labr.				3				
		Magdeln. w. Belir prot			3						
	Killkear	Thos. Keraughty pa	labr.		1						
		Hugh Mulvihill pa	labr.		1						
11——69		10———70		5	56	6	30		7	1	12
[f.385] Kilmctranny	Killkear	W. McMaster prot	farmr.	2		3			1		1
		Hugh McMaster prot	labr.	1							
		Jas. Ruttledge prot	labr.								
		Rogr. McDonaugh pa	labr.		1						
		Mary wd. McManus pa									
Killmctranny	Cloughveenah	Patt. Healy pa	labr.				1				
		Darby McDonaugh pa	labr.		3		1				
		Bartholy Cureen pa	labr.				2				
		Micl. Killaghan pa	labr.		2						
		Bridgt. wd. McDermott pa									
		Terance McManuss pa	Pedlar								
		Chas. Brenon pa	Merc		2				1		1
		Patt. McDermott pa	labr.								
		Bridgt. wd. Mullany pa			1		1				
		Chas. fflinn pa	Smith		2		1				
	Clystukee	Jas. Langdon pa	labr.		1						1
		Bryn. Quinane pa	labr.		1						
		Willm. fflinn pa	labr.		1						
		Bridgt. wd. Forlan pa									
		Edmond McDermott pa	labr.						1		
		Thos. Reaney pa	labr.								

Com~Sligoe Parish of	Place of Abode	Names and Religion	Proffession	Children under 14 Prot.	Children under 14 Paps.	Children above 14 Prot.	Children above 14 Paps.	Men Servts Prot.	Men Servts Paps.	Women Servts Prot.	Women Servts Paps.
	Knockmore	James Conaughton pa	labr.						1		1
		Henry McGouglan pa	labr.		1						1
		Bridgt. Fanane wd. pa			3						1
		Edmond McGloughlin pa	labr.		2						1
		Peter Killykoole pa	labr.								
		J. Coony pa	labr.		3						
		Cha Conilan pa	labr.		1						1
	Doreenashee	Patt Coony pa	labr.								
		Chas. McManus pa	labr.		1						
		Foran McManus pa	labr.								
		Patt. Moran pa	labr.		3		1				
		Hugh McManuss pa	labr.								
		Murthough Horisk pa	labr.				2				
	Caricknagrass	Patt. Healy pa	labr.		2						
		Owen Conlian pa	labr.								
		Jas. McCormack pa	labr.		1						
		Morgan Gaffiny pa	labr.		1						
		Bartholy Noon pa	labr.								
		Chas fflinn pa	labr.		1						1
		Micl. Conbane pa	labr.		1						1
6——72 it could be but 76		6——79		3	34	3	9		4		9
[f.386] Kilmactrany	Ballinculline	Pat. Connilan pa	farmr.		2						
		Js. Brennan pa	farmr.						1		1
		Cath. McDruy w: pa	farmr.				2				1
		Loghn. Connilan pa	farmr.						1		
		Bry. Connilan pa	farmr.		1		1		1		
		Conn. Connilan pa	labr.								
		Cath. Finane ww. pa	begr								
	Coolmoorna	Bry. Connilan pa	farmr.		2						1
		Bry. Keana pa	farmr.		3		2				
		Dom. McManus pa	farmr.		2						1
		Wm. Keane pa	labr.		3		5				
		J. Murray pa	labr.		3						1
		Ter. Mullany pa	farmr.		3						1
		Edwd. Conbane pa	farmr.		2						
		Pat. Keana pa	farmr.		2						
		Mary Sweeny pa	farmr.		2						
	Killamoy	Bridt. McDonogh w: pa	begr								
		Tim McHugh pa	farmr.		1		2		1		1
		Wm. Tigue pa	farmr.		2						1
		Marg. Mcdonagh w:	beggar								
		Pat. Trinon pa	Cooper						1		1
		Ch. Loghna pa	labr.		1		1				2
		Hon. Loghlin w: pa	beggar		3						
		Jn. Cassedy pa	labr.		1						
		Mary Kerin wd. pa						2			
		Ow. McLan pa	labr.		1		1				
		Michl.Longan pa	labr.								
		Lau: Duffy pa	labr.		1						

Com~Sligoe Parish of	Place of Abode	Names and Religion	Proffession	Children under 14 Prot.	Paps.	Children above 14 Prot.	Paps.	Men Servts Prot.	Paps.	Women Servts Prot.	Paps.
		Nich. Green pa	labr.								
		Fran. Brennan pa	labr.								
		Patt.Flin pa	labr.		2				1		
		Hu. Vanummy pa	labr.		1		1				
		Pet. McHugh pa	labr.		3						
		Miles Higgins pa	labr.		1						
		Tha. Cullane pa	labr.		1						
		Ambr. McDonogh pa	labr.								
		Bry. Mcneal pa	labr.		2						
		Mich. Redican pa	labr.		2						
		Michl. Higgins pa	labr.		1						
		Pat. McDermot pa	labr.		1						1
		Th. Lavin pa	labr.		2		1				
76 as there are 6 wds 82					51		17		6		12
[f.387] Killmctranny	Killanoy	John Keir pa	labr.								
		Mary Flanagan pa	beggar				2				
		J. Ledan pa	labr.		3						
		Rog. McManis pa	labr.		1						
		J. Mcdonagh pa	labr.		4						
		Fran. Dowd pa	labr.								
	Ballinashee	Bry. Connilan pa	farmr.		1		1				
		Martn. Ultugh pa	farmr.		1						
		Laur. Noon pa	labr.		1						
		Darby Noon pa	labr.								
		Jn. McCormick pa	farmr.		1						
		Js. Moverigh pa	farmr.		2						
		Js Connilan pa	farmr.		1		1				
		Th. Healy pa	labr.				1				
		Darby Conoghan pa	labr.		2						
		Far. Connilan pa	farmr.		2						
		Anw Gafney pa	weavr.								
		Anw Connilon pa	labr.								
	Straduff- mountain	J. Gordon pa	Cooper								2
		Ths. Taylor pa	farmr.		3		1				
		Js. Kerin pa	labr.		2						
		Dau Horan pa	labr.		3						
		Pet. Doodican pa	labr.								
		Petr. Conr[4] pa	Priest						1		1
		Wm. Conr pa	farmr.		2						1
		Mic. Conr pa	farmr.		3				1		
		Conr McManus pa				2					1
		54			34		6		2		5

[verso] Kilmactranny

NOTES

1. Less 1781 acres of Lough Arrow and smaller loughs (*General Alphabetical Index*).

2. Lewis, 'Kilmactrany'.

3. A townland owned by the King family (N.L.I., Maps of the estate of Sir Gilbert King MS 16 F 9).

4. Peter O'Connor was the parish priest of Kilmctranny. He was a supporter of the Rev. William (alias Augustine) O'Kelly, prior of St. Mary's, Roscommon in 1748 to succeed Patrick French as bishop of Elphin (Fenning 'Diocese of Elphin', p.166).

KILROSS, COUNTY SLIGO

INTRODUCTION: *The parish of Kilross is in the barony of Tirerrill, 2¹/₂ miles east of Collooney. It covers 3,932 statute acres.*[1] *There was an 'abundance of limestone'.*[2]

The name of the incumbent of Kilross is not known.

OCCUPATIONS

Ale seller	1	Farmer	48	Saddler	1
Beggar	13	Herd	8	Servants, household	67
				Smith	1
Broguemaker	2	Labourer	33	Tailor	1
Cottier	3	Quack	1	Weaver	4

Com~Sligoe Parish of	Place of Abode	Names and Religion	Proffession	Children under 14		Children above 14		Men Servts		Women Servts	
				Prot.	Paps.	Prot.	Paps.	Prot.	Paps.	Prot.	Paps.
[f.388]Killross	Tullymore[3]	John Armstrong prot	farmr.	3		2			4		3
		Jane Armstrong ww. pro	farmr.	1		2					
		Jas. Chapman pro	farmr.	1		1			1		
		Patt. Neelany pa	labr.				2				
		Wm. Honegon pa	labr.		1		1				
		Thos. Keellanghan pa	farmr.		1		1				
	Tullybeg	Wm. Hart pa	farmr.		1						1
		Dav. McHenry pa	farmr.		2				1		
		Win. Mchenry ww. pa	beggar								
	Cartron	Thos. McConboy prot	weaver	2		3			1		
		Jas. Kenney pa	labr.		2						
	Ballygrana	Timo. Grey pa	herd		2						
		Mat. McHenry pa	labr.		1						
	Ballygawly	Owen Ultagh pa	Quack				3				1
		Jn. Fury pa	labr.								
		Walter Carter pro	farmr.	2					1		
		Jn. Logheed pro	farmr.						1		
		Jn. Taylor pro	farmr.	3						1	
		Thos. Taylor pro	farmr.								1
		Wm. Kilcleen pa	farmr.		3						2
		Thos. Carty pa	labr.		4						
		Maur. Davy pa	labr.		2		1				1
		Hugh Davy widr. pa	herd						1		
		Nich. Quin pa	weaver		2		2				
		Rogr. Carbry pa	farmr.		2		2				
		Dom. Wemny pa	Brogue- maker		3						
		Jas. Kilguir pa	farmr.		4						
		Cormick Kilgir pa	farmr.		1						
		Cath. Devanny pa	farmr.				2				
		Ter. Devanny pa	farmr.		1		1				
		Bry. Lenany pa	labr.				2				
		Bry. Hart pa	labr.		4						
		Mich. Caleary wr. pa	labr.				1				
		Jn. Wemny pa	labr.								
		Mary Connel ww. pa	beggar		2						
	Knockatober	Jas MacNiff pa	herd		3						
		Laur. Fallon pa	labr.		2						
		Alice Oats widw. pa	beggar								
	Kilross	Jas. Healy pa	herd		3		1				
		Thady Flin pa	Smith		2						
		Aug. Scanlan pa	labr.		2						1
15 - 61		16 - 62		12	52	8	17		10	1	10
[f.389]Kilross	Kilross	Oliv. Farrel pro:	ale seller						1	1	
		Richd. Nicholson pa	herd	2		1					1
	Douray	Wm. Christian pro	farmr.			4					
		Ch. Bryardun pa	farmr.		3				1		2
		Jn. Kenny pa	farmr.		2						
		Ter. Bartly pa	farmr.		2				1		1

Com~Sligoe Parish of	Place of Abode	Names and Religion	Proffession	Children under 14 Prot.	Paps.	Children above 14 Prot.	Paps.	Men Servts Prot.	Paps.	Women Servts Prot.	Paps.
		Owen Flin pa	labr.		2						
		Patt. Glin pa	labr.								1
		Alice Flin ww. pa	beggar								
		Jas. Casey pa	farmr.				3				
		Cath. Casey widw. pa:	beggar								
		Mary Glin Widw. pa	farmr.		1		3				
		Mary Donelan ww. pa	farmr.		1		2				
		Bridgt. Conlane ww. pa	beggar								
	Caranduffy	And. Donoghy pro	farmr.	6					1	1	
		Ow. McHugh pa	herd		1		1				
		Jn. McAuly pa	labr.		4						
	Cartronduffy	Rob. Reed pro:	farmr.	3					2		2
		Geo. Reed pro:	Cottier								1
	Tullymoremead	Jas. Reed pro	farmr.	5		2			3		2
		Thos. Sullivan pa	labr.								
		Rob. Hinde pa	Saddler		1						
	Doonamurray	Fleming Phibbs pro	farmr.	4					2		2
		Jas. Cone pa	labr.								
		Mark Cone pa	labr.						1		1
		Mary Cone ww. pa	beggar								
		Thad. Quinane pa	labr.		1						1
		Jn. Johnston pa	labr.								
	Clooneenroe	Denis Mulvany pa	herd				3				1
		Thos. Tigue pa	labr.		1		4				1
	Arnisbrack	Jas. Napier pro:	farmr.	4					1		1
		Bryan Bern pa	farmr.		4						
		Deny. Brennan pa	farmr.		3		1				
		Jas. Kimmitt pa	farmr.		2				1		1
		Robt. Kimmitt pro	labr.								
		Ed. Kimmitt pa	farmr.		2						
		Thos. Kimmitt pa	labr.		3						
		Tho: Kimmitt pa	labr.		1						
		Eliz. Geelan ww. pa	beggar								
		Connr. Tigue pa	farmr.		2				1		
		Jn. Kimmitt pa	farmr.		3		1				
	20 - 55	20 - 58			24	38	7	18	15	2	18
[f.390]Killross	Arnisbrack	Ch. O'Connor pa	weaver		2		1				
		Jn. Quinane pa	Taylor								
		Jn. Phillips pa	labr.		1		1				
	Castledargan	Wm. Ormsby pro	farmr.					1			3
		Peter Bern pa	herd		1						
		Michl. Horoghy pa	labr.		4						
		Steph. Ormsby pro	farmr.			6			1		1
		Wm. Carthy pa	labr.				2				
		Hugh Carthy pa	labr.								
		Jn. Philips pa	labr.		1		1				
		Jn. Quinane pa	broguemaker								
		Marg. Timon pa	beggar								
		Ann Timon pa	beggar								

Com~Sligoe Parish of	Place of Abode	Names and Religion	Proffession	Children under 14		Children above 14		Men Servts		Women Servts	
				Prot.	Paps.	Prot.	Paps.	Prot.	Paps.	Prot.	Paps.
		Sam Lockart pro	farmr.	3							1
		Jas. Healy pa	farmr.		2						
		Alexr. Lockart pro	farmr.	2					1		1
		Jas. Lyndsey pro	farmr.								1
		Hump: Gilmer pro	farmr.	3							
		Alice Lockart ww. pro	beggar								
		Jas. Lockart prot	farmr.	2							
		Petr. Mulkeeran pa	farmr.		1		1				
		Edmd. Giraghty pa	labr.		1						
		Mary fflaharty w. pa	beggar								
		Jane Lockart wid: pro	beggar								
	Cloghbrack	Peter Harrison pa	farmr.		2		2				
		Jas. Dolan	farmr.		3						
		Own. Donoghoo pa	farmr.		1		2				
		Wind. Feeny widw. pa	farmr.		1		3				
		Bridgt. Coil widw. pa	farmr.								1
		Patt. Kelly pa	weaver								
	Legnenerunagh	Arth. Dogherty pa	Cottier								
		Jn. Kelly pa	Cottier		1						
		Joseph Reed prot	labr.	1							
		Patt. Russel pa	labr.								
		19 - 48 18 - 45		11	21	6	13	1	2		8

NOTES

1. Less 79 acres of water (*General Alphabetical Index*).

2. Lewis, 'Kilross or Kilrasse'.

3. Townland owned by the Coopers of Markree, Co. Sligo. Tullymore was said to be 'good arable for tillage, sheep or fattening light cowes'. Part was moory and sour but 'very reclaimable' with limestone gravel 'on the spot' (N.L.I., Survey of lands owned by Rt. Hon. Joshua Cooper, 1788 MS 21 F 2/2).

BALLYSUMAGHAN, COUNTY SLIGO

INTRODUCTION: *The parish of Ballysumaghan was in the barony of Tirerrill on the road from Sligo to Drumsna. It had 4,216 acres.*[1] *Lewis says that the soil was a good deep loam, with a large tract of bog and several good limestone quarries.*

The incumbent was the Rev. John Holmes, who held the parish with that of Ballynakill, County Galway and County Roscommon from 1729 (see Ballynakill, County Galway and County Roscommon).

OCCUPATIONS

Beggar	8	Gentleman	1	Ploughman	1
Cottier	6	Herd	13	Servants, household	40
Farmer	32	Labourer	23		

Com~Sligoe Parish of	Place of Abode	Names and Religion	Proffession	Children under 14 Prot.	Paps.	Children above 14 Prot.	Paps.	Men Servts Prot.	Paps.	Women Servts Prot.	Paps.
[f.391] Ballysumaghan	Guiddaun	Wm. Farrel pro:	farmr.	3		3		1	2		1
		Edmd. Moony pa	plowmn.				2				
		Hu. Gauran pa	labr.	1							1
		Carabry McGan pa	labr.		4		1				
		Edmd. Flaharty pa	labr.		2						
		Tha. Kimmitt pa	labr.				1				
		Luke McGan pa	labr.		1						
		Wm. McGauran pa	Herd		1						
	Killyalloe	Martn. Johnston pro:	farmer	2		4					1
		Alexr. Johnston pro:	farmr.	3							1 1
		Pat. Banaghan pa	herd				2	1			1
	Ardleebeg[2]	Pat. Walker pro:	farmr.	1							
		Jas. Hart pa	farmr.		2						
		Jn. Kelly pa	farmr.		2				2		
		Andw. Meeghan pa	herd		3				1		
	Lecarrow	Mich. Tigue pa	herd				1				
	Lurga Jas.	Mulvihill pa	farmr.		4		1				
		Connor Mulvihil pa	farmr.		2						1
		Pat. Goolrick pa	labr.		2						
		Ow. Mulvihil pa	herd		1						
		Dom. Banaghan pa	farmr.		2				2		
		Wm. Kimmitt pa	farmr.		3		2				
		Pat. Kimmitt pa	farmr.		1						1
		Rogr. Connilan pa	farmr.		1		1				
	Cloonela	Fr. Conbolue pa	farmr.				1				1
		Martin Roddy pa	farmr.		2						1
		Nich. Walker prot:	labr.								
		Margt. Bright prot: ww.	beggar								
		Ann Johnston ww. pro:	beggar			1					
	Culticloghane	Mat. McCormick pa	herd		2						
		Sar. Kilcleen ww. pa	cottier				2				
	Caracrin Robt.	Burrows pro:	Gent	5		1		1	1	1	1
		Jane Burrows widw. pro:	farmr.			2			1		
		Js. McDonnel pa	labr.		4						
		Dens. McDonnel pa	labr.		3						
		Bridg. Gouloghty ww. pa	beggar								
		Cath. Cleary ww. pa	beggar								
		Cath. Clery ww. pa	cottier		1		2				
		Edmd Cullian pa	labr.		4		1				
	Doonalla	Jas. Connilan pa	herd								
	Falnashammer	Ow. Guane pa	herd				1				
15		16 - 60		14	45	11	18	2	10	1	10
[f.392] Ballysumaghan	Falneshammer	Bry Greaghan pa	labr.		2		3		1		2
	1st Knock-negee[3]	Rogr. Macavah pa	herd		3						
		Js. Sheridan	labr.								

Com~Sligoe / Parish of	Place of Abode	Names and Religion	Proffession	Children under 14		Children above 14		Men Servts		Women Servts	
				Prot.	Paps.	Prot.	Paps.	Prot.	Paps.	Prot.	Paps.
	2nd Knock-negee	Mark Flanagan pa	labr.								
		Js. Flanagan pa	herd		1		2				
		Ric. McAndrew pa	labr.		2						
		Tim. Brislan pa	labr.		1		1				
		Bar. Healy pa	labr.				2				
		Toby Phibbs pro:	farmr.	2							1
	Ballysum-maghan	Ch. Higgins pa	farmr.						1		1
		Win. Higgins widw. pa	cottier								
		Bry. McAuly pa	labr.		3						
		Den. McAndrew pa	farmr.				2				
		Margr. McAuly ww. pa	beggar								
		Cath. Kimit ww. pa	cottier		2						
		Mary Mulvihil ww. pa	beggar								
		Bridgt. Esker ww. pa	beggar								
		Ow. Keveny pa	farmr.		2						
		Bry. Brehon pa	farmr.		1						
		Pat. Tigue pa	labr.		1						
		Wind. McAuly ww. pa	farmr.		2						
		Mary Mullan ww. pa	cottier				1				
	Drummee	Pat. Grey pa	farmr.		2						
		Th. Clerkan pa	farmr.				2				
		Wm. Bright pro:	farmr.	2							
		Th. Bright pro:	farmr.	1							
		Dav. Middleton pro:	farmr.						1		1
		Mich. Duneen pa	labr.		1						
		Morgn. Monaghan pa	labr.		1						
	Culticarican Lavally[4]	Conr. Coyl pa	herd		2		1				
		Pat. Tursany pa	herd						1		
		Jas. Geelan pa	labr.		2						
	Strananagh[5]	Edm. Meeghan pa	farmr.		2				1		1
		Mich. Meeghan pa	farmr.		5				1		
		Js. Meehan pa	farmr.		5				1		1
		Mich. Meehan pa	farmr.		1				1		1
		Pat. Connilan pa	herd		2				1		
		Jn. Meeghan pa	farmr.		1						
		Thos. Flin pa	farmr.		3		2				
		Mich. Tonry pa	labr.		1						
		Bridt Horisk ww. pa	cottier				1				
		8 - 66		5	48		18		8		8
[f.393] Ballysumaghan	Strananagh	Ann Wick ww pro:	beggar	1							
		Mich. Mullany wr. pa labr.									

[one blank page]

[verso] Ballysumaghan

[f394] Com~Sligoe Parish of	Place of Abode	Names and Religion	Proffession	Children under 14		Children above 14		Men Servts		Women Servts	
				Prot.	Paps.	Prot.	Paps.	Prot.	Paps.	Prot.	Paps.
Shancoe		Heads of families Protestants	papists								
Brought from	page 1	6	74	6	58	3	23		12	2	14
	page 2	8	46	10	54	8	23		11		18
	Total	14	120	16	112	11	46		23	2	32
Protestants 43	papists 333										
Aughanagh											
Brought from from	page [1]	9	51	8	56		10	4	11	2	12
	page 2	11	68	5	48	1	20		10		12
	page 3	12	65	3	62	4	15	2	3	1	7
	page 4		29		24		8		1	1	2
	Total	32	213	16	190	5	53	6	25	4	33
Protestants 63	papists 514										
Kilmacallane											
Brought from	page 1	22	60	18	46	10	21		18	1	16
	page 2	4	79	2	67		27		7	1	7
	page 3	11	76	6	61	12	13	1	5		8
	page 4	10	63	6	45	4	12		9		13
	page 5	12	67	5	46	13	28	2	7	1	8
	page 6	12	62	6	43	12	15	3	6	5	7
	page 7	3	11	1	5	4	4		2		3
	Total	74	418	44	313	55	120	6	54	8	62
Protestants 187	Papists 967										
Taunagh											
Brought from	page 1	5	69	5	49	5	11	4	9		13
	page 2	11	63	14	49	7	23		9	2	7
	page 3	1	12		7	2	4		2		
	Total	17	144	19	101	14	38	4	20	2	20
Protestants 56	papists 323										
Kilvicdoon											
Brought from	page 1	12	70	11	46	2	16	1	6	1	10
	page 2	2	80	2	32	2	12		1		6
	page 3	2	61	1	33		23		9		11
	Total	16	211	14	111	4	51	1	16	1	27
Protestants 36	papists 416										
Drumcollum		Heads of families Protestants	papists								
Brought from	page 1	8	68	15	50	5	18	1	5	2	12
	page 2	22	58	24	32	9	31	2	10	1	18
	page 3	17	61	16	55	18	21	1	10	1	12
	page 4	17	44	15	43	5	16		23		14
	Total	64	231	70	180	37	86	4	48	4	56
Protestants 179	Papists 601										

Com~Sligoe / Parish of	Place of Abode	Names and Religion	Proffession	Children under 14 Prot.	Paps.	Children above 14 Prot.	Paps.	Men Servts Prot.	Paps.	Women Servts Prot.	Paps.
Ballinakill											
Brought from	page 1	16	60	13	59	4	18		9	2	10
	page 2	8	26	7	25	6	15		2	3	12
	Total	24	86	20	84	10	33		21	5	22
Protestants 59	Papists 246										
Kilmactranny											
Brought from	page 1	6	76	4	33		9		3		12
	page 2		82		40		15		7		10
	page 3	10	70	5	56	6	30		7	1	12
	page 4	6	79	3	34	3	9		4		9
	page 5		82		51		17		6		12
	page 6		54		34		6		2		5
	Total	22	443	12	248	9	86		29		60
Protestants 44	Papists 866										
Kilross											
Brought from	page 1	16	62	12	52	8	17		10	1	10
	page 2	20	58	24	38	7	18		15	2	18
	page 3	18	48	11	21	6	13	1	2		8
	Total	54	168	47	111	21	48	1	27	3	36
Protestants 126	Papists 390										
Ballysumaghan											
Brought from	page 1	15	60	14	45	11	18	2	10	1	10
	page 2	8	66	5	48		18		8		8
	page 3	1	1	1							
	Total	24	127	20	93	11	36	2	18	1	18
Protestant 68	Papists 292										

	Protestants	Papists	Proffession
Shancoe	43	333	about 1 to 8
Aughanagh	63	514	1 to 8
Kilmacallane	187	967	1 to 5$\frac{1}{2}$
Taunagh	56	323	1 to 6
Kilvicdoon	36	416	1 to 11$\frac{1}{2}$
Drumcollum	179	601	1 to 3$\frac{1}{2}$
Ballinakill	59	246	1 to 4
Kilmactranny	44	866	1 to 19$\frac{3}{4}$
Killross	126	390	1 to 3
Ballysummaghan	58	292	1 to 5
Total	851	4948	1 to 5$\frac{8}{10}$

5799

[Edward Synge's writing]

This is the abstract of all the other Parishes & to be bound next after the Particulars to be placed in the same order in the Book in which they lye in this Paper

NOTES

1. Including 14 acres of Castle Lough (*General Alphabetical Index*).

2. Ardlimore and Ardlibeg were leased by Francis Savage in the mid-eighteenth-century from the O'Hara family (N.L.I., List of Townlands and their proprietors, O'Hara Papers, MS 20,397).

3. The townland of Knocknegee was leased by Francis Savage in the mid-eighteenth century from the O'Hara family (ibid).

4. The townland of Lavally was leased in the mid eighteenth-century by Francis Savage from the O'Hara family (ibid).

5. The townland of Stranagh was rented by Francis Savage in the mid-eighteenth century from the O'Hara family (ibid).

SLIGO, ST. JOHN'S, COUNTY SLIGO

INTRODUCTION: *The parish of St John's which includes the sea port town of Sligo was in the barony of Upper Carbery. The parish covered 7,256 statute acres.*[1]

The borough was created by James I in 1613 with a portrieve and twelve burgesses.[2] *Two MPs were returned to parliament.*[3] *In about 1620, the town was granted the right to have a market and licence was granted to export various manufactured goods from the port.*[4] *The local Anglo-Irish families, the Wynnes, the Coopers, the Ormsbys and the Gores were members of Sligo council from the early eighteenth century.*[5] *Much of the land in Sligo town was owned by the Temple (later Palmerston) and Wynne families. This included parts of the town, and the town's fairs and markets, tolls and customs.*[6] *Madam Wynne, a pensioner of Sligo was perhaps the widow of Owen Wynne (1664-1737).*[7]

Lord Cork mortgaged land in the neighbouring parish of Ahamlish in the early seventeenth-century to Andrew O'Crean, whose family supported the O'Conor Sligo. Four Roman Catholic members of the O'Crean family were in Sligo town in 1749: John Crean, soapboiler, William and Lawrence Crean, cottiers, and Widow Sisley Crean, shopkeeper.[8]

In the mid-eighteenth century, Sligo was thought to be an 'improving town' but except for the barracks there were only 15 slated houses. Not more than 20 men of business in the town could afford to pay out £50 to construct a slated house.[9] *The rest of the town would have been cabins. In 1733, Henry Hatch, Palmerston's Dublin agent, believed that the town was 'thriving' and that six troopers of dragoons and two companies of foot were stationed in the barracks, whose pay exceeded £7000.*[10] *However in 1738 the army was said by John Irwin, a disgruntled resident, not to contribute to the town's wealth, but only to the income of farmers in the countryside.*[11]

As well as troops stationed in the town (who do not figure in the Census, except for the barrack master) the trade of the town was almost entirely dependent in one way or another on the port. Imports of goods from the continent and exports of oats, oatmeal and butter in return were watched by the Collector of the port and his tide waiters and gaugers.[12]

The parish was united to that of Calry in 1681.[13] *The rector and vicar of St. John's parish, Sligo in 1749 was the Rev. Eubule Ormsby who was instituted in 1730. The patron was the bishop.*

OCCUPATIONS

Ale keeper	1	Collector	1	Gauger	1	Merchant	11	Reedmaker	2	Staymaker	2
Ale seller	10	Comber	3	Gentleman	15	Miller	6	Retailer	1	Surgeon	1
Apothecary	3	Combmaker	1	Gentlewoman	1	Millwright	1	Saddler	4	Surveyor	1
Bailiff	1	Confectioner	1	Glazier	2	Nailer	2	Sawyer	11	Tailor	22
Baker	9	Cooper	9	Glover	6	Old woman	1	Schoolmaster	3	Tanner	5
Barrack master	1	Cottier	295	Haberdasher	1	Overseer	1	Schoolmistress	2	Tide officer	3
Bellman	1	Cowboy	4	Harnessmaker	1	Painter	1	Servant	2	Tinker	2
Blacksmith	1	Currier	2	Hatter	2	Paver	1	Servants household	437	Upon Charity	5
Boatman	4	Distiller	2	Horserider	1	Peddler	1			Vestry Clerk	1
Broguemaker	19	Doctor	1	Huckster	1	Pensioner	15	Shepherd	1	Watchmaker	2
Butcher	16	Dyer	1	Innkeeper	7	Piper	1	Shoemaker	13	Weaver	74
Cabinetmaker	1	Farmer	260	Joiner	6	Plowmaker	1	Shopkeeper	29	Weighmaster	1
Carman	5	Farmer/esquire	1	Labourer	244	Poor woman	2	Slater	1	Wheelwright	5
Carpenter	7	Fisherman	23	Leather cutter	1	Postmaster	1	Smith	20	Wigmaker	6
Cattler	1	Flaxdresser	2	Maltster	3	Presser	1	Snuffmaker	1	Woolcomber	1
Chandler	1	Gaoler	1	Mantua maker	1	Pumpmaker	2	Soapboiler	1	Yarn merchant	1
Clothier	2	Gardener	7	Mason	11	Quilter	1	Spinner	2		

Com~Sligoe Parish of Sligoe	Place of Abode	Names and Religion	Proffession	Children under 14 Prot.	Paps.	Children above 14 Prot.	Paps.	Men Servts Prot.	Paps.	Women Servts Prot.	Paps.
[f.396]	Sligoe	Wm. Barton[14] & Wife prot	Cooper	3		2				2	
	Do	Bridget Moran papt	———								
	Do	Elizabeth Hipson pro	———								2
	Do	Mary Brown prot	——								
	Do	Thos. Carter & Wife prot	Shoomakr.	1				1	1		
	Do	Mark Carter prot	———								
	Do	Jas. Little & Wife prot	Baker	1							
	Do	John Hamilton & Wife prot	Sailor	1							
	Do	Jon. Lindsey & Wife prot	Distiller	1		2					1
	Do	Fras. Carrol[15] & Wife prot	In-keepr	1							1
	Do	Law. Vernon[16] prot	Farmr			2					3
	Do	Jas. Mason prot	Baker								
	Do	Thos. Parke & Wife prot	Wig-makr.	2							
	Do	Ann Cummin pro	Ale-keepr.	3							
	Do	Thos. Gore pro	Labourer	1							
	Do	Joan Higgin papt	Shop-keepr.								
	Do	Thos. Higin papt	Taylor		3						
	Do	Juggy Higin papt	———								
	Do	Dolly & Mary Naughton papt									
	Do	Jas. Mulloy & Wife papt	Boatman								
	Do	Bridget Gore papt	——		1						
	Do	Samus Debutt[17] pro	Gent	0				1	1		0
	Do	Mary Debutt pro	Gent					1	1		
	Do	Joshua Debutt & Wife pro	Distiller	1							2
	Do	Mary Debutt: pro:	Gent								
	Do	Thos. Knox[18] & Wife pro	Mercht.	1				1		3	
	Do	Mary Martin pro		2							
	Do	Abrahm. Martin[19] & Wife pro	Tanner	3		1					2
	Do	Catherin Jameson pro		1							1
	Do	Thos. Jameson prot	Farmer								
	Do	George Shaw & Wife pro	Farmer	1							
	Do	Mary Wood pro	Baker								1
	Do	Jon. Edwds & Wife pro	Ale-seller	1		1					3
	Do	Thos. McIntire & Wife pap	Taylor		1				2		1
	Do	Jon. Allingam & wife papt	Taylor		1						
	Do	Jon. Lekins & Wife pro	Shoomakr.					4			
	Do	Ann Kelly prot	——								1
	Do	George Driffas & Wife pro	harnishmakr.								
	Do	Henry Glinn & Wife pro	Butcher	3							
	Do	Ann Gallagher pro	Schoolmrs.	1							
	Do	Jas. Young & wife prot	Sadler	2							1
		48 protests - 13 papists		30	6	8		8	5	5	19
[f.397]Sligoe	Sligoe	Margt. Clark prot	Ale seller	2							1
	Do	Holbert Cuningham & Wife pro	Joyner	1							
	Do	Mrs Hart pro	Schoolmrs	1							1
	Do	Mr Stenson & Wife pro	Taylor								1
	Do	Chas. Holms & Wife pro	Wig-makr.	2							
	Do	Mrs Thomson: pro:	——							1	0
	Do	Hugh Coffrey & Wife papt	Butcher		1						

Com~Sligoe Parish of Sligoe	Place of Abode	Names and Religion	Proffession	Children under 14		Children above 14		Men Servts		Women Servts	
				Prot.	Paps.	Prot.	Paps.	Prot.	Paps.	Prot.	Paps.
	Do	Eleanor Doyle pap	Baker	1							
	Do	Wm. Gibson20 & Wife pro	Shop-keepr.	2		2		1		1	1
	Do	Thos. Tressey pap	baker								
	Do	Wm. Sinclar & Wife pro	Snuff-makr.								
	Do	Joseph Burness prot	Baker	2							
	Do	Joseph Bell & Wife pro	Glover	5							
	Do	Wm. Bell & Wife pro	Glover	5							
	Do	Caleb Bell21 & Wife pro	Glover								
	Do	Thos. Bell & Wife pro	Glover							1	
	Do	Peter Bolan22 papt	Shop-keepr.								
	Do	Owen Connor & Wife papt	Labour.				1				
	Do	Thos. Casey papt	Shop-keepr.						1		
	Do	John Crean & Wife papt	Soapboiler		2				1		1
	Do	Edwd. Corkran23, papt	Mercht.						4		
	Do	Widdow Corkran pap	Gent		4						3
	Do	Ellis Dorman pro	Gent								
	Do	Richd. Tyler prot	Apothecary	1							1
	Do	Fras. Hall & Wife pro	postmasr.	3		1				1	
	Do	Edwd. Killroy & Wife papt	Cotter								
	Do	Mrs. Sinclare prot	Gent	3							
	Do	Joseph Davey24 & Wife pro	Mercht.	2				1		1	1
	Do	Bryn. McManus & Wife pro	Taylor								
	Do	Walter Welsh & Wife pap	Taylor								
	Do	Lawrence Welsh papt	Taylor								
	Do	Widdw Hart papt	Gent		1						
	Do	Thos. Murray pro	Sadler								
	Do	Adam Guthry & Wife pro	Farmer	2	1			1			2
	Do	Wm. Crean & wife pap	Cotter		1		2				
	Do	John Scott & Wife pro	Painter	1							
	Do	John McClurn & Wife pro	Cabinetmakr.	1							
	Do	Jas. Glancey & Wife pro	Cotter		1						
	Do	John Fahy25 & wife pap	Weaver		2						1
	Do	Neal McGurk & Wife papt	Dyer								
	Do	Dudly Connor & Wife papt	Labourer		1						
		36 Protests - 32 pap		34	13	2	3	3	6	5	13
[f.398]Sligoe	Sligoe	Isabell Morgan prot	Quilter	1							
	Do	Widw. McCarnick pap	Cotter		3						
	Do	Widdw Dignan pap	Mantua makr.								
	Do	Thos. Burrows & Wife pro	In-keepr.	4		1		3	2		
	Do	Widw. Raghnine papt	Shopkeepr		2						
	Do	Moses Kirkpatrick & Wife pro	In-keepr.	3							1
	Do	Widdow Gore26 prot	Gent								
	Do	Mr Babington27 & Wife pro	Tide officer	1							2
	Do	Mr Little & Wife pro	Gaoler	1						1	
	Do	James Williams prot	Weaver	1		1					
	Do	John Clemens prot	Watchmakr.								
	Do	Jane Walker, widw. prot	Shop-keepr.							1	
	Do	Eleanor Carrel papt	Hugster		1						
	Do	Widw. Willson prot	Shop-keepr.								1

Com~Sligoe Parish of	Place of Abode	Names and Religion	Proffession	Children under 14		Children above 14		Men Servts		Women Servts	
				Prot.	Paps.	Prot.	Paps.	Prot.	Paps.	Prot.	Paps.
	Do	John King[28] & Wife pro	Shop-keepr.	1		3			4		1
	Do	Thos. Burrows & Wife pro	Shop-keepr.	1						1	
	Do	Stephen McGlin & wife pap	Staymakr.		2						1
	Do	Laurence Crean & Wife pap	Cotter		1						
	Do	Thady Teig & wife papt	Shop-keepr.		3		1				
	Do	Aylee King wife prot	Shop-keepr.			1			2		4
	Do	Widw. Sisly Crean[29] pap	Shop-keepr.				2				
	Do	Michl. Brunan & Wife pap	Shop-keepr.		1						1
	Do	Jas. Burrows & Wife pro	Ale seller	3					4		2
	Do	Arthur Vernon & Wife pro	Chandler	1							2
	Do	Jane Burn prot	Shop-keepr.	1							1
	Do	Jane Jameson prot	Shop-keepr.								1
	Do	Archibald Egelston[30] pro	Shop-keepr.	4		1			0	1	
	Do	Robt. Buntien & Wife pro	Gent								
	Do	Paul Garraghy & Wife pap	Shop-keepr.						1		
	Do	Owen McDonagh pap	Cotter								1
	Do	Bartly Killwee & Wife pap	Gardnr.		2						1
	Do	Patrick Mcdonogh & Wife pap	Cotter		2						
	Do	Henry Turbot & Wife pro	Cotter			1					
	Do	John Mitchel & Wife pro	Wheelwright			1				1	
	Do	John Crafford & Wife pro	Ale seller							1	
	Do	John Gibson[31] & Wife pro	Shop-keepr.								1
	Do	John Higin & Wife pap	Ale seller						1		
	Do	Chas. Jeffry & Wife pro	Tide officer	1						1	
	Do	Walter Kelly & Wife pro	Cotter	1							
	Do	Wm. Barret[32] & Wife pro	Ale seller	2					1		1
	Do	Barret Knott[33] & Wife pro	Farmer	2				1			2
shoud be 44 — 22		pro: 49 - pap 22		28	17	9	3	4	15	7	23
[f.399]Sligoe	Sligoe	Eleanor Nugent papt	Ale Seller								1
	Do	Garret Finly & Wife pro	Cotter								
	Do	Jams Murray & Wife pro	Shoomakr.								1
	Do	Wm. Griffin & Wife pro	Slater			1					
	Do	Danl. Sweeny & Wife pap	Labourer		1						
	Do	George Brown & Wife pro	Shop-keepr.	1							1
	Do	Edwd. Carrol & Wife pro	Gardener	1		1					
	Do	Peter McDonogh & Wife pap	Cotter								
	Do	Andw. Healey & Wife pap	Shop-keepr.		1						
	Do	Edwd. Bradican & Wife pap	Boat-man		2				1		2
	Do	Andw. Vanvick & Wife pro	Weaver	3							
	Do	Robt Jolly & Wife pap	Shop-keepr.								1
	Do	Martin Crean & Wife pap	Yarn Mercht..								
	Do	John Crofton pro: Wife pap	Farmer	1		3					2
	Do	Robt. Parke & Wife pro	Glazier	2				1			
	Do	Peter Shuttleworth & Wife pro	Sailor	2						1	1
	Do	Elizabeth King widw. pro	Farmer	2							1
	Do	Fras. Ellis & Wife pro	Sailor	3							1
	Do	Robert Ormsby[34] pro	Apothecary					1			
	Do	Saml. Pickering & Wife pro	Shop-keepr.								1
	Do	Henry Farrel[35] & Wife pro	Doctor						1		3

Com~Sligoe Parish of	Place of Abode	Names and Religion	Proffession	Children under 14 Prot.	Paps.	Children above 14 Prot.	Paps.	Men Servts Prot.	Paps.	Women Servts Prot.	Paps.
	Do	Chas Martin & Wife pro	Tanner								2
	Do	Eleanor King widw. pro	Farmer	1							
	Do	Peter Egan & Wife pro	Shop-keepr.	1							1
	Do	Susanna Greenlaw[36] widw. pro	Shop-keepr.	2				1		1	
	Do	Jane Lindsay prot	———								
	Do	Murtagh Geoghagan & Wife pap	Farmer						2		3
	Do	Patrick Gean & Wife pap	Farmer								
	Do	Mr. Sterling & Wife pap	Farmer								
	Do	Edwd. Egan & Wife pap	Haberdasher		3						
	Do	Widow Bruen papt	Shop-keepr.		2					1	1
	Do	Wm. Duke & wife prot	Apothecary	2		1				1	1
	Do	Jon. Lynchaghan[37] & Wife pap	Shop-keepr.		2		1				2
	Do	Robt. Rork & Wife pro	Shop-keepr.	1							
	Do	Arthur Williams: pro	Watchmakr.			2					
	Do	Joseph Noriss & Wife pro	Tinker	2							
	Do	Wm. Woolsey & Wife pro	Baker								
	Do	CÆzar Truby & Wife pro	Confectioner	2							
	Do	Chas. Matthews & Wife pro	Shop-keepr.	3							
	Do	Wm. Wyer protestant	Weighmaster								
		pro: 46: pap 25		29	11	8	1	3	6	4	24
[f.400]Sligoe	Sligoe	Widdw. Hill protest	Pensioner			2					
	Do	Madm. Wynne prot	Pensioner	6		2		2		1	2
	Do	Jon. Jones & Wife papt	Cotter		1						
	Do	Richd. Mee & Wife prot	Ale seller								1
	Do	Wm. McBride & Wife pro	Sailor			1					
	Do	Widw. Wingle pro	upon Charity	1							
	Do	Widw. Gracey prot	upon Charity								
	Do	John Underwood & Wife pro	Cotter								1
	Do	Jon. Withers & Wife pro	Pensionr.	3		1					
	Do	Thos. Mullin[38] & Wife pro	Weaver	4							2
	Do	Wm. Turbet	upon Charity								
	Do	Mr. Mullin & Wife pro	Weaver	1						1	1
	Do	Barthy Doodican & Wife papt	Cotter		3						3
	Do	Jas. Ô Hara & Wife papt	Wigmakr.		1					1	
	Do	Wm. Phillips[39] & Wife pro	In-keepr.			2		1	2		2
	Do	Robt. Lynch & Wife papt	hatmakr.		2		1	2			
	Do	Josseph Hudson & Wife pro	Weavr.	2							
	Do	Jas Grimes & Wife pro	Weavr.	1							
	Do	Mr. Drean & Wife pro	Cotter								
	Do	Widdow Moor prot	Ale seller	2							1
	Do	Mrs Crafford pro	Cotter			1					1
	Do	Jon Crafford & Wife pro	Farmer						1		1
	Do	Bryn. ô Donnel & Wife papt	Cotter								
	Do	Owen McGowan & Wife papt	Labor.								
	Do	Mary Cashore prot	Cotter	1							
	Do	Pat Scanlan pap	Cotter		2						
	Do	Chas. Smith[40] & Wife pro	Gauger	3						1	2
	Do	Law. Peters & Wife pro	Sailor			1					1
	Do	Jon. Shannon & Wife pro	Labour.								

Com~Sligoe Parish of	Place of Abode	Names and Religion	Proffession	Children under 14 Prot.	Paps.	Children above 14 Prot.	Paps.	Men Servts Prot.	Paps.	Women Servts Prot.	Paps.
	Do	Hugh Shannon & Wife pro	Weavr.	3				2			
	Do	Col. Gore prot	Gent			3		2		2	2
	Do	Thos. Allexandr.	Gardner								
	Do	Robt. Allexandr pro	——								
	Do	Jane Pokin prot	Charity								
	Do	Jon. Pokin prot	Woolcombr.	4							
	Do	Col. Irwin[41] & Wife pro	——			1			2	2	2
	Do	Miss Coddin pro	Gent								
	Do	Mary McAnair pro	——								
	Do	Jon. Blakeney & Wife pro	Spining -								
	Do	Arthur White & Wife pro	Flaxdressr.	1							
		pro:51 - pap 13		32	9 1	4	1	9	5	8	22
[f.401]Sligoe	Sligoe	Widdow White prot	Flaxdressr.			1					
	Do	Michl. Dinny & Wife pap	Farmer				2				
	Do	Widdw. Waters prot	upon Charity			2					
	Do	Widdw. Mcdullagh pro	Spinner								
	Do	Peter Gunlisk & Wife papt	butcher		4						
	Do	Jas. Dyer & Wife papt	Labourer		1						
	Do	David Boyd[42] pro	Cotter	3		1					
	Do	Thos. Dean & Wife pro	barack mr.			2			1	1	
	Do	Catherine Hudson pro	Cotter	3							
	Do	Jon. Caulfield & Wife pro	Mason	3				1			1
	Do	Jas. Mullan & Wife pro	Cotter	1							
	Do	Widw Griffin pro	Cotter	2							
	Do	Deborah Griffin pro	——								
	Do	Catherine Griffin	——								
	Do	Edwd Killfeder & wife pap	Cotter		3						
	Do	Simon Fury & Wife pro	Mason	1							
	Do	Catherine Scanlan pap	Cotter								
	Do	Michl. Gawney & wife pap	Joyner		3						
	Do	Robt. Wyer & Wife pro	Weaver	2							
	Do	Wm. Bell & Wife pro	Shoomakr.	1							
	Do	Jas. Gibson prot	joyner			1					2
	Do	Widdw Remon pro	Ale seller	1							1
	Do	Geo. McFadin & Wife pro	Shoomakr.	1		2					
	Do	Michl. Scott & Wife pro	Cotter								
	Do	Jas. Wallis[43] & Wife pro	Cotter			1					
	Do	Jas. Wallis Senior & Wife pro	Cotter								
	Do	Widdw. Stratford pro	Cotter			2					
	Do	Wm. Griffin & Wife pro	Glazier	4		3					
	Do	Joseph Thos. & Wife pro	Schoolmaster	3							2
	Do	Rogr. Horoghy[44] & Wife pap	Shop-keepr.		5		1		1		1
	Do	Peter Gallaghr. & Wife pap	Wheelwright		1				2		1
	Do	Jas. Hetherington & Wife pro	Cattler	2							
	Do	Harry McDermot & Wife pap	joyner		2						
	Do	Wm. Barret prot	Gent						1		
	Do	Terence Golrick & Wife pap	Cotter		1						
	Do	Jas. Flinn & Wife pap	Cotter								1
	Do	Morgn. McCarrick pap	Mercht..		1						2

Com~Sligoe Parish of	Place of Abode	Names and Religion	Proffession	Children under 14		Children above 14		Men Servts		Women Servts	
				Prot.	Paps.	Prot.	Paps.	Prot.	Paps.	Prot.	Paps.
	Do	Widw. Smith papist	Cotter		2						
	Do	Mary Gallagher pap	Cotter		1						
	Do	Terence Ô Brien & Wife pap	Taylor		1						2
	Do	Peter Egan & Wife pap	Mercht..								1
shoud be 38— 28		prot 35.pap 31		27	25	15	3	1	5	1	14
[f.402]Sligoe	Do	Danl. Gallaghr & Wife pap	Wheelwright		4				2		1
	Do	Edwd. Welsh & Wife pap	blacksmith				1				
	Do	Widdow Dowdle pap	Cotter								1
	Do	Pat. Hart & Wife pap	Farmer		2		1		1		
	Do	Edwd. Gimlisk & Wife pap	Leather cuttr.								
	Do	Jas. Groky & Wife papt	Cotter								
	Do	Richd. Henry & Wife papt	Cotter		1						
	Do	Wm. Doyl & Wife pro	Wig-makr.			1					
	Do	Gregory Scanlan & Wife pap	Clothier								
	Do	Thady Hart & Wife papt	Cotter								
	Do	Peter Higin & Wife papt	Taylor		1						
	Do	Thady Egan[45] & Wife pap	brogmkr.		1						
	Do	Bryn. Nolan pap	brogmkr.		1						
	Do	Owen Mullowmoe pap	Cotter								
	Do	Thady Connely & Wife papt	brogmkr.		1						
	Do	Bartly Gallaghr & Wife pap	brogmkr..								
	Do	John Mullan & Wife pap	Cotter								
	Do	Thos. Healy & Wife pap	Smith								
	Do	Fras. Dowd pap	Cotter		1						
	Do	Wm. McSharry & Wife papt	Cotter		4						
	Do	Michl. Egan & Wife papt	Glover								
	Do	Fras. Ormsby & Wife papt	Labor.								
	Do	Rogr. Geraghty & Wife pap	butcher				2				
	Do	Fras. Murphy & Wife pap	Cotter		1						
	Do	Jon. Kivill & Wife papt	Cotter		2						
	Do	Thos.McCarick & Wife pap	Cotter		2						
	Do	Jas. McKim & Wife pap	Weavr.								
	Do	Barnaby Kenery & Wife pro	Cotter	1							
	Do	Jon. McKinsey & Wife pro	Weavr.			2				1	1
	Do	Jas. McGowran & Wife pap	Mercht..		1						
	Do	Jon. Connor & Wife pap	Brogmkr.		1						
	Do	Patrick Nolan & Wife papt	paver								
	Do	Jon. Hart papt	Labor.		1						
	Do	Patrick Conellan pap	Labor.								
	Do	Thos. fflin & Wife pap	Labor.								
	Do	Hugh Conelly & Wife papt	Taylor		1						
	Do	Wm. fflin & Wife pap	Labor.		2						
	Do	Timothy Brien & Wife pap	Cottr.		1						
	Do	Denis Creaghan & Wife pap	Labor.		2						
	Do	Wm. Mullin prot	Weavr.	1							
	Do	Edwd. Bell & Wife prot	Glover								
		prot 11 —— pap 63		2	30	3	4	-	3	1	3
[f.403]Sligoe	Sligoe	Pat. Devany & Wife papt	Cotter		2						
	Do	Pat. Carroll & Wife pap			1						

Com~Sligoe Parish of	Place of Abode	Names and Religion	Proffession	Children under 14		Children above 14		Men Servts		Women Servts	
				Prot.	Paps.	Prot.	Paps.	Prot.	Paps.	Prot.	Paps.
	Do	Philip Lonican & Wife pap	Labourer								
	Do	Jon. Cowen & Wife pap	Labourer								
	Do	Daniel Brunan & Wife pap	Cotter								
	Do	Andw. McGowray & Wife pap	Labourer		1						
	Do	John Coss & Wife pap	Cotter								
	Do	Mary Coss papt	Cotter		1						
	Do	Mary Bolan pap	Cotter								
	Do	Pat. McAnolty & Wife papt	Weaver								
	Do	Danl. Folan & Wife papt	Cotter		1						
	Do	Michl. Finacan & Wife pap	Cotter		1						
	Do	John Willis & Wife prot	Cotter	1	0					2	0
	Do	Matt. Welsh & Wife pap	Labourer		2		1				
	Do	Michl. Hara & Wife pap	Cotter		1						
	Do	Coleman Daily & Wife pap	Labourer		1						
	Do	James Folan & Wife pap	Cotter		1						
	Do	Pat. Linany & Wife pap	Labourer		1						
	Do	Bryn. Higin & Wife pap	Labourer		1						
	Do	Jon. Willis & Wife pro	Broguemakr.								
	Do	Nicholas Hunt & Wife pap	Labourer		1						
	Do	George Anderson & Wife pro	Weaver	1		1					
	Do	Widow Davies prot	Cotter	3							
	Do	Wm. Homersly & Wife pro	Weaver	2				2			
	Do	John Hudson & Wife pro	Weaver	2							
	Do	Manus McDaniel & Wife pap	Labourer		1		2				
	Do	Patt. Quinn & Wife pro	Weaver	3							1
	Do	Jas. Stewart & Wife pro	Sailor	4							
	Do	John Farqusson & Wife pro	Taylor								
	Do	Thos. Mooney & Wife pap	Labourer								
	Do	Thos. Mullhern[46] & Wife pap	Presser								
	Do	Phelim Conor & Wife pap	Labourer		1						
	Do	Garret McCowan & Wife pap	Broguemakr.		2				2		
	Do	John. McGinery & Wife pap	Labourer		1						1
	Do	Peter Ryly & Wife pap	Weaver		2						
	Do	Wm. Denerton & Wife pro	Cotter								
	Do	Eleanor Lenard pro	Cotter			2					
	Do	Hugh Gallanagh & Wife pap	Labourer								
	Do	Neal Gallana & Wife pap	Labourer		1						
	Do	Michl. McGowan & Wife pap	Labourer		1						
	Do	Bryn Canagh & Wife pap	Butcher		1						
		pro 19 — papt 58		16	25	3	3	2	2	2	2
[f.404]Sligoe	Sligoe	Dinis McTiere & Wife pap	Labor.								
	Do	Patrick Herny & Wife pap	brogmakr.								
	Do	Mrs Price prot	Cotter	3							
	Do	Luke Daily & Wife pap	Weavr.		2						1
	Do	Peter Donoghy & Wife pap	Labor.								
	Do	Nichs Caulfield pro	Mason								
	Do	Catherine Leadon pap	Cotter								
	Do	Willm. Caulfield pro & Wife pap	Mason	1							
	Do	Daniel Breaghan & Wife pap	Weavr.		2						

Com~Sligoe Parish of	Place of Abode	Names and Religion	Proffession	Children under 14		Children above 14		Men Servts		Women Servts	
				Prot.	Paps.	Prot.	Paps.	Prot.	Paps.	Prot.	Paps.
	Do	Bryn Feeny & Wife pap	brogmakr.		2						
	Do	Wm. Ferny & Wife pap	brogmakr.		1						
	Do	Wm. Edwds & Wife pro	Shoomakr.								
	Do	Manus Finican & Wife pap	Tinker		2						
	Do	Ann Boid prot	baker	1							
	Do	John Egan pap	brogmkr.						3		
	Do	Martin Kelly & Wife pap	Carpentr.								
	Do	Jon. White & Wife pro	Tanner			1					
	Do	Widdow Hudson pro	In keepr.			2			2		1
	Do	Dinis Holly & Wife pap	Cotter		4						
	Do	Domnick Teig	Smith								
	Do	Martin Giblan	Cooper								
	Do	Ambrose Gillgan[47] pap	Cotter						2		1
	Do	Widdow Jones pro	Cotter	1							
	Do	Hugh Hall & Wife pap	Pedlar		3						
	Do	Catherin McDermt. pap	Cotter				1				
	Do	Bridgt. Conellan pap	Cotter		1						1
	Do	Martin Mallon & Wife pap	Cotter								1
	Do	Henry McCarrick pro & Wife pap	Carpentr.	1							1
	Do	Widdw. McCarrick pap	In keepr.				1				1
	Do	Eneas Breheny & Wife pap	Labor.		1						
	Do	Owen Gallagher & Wife pap	Farmr.		2				1		
	Do	Jeremiah Fury Esqr & Wife pro	Farmr.	1	3	1					
	Do	Pat. Giblan & Wife pap	Cotter		1						1
	Do	Michl. Burrows & Wife pro	Mercht..	3							1
	Do	John Gibson[48] pro	Farmr.								
	Do	Arthr. Martin & Wife pro	Farmr.	3					1		1
	Do	Georg. Skelton & Wife pro	Wig-makr								
	Do	Arthur Tyler & Wife pro	Farmr.								
	Do	Wm. Egan & Wife pap	Shoomakr.		4		2				
	Do	John Black pro	Smith						1		
		pro 23; papt 43		14	25	6	4	-	11	-	10
[f.405]Sligoe	Sligoe	Thos. Lyons & Wife pap	Labor.								
	Do	Richd. Cole & Wife pro	Smith	2							
	Do	Owen Marriutt & Wife pap	Taylor		2						
	Do	Saml. Price pro	Taylor				2				
	Do	Green Fury & Wife pap	Weavr.								
	Do	Peter Climate & Wife pro	Weavr.			2					
	Do	Dinis Climate & Wife pap	Cotter		1						
	Do	Widdw ffeeneh pap	Cotter								1
	Do	Martin Sweeny pap	Cotter		4						
	Do	Owen Sweeny & Wife pap	Labor.		1						
	Do	Michl. McDonogh[49] papt	Farmr.								
	Do	Geo. Burrows & Wife pro	Carpenr.	4					2		1
	Do	Anthony Lenox pap Wife protestant	Clothier						2		
	Do	Jas. Mcdonogh & Wife pap	Farmr.		1						
	Do	Mathew Connor pap	Cotter								
	Do	Mr Sweeny pap	Cotter								

Com~Sligoe Parish of	Place of Abode	Names and Religion	Proffession	Children under 14		Children above 14		Men Servts		Women Servts	
				Prot.	Paps.	Prot.	Paps.	Prot.	Paps.	Prot.	Paps.
	Do	Michl. Clery & Wife pap	Labor.		1						
	Do	Fras. Tullock & Wife pro	butcher								
	Do	Widdw. Owens pap	Cotter		2						
	Do	Mathew Dignan & Wife pap	Carman				1				
	Do	Jas. Gallanagh & Wife pap	Carman						1		
	Do	Chas. Riley[50] & Wife pro	Weavr.	7							1
	Do	Bartholomew Winard. & Wife pap	Reedmakr.								
	Do	Jas. Brown & Wife pro	Smith					1			
	Do	Jas. Carr & Wife pro	Smith	5							
	Do	Hugh Brenan & Wife pap	Labor.								
	Do	Bryan Kean & Wife pap	Weavr.		4						1
	Do	Thady May & Wife pap	Taylor								
	Do	Owen Gallagher & Wife pap	Labor.		3						
	Do	Cormuck Coningham & Wife pap	Labor.		1						
	Do	Edwd. Gallaghr & Wife pap	Labor.		3						
	Do	Jas Collogh & Wife pap	Labor.		2						
	Do	Own. Healy & Wife pap	Labor.		2						
	Do	Danl. McDermot & Wife pap	Labor.								
	Do	Michl. McKieve & Wife pap	Labor.		1		1				
	Do	Bryan Dermott & Wife pap	Labor.								
	Do	Jas Flemon & Wife pap	Cotter		1						
	Do	Thos. McSharry prot Wife papist	Cotter								
	Do	Luke Narey & Wife pap	Labor.		1						
	Do	Widw. Sheal pap	Cotter		1						
		pro 17— pap 55		18	31	4	2	1	5		4
[f.406]Sligoe	Sligoe	George Brooks & Wife pro	Shoomakr.								1
	Do	Danl. Carrol & Wife pap	Cottr.		2						
	Do	Wm. Mcfadine & Wife pap	Labor.								
	Do	Michl. Carrick papt	Labor.				1				
	Do	Edwd Lions & Wife pap	Labor.		3						
	Do	John Creaghan & Wife pap	Cotter				2				
	Do	Phelim Conor & Wife pap	Labor.		2						
	Do	Pat. Jordan & Wife pap	brogmakr.								
	Do	James Owen & Wife pap	Bailiff	1							
	Do	Pat. Haley & Wife pap	Labor.		1						
	Do	Bryn. Wine & Wife pap	butcher		1						
	Do	Edwd Rice & Wife prot	Cotter	2							
	Do	Cuthbert Harrison & Wife pro	butcher	1							
	Do	Jon Carrol & Wife pro	Currier								
	Do	Anthony Garvey & Wife pap	Baker								
	Do	Rogr. Conelan & Wife pap	Weavr.								
	Do	Jon. McKim & Wife pro	Weavr.								
	Do	Wm. Fullerton & Wife pro	Weavr.								
	Do	Jas. Long & Wife pro	Sadler			1					
	Do	Jas. Risy & Wife pap	Combmakr.								
	Do	Thos. Cormack & Wife pro	Weavr.	1							
	Do	Hugh McNass & Wife pap	Joyner								
	Do	Jon. Cambell & Wife pro	Cotter	2							1

Com~Sligoe Parish of	Place of Abode	Names and Religion	Proffession	Children under 14		Children above 14		Men Servts		Women Servts	
				Prot.	Paps.	Prot.	Paps.	Prot.	Paps.	Prot.	Paps.
	Do	Widw. McGuire pap	Cotter		2						
	Do	Mrs Jackson pro	Gent						1	2	
	Do	Wm. Cumin & Wife pro	Shoomakr.		2						
	Do	Widow Hughes[51] pro	In keepr.							1	1
	Do	Mr. Bell & Wife pro	Pensionr.								
	Do	John Blakeney & Wife pro	Gardenr.	3							
	Do	Geo. Mathews & Wife pro	Hatter								
	Do	Thos. Morison & Wife pro	Cotter	3							1
	Do	Nichos. Glanvill & Wife pro	Pensionr.	2							
	Do	Mathias Mathews & Wife pro	Shoomakr.	3							
	Do	Widdw Cullane pap	Cotter								
	Do	Wm. Edwds & Wife pro	Schoolmasr.								
	Do	Widdw Hamilton pro	Cotter			3					
	Do	Peter Brown[52] & Wife pro	Boatman	4							
	Do	Thos. Brown[53] & Wife pro	Tide officer	3							1
	Do	Wm. McTear & Wife pap	Fisherman		3		2				1
	Do	Thos. Willson & wife pro	Fisherman			1					
		pro: 44 - pap 30		25	14	7	5	-	1	3	6
[f.407]Sligoe	Sligoe	Mackin Camell & Wife pro	Pensionr			1					
	Do	Wm. Gowna & Wife pap	Retailer		1						
	Do	Frans. Dunlevey & Wife pap	ffishermn		3						
	Do	Jacob Bany & Wife pro	Sailor								
	Do	Wm. McGowan & Wife pap	Sailor								
	Do	Bryn Clery & Wife pap	Mason								
	Do	Thos. Mulloy & Wife pap	Fisherman		1						
	Do	Martin Devany & Wife pap	Fisherman		2						
	Do	Bryn Calaghan & Wife pap	Fisherman		3						
	Do	Wm. Mcgrearty & Wife pap	Fisherman				2				
	Do	Loghlin Gillgan & Wife pap	Fisherman		2						
	Do	Pat. Devany & Wife pro	Fisherman								
	Do	Chas. Conell & Wife pap	Fisherman		2						
	Do	Neal McCaffry & Wife pap	Carpenter		2					1	
	Do	John Tidd & Wife pro	Farmer	2							
	Do	John Brill & Wife pap	Fisherman			1					
	Do	Thos. Skivinton & Wife pro	Cotter	1							
	Do	Jas. Keevan & Wife pap	Labourer								
	Do	Hugh Conellan & Wife pap	Miller[54]		3						
	Do	Jas. McBrill & Wife pap	Fisherman		0					1	
	Do	Edmd. Murphy & Wife pap	Fisherman								
	Do	Michl. McGrory & Wife pap	Fisherman		1						
	Do	Frans Coner papt	Labourer								
	Do	Cormuck Fury & Wife pap	Fisherman		2						
	Do	Frans. Killaspick & Wife pap	Fisherman		1						
	Do	Frans Mcgowan & Wife pap	Taylor		1						
	Do	Phelim McDonell & Wife pap	Fisherman		1						
	Do	Jon. Langan & Wife pap	Carpenter								
	Do	Owen Brislan & Wife pap	Fisherman		1						
	Do	Widow McLinn									
	Do	Widdow Ryley pap	Cotter								

Com~Sligoe Parish of	Place of Abode	Names and Religion	Proffession	Children under 14		Children above 14		Men Servts		Women Servts	
				Prot.	Paps.	Prot.	Paps.	Prot.	Paps.	Prot.	Paps.
	Do	Widdw Cummin pro	Farmer	3							
	Do	Widw Nary pap	Cotter		1						
	Do	Wm. Crafford & wife pap	Millwright				1				
	Do	Jon. McFarson & wife pap	Sailor								
	Do	Mr. Cross[55] & Wife pro	Surveyor	1		2			2		1
	Do	Mr. Sandfort[56] pro	Collector								
	Do	Terence Gallagher & wife pap	Fisherman		0		1				
	Do	John Battersby & wife pap	Sailor		2						
	Do	Jas. Doverisk & wife pap	Sailor		3						
	Do	Law. McLinn & wife pap	Cooper		1						
	Do	Widw. McNaburn pap	Cotter				2				
		pro: 14 - pap 63		7	34	1	6	-	3	1	1
[f.408]Sligoe	Sligoe	Edwd. March & wife pap	Tanner		1						
	Do	Thady Goverty & Wife pro	Comber	1							
	Do	Dinis Carrway & wife pap	Labor.		2						
	Do	Jon. Mullarky & wife pap	Fisher								
	Do	Pat. Killeowen & wife pap	ffisher		2						
	Do	Benjamin Clark & Wife pro	Boatman								
	Do	Wm. Foster & Wife pro	ffisher	4							
	Do	George Smith & Wife pro	Sadler	1							
	Do	Wm. Evans & Wife pro	Cotter	1							
	Do	Mr. Shells & Wife pro	Cotter	1							
	Do	Jon. Harkan & wife pap	Carpenr.		3						
	Do	Wm. Clery & wife pap	Labor.								
	Do	Henry Stinson & Wife pro	Pensionr.								
	Do	Wm. Maley pap	Cotter								
	Do	Fras. McGowan pap	Cotter								
	Do	Jenkins Gravel & Wife pro	Comber	3							
	Do	Peter Black & wife pap	butcher								
	Do	John Clery pap	Cotter		4						
	Do	Danl. Carbry pap	Cotter		4						
	Do	Fras. Genery & Wife pro	Cotter	3							
	Do	John Noon & wife pap	Labor.		2						
	Do	Jas. Muckleree & Wife pro	butcher	4		3					
	Do	Thos. Anderson & Wife pro	Cotter	1							
	Do	John Gonegal & wife pap	Reedmakr.		2						
	Do	Wm. Wisely & Wife pro	Cotter								
	Do	Widdw. Glancy pap	Cotter								
	Do	Michl. Harkan & wife pap	brogmakr.		1				2		
	Do	Owen Mullican & wife pap	Cotter		1						
	Do	Aneas Booy & wife pap	Plowmakr.								
	Do	Mary Brien pap	Cotter								
	Do	Geo Shipton & Wife pro	Pensionr.	1							
	Do	Thady Meaghr & wife pap	Weavr.		0		1				1
	Do	Widw. Jonins pap	Cotter		0				1		
	Do	Peter Black & wife pap	Labor.								
	Do	Danl. Harkan & wife pap	brogmakr.								
	Do	Patrick Early & wife pap	Labor.		1						
	Do	Jon. Tenson & Wife pro	Nailer	3							

Com~Sligoe Parish of	Place of Abode	Names and Religion	Proffession	Children under 14		Children above 14		Men Servts		Women Servts	
				Prot.	Paps.	Prot.	Paps.	Prot.	Paps.	Prot.	Paps.
	Do	Owen Moor & wife pap	Carman		1						
	Do	Jon. Crooks & Wife pro	Mason					1			2
	Do	Jas. Graham & wife pap	Cotter				1				
	Do	Widw. Neal pap	Cotter		1						
		prot 29 - pap 44		23	25	3	2	1	3		3
[f.409]Sligoe	Sligoe	Terence Slany & wife pap	Labour.		1						
	Do	Wm. Reed & Wife pro	Weaver								
	Do	Jas Reed prot	Weavr.		2	1		0			
	Do	Pat Walsh & wife pap	Carman		1						
	Do	Owen Gallaghr.& wife pap	Fisher		2						
	Do	Thady McManamana & wife pap	Mason								
	Do	Walter Kelly & wife pap	Labour.		1						
	Do	Danl. Flaherty & wife pap	Labour.		2						
	Do	Paul Conellan & wife pap	weavr.		1						
	Do	Owen Judge & wife pap	Labourer		1						
	Do	James Gillan & wife pap	Carman		1						
	Do	Pat. Conor & wife pap	Labour.		2						
	Do	Martin Mologhory & wife pap	Labour.		1						
	Do	David Tricel & Wife pro	joyner	1							
	Do	Thos. Sanders & Wife pro	Cotter		2						
	Do	Jon. Kerine & wife pap	brogmakr.		2				4	1	
	Do	John Clery & wife pap	Labour.		2						
	Do	Danl. Carby & wife pap	Labour.		1						
	Do	Pat. Carney & wife pap	Labour.		2						
	Do	Widdow Conelly pro	Cotter				1				
	Do	Pat. Killgallen & wife pap	Smith		1						
	Do	Widdow Gardner pro	Cotter	1		2					
	Do	Danl. Davies & Wife pro	Weavr.			1					
	Do	Mrs. Gunegal pro	Cotter		1						
	Do	Mary Smith pro	Cotter								
	Do	Michl. Hart & wife pap	Cotter		2						1
	Do	Owen Gawna & wife pap	Wheelwrite		3						
	Do	Andw. Ormsby57 & Wife pro	Labour.	2					1		
	Do	Bryn. Curley & wife pap	Labour.								
	Do	Saml. Henesy & Wife pro	Smith	1		3					
	Do	Dorothy Peters & Wife pro	Cotter			1					
	Do	Jas. Wisely & Wife pro	Weavr.	1							
	Do	Jas. Stewart & Wife pro	pensionr.								
	Do	Wm. Davies & Wife pro	Cotter								
	Do	Widdw. Black pro	Cotter	1							
	Do	Michl. Harken & wife pap	brogmakr.		3				1		
	Do	George Davies & Wife pro	Pensionr.								
	Do	Jas. McGowan & Wife pro	Smith	1				2			1
	Do	Joseph McGowan & Wife pro	Carpenter	1		1					
	Do	Dinis McDonell & Wife pro	Butcher	1							
		prot 90 - papt 43		10	32	10	1	3	6	1	2
[f.410]Sligoe	Sligoe	Robert Ginis papist Wife protestant	Taylor		3						1
	Do	Robt. Rottly & wife pap	Cotter								
	Do	Michl. Gregan papt	brogmakr.								

Com~Sligoe Parish of	Place of Abode	Names and Religion	Proffession	Children under 14 Prot.	Paps.	Children above 14 Prot.	Paps.	Men Servts Prot.	Paps.	Women Servts Prot.	Paps.
	Do	Pat. Colins & wife pap	Labour.		1						
	Do	Thos. Conelan & wife pap	Labour.		1						
	Do	Neal Rosniane & wife pap	Labour.		2						
	Do	Fras. Lally & wife pap	Cooper		1						
	Do	Widdw. Mulhern pap	Cotter		2						
		Widw. Porter pro									
		Widdow Layng	Cotter								
	Do	Conor McManus & Wife pap	Labour.		2						
	Do	Widw. Costello papt	Cotter		2						
	Do	Widdow Teig pap	Cotter								
	Do	Elizabeth Kelly pap	Cotter								
	Do	Peter Rogers & Wife pro	Butcher	1							
	Do	Chas. Kerin & Wife pap	Labour.		4						
	Do	Mrs Smith prot	Cotter	1							1
	Do	Terence McManus & Wife pap	Cotter		1						
	Do	John Frizel & Wife pro	Pensionr.								
	Do	Jon. Scot & Wife pap	Cotter		1		1				
	Do	Jon. Mcdeonogh & Wife pap	horsrider		1						
	Do	John Quinn & Wife pap	Staymakr.				1				
	Do	Francis McCarrick & Wife pap	Labour.		1						
	Do	Sanders Curry & Wife pro	Cotter								
	Do	Thos. Hamealy & Wife pro	Sawyer								
	Do	Walter McCally prot his wife a papist	Weavr.	1		2		1			
	Do	Maurice Patton & Wife pro	Farmer	2					2		0
	Do	Fras Ekins[58] protestant	Schoolmasr.			3					
	Do	Thos. Hart & Wife pro	Taylor		1						
	Do	David Carter & Wife pro	Shoomakr.	1							1
	Do	Doctor Edgar & Wife pro	Surgeon			3				1	
	Do	John Palmer prot	Cooper	2							1
	Do	Pat. Devany & Wife pap	Cotter		1						
	Do	Widdow Crooks pro	Cotter								
	Do	Jas. Nally & Wife pro	Mason	2				1	1		
	Do	Pat. Kenedy & Wife pro	Smith	4				1		1	
	Do	Thos. Williamson & Wife pro	Mercht..	1							
	Do	Miles Burk & Wife pro	pensionr.								
	Do	John Withers & Wife pro	pensionr.	1							
	Do	Thos. Withers & Wife pro	Shoomakr.					1			
	Do	Robt. Hewit & Wife pro	Shoomakr.	4							
	Do	Widdw. Allen protestant	Cotter	2		1					
		prot 37 - pap 35		22	24	9	2	4	3	2	4
[f.411]Sligoe	Sligoe	John Smith & Wife pro	Nailer	3							
	Do	Widdw McDonagh pro	Cotter	1		1					
	Do	Saml. Shaw & Wife pro	Mercht..	4		1					
	Do	Wm. Gill & Wife pro	Smith	2		1					
	Do	Widdw Burk prot	Cotter	3							
	Do	Widdw Gill prot	Cotter			2					
	Do	Widdw Tidey prot	Cotter			2					
	Do	Thos. Hollyday & Wife pro	Cotter	1		2					
	Do	Mrs Kelly papt.	Cotter								1

Com~Sligoe Parish of	Place of Abode	Names and Religion	Proffession	Children under 14		Children above 14		Men Servts		Women Servts	
				Prot.	Paps.	Prot.	Paps.	Prot.	Paps.	Prot.	Paps.
	Do	John Lambert & Wife pro	Comber	4							
	Kelticahill	Cormuck Daily & Wife pap	Cotter		1						
	Do	Pat. Shuredan & Wife pap	Labor.		1						
	Do	Farel Hara & Wife pap	Labor.		2						
	Do	John Delin & Wife pap	Labor.		1						
	Do	Teig Mullican & Wife pap	Labor.		1						
	Do	Dinis Keregan pap	Labor.								
	Do	Own. Kelly & Wife pap	Labor.		3						
	Do	Luke Brunn & Wife pap	Labor.								
	Do	Thos. Fox & Wife pap	Labor.		4						
	Do	Peter Keregan & Wife pap	Weavr.		1						
	Do	Darby Gelan & Wife pap	Labor.								
	Do	Hugh Haley & Wife pap	Cowboy		1		2				
	Do	Wm. Henesy & Wife pro	ffarmer								1
	Do	Andw. Henesy & Wife pro	ffarmer	3					2		1
	Do	Warren Henesy & Wife pro	ffarmer								
	Do	Jon Henesy & Wife pro	ffarmer	4							
	Do	Sanders Irwin & Wife pro	ffarmer	1							
	Do	Richd. Feleson & Wife pro	Weavr.	2							
	Do	Saml. Lindsey & Wife pro	Cooper	2							
	Do	David Lindsey	Farmr.	4							1
	Sligoe	Jas. Killaher & Wife pap	Labor.		2						
	Do	Michl. Donbar & Wife pap	Labor.		4						
	Do	Jas. McDonoghy & Wife pap	Labor.		1						
	Do	Thady Flanagan & Wife pap	Labor.				1				
	Do	Michl. Keaghran & Wife pap	Labor.		2						
	Do	Jas. Kelly & Wife pap	Labour.		3						
	Do	Peter Lynagh & Wife pap	Taylor		1						
	Do	Wm. Jinks & Wife pap	Labour.								
	Do	Pat. Kerin & Wife pap	Labour.								
	Do	Thos. Killfeder & Wife pap	Labor.								
	Do	Jas. Gillgan & Wife pap	Labor.		1						
		pro 30 - pap 46		34	29	9	3	-	2	-	4
[f.412]Sligoe	Sligoe	Michl. Cunbane & Wife pap	Weaver		1						
	Do	John Teige & Wife pap	Labour.		2						
	Do	Robt Clark & Wife pro	Servt.	3							
	Do	Anthony Burnet & Wife pro	Smith			2					
	Do	Dinis Hara & Wife pap	Labor.								
	Do	Pat. Bolan & Wife pap	Labor.		2						
	Do	Holbert Jordan[59] & Wife pap	Labor.		2						
	Do	Gillduff Fihilly & Wife pap	Labor.		2						
	Do	Jasper Lester pro & wife papist	piper								
	Do	Maurice Conmee & Wife pap	Labor				4				
	Do	Richd. McGinis & Wife pap	Labor.		1						
	Do	Bartly Flattelly & wife	Labor.		4						
	Do	David May & Wife pap	Labor		1						
	Do	Jon. Daily & Wife pap	Labor.		4						
	Do	Murtagh Dyer & Wife pap	Weavr.				1				
	Do	Owen Scan & Wife pap	Labor.								

Com~Sligoe Parish of	Place of Abode	Names and Religion	Proffession	Children under 14		Children above 14		Men Servts		Women Servts	
				Prot.	Paps.	Prot.	Paps.	Prot.	Paps.	Prot.	Paps.
	Do	Jon Winterscale[60] & Wife pro	Tanner	2				1			
	Do	Robt. Hegarty[61] & Wife pap	Labr.		4		1				
	Do	Thos Welsh & Wife pap	Weavr		2						
	Do	Jon Taylor & Wife pap	Gardener		3						
	Do	Robt Tucker & wife pro wife papist	butcher			2					
	Do	Peter Tuckr prot wife pap	Cellerman								
	Do	Thos Clanoge & wife pap	Labor		1						
	Do	Pat Grogely & Wife pap	Taylor								
	Do	Miles Costello & wife pap	Labor.								
	Do	Jas. Cunigan & Wife pap	Labor				1				
	Do	Thos. Hart & Wife pap	Weavr.		2						
	Do	Henry Morgan & Wife pro	Weavr.	1							
	Do	Henry Costello[62] & wife pap	Labr.	2					2		
	Do	Thos. Morgan & wife pro	Weavr.	2							
	Do	Hugh Wood &Wife pap	Labor		1						
	Do	Thos. Tankerd & Wife pap	Labor		1						
	Do	Chas Helly & wife pap	butcher		2						
	Do	Thos Kathron & Wife pro	Curryer	0		1					
	Do	Widw Palmer pro	Cotter	2							
	Do	John Anderson pro	Wigmakr.	3							
		pro 21 pap 59		18	41	5	7	1	2		
[f.413] Sligoe		Thos. Winterscale & Wife pro	butcher	2		1					
	Do	Jon. Brown & Wife pro	Cooper	2		1					
	Do	Fras Irwin & Wife pro	pensionr.								
	Do	Michl. Stanley & Wife pro	Vestry Clk	1		1				1	
	Do	John Higin	Farmer								
	Do	Widw Hart	Cotter		4						
	Do	Jas. Kelly	Butcher		3						
	Do	John Egan & Wife pro	Cotter	2		1					
	Ballytivena[63]	Michl. Cox & Wife pap	Labour.		1						
	Do	Archibald Johnson & Wife pro	Cotter	1							
	Do	Luke Devany & Wife pap	Labour.								
	Do	Bryan Cahillery & Wife pap	Labor.				2				
	Do	Michl. Conellan & Wife pap	Labour.		1						
	Do	Jas. Lanoge & Wife pap	Labour.		1						
	Do	Thos. Quinn & Wife pap	Labour.								
	Do	Owen Kithcart & Wife pap	Labour.								
	Do	John McGlaughlin & Wife pap	Smith		1						
	Do	Thos. Conor & Wife pap	Labour.		1						
	Do	Adam Johnson & Wife prot	Labour.	1							1
	Do	Wm. Griffiths & Wife pro	Farmer	4		1			5		3
	Do	Richd. Robison & Wife pro	Labour.	3							
	Do	Jas. Gillgan & Wife pro	Weaver	4					2		
	Do	Wm. Allin & Wife pro	Weavr.	3				2			
	Do	Jas. Carty & Wife pap	Labour.		1						
	Do	Edwd.Heneken & Wife pap	bleacher		4						
	Do	Owen Branally & Wife pap	broguemakr.		3						
	Do	Robt.Lenox& Wife pap	Miller		4						

Com~Sligoe Parish of	Place of Abode	Names and Religion	Proffession	Children under 14		Children above 14		Men Servts		Women Servts	
				Prot.	Paps.	Prot.	Paps.	Prot.	Paps.	Prot.	Paps.
	Do	Mathew Pye & Wife pro	Weaver								
	Rathraghan	Jas. Quigly & Wife pap	Labour.		1						
	Do	Richd. Lonican & Wife pap	Labour.		2		3				
	Do	Dinis Conelly & Wife pap	Labour.		1						
	Do	Joseph Conor & Wife pap	Labour.								
	Do	Thady Hargidan & Wife pap	Labour.		1						
	Do	Jas. Gillgan & Wife pap	Weaver		1						
	Do	Patrick Gillan & Wife pap	Weaver		3						
	Do	Roger Caveny & Wife pap	Weaver		4			3			
	Do	Bernard McNeese & Wife pap	Weaver		3						
	Do	Patrick McAnris & Wife pap	Weavr.		2			1	1		
	Do	Walter Lindsey & Wife pro	Weaver	1				2			
	Do	Michl. Cowen & Wife pap	Weaver		3				1		
	Do	Jon. Carrol & Wife pap	Weaver		4		1				
		pro 26 pap 55		24	49	5	6	5	12	-	5
[f.414]Sligoe	Rathragen	Arthur McCowan & Wife pro	Weaver	4				5			
	Do	Andw. Montgomery & Wife pro	Weavr.	3				4			
	Do	George McCallagh & Wife pro	Weaver	1							
	Do	Robt. McCollogh & Wife pro	Weaver					1			
	Do	Patrick Gallagher & Wife pap	Weavr.		2				1		
	Do	Chas. Ryly & Wife pap	Weaver		2				1		
	Do	Patrick Cran & Wife pap	Weavr.		4						
	Do	Thos. Killerbran & Wife pap	Cowboy		4		1				
	Shannon[64]	Michl. Lenox & Wife pap	Miller		2				2		1
	Do	Bryan Rogers & Wife pap	Labor.		1						
	Do	Thos. Mark & Wife pro	Shoomakr.	3							
	Do	Barthy McSharry & Wife pap	Farmr.		2						
	Do	Darby McSharry & Wife pap	Farmr.		2						
	Do	Jon. Mullinkilly & Wife pap	Labour.		1						
	Do	Owen Mahon & Wife pap	Labour.		2						
	Do	Wm. McNabinn & Wife pap	Farmer		3						
	Carncash[65]	Jas. Dean & Wife pap	Farmer		2						
	Do	Terence Whorisk & Wife pro	Farmer								
	Do	Thos. Whorisk & Wife pap	Laborr.		2						
	Do	Bryn. Finigan & Wife pap	Labor.		1						
	Do	Bryn Mullvihill & Wife pap	Labour.		2						
	Do	Edmund Cuyllkin & Wife pap	Smith		1						
	Do	Luke Finane & Wife pap	Cotter		1						
	Do	Andw. Stuart[67] & Wife pro	Farmer	6							1
	Carrowlusk	Patrick Roonian & Wife pap	Cotter		2						
	Do	Edwd. Gillgan & Wife pap	Cotter		3						
	Do	Hugh Joy & Wife pap	Cotter		3						
	Do	Jon. Hart & Wife pap	Cotter		1						
	Do	Bartly Gillgan & Wife pap	Cotter		4						
	Do	Roger Conor & Wife pap	Cotter		2						
	Do	Thady Brett & Wife pap	Cotter		5						
	Do	Patrick Digean & Wife pap	Cotter		2						
	Do	Bartly Gellan & Wife pap	Cotter		1						
	Fermoyle	Dinis Conor & Wife pap	farmer		0		1				

Com~Sligoe Parish of	Place of Abode	Names and Religion	Proffession	Children under 14		Children above 14		Men Servts		Women Servts	
				Prot.	Paps.	Prot.	Paps.	Prot.	Paps.	Prot.	Paps.
	Do	Conel Conor & Wife pap	farmer		1						
	Do	Peter Scanlan & Wife pap	Cotter								
	Do	Thos. Connolly & Wife pap	Cotter		2						
	Do	Bryan Helly & Wife pap	Cotter		1						
	Do	Roger Connor & Wife pap	Cotter								
	Do	John Hart & Wife pap	Cotter		1						
	Do	Hugh McLaughlin & Wife pap	Mason		3						
		pro 12: pap 70		17	65	-	2	10	4	-	2
[f.415]Sligoe	Donally	Terence Ryly & Wife pap	Weaver								
	Do	Thos. Nelson & Wife pap	Labour.								
	Do	Thady Hargidan & Wife pap	Labour.		2						
	Do	Michl. Caveny & Wife pap	Labour.		2						
	Do	Mark McGowan & Wife pap	Labor.		1						
	Do	Mr Dodwell & Wife pro	Farmer	3					2		2
	Bar-roe68	Joas. Corkran & Wife pap	Labourer		2						
	Do	Peter Bary & Wife pap	Labor.		2						
	Do	Hugh Kerageen & Wife pap	Labour.		1						
	Do	Redmund Fleming & Wife pap	Labour.		1						
	Do	John Gallaghr & Wife pap	Cotter		1						
	Do	Dudly Golrick & Wife pap	Labor.		1						
	Do	Allexandr Sweeny pap	Labor.		2						
	Do	Richd. Colkin & Wife pap	Labour.								
	Do	Pat. Conolly & Wife pap	Labour.		2						
	Do	Jon. Henderson & Wife pap	Farmr.	4							
	Do	Wm. McGowan & Wife pro	Farmr.	1		1			1		2
	Do	John McGowan & Wife pro	Farmr.	3					1		2
	Ballynode	Edwd. Owens & Wife pro	Matster								
	Do	John Gillan & Wife pro	Labor.								
	Do	Thos. Doodican & Wife pap	Labor.		1						
	Do	George Moor & Wife pro	ffarmer	2					1		1
	Do	Patrick Coony & Wife pap	Mason				0				
	Do	Jon. Coony & Wife pap	Labor.		1						
	Do	Henry Hart & Wife pap	Labor.								
	Do	Loghlin McGiverty & Wife pap	Labor.		1						
	Do	Terence Hargidan & Wife pap	Labor.		2						
	Do	John Short & Wife pap	Labour.		2						
	Do	Jas. Griffin & Wife pap	Weaver		3						
	Do	Anthony Hart & Wife pap	Labour.		2						
	Do	Thos. Teig & Wife pap	Labour.		1						
	Do	Pat. Hilly & Wife pap	Labour.		1						
	Do	Thos. Hilly & Wife pap	Labour.		2						
	Do	Robt. Boulton & Wife pro	Cooper	4		1					1
	Do	Hugh McTanist & Wife pap	Labor.								
	Do	Rogr. Conor & Wife pap	Labor.		1						
	Do	Bryn. Ferry & Wife pap	Labor.								
	Do	Michl. Ganley & Wife pap	Labor.		5						
	Do	Peter Quinlisk & Wife pap	Labor.		1						

Com~Sligoe Parish of	Place of Abode	Names and Religion	Proffession	Children under 14		Children above 14		Men Servts		Women Servts	
				Prot.	Paps.	Prot.	Paps.	Prot.	Paps.	Prot.	Paps.
	Carricknellist & Barrynamonow	Fras. Cunigan & Wife pap	Farmer		3						
	Do	Jas. Cunigan & Wife pap	Farmr.		4						
		pro 14 pap 66		17	47	2	-	-	5	-	8
[f.416]Sligoe	Carricknellist & Barrynamonow	John Cunigan & Wife pap	Farmer		2						
	Do	Pat. Cunigan & Wife pap	Farmer		3						
	Do	Bartly Cunigan & Wife pap	Farmer		1						
	Do	Michl. Ô Hara & Wife pap	Farmer		3						
	Do	Michl. Ô Boey & Wife pap	Farmer		4						
	Do	Andw. Ô Bory & Wife pap	Farmer								
	Do	Jas. Ô Bary & Wife pap	Farmer								
	Do	Hugh Ô Bary & Wife pap	Farmr.		3						
	Do	Pat. Haley & Wife pap	Farmr.		2						
	Do	Andw ffeeny & Wife pap	Farmer		3						
	Do	Edmund ffeeny & Wife pap	Farmr.		2				1		1
	Do	Peter Feeny & Wife pap	Farmer								
	Loghkinittin	John Peacock & Wife pro	Farmer								
	Do	Patrick Phillips & Wife pro	Farmr.	3							
	Do	Wm. Muns & Wife pro	Farmer	3							
	Do	Terence Golrick & Wife pap	Farmer		1						
	Do	Pat. Golrick & Wife pap	Farmr.		3						
	Do	John Teraghty & Wife pap	Weavr.		2						
	Do	Owen Devany & Wife pap	Farmr.		3		2				
	Tully	Fras. Brunan & Wife pap	weavr.		2						
	Do	Jas. Brunan & Wife pap	Farmer		3						
	Do	Luke Brunan & Wife pap	Farmer		2						
	Do	Jon. Oats & Wife pap	Farmer		1						
	Do	Thos. Meelican & Wife pap	weaver		2						
	Do	Thady Mally & Wife pap	Farmer		2						
	Do	Fras. Brunan & Wife pap	Farmer								
	Do	Thos. Brunan & Wife pap	Farmer		3						
	Do	Pat. McDonogh & Wife pap	Labor.		1						
	Do	Edwd. Feris & Wife pap	Farmr.		2						
	Do	Farrel Hargidan & Wife pap	Labor.		4						
	Do	Andreas Mullican & Wife pap	Smith		3						
	Do	Pat. Mullican & Wife pap	Labor.		4						
	Do	Thos. Mullican & Wife pap	Farmer		3						
	Cloghermore	Thady Oats & Wife pap	Farmr.		1						
	Do	John Hargidh. & Wife pap	Farmer		1						
	Do	Peter McDonoghy & Wife pap	Farmr.				3				
	Do	Patrick Dyer & Wife pap	Farmer				1				
	Do	Pat. Breeaghn & Wife pap	Farmer		3						
	Do	Pat. Scanlan & Wife pap	Farmer		1				3		
	Do	Dinis Moolican & Wife pap	Cowboy		3						
	Do	Owen McTanes & Wife pap	Taylor		2						
		pap 76 pro:6 pap 74		6	75	-	6	-	4	-	1
[f.417]Sligoe	Cloghermore	Dinis Carty & Wife pap	Weaver								
	Do	Michl. Carty & Wife pap	Labour.		1						
	Do	Dinis Derig & Wife pap	Labour.		2				1		

Com~Sligoe Parish of	Place of Abode	Names and Religion	Proffession	Children under 14 Prot.	Children under 14 Paps.	Children above 14 Prot.	Children above 14 Paps.	Men Servts Prot.	Men Servts Paps.	Women Servts Prot.	Women Servts Paps.
	Corwollick	Cormuck Brinan & Wife pap	Labour.		1				1		
	Do	Widw. Young protest	Cotter			1					
	Callgagh	Mr Edwd Martin[69] & Wife pro	Farmer					1	1	1	2
	Do	Teig Dillan & Wife pap	Cotter		3		3				
	Do	John Oats & Wife pap	Cotter		3						
	Do	Nichols Linany & Wife pap	Cotter				2				
	Do	David Wyer & Wife pro	Farmr.	2		1					1
	Do	Teig Kileslean & Wife pap	Cotter		1				1		
	Do	Bryn. Brunan & Wife pap	Cotter		1				1		
	Do	John Brynan protestant Wife papist	Taylor		1						
	Do	Bryn. Feenan & Wife pap	Labour.								
	Do	Phelim Carbry & Wife pap	Farmr.		3						
	Do	Rogr. Carbry & Wife pap	Farmr.		3						
	Do	Conor Gellan & Wife pap	Farmr.		2						
	Do	Hubert Farel & Wife pap	Farmr.		4						
	Do	Pat. Martin & Wife pap	Farmer		2						
	Do	Bartly Lonican & Wife pap	Farmer								
	Do	John Lonican & Wife pap	Farmer								
	Do	Thady Monaghn & Wife pap	Farmer		2						
	Do	Rogr. Scanlan & Wife pap	Farmr.		4						
	Do	Jon. Brunn & Wife pap	Farmer		1						
	Do	Hugh Hart & Wife pap	Farmer				3				
	Do	Michl. Hart & Wife pap	Labour.		2						
	Do	Bartly Hart & Wife pap	Farmr.		2						
	Do	Michl. Golrick & Wife pap	Farmr.		1						
	Shannon Knox	Robt. Carr & Wife pro	Labour.								
	Do	Dinis Nicole & Wife pap	Labour.		1						
	Do	Hugh Wood & Wife pro	pensionr.	4							
	Faughts[70]	Jas. Henesy & Wife pro	Farmer			3			1		1
	Do	John Henesy & Wife pro	Farmer	3					1		1
	Do	Saml. Henesy & Wife pro	Farmer	2					1		1
	Do	John Lindsay & Wife pro	Wheelright		3						
	Part of Sligo	Mr Mitchellburne Knox[71] & Wife pro	Mercht.			1		2		3	1
	Do	Mr John Knox[72] & Wife pro	Mercht.			2			1		2
	Hazlewood	Col. Wynne[73] & Wife pro	———	2		2		12		10	10
Servts undr Col. Wynne	Do	Wm. Kelly & Wife pap	Gardner								
	Do	Wm. Kelly & Sister	Cotter								
	Do	Thos. Daily & Wife pro	Cotter	1							
pap 55		pro. 26 pap 53		17	40	10	8	15	9	4	19
[f.418]	Hazlewood	John Early & Wife pro	Cotter	3		1					
	Do	Owen Ternan & Wife pap	Cotter		3		2				
	Do	Pat. Gallagher & Wife pap	Cotter								
	Do	Dinis Carrol & Wife pap	Cotter		2		3				
	Do	Thady Derrig & Wife pap	Cotter		3						
	Do	Fras. Brenan & Wife pap	Cotter								
	Do	Pat. Kenedy & Wife pap	Cotter		2						
	Do	Patt. Flanelly & Wife pap	Cotter		2						
	Do	Miles May & Wife pap	Cotter		1						

Com~Sligoe Parish of	Place of Abode	Names and Religion	Proffession	Children under 14		Children above 14		Men Servts		Women Servts	
				Prot.	Paps.	Prot.	Paps.	Prot.	Paps.	Prot.	Paps.
	Do	Luke Fenan & Wife pap	Cotter		3						
	Do	John Derrig & Wife pap	Cotter				1				
	Do	Michl. Derrig & Wife pap	Cotter		5						
	Do	Patt. Derrig & Wife pap	Cotter		2						
	Do	Patt. Navin & Wife pap	Cotter				1				
	Do	Edwd. Mullroony & Wife pap	Cotter				1				
	Do	Jas. Hargidan & Wife pap	Cotter		2		1				
	Do	Hugh Comen & Wife pap	Cotter		3		2				
	Do	Jas. Daily & Wife pap	Cotter								
	Do	Dinis Carrol & Wife pap	Cotter		2		1				
	Do	Rogr. Hart & Wife pap	Cotter								
	Do	Phelim Moran & Wife pap	Cotter		3						
	Do	Peter Carrol & Wife pap	Cotter		4						
	Do	Thos. Camel & Wife pro	Cotter	3							
	Do	Andw. Murtagh	Cotter							2	
	Do	Wm. Morrison & Wife pro	Cotter	3		3					
	Do	Michl. Hargidan & Wife pap	Cotter		3		2				
	Do	Timothy Dillan pap	Cotter		2		3				
	Do	Jas. Mcdermot & Wife pap	Cotter		1						
	Do	John Moor & Wife pro	Servt.	2							
	Do	Jas. McDaniel & Wife pro	Cotter	5							2
	Do	Widw Dillan pap	Cotter								
	Do	Chas. Kelly & Wife pap	Cotter		1						1
	Road To Tullynegrackin	Jon. Quinlisk & Wife pap	Labour.		2						
	Do	Peter Taness & Wife pap	Labour.		4						
	Do	Daniel Scanlan & Wife pap	Labour.		3						
	Do	Pat. Kelly & Wife pap	Labour.								
	Do	Adam Midleton & Wife pro	Labour.	3							
	Do	Patrick Ternan & Wife pap	Taylor		2						
	Do	Chas. Carty & Wife pap	Smith		3						
	Do	John Mucklehony & Wife pro	Labour.								
	Do	Cormuck Murphy	Labour.		3						
		pap 63 pro: 15 pap 65		19	61	4	17	-	-	2	3
[f.419]Sligoe	Road to Tullynegrackin	Wm. Charlesworth & Wife pro	Farmer	2	0						
	Do	John Armstrong[74] & Wife pro	Farmer	3		1					
	Do	Jas. Graham & Wife pro	Farmer	3							
	Do	Jas Parke & Wife pro	Farmer	1							
	Coolbegg	Jas. Brackall & Wife pap	Cotter								
	Do	Thos. Jinks & Wife pap	Cotter								
	Drimishibole	Edwd Hart & Wife pap	Farmer		4		1			1	1
	Do	Pat. Hart & Wife pap	Farmer		3					1	
	Do	John Hart & Wife pap	Cotter								
	Do	Jas. Hany & Wife pap	Farmr.		1						
	Do	Michl. Hany & Wife pap	Farmr.		1						
	Do	Thady McGloghtin & Wife pap	Farmr.		3						
	Do	Jon. Muckloure & Wife pap	weavr.		3						
	Do	Hugh Hart & Wife pap	Farmr.		2						1
	Do	Jon. Hany & Wife pap	Farmr.		1		3				1

Com~Sligoe Parish of	Place of Abode	Names and Religion	Proffession	Children under 14 Prot.	Children under 14 Paps.	Children above 14 Prot.	Children above 14 Paps.	Men Servts Prot.	Men Servts Paps.	Women Servts Prot.	Women Servts Paps.
	Do	Jas. Mcguin & Wife pap	Farmr.				2				
	Do	John Davey pap	Farmr.								
	Do	Pat. Feeny & Wife pap	Farmr.								
	Do	Bryn. Gera & Wife pap	Farmr.				3				
	Do	Darby Callan & Wife pap	brogmakr.		1						
	Do	Michl. McDonogh & Wife pap	Labor.		2						
	Do	Thos. Hargidan & Wife pap	Farmr.								
	Do	Jon. Conillan & Wife pap	Farmr.		2						
	Do	Morgan Moran & Wife pap	Farmr.		2						
	Do	Michl. Moran & Wife pap	Farmr.		3						
	Do	Mattw. Jinks & Wife pap	Farmr.		2						
	Do	Hugh Killaher & Wife pap	Farmr.								
	Do	Pat. Manean & Wife pap	Farmr.		1						
	Do	Owen Meenan & Wife pap	Farmr.		2						
	Do	Pat. Hargidan & Wife pap	Farmr.		3						
	Do	Martin Hargidan & Wife pap	Farmr.								
	Do	Pat. Mcsharry & Wife pap	Labour.				1				
	Do	Thady McGloghlin & Wife pap	Farmr.		2						
	Do	Pat. Brinan & Wife pap	Farmr.		2						
	Carrownaready	Daniel Ternan & Wife pap	Farmr.								
	Do	Pat. Kelly & Wife pap	Farmr.		3						
	Do	Jon. Kelly & Wife pap	Farmr.		2						
	Do	Miles Sweeny & Wife pap	Cotter				1				
	Do	Thos. Scanlan & Wife pap	Farmr.		3						
	Do	Darby Conillan & Wife pap	Farmr.		2						
	Do	Dudly Scanlan & Wife pap	Cowboy		1						
	pro 8. pap: 73			9	51	1	11	-	2	-	3
[f.420]Sligoe	Carowna-madow	Patt. Hany & Wife pap	Labour.		1						
	Do	Michl. Don & Wife pap	Farmr.		2						
	Do	Jas. Dogherty & Wife pap	Labour.		2						
	Do	Bryn Hara	Labour.								
	Do	Widw. McGowaran pap	ffarmr.		4						
	Do	Mathew Dier & Wife pap	Labour.		2						
	Aghamore	Mr Gilbert Trimble & Wife pro	Farmer		1			4			3
	Do	Fras. Dyer & Wife pap	Labour.								
	Do	Jas. Davey & Wife pap	Labour.		2				3		
	Do	Peter McNella & Wife pap	ffarmr.		4				1		
	Do	Murtagh McHugh & Wife pap	Gardener		4						
	Carrickhenny	Owen Monoghan & Wife pap	farmr.		1						
	Do	Pat. McLenough & Wife pap	Labour.								
	Do	Henry Monoghan & Wife pap	ffarmr.				1				
	Do	Jon. Hart & Wife pap	farmr.		2						
	Do	Darby Oats & Wife pap	farmr.								
	Do	John Hart & Wife pap	farmr.		3						
	Do	Jon. Cullan & Wife pap	farmr.		3						
	Do	Jas. Nelan & Wife pap	farmr.		3						
	Do	Dinis Lynch & Wife pap	farmr.								
	Do	Dan. Lynch & Wife pap	farmr.		1						
	Do	Wm. Morison & Wife pro	ffarmr.								

Com~Sligoe Parish of	Place of Abode	Names and Religion	Proffession	Children under 14		Children above 14		Men Servts		Women Servts	
				Prot.	Paps.	Prot.	Paps.	Prot.	Paps.	Prot.	Paps.
	Carrowgu-bedagh	Thos. Walker & Wife pro	Labour.	3							
	Do	Pat. Devany & Wife pap	Labor.		2						
	Do	Thos. Mihan & Wife pap	Labor.		2						
	Do	Thady Oats & Wife pap	farmer		1						
	Do	Jon. Bolan & Wife pap	farmer		2						
	Do	Darby Bree & Wife pap	farmer		3						
	Do	Owen McSharry & Wife pap	farmr.								
	Do	Wm. McSharry & Wife pap	Labor.		2						
	Do	John Moor & Wife pro	ffarmer	2							
	Carrowroe	Thos. Granaghan & Wife pro	farmr.	3		3					
	Do	Danl. McVahy & Wife pap	Labour.		3						
	Do	Thady Davey & Wife pap	Labour.		3						
	Do	Rogr. Conelan & Wife pap	Labour.								
	Do	Wm. Finagan & Wife pap	Labour.	1							
	Do	Jon. Sesknan & Wife pap	Labor.								
	Do	Redmd. Murphy & Wife pap	farmr.		1		2				
	Do	Martin Cranoge & Wife pap	Labour.		3						
	Do	Owen Fenan & Wife pap	Labour.				1				
	Do	Jon. Hever & Wife pap	Labour.		1		1				
		pro 10 - pap 71		8	58	4	5	-	8	-	3
[f.421]Sligoe	Carrowroe	Wm. Duglas & Wife pro	Weavr			1					
	Do	John Davey pap	Labour.								
	Do	Jon. Brown & Wife pro	Cotter								
	Do	Wm. Brown & Wife pap	Labor.								
	Do	Edmd Feeny & Wife pap	Labor.				2				
	Do	Geo. Ormsby & Wife pro	Cotter								
	Ballydoogan	Danl. Waters & Wife pap	Farmr.								
	Do	Miles McFadine & Wife pap	Labour.								
	Do	Conor Scanlan & Wife pap	farmer		1						
	Do	Daniel Navin & Wife pap	farmer		1						
	Do	Michl. Killfeder & Wife pap	farmer		2						
	Do	Wm. Lenaghan & Wife pap	farmer								
	Do	Brian Kelly & Wife pap	Labor.		1						
	Do	Law: Waters & Wife pap	Labor.		2						
	Do	Wm. Patten & Wife pro	farmer	3							
	Do	Wm. Howley & Wife pap	Labour.		2						
	Do	Bryn. Manin & Wife pap	Labour.		2						
	Do	Bryn. Meaghan & Wife pap	Farmer		3						
	Do	Michl. Devany & Wife pap	Labor.								
	Do	Thos. Tankard pap	farmer		3						
	Do	Thos. fflin & Wife pap	Farmr.		2					1	1
	Do	Wm. Buntien[75] & Wife pro	Farmr.	3						1	1
	Willybrook	Council Ormsby & Wife[76] protest	Gent	4				1		4	
	pt Sligoe	Mrs Booth[77] protest	Gent			nieces 2			3		1
		pap 32 prot: 13: pap 30		10	19	3	2	1	3	6	3
[f.422]Sligoe	Drimoghan	Michl. Kilcullen & Wife Paps	Smith		4						
	Do	Teady Haro & Wife Paps	pumpmaker		1				1		
	Do	Teady Fenny & Wife Paps	Labour.								
	Do	Daniel Feenan & Wife Paps	farmer		2		1				

Com~Sligoe Parish of	Place of Abode	Names and Religion	Proffession	Children under 14		Children above 14		Men Servts		Women Servts	
				Prot.	Paps.	Prot.	Paps.	Prot.	Paps.	Prot.	Paps.
	Do	Chas. McSharry & Wife Paps	farmer		2						
	Do	Jas. Fonly & Wife Paps	farmer		2		1		3		1
	Do	Patt. Kunigham & Wife Paps	farmer		2				1		
	Do	Michl. Kunigham & Wife Paps	farmer		3						
	Do	Willm. Kunigham & Wife Paps	farmer		6				1		
	Do	Michll. Meenan & Wife Paps	farmer		4						
	Do	Anthony Kunigham & Wife Paps	farmer		2						
	Do	Mable Feenan widow pap	Cottier		1		1				
	Do	John Kunigham & Wife Paps	Cottier		1						
	Do	Chas. McDermot & Wife Paps	Labourer		1						
	Do	Dudly Brady & Wife Paps	Labourer		1						
	Do	Mathew Verdon & Wife Paps	farmer		2						
	Do	Patt. Gugglean & Wife Paps	farmer		1						
	Do	Patt. Kunigham & Wife Paps	Labourer		2						
	Do	Connor McGaivan & Wife Paps	Cottier								
	Barnaslye	Bryan Gilgan & Wife Paps	Cottier				2				
	Do	Mark Neallan & Wife Paps	Cottier								
	Do	Hugh Brenan & Wife Paps	Cottier								
	Do	Dinnis McSharry & Wife Paps	Cottier		1						
	Do	John Fin & Wife Paps	Cottier		5						
	Do	Michl. Rorke & Wife Paps	Cottier								
	Do	Henry Battle & Wife Paps	Cottier		3						1
	Do	Felix Hartt & Wife Paps	Cottier		3						
	Do	Owen Battle & Wife Paps	Cottier		1						
	Do	Jams. Gublean & Wife Paps	Cottier		2						
	Common	Mrs. Ormsby and Mr Fountaineer	Gentlewomen					1	3	1	3
	Do	Mark Henry & Wife Paps	Cottier		1		2				
	Do	John Killbride & Wife Paps	Cottier		3						
	Do	Roger Noon & Wife Paps	Cottier								
	Do	James Gilgan & Wife Paps	Cottier						1		
	Do	Patt. Cock & Wife Paps	Cottier		1				1		
	Do	Patt. Connel & Wife Paps	Cottier		1						
	Do	Hugh Caveny & Wife Paps	Smith		4				1		
	Do	David Taylor & Wife prot	Miller	2					1		
	Do	Jams. Carter & Wife prots	Miller	1							
	Do	Patt. Moran & Wife Paps	Cottier		3						
	Do	Mark Malvin & Wife Paps	Labourer		2		1				
		prot 6 pap 75		3	67		8	1	13	1	5
[f.423]Sligoe	Tully	Willm. Ryney & Wife pro	overseer								
	Do	Edwd. Connely & Wife Paps	Cottier		1						
	Do	Lawrence Gillan & Wife Paps	Labourer								
	Do	Edwd Connel & Wife Paps	Labourer		3		2				
	Strandhill	Edwd Welsh & Wife Paps	farmer		1		2		1		2
	Do	Anthony Higgan & Wife Paps	Cottier		1		1		0		0
	Do	James Dugan & Wife Paps	Maulster								
	Do	Jas. McGlaughlin & Wife Paps	Cottier				2				
	Do	Peter Geeyen & Wife Paps	Cottier		1						
	Do	Bryan Carren & Wife Paps	Cottier		2						
	Do	Daniel Flannelly pap	Labourer								

Com~Sligoe Parish of	Place of Abode	Names and Religion	Proffession	Children under 14 Prot.	Paps.	Children above 14 Prot.	Paps.	Men Servts Prot.	Paps.	Women Servts Prot.	Paps.
	Inchymulclye[78]	Bryan McGevene & Wife Paps	Cottier		2						
	Oyster Island[79]	Michl. Gilgan & Wife Paps	Cottier		1						
	Carrow Bunnan[80]	John Ward & Wife Paps	Labourer								
	Carrownadough	Bryan Follon & Wife Paps	Sheepherd		3						
	Scardon	Frans. Gilgan & Wife Paps	farmer		3						
	Do	Daniel Ternan & Wife Paps	farmer		2						
	Do	Redmond Gilgan & Wife Paps	Labourer		3						
	Do	Martin Janings & Wife Paps	Labourer								
	Do	John Kelly & Wife Paps	Pumpmaker		4		2				
	Do	Willm. Welsh & Wife Paps	farmer		2						
	Do	Thos. Battle & Wife Paps	farmer		3						
	Do	John Cavanough & housekeeper	Cottier								
	Do	Michl. Gilgan & Wife Paps	farmer		1						
	Do	Jas. Gilgan & Wife Paps	farmer		1				1		
	Do	Paul Gilgan & Wife Paps	farmer		4						
	Do	John Gilgan & Wife Paps	farmer		2		1				
	Do	Elice Gilgan widow pap	Cottier		1						
	Do	Daniel. McCarmock & Wife Paps	Cottier		2						
	Do	Thos. Cavanagh & Wife Paps	Labourer		2						
	Do	Willm. Sanders, Wife & mother in law. prot	farmer	2					2		2
	Do	Jams Gilgan & Wife Paps	farmer		1						
	Do	David Carter & Wife pro	farmer						1		1
	Do	Patt. Benson & Wife pro	farmer	1							
	Do	Luke Gilgan & Wife Paps	farmer		1		1				1
	Do	Michl. Gilgan & Wife Paps	farmer								
	Rathmcallick	Felix McGlaughlin & Wife Paps	Labourer								
	Do	Hugh Mcsharey & Wife Paps	Smith		4				1		1
	Do	Owen Caroly & Wife Paps	Labourer		3						
	Do	Patt. Sinke & Wife Paps	Labourer		1						
		Margret Runian widow	Cottier		2						
6pro 9 pap 71		pro 8 - pap 60		3	57		11		6		7
[f.424]	Cartron na Bruey	Ann Gilgan widow papt	Cottier				3				
	Do	John Gunan & Wife Paps	Cottier		2				2		
	Carrowkeel	Daniel Devany & Wife and one old woman Paps	Cottier		3						1
	Do	Peter Kearrickan & Wife Paps	Cottier		2				1		
	Grangeormsby	Dinnis Kearrickan & Wife Paps	Cottier		2				1		
	Do	Michl. Kearrickan his wife & mother Paps	Cottier								
	RathmcCarrick	Loughlin Feenan & Wife Paps	farmer								
	Do	Owen Clark & Wife Paps	Cottier		3						
	Do	Jams Cavanagh widower papt	farmer				3				
	Do	Daniel Cavanagh & Wife Paps	farmer		1						
	Do	John Gilgan & Wife Paps	Cottier		1						
	Do	Martin Sinke & Wife Paps	Labourer		2						
	Do	Darby Feeny & Wife Paps	farmer								
	Do	Teady Runian & Wife Paps	farmer		1						
	Do	Bartt. Nealan & Wife Paps	farmer		4						

Com~Sligoe Parish of	Place of Abode	Names and Religion	Proffession	Children under 14		Children above 14		Men Servts		Women Servts	
				Prot.	Paps.	Prot.	Paps.	Prot.	Paps.	Prot.	Paps.
	Do	Andrew Nealan & Wife Paps	farmer		2						
	Do	Manas ô Bree & Wife Paps	Labourer		2						
	Do	Lawrence McHugh & mother Paps	farmer								
	Do	Dinnis Manoghan & Wife Paps	Cottier		4						
	Do	Will. Neary & Wife Paps	Cottier		1		2				
	Do	Michll. Dwyer & Wife Paps	Labourer		2						
	Do	Owen Healy[81] & Wife Paps	Labourer								
	Do	Will. Boanan & mother Paps	Labourer								
	Do	Peter Gunan & Wife Paps	Cottier		2						
	Barney Sray	Jams Gilgan & Wife Paps	Cottier		1				1		
	Balydugan	Thos. Flynn	farmer		2				1		2
	Do	Will. Bonton wife & mother pro	farmer	3					1	1	2
	Do	Andrew Murren & Wife Paps	Cottier		1						
	Do	Murtough Cough & Wife Paps	Labourer		1						
	Do	Bryan Meean & Wife Paps	Labourer		2						
	Do	Will. Patten & Wife pro	farmer	3		1					
	Do	Fran. Bell & Wife pro	farmer					1	3		1
	Do	Therince Conellan & Wife Paps	Cottier		2						
	Do	Jams. Kelly & Wife Paps	Cotier								
	Do	Teady Navin & Wife Paps	farmer				1				1
	Do	Andrew Mcdonogh widower papt	farmer	2		3		1			
	Do	Margret Healy widow & mother Paps	Cottier								
	Do	Dinnis Sweeny & Wife Paps	Labourer		1						
	Do	Thos. Stanard widower & mother Paps	farmer		2						
	Do	Bryan Meoughan & Wife Paps	farmer		2						
pro 7 - 75		pro 6 pap 76		6	50	1	12	1		11	7
[f.425]Sligoe	Ballydugan	Cormack Cullinan & Wife Paps	Labourer				2				
	Do	Michl. Breanny & Wife Paps	Cottier				1				
	Do	Cormack Boughan & Wife Paps	Labourer		1						
	Do	Ann Koxs widow Paps	Cottier		2						
	Do	Honour McGoan and Brigitt Teige widows	Poor woman								
	Pap. 9	pap 10					3	3			
[f.426]Sligoe	Carrowmore	John Teige & wife Paps	Weaver		1		1				
	Do	Loghlen Gooran & wife Paps	farmer		3				1		
	Do	Micheal Conner & wife Paps	Smith		1						
	Do	Maurice Gooran & wife Paps	farmer		1				1		2
	Do	Teige Mcdonnagh & wife Paps	farmer		3						
	Do	Teige Devany & wife Paps	Labourer		1						
	Do	Farrell Mahide & wife Paps	farmer		2						1
	Do	Dudley Mcdonogh & wife Paps	Labourer		1		2				
	Do	Thos. Douglass & wife Paps			1						
	Do	James Killfeder & wife Paps	Farmer		3						
	Do	Thos. Canny & wife Paps	Farmer		3						2
	Do	Patrick Stauton & wife Paps	Labourer		2				1		
	Do	Jams Slany & wife Paps	Farmer								
	Do	Willm. Quin & wife paps	weaver		2						

Com~Sligoe Parish of	Place of Abode	Names and Religion	Proffession	Children under 14		Children above 14		Men Servts		Women Servts	
				Prot.	Paps.	Prot.	Paps.	Prot.	Paps.	Prot.	Paps.
	Do	John Killfeder & wife paps	Farmer		2		1				
	Do	Owen Gooran & wife paps			1	0					
	Do	Peter Bree & wife paps	Farmer		2		1				
	Do	John Grady & wife & mother in law Farmer			1						
	Do	Miles McFadden & wife paps	Farmer		2						
	Do	Owen Banaghan & wife paps	Labourer		2						
	Do	Andrew Dyer & wife paps	Farmer		1		1				1
	Do	Dudley Shanlon & wife paps	Farmer		2				1		
	Do	Mark Meenan & wife paps	Farmer		4				2		
	Do	thos. McManus	Weaver								
	Do	Patrick Killfeder Paps	Labourer								
	Clover Hill	Rogr. Chambers & wife pro	Gent. farmer	3		4			2		2
	Do	Darby Meenan his wife and sis in law	Herd								
	Do	Owen McManus & wife paps	Farmer				4	+	2		
	Do	Geo. Irwin & wife ye man a Prot: & wife Paps	Farmer						1		
	Do	Barby Brenan & wife paps	Farmer		3		2				
	Do	Law. Brenan wife & mother paps	Farmer		1		1				
	Do	John Conry, wife & mother pap	Farmer				1				
	Do	Thos. Kenedy & wife paps	Farmer								
	Do	Darby Meenan & wife paps	Labourer		4						
	Do	Patt. Brenan & wife paps	Farmer		3				1		
	Do	Mark McSharry & wife paps	Farmer		4						
	Carrowkeel	Peter Managhan & wife paps	Labourer		1						
	Do	Patt. Teige & wife paps	Cottier		4						
	Do	Patt McDaniel & wife paps	Labourer		2						
	Do	Willm. McGlone & wife paps	Labourer		1						
	Do	Jams. Gellan[82] & wife paps	Labourer		2						
		3 prot 84 Paps		3	66	4	14		12		8
[f.427]	Carrowkeel	Geo. Rhea & wife paps	Weaver				3				
	Do	Hugh Kechrane & wife paps	ffarmer								
	Do	Thady Keckrane & wife paps	ffarmer		5						
	Do	Peter. McGlone & wife paps	Farmer		4						
	Do	Jams. McLaghlin & wife paps	Farmer		2		2		1		
	Do	Edwd. Mucklehoney & wife pro	Farmer								
	Do	Geo. Irwin & wife Prot & widow Papist		3							
		pro 4 - pap 12	Tot	3	11		5		1		
[f.428]Sligoe	Breeogue	Teady Feighney & wife paps	Farmer		3		3		1		
	Do	Chars. Blake & wife pro	Farmer	3		4					1
	Do	Thomas Daniel & wife paps	Farmer		2		1				
	Do	Aney McSharry widow paps	Cottier				4				
	Do	Loughlin Bunian widower paps	Cottier				1				
	Do	Rogr. Runian & wife paps	Farmer		2						
	Do	Margret Daniel widow paps	Cottier		2						
	Do	Thos. Curreen & wife paps	Farmer				3				
	Do	Owen Bree & wife paps	Farmer		1						
	Do	Margret Mulligan widow Papist	Cottier				1				

Com~Sligoe Parish of	Place of Abode	Names and Religion	Proffession	Children under 14		Children above 14		Men Servts		Women Servts	
				Prot.	Paps.	Prot.	Paps.	Prot.	Paps.	Prot.	Paps.
	Do	Gilbert Keivelaghan & wife paps	Cottier								
	Do	Teady Gaffeny & wife paps	Cottier								
	Do	Honor Curreen widow paps.	Cottier		2						
	Do	John White & wife pro	weaver	2							
	Do	Owen Feighney & wife paps	Cottier		2		2				
	Do	Mathew Cawley & wife paps	Farmer		3						
	Do	Martin Hartt & wife paps	Farmer		3				1		
	Do	Edmond Cavenagh widower paps	Farmer		1		3				
	Do	Martin Gawran widower Paps.	Cottier		3						
	Do	Anthony Barry widower Protestant	Cottier								
	Do	Andrew Connelan & wife & his father paps	Farmer		1		1				
	Do	Catherine Connelan paps	Cottier		1		1				
	Do	Bryan Burns & wife paps	Farmer		2						
	Do	Mary Gillan widow paps	Cottier				2				
	Do	Patt. Gillan & wife paps	Cottier				1				
	Do	Shering McSwine & wife paps	Cottier		2						
	Do	Bartly Cunigham & sister paps	Farmer						1		
	Do	John Bealan & wife paps	Cottier		1						
	Do	Patt. Henican & wife paps	Miller		1		2				
	Do	Patt. Bealan[83] & wife paps	Cottier		6						
	Do	Patt. Healy & wife paps	Cottier		1						
	Do	Chars. Ward & wife paps	Cottier				3				
	Do	Edmond McGuin & mother paps	Cottier								
	Knocknahur	Hugh McGlaghlin & wife paps	Farmer		2		2				
	Do	Hugh Cunigham & wife paps	Cottier		1						
	Liscennacouran	Bartly Gunan & wife paps	Cottier								
	Duloghan	Jas. Banan & wife paps	Cottier		1						
	Do	Jas. Meenan & wife paps	Cottier		3						
	Carrowcrin[84]	Patt. Darsey & wife paps	Maulster		8						
	Do	Patt. McGeryan & wife paps	Cottier		4						
	Bree	Daniel Mulligan & wife paps	Cottier		2						
		Pr. 5 pa. 70 Pro: 6 Papists 76		5	60	4	30		3		1
[f.429]Sligo	Kilmakowen	Arthur Nicholson & wife pro	farmer	4		2		2	3		2
	Do	Widow Nanon Protestant	farmer			1					
	Do	Andrew Samin & wife pro	farmer	2							1
	Do	John Panion & wife pro	farmer						1		1
	Do	Widow O'Hara	Cottier			1					
	Do	Katherine Connor widow Papist	Cottier		2		1				
	Do	Thomas Golrick and wife Papist	Cottier				2		1		1
	Do	Dennis McSharry and wife Papist	farmer		3						
	Do	Archibald Robinson and wife prott	farmer	4		1			1		
	Do	Jams Gilgin & wife paps	Cottier		3						
	Do	Carmick Mooney & wife paps	Cottier		3						
	Do	Henry Ward and wife paps	Cottier								1
	Do	Ambrose Kevilichan & wife's mother	farmer		1		1				1
	Do	Owen Mungan & wife paps	farmer				3				

Com~Sligoe Parish of	Place of Abode	Names and Religion	Proffession	Children under 14		Children above 14		Men Servts		Women Servts	
				Prot.	Paps.	Prot.	Paps.	Prot.	Paps.	Prot.	Paps.
	Do	Will. Teige wife & mother in law paps	farmer								
	Do	Thos. Kilray & wife pro	farmer	1					1		1
	Do	Henry Kilray & mother Prot.	farmer								
	Do	Dinnis Carty & wife paps	farmer				1				
	Do	John Carty & wife paps	farmer		1						
	Do	Martin Curreen & wife paps	farmer		3				1		1
	Do	John Banaghan, wife and mother pap	Labourer		3						
	Do	Mary Casany widow paps	Cottier				2				
	Do	Paul McAwee & wife and father paps	Cottier		2						
	Do	Manus Gawran & wife paps	farmer		2						
	Do	Rogr. Skanlan & wife paps	farmer			1					
	Do	Bryan Neal & wife paps	Cottier		1						
	Do	Michl. Murrhan & wife paps	farmer		1		2				
	Do	Michll. Mcdonnagh & wife paps	Cottier		2						
	Do	Jas. McDaniel & wife paps	Cottier		3						
	Do	Peter McSharry & wife paps	Cottier		3						
	Cullinamore	Jams Flannelly & wife paps	Cottier		2		1				
	Do	Christopher Flannelly & wife paps	Cottier		1						
	Do	Michl. McGlaghlin & wife paps	Cottier		1						
	Do	John McGlaghlin & wife paps	Cottier		1						
	Do	John Ward & wife paps	Cottier		2						
	Do	Daniel McGlaghlin & wife paps	Cottier		5						
	Do	John Ward & wife paps	Cottier		2						
	Drimerose Grange	Teady McDonnagh & wife paps	farmer		1		4		3		3
	Do	Thos. Devaney & wife paps	Cottier		3						
	Do	Patt. Calpion & wife paps	Cottier		1				1		
	Do	Rogr. Parke[85] & wife pro	Cottier	1		1					1
	Pa 67 pro 15 pap in Number 65			12	52	6	18	2	11	1	13

[verso f.249]

1525 Protestants in the parish of Sligoe
35603 papists in the same parish

NOTES

1. Including 750 acres of Lough Gill (*General Alphabetical Index*).

2. Ibid.

3. *History of the Irish Parliament*, ii, 323-4.

4. Wood-Martin, *Sligo*, iii, 95.

5. T. O'Rorke, *History of Sligo: town and county* (2 vols, Dublin, 1890, i, 326-8). (Henceforth O'Rorke, *History of Sligo*).

6. Winston Guthrie Jones, *The Wynnes of Sligo and Leitrim* (Manorhamilton 1994), p.36. (Henceforth Guthrie, *The Wynnes of Sligo*).

7. Census, f.399.

8. Wood-Martin, *Sligo*, ii, 150; Census ff 297, 398.

9. John Irwin to Lord Palmerston, 30 January 1738 (Southampton University, Broadlands Papers, MS BR143/37).

10. Henry Hatch, Dublin to Palmerston, 20 August 1733 (Southampton University, Broadlands Papers MS BR141/1/3).

11. John Irwin to Lord Palmerson, 30 January 1738 (Southampton University, Broadlands Papers, MS BR143/37).

12. In 1756, £1208.11.4d was paid in duty on imported goods and £26.11.7d on exports (Wood-Martin, *Sligo*, iii, 229).

13. Lewis, 'John's (St.)'.

14. William Barton lived in a slated house (John Irwin to Lord Palmerston, 30 January 1738 (Southampton University, Broadlands Papers MS BR143/1/37)).

15. Possibly the 'one Carroll' referred to in note 67 by Thomas Mulhern (N.A., P.R.O., CUST 1/48 f.67).

16. Lawrence Vernon was recorder of Sligo in 1732, ballast master in 1730, when he led the improvement of the port, and was provost of Sligo from 1734 to 1753. He was a tenant of the Palmerston estate in 1772 (Wood-Martin, *Sligo*, iii, 109, 230; N.A, P.R.O., CUST 1/31 f.59; Account of a Years Rent due 1772 (Southampton University, Broadlands Papers MS BR57/60)).

17. Samuel Debutts was a son of John Debutts, merchant. Mary Debutts was his sister. They were a successful Sligo family. Lawrence Debutts, a distiller, was leased land by the Temple family in 1687. John Debutts had been Provost of Sligo. Samuel was clearly prosperous: he paid for the building of a new Custom House in Sligo in the 1740s (Burke *LGI* (1958); Southampton University, Broadlands Papers MS BR57/60; N.A., P.R.O., CUST 1/31 f.9).

18. Thomas Knox, according to the report of Robert Stephenson in 1755, established a bleachyard in the previous year for which he received a salary in 1748 from the trustees of the Linen Board. It had a wash-mill, rubbing-boards, beetling engine, kieves, furnaces &c. (Robert Stephenson, *The Inquiry into the State and Progress of the Linen Manufacture continued Number II* (Dublin 1758), p.256). (Henceforth Stephenson, *Inquiry*).

19. Abraham Martin witnessed the will of James Soden 24 April 1763 (*Abstracts of Wills,* ii, 314).

20. William Gibson was a tenant of the Palmerston estate and lived in a slated house (John Irwin to Lord Palmerston, 30 January 1738 (Southampton University, Broadlands Papers MS BR143/1/37)).

21. The will of Caleb Bell of Sligo was proved in 1760 (N.L.I., Index to Diocesan Wills, Elphin, mic. p.1727).

22. The will of Peter Boland, merchant of Sligo was proved in 1790 (N.L.I., Index to Diocesan Wills, Elphin, mic. p.1727).

23. Robert Stephenson, in his inspection of linen manufacture in Sligo in 1750, said that the factory of Edward Corkran had been established for many years and 'was the first introduction of weaving in this county'. Corkran also had four bleachyards and a mill. He did 'a considerable amount of business' (Stephenson, *Inquiry* , p. 256).

24. Joseph Davey had a long-running feud with the Board of Customs. In October 1746 he complained to the Board that his ship laden with butter was detained by the surveyor and he was asked to pay duty for more butter than was shipping and 'other unwarrantable proceedings'. In November that year he kept a ship of rock salt undischarged for more than two months and 'abused and scurrilously traduced the Port Officers'. He was told to behave himself to the King's Officers in a civil manner. He made a further complaint against the surveyor in March 1746/7 which was not upheld (N.A., P.R.O., CUST 1/31 f.9; 1/41 ff. 49, 70, 36).

25. John Fahy lived in a slated house (John Irwin to Lord Palmerston, 30 January 1738 (Southampton University, Broadlands Papers MS BR143/1/37)).

26. Mrs Gore was a tenant of the Palmerston estate. She was described by Henry Temple's agent as a 'common object of charity' Francis Corkran to Henry Temple, 2 January 1740 (Southampton University, Broadlands Papers MS BR143/1/2)).

27. Matthew Babington began work in the customs in 1741. He was sent from Londonderry to Sligo as a tidewaiter in February 1747/8. (N.A., P.R.O., CUST 1/31 f.9; 1/32 f.96; 1/44 f.28).

28. John King, merchant of Sligo was reported to have imported 815 bushels of white salt and other goods without paying duty. He was a tenant of the Palmerston estate in 1772 (N.A., P.R.O., CUST 1/31 f.9; 1/43 ff 104, 134; Southampton University, Broadlands Papers MS BR57/60).

29. Widow Crean was a tenant of the Palmerston estate. (Francis Corkran to Henry Temple 2 January 1740 (Southampton University, Broadlands Papers MS BR143/1/2)).

30. Archibald Egelston was a tenant of the Palmerston estate (Account of a Years Rent due, 1772 (Southampton University, Broadlands Papers MS BR57/60)).

31. John Gibson was a tenant of the Palmerston estate (John Irwin to Lord Palmerston, 30 January 1738 (Southampton University, Broadlands Papers MS BR143/1/37)).

32. William Barrett married Elizabeth Phibbs in 1749 (N.L.I, Marriage Licence Bonds Diocese of Elphin, mic. p.1881).

33. Barrett Knott witnessed the will of James Soden, 24 April 1763 (*Abstracts of Wills*, ii, 314).

34. Robert Ormsby leased the point of Ballytivnan from the Palmerston estate (Account of a Years Rent due, 1772 (Southampton University, Broadlands Papers MS BR57/60)).

35. Henry Farrell married Mary Duany in 1747. He witnessed the memorial of the will of Richard Gore, of Sligo 12 February 1752 (N.L.I, Marriage Licence Bonds Elphin mic. p.1881; *Abstracts of Wills*, ii, 135).

36. Probably the widow of John Greenlaw, a boatman (N.A., P.R.O., CUST 1/42 f.131).

37. A widow Mary Lynchaghan was a tenant of the Palmerston estate (Account of a Years Rent due, 1772 (Southampton University, Broadlands Papers MS BR57/60)).

38. Thomas Mullin was a tenant of the Palmerston estate (Account of a Years Rent due, 1772 (Southampton University, Broadlands Papers MS BR57/60)).

39. William Phillips was a tenant of the Palmerston estate and lived in a slated house (John Irwin to Lord Palmerston, 30 January 1738 (Southampton University, Broadlands Papers MS BR143/1/37)).

40. Charles Smith came from Killibeggs to Sligo in 1743 where he had been the eldest supernumerary gauger in Ulster. He was made a full gauger in 1743 (N.A., P.R.O., CUST 1/35 f.87).

41. Col. John Irwin was a tenant of the Palmerston estate. He and his brother caused much difficulty to Henry Temple during the 1720s and 1730s, claiming part of Castlegarran in the parish of Drumcliff (Henry Hatch to Lord Palmerston, 20 August 1733; Robert Roberts to Lord Palmerston, 14 July 1726, 15 September 1733; Robert Roberts to Lord Palmerston, 14 July 1724 (Southampton University, Broadlands Papers MS BR141/1/f.3, 4; BR142/f.22)).

42. David Boyd was a tenant of the Palmerston estate (Account of a Years Rent due, 1772 (Southampton University, Broadlands Papers MS BR57/60)).

43. Possibly James Wallace who in 1749 was fined £8 for concealing 229 gallons of pot ale and in 1749/50 £9 for concealing 198 gallons of ale (N.A., P.R.O., CUST 1/48 f.136).

44. Roger Horroghy was a tenant of the Palmerston estate (Account of a Years Rent due, 1772 (Southampton University, Broadlands Papers MS BR57/60)).

45. A Thady Egan was a tenant of the Palmerston estate (Account of a Years Rent due, 1772 (Southampton University, Broadlands Papers MS BR57/60).

46. Thomas Mulhert, clothier, said that the officer of Excise had seized a pan belonging to him for a fine laid on 'one Carroll' (N.A., P.R.O., CUST 1/48 f.67).

47. Ambrose Gilligan OP was listed in 1743 as living in Sligo (Beirne, (ed.) *Diocese of Elphin*, p. 125).

48. John Gibson was a tenant of the Palmerston estate (Account of a Years Rent due, 1772 (Southampton University, Broadlands Papers MS BR57/60)).

49. Possibly Michael McDonnagh, listed in the State of Popery returns 1731 and in 1762. He died in 1763 (Beirne, (ed.) *Diocese of Elphin*, p.125).

50. The will of Charles Reilly of Sligo was proved in 1792 (N.L.I., Index to Diocesan Wills Elphin, mic. p.1727).

51. Probably Elizabeth Hughes who, in the opinion of the collectors, had been injured by a prosecution, probably for selling without a licence (N.A., P.R.O., CUST 1/48 f.136).

52. Peter Brown, a boatman of Drogheda was sent to Sligo to succeed George Throp who had been dismissed (N.A., P.R.O., CUST 1/44 f.56).

53. Thomas Brown tidewaiter in the port of Sligo was allowed his expenses when he was on board the 'Penguin' from Newfoundland stranded at Killala in January 1748/9 being 23 days, during which time he was dangerously ill of a flux (N.A., P.R.O., CUST 1/47/69).

54. There were mills below the bridge in Sligo, owned in the eighteenth century by the Martin family (McTernan, *In Sligo*, p. 373).

55. William Cross was the port surveyor. In May 1747 he came to Sligo in exchange for the previous surveyor, William Miller who was sent to Dundalk. Cross was told he must perform better than his predecessor (N.A., P.R.O., CUST 1/42 f. 99).

56. In 1756 the salary of James Sandford as collector of Sligo port was £24.1s.3d quarterly, with £7. 10s.0d for a clerk. (N.L.I., Account of HM revenue including collectors fees for the quarter ended 2 March 1756, MS 10,128).

57. Andrew Ormsby was a tenant of the Palmerston estate (Account of a Years Rent due, 1772 (Southampton University, Broadlands Papers MS BR57/60)).

58. Francis Ekins may have been the only one of the five schoolmasters in Sligo who held a degree from Trinity College Dublin. However this is speculative, as he would have been 92 in 1748. Francis Ekins was born in Co. Galway, a son of Walter Ekins. He entered TCD in 1676 aged 18 and took BA in 1681 (*Alumni Dubliniensis*).

59. Hubert Jordan was a tenant of the Palmerston estate (Account of a Years Rent due, 1772 (Southampton University, Broadlands Papers MS BR57/60)).

60. John Winterscale was a tenant of the Palmerston estate. His plot in Holborn Street, Sligo town was owned by Joshua Cooper of Markree (Account of a Years Rent due 1772 (Southampton University, Broadlands Papers MS BR57/60; N.L.I., MS 750/40)).

61. Robert Heagarty was a tenant of the Palmerston estate (Account of a Years Rent due, 1772 Southampton University, Broadlands Papers MS BR57/60).

62. Henry Costello was a tenant of the Palmerston estate (Account of a Years Rent due, 1772 (Southampton University, Broadlands Papers MS BR57/60)).

63. 'Thos Corkran Part of Rathbroghan 65a Good Arable fit for Fattening tillage or Meadow ditto the Bleach Green 10a 1r 25p, Mr Wm. Griffith part of Ballytivnan & Rath Brgn.' 172a 0r 12p (He paid £10. rent on 6 May 1749). 'The same as above but that there are some bottoms, Mr Robert Bolton Ballytivnan 13a 1r 11p. The same as Mr Corkrans, James Crawford 19a 3r 19p. The same but that the part next the Greenfort is a bogy bottom' (N.L.I., MS 750/3; MS 5790/363).

64. 'Arable and Pasture. Good for Tillage or Meadow' (N.L.I., MS 750/13).

65. Mills at Rathbragan had been in existence since the early sixteenth-century. The Strafford Survey reported a 'good English mill' at Rathbraghan, the next door townland, in the 1630s. In 1722 the mills at Rathbragan for grinding corn and tucking cloth became the property of the Wynne family (Wood-Martin, *Sligo*, iii, 240; McTernan, *In Sligo*, pp 372-3).

66. 'Arable and Pasture 95 3 30 Very good for Tillage or Sheep. Bog 26 2 23. This bog is... mangled very much in turf holes' (N.L.I., MS 750/11).

67. Andrew Stuart rented land at Carncash for £15.1s.11d, 21 March 1749 (N.L.I., MS 5790 f.358).

68. 'William McGowans part 36 3 16 Arable and Pasture fitt for Tillage some part thereof Rushy and Sour;John McGowans part 37 2 36 Ditto... well Inclosed and Divided Limestone Gravel convenient; William Hendersons part 6 0 22 Part of this Moory Limestone Gravel Convenient; Roger Hendersons part 19 2 28. This is the same as ye first above and well inclosed & divided; John Hendersons part 19 2 20 Ditto' (N.L.I., MS 750 f.4).

69. Edward Martin, a farmer of Callgagh was agent to Owen Wynne III. He was a coroner of Ireland in 1746 and he lived in a slated house in the town. In 1753 he became a burgess of the town. He was Provost from 1760 to 1768 (Watson *Almanack*;Account of a Years Rent due, 1772 (MS BR 57/60); John Irwin to Lord Palmerston, 30 January 1738 (Southampton University, Broadlands Papers, MS BR143/1/37); Wood-Martin, *Sligo*, iii, 101, 439).

70. 'Arable and Pasture 62 2 36 Good for tillage &c, Green Pasturable Bottom 2 0 0; Reclaimable Green Moory Pasture 32 2 35. This is very Reclaimable the Limestone Gravel on the Spot; Mixed Moory & Dry Mangled Bog 9 2 8. This is also Reclaimable Mangled Bog 12 2 25. This is very much Mangled and Cutt away in Holes (N.L.I., MS 750 f.5).

71. Mitchellburne Knox was a man of some importance in Sligo. He was elected to Sligo council in 1715 and became Provost in 1722. He lived in a house with a slated roof, which indicated wealth, as in 1738 there were said to be only 15 slated houses in the town. Apart from his business as a merchant, he made money by assessing salvage money on wrecks off the Sligo coast. He and Thomas Knox witnessed the will of Richard Gore who died in 1752 (O'Rorke, *History of Sligo*, i, 328; Wood-Martin, *Sligo*, iii, 47; John Irwin to Lord Palmerston, 30 January 1738 (Southampton University, Broadlands Papers, MS BR143/1/37); N.A., P.R.O., CUST 1/35 f.13; 1/31 f.246; *Abstracts of Wills* ii,135).

72. John Knox owned 400-500 acres of woods at Rockwood of oak, ash, birch, sally [willow] and alder which were by Lough Gill. He put them up for sale in 1744. He was elected to Sligo council in 1750. He too lived in a slated house in the town (*Dublin Courant*, 25-29 Dec. 1744; O'Rorke, *History of Sligo*, i, 328; John Irwin to Lord Palmerston, 30 January 1738 (Southampton University, Broadlands Papers, MS BR143/1/37)).

73. Owen Wynne III (1686-1755) was High Sheriff of Sligo in 1723 and 1725. His wife was a daughter of John ffolliott of Donegal. Their daughter Hannah married William Ormsby of Willowbrook, Sligo, enlisted in brigadier Cope's Regiment of Dragoons 1701/2; lieutenant 1710/11; captain lieutenant 1737; captain 1741 in Colonel Brown's Regiment. In 1753 he was a major in the 9th regiment of Dragoons. He leased the island of Inishmurry from the Palmerston estate, probably for grazing cattle (Guthrie-Jones, *Wynnes of Sligo*, pp 40-3; N.A., P.R.O., WO 64/9 f.174; Southampton University, Broadlands Papers MS BR57/60).

74. John Armstrong was renting land at Tullymore, Sligo from Joshua Cooper of Markree in 1788. It was 'Good arable for tillage sheep or fattening light cowes' (N.L.I., MS 21 F 2/2).

75. William Buntein and his wife lived in a slated house (John Irwin to Lord Palmerston, 30 January 1738 (Southampton University, Broadlands Papers, MS BR143/1/37)).

76. William Ormsby, son and heir of Francis Ormsby of Willybrook [Willowbrook]. He married Hannah Wynne, daughter of Owen Wynne III William Ormsby, son and heir of Francis Ormsby of Willybrook [Willowbrook]. He was a student at the Inner Temple in 1736 and admitted to the King's Inns in 1741. He married Hannah Wynne, daughter of Owen Wynne III (*King's Inns Admission Papers*; Guthrie-Jones, *The Wynnes of Sligo* p.40).

77. Mrs Booth lived in a slated house in the town (John Irwin to Lord Palmerston, 30 January 1738 (Southampton University, Broadlands Papers, MS BR143/1/37)).

78. Probably the island of Inishmurray, which was owned by the Temples. Six families were living there in 1787. It had a reputation for having the 'best kelp in Ireland' (Beaufort, *Journal*, TCD MS 4026/2 f.57).

79. A pier was built on Oyster Island, but so badly that by 1787 it was in ruins (Beaufort, 'Journal', TCD MS 4026/2 f.58).

80. Townland owned by the Cooper family of Markree. Said to be arable and pasture good for tillage, fattening light cows or sheep. There was some 'dry bog interspd. with vains of Green Pastre on ye Hill of Knocknarea' (N.L.I., MS 21 F 2/24).

81. Owen Healy was a tenant of the Palmerston estate (Account of a Years Rent due, 1772 (Southampton University, Broadlands Papers MS BR57/60)).

82. James Geilan had been a tenant of the Palmerston estate but was dead in 1772 (Account of a Years Rent due, 1772 (Southampton University, Broadlands Papers, MS BR57/60)).

83. A Patrick Bealan was a tenant of the Palmerston estate in 1772 (Account of a Years Rent due, 1772 (Southampton University, Broadlands Papers, MS BR57/60)).

84. Townland owned by the Coopers of Markree, co. Sligo. Said to be good for tillage or sheep (N.L.I., MS 21 F 2/23).

85. Roger Park was a tenant of the Palmerston estate in 1772 (Account of a Years Rent due, 1772 (Southampton University, Broadlands Papers, MS BR57/60)).

DRUMCLIFF COUNTY SLIGO

INTRODUCTION: *The parish of Drumcliff is in the barony of Lower Carbery, 3 miles north-north-west from Sligo on the main road to Ballyshannon. It had 26,598 statute acres including 112 acres of Glencar Lake and 66 acres of small loughs.*[1] *By 1749, Drumcliff was a centre for weaving, with 27 weavers and 3 bleachers working in the parish. The wealthy Sligo merchant, Mitchellburne Knox, brought looms into the district.*[2]

The incumbent of Drumcliff was the Rev. Edward Munns, who had been appointed archdeacon of Elphin in 1743. He held the parish with that of Ahamlish. He lived in the parish. The rectory was impropriate in the Wynne family.

OCCUPATIONS

Occupation	Count	Occupation	Count	Occupation	Count
Aleseller	5	Dairyman	5	Pincher	1
Bailiff	1	Eelseller	2	Pumpmaker	2
Blacksmith	3	Farmer	18	Scaler	1
Bleacher	3	Gardener	1	Servants, household	255
Boatman	4	Garner	1	Shepherd	1
Broguemaker	1	Innkeeper	1	Shoemaker	1
Church Clerk	1	Labourer	55	Smith	4
Cleric	1	Landholder	282	Tailor	8
Cooper	4	Mason	1	Tiler	3
Cottier	80	Miller	5	Weaver	26
Cowboy	6	Overseer	2	Weaver and landholder	1
Cowherd	36				

Com~Sligoe / Parish of	Place of Abode	Names and Religion	Proffession	Children under 14 Prot.	Paps.	Children above 14 Prot.	Paps.	Men Servts Prot.	Paps.	Women Servts Prot.	Paps.
[f.430] Drumcliff	Kinatogher	Dinis Coragan & wife paps	Lad.houldr.						1		
	Do	John Coragan & wife paps	Lad.houldr.		1				0		
	Do	Darby Mulvany & wife paps	Lad.houldr.		1				2		
	Do	Teady Feeny & wife paps	Lad.houldr.								
	Do	Farfass Mulconrey & wife paps	Cow herd								
	Do	John Gealan & wife paps	Deryman				1				
	Do	Thos. Hauraghlan & wife paps	Deryman				1				1
Do	Lower Rosses³	Darby Kinlaghn & wife paps	Lad.houldr.		2						
	Do	Laghlin Gowran & wife paps	Lad.houldr.								
	Do	Petter Gealon & wife paps	Lad.houldr.		1		2				
	Do	Darby Kinorlean & wife paps	Lad.houldr.		1						
	Do	Diness ffeeny & wife paps	Lad.houldr.								
	Do	Patt. ffeeny & wife paps	Lad.houldr.		2		1				
	Do	Owen ffeeny & wife paps	Lad.houldr.		2		1				
	Do	Wm. Gealan & wife paps	Lad.houldr.		2		1				
	Do	John Gilgan & wife paps	Lad.houldr.		1		2				
	Do	Patt. ffeeny & wife paps	Lad.houldr.		3						
	Do	Andr. Gealan & wife paps	Lad.houldr.		3						
	Do	Darby Gealan & wife paps	Lad.houldr.								
	Do	Jams Gealan & wife paps	Lad.houldr.		4		1				
	Do	Bartly Finagan & wife paps	Lad.houldr.		2						
	Do	Domnick Kinerlen & wife paps	Labour.		2						
	Do	John Kinlogh & wife paps	Lad.houldr.		2						
	Do	Michl. Gilgan & wife paps	Labour		1						
	Do	Thos. Gealan & wife paps	Lad.houldr.		1						
	Do	Patt. Gealan & wife paps	Cowherd		2						
	Do	Patt. Gilgan & wife paps	Labour		1						
Do	Roses uper	Thos. Devany & wife paps	Lad.houldr.		1						
	Do	Mick. Gealan & wife paps	Lad.houldr.		2						
	Do	Wm.Caran & wife paps	Cowherd				2				
	Do	Widw. Devany paps	Cottor		2						
	Do	Thos. Kinlagh & wife paps	Taylor		2						
	Do	John Kinlaghan & wife paps	Labourer		1		1				
	Do	Bartly Crad & wife paps	Weaver								
	Do	Thos. Conaghan & wife paps	Lad.houldr.				2				
	Do	Owen Gealan & wife paps	Lad.houldr.		1						
	Do	Charles Geal & wife paps	Lad.houldr.		1				1		
Do	Roses Gealan	Edwd. Smith & wife prots.	Lad.houldr.						1		1
	Do	Jams Boyd & wife prots.	Lad.houldr.	2							
	Do	Edmd. Gealan & wife paps	Lad.houldr.		2		1				
	Do	Thos. Caran & wife paps	Lad.houldr.		1						
		prots 4 - paps 77		2	47		16		4		4
[f.431] Drumcliff	Magheramore	Darby Coman & wife paps	Lad.houldr.		3						
	Do	Richd. Harken & wife paps	Lad.houldr.		2						
	Do	Owen Hart & wife paps	Lad.houldr.		5						
	Do	Wm. McSharey & wife paps	Lad.houldr.				1				
	Do	Jams. McGrorarey & wife paps	Miller		2						

Com~Sligoe Parish of	Place of Abode	Names and Religion	Proffession	Children under 14 Prot.	Paps.	Children above 14 Prot.	Paps.	Men Servts Prot.	Paps.	Women Servts Prot.	Paps.
	Do	Jams. McGoan & wife paps	Labourer								
	Do	Michl. McGoan & wife paps	Deryman		1						
	Do	Terance Boyl & wife paps	Labourer								
	Do	Charles Dogan & wife prots	Bleacher			1			1		1
Do	Clunidarar[4]	Robt. Shaw[5] widw. protes	farmer	5		2			1		1
	Do	Saml. Shaw & wife prot	Lad.houldr.			3		1			1
	Do	Arter Osburn & wife prot	Cooper	2							
	Do	Jams Karr & wife prot	farmer	4		2					
	Do	Patt. Dan & wife prots	Weaver	1							
	Do	Jams McKoen & wife paps	Labourer		2						
	Do	Farall Galagher & wife paps	Smith		2		2				
	Do	David Friezr & wife prots.	Weaver								
	Do	Domnick Tugera & wife paps	Labourer								
Do	Drum	Robt. Cuningham[6] & wife prots	farmer					1			1
	Do	Saml. Cuningham & wife prots	Lad.houldr.	5							
	Do	Jams Doney & wife prots	Labourer	3							
	Do	Bartly McSharey & wife paps	Labourer								
	Do	Teady Bofin & wife paps	Cowherd				1				
Do	Racormick	Morass Kinlaghan & wife paps	Lad.houldr.				1				
	Do	Thos. Kinloghan & wife paps	Lad.houldr.		2						
	Do	Michl. Gealan & wife paps	Lad.houldr.		2						
	Do	Phillip Kinlaghan & wife paps	Lad.houldr.		2						
	Do	Wm. Fegliny & wife paps	Lad.houldr.		1						
	Do	Coner McGolrick & wife paps	Cowherd				2				
	Do	Thos. McGolrick & wife paps	Labourer								
	Do	Milles Jonins & wife paps	Taylor		2						
	Fiagheradarne	Jams Boyl & wife paps	Inkeeper		3		1				
	Do	Teady Kearan & wife paps	Lad.houldr.		1						
	Do	Terance Cunen & wife paps	Lad.houldr.		3						
	Do	Murtagh Coner & wife paps	Lad.houldr.		1						
	Do	Bartly Geeing widr. pap	Lad.houldr.		1						
	Do	Hugh Gaghan & wife paps	Smith								
Do	Tully	Hugh Sheal & wife paps	Labourer		1						
	Do	Michl. Tugara & wife paps	Labourer		2						
	Do	ffardo. McGoan & wife paps	Labourer		3						
	Kinatogher	Bryn. Caragan & wife paps	Lad.houldr.		1				1		
Prots 20 pa 59		prot 14 - pap 62		20	42	8	8	2	3		4
[f.432] Drumcliff	Lisnalurg[7]	Jams. Brinan & wife pap	Labourer		1		1				
	Do	Michl. Corad & wife pap	Labourer		2						
Do	Tysan[8]	Michl. Hart & wife pap	Cowherd		2						
	Do	Wm.Devany & wife pap	Labourer		1		1				
Do	Rahaperny[9]	Wm. Hara & wife prot	Overseer[10]	2		1					
	Do	Owen McGanior & wife prot	Overseer				2				
	Do	Cormuck Nickeson & wife pap	Labourer		2						
Do	Kiltecolly[11]	John Hunter[12] & wife prot	Weaver	4							
	Do	Ellenr. Clary[13] widow pap	Lad.houldr.		2		1				
	Do	Jams. Mcnaburn & wife pap	Labourer		1						
	Do	John McGines & wife pap	Lad.houldr.		2						
	Do	John Feeny & wife pap	Lad.houldr.		2						

| Com~Sligoe | Place of | Names and Religion | Proffession | Children under 14 | | Children above 14 | | Men Servts | | Women Servts | |
Parish of	Abode			Prot.	Paps.	Prot.	Paps.	Prot.	Paps.	Prot.	Paps.
	Do	Owen Lengan & wife pap	Lad.houldr.				2				
	Do	Phillip Lengan & wife pap	Lad.houldr.		1						
Do	Killselagh Lowr[14]	Robert Lyndsay & wife prot	Lad.houldr.	2			1				
	Do	Robt Shaw & wife prot	Lad.houldr.				2				
	Do	Diness Hart & mothr.	Cowherd								
Do	Killselagh Upr	Jams Wier & wife prot	Lad.houldr.			2			1		1
	Do	Jams Potter & wife prot	Lad.houldr.	2				1	1		2
	Do	Bry. McCormick & wife pap	Weaver		2						
	Do	Bartly Gealan & wife pap	Labourer		2						
	Do	Bry. Mccormick & wife pap	Weaver		2						
Do	Killselagh Dignan	Luck Coner & wife pap	Lad.houldr.		2						
	Do	Terance Coner & wife pap	Lad.houldr.		2		2				
	Do	Thos. Hargitan & wife pap	Lad.houldr.		2		1				1
	Do	Patt. Mulroony & wife pap	Labourer		2		1				1
	Do	Wm. Mulroony & wife pap	Lad.houldr.								
Do	Farnacarny	Allixandr Comble & wife pap	Aleseller						2		2
	Do	Owen Ward & wife pap	farmer		1				1		1
	Do	Allixandr Robison & wife prot	Aleseller	1					1		1
	Do	Petter Hart & wife pap	Aleseller		1				1		1
	Do	Bry. Dowen & wife pap	Labourer				2				
	Do	Widw. McDonel paps	Aleseller				2				
	Do	John Killcollen & wife pap	Labourer		1						
Do	Gortnagrally	Michl. Conor & wife pap	farmer				3				
	Do	Mark Shery & wife pap	Weaver		2						
	Do	Patt. McKelson & wife pap	Lad.houldr.		1						
	Do	Bry. Cered & wife pap	Labourer		1						
	Do	Frances Laneghan & wife pap	Lad.houldr.		2						
	Do	Bry. Lanaghan & wife pap	Cottor			1					
	Do	Peter Carrick & wife pap	Lad.houldr.		2						
Prots. 14.		Prots 12 - paps. 66		11	41	13	12	1	7	-	10
[f.433] Drumcliff	Ballymulan	Martin Gourum & wife pap	Labour		3		3				
		Patt. Gilgan & wife pap	Labour				1				
	Do	Michl. Gilgan & wife pap	Boatman		2						
	Do	Patt. Gourvan & wife pap	Labour		1						
	Do	Andw. Gaumy & wife pap	Pumpmakr		4		1				
	Do	Mich. Kinlaghan & wife pap	Cowherd		1		1				
	Do	John Hall & wife prots	Milor	3							
	Do	David. Furey & wife pap	Boatman		7						
	Do	Teady Crowley & wife pap	Labour		4		1				
	Do	Con. O'Donel[15] & wife pap	Bleachr.		2						
	Do	Jams Haron & wife pap	Labour		1						
	Do	Bartly Keenan & wife pap	Labour		3						
	Do	John Muleesan & wife pap	Labour								
	Do	Ever Luard & wife pap	Garner			1			4		4
Do	Creggs[16]	Mr Phillip Birn Prot	farmer						4		4
	Do	James Chambers & wife prot	Gardener	3							
	Do	Patt. Kinlaghan & wife pap	Labour				1				

Com~Sligoe / Parish of	Place of Abode	Names and Religion	Proffession	Children under 14		Children above 14		Men Servts		Women Servts	
				Prot.	Paps.	Prot.	Paps.	Prot.	Paps.	Prot.	Paps.
	Do	Owen Kinlaghan & wife pap	Tiler		1						
	Do	Phillip Kinlaghan & wife pap	Tiler								
	Do	Teady Kinlaghan & wife pap	Tiler		3						
	Do	Loghlin Kinlaghan & wife pap	Tayler		1						
	Do	Luck Finackan & wife pap	Labour		2						
	Do	Edwd. Mony & wife pap	Labour		3						
	Do	Brian Finaghan & wife pap	Labour		3						
	Do	John Bofin & wife pap	Labour		2						
	Do	Jon. Finackan & wife pap	Labour		1						
	Do	Domnick O'Fin & wife pap	Labour								
	Do	Bry. Dowen & wife pap	Smith		2						
	Do	Lorance O Hara & wife pap	Labour		1						
Do	Mulinakeny	John Gilgan & wife pap	Tayler		2						
	Springfield	Jams. Killale & wife pap	Labour		2		2				
	Do	Naghtin O'Donel & wife pap	Bleachr.		2						
	Do	Jams Gilgan & wife pap	Labour		2						
	Do	Dinis Conaghan & wife pap	Labour		2						
	Balinvoer	Hugh Rice & wife pap	Cooper		2						
	Do	Thom. Feghney & wife pap	Labour		1						
	Do	Patt. Keran & wife pap	Taylor								
	Lisnalurg	Bartly Sweeny & wife pap	Labour		1						
	Do	Fency McGlaghlin & wife pap	Mason		2						
	Do	Charless Gilgan & wife pap	Labour		1						
	Do	Teady Longan & wife pap	Smith								
		prots 5 paps 76		6	65	1	10		8		8
[f.434] Drumcliff	Newtown Drumcliff	Teady Quin & wife pap	Beliff		2						
	Do	John Carty & wife pap	Cowherd		1						
	Broadcullen	Thos. Ora & wife prots	Pincheur[?]			1					
	Do	Thos. Hall & wife prots	Church Clerk	2		2			1		1
	Do	Owen Feeny & wife pap	Labourer		3		1				
	Do	Mathw. Feres & wife pap	Cowherd		2						
	Balinagalagh[17]	Owen Scandlan & wife pap	Lad.houldr.		2		2				
	Do	Pat. Togara & wife pap	Lad.houldr.		3						
	Do	Mathw Doud & wife pap	Lad.houldr.								
	Do	Dainel Lagan & wife pap	Lad.houldr.		1						
	Do	Luck Whorisk & wife pap	Lad.houldr.		1						
	Do	Rogr. McShary & wife pap	Cottor		3						
	Do	Roger Whorisk & wife pap	Cowherd		2		1		1		
	Do	John McTogara & wife pap	Cowherd		4						
	Do	Patt. Comen & wife pap	Cottor		2		1				
Do	Lislahelly	Jams. Gilmr & wife prot	farmer	5					2		2
	Do	Diness Coner & wife pap	Lad.houldr.						1		1
	Do	John Kenney & wife pap	Cottor		2						
	Do	Owen. Coner & wife pap	Cooper		3		2				
Do	Tormore[18]	Patt. Mcshary & wife pap	Lad.houldr.		4		2				
	Do	Robt. Lynch & wife pap	Lad.houldr.								
	Do	Jams Lynch & wife pap	Lad.houldr.								
Do	Glanmidle	Bartly Coner & wife pap	Lad.houldr.		2		2				

Com~Sligoe Parish of	Place of Abode	Names and Religion	Proffession	Children under 14 Prot.	Paps.	Children above 14 Prot.	Paps.	Men Servts Prot.	Paps.	Women Servts Prot.	Paps.
	Do	Patt. Coner & wife pap	Cowherd		2						
	Do	Dainel Coner & wife pap	Cowherd		1						
	Do	Wm. Shaw & wife prots	farmer	3		2					
Do	Drom	Jams Henderson[19] widwr prots	Lad.houldr.		4						
	Do	George Farbis & wife prots	Lad.houldr.	3		1					
	Do	John Stuard & wife prot	Lad.houldr.	2					1		1
	Do	Wm. Young & wife Prot	Weaver	3					1	1	1
	Do	Wm. White wid. prots	Lad.houldr.			1					
Do	Castlegall	Terance Horan & wife pap	Cowherd		4						1
	Do	John Cunon & wife pap	pumpmaker		2						
	Do	Teady Mcshary & wife pap	Taylor		4				1		
	Do	Roger Teag & wife pap	Labourer								
Do	Magheramore[20]	Bartly Teag & wife pap	Labourer		1						
	Do	Daniel Horan & wife pap	Cowherd		1						
	Do	Terance Turisk & wife pap	Labourer		1						
	Do	Bryn. Turisk & wife pap	Lad.houldr.				1				
	Do	Mark Dinin & wife pap	Lad.houldr.								
	Do	Owen Horkan & wife pap	Lad.houldr.		3						
		Prots 16 paps 64		18	56	11	12		8	1	7
[f.435] Drumcliff	Gortnagrally[21]	John Coner & wife pap	Land.houldr.		1				1		1
Do	Ballygilgan[22]	George Lindsay paps & wife prot	Land houldr.	2		3					1
	Do	Richard Brockes & wife prots	Land houldr.	2		1					1
	Do	David Lyndsey & wife prots	Weaver	1							1
	Do	James Lyndsey & wife prots	Boatman	3							
	Do	Wm. Cuningham & wife prots	Weaver	2							
	Do	Mathias Andrew & wife prots	Weaver								
	Do	George Blear & wife prots	Cooper	2		2					1
	Do	Wm. Walles & wife prots	Miller	3		1					1
	Do	Cormick Togara & wife pap	Land houldr.		2		3				
	Do	Mally Cam wid. paps	Land houldr.		1		5				
	Do	Hugh Gealan & wife pap	Land houldr.		1		2				
	Do	Daniel Dunn & wife pap	Land houldr.		1						
	Do	Patt. Denen & wife pap	Cowherd		1						
	Do	Mathias Camble & wife pap	Cottor		2						
	Do	Wm. Rickey & wife prots	Labourer	1							
	Do	Murtagh Whorisk & wife pap	Cowherd		3						
	Do	Roger Carney & wife pap	Cottor		3		4				
	Do	Farall Kilvary & wife pap	Labourer		3						
	Do	John Roy & wife pap	Labourer		2						
	Do	Hugh Pue & wife pap	Cottor								
	Do	Daniel Roy & wife pap	Cottor		3		1				
	Do	Cormick Hart & wife pap	Aleseller		5		1		1		1
	Do	Mich. Mulack & wife pap	Cottor		4		1				
Do	Drumcliff	Revd Mr Edwd Munn[23] & wife prots	Cleric	2			5	2	2	2	2
	Do	John Rooss & wife prots	Weaver	3		1					
	Do	Andr Keaven & wife pap	Weaver		3				2		1
	Do	Laghlin Carty & wife pap	Taylor		1		2				

Com~Sligoe Parish of	Place of Abode	Names and Religion	Proffession	Children under 14		Children above 14		Men Servts		Women Servts	
				Prot.	Paps.	Prot.	Paps.	Prot.	Paps.	Prot.	Paps.
	Do	John Hany & wife pap	Labourer		1		1				
	Do	Thos. Costelo & wife pap	Boatman		4		1				
	Do	Patt. Donely & wife pap	Cowherd		1		3				
	Do	Barthow Hoy & wife pap	Labourer		2						
Do	Clunmull	Wm. Regan & wife pap	Deryman		1		2				1
	Do	Peter. O'Hara & wife pap	Shepherd		1		2		1		
Do	Clunin	Terance Galagher & wife pap	Labourer								1
	Do	Hugh Conaghan & wife pap	Cottor								1
Do	newtown Drumcliff	Jams Shaw & wife prots	Land houldr.	1				1			1
	Do	George Young & wife prots	Weaver			1			1	2	
	Do	Roger Feeny & wife pap	Land houldr.		2		3				
	Do	Michl. Kegan & wife pap	Land houldr.		1		3				
	Do	Patt. Lagan & wife pap	Cottor								
		Prots 26 paps 55		22	51	9	39	3	8	4	14
[f.436] Drumcliff	Lisadelmonin	Dimkin Hagan & wife protest.	Lad.houldr.			3					
	Do	Teady Hart & wife pap	Cowherd				3				
	Do	Ellonr.Trumble widw pap	Lad.houldr.			1					
	Do	Michl. Mulvany & wife pap	Cottor		2						
	Do	Brigit Cragon wid. papt	Land.houldr.		1						
	Do	Willm. Wear & wife prot	Land.houldr.	5					1		1
	Cloghbolly	Fardo.Killmehel & wife pap	Land.houldr.		2		2				
	Do	Martin Feghny & wife pap	Land.houldr.		1						2
	Do	Diniss McDermod & wife pap	Land.houldr.		1		2				
	Do	Owen Killmehel & wife pap	Cottor		1		1				
	Do	John Millon & wife prot.	Cottor	1							
	Do	Daniel Carvey & wife pap	Land.houldr.		2						
	Do	Owen Whoran widwr. pap	Land.houldr.		4						
	Do	Teady Togher & wife pap	Land.houldr.		2		1				
	Do	John Dogherty & wife pap	Land.houldr.		2		3				
	Do	Manice McMeka & wife pap	Land.houldr.		1		5				
	Do	Patt. Lydon & wife pap	Lad.houldr.		2						
	Do	Willm. Lydon & wife pap	Lad.houldr.		2		1				
	Do	Jams Whoran & wife pap	Lad.houldr.		2		1				
	Do	Jams Judge & wife pap	Cottor		3						
	Do	Margrit McCormack wid. pap	Lad.houldr.		2		1				
	Do	Terance Lydan & wife pap	Cottor								
Do	Cloghcor	Thos. Costole & wife pap	farmer		2		2		1		
	Do	Terance McDermot & wife pap	Cottor		1						
	Do	Jams. Murphey & wife pap	Cottor								
	Do	Patt. Moony widr. papt	Lad.houldr.						1		1
Do	Labolly	John Hart & wife pap	Lad.houldr.		3				1		1
	Do	Darby Carney & wife pap	Lad.houldr.		1		2		1		1
	Do	Patt. McNickal & wife pap	Lad.houldr.		1		3				
	Do	Margrit Gealan wid. papt	Lad.houldr.				3				
	Do	Jams Welsh & wife pap	Lad.houldr.				2				
	Do	Cormick Welsh & wife pap	Lad.houldr.		2		2				
	Do	Diness Hart & wife pap	Cottor		1						1
	Do	Thos. Hart & wife pap	Cottor		1						

Com~Ros Parish of	Place of Abode	Names and Religion	Proffession	Children under 14		Children above 14		Men Servts		Women Servts	
				Prot.	Paps.	Prot.	Paps.	Prot.	Paps.	Prot.	Paps.
	Do	Owen Kilcollen & wife pap	Cottor		1		2				
	Do	Willm. Glanes & wife pap	Cottor						1		
	Ardtamon Riasby	Richd. Cashell & wife pap	Land.houldr.		1				1		
	Do	John Togher & wife pap	Cottor		1				1		1
	Do	Peter Corkran & wife pap	Cottor		2				1		1
	Do	Richd. Costelo & wife pap	Lad.houldr.		2				1		
Do	Part of Drumcliff	Jams Farrel & wife pap	Lad.houldr.		2		1		1		1
		prots 5 - paps 71		6	51	4	37		11		10
[f.437] Drumcliff	Donforc	Mr Willm. Jones prot	farmer	1		2			2	1	2
	Do	mary Hart wid. papt	Cowherd		2		2				2
	Balinphill	Saml. Youen & wife prots	Land.houldr.						1		1
		Sam Youen jun. & wife prots	Scaler	1					1		1
		Willm. Youen & wife prots	Landhouldr.	2							
		Saml. Tayler & wife prots	Landhouldr.			1			1		
		George Tayeor & wife prots	Landhouldr.								
		John Walker & wife prots	Landhouldr.	1	3				1		1
		Frances Walker & wife prots	Landhouldr.								1
		Thos. McKin widr. protest.	Landhouldr.	1		4		1			1
		Wm. McKim & wife prots	Landhouldr.	1					1		1
		Davd. Gilmr & wife prots	Shoemaker	1		2					
		Thos. Blear & mothr. prots	Cotor			2			1		
		John Smith & wife prots	Cotor	1							
		Nicklass Mulaney widr. paps	Cowherd		1		2				
		Lorance Pue & wife papt.	Weaver		3						
	Newtown Donforc	Luck Nickal & wife papt.	Landhouldr.		2						
		Roger Gealan & wife papt.	Landhouldr.								1
		Luck Boil & wife papist	Landhouldr.		1						
		Danl. Hart & wife papt.	Landhouldr.		2						
		Jams Nickal widr. papist	Landhouldr.				1				
		Hugh Hart & wife papist	Landhouldr.		1						
		manice Kinelahan & wife papt.	Landhouldr.		1						
		Thos. Smith & wife Protest.	Weaver						1		
	Cargan	Hugh Killmarten & wife papt.	Landhouldr.		3		4				
		Willm. Killmarten & wife papt.	Landhouldr.		3					1	
		Peter Sweeny & wife papist	Landhouldr.		2				1		1
		John Hart & wife papist	Landhouldr.				1		1		
	Ardtrassna	Willm. Waran & wife protest.	farmer	5					1		1
		John Waran & wife protest.	Landhouldr.	4					1		1
		Patt. Killeol & wife papist	Cowherd		2		3				
		Owen Kinerlahan & wife papt.	Weaver		2		3				
		Patt. Glanen & wife papisst	Cowherd		1						
	Lissadell monin	Willm. Sigans & wife protest	Landhouldr.	1					1		1
		Robt. Sigans & wife protest.	Landhouldr.	2					1		1
		Willm. Flanally & wife papt.	Landhouldr.		3				1		1
		Daniel Gealon & wife papt.	Landhouldr.		3		3				
		Manice Gealan & wife papt.	Landhouldr.		1		4				
		Jams Carrual & wife papt.	Landhouldr.		1		1				
		thos. Kinerlahon & wife papt.	Landhouldr.		2		2				
		Owen Gealan & wife papt.	Landhouldr.		2		2				
		prots 33 paps 42		21	41	11	28	1	16	2	17

Com~Sligoe Parish of	Place of Abode	Names and Religion	Proffession	Children under 14 Prot.	Children under 14 Paps.	Children above 14 Prot.	Children above 14 Paps.	Men Servts Prot.	Men Servts Paps.	Women Servts Prot.	Women Servts Paps.
[f.438] Drumcliff	Cloonagh	Daniel Brian & wife papt.	Ladhouldr.							1	
		Peter Muldirig & wife papt.	Ladhouldr.		1						
		Jams Donleavey & wife papt.	Ladhouldr.		2						
		Teady Donely & wife papt.	Ladhouldr.		2		1				
		Thos. McCormuck & wife papt.	Ladhouldr.		2						
		Mills Costelo & wife papt.	Ladhouldr.		1						
Do	Gortarouey	James Mordagh & wife papt.	Ladhouldr.	4							
		Jams Smith widr. Prot	Ladhouldr.			1					1
		Jams Barbr & wife prot.	Ladhouldr.	3							
		David Haroson & wife prots	Ladhouldr.	1		1					
		Jams. Haron & wife papt.	Ladhouldr.				1				
		Owen Regan & wife papt.	Ladhouldr.		3		1				
		Phelm. Cristial & wife papt.	Ladhouldr.				2				
		Patt. Regan & wife papt.	Ladhouldr.		2						
		Terance Rourk & wife papt.	Cottor		2						
		Bartly Me & wife papt.	Cottor								
		Manice McShary & wife papt.	Cowherd		3		3				
		Willm. Rickey widr prot	Cottor	1							
Do	Orlar[24]	Henry Seely & wife prot.	farmer						3		3
		Bry. Mcnaburn & wife papt.	Cowherd		1						
	Bruanbin	Neal Keanry & wife papt.	Cottor		1						
		Anthony Donlevey & wife papt.	Cottor		2						
		Rogr. Conr. & wife papt.	Cottor		2						
		Edmd. Kelly & wife papt.	Cowherd		2		3				
		Ranel Kelly & wife papt.	Cottor		4						
		Ranel Mulconrey & wife papt.	Cottor		1						
	Culadrumenbar[25]	Jams Barbr. & wife Prot	Landhouldr	3	~~3~~	1			1		1
	Do	Robt Barbr & wife prots	Ladhouldr	4					1		1
	Do	Joseph Barbr & wife prots	Ladhouldr	3					1		1
	Do	Faral mcGoan & wife paps	Cottr				1				
	Culadrum Gilmr	David Lyndsay & wife prots.	Ladhouldr.						1	2	
		Rogr. Park[26] & wife prots	Ladhouldr.	1					1		1
		George Vance & wife prots	Ladhouldr.	1					1		1
		Charles Camble widr. papt	Ladhouldr.		3				1		1
		John Hoy & wife papt.	Ladhouldr.						1		
		Michl. Hoy & wife papt.	Ladhouldr.		2						
		Hugh hoy & wife papt.	Cottor								
		Patt. Feeny & wife papt.	Ladhouldr.		3						
	Rahelly	John Barbr & wife prot.	farmer	1		3		1	1		
		Wm. Barbr. & wife prots	Ladhouldr.	3							
		John Gealan & wife papt.	Ladhouldr.		1						
Prots 26		prots 34 papts 53		25	40	6	12	1	13	2	10
[f.439] Drumcliff	Artakilliny	Irwin Gilmr & wife prots	farmer	1						1	1
		Jams Harasson & wife prots	Ladhouldr.					1			
		Mathw. Oates & wife papt.	Ladhouldr.		2		1				
		Jams Mulvany & wife papt.	Ladhouldr.		2		2				
		farall McGoan & wife papt.	Ladhouldr.				2				
		Michl. Lydon & wife papt.	Ladhouldr.								1

Com~Sligoe Parish of	Place of Abode	Names and Religion	Proffession	Children under 14 Prot.	Paps.	Children above 14 Prot.	Paps.	Men Servts Prot.	Paps.	Women Servts Prot.	Paps.
Do	Ballyconel	Own McGaragh wid. paps	Cottor				1				
		John Jones & wife papt.	Ladhouldr.	3				2			1
		Bry. Heally & wife papt.	Ladhouldr.		2						
		John McMarten & wife papt.	Ladhouldr.								
		Patt. Marten & wife papt.	Ladhouldr.		2				1		
		Laghlin Carney & wife papt.	Landhouldr.		1		4				
		Michl.Conaghan widr. papt	Ladhouldr.				4				
		Patt. Heraghty & wife papt.	Ladhouldr.								
		Robt. Butler & wife papt.	Ladhouldr.				3				
		thos. Costelo & wife papt.	Ladhouldr.		1						
		Teady Cerad & wife papt.	Ladhouldr.		2		2				
		Roger Costelo & wife papt.	Ladhouldr.		1		1				
		Wm. McMarten & wife papt.	Ladhouldr.		1						
		Jams. Heraghty & wife papt.			3						
		Mortagh Heraghty & wife papt.			3						
		Andr. Gealan & wife papt.			1		1				
		Tyrance Glancy & wife papt.	Ladhouldr.								
		Hugh Feeny & wife papt.	Cottor		1						
		Edmd. Carty & mothr. papt.	Cottor						1		
		Daniel Mehan & wife papt.	Ladhouldr.		1						
		Diness Keghran & wife papt.	Ladhouldr.		2		1				
		James Heraghty & wife papt.	Ladhouldr.		1		1				
		Edmd. Glaghlin & wife papt.	Cottor		1						
		Rogr Glaghlin & wife papt.	Cottor				2				
		Gregory Kelly & wife papt.	Cottor		3						
		Owen Hart & wife papt.	Cottor		2						
		Hugh Whorisk & wife papt.	Cottor		1		2				
		Betty O'Hara widw papt	Cottor				1				
		Hugh Conaghan & wife papt.	Cottor		2		2				
		Bry. Hart & wife papt.	Cottor								
	Cloonagh	Phelem McCana & wife papt.	Ladhouldr.		3		2				
	Do	Owen Heally & wife papt.	Ladhouldr.		4						
	Do	Owen McCormuck wife paps	Ladhouldr.		3						
		Danl. Killrow & wife papt.	Ladhouldr.		2						
		thos. Whorisk & wife papt.	Ladhouldr.		2						
		prots 6 pap 73		4	49		32	3	3		3
[f.440] Drumcliff	Raghley	Patt. Hart & wife papist	Landhouldr.		1				1		1
		Michl. Hart & wife papist	Landhouldr.		1		1				
		Owen Cristea & wife papt.	Landhouldr.				4				
		Diness Hart & wife papt.	Landhouldr.						1		1
		Michl. Hart & wife papt.	Landhouldr.						1		1
		Jams Moony & wife Papist	Cottor		1		1				
		John Hopeny & wife papt.	Cowboy				2				
	Kilmacanan	Charles Goan & wife papt.	Landhouldr.		2				2		1
		Daniel Carvey & wife papt.	Landhouldr.		3						
		Izabbla Milon wid. protes	Landhouldr.			2					
		Owen Toghr & wife papt.	Landhouldr.		2		1				
		Darby Mcmorow & wife papt.	Landhouldr.		4						
		Patt. Heraghty & wife papt.	Landhouldr.		3		1				

Com~Sligoe / Parish of	Place of Abode	Names and Religion	Proffession	Children under 14 Prot.	Children under 14 Paps.	Children above 14 Prot.	Children above 14 Paps.	Men Servts Prot.	Men Servts Paps.	Women Servts Prot.	Women Servts Paps.
		Hugh Heraghty & wife papt.	Landhouldr.		2			1			
		Wm. McNickal & wife papt.	Landhouldr.		1						
		Edwd. McGolrick & wife papt.	Cottor		3						
		Terance McGolrick wid. papt	Cottor		4						
		Jams Carney & wife papt.	Blacksmith		4						
		Ned. Carney & wife papt.	Cowboy		4						
Do	Radidle	Lorance Gelan & wife papt.	Landhouldr.		2		2	3			
		Wm. Gelan & wife papt.	Landhouldr.		2			1			1
		thos. Gealn & wife papt.	Cottor		2						
		Cathren Culkin & wife papt.	Cottor				1				
		Phellem Culkin & wife papt.	Weaver								1
Do	Balintamble	Gilbert Ormsby & wife protes	farmer	1				1			1
		Hugh Togher & wife papt.	Landhouldr.		1						
		Henrey Hart & wife papt.	Cottor								1
		Hugh Cerad & wife papt.	Landhouldr.		4						
		Coner McDermot & wife papt.	Landhouldr.		1		1				
		Roger McGlaghn & wife papt.	Cottor		2		1				
		Terance O'Hara & wife papt.	Cottor		1						
		Dainel McGlaghlin & wife papt.	Weaver				4				
		Teady Keaveny & wife papt.	Cowboy				3				
		Mark Corkran & wife papt.	Weaver								
Do	Balinadan	Bartly Costello & wife papt.	farmer					1			1
		John Hart & wife papt.	Cowboy		4						
		Patt. Gealan & wife papt.	Cottor		2						
		Hugh Heraghty & wife papt.	Cottor		4						
		Patt. Hauk & wife papt.	Cottor		4						
		Charles Costelo & wife papt.	Cottor								
		Euness Heraghty & wife papt.	Cottor		4						
pap 77		prots 3 paps 78		1	67	2	22	11			9
[f.441] Drumcliff	Balinadan	mary Curtan wid. papt	Cottor		1		1				
		Bryan Horaghly & wife papt.	Cottor		3						1
		Teady Cerad & wife papt.	Cottor		3						1
Do	Liscornagark	David Henery & wife prots	Ladhouldr.	4							
		nathanl Wallys & wife papt.	Milor	2							
		Patt. Heally & wife papt.	Ladhouldr.		2						1
		Bryan Grady & wife papt.	Ladhouldr.				1	1			1
		Roger Feeny & wife papt.	Ladhouldr.		2			1			
		Michl. Feeny & wife papt.	Ladhouldr.					1			
		Owen Mccerad & wife papt.	Ladhouldr.		2						
		Thos. Kinerlahan & wife papt.	Ladhouldr.				1				
		Patt. Mulackan & wife papt.	Ladhouldr.								1
		Bry. McCerad & wife papt.	Ladhouldr.		1						
		Laghlin Killvany & wife papt.	Ladhouldr.				1				
		Patt. Cerad & wife papt.	Ladhouldr.		1		1				
		Bry. McShary & wife papt.	Ladhouldr.		1		1	1			
		Patt. Cunagan & wife papt.	Ladhouldr.		2						
		Owen McShary & wife papt.	Cowboy		3						
		Bry. Mcgoan & wife papt.	Cottor								
		Andr. Blear & wife papt.	Cottor								1

Com~Sligoe Parish of	Place of Abode	Names and Religion	Proffession	Children under 14 Prot.	Paps.	Children above 14 Prot.	Paps.	Men Servts Prot.	Paps.	Women Servts Prot.	Paps.
Do	Carunagark	Else Donlevey wido. papt.	Cottor				1				
		Owen Pue & wife papt.	Cottor		1		1				
		John Cohool & wife papt.	Cottor		1		1				
		Gabril Donlevey & & mothr. papt.	Cottor				2				
		Anthony Denlevy & wife papt.	Cottor		2						
		Michl. Hart & wife papt.	Cottor		1						
		Bry. Hart & wife papt.	Ladhouldr.				2				
		Jams. Glanaghey & wife papt.	Ladhouldr.		2		2				
		Garat Dougherty & wife papt.	Ladhouldr.		2		1				
		Mick. Mcmickal & wife papt.	Ladhouldr.		2						
		Hugh Gealan & wife papt.	Ladhouldr.		3						
		Terance Boiel & wife papist	Ladhouldr.		1						
		Pat. Boiel & wife papist	Ladhouldr.		1						
		Cormuck Mickal widor. pap	Landhouldr.		2						
		Lorance Roonian widr. papt.	Cottr.		2						
		Luck Mulvany & wife papt.	Cottor		3						
		Jams Killrow & wife papt.	Cowboy		2					1	
		Sara Donlevey wido. paps	Cottor		2						
		Mary Browen wido. paps.	Cottor				1				
		Hugh Jones & wife prots.	Cottor		1		1				
		Prots 6 paps 68		7	45	1	17		5		6
[f.442] Drumcliff	Barnadara	Thos. Wallis & wife prots.	Miller	3		1					
		Jams ffeeny & wife papt.	Ladhouldr.				1				
		Bry. McGaraghey & wife papt.	Cowherd				2				
		Donel Brandon & wife papt.	Ladhouldr.		2						1
		Wm. Gealan & wife papt.	Ladhouldr.		3						
		John Lagan & wife papt.	Ladhouldr.		2						
		Michl. Gealan & wife papt.	Ladhouldr.		2						
		ffardo ffreel & wife papt.	Ladhouldr.		1						
		Marten Feeny & wife papt.	Ladhouldr.		1						
		Domnick Freel & wife papt.	Ladhouldr.		2						
		Bry. McGoan & wife papt.	Ladhouldr.							1	
		John Cunan & wife papt.	Cowherd		2						
		Michl. Hoy & wife papt.	Ealseller[27]		3		2				
		Patt. Brinan & wife papt.	Ealseller		2						
		Mathw. Lemin & wife papt.	Ladhouldr.		3						
		Owen Douey & wife papt.	Taylor				3				
		Owen Feeny & wife papt.	Weaver & Landhouldr.				3				
		Diness Feeny & wife papt.	Ladhouldr.		4		2				
		John Feeny & wife papt.	Ladhouldr.		1						
		Owen McNaburn & wife papt.	Ladhouldr.		2						
Do	Brodcullen	Wm. Pey & wife prots	Weaver			1					
		Olifor Pey & wife prots	Weaver	3		1					
		Wm. Cuningham & wife prots	Ladhouldr.	2							
		Robt. Young & wife prots	Ladhouldr.	3							
		John Young & wife prots	Weaver								
		John Jackson & wife prots	Weaver	1		2					
		John Jackson & wife prots	Ladhouldr.	2							

Com~Sligoe Parish of	Place of Abode	Names and Religion	Proffession	Children under 14		Children above 14		Men Servts		Women Servts	
				Prot.	Paps.	Prot.	Paps.	Prot.	Paps.	Prot.	Paps.
		Thos. Ward & wife papt.	Ladhouldr.		3						
		Patt. Gealan & wife papt.	Cowherd		3						
		John Mehan & wife papt.	Ladhouldr.		2						
		Roger Gealan & wife papt.	Ladhouldr.		1						
		ffrances West & wife prots	farmer	4					2		2
		Patt. Finan & wife papt.	Ladhouldr.		2						1
		Patt. Cristal & wife papt.	Ladhouldr.								
Do	Ballymulan	Allixandr. Little & wife prots	Ladhouldr.		3		1		1		
		George Lyndsay & wife prots	Lad.houldr	5					1		1
		Archbl. Little & wife prots	Ladhouldr.	1					1		1
		Samnl. Barbr. & wife prots	Ladhouldr.	2					1		1
		Umphrey Hunter & wife prots	Weaver	1		1					
		Robt. Hunter & wife prots	Weaver	1		1					
		Mary Gregg widw. prots.	Ladhouldr.			1					
Prots 31		prots 32 paps 50		28	41	41	13	1	5	2	7
[f.443] Drumcliff	Rahelly	Laughlin Conaghhn & wife paps.	Ladhouldr.		4						
		Jams. Fearnon & wife paps.	Cottor		1		1				1
		Jams Giblan & wife paps.	Blacksmith		1						
		Michl. Farel & wife paps.	Cowherd		3				1		
Do	Castlegaran	Waltr Finagan & wife paps.	Broagmaker		3				1		
		John Lydan & wife paps.	Cottor		1						
		Owen Keasey & wife paps.	Ladhouldr.		1						
		Michl. Feeny & wife paps.	Ladhouldr.		2				1		1
		Charless Haran & wife paps.	Ladhouldr.		2		2				
		Marke Feeny & wife paps.	Ladhouldr.		2		2				
		Rogr. Farel & wife paps.	Ladhouldr.								
		thos. Haran & wife paps.	Ladhouldr.		2		2				
		Bry: McDermod & wife paps.	Blacksmith		4		1				
Do	Muninanean[28]	Roger Farel & wife paps.	Ladhouldr.		1		1				1
		Brian McGoan & wife paps.	Ladhouldr.		2		3				
		Luck Carty & wife paps.	Ladhouldr.				2				
		Diness Whorisk & wife paps.	Cowherd				1				
		Manice Feeny & wife paps.	Cowherd		2						
		Hugh Whorisk & wife paps.	Taylor		2		1				
		Jams ffeeny & wife paps.	Ladhouldr.		2						
		Patt. Towey & wife paps.			2						1
		Michl. Towey & wife paps.	Ladhouldr.		2						
		Patt. Whorisk & wife paps.	Ladhouldr.		3						1
Do	Muninanean	Mick McGoan & wife paps.	Ladhouldr.				2				
		Widw Feeny papt	Ladhouldr.		2						
		Jams Feeny & wife paps.	Cowherd		3						
Do	Bunanally	Wm. Gregor & wife prot	Ladhouldr.	3	~~6~~	3			1		1
		Hugh Greg & wife prot	Ladhouldr.	6					1		1
		Wm. Greg & wife prots	Ladhouldr.	2							1
		Reaf Scoot & wife prots	Cottor	2							1
		Darby Feeny & wife paps.	Cowherd		4						
	Dunauney[29]	Wm. Gilmr & wife prots	farmer	1					2		4
		John Feeny & wife paps.	Cowherd			1					
		Michl. Garagh & wife paps.	Deryman								2

Com~Sligoe Parish of	Place of Abode	Names and Religion	Proffession	Children under 14		Children above 14		Men Servts		Women Servts	
				Prot.	Paps.	Prot.	Paps.	Prot.	Paps.	Prot.	Paps.
		Michl[?] & wife paps	Ladhouldr.		1						
		Terance Roirk & wife paps.	Ladhouldr.		1						
		Bartly Lydan & wife paps.	Ladhouldr.		2						
		John Hart & wife paps.	Ladhouldr.		1						
		Jams Tymon & wife paps.	Cowherd		1						
		Teady Mcnaburn & wife paps.	Ladhouldr.		1						
Pap 69		prots 10 paps 68		14	60	4	18	7̶	7		15

[verso]

County of Sligoe Parish of	Place of Abode	Names and Religion		Proffession	Children under 14		Children above 14		Men Servts		Women Servts	
		Prot.	Paps		Prot.	Paps.	Prot.	Paps.	Prot.	Paps.	Prot.	Paps.
Drumcliff												
	No 1	4	77		2	47		16		4		4
	No 2	14	62		20	42	8	8	2	3		4
	No 3	12 .	66		11	41	13	12	1	7	-	10
	No 4	5	76		6	65	1	10		8		8
	No 5	16	64		18	56	11	12		8	1	7
	No 6	26	55		22	51	9	39	3	8	4	14
	No 7	5	71		6	51	4	37		11		10
	No 8	33	42		21	41	11	28	1	16	2	17
	No 9	34	53		25	40	6	12	1	13	2	10
	No 10	6	73		4	49		32	3	3		3
	No 11	3	78		1	67	2	22		11		9
	No 12	6	68		7	45	1	17		5		6
	No 13	32	50		28	41	41	13	1	5	2	7
	No 14	10	68		14	60	4	18		7		15

[in Edward Synge's hand]
N.B. this is wrong cast up
    the No of Prots is but   206
        Paps   903

NOTES

1. *General Alphabetical Index*

2. M'Parlan, *Statistical Survey*, p. 28.

3. Townland owned by the Coopers of Markree, said to be arable pasture which was 'choice for tillage or sheep, the Sea Wrack convenient'. The bogs were 'of little value and '[one] is distroyed by blowing sand' (N.L.I., MS 21 F 2/38).

4. Clunidara [Cloonderry] townland was owned by the Gore family (P.R.O.N.I.,D/4131).

5. Robert Shaw rented land from Owen Wynne for £3.18s.1d (N.L.I., MS 5790/357).

6. Robert Cunningham rented land from Owen Wynne for £1.8s.0d (N.L.I., MS 5790/.358).

7. Townland owned by the Wynne family which was accounted as 'good for tillage or fattening Note there is a bleach green thereon. Also well inclused'. (N.L.I, 750/2).

8. Townland leased by the Wynne family from the O'Hara family (N.L.I., MS 20,397).

9. Townland leased by the Wynne family from the O'Hara family (N.L.I., MS 20,397).

10. Overseers were appointed by justices of the peace and were responsible for collecting and accounting for the poor rate (Holdsworth, p.83, 84).

11. Townland owned by the Wynne family described in 1760 as 'Arable & Pasture Good for Tillage or Sheep, ditto Profitable Moor. Very Reclaimable the Limestone Gravel on the Spot. Ditto Dry Mangled Bog. The same when the turf is cut off' (N.L.I., MS 750/21)

12. John Hunter rented 18 a 3 r 19 p arable and pasture land in 1749 for 10s a half year from Owen Wynne (N.L.I., MS 5790/358).

13. Widow Clery rented 1a.3r.0p from Owen Wynne in 1749 at £1.3s.0d (N.L.I., MS 5790/356).

14. Kinsellagh Upper and Lower (or North and South) were part of the Wynne estate. The land was partly arable pasture 'Good for tillage or Fattening light Cowes or Sheep. Part of it was moor which was 'very reclaimable the Limestone Gravel on the spot' and bog 'Good for Turf only untill it is cutaway and then may be reclaimable' (N.L.I., MS 750/23).

15. Con O'Donnel rented bleachyards from Owen Wynne (N.L.I., MS 5790/358).

16. A Wynne townland 'Good for Tillage or Sheep' (N.L.I., MS 750/16).

17. Townland owned by the Gore family (P.R.O.N.I., D/4131).

18. Townland owned by the King family (N.L.I., MS 16 F 9).

19. James Henderson rented land from Owen Wynne in 1749 for £2.0s.0d (N.L.I., MS 5790/358).

20. Townland leased by the O'Hara family from the Wynne family (N.L.I., MS 20,397).

21. Townland owned by the King family (N.L.I., MS 16 F 9).

22. Townland leased by the O'Hara family from the see of Elphin (N.L.I., MS 20,397).

23. Edward Munns was born in County Roscommon and educated by Mr Jones at Bishop Hodson's School, Elphin. He entered TCD in 1700 aged 18 and graduated BA in 1705. He was instituted vicar of Boyle 1718-29, of Kilgeffin 1729-30 and of Drumcliffe 1730 until his death in 1756. He was Archdeacon of Aghadoe 1734-6 (Leslie, 'Elphin' p.32).

24. Townland owned by the Coopers of Markree. The land was arable and pasture good for tillage or fattening, but the bottom land was subject to flooding. The bog was said to be 'very reclaimable' (N.L.I., MS 21 F 27).

25. Townland owned by the Gore family (P.R.O.N.I., D/4131).

26. A Roger Parke, gentleman lived at Court and Tinid in the mid-seventeenth century (*Census of Ireland*).

27. Dozens of eel weirs were built to trap eels as they swam up the rivers (OS 6":1 mile map County Roscommon 1838, Sheet 34, 52).

28. Townland owned by the Wynne family and leased by James Soden of Killcash, parish of Ahamlish (See Census f. 446).

29. Townland owned by the Gore family (P.R.O.N.I., D/4131).

AHAMLISH COUNTY SLIGO

INTRODUCTION: *Ahamlish is in the barony of Lower Carbery. It is the furthest parish to the north in the diocese, separated from Drumcliff by the great cliff of Ben Bulben, and bordered by the sea and the parish of Rossinver in the diocese of Ardagh. It covered 16,413 statute acres.[1] Lewis says that the land was made up of arable, bog and waste.[2] Land formerly owned by the O'Connor Sligo passed to the earl of Stafford and then to the Temples who became viscounts Palmerston.[3] The main occupation was farming. There was one mason who may possibly have worked on the limestone quarries on Ben Bulben. There was a fair at Cliffony four times a year.[4]*

The parish was held with that of Drumcliff. The church of Ireland incumbent was the Rev. Edward Munns, archdeacon of Elphin (see Drumcliff). He lived in Drumcliff.

OCCUPATIONS

Broguemaker	1	Gentleman farmer	3	Servants, household	25
Cottier	10	Labourer	2	Tailor	1
Cowherd	1				
Farmer	102	Mason	1	Weaver	1

Com~Sligoe Parish of	Place of Abode	Names and Religion	Proffession	Children under 14 Prot.	Children under 14 Paps.	Children above 14 Prot.	Children above 14 Paps.	Men Servts Prot.	Men Servts Paps.	Women Servts Prot.	Women Servts Paps.
[f.444] Aghamplish	Carowymore	Bryan Curk & wife Pap	Farmer		3						
	Ditto	Thady Curk & wife Pap	Farmer		3						1
	Ditto	Thady Ô'Connor[5] & wife Pap	Farmer		1		2				
	Ditto	Daniel Heraghty & wife Pap	Farmer				2				
	Ditto	John Heraghty & wife Pap	Farmer		1						
	Ditto	Cormack Hart & wife Pap	Farmer		3						
	Ditto	Widow McGuan Paps	Farmer				3				
	Ditto	Jas. McGarmick & wife Pap	Farmer		1						
	Ditto	Patt. Hartt & wife Pap	Farmer		4						
	Ditto	Terence McDonagh & wife Pap	Farmer		3		2				
	Ditto	Teige Hargadan & wife Pap	Farmer		3						
	Ditto	Michll. Leadon & wife Pap	Farmer		3						
	Ditto	Patt. Vomny & wife Pap	Farmer		2		1				
	Ditto	Terence Vomny & wife Pap	Farmer		3						
	Ditto	John McCornan & wife Pap	Farmer		3						
	Ditto	Jas. McCornan & wife Pap	Farmer		3						
	Ditto	Patt. Freoh & wife Pap	Farmer		1						
	Ditto	Connor Marday & wife and sister Pap	Farmer								
	Ditto	Domk. Leadon & wife Pap	Farmer		2						
	Ditto	Patt. Loghnan & wife Pap	Farmer		1						
	Ditto	Dennis Killpheder & wife Pap	Farmer		2						
	Ditto	Patt. Leadon & wife Pap	Farmer				4				
	Ditto	Patt. Dogherty widower pap	Labourer		1						
	Ditto	Darby Corigan & wife Pap	Farmer		4						
	Ditto	Step: Mccormack & wife Pap	Brogmaker		3						
	Cartron	Rogr. O'Connor & wife Pap	Farmer		5						1
	Ditto	John Hart & wife Pap	Tailor		1		2				
	Ditto	Bryan McGreeny & wife Pap	Cottier		2						
	Ditto	Mark Hargadon & wife Pap	Cottier								
	Ditto	Bryan Cuningham widower paps	Farmer		2						1
	Ditto	Roger Ward & wife Pap	Farmer		1						
	Ditto	John Harkon & wife Pap	Farmer		3						
	Ditto	Connor Common & wife & father Paps	Farmer		1						
	Ditto	Edmond Loghnan & wife Pap	Farmer 3								
	Ditto	John McAndrew & wife Pap	Farmer		2		2				
	Ditto	John Gallagher & wife Pap	Farmer				1				
	Ditto	Owen Common & wife Pap	Farmer		3						
	Ditto	Felix Gallagher & wife Pap	Farmer		2		1				1
	Ditto	James Gallagher & wife Pap	Farmer		3						1
	Ditto	Thos. Kenedy & wife Pap	Farmer		3		1				
	Ditto	Thady Killbarn & wife Pap	Farmer				2				
		No 81 paps			81		23				5
[f.445] Aghamplish	Cliffony	Geor. McLoghnan & wife Pap	Farmer				2				
	Ditto	And. McLoghlin & wife Pap	Farmer								1
	Ditto	Chas. Brehony & wife Paps	Farmer				2				
	Ditto	Connor Whorisk & wife Paps	Farmer				2				

Com~Sligoe / Parish of	Place of Abode	Names and Religion	Proffession	Children under 14 Prot.	Paps.	Children above 14 Prot.	Paps.	Men Servts Prot.	Paps.	Women Servts Prot.	Paps.
	Ditto	John Coonagher & wife & mother Paps	Farmer		1						
	Ditto	Sarah Cullen widow Paps	Farmer		2						
	Ditto	Felix Gunigill Widower Paps	Farmer				2				
	Ditto	John Ward & wife Paps	Cowherd								
	Caden Revagh	Jas. McTeir & wife Paps	Farmer		1				1		
	Ditto	Hugh Gallagher & wife Paps	Farmer		1				1		
	Ditto	Jas. Gardener & mother sister and Brother paps	Farmer		1						
	Ditto	Daniel Coonaghan & wife Paps	Mason		2		1				
	Ditto	Edmd. Gallagher & wife Paps	Farmer				3				
	Ditto	Jas. Burke & wife Paps	Farmer		2		1				
	Ditto	Bryan Sweeny & wife and mother Paps	Farmer		1		2				
	Ditto	Dinnise Murertier & wife Paps	Weavr		2						
	Ditto	John Mulherro & wife Paps	Farmer								
	Carn	Domk. Farrell & wife Paps	Cottier		1						
	Ditto	John Finellan, wife & mother Paps	Cottier								
	Ditto	Willm. Soden & wife prots	Cottier	2							
	Ditto	Frans. Gillon & wife Paps	Cottier								
	Dromfad	John Mallion & wife Paps	Cottier		1						
	Ditto	John Martin & wife Paps	Cottier		2						
	Ditto	Willm. Fenigan & wife Paps	Cottier		1						
	Stridagh	Jas. Jones[6] & wife prots	Farmer	3		1			3	1	2
	Ditto	Bartly Pew & wife Paps	Farmer								
	Ditto	Richd. Pew & wife Paps	Farmer								
	Ditto	Patt. Bruen & wife Paps	Farmer				2				
	Ditto	Jas. Whorisk & wife Paps	Farmer		1		1				
	Ditto	Jas. Guan & wife Paps	Farmer		2		1				
	Ditto	Jas. Meeaghan & wife Paps	Farmer		2						
	Ditto	Jas. Bruen & wife Paps	Farmer		1						
	Agharow	John Heraughty & wife Paps	Farmer				2				1
	Ditto	August Finigan & wife Paps	Farmer		1		2				
	Ditto	Owen Feighney & wife Paps	Farmer		2						
	Ditto	Thos. Feighney & wife Paps	Farmer		2						
	Ditto	Bryan Corrill & wife Paps	Farmer		2						
	Ballyscannell[7]	Domk. Connor & wife Paps	Farmer		1		1				
	Ditto	Luke Carrell & wife Paps	Farmer				2				
	Ditto	Bryan Carrell & wife Paps	Farmer								
	Ditto	Hugh Hartt & wife Paps	Farmer		2						
[verso] 1120		Prot 81 Paps Papists in the Parish of Aghamplish 57 Protestants in the Parish of Aghamplish		5	34		26	5	1	4	
[f.446] Aghamplish	Dunsaskin	Jas. Whorisk & wife Paps	Farmer				2				
	Ditto	Dinnis Heraghty & wife Paps	Farmer								
	Ditto	John Murphy & wife Paps	Farmer				1				
	Lislary	Willm. Diven & wife Paps	Farmer		2						
	Ditto	Neal Devin & wife Paps	Farmer		3						
	Ditto	John Waters widower Paps	Farmer		2						

Com~Sligoe Parish of	Place of Abode	Names and Religion	Proffession	Children under 14		Children above 14		Men Servts		Women Servts	
				Prot.	Paps.	Prot.	Paps.	Prot.	Paps.	Prot.	Paps.
	Ditto	Murt. Dolan & wife Paps	Farmer		3						
	Ditto	Eneas Mulderrigg & wife Paps	Farmer								
	Ditto	Jas. Dogherty & wife Paps	Farmer		1						
	Ditto	Willm. Gillan & wife Paps	Farmer								
	Ditto	Patt. McCan & wife Paps	Farmer		1						
	Ditto	Dinnis Guan & wife Paps	Farmer		1						
	Aronaglass	Eneas Mulderrigg & wife Paps	Farmer								
	Ditto	Mark McConnor & wife Paps	Farmer		1						
	Ditto	Luke Killmartin & wife Paps	Farmer								
	Ditto	Owen Feeny & wife Paps	Farmer		2						
	Ditto	Thos Roagon & wife Paps	Farmer		2						
	Ditto	Mark. McSharry & wife Paps	Farmer								
	Ditto	Thos. Gemison & wife prots	Farmer	1							
	Ditto	Owen Ô Horoe & wife Paps	Farmer		1						
	Ditto	John Andrew & wife Paps	Farmer				2				
	Ditto	Daniel McSharry & wife Paps	Farmer				3				
	Ditto	Willm. Carroll & wife Paps	Farmer		1						
	Ditto	Daniel Harkan & wife Paps	Farmer		3						
	Ditto	Jas. Killmartin & wife Paps	Farmer				2				
	Ditto	Teige Ô Swory & wife Paps	Farmer		1						
	Ditto	Patt. McGoan & wife Paps	Farmer		2						
	Gorthelick	Owen Clark & Aunt Paps	Farmer								
	Ditto	Pat. Killaher & wife Paps	Farmer		1						
	Killcash	Jas. Soden[8] prots Gent	Farmer								
	Ditto	Rebecca Sodon widow prot									
	Ditto	John Soden & wife Prot Gent	ffarmer	1							
	Ditto	Thos. Soden[9] & wife Prot	Gent ffar.						2		2
	Ditto	Daniel Whorisk & wife Paps	Labourer		2						
	Ditto	Dinnis McKirery & wife Paps	Cottier		3						
	Derrylelias	Patt. Sweeny widower Pap	Farmer								
	Ditto	Laghman Healy & wife Paps	Farmer		4						1
	Ditto	Henry Crean & wife Paps	Farmer		1						
	Ditto	Fran. Crean & wife Paps	Farmer		3						
	Ditto	Anto. Crean & wife Paps	Farmer		1						
	Ditto	Widow Sweeny Pap	Farmer		2		1				
Ditto		8 Prots 71 Paps No		2	43		11		2		3
[f.447] Aghamplish	Ballyscannill	Michl. Hartt & wife Paps	Farmer		2						
	Ditto	Michl. Hartt & mother Paps	Farmer								
	Ditto	Bryan Hartt & wife Paps	Farmer		2				1		
	Ditto	John Healy & wife Paps	Farmer								
	Ditto	Michl. Guan & wife Paps	Farmer		1						
	Ditto	Faraigh Guan & wife Paps	Farmer		1						
	Ditto	Willm. Carrell & wife Paps	Farmer								
	Ditto	John Carritt widower Paps	Farmer								
	Ditto	Henry Healy & wife Paps	Farmer								
	Ditto	Rogr.Finigan & wife Paps	Farmer		2						1
	Ditto	Jas. Dyer & wife Paps	Farmer		1						
	Ditto	Thos. Corrill & wife Paps	Farmer		1		1				
	Ditto	Domk. Bruan & wife Paps	Farmer								

Com~Sligoe Parish of	Place of Abode	Names and Religion	Proffession	Children under 14 Prot.	Children under 14 Paps.	Children above 14 Prot.	Children above 14 Paps.	Men Servts Prot.	Men Servts Paps.	Women Servts Prot.	Women Servts Paps.
	Ditto	Dinnis Martin & wife Paps	Farmer		1		1				
	Ditto	Peter Geilane & wife Paps	Farmer		1						
	Ditto	Henry Grady & wife Paps	Farmer		1						
	Ditto	Dinnis Grady & wife Paps	Farmer		2		1				
	Ditto	Patt. Grady & wife Paps	Farmer		2						
	Ditto	Willm. Grady & wife Paps	Farmer		1						
	Ditto	Owen Grady & wife Paps	Farmer		1						
	Ditto	Ullick Herbertt & wife Paps	Farmer				1				
	Ditto	Willm. Gallagher & wife Paps	Farmer								
	Ditto	Edmd. Smith & wife Paps	Farmer		1						
	Ditto	Jas.Feeny & wife Paps	Farmer		1						
	Ditto	Bartt. Connor & wife Paps	Farmer								
	Ditto	Patt. Hoy & wife Paps	Farmer		1						
	Dunsasken	Luke Guan & wife Paps	Farmer		2						
	Ditto	John Dyer & wife Paps	Farmer		1						
	Ditto	Owen Dyer & wife Paps	Farmer		1						
	Ditto	Felix Hartt & wife Paps	Farmer								
	Ditto	Peter Corrill & wife Paps	Farmer								
	Ditto	Farrill Dermott & wife Paps	Farmer								
	Ditto	Thos. Waters widower Paps	Farmer								
	Runrow	Patt. McCanna & wife Paps	Farmer		3		2				
	Ditto	Chas. Whorisk & wife Paps	Farmer		2		1				
	Ditto	Connor Runian & wife Paps	Farmer		1						
	Ditto	John McNaburn & wife Paps	Farmer		3		1				
	Ditto	Thos. Gillan & wife Paps	Farmer		1						
	Ditto	Patt. Cearagon & wife Paps	Farmer				2				
	Ditto	Cormk. Kired & wife Paps	Farmer		3						
	Ditto	Terince Waters & wife Paps	Farmer		1		2				
		80 Papists in No			40		12	1		1	
[f.448]	Killesloge	Cris Donlevy & wife Paps	Farmer		2				2		2
	Ditto	Charles Hartt and wife Paps	Farmer		4				2		2
	Ditto	Patt McNalty & wife Paps	Cottier		3		2				
	Ditto	Jams McAndrew & wife Paps	Cottier				1				
	Ditto	Dinnis McCommon & wife Paps	Cottier		1						
	Ballygorman	Dins McCannon & wife Paps	Cottier		3						
	Ditto	Terence McCannon & wife Paps	Cottier		2		2				
	Ditto	Willm. Killy & wife Paps	Cottier				3				
	Ditto	Patt. Boyle & wife Paps	Cottier				2				
	Ditto	Mary McAndrew Paps widow	Cottier		1						
	Mullaghmore	Edmd. Magill & wife Paps	Cottier		2		1				
	Ditto	John McAndrew & wife Paps	Cottier		3						
	Ditto	Catherine Freeny Paps widow	poor woman		1						
	Ditto	Chas. McInnisty & wife Paps and sister	Cottier								
	Ditto	Edmd Killmartin Paps and wife	Cottier		1						
	Ditto	Jas. McKiy & wife Paps	Cottier		3						
	Ditto	Bryan Common wife Paps	Cottier								
	Ditto	Darby Common & wife	Cottier								
	Ditto	Patt. McCannon his wife and Aunt Paps									

Com~Sligoe Parish of	Place of Abode	Names and Religion	Proffession	Children under 14		Children above 14		Men Servts		Women Servts	
				Prot.	Paps.	Prot.	Paps.	Prot.	Paps.	Prot.	Paps.
	Grellagh	Owen Connell & wife Paps	Farmer				3				
	Ditto	Law. Connelly & wife Paps	Farmer		2						
	Ditto	Edmd. Mcglain & wife Paps	Farmer		2						
	Ditto	Owen Hartt & wife Paps	Farmer		3		1				
	Ditto	Jas. Meehan & wife Paps and mother in law	Farmer								
	Ditto	Thos Pew his wife Paps & mother	Miller				1				
	Ditto	Patt Congill & wife Paps	Miller		2						
	Castle Gall	Michl. Burke & wife Paps	Cottier								1
	Ditto	Thos. Burke his wife Paps 2 brothers, sister	Cottier								
	Ditto	Edmd. Burke & wife Paps and brother	Cottier		3						
	Ditto	Bryan Higgan, wife and old woman Paps	Cottier		2		3				
	Ditto	Neal Mulloge & wife Paps	Smith		2						
	Bundooff	Jas. Killmartin & wife Paps					4				
	Ditto	Peter McHugh & wife Paps			2						
	Ditto	Terance McHugh & wife Paps			2						
	Ditto	Daniel McHugh & wife Paps			1						1
	Ditto	James Leadon & wife Paps					1				
	Ditto	John Vemney & wife Paps	Cottier		2						
	Ditto	Roger Brellaghan & wife Papists			1		1				
	Ditto	John McGagloen & wife Paps mother in law	Broguemaker		1						
	Ditto	Willm Gillmartin and wife Paps	Cottier		2						
	Ditto	Thos Cavenagh & wife Pap ists		2					1		
		90 Papists in No		0	55	0	27 [ms damaged]				
[f.449]	Bundooff	Murt.Connor & wife Paps		2							
	Ditto	John Hargadon & wife Paps	Cottier				2				
	Ditto	Hugh Meeghan & wife Paps	Farmer		4						
	Ditto	Thos. Meeghan & wife Paps	Farmer		2		2				
	Ditto	John Vemney & wife Paps	Farmer		3						
	Ditto	Daniel McVemney & wife Papists					2				
	Ditto	Patt. McGuan & wife Paps	Cottier		1		2				
	Ditto	Giles Rorke widow Pap	poor woman				1				
	Ditto	Mary Somny widow					2				
	Ditto	Willm. Burke & wife Paps	Farmer				2				
	Ditto	Daniel McGuan & wife Paps	Farmer				2				
	Ditto	Bryan McGuan & wife Paps	Farmer		2		3				
	Ditto	Hugh Killmartin & wife Papt	Farmer		1						
	Ditto	Terence Leadon & wife Papist	Farmer		2		2				
	Ditto	Ter. McGuan & wife Pap	tFarmer		2		3				
	Ditto	Dinas Gorman & wife Pap	tFarmer		3		1				
	Ditto	Bryan Gorman & wife Papist	Farmer		2						
	Ditto	Terence Gorman & wife Paps	Cottier								
	Ditto	Mau. Gonigill & wife Paps	Cottier								
	Ditto	Michl. Gonigill & wife Pap	Farmer		3		1				
	Ditto	Owen Hartt & wife Paps	Farmer		1						

Com~Sligoe / Parish of	Place of Abode	Names and Religion	Proffession	Children under 14		Children above 14		Men Servts		Women Servts	
				Prot.	Paps.	Prot.	Paps.	Prot.	Paps.	Prot.	Paps.
	Ditto	Patt Tranisk & wife Paps	Cottier		2						
	Creevykeel	Owen Linany & wife Paps	Farmer		3						
	Ditto	Michl. Hartt & wife Paps			1						
	Ditto	John Linany & wife Paps	Farmer				3				
	Ditto	Edmd. Linany & wife Paps	Farmer		1						
	Ditto	Faril Killyfeder & wife Paps	Farmer		2						
	Ditto	Terence Gunigal & wife Paps	Farmer		3						
	Ditto	Patt. Killpheder & wife Paps	Farmer		1						
	Ditto	Thady Killy & wife Paps	Cotter		3						
	Ditto	Evor Linany & wife Paps	Cottier		2						
	Ditto	Teren. McInisk & wife Paps	Cottier		2						
	Ditto	Mary McMorris widow					2				
	Ditto	Chas Ô Connor & wife Paps					4				1
	Ditto	Bryan Ô Connor & wife Paps			3						
	Ditto	Ant. McNeale & wife Pap	Farmer		3		1				
	Ditto	Owen Gilloon & wife Paps his mother sistr & bror.	Cottier		2						
Papt 79		77 Paps in No.			58		46	[ms damaged]			
[f.450] Aghamplish	Derrylelians	John Harken & wife	Farmer		2						
	Gurthaderry	John McMarry & wife Paps	Farmer		1						
	Ditto	Hugh Glaney & wife Pap	Farmer		1						
	Carranamadew	Hugh McGoan & wife Pap	Farmer		1						
	Ditto	Daniel McCadan & wife Prot	Farmer			2			2	1	
	Ditto	John Kelly & wife Pap	Farmer								
	Ditto	Chas Kelly & wife Papt	Farmer		1						
	Ditto	John McGoan & wife Pap	Farmer		1						
	Ditto	Widow Loagan Papt	Farmer				1				
	Ditto	Thady Christy & wife Pap	Farmer		1						
	Newtown	John Downey & wife Prot and nephew	Farmer								
	Ditto	Henry Downey & wife Prot	Farmer	1							
	Ditto	Connor Killmartin & wife Pap	Farmer		2		3				
	Ditto	Daniel Killmartin & wife Papist	Farmer		2						
	Killcarrow	Hugh Hargadon & wife Papt	Farmer				3				
	Ditto	Willm Killmartin & wife Pap	Farmer		3		1				
	Ditto	Luke Killmartin & wife Pap	Farmer		2		3				
	Ditto	Patt Killmartin & wife Pap	Farmer								
	Ditto	Jas. Hargadon & wife Pap	Farmer		2						
	Ditto	Widow Toughell Papist	Farmer				1				
	Ditto	Patt. Leadon & wife Pap	Farmer		1		2				
	Ditto	Willm Killmartin & wife Papt	Farmer								
	Old Grange	Edm. Soden Esqr & wife[10] Protestants	Gent. ffarmr			1		2	3	1	4
	Ditto	John Baird & wife Prot	Farmer	2		3		1			
	Ditto	Jas. Mason & wife Prot	Clothier	1				1			1
	Ditto	Edwd Carre & wife Prot	weaver								
	Ditto	Terence Brine & wife Pap	Mercht.		2						1
	Ditto	Owen Feeny & wife Pap	Mason		2						
	Dittro	Thady Brawley & wife Pap and mother in law	Miller		3				1		

Com~Sligoe Parish of	Place of Abode	Names and Religion	Proffession	Children under 14		Children above 14		Men Servts		Women Servts	
				Prot.	Paps.	Prot.	Paps.	Prot.	Paps.	Prot.	Paps.
	Ditto	Thos Runian & wife Pap	Shopkepr								1
	Moneygold	Jas Soden, wife & mother Protestants	Gent	2					4		4
	Ditto	Patt Mullany & wife Pap	Cottier		1		2				1
	Ditto	Terence Kivelaghan & wife Paps	Farmer			3					
	Ditto	Owen Fenly & wife Pap and a mother in law	Farmer		1		1	[Ms damaged]			
	Ditto	Cormack Sheal & wife Pap	Cooper		2						
	Ditto	Jas McGoan & wife Pap	Cottier		2						1
	Ditto	Jas McDermoot & wife Pap	Smith		3				2		
	Ditto	Daniel mcGoan & wife Paps	Cottier		1						
	Derry	Martin Gilan & wife Paps	Cottier		2				1		
		18 Prots 62 Paps		6		17		13			
				[ms damaged]							

[verso]

57 protestants in the parish of Aghamlis
1120 papists in the same parish

NOTES

1. Including 22 acres of Cloontylough (*General Alphabetical Index*).

2. Lewis, 'Ahamplish'.

3. Wood-Martin, *Sligo*, ii, 20, 141.

4. M'Parlan, *Statistical Survey*, pp 27-9.

5. Descendant of the O'Connor Sligo who had owned part of the parish. By the early seventeenth century their power had been greatly lessened with the payment of an large jointure to the Countess of Desmond (O'Rorke, *History of Sligo*, ii, 21).

6. James Jones was the uncle of Edward Jones, gentleman of Stridagh who died 1757/8. James had a son, Thomas (*Abstracts of Wills*, ii, 223).

7. Edward Jones of Stridagh owned the freehold of Ballyscannill (*Abstracts of Wills*,.ii, 223).

8. James Soden was born at Glasslough, Co. Monaghan, a son of Edmund Soden an attorney and Margaret Knox. He entered Trinity College, Dublin in 1724, aged 19 but seems not to have taken a degree. The Soden family owned the estate of Grange, Runroe and Carbury in Sligo and Ahamlish and houses in Sligo, leased by Benjamin Burton. They also leased the farm of Monynean, Drumcliff from Owen Wynne and Moneygold, Derry and Lyle, the island of Dernish, Cloontyproclish and the west part of Drumfad from Lord Palmerston. James married Jane Wynne and died in 1763 (*Alumni Dubliniensis; Abstracts of Wills*, ii,154-5 ; Southampton University, Broadlands Papers MS BR57/60).

9. Thomas Soden witnessed the will of Edward Jones of Stridagh in 1757. His farm was called Kitkat (*Abstracts of Wills*, ii, 223).

10. Thomas Soden gentleman lived in Grange in the mid-seventeenth century (*Census of Ireland*).

Abbytown [?Abbeycartron]	Roscommon	Ardleebeg	Ballysumaghan
Acres	Roscommon	Ardmore	Killukin
Aghadangen	Lissonuffy	Ardmoyle	Kilnamanagh
Aghaderry	Tibohine	Ardmuln [Ardmullen]	Cam/Kiltoom
Aghadriston	Tibohine	Ardnakinene	Kilmore
Aghagad Begg	Fuerty	Ardrologh	Kilmacumsy
Aghalour	Tibohine	Ardsallagh	Roscommon
Aghalurchy	Cloonfinlough	Ardsallagh	Aughrim
Aghamore	Sligo	Ardtrassna	Drumcliff
Aghamore	Lissonuffy	Ardvone	Rahara
Aghamult	Roscommon	Arm	Kilkeevan
Agharow	Ahamlish	Arnisbrack [Arnasbrack]	Kilross
Aghdrishan	Kilteevan	Aronaglass	Ahamlish
Aghrane [or Castlekelly]	Athleague	Artakilliny	Drumcliff
Ahagad	Fuerty	Arttermon Righy	Drumcliff
Ahairriscull	Kilmore	Athleague Town	Athleague
Ahanasourn [Aghnasourn]	Kilbryan	Athlone [see Big Meadow]	Athlone, St.
Ahascragh	Ahascragh		Peter's
Ahernagulta	Ardcarn	Attin	Creeve
Ally Knockan called Cartron	Tisrara	Attingrenbeg [Attiagnygrana]	Creeve
Amore [Uma]	Roscommon	Attiogh [Atteagh]	Kiltoom
Anaghbeg	Cloonygormican	Atty Knockan [Attiknockan]	Tisrara
Anaghmona	Kilteevan	Aughagorula [Aghagowla]	Boyle
Anaghmore	Killukin	Aughagrange	Boyle
Anahbeg	Ahascragh	Aughanaugh [Aghanagh]	Aghanagh
Anaugh	Kilmacallan	Aughcar	Boyle
Anaughloy	Kilmactranny	Aughlard [Aughlahard]	Cloonfinlough
Annagh [Annaghbeg]	Tumna	Aughoo	Drumcolumb
Annaghmonahan [Annamona]	Tumna	Aughwerny	Cloonfinlough
Antriol'Beg	Cloontuskert	Aurigna [Arignagh]	Kilmactranny
Anughgila	Kilkeevan	Baladerouth	Aghanagh
Anughvaghery	Kilkeevan	Balenepark	Kilkeevan
Araghty	Athleague	Balibane [Ballybaun]	Ahascragh
Ardaghcullen	Killukin	Balimagarra	Tibohine
Ardaghcullen	Cloonygormican	Balinadan	Drumcliff
Ardass	Kilkeevan	Balinagalagh [Ballynagalliagh]	Drumcliff
Ardcarn	Ardcarn	Balinphill [Ballinphull]	Drumcliff
Ardcomber	Drumcolumb	Balintamble	Drumcliff
Ardcouhil [Ardchamoyle?]	Tumna	Balinvoer [Ballinvoher]	Drumcliff
Ardenish	Ardcarn	Ballagbah [Ballaghbawbeg]	Baslick
Ardgallagher	Kilmore	Ballaghbuy	Boyle
Ardgower	Ardcarn	Ballaglidagey	Kilcroan
Ardhenagh [Ardkeenagh]	Kilcooley	Ballenfoll	Kilmeane
Ardkeel	Roscommon	Balliboggan [Ballyboggan]	Ahascragh
Ardkeena [Ardkeenagh]	Estersnow	Balliglass, Galway	Ahascragh
Ardkorkey	Estersnow	Balliglass, Roscommon	Tibohine
Ardleckny [Ardleckna]	Aughrim	Ballilion [Ballylion]	Cam
Ardlee [Ardloy]	Tawnagh	Ballinaboy	Kilteevan

Ballinaddy	Shankill	Ballygilgan	Drumcliff
Ballinafad	Cloonfinlough	Ballyglass	Baslick
Ballinagar	Kilcorkey	Ballyglass [Ballyglass Upper]	Cloonygormican
Ballinahoune	Kilbegnet	Ballyglass [Middle & North]	Kilcroan
Ballinakill	Ballynakill, co. Sligo	Ballyglass	Killukin
		Ballyglass [Ballyglass Lower]	Cloonygormican
Ballinary	Kilmactranny	Ballygrana [Ballygrania]	Kilross
Ballinascarrow	Fuerty	Ballyhobert [Ballyhubert]	Lissonuffy
Ballinashee	Kilmactranny	Ballyleague	Cloontuskert
Ballinboher	Estersnow	Ballymacinily	Ogulla
Ballincullin	Kilmactranny	Ballymackerily	Cloonygormican
Ballindall	Roscommon	Ballymartin [Beg + More]	Roscommon
Ballindrimly [Ballindrumlea]	Kilkeevan	Ballymore [or Corbally]	Boyle
Ballindullighans	Baslick	Ballymulan	Drumcliff
Ballinfall [Ballinphuill]	Boyle	Ballymuny [Ballymurray]	Elphin
Ballinfull	Tibohine	Ballymurry [Ballymurray]	Kilmeane
Ballinkilleen	Killukin	Ballynagard	Roscommon
Ballinlass	Killeroran	Ballynahaen	Taghboy
Ballinlegg [Ballinligg]	Kilmactranny	Ballynamore	Killian
Ballinlegg [Ballinligg]	Fuerty	Ballynasagarl	St John's
Ballinlugg [Ballinlag]	Kilmeane	Ballynode	Sligo
Ballinooker	Kilnamanagh	Ballynvill [Ballinvilla]	Killumod
Ballinroe	Boyle	Ballyoughter	Shankill
Ballinscarra	Aghanagh	Ballyrush	Kilmacallan
Ballintemple	Cloonfinlough	Ballyscannill [Ballyscannell]	Ahamlish
Ballintober	Ballintober	Ballyshearone	Creeve
Ballintruffy	Shancough	Ballysumaghan	Ballysumaghan
Ballintrugan	Fuerty	Ballytivena	Sligo
Ballinturly	Fuerty	Ballytouhy [Bellytoohey]	Termonbarry
Ballinvernun	Kilmacallan	Ballytrassna [Ballytrasna]	Boyle
Ballinvoher	Roscommon	Ballyvahan	Kiltrustan
Balliwelahan	Creeve	Ballywellaher	Creeve
Ballough	Rahara	Balnafad	Aghanagh
Ballybegg	Ogulla	Balraughbo	Killadoon
Ballybohan	Roscommon	Balydugan [Ballydougan]	Sligo St. Johns
Ballybrehan	Cloonygormican	Balymackert	Ballintober
Ballybrehan	Kilcooley	Balymulan [Ballymullany]	Aghanagh
Ballybride	Roscommon	Banavane	Ahascragh
Ballybroghten [Ballybroghan]	Kilcooley	Bar-roe [Barroe]	Sligo
Ballycahir	Oran	Barcoe	Killadoon
Ballycleare [Ballyclore]	Cloontuskert	Barnacullin [Barnacullen] Rahara	
Ballyconbeg [Ballyconboy]	Kilcorkey	Barnadara [Barnaderg]	Drumcliff
Ballyconnel [Ballyconnell]	Drumcliff	Barnadarah	Killadoon
Ballycummin	Kilmore	Barnaslye	Sligo
Ballydaly	Cloonygormican	Barnecaly [Barnadawley]	Tibohine
Ballydaly	Killukin	Barnobuy [Barnaboy]	Kilnamanagh
Ballydoogan	Sligo St Johns	Barrynamonow	Sligo
Ballydooly [Ballydooley]	Oran	Barts Cartron	Roscommon
Ballyduffy	Lissonuffy	Beabramully	Athlone, St. Peter's
Ballyerter	Ahascragh		
Ballyfinigan [Ballyfinegan]	Ballintober	Beggantown	Kiltoom
Ballyfuron	Taghboy	Behy	Tawnagh
Ballygalda [or Trust]	Roscommon	Belagh [Bellaugh]	Athlone, St. Peter's
Ballygawly	Kilross		

Bellamon [Ballymoe]	Drumatemple, co. Galway	Canalough	Ballynakill, co. Sligo
Belragh	Aughrim	Capalishin [Cappalisheen]	Kiltoom
Biggberries	Kiltoom	Carabehy	Tibohine
Bigmeadow	Athlone, St. Peter's	Caracrin	Ballysumaghan
		Caracummeen [Corracommeen	]Tibohine
Blindwell	Athleague	Carageen [Carrigeencarragh]	Estersnow
Bockil	Tibohine	Caranduff	Kilross
Boganfin [Bogganfin]	Kiltoom	Caranspirawn	Aghanagh
Boher	Killukin	Cararruddy	Tibohine
Bonnapreaghan	Killenvoy	Caraward	Lissonuffy
Bowagh [Bohagh]	Ballintober	Carbohill	Cloonfinlough
Boxford	Fuerty	Carenlass	Bumlin
Boyanagh	Elphin	Cargan	Drumcliff
Boyle	Boyle	Cargeen	Kilmeane
Bracklon	Ballintober	Cargeens	Dunamon
Bracklon [Brackloon]	Fuerty	Cargen	St John's
Braclone [Brackloon]	Tumna	Carginboy	Kilmactranny
Braiscan	Kilcorkey	Caricknagrass	Kilmactranny
Breadough [Bredagh]	Dysert	Caricknahoran	Aghanagh
Bredah [Bredagh]	Killasolan	Carinkill	Ogulla
Bree	Sligo	Carinonduffy	Kilross
Breeogue	Sligo	Carkar	Kilcooley
Brenabegg [Breanabeg]	Kilkeevan	Carkar	Cloonygormican
Brickliffe [Bricklieve]	Drumcolumb	Carn [Carns]	Ahamlish
Bridogue	Kilnamanagh	Carnagarrow	Ogulla
Broadcullen	Drumcliff	Carnagh [East and West]	St John's
Bryanfield [Brierfield]	Cloonygormican	Carnagullah	Kiltrustan
Bryanmore [Bryan More]	Tibohine	Carnan	Drumatemple
Buckfield	Fuerty	Carncash	Sligo
Bunadolan	Aghanagh	Carne [Carns]	Ogulla
Bunanally	Drumcliff	Carneha	Tawnagh
Bunariby [Bunnaribba]	Athlone, St. Peter's	Carnekill [Carnekitt]	Ogulla
		Carnespin	Aughrim
Bunreagh	Killumod	Carnrawer	Killumod
Bunyerda [Bunnageddy?]	Lissonuffy	Caroclauah	Killadoon
Bunymuck [Bunnamucka]	Killukin	Carogarive	Tibohine
Cabragh	Shancough	Carokeel	Tibohine
Caden Revagh	Ahamlish	Caromore	Ardcarn
Cahir	Kilross	Caronhard	Tibohine
Calbrah	Killasolan	Caronoknehan	Tibohine
Calbrahpally	Killasolan	Caronurlar	Elphin
Caldragh	Kiltrustan	Carowmore	Killumod
Caldrimoran	Shankill	Carowmore	Kilmore
Callenemona	Cloontuskert	Carownamadow	Sligo
Callgagh [Caltragh]	Sligo	Carowymore	Ahamlish
Callow	Kilnamanagh	Carragarra	Oran
Calltrough	Kilmacumsy	Carrakeel	Kilmore
Caloughtra	Kilmactranny	Carranalbanagh	Boyle
Cam	Cam	Carregbegg	Tisrara
Cambo [Canbo]	Estersnow	Carren	Sligo
Camderry	Kilbegnet	Carrick	Ballynakill co. Sligo
Camlin	Kilcolagh		
Cams	Tawnagh	Carrick	Cam

Carrickhenny	Sligo	Carruclogher [Carrowclogher]	Cloonfinlough
Carricknellist & Ballynamonow	Sligo	Carrumoneen	Cloonfinlough
Carrigens	Kilcooley	Carrygurrow	Cloonygormican
Carrokeeny	Kiltoom	Carthrone	Kilbegnet
Carromore	Killadoon	Cartoun	Tibohine
Carromore	Boyle	Cartron na Bruey	Sligo
Carronaff	Killukin	Cartron	Aghanagh
Carronard	Cloonfinlough	Cartron	Ahamlish
Carrow Bunnan	Sligo	Cartron	Elphin
Carroward	Kilbride	Cartron	Killumod
Carrowbane	Cloonygormican	Cartron	Kilmore
Carrowbane	Kilbride	Cartronduffy	Kilross
Carrowcarn	Kilmacumsy	Caruard [Carroward]	Tisrara
Carrowcolly	Kilmacumsy	Carubane	Ballintober
Carrowcrin	Sligo	Carugarry	Baslick
Carrowduff [Lower and Upper]	Cloonygormican	Carugary	Baslick
Carrowgarry	Kilmacumsy	Carukeel	Kilkeevan
Carrowgubedagh	Sligo	CaruMonough	Rahara
Carrowintod	Kilmacumsy	Carumore	Kilkeevan
Carrowirin	Kilbride	Carunagark	Drumcliff
Carrowkeel	Aghanagh	Carunderty	Taghboy
Carrowkeel	Kilnamanagh	Carunthleave	Tisrara
Carrowkeel	Ballynakill, co. Sligo	Carureagh	Ballintober
		Carventerof	Taghboy
Carrowkeel	Sligo	Carventerof [Carrowntlieve]	Tisrara
Carrowkeel	Dunamon	Cashel	Killukin
Carrowkeel	Tawnagh	Cashill	Kilkeevan
Carrowkeely	Cloonygormican	Cashill	Boyle
Carrowkeely	Kilcooley	Cashvughbeg	Cam
Carrowlusk	Sligo	Caslinode	Bumlin
Carrowmongue	Shankill	Casorogisha	Ardcarn
Carrowmore	Killumod	Castle Douglass	Drumcolumb
Carrowmore	Roscommon	Castlebaldwin	Kilmacallan
Carrowmore	Shankill	Castleblakeney	Killasolan
Carrowmore	Sligo	Castlecoote	Fuerty
Carrownadough	Sligo	Castlegar [East and West]	Ahascragh
Carrownagelty	Kilmacallan	Castlegaran [Cashelgarran]	Drumcliff
Carrownagleragh	Aughrim	Castleplunket	Baslick
Carrownamada	Kilmeane	Castlereagh	Kilkeevan
Carrownamadra [Carrowmaddy]	]St John's	Castleteehon	Baslick
Carrownaready	Sligo	Castleteehon	Fuerty
Carrowngagh	Estersnow	Caugher [Caher]	Kilkeevan
Carrownure [Lower and Upper]	St John's	Cavetown [or Ballynahoogh]	Estersnow
Carrownvalley	Killukin	Churchborough	Killenvoy
Carrowpadan [Carrowphadeen]	St John's	Clare	Cloonfinlough
Carrowreagh	Aughrim	Clasheganny	Killukin
Carrowreagh	Kilcorkey	Classlaher	Rahara
Carrowreagh	Kilnamanagh	Cleboy	Ballintober
Carrowreagh	Killumod	Cleen	Ardcarn
Carrowrevagh	Athleague	Cleevery	Aghanagh
Carrowroe	Roscommon	Clegarna	Tibohine
Carrowroe	Sligo	Cleragh	Tibohine
Carrowstellan	Fuerty	Cliffony [Newtown Cliffony]	Ahamlish
Carrowtuckeen	Kilbryan	Clignah [Clegna]	Ardcarn

Cloancannon	Athleague	Clooncoan	Kilmore
Cloghan	Taghboy	Clooncommonmore	Kilmore
Cloghbolly [Cloghboley]	Drumcliff	Cloonconnoo	Oran
Cloghbrack	Kilross	Clooncouse	Kilkeevan
Cloghbrack	Kilbride	Clooncurr	Cloonygormican
Cloghcor	Drumcliff	Clooncurr	Kilcooley
Clogher	Estersnow	Cloondaharabegg	Kilkeevan
Clogher	Killasolan	Cloondaharabegg	Kilkeevan
Clogher	Ahascragh	Cloondaharamore	Kilkeevan
Clogher	Kilmore	Cloondara [Cloondarah]	Tisrara
Cloghermore	Elphin	Cloondart	Tibohine
Cloghermore	Sligo	Cloone Cranon	Elphin
Cloghfin	Aghanagh	Clooneagh	Tibohine
Cloghorny	Killenvoy	Clooneagh [Clooneigh]	Kilcooley
Cloghr Begg [Clogher Beg]	Elphin	Cloonebern	Killukin
Cloheen	Tumna	Cloonecalgan	Oran
Clonacose[Clooncouse]	Tumna	Cloonedilern	Tisrara
Clonbanough [Cloonbanniv]	Ahascragh	Cloonedirha	Drumatemple
Clonbounogh [Cloonbunny]	Tibohine	Cloonee	Drumatemple
Cloncagh [Clooncah]	Kilteevan	Clooneen	Ballynakill, co.
Clonconny [Cloonconny]	Elphin		Sligo
Cloncovanagh	Kiltrustan	Clooneen	Kilnamanagh
Cloncraff	Kilteevan	Clooneen	Kilmactranny
Clongoonagh [Cloongoonagh]	Tumna	Clooneenroe	Kilross
Clonmane [Cloonmeana]	Tumna	Cloonekillaron	Kilcooley
Clonmoghan [Cloonmahan]	Elphin	Cloonekillen	Kilcooley
Clonmullen [Cloonmullin]	Tibohine	Cloonekillen	Cloonygormican
Clonsheevan [Cloonskeeven]	Tumna	Cloonela [Cloonelly]	Ballysumaghan
Clonskee	Ahascragh	Cloonera	Kilbride
Clontorsart [Cloontowart]	Tibohine	Cloonerafield	Kilkeevan
Clonvillane	Elphin	Clooneran	Kilkeevan
Cloomaguinen	Kilnamanagh	Cloonerk	Kilbride
Cloon Quin [Cloonyquin]	Elphin	Cloonery [Cloonearagh]	Cloonfinlough
Cloonadra [Cloonaddra]	Cloontuskert	Cloonfad	Termonbarry
Cloonaff	Kilkeevan	Cloonfad	Tibohine
Cloonagh	Taghboy	Cloonfellan	Kilteevan
Cloonagh	Ballintober	Cloonfinglas	Tibohine
Cloonagh	Drumcliff	Cloonfinlogh	Cloonfinlough
Cloonagrason [Cloonagrassan]	Drumatemple	Cloonforest [Cloonfower]	Kilkeevan
Cloonalis	Kilkeevan	Cloonfree	Cloonfinlough
Cloonaraget	Tibohine	Cloonheen [Clooneigh]	Kilteevan
Cloonaraget	Tibohine	Cloonibrig	Killeroran
Cloonard	Tibohine	Cloonicaly	Tibohine
Cloonarra	Tibohine	Cloonican	Kilkeevan
Cloonasker	Shankill	Cloonikelly	Athleague
Cloonaugh	Ballynakill, co.	Cloonikerny	Ballintober
	Sligo	Clooniquin	Fuerty
Cloonbiker	Ardcarn	Cloonkeen	Kilkeevan
Cloonbrislane	Tumna	Cloonkillaron	Cloonygormican
Clooncagh	Tisrara	Cloonkillaron [Cloonkerin]	Kilcooley
Clooncannon [Cloncannon]	Ahascragh	Cloonlative [Cloonlative]	Kilkeevan
Clooncarran	Lissonuffy	Cloonlion [Cloonylyon]	Killeroran
Clooncaugh	Kilkeevan	CloonLoughnan	Tisrara
Clooncaugh	Cloonfinlough	Cloonmane [Cloonmeane]	Kilmore

CloonMcmileen	Kilnamanagh	Coolback	Drumcolumb
Cloonminly	Kilteevan	Coolbegg [Cuilbeg]	Sligo
Cloonmore	Kilteevan	Coolboy	Drumcolumb
Cloonmore	Termonbarry	Cooldavin	Tibohine
Cloonmurry [Cloonmurray]	Killukin	Coolefobole [Collaphubble]	Kilmeane
Cloonmustard [Cloonmustra]	Cloontuskert	Coolegary [Coolagarry]	Tibohine
Cloonoe	Lissonuffy	Coolgarry [Coolagarry]	Cam
Cloonown	Athlone, St.	Cooll Derry [Coolderry]	Tisrara
	Peter's	Coolmeen	Fuerty
Cloonreane	Cloonfinlough	Coolmoorna	Kilmactranny
Cloonrebracken	Bumlin	Coolshanghting	Cloontuskert
Cloonredoon [Cloonradoon]	Bumlin	Coolskeagh	Drumcolumb
Cloonree	Kilkeevan	Cooltacker	Cloonfinlough
Cloonruff	Athleague	Coopers Hill [or Gobbodagh]	Drumcolumb
Cloonsaghn [Cloonshangan]	Estersnow	Coot Hall [Cootehall]	Tumna
Cloonscarbry	Killian	Coote Hall	Ardcarn
Cloonsellagh [Cloonsillagh]	Kilmore	Coots Cartron	Roscommon
Cloonselliff	Kilkeevan	Coraducy	Aghanagh
Cloonshanagh	Kilmore	Corbally [East + West]	Creeve
Cloonshanovil [Cloonshanville]	Tibohine	Corbeghurlingh	Athleague
Cloonshee	Cloonfinlough	Corboe	Kilbride
Cloonslanner	Cloonfinlough	Corboly [Corboley]	Killenvoy
Cloonsreen	Killukin	Corclare	Aughrim
Cloonsuck	Kilkeevan	Cordrehid	Killukin
Cloonsweeny	Killian	Cordrohit	Lissonuffy
Cloontarnse	Kilkeevan	Cordromin [Cordrumman]	Bumlin
Cloontorsart [Cloontowart]	Tibohine	Cordromin [Cordrumman]	Kiltrustan
Cloontrask	Kilkeevan	Corelea	Cam
Cloonwindin	Kilkeevan	Corgowan	Kilglass
Cloony Shead	Tisrara	Coristoonabeg	Drumatemple
Cloonybryn [Cloonybrien]	Ardcarn	Coristoonamore	Drumatemple
Cloonycarrow	Kilnamanagh	Corlack	Kilbegnet
Cloonyleg	Tisrara	Corlack	Kilcroan
Cloughoge	Aghanagh	Corlare	Kilmore
Cloughveana	Kilmactranny	Corlasheen	Killadoon
Clountouscort	Cloontuskert	Corlesheen	Kilmacallan
Clouroghan	Elphin	Corlis	Aughrim
Clover Hill	Sligo	Cormagrine	Termonbarry
Cluggernah	Lissonuffy	Cornafeigh	Estersnow
Clunidarar	Cloonfinlough	Cornamilta	Boyle
Clunin [Clooneen]	Drumcliff	Cornamucla [Cornamucklagh]	Ahascragh
Cluniragh	Cloonfinlough	Cornamucla	Ahascragh
Clunmull	Drumcliff	Cornamuhala	Killadoon
Clystukee	Kilmactranny	Cornamukolah	Killadoon
Cogglekeeny [Coggalkeenagh]	Lissonuffy	Cornasee	Kiltoom
Cogglemore [Coggalmore]	Lissonuffy	Cornecask	Athleague
Cogglestack [Coggalstack]	Lissonuffy	Corneflyne	Kilmore
Cogill	Kilbride	Cornegee	Cam
Colclogernogh	Kiltrustan	Cornegrine	Termonbarry
Common	Sligo	Cornehulty	Tibohine
Comouge	Elphin	Cornelee	Cam
Coola	Ballynakill, co.	Cornemant [Cornemart]	Killenvoy
	Sligo	Cornepalace [Cornapallis]	Tisrara
Coolalongfal	Aghanagh	Cornespineoge	Aughrim

Cornetatan [Corrantoban]	Kiltoom
Cornetstown	Elphin
Corneveigh [Cornaveigh]	Estersnow
Cornonant [Cornananta]	Killeroran
Cornsleyrany	Ogulla
Coroongh	Kilmacumsy
Corramore [or Gorteencloogh]	Athleague
Corranageelogue	Oran
Corrane [Corraun]	Termonbarry
Correa [Corry]	Kilmeane
Correagh	Kilcooley
Correagh	Cloonygormican
Correlfin	Kilbride
Correnamady	Creeve
Corriduane	Kilkeevan
Corrill [Correal]	Fuerty
Corrobane	Kilmore
Corroghohil [North + South]	Tibohine
Corroghroe	Lissonuffy
Corrohnenagh	Kilbegnet
Corronell	Killukin
Corroughboy	Cam
Corrow Derry	Kiltoom
Corrowduff	Cam
Corrowmoragh	Kiltoom
Corry	Kiltrustan
Corry	Cloontuskert
Corscagh [Corskeagh]	Kiltrustan
Cortline	Cloonfinlough
Cortoles	Killukin
Coruntober	Cam
Corvoghlow	Athleague
Corwollick [Corwillick]	Sligo
Coun Kell	Kilglass
Creaghtae [Creta]	Kiltrustan
Creevah	Ardcarn
Creevaugh	Kilmactranny
Creeve	Shankill
Creeve	Oran
Creeve	Creeve
Creevelan [Creevolan]	Creeve
Creeverae	Killian
Creevmully	Fuerty
Creevy	Tibohine
Creevykeel	Ahamlish
Cregagh [Cregga]	Kiltrustan
Cregalahan [Creglahan]	Kilkeevan
Cregamean [Creggamean]	Kilkeevan
Cregan	Ahascragh
Cregancorr	Kilkeevan
Cregane	Lissonuffy
Cregawon	Kilcroan
Creggan	Kilbegnet
Creggany	Athleague

Creggs	Kilbegnet
Creggs	Drumcliff
Cregisten	Kilkeevan
Creviquin	Roscommon
Crogane	Killian
Croghan	Killukin
Crosna	Ardcarn
Culadrumen br.	Drumcliff
Culadrumen Gilmr.	Drumcliff
Culespudane	Athleague
Culivacken	Cloonfinlough
Cullalusset	Kilgefin
Culleclych	Cloontuskert
Cullegh	Bumlin
Cullidim	Drumcolumb
Cullidion	Ballynakill, co. Sligo
Cullinamore [Culleenaghmore]	Sligo
Cullmore [Cuilmore]	Ardcarn
Cullsheahern	Aghanagh
Culnecallagh	Cloontuskert
Culoughtra	Kilmactranny
Culticarican	Ballysumaghan
Culticloane	Ballysumaghan
Cultidion	Ballysumaghan
Cultilogh	Aghanagh
Cummin	Clooncraff
Curgullin	Kilmore
Curgullin [Corgullion]	Kilmore
Curnaglick	Boyle
Curnecarta	Boyle
Currabegg	Athleague
Curraghsalla	Tibohine
Curramore	Kiltoom
Curriturpane [Curreentorpan]	Tibohine
Curroghsallow [Curraghsallagh]	Tibohine
Curry	Clooncraff
Curry	Kilmore
Currys	Aughrim
Curska	Tibohine
Dackloon [Dacklin]	Killumod
Dailoon	Kiltrustan
Dangan	Kilmore
Darham	Kilbride
Derefada	Taghboy
Derelea	Kilmactranny
Derreen	Ardcarn
Derreen [Derrinea]	Tibohine
Derridaragh	Cloonfinlough
Derrifucal	Kilglass
Derrim'stirr	Kilglass
Derrimacarbry [Derrycarbry]	Kilteevan
Derrinasugh [Derrenasugh]	Tumna
Derrine [Derreen]	Kilkeevan

Derrinlarg [Derrinlurg]	
Derrinomekan	
Derrinturk	
Derry	
Derrycough [Derrycoagh]	
Derrycumsy	
Derrycunny	
Derryfattan	
Derryhanilly	
Derryhubbert	
Derryhuppo [Derryhippoo]	
Derrykirken	
Derrykirken	
Derrylelias	
Derrynaseer	
Derryskinan	
Derryskinan	
Derygree	
Derymilan [Derrymoylin]	
Dignan	
Dill	
Dillonsgehane	
Dillonsgrove	
Dillonstrily	
Dingowen	
Dleamr.Slatogh	
Donally [Doonally]	
Donamaddy	
Donforc [Doonfore]	
Dooaune	
Doon	
Doon	
Doon	
Doon Sheheen	
Doonalla [Doonally]	
Doonamurry [Doonamurray]	
Doonardbeg [Doonardbeg]	
Doonardmore [Doonardmore]	
Dooneen	
Doonguillah [Doongelah]	
Doonicorneen	
Doreenashee	
Doughel [Doughil]	
Douray	
Draniadralane	
Dreemore [Drumore]	
Drimangh [Drimnagh]	
Drimatemple [Drumatemple]	
Drimdoe [Drumdoo]	
Drimdulan	
Drimercash	
Drimernod	
Drimerose Grange	
Drimilidane	

Tisrara
Tibohine
Kilteevan
Ahamlish
Kilnamanagh
Kilbride
Roscommon
Killukin
Lissonuffy
Lissonuffy
Kilbegnet
Kilcooley
Cloonygormican
Ahamlish
Tumna
Ardcarn
Ahamlish
Ardcarn
Termonbarry
Drumcliff
Tumna
Lissonuffy
Baslick
Lissonuffy
Elphin
Kilglass
Sligo
Kilbegnet
Drumcliff
Kilglass
Killukin
Boyle
Cloonygormican
Kilmacallan
Ballysumaghan
Kilross
Kiltrustan
Kiltrustan
Kilcolagh
Aghanagh
Lissonuffy
Kilmactranny
Cloonfinlough
Kilross
Ballynakill, co.
  Sligo
Kilmactranny
Ogulla
Drumatemple
Boyle
Kilkeevan
Killukin
Killukin
Sligo
Drumcolumb

Driminagh
Driminirlow [see Drumharlow]
Drimishibole [Drumaskibbole]
Drimlogh
Drimoghan
Drimsallagh [Drumsillagh]
Drimtreemanane
Driney
Drissoge
Drissugan [Drishaghaun]
Drom
Dronifad [Drumfad]
Drumbalon [Drumboylan]
Drumbrick
Drumcliff
Drumcollam
Drumcormack
Drumcuny
Drumdony
Drumduff
Drumenagh [Druminagh]
Drumharlow
Drumlaughn
Drumlion
Drumlish
Drummee
Drummod
Drummone
Drummoodan
Drummore
Drummot [Drummad]
Drumoo Cull
Drumoo Cull
Drumore
Drumsoughla [Drumsoghal]
Drynogh
Dubarn
Duloghan
Dunamon
Dunauney [Doonierin]
Dundermott [Dundermot]

Dunsasken [Doonshaskin] Ahamlish
Durafad
Eastersnow
Edon [Eden]
Elphin Town
Emlagh
Emlagh
Emlagh
Emlagh
Emlaghbegg
Emlaghglassen

Emlaghnagry [Emlaghnagree]

Ogulla
Tumna
Sligo
Kilkeevan
Sligo
Tumna
Tumna
Tibohine
Killukin
Baslick
Drumcliff
Ahamlish
Tumna
Ardcarn
Drumcliff
Drumcolumb
Ardcarn
Ardcarn
Aghanagh
Kilbride
Tibohine
Tumna
Aghanagh
Killukin
Shancough
Ballysumaghan
Clooncraff
Kilglass
Aughrim
Tumna
Tibohine
Kilmacallan
Aghanagh
Kilmactranny
Kilmactranny
Lissonuffy
Tisrara
Sligo
Dunamon
Drumcliff
Drumatemple, co.
  Roscommon

Shancough
Ardcarn
Tibohine
Elphin
Baslick
Elphin
Tawnagh
Kilkeevan
Oran
Ballynakill, co.
  Roscommon
Oran

Emlaughmore	Oran	Glaikagh	Shancough
Enagh	Killukin	Glan Thomas	Elphin
Eriblagh [Erriblagh]	Creeve	Glanacaka	Drumcolumb
Erizan	Tibohine	Glanamiltogue	Cloonfinlough
Errew [Erra]	Lissonuffy	Glanegon	Kilmeane
Errinagh [Erenagh]	Cloontuskert	Glanmidle [?]	Drumcliff
Erris	Boyle	Glanvella [Glenvela]	Baslick
Errit	Tibohine	Glebe	Bumlin
Errosuch	Ardcarn	Glen	Ballynakill, co.
Estersnow	Estersnow		Sligo
Falneshammer	Ballysumaghan	Glooria	Ardcarn
Falsk	Killukin	Glorey	Estersnow
Fanagh	Ardcarn	Glynisk	Ballynakill, co.
Farbreagues	Kilmeane		Galway
Farnacarny	Drumcliff	Gobbertasnan	Tumna
Farnbeg	Bumlin	Gorloose [Garryglass]	Bumlin
Farnikelly	Fuerty	Gorrynegron [Garrynagran]	Taghboy
Farraragh [Newtown Farragher]	Cloonygormican	Gort [Gilliaghan & Gort]	St John's
Fass	Estersnow	Gort Ganny [Gortaganny]	Rahara
Faughts	Sligo	Gortacousane [Gortacoosan]	Killeroran
Feeragh-beg	Kilmore	Gortarouey [Gortarowey]	Drumcliff
Feeraghmore [Fearagh]	Kilmore	Gorteenfadda	Kilbegnet
Ferenykelly	Fuerty	Gorteenruckane	Athleague
Ferenykelly	Cam	Gortgalline	Cloontuskert
Fermoyle	Sligo	Gortgrassagh	Tumna
Fevagh [Feevagh]	Dysert	Gorthelick	Ahamlish
Fiagherdarne	Drumcliff	Gortiganny	Tibohine
Fiegh	Tibohine	Gortlech [Gortleck]	Tumna
Finisklin	Estersnow	Gortmore	Kilbegnet
Flask [Flaskaghbeg]	Elphin	Gortmore	Fuerty
Flask More [Flaskaghmore]	Elphin	Gortmorris	Kilbegnet
Forsonough	Tisrara	Gortnabloisk	Kilmeane
Fox Hill	Kilmacallan	Gortnagorr	Shankill
Fox Tail	Shankill	Gortnagrally [Gortnegrelly]	Drumcliff
Foxbourough	Elphin	Gortnalawn [Gortylean]	Kilbegnet
Frankfort	Kilkeevan	Gortnalowee	Kilbegnet
French Park	Tibohine	GortnaMonsogh	Rahara
Fuerty	Fuerty	Gortnareask	Baslick
Furea	Taghboy	Gortnaselagh [Gortnasillagh]	Baslick
Furoo	Kilbegnet	Gortnecligh [Gortnacloy]	Kilmacumsy
Gallagh	Cloontuskert	Gortnegnanagh	Shankill
Gallowshill	Athlone, St.	Gorvogh	Kilbegnet
	Peter's	Gorvogh	Kilbegnet
Gallowstown [or Lisnacroghy]	Roscommon	Gowla	Ahascragh
Galy	Killenvoy	Grallagh	Tibohine
Ganavine [Ganaveens]	Killian	Grallagh	Boyle
Gannenomer [Glenammer]	Athleague	Granaghan Martin	Lissonuffy
Ganvins [Glenfin]	Rahara	Graney [Granny]	Estersnow
Gardenstown	Cloontuskert	Grange	Cam
Garinford [Garryphort]	Cam	Grange	Kiltrustan
Garroloher [Garrowlougher]	Tumna	Grange	Ahamlish
Garuagh [Garoke]	Bumlin	Grange	Cloonygormican
Garvogue	Shancough	Grangebegg [Grange Begg]	Boyle
Gillstown	Kilglass	Grangemore	Boyle

Grangeormsby	Sligo
Grellagh	Ahamlish
Grevirk [Grevisk]	Ardcarn
Gubeglannow	Cloonygormican
Guiddaun [Gaddan]	Ballysumaghan
Guranmore	Kilbegnet
Gurrane	Kilbegnet
Harkfree	Estersnow
Harkhill	Estersnow
Harraslowr [Harristown]	Kilkeevan
Hazlewood [Demesne]	Sligo
Heapstown	Kilmacallan
Highlake [or Ardlaghneenmore]	Cloonygormican
Hollywell	Kilbride
Holybrook [Ballyhealy]	Aghanagh
Holymount [or Knockacurren]	Ardcarn
Husetown [Hughestown]	Tumna
illteshinoge	Kilmore
Imalagh	Tumna
Inchroe [Gortfree & Inchiroe]	Cam
Inchymulclye	Sligo
Innfield	Ballintober
Ironheragh	Tumna
Irvillah	Ahascragh
Isherbane [Eskerbaun]	Cam
Iskermon	Ahascragh
Issey	Ballynakill, co. Galway
James Town	Taghboy
Keaulgaru [?]	Shancough
Keelogues	Kilbryan
Keelogues	Killenvoy
Keenagh	Athleague
Keilbogg	Termonbarry
Keilgraffy	Kilgraff
Keillmore	Clooncraff
Kellenrivagh	Killenvoy
Kellnaghmore	Kilmore
Kellnamanagh [Kilnamanagh] Peter's	Athlone, St.
Kellybrook	St John's
Kelticahill	Sligo
Kelticuneen	Tumna
Kilbegnett	Kilbegnet
Kilcarwran [Kilcanoran]	Aughrim
Kildallogue[Kildalloge]	Kiltrustan
Kilfagna [Kilfaughna]	Ardcarn
Kilgarive [Kilgarve]	Tibohine
Kilglass	Ahascragh
Kilienoroe	Lissonuffy
Kilinirvan	Dysert
Kilkean	Kilmactranny
Killadoon	Killadoon
Killamoy	Kilmactranny
Killappoge	Killumod
Killaquin	Killukin
Killar [Killerr]	Drumatemple
Killasolane [Killosolan	Killasolan
Killbarry	Termonbarry
Killbrine [Kilbryan]	Kilbryan
Killcar	Cam
Killcarrow [Kilcar]	Ahamlish
Killcash	Ahamlish
Killcegan	Kilglass
Killcock [Kilcock]	Kilmore
Killcola [Kilcolagh]	Kilcolagh
Killcooley [Kilcooley]	Kilcooley
Killcorky [Kilcorkey]	Kilcorkey
Killcosh [Kilcoosh]	Kilmeane
Killearny [Killarney]	Roscommon
Killeen	Ardcarn
Killegan	Kilglass
Killeghan	St John's
Killenboy [Killeenboy]	Kilteevan
Killenordenmore [Killinorden]	Bumlin
Killenvoy [Killinvoy]	Taghboy
Killerny	Cam
Killeslogh	Ahamlish
Killevoy	Aughrim
Killiloge	Drumcolumb
Killinagh [Beg and More]	Elphin
Killincirvane	Dysert
Killindeeny [Killeendeema]	Rahara
Killinolough	Dysert
Killinoroe	Lissonuffy
Killisteen	Kilbryan
Killkear [Kilkere]	Kilmactranny
Killmacroy [Kilmacroy]	Boyle
Killmcums [Kilmacumsy]	Kilmacumsy
Killmore	St John's
Killmore [Kilmore]	Kilmore
Killmore [Kilmore]	Kilkeevan
Killnamanagh	Kilnamanagh
Killnamanagh [Kilnamanagh]	Kilnamanagh
Killnatreen	Killumod
Killne Grall [Kilnagralta]	Tisrara
Killnemunah	Aughrim
Killraddan	Aughrim
Killselagh Dignan	Kilcroan
Killselagh [Kilsellagh]	Drumcliff
Killselagh Lowr	Drumcliff
Killselagh Upr	Drumcliff
Killsheehre	Aghanagh
Killtabrannuck [Kiltybrannock]	Boyle
Killtinighan	Boyle
Killtultoge [Kiltultoge]	Cloonygormican
Killucloghane	Kiltrustan
Killucloghane	Kiltrustan

Killucuan	Elphin
Killugan	Kilglass
Killukin	Killukin
Killumod	Killumod
Killvoney	Tisrara
Killvoy [Kilvoy]	Shankill
Killyaloe	Ballysumaghan
Killynagh	Elphin
Killyon	Killian
Kilmacanan	Drumcliff
Kilmaculril [Kilmacarril]	Tumna
Kilmakowen	Sligo
KilmcNanay [Kilmacanenenny]	Lissonuffy
Kilmore	Bumlin
Kilmore	Athleague
Kilmurtagh	Cloontuskert
Kilnebrady	Shankill
Kilnebrady	Shankill
Kilrahiscra	Killeroran
Kilree	Ogulla
Kilross	Kilross
Kilruddan [Kilroddan]	Tibohine
Kilscagh	Kiltrustan
Kilteam	Kilteevan
Kilteboe	Tibohine
Kiltebranly	Tibohine
Kiltecolly [Kiltycooly]	Drumcliff
Kilteevan	Kilteevan
Kiltemane [Kiltimean]	Tibohine
Kiltibeg	Termonbarry
Kiltilogh	Kilmacallan
Kiltoom	Kiltoom
Kiltrustan [Kiltrustan]	Kiltrustan
Kilultough [Killultagh]	Cloonfinlough
Kinard	Clooncraff
Kinatogher [Kiltogher]	Drumcliff
Kinclare	Shankill
Kinclare	Killasolan
Kingsbura [Kingsborough]	Killadoon
Kingsland	Kilnamanagh
Kirlogh	Kilmore
Kislree	Ogulla
Knocadalton [Knockadalteen]	Killadoon
Knocbreeni	Drumcolumb
Knockabro [Knockavroe]	Boyle
Knockadangan	Athleague
Knockado [Knockadoo]	Boyle
Knockagaher	Shancough
Knockananima	Killukin
Knockanarrow	Aghanagh
Knockanum	Killukin
Knockatober	Kilross
Knockbrack	Killenvoy
Knockbranah	Ballynakill, co. Sligo

Knockdonel	Ardcarn
Knockdumdonel	Kilmeane
Knockglass	Kilcolagh
Knockhall	Kilcolagh
Knocklaght	Ballintober
Knockmeane [Knockmeane]	Kilmeane
Knockmore	Kilmactranny
Knockmurry	Kilkeevan
Knocknagawna	Kilmore
Knocknagee	Ballysumaghan
Knocknahur [North + South]	Sligo
Knocknashana	Tumna
Knocknenoole [Knocknanool]	Kiltoom
Knockonyconner	St John's
Knockraver [Knockrawer]	Drumcolumb
Knockro	Kilkeevan
Knockroe	Aghanagh
Knockroe	Estersnow
Knockroghery [Knockcroghery]	Killenvoy
Knockrow [Knockroe]	Killumod
Knockrush [Knockarush]	Boyle
Knockvicar	Ardcarn
Labolly	Drumcliff
Lack [Lacken]	Termonbarry
Lacken	Rahara
Lacken	Cloonfinlough
Lagane [Lacken]	Aughrim
Laghhorris	Creeve
Lahardon [Lahardan]	Killadoon
Lanfoot	Shankill
Lanortan	Ahascragh
Laranon	Ogulla
Laraugh [+ Ross?]	Oran
Larganroe	Kiltrustan
Largonroe	Kiltrustan
Lattoon	Ahascragh
Laughill	Tumna
Lavagh	Kilglass
Lavally	Kiltrustan
Lavally	Ballysumaghan
Leabegg	Drumatemple
Leagh	Kilbegnet
Leam	Boyle
Leamore	Ballynakill, co. Roscommon
Lecarow	Aghanagh
Lecarrow	Kilglass
Lecarrow	Ballysumaghan
Legatinly [Leggatinty]	Tibohine
Legnagun	Boyle
Legnenerunagh	Kilross
Leitrim	Kilbride
Lekurue	Ballintober
Lenigin	Creeve
Lesineniren [Lisheenanierin	Cloonfinlough

Letreen [Lettreen]	Kiltrustan	Lisscom	Cam
Letrym [Leitrim]	Tibohine	Lissdallun [Lisdaulan]	Killenvoy
Lickane [Lackan]	Kilcolagh	Lissgarrow	Killenvoy
Lignashamur	Killukin	Lissheen [Lisheen]	Kiltrustan
Lillibrook [Lillybrook]	Aghanagh	Lissicone	Aghanagh
Line Mallow	Tisrara	Lissinivicane	Baslick
Linenoran	Aughrim	Lissinsellagh [Lisnasillagh]	Athleague
Linnabull	Creeve	Lisslody [Lisliddy]	Kilkeevan
Lisadely	Tibohine	Lissmacool [Lismacool]	Kilmacumsy
Lisadurn	Roscommon	Lissmaho [Lismaha]	Tisrara
Lisahark	Tibohine	Lissmoile [Lismoyle]	Cam
Lisaloy	Baslick	Lissnabull [Lisnaboll]	Kilmacumsy
Lisalvay	Baslick	Lissnagirra [Lisnagirra]	Athleague
Lisananny	Tibohine	Lissnalane [Lisnalarnnow]	Athleague
Lisavilly [Lissavilla]	Aughrim	Lissne Gobrough	Tisrara
Lisawrogy	Killian	Lissnelew	Athleague
Lisbanagher	Aghanagh	Lissnesellagh	Athleague
Lisbane [Lisbaun]	Kiltoom	Lissonuffy	Lissonuffy
Lisboy	Kilkeevan	LissPhelim	St John's
Lisbride	Roscommon	Lissphilip [Lisphilip]	Kilmacumsy
Liscennacouran	Sligo	Lissryan	Bumlin
Lisconney [Lisconny]	Drumcolumb	Listrumneal	Tibohine
Liscoonagark	Drumcliff	Lisvaddy	Aughrim
Liscorky	Kilcooley	Little Berries	Kiltoom
Lisdaly	Killumod	Littleknockdo	Boyle
Lisdoo	Tibohine	Loghboy	Aughrim
Lisdorn	Roscommon	Loghkinittin [Louganelteen?]	Sligo
Lisergool [Lissergool]	Tibohine	Loghoghgloss	Kilbegnet
Lisfflin	Cam	Logitean	Aughrim
Lisgallin	Fuerty	Longfield	Rahara
Lisgamon	Athleague	Longford	Kilkeevan
Lisgobban	Kilbride	Lorgan	Killasolan
Lishnageeragh	Ballynakill, co. Galway	Loughglin [Loughglinn]	Tibohine
		Loughteask	Elphin
Lishugh	Aughrim	Lower Rosses	Drumcliff
Lislahelly	Drumcliff	Lowfield	Kilmore
Lislary	Ahamlish	Lowpark [Lowparks]	St John's
Lismaho	Tisrara	Luarton	Ardcarn
Lismak	Tisrara	Lugnamuddy [or Cashelfinoge]	Boyle
LismcEgan	Kiltrustan	Lurga	Ballysumaghan
Lismehie [Lismeehy]	Lissonuffy	Lustea [Lustia]	Tumna
Lismuliff	Ogulla	Lyskyle	Killian
Lisnalurg	Drumcliff	Lyskyle [Liscuil]	Killian
Lisnalurg	Drumcliff	Lysterfield	Cam
Lisneane	Ogulla	Macmoyne [Mocmoyne]	Boyle
Lisneville [Lissaneaville]	Fuerty	Magheramore	Drumcliff
Lissacgan	Ahascragh	Maherlack [Magheralackagh]	Kilmactranny
Lissadel monin	Drumcliff	Mahon Slatogh	Kilglass
Lissadell monier [Lissadill]	Drumcliff	Maludeen [Moheedian]	Creeve
Lissafobble [Lissaphobble]	Lissonuffy	Mantua [Mantuar]	Shankill
Lissaniska	Ballynakill, co. Galway	Martins Trily	Lissonuffy
		Martry	Creeve
Lissanriagh	Cloontuskert	Meanagh	Bumlin
Lisscoffy	Athleague	Meeanah	Killeroran

Meelick	Kilmore	Nadneveagh	Kilcooley
Meeorane	Tumna	New Town	Drumcliff
Meery [Meera]	Tumna	Newpark, part of	Kiltoom
Mianagh	Bumlin	Newtown	Kilteevan
Mihane [Meehaun]	Killenvoy	Newtown	Shankill
Milltown Fallon [Milltown]	Dysert	Newtown	Oran
Milltown Pass	Kiltoom	Newtown	Bumlin
Mivanon	Kiltoom	Newtown	Kilbride
Moat	Kilbegnet	Newtown	Termonbarry
Mogh	Tumna	Newtown Donforc	Drumcliff
Moher	Cloonfinlough	Oagham	Tawnagh
Moher	Cloontuskert	Oakport [Demesne]	Ardcarn
Monastirhnaleer [or Abbey Grey]	Athleague	Ochorin	Tibohine
Moneene	Cloontuskert	Ogila	Ogulla
Moneygold	Ahamlish	Oldcalleland	Ogulla
Monksland	Athlone, St. Peter's	Oran	Oran
		Orlar	Drumcliff
Monyboy	Kilcooley	Osna	Tumna
Monylough	Elphin	Oughtanboy	Aghanagh
Monymore [Moneymore]	Kilmeane	Ownagh	Elphin
Moor	Killadoon	Oxhill	Ardcarn
Moore	Kilkeevan	Oxhill in Ardcarn	Ardcarn
Mooyglass	Kilglass	Oyster Island	Sligo
Mosshill	Clooncraff	Padween	Kilbryan
Mote	Kilmeane	Pargaruff	Baslick
Mount Thady	Killukin	Peake	Kilcorkey
Mountalbot	Athleague	Polleher	Cam
Mountalbott	Tisrara	Polleher	Cam
Moyglass	Kilmore	Port	Ahascragh
Moyliss	Fuerty	Portron	Killenvoy
Moyne	Tibohine	Pulbaun	Athleague
Mt. Dillon	Lissonuffy	Pullowen	Kilbryan
Muckinagh	Kilmore	Pulneronylane	Bumlin
Mucklon	Taghboy	Qurafad	Shancough
Muff	Fuerty	Raconilly	Cloonygormican
Mulinakeny	Drumcliff	Racormick	Drumcliff
Mulladoe	Kilkeevan	Racormick	Drumcliff
Mullaghmore	Ahamlish	Radidle	Drumcliff
Mullaghmore	Ballynakill, co. Sligo	Radiveen	Kilbryan
		Rafowdagh	Baslick
Mullaughkirk	Shancough	Rafowdagh	Baslick
Mullimore	Killukin	Raghley	Drumcliff
Mullin	Tibohine	Rah	Oran
Mullinashe	Tibohine	Rahaperny	Drumcliff
Mulliveheran	Bumlin	Rahara	Rahara
Mullogh M'Cormick	Kilglass	Raheens	Elphin
Mulloughadogh	Taghboy	Rahelly	Drumcliff
Mullowginnan	Killukin	Rahoverin	Drumatemple
Mullymucks	Kilbride	Rakery	Tibohine
Mungagh	Kilkeevan	Ranagh	Oran
Muninanean	Drumcliff	Ranagligh	Ogulla
Munnila	Tawnagh	Ranarooanah	Kilmore
Munnyduff	Kilmore	Rardeevin	Baslick
Muterre	Kilmactranny	Rardinghra	Creeve

Place	Parish	Place	Parish
Ratallin	Kilcolagh	Ruskey	Termonbarry
Rathconnor	Kilbride	Sallymount	Kilbride
Rathledge	Kilkeevan	Scardane	Athleague
RathmcCarrick	Sligo	Scardon	Sligo
Rathmeigh	Ballintober	Scormore	Kilmacumsy
Rathmore	Killukin	Scrabbagh	Kilmore
Rathmoyle	Baslick	Scregg	Killenvoy
Rathnesoliagh	Ballintober	Scregg	Killukin
Rathraghan	Sligo	Scrimoge	Bumlin
Rathroe	Shankill	Scrine	Kilmeane
Ratra	Tibohine	Shanbally	Kilmacumsy
Rawkinerly	Kilcorkey	Shanco	Drumatemple
Rawneclerg	Kilcorkey	Shancoe	Shancough
Rawnegligh	Ogulla	Shannon	Sligo
Reaugh	Cloonfinlough	Shannon Knox	Sligo
Rin [Rinn]	Ardcarn	Shanvalladin	Dunamon
Rinnebol etc.	Kilcolagh	Shanwallybone	Tumna
Rockbrook	Ballynakill, co. Sligo	Sheeawne	Cloontuskert
		Sheegory	Boyle
Rockfield	Fuerty	Skehingen	Cloonygormican
Rockingham	Ardcarn	Skenivar	Kilmacumsy
Rocksavage	Athleague	Skey	Kilmore
Rocksboro'	Kilbride	Slalogh Begg	Kilglass
Rodyn	Aughrim	Sleevengee	Roscommon
Roo	Kilmore	Slieveagh	Kilnamanagh
Rooaune	Kilglass	Slieveroe	Kilnamanagh
Rookwood	Athleague	Sligo	Sligo
Rooscagh [Rooskagh]	Athlone, St. Peter's	Sliveformagh	Ardcarn
		Smutterna	Kilbryan
Roscommon	Roscommon	Snipehill	Ballintober
Roses Gealan	Drumcliff	Soohy	Ballynakill, co. Sligo
Roses uper	Drumcliff		
Rosmilan	Kilbegnet	Springfield	Tawnagh
Ross Begg	Elphin	Sraduff	Kilmactranny
Rosses	Aghanagh	St.John's	St John's
Rossmeen	Ballintober	Stonypark	Roscommon
Rossmore	Ballynakill, co. Sligo	Straduff-mountain	Kilmactranny
		Strananagh	Ballysumaghan
Rossmore [East + West]	Elphin	Strandhill	Sligo
Rover Kelly [Roverkilly]	Rahara	Street	Bumlin
Runabehee	Kilnamanagh	Stridagh	Ahamlish
Runaleakan	Killadoon	Strokestown	Bumlin
Runatruhan	Killadoon	Taghwinnagh	Boyle
Runifarny	Kilglass	Tannoor	Killumod
Runimullin	Kilnamanagh	Tansyfield	Elphin
Runiradane	Kilnamanagh	Tanzyfort	Aghanagh
Runnibocan	Oran	Tapp	Killadoon
Runnymead [Runnamoat]	Cloonygormican	Tarmonbegg	Kilkeevan
Runoghue	Elphin	Tarmonmore	Kilkeevan
Runrow	Ahamlish	Taughill	Kilkeevan
Rusheen	Ardcarn	Taughnara	Kilkeevan
Rusheen	Drumcolumb	Taughnuse	Kilkeevan
Rushill	Aughrim	Taulagh	Killukin
Rushine	Baslick	Taunadrisoge	Tibohine

Taunirover	Tibohine	Tullaboy	Estersnow
Tawnacarrow	Boyle	Tullahan	Kilnamanagh
Tawnnatasky	Boyle	Tullavahan	Estersnow
Tenecreevy	Tibohine	Tullileag	Tibohine
Termore	Kilmacumsy	Tullin	Kiltrustan
Thurwough	Kilmacumsy	Tullineshinaham	Ardcarn
Tibohin	Tibohine	Tullinuer	Kilmactranny
Ticooly [Carr + O'Kelly]	Killasolan	Tullnahirk	Aughrim
Tiernemunter	Ardcarn	Tully	Elphin
Timanagh	Ballintober	Tully	Kilcorkey
Time	Cam	Tully	Killukin
Timoney	Ogulla	Tully	Kilbride
Tintagh	Boyle	Tully	Sligo
Toberowry	Elphin	Tully	Drumcliff
Toberumkee	Drumatemple	Tully	Killadoon
Toberumkee	Oran	Tully	Kilmore
Tobervaddy	Fuerty	Tully	Kilross
Togherfin	Kilmeane	Tullybeg	Tumna
Tohercoll	Taghboy	Tullyleige	Kilross
Tomna	Tumna	Tullymore	Kilross
Toneroe	Kilnamanagh	Tullymoremead	Tibohine
Tonilamony	Fuerty	Tullynashoge	Sligo
Tonnagh	Aghanagh	Tullynegrackin [North + South]	Kilmeane
Tonregee	Kilbride	Tullyroe	Lissonuffy
Toomelidane	Drumcolumb	Tullyvarran	Ogulla
Toomrilan	Ahascragh	Tulsk	Kilmore
Tormore	Drumcliff	Tuluscan	Cloonfinlough
Torpane	Taghboy	Tumeever	Kilgefin
Toruck	Taghboy	Tumegranel	Lissonuffy
Torville	Roscommon	Tunereevacomen New	Lissonuffy
Torymartin	Killukin	Tureen	Kilcroan
Tourenagh	Ballintober	Turlagh	Tibohine
Tournagee	Kilnamanagh	Turlogh	Shankill
Traghnadarne	Drumcliff	Turlogh	Aughrim
Treily	Cloontuskert	Twomore	Drumcliff
Trien	Cam	Tysan	Killadoon
Trien	Kilkeevan	Umercroe	Killadoon
TrineesevaLynch	Lissonuffy	Umercroe	Bumlin
Trinegry	Estersnow	Upper Ballyfeeny	Taghboy
Trinemacmurtagh	Drumcolumb	Wheremore	Tawnagh
Trinemarly	Estersnow	Whitehill	Kilkeevan
Trinescrabba	Aghanagh	Willsgrove	Sligo
Trumane	Athleague	Willybrook	Ardcarn
Tubberpatrick	Kiltrustan	Wrenn	
Tuberelvy	Baslick		
Tubermurry	Shankill		
Tulla	Killeroran		